APPLICATIONS OF MATLAB IN SCIENCE AND ENGINEERING

Edited by **Tadeusz Michałowski**

Applications of MATLAB in Science and Engineering
Edited by Tadeusz Michałowski

Published by InTech
Janeza Trdine 9, 51000 Rijeka, Croatia

Publishing Process Manager Davor Vidic

Technical Editor Teodora Smiljanic

Cover Designer InTech Design Team

Additional hard copies can be obtained from orders@intechopen.com

Applications of MATLAB in Science and Engineering, Edited by Tadeusz Michałowski
p. cm.
ISBN 978-953-307-708-6

For EU product safety concerns:
IN TECH d.o.o., Prolaz Marije Krucifikse Kozulić 3, 51000 Rijeka, Croatia,
info@intechopen.com or visit our website at intechopen.com.

Meet the editor

Dr. Tadeusz Michałowski is a Professor at Cracow University of Technology (Kraków, Poland). He is a Member of Committee of Analytical Chemistry at Polish Academy of Sciences, 1996-2007. Professor Michałowski's areas of interests include electrochemistry and spectrometric methods of analysis, titrimetry, mathematical modelling, calibration methods and his main scientific achievements are discovery of generalized electron balance (GEB); formulation of generalized approach to electrolytic systems (GATES), formulation of generalized equivalence mass (GEM), and new resolution of many problems involved with analytical chemistry and physical chemistry in area of electrolytic systems.

Contents

Preface

MATLAB (**Mat**rix **Lab**oratory) is a matrix-oriented tool for mathematical programming, applied for numerical computation and simulation purposes. Together with its dynamic simulation toolbox Simulink, as a graphical environment for the simulation of dynamic systems, it has become a very powerful tool suitable for a large number of applications in many areas of research and development. These areas include mathematics, physics, chemistry and chemical engineering, mechanical engineering, biological and medical sciences, communication and control systems, digital signal, image and video processing, system modeling and simulation, statistics and probability. Generally, MATLAB is perceived as a high-level language and interactive environment that enables to perform computational tasks faster than with traditional programming languages, such as C, C++, and Fortran.

Simulink is integrated with MATLAB as MATLAB/Simulink, i.e., data can be easily transferred between the programs. MATLAB is supported in Unix, Macintosh, and Windows environments. This way, Simulink is an interactive environment for modeling, analyzing, and simulating a wide variety of dynamic systems.

The use of MATLAB is actually increasing in a large number of fields, by combining with other toolboxes, e.g., optimization toolbox, identification toolbox, and others. The MathWorks Inc. periodically updates MATLAB and Simulink, providing more and more advanced software. MATLAB handles numerical calculations and high-quality graphics, provides a convenient interface to built-in state-of-the-art subroutine libraries, and incorporates a high-level programming language. Nowadays, the MATLAB/Simulink package is the world's leading mathematical computing software for engineers and scientists in industry and education.

Due to the large number of models and/or toolboxes, there is still some work or coordination to be done to ensure compatibility between the available tools. Inputs and outputs of different models are to-date defined by each modeler, a connection between models from two different toolboxes can thus take some time. This should be normalized in the future in order to allow a fast integration of new models from other toolboxes. The widespread use of these tools, is reflected by ever-increasing number of books based on the MathWorks Inc. products, with theory, real-world examples, and exercises.

This book presents a review of some activities in modeling and simulation processes.

Chapter 1 is devoted to the Generalized Approach To Electrolytic Systems (GATES), applicable for resolution of electrolytic systems of any degree of complexity with use of iterative computer programs (e.g., one offered by MATLAB) applied to the set of non-linear equations, where all physicochemical knowledge can be involved. The Generalized Electron Balance (GEB), immanent in formulation of all redox systems, is considered in categories of general laws of the matter preservation.

MATLAB programs are also related to biological sciences. Chapter 2 presents the Odefy toolbox and indicates how to use it for modeling and analyzing molecular biological systems. The concepts of steady states, update policies, state spaces, phase planes and systems parameters are also explained. Applicability of Odefy toolbox for studies on real biological systems involved with stem cell differentiation, immune system response and embryonal tissue formation is also indicated.

Much of the data obtained in molecular biology is of quantitative nature. Such data are obtained with use of 2D microarrays, e.g., DNA or protein microarrays, containing 104 - 105 spots arranged in the matrix form (arrayed) on a chip, where e.g., many parallel genetic tests are accomplished (note that all variables in MATLAB are arrays). For effective handling of the large datasets, different bioinformatic techniques based on matrix algebra are applied to extract the information needed with the use of MATLAB. A review of such techniques in provided in Chapter 3.

A reference of MATLAB to physical sciences is represented in this book by a series of chapters dealing with electrical networks, communication/information transfer and filtering of signals/data. There are Chapters: 4 (on a hysteresis voltage control technique), 5 (on hysteresis current controlled inverters), 6 (on voltage source converter), 7 (on power transmission networks), 8 (on fading in the communication channel during propagation of signals on multiple paths between transmitter and receiver), 9 (on wireless video communication), 10 (on active RC-filters done to diminish random fluctuations in electric circuits caused by thermal noise), 11 (on comb filter, used for decimation, i.e., reduction of a signal sampling rate), 12 (on fractional delay filters, useful in numerous signal processing), and 13 (on tuning methods).

MATLAB is an interactive environment designed to perform scientific and engineering calculations and to create computer simulations. Simulink as a tool integrated with MATLAB, allows the design of systems using block diagrams in a fast and flexible way (Chapter 14). In this book, it is applied for: mechanical systems (Chapter 15); hydraulic and electromagnetic actuators (Chapter 16); control of the motion of wheeled mobile robot on the rough terrain (Chapter 17); comparative study on spur gears with symmetric and asymmetric teeth (Chapter 18); thermal and mechanical models for welding purposes (Chapter 19). A toolbox with stochastic Markov model is presented in Chapter 20.

Some operations known from statistical data analysis are also realizable with use of MATLAB, namely: cluster analysis (modulation recognition of digital signals, Chapter 21) and pattern recognition (digital image watermarking, Chapter 22).

The last two chapters discuss the registration of radioactive iodine along the gastrointestinal tract (Chapter 23), and acid-base neutralization in continuously stirred tank reactor (Chapter 24).

Tadeusz Michałowski
Cracow University of Technology, Cracow
Poland

1

Application of GATES and MATLAB for Resolution of Equilibrium, Metastable and Non-Equilibrium Electrolytic Systems

Tadeusz Michałowski
Faculty of Chemical Engineering and Technology, Cracow University of Technology, Cracow, Poland

1. Introduction

The Generalized Approach To Electrolytic Systems (GATES) (Michałowski, 2001, 2010) provides the possibility of thermodynamic description of equilibrium and metastable, redox and non-redox, mono-, two- and three-phase systems, with the possibility of all attainable/pre-selected physicochemical knowledge to be involved, with none simplifying assumptions done for calculation purposes, where different types of reactions occur in batch or dynamic systems, of any degree of complexity. The Generalized Electron Balance (GEB) concept, devised and formulated by Michałowski (1992), and obligatory for description of redox systems, is fully compatible with charge and concentration balances, and relations for the corresponding equilibrium constants. Up to 1992, the generalized electron balance (GEB) concept was the lacking segment needed to formulate the compatible set of algebraic balances referred to redox systems. The GEB is also applicable for the systems where radical species are formed. Shortly after GEB formulation, the GATES involving redox systems of any degree of complexity, was elaborated.

In this chapter, some examples of complex redox systems, where all types of elementary chemical reactions proceed simultaneously and/or sequentially, are presented. In all instances, one can follow measurable quantities (potential E, pH) in dynamic and static processes and gain the information about details not measurable in real experiments; it particularly refers to dynamic speciation. In the calculations made according to iterative computer programs, e.g., MATLAB, all physicochemical knowledge can be involved and different "variations on the subject" are also possible; it particularly refers to metastable and non-equilibrium systems. The Generalized Equivalent Mass (GEM) concept, also devised (1979) by Michałowski (Michałowski et al., 2010), has been suggested, with none relevance to a chemical reaction notation. Within GATES, the chemical reaction notation is only the basis to formulate the expression for the related equilibrium constant.

2. GEB

In order to formulate GEB for a particular redox system, two equivalent approaches were suggested by Michałowski. The first approach (Michałowski, 1994; Michałowski and Lesiak,

1994a,b) is based on the principle of a "common pool" of electrons, introduced by different species containing the electron-active elements participating redox equilibria. The disproportionation reaction is a kind of dissipation of electrons between the species formed by dissipating element, whereas the transfer of electrons between two (or more) interacting elements in a redox system resembles a "card game", with active elements as gamblers, electrons - as money, and non-active elements - as fans.

The second approach (Michałowski, 2010) results from juxtaposition of elemental balances for hydrogen (H) and oxygen (O). For redox systems, the balance thus obtained is independent on charge and concentration balances, whereas the related balance, when referred to non-redox systems, is the linear combination of charge and concentration balances, i.e. it is not a new, independent balance (Fig. 1). Any non-redox system is thus described only by the set of charge and s concentration balances, together s+1 linearly independent balances. Any redox system is described with use of charge, electron (GEB) and s concentration balances, together s+2 linearly independent balances. Charge balance results from balance of protons in nuclei and orbital electrons of all elements in all species forming the electrolytic system considered.

For redox systems, the balance obtained according to the second approach can be transformed (Michałowski, 2010) into the form ascribed to the first approach. In the second approach, we are not forced to calculate oxidation degrees of elements in particular species; it is an advantageous occurrence, of capital importance for the systems containing complex organic compounds, their ions and/or radicals.

The principles of minimizing (zeroing) procedure, realized within GATES according to iterative computer program, are exemplified e.g., in (Michałowski, 1994; Michałowski and Lesiak, 1994a).

Fig. 1. The place of electron balance (GEB) within elemental balances.

3. General characteristics of electrolytic systems

Electrolytic systems can be considered from thermodynamic or kinetic viewpoints. The thermodynamic approach can be applied to equilibrium or metastable systems. In equilibrium systems, all reaction paths are accessible, whereas in metastable systems at least one of the reaction paths, attainable (virtually) from equilibrium viewpoint, is inaccessible, i.e. the activation barriers for some reaction paths are not crossed, and the resulting reactions cannot proceed, under defined conditions. It particularly refers to aqueous electrolytic systems, where less soluble gaseous species, such as H_2 or O_2, can virtually be formed, provided that this process is not hampered by obstacles of different nature. However, formation of the presupposed gas bubbles in the related solution, needs a relatively great expenditure of volumetric work, $\Delta L = -\int p \cdot dV$, made against the surrounding solution, by gas molecules forming the bubble. The ΔL value can be recalculated on an overvoltage ΔU = ΔL/q, where q is the charge consumed/released in the (virtual) reduction/oxidation process. Owing to the fact that the particular bubble assumes a macroscopic dimension, ΔL and then ΔU values are high. Particularly, ΔU referred to the (presupposed) formation of O_2, cannot be covered by the oxidation potential of MnO_4^{-1} in aqueous medium and the (virtual) reaction $4MnO_4^{-1} + 4H^{+1} = $ $4\mathbf{MnO_2} + 3O_2 + 2H_2O$ does not occur, even at elevated temperatures. Another kind of obstacles resulted from formation of a hydroxide/oxide layer on surface of a metal (e.g., Mg, Al) introduced into pure water; these layers protect further dissolution of the metal and formation of H_2.

One can distinguish static (batch) and dynamic electrolytic systems, resolvable within GATES. The dynamic process, most commonly applied in laboratory practice, is the titration, where titrant (T) is added into titrand (D), and the D+T system is thus formed. In D+T systems considered in chemical analysis, different (acid-base, redox, complexation or/and precipitation, extended on two- and three-phase (liquid-liquid extraction systems) types of reactions may occur simultaneously and/or sequentially and, moreover, a particular type of a reaction, e.g., complexation, can be exemplified by different representatives, e.g., different ligands.

Modelling the electrolytic systems consists of several interacting steps, indicated in Fig. 2. The collected preliminary data are of qualitative and quantitative nature. The qualitative aspect refers to specification of particular components (species), whereas quantitative aspect relates to equilibrium constants, involving particular species of the system. Later on, only the steps involved with calculations, data handling and knowledge gaining will be discussed.

4. Rules of conservation

In chemical systems, one can refer to different rules of conservation, due to elements, protons, electrons and external charges of species – particularly the species entering the electrolytic systems, where none nuclear transformations of elements occur. Some rules of conservation are interrelated, and this fact is referred to systems of any degree of complexity. This way, the problem of interdependency of the balances arises. Starting from the rules of conservation viewpoint, it is assumed, that any electrolytic system, composed of condensed (liquid, liquid+solid, liquid1+liquid2, or liquid1+liquid2+solid) phases (Michałowski and Lesiak, 1994a) is separated from its surroundings by diathermal walls, that enable any process in the closed system to proceed under isothermal conditions. In such systems, the mass transport can occur only between the phases consisting such a system. In thermodynamic considerations of dynamic electrolytic systems it is also assumed that all the processes occur in *quasistatic* manner.

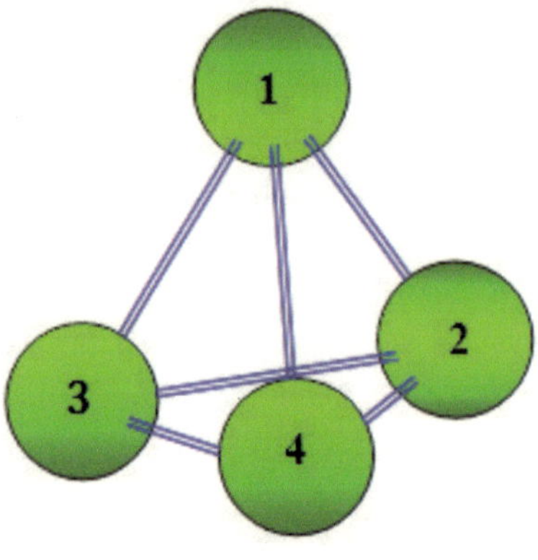

Fig. 2. Steps of modelling any electrolytic system: 1 - Collection of preliminary data; 2 - Preparation of computer program; 3 - Calculations and data handling; 4 - Gaining of knowledge.

As were stated above, the linear combination of elemental balances for hydrogen (H) and oxygen (O), referred to redox systems in aqueous media, provides the balance equivalent to GEB, in its primary form. In formulation of the balances, formation of hydrated forms $X_i^{z_i} \times n_i H_2O$ ($n_i \geq 0$) of ionic ($z_i \neq 0$) and/or nonionic ($z_i=0$) species $X_i^{z_i}$ is admitted in considerations. The GEB, referred to a redox system, is fully compatible with other (charge and concentration) balances related to this system and is linearly independent from that balances.

5. Formulation of GEB

5.1 Batch redox systems

5.1.1 Fenton reagent

The Fenton reagent is usually obtained by mixing $FeSO_4$ and H_2O_2 solutions. In order to describe this redox system quantitatively, let us consider the monophase system (solution) of volume V_0 [L], composed of N_{01} molecules of $FeSO_4 \cdot 7H_2O$, N_{02} molecules of H_2O_2 and N_{0W} molecules of H_2O introduced with H_2O_2 solution (e.g., perhydrol), and N_W molecules of H_2O as the solvent. The solution: H_2O (N_1), H^{+1} (N_2, n_2), OH^{-1} (N_3, n_3), OH (N_4, n_4), H_2O_2 (N_5, n_5), HO_2^{-1} (N_6, n_6), HO_2 (N_7, n_7), O_2^{-1} (N_8, n_8), O_2 (N_9, n_9), Fe^{+2} (N_{10}, n_{10}), $FeOH^{+1}$ (N_{11}, n_{11}), $FeSO_4$ (N_{12}, n_{12}), Fe^{+3} (N_{13}, n_{13}), $FeOH^{+2}$ (N_{14}, n_{14}), $Fe(OH)_2^{+1}$ (N_{15}, n_{15}), $Fe_2(OH)_2^{+4}$ (N_{16}, n_{16}), $FeSO_4^{+1}$ (N_{17}, n_{17}), $Fe(SO_4)_2^{-1}$ (N_{18}, n_{18}), HSO_4^{-1} (N_{19}, n_{19}), SO_4^{-2} (N_{20}, n_{20}), where N_i is the number of entities X_i with mean number n_i of hydrating water particles attached to it, $n_i \geq 0$. Balances for H and O are as follows:

$$\begin{gathered} 2 \cdot N_1 + N_2 \cdot (1+2n_2) + N_3 \cdot (1+2n_3) + N_4 \cdot (1+2n_4) + N_5 \cdot (2+2n_5) + N_6 \cdot (1+2n_6) + \\ N_7 \cdot (1+2n_7) + N_8 \cdot 2n_8 + N_9 \cdot 2n_9 + N_{10} \cdot 2n_{10} + N_{11} \cdot (1+2n_{11}) + N_{12} \cdot 2n_{12} + \\ N_{13} \cdot 2n_{13} + N_{14} \cdot (1+2n_{14}) + N_{15} \cdot (2+2n_{15}) + N_{16} \cdot (2+2n_{16}) + N_{17} \cdot 2n_{17} + N_{18} \cdot 2n_{18} + \\ N_{19} \cdot (1+2n_{19}) + N_{20} \cdot 2n_{20} = 14 \cdot N_{01} + 2 \cdot N_{02} + 2 \cdot N_{0W} + 2 \cdot N_W \end{gathered} \tag{1}$$

$$N_1+N_2 \cdot n_2+N_3 \cdot (1+n_3)+N_4 \cdot (1+n_4)+N_5 \cdot (2+n_5)+N_6(2+n_6)+N_7(2+n_7)+ N_8 \cdot (2+n_8)+N_9 \cdot (2+n_9)+N_{10} \cdot n_{10}+N_{11}(1+n_{11})+N_{12} \cdot (4+n_{12})+N_{13} \cdot n_{13}+ N_{14} \cdot (1+n_{14})+N_{15} \cdot (2+n_{15})+N_{16} \cdot (2+n_{16})+N_{17} \cdot (4+n_{17})+N_{18} \cdot (8+n_{18})+ N_{19}(4+n_{19})+N_{20} \cdot (4+n_{20})=11 \cdot N_{01}+2 \cdot N_{02}+N_{0W}+N_W \quad (2)$$

From (1) and (2) we have

$$-N_2+N_3+N_4+2N_5+3N_6+3N_7+4N_8+4N_9+ N_{11}+8N_{12}+N_{14}+ 2N_{15}+2N_{16}+8N_{17}+16N_{18}+7N_{19}+8N_{20}=8N_{01}+2N_{02} \quad (3)$$

Adding the sides of (3) and:

$$+N_2-N_3-N_6-N_8+2N_{10}+N_{11}+3N_{13}+2N_{14}+N_{15}+4N_{16}+N_{17}-N_{18}-N_{19}-2N_{20}=0$$

$$6N_{01}=6N_{12}+6N_{17}+12N_{18}+6N_{19}+6N_{20}$$

after cancellation of similar terms, one obtains the relation

$$N_4+2N_5+2N_6+3N_7+3N_8+4N_9+2N_{10}+2N_{11}+2N_{12}+ 3N_{13}+3N_{14}+3N_{15}+6N_{16}+3N_{17}+3N_{18}=2N_{01}+2N_{02} \quad (4)$$

Dividing the sides of (6) by $N_A \cdot V_0$, we get the simple form of GEB related to this system

$$[OH]+2 \cdot ([H_2O_2]+[HO_2^{-1}])+3 \cdot ([HO_2]+[O_2^{-1}])+4 \cdot [O_2]+ 2 \cdot ([Fe^{+2}]+[FeOH^{+1}]+[FeSO_4])+3 \cdot ([Fe^{+3}]+[FeOH^{+2}]+[Fe(OH)_2^{+1}]+ 2 \cdot [Fe_2(OH)_2^{+4}]+[FeSO_4^{+1}]+[Fe(SO_4)_2^{-1}])=2 \cdot C_{01}+2 \cdot C_{02} \quad (5)$$

where $[X_i] = N_i/(N_A \cdot V_0)$, $C_{0j} = N_{0j}/(N_A \cdot V_0)$. Hydrating water particles at the corresponding species X_i are omitted in (5), for simplicity of notation. Eq. (5) involves only the elements participating redox equilibria; the electrons of sulfur in sulfate species do not participate the redox equilibria. Note that the radical species (OH, HO_2) are involved in (5), and O_2 is the biradical.

For redox systems, the balance obtained according to the second approach can be transformed into the form ascribed to the first approach. However, in the second approach we are not forced to define/calculate oxidation degrees of elements; it is a very advantageous occurrence, of capital importance for the systems with complex organic compounds, their ions and/or radicals.

5.1.2 A generalizing notation

Let us consider the electrolytic system, where the species of $H_pO_qX_r^{+z} \cdot n_{pqrz}H_2O$ type ($z = z_{pqrz} = 0, \pm1, \pm2,\ldots$; $n_{pqrz} \geq 0$) are formed after introducing the substance $H_PO_QX_R \cdot nH_2O$ into water. From comparison of the elemental balances, we get the equation (Michałowski, 2010)

$$\sum_{pqrz} (r \cdot Z_X+p-2q-z) \cdot [H_pO_qX_r^{+z} \cdot n_{pqrz}H_2O]=(R \cdot Z_X+P-2Q) \cdot C \quad (6)$$

where Z_X is the atomic number for the element X; the set of indices (p,q,r,z) covered by the sum in (6) is different from: (2,1,0,0) for H_2O, (1,0,0,1) for H^{+1}, and (1,1,0,–1) for OH^{-1}. It is assumed that $H_PO_QX_R \cdot nH_2O$ does not react (as oxidizing or reducing agent) with water, i.e. products of water oxidation or reduction are not formed. For example, after introducing Br_2 (X = Br; P=Q=n=0, R=2; $Z_X = Z_{Br} = 35$) into water, the following bromine species are formed as hydrates in the disproportionation process: $HBrO_3$ (p=r=1, q=3, z=0), BrO_3^{-1} (p=0, r=1, q=3, z=–1), HBrO (p=q=r=1, z=0), BrO^{-1} (p=0, q=r=1, z=–1), Br_2 (p=q=z=0, r=2), Br_3^{-1} (p=q=0, r=3, z=–1), Br^{-1} (p=q=0, r=1, z= -1). Applying Eq. 6, we get (Michałowski, 1994)

$$(Z_{Br}-5)([HBrO_3]+[BrO_3^{-1}])+(Z_{Br}-1)([HBrO]+[BrO^{-1}])+2Z_{Br}[Br_2]+ (3Z_{Br}+1)[Br_3^{-1}]+(Z_{Br}+1)[Br^{-1}]=2Z_{Br}\cdot C \qquad (7)$$

where C [mol/L] is the total concentration of Br_2. In (7), hydrating water particles are omitted, for simplicity.

For comparative purposes, one can refer to (a) Br_2 (C) + KBr (C_1); (b) NaBrO (C_2); (c) $KBrO_3$ (C_3) + KBr (C_1) solutions. In all instances, the left side of (7) is identical, whereas the right side is as follows: $2Z_{Br}C + (Z_{Br}+1)C_1$ for (a); $(Z_{Br}-1)C_2$ for (b); $(Z_{Br}-5)C_3 + (Z_{Br}+1)C_1$ for the case (c).

5.2 Dynamic redox systems

In physicochemical/analytical practice, a dynamic system is usually realized according to titrimetric mode, where V mL of titrant (T) is added into V_0 mL of titrand (D). Assuming additivity in volumes, V_0+V of D+T system is thus formed. In common redox titrations, two or more elements, represented by different species, can participate redox equilibria.

5.2.1 $FeSO_4+H_2SO_4+KMnO_4$

This system be referred to titration of V_0 mL D, composed of $FeSO_4$ (C_0) + H_2SO_4 (C_1), with V mL of C mol/L $KMnO_4$ as T. The electron balance (GEB) has the form (Z_1 = 25 for Mn, Z_2 = 26 for Fe):

$$(Z_1-7)[MnO_4^{-1}] + (Z_1-6)[MnO_4^{-2}] + (Z_1-3)([Mn^{+3}] + [MnOH^{+2}] + \gamma_1[MnSO_4^{+1}] + \gamma_2[Mn(SO_4)_2^{-1}]) + (Z_1-2)([Mn^{+2}] + [MnOH^{+1}] + [MnSO_4]) + (Z_2-2)([Fe^{+2}] + [FeOH^{+1}] + [FeSO_4] + (Z_2-3)([Fe^{+3}] + [FeOH^{+2}] + [Fe(OH)_2^{+1}] + 2[Fe_2(OH)_2^{+4}] + [FeSO_4^{+1}] + [Fe(SO_4)_2^{-1}]) - ((Z_2-2)C_0V_0 + (Z_1-7)CV)/(V_0+V) = 0 \qquad (8)$$

The symbols: γ_1 and γ_2 in (8) are referred to the pre-assumed sulphate complexes (see Fig. 18A); γ_1 = 1, γ_2 = 0 if only $MnSO_4^{+1}$ is pre-assumed, and $\gamma_1 = \gamma_2 = 1$ if both ($MnSO_4^{+1}$ and $Mn(SO_4)_2^{-1}$) complexes be pre-assumed.

5.2.2 $KIO_3+HCl+H_2SeO_3(+HgCl_2)$+ ascorbic acid

An interesting/spectacular example is the titration of V_0 mL of D containing KIO_3 (C_0 mol/L) + HCl (C_a mol/L) + H_2SeO_3 (C_{Se} mol/L) + $HgCl_2$ (C_{Hg} mol/L) with V mL of C mol/L ascorbic acid ($C_6H_8O_6$) as T. For example, the electron balance (GEB) referred to this system can be written as follows (Michałowski, 2010):

$$(Z_1+1)[I^{-1}]+(3Z_1+1)[I_3^-]+2Z_1([I_2]+\alpha\cdot[\mathbf{I_2}])+(Z_1-1)([HIO]+[IO^{-1}])+(Z_1-5)([HIO_3]+[IO_3^{-1}])+ (Z_1-7)([H_5IO_6]+[H_4IO_6^{-1}]+[H_3IO_6^{-2}])+(Z_2-2)([Hg^{+2}]+[HgOH^{+1}]+[Hg(OH)_2])+ (Z_2-2+Z_1+1)[HgI^{+1}]+(Z_2-2+2(Z_1+1))[HgI_2]+(Z_2-2+3(Z_1+1))[HgI_3^{-1}]+ (Z_2-2+4(Z_1+1))[HgI_4^{-2}]+2\gamma\cdot(Z_2-1)([Hg_2^{+2}]+[Hg_2OH^{+1}])+Z_3([C_6H_8O_6]+[C_6H_7O_6^{-1}]+ [C_6H_6O_6^{-2}])+(Z_3-2)[C_6H_6O_6]+(Z_4+1)[Cl^{-1}]+2Z_4[Cl_2]+(Z_4-1)([HClO]+[ClO^{-1}])+ (Z_4-3)([HClO_2]+[ClO_2^{-1}])+(Z_4-4)[ClO_2]+(Z_4-5)[ClO_3^{-1}]+(Z_4-7)[ClO_4^{-1}]+ (Z_1+Z_4)[ICl]+(Z_1+2(Z_4+1))[ICl_2^{-1}]+(2Z_1+Z_4+1)[I_2Cl^{-1}]+(Z_2-2+Z_4+1)[HgCl^{+1}]+ (Z_2-2+2(Z_4+1))[HgCl_2]+(Z_2-2+3(Z_4+1))[HgCl_3^{-1}]+(Z_2-2+4(Z_4+1))[HgCl_4^{-2}]+ (Z_5-4)\{[H_2SeO_3]+[HSeO_3^{-1}]+[SeO_3^{-2}])+\beta\cdot(Z_5-6)([HSeO_4^{-1}]+[SeO_4^{-2}])- ((Z_1-5)C_0V_0+\gamma(Z_2-2+2(Z_4+1))C_{Hg}V_0+Z_3CV+(Z_4+1)C_aV_0+\beta(Z_5-4)C_{Se}V_0)/(V_0+V)=0 \qquad (9)$$

where Z_1, Z_2, Z_4, Z_5 are atomic numbers for I, Hg, Cl and Se, respectively; Z_3 is the number ascribed to ascorbic acid. The following terms were introduced in there:

- α = 1, valid under assumption that solid iodine (**I_2**) is present in the system considered; α = 0, for a system not saturated against solid iodine (I_2 refers to soluble form of iodine);
- β = 1 refers to the case, where Se(VI) species were involved; at β = 0, the Se(VI) species are omitted;
- γ = 1 refers to the case, where Hg(I) species were involved; at γ = 0, the Hg(I) species are omitted.

6. Charge and concentration balances

The set of balances referred to non-redox systems consists of charge and concentration balances. For redox systems, this set is supplemented by electron balance (GEB). For example, the charge and concentration balances referred to C mol/L Br_2 (see section 5.1.2)

$$[H^{+1}]-[OH^{-1}]-[BrO_3^{-1}]-[BrO^{-1}]-[Br_3^{-1}]-[Br^{-1}]=0 \quad (10)$$

$$[HBrO_3] + [BrO_3^{-1}] + [HBrO] + [BrO^{-1}] + 2[Br_2] + 3[Br_3^{-1}] + [Br^{-1}] = 2C \quad (11)$$

are supplemented by Eq. (7), i.e. (7), (10) and (11) form the complete set of balances related to aqueous solution of Br_2 (C mol/L).

Charge and concentration balances referred to the systems 5.2.1 and 5.2.2 are specified in (Michałowski and Lesiak, 1994b, Michałowski et al., 1996) and (Michałowski and Lesiak, 1994b, Michałowski, 2010), respectively. For example, the species involved in the system 5.2.2 enter s+2 = 7 balances: GEB, charge balance, and five concentration balances; K^{+1} ions, as a sole potassium species in this system, enters simply the related charge balance, i.e. concentration balance for K^{+1} is not formulated. Generally, concentration balances are not formulated for the species not participating other (acid-base, complexation, precipitation or redox) equilibria in the system considered.

7. Equilibrium constants

Different species in the system are interrelated in expressions for the corresponding equilibrium constants, e.g., ionic product of water, dissociation constants (for acidic species), stability constants of complexes, solubility products, standard potentials (E_{0i}) for redox reactions, partition constants in liquid-liquid extraction systems. Except E_{0i}, all equilibrium constants are formulated immediately on the basis of mass action law.

The redox systems are completed by relations for standard potentials (E_{0i}), formulated on the basis of the Nernst equation for potential E, referred to i-th redox reaction notation, written in the form $... + z_i e^{-1} = ...$, where $z_i > 0$ is the number of electrons (e^{-1}) participating this reaction. First, the equilibrium constant (K_{ei}) for the redox reaction is formulated on the basis of mass action law and then the relations:

$$K_{ei} = 10^{z_i \cdot E_{0i}/S} \quad \text{and} \quad [e^{-1}] = 10^{-E/S} \quad (12)$$

are applied, where S = $RT/F \cdot \ln 10$, and T, R, F are as ones in the Nernst equation. Both types of constraints, i.e. balances and the expressions for equilibrium constants, are of algebraic nature. It enables to consider the relations as common algebraic equations, nonlinear in their nature.

In order to avoid inconsistency between the equilibrium constants values found in literature, the set of independent equilibrium constants is required. One should also be noted that some species are presented differently, see e.g., pairs: AlO_2^{-1} and $Al(OH)_4^{-1}$; $H_2BO_3^{-1}$ and $B(OH)_4^{-1}$; IO_4^{-1} and $H_4IO_6^{-1}$, differing in the number of water molecules involved. The species compared here should be perceived as identical ones and then cannot enter the related balances, side by side, as independent species.

The balances and complete set of interrelations resulting from expressions for independent equilibrium constants are the basis for calculations made according to an iterative computer program, e.g., MATLAB. The results thus obtained can be presented graphically, at any pre-assumed system of coordinates, in 2D or 3D space.

The procedure involved with the terms β and γ expresses the principle of "variation on the subject" applied to the system in question. The system considered in 5.2.2 is described with use of the set of 36 independent equilibrium constants in the basic version, i.e. at $\beta=\gamma=0$. More equilibrium data are involved, if some "variations on the subject" be done, i.e. when some reaction paths are liberated. In the "variations" of this kind, further physicochemical data are applied (see section 11.2).

8. Calculation procedure

The balances, related to a dynamic system and realised according to titrimetric mode, can be written as a set of algebraic equations

$$F_k(\mathbf{x}(V))=0 \tag{13}$$

where $\mathbf{x}(V) = [x_1(V), \dots , x_n(V)]^T$ is the vector of basic (independent, fundamental) variables $x_i = x_i(V)$ (scalars) related to a particular V–value, i.e. volume of titrant added. The number (n) of variables is equal to the number of the balances. At defined V–value, only one vector, $\mathbf{x} = \mathbf{x}(V)$, exists that turns the set of algebraic expressions $F_k(\mathbf{x}(V))$ to zero, i.e. $F_k(\mathbf{x}(V)) = 0$ (k=1,...,n) and zeroes the sum of squares

$$SS(V)=\sum_{k=1}^{n}(F_k(\mathbf{x}(V)))^2=0 \tag{14}$$

for any V–value. If $\mathbf{x}_s(V)$ is the vector referred to starting (s) values for basic variables related to a particular V–value, then one can expect that $\mathbf{x}_s(V) \neq \mathbf{x}(V)$ and

$$SS(V)=\sum_{k=1}^{n}(F_k(\mathbf{x}_s(V)))^2>0 \tag{15}$$

The searching of $\mathbf{x}(V)$ vector values related to different V, where $F_k(\mathbf{x}(V)) = 0$ (k=1,...,n), is made according to iterative computer programs, e.g., MATLAB. The searching procedure satisfies the requirements put on optimal $\mathbf{x}(V)$ values, provided that SS value (Eq. 15) is lower than a pre–assumed, sufficiently low positive δ–value, $\delta>0$, e.g., $\delta = 10^{-14}$. i.e.

$$SS(V)=\sum_{k=1}^{n}(F_k(\mathbf{x}(V)))^2<\delta$$

However, the iterative computer programs are (generally) designed for the curve-fitting procedures where the degree of fitting a curve to experimental points is finite. In this case, the criterion of optimisation is based on differences SS(V,N+1) – SS(V,N) between two successive (Nth and N+1th) approximations of SS(V)–value, i.e.

$$|SS(V,N+1)-SS(V,N)|<\delta \tag{16}$$

at a sufficiently low δ–value. However, one should take into account that the inequality (16) can be fulfilled at local minimum different from the global minimum. It can happen if the starting values $\mathbf{x}_s(V)$ are too distant from the true value $\mathbf{x}(V)$ where the equality (14) is fulfilled. In this case, one should try (repeat) the calculations for new $\mathbf{x}_s(V)$ values guessed.

The choice of δ–value depends on the scale of analytical concentrations considered. To 'equalise' the requirements put on particular balances, it is advised to apply 'normalised' balances, obtained by dividing the related balance by total (analytical) concentration involved in this balance.

In all simulated titrations considered below, the following regularities are complied:

1. The independent variables $x_i = x_i(V)$ are introduced as the (negative) powers of 10 (as the base number);

For any [X] > 0 one can write $[X] \equiv 10^{\log[X]} = 10^{-pX}$, where pX = – log[X]. One should be noted that [X] > 0 for any real pX value, $pX \in \Re$. It particularly refers to protons ($X = H^+$) and electrons (Eq. 12). Such choice of the basic variables improves the course of iteration procedure.

2. The changes in the system are made according to titrimetric mode, with volume V taken as the steering variable.
3. It is advisable to refer the fundamental variables to the species whose concentrations predominate at the start for calculations.

The minimizing procedure starts at the V–value, $V = V_s$, that appears to be 'comfortable' from the user's viewpoint, where the starting $\mathbf{x}_s(V)$ values are guessed. Then the optimisation is realised, with negative step put on the V–variable, up to V = V(begin) close to zero value. The possible changes in the phase composition during the iteration procedure should also be taken into account. It particularly refers to formation/disappearance of a solid phase(s) or a change in equilibrium solid phase; the latter problem is raised in section 12. For this purpose, the expressions identical with the forms of the corresponding solubility products should be 'peered' during the simulated procedure. In the system considered in section 5.2.2, the solid iodine, $\mathbf{I_2}$, is formed within defined V-range.

The results thus obtained enable to calculate all variables of interest. It refers both to fundamental variables such as E, pH and concentrations, and other concentrations of interest. For example, the Br_2 + H_2O (batch) system is described by three balances: (7), (10), (11). In this case, one can choose three fundamental variables: pH, E and pBr, involved with concentrations and referred to negative powers of the base 10: $[H^{+1}] = 10^{-pH}$, $[e^{-1}] = 10^{-E/S}$ (Eq. 12), $[Br^{-1}] = 10^{-pBr}$. Three independent variables involved in three balances give here a unique solution for (x_1, x_2, x_3) = (pH, E, pBr), at a pre-assumed C value (Eq. 11). On this basis, one can calculate concentrations of all other species, e.g.:

$$[BrO_3^{-1}]=10^{6A(E-1.45)+6pH-pBr};[Br_2]=10^{2A(E-1.087)-2pBr} \tag{17}$$

where the fundamental variables are involved; A = 1/S (Eq. 12).

In a simulated titration, as a representation of dynamic system, the set of parameters involve: volume V_0 of D and concentrations of reagents in D and T. Volume V of T is a steering variable/parameter value, at a given point of the titration.
The results of calculations provide the basis for graphical presentation of the data, in 2D or 3D space, that appears to be very useful, particularly in the case of the titrations. The curves for concentrations of different species X_j as a function of volume V are named as speciation curves, plotted usually in semi-logarithmic scale, as the $\log[X_j]$ vs. V relationships. For comparative purposes, it is better to graph the plots as the function of the fraction titrated

$$\Phi = \frac{C \cdot V}{C_0 \cdot V_0} \tag{18}$$

where C_0 is the concentration [mol/L] of analyte A in D of initial volume V_0, V is the volume [mL] of T added up to a given point of titration, C [mol/L] - concentration of a reagent B (towards A) in T; e.g., for the D+T system presented in section 5.2.2 we have: A = IO_3^{-1}, B = $C_6H_8O_6$. The course of the plots E = E(V) and/or pH = pH(V) (or, alternately, pH = pH(Φ) and/or E = E(Φ)) is the basis to indicate the equivalence point(s) according to GEM (Michałowski et al., 2010), with none relevance to the chemical reaction notation.
The plots pH = pH(V) and/or E = E(V) can also be obtained experimentally, in potentiometric (pH or E) titrations. Comparing the experimental plots with the related curves obtained in simulated titrations, (a) one can check the validity of physicochemical data applied in calculations, and (b) to do some "variations on the subject" involved with reaction pathways and/or incomplete/doubtful physicochemical data.

9. Graphical presentation of the data referred to redox systems

9.1 Aqueous solutions of Br_2 (batch system)

The properties of aqueous bromine (Br_2, C mol/L) solutions, considered as a weak acid, are presented in Figures 3a-d, for different C values (Eq. (11)). As wee see, E decreases (Fig. 3a) and pH increases with decrease in C value. The pH vs. E relationship is nearly linear in the indicated C-range (Fig. 3c). The Br_2 exists as the predominating bromine species at higher C values (Fig. 3d); it corresponds with the speciation plots presented in Fig. 4.

9.2 Examples of redox titration curves

9.2.1 Titration in Br_2+NaOHandHBrO+NaOHsystems

As a result of NaOH addition into the solution of (a) Br_2, (b) HBrO, acid-base and redox reactions proceed simultaneously; a decrease in E is accompanied by pH growth, and significant changes in E and pH at equivalence/stoichiometric points occur, see Figs. 5a,b. Both titrations are involved with disproportionation reactions, formulated on the basis of speciation curves (Fig. 6). From comparison of ordinates at an excess of NaOH we have $\log[BrO_3^{-1}] - \log[BrO^{-1}] \approx 4$; i.e. $[BrO_3^{-1}]/[BrO^{-1}] \approx 10^4$, and then the effectiveness of reaction

$$3Br_2 + 6OH^{-1} = BrO_3^{-1} + 5Br^{-1} + 3H_2O \tag{19}$$

exceeds the effectiveness of reaction

$$Br_2 + 2OH^{-1} = BrO^{-1} + Br^{-1} + H_2O$$

by about 10^4. Note that the stoichiometries of both reactions are the same, 3 : 6 = 1 : 2. Concentration of Br^{-1} ions, formed mainly in reaction (19), exceeds $[BrO_3^{-1}]$ by 5, at higher pH values.

9.2.2 Titration in I_2+NaOH system

The iodine speciation curves related to titration of V_0 = 100 mL of D containing iodine (I_2, 0.01 mol/L) with V mL of C = 0.1 mol/L NaOH are presented in Fig. 7. Owing to limited solubility of iodine in water, at V = 0, a part of iodine remains as a solid phase, s < C_0. This two-phase system exists up to V = 11.2 mL; for V > 11.2 mL we have $[\mathbf{I_{2s}}] = 0$. In the course of further titration, concentration $[I_2]$ of dissolved iodine decreases as the result of advancing disproportionation. After crossing the stoichiometric point, i.e. at an excess of NaOH added, the main disproportionation products are: IO_3^{-1} and I^{-1}, formed in the reaction

$$3I_2 + 6\,OH^{-1} = IO_3^{-1} + 5I^{-1} + 3H_2O \qquad (20)$$

From Fig. 6 it results that, at an excess of NaOH added, the effectiveness of reaction (20) exceeds the one for reaction

$$I_2 + 2\,OH^{-1} = IO^{-1} + I^{-1} + H_2O$$

by about $2.5\cdot10^9$. The E = E(V) and pH = pH(V) curves related to titration of iodine (I_2) in presence/absence of KI in D with NaOH admixtured (or not admixtured) with CO_2 as T are presented in Figures (5) and (6). The titration curves related to liquid-liquid extraction systems (H_2O+CCl_4) were considered in (Michałowski, 1994a).

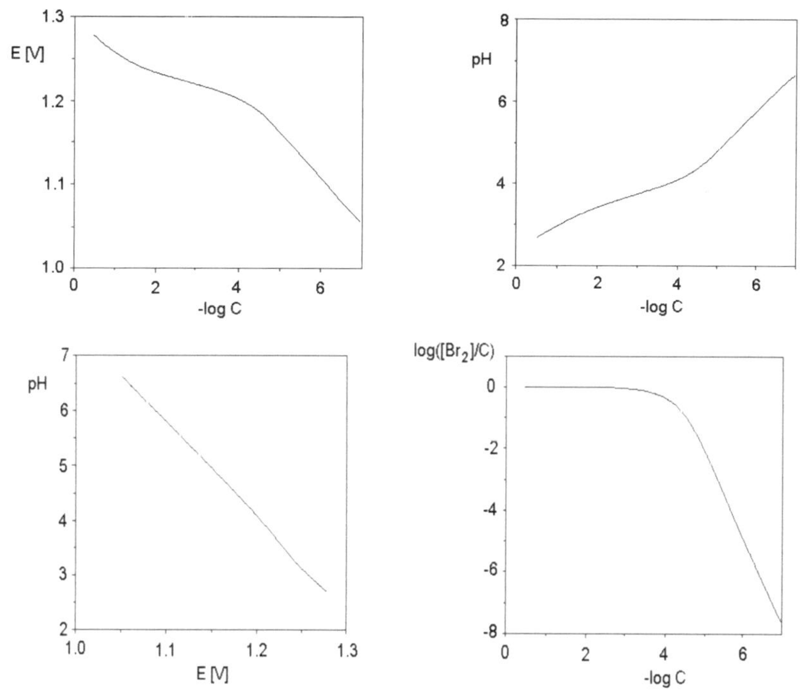

Fig. 3. The curves involved with C mol/L Br_2 solutions in pure water, plotted at the coordinates indicated [4].

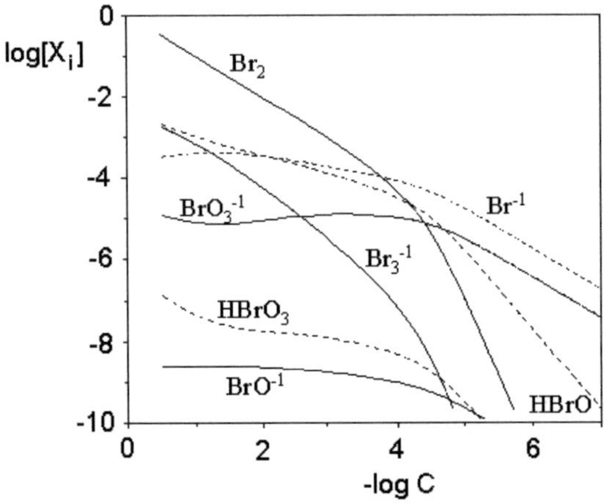

Fig. 4. Concentrations of (indicated) bromine species at different –logC values for C mol/L Br_2.

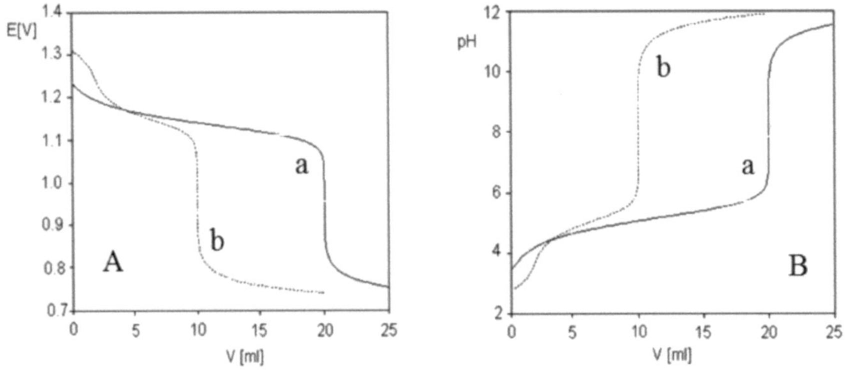

Fig. 5. Theoretical titration curves for: (A) E = E(V) and (B) pH = pH(V), at V_0 = 100 mL of C_0 = 0.01 mol/L (a) Br_2, (b) HBrO titrated with V mL of C = 0.1 mol/L NaOH.

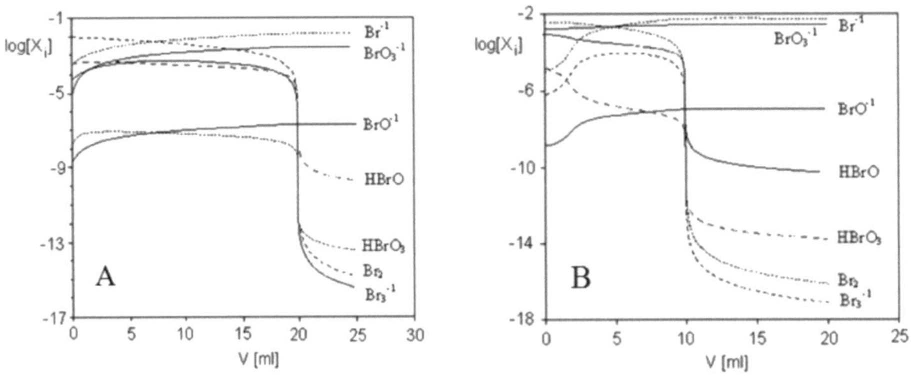

Fig. 6. Speciation of bromine species during titration of V_0 = 100 mL of C_0 = 0.01 mol/L (A) Br_2, (B) HBrO titrated with V mL of C = 0.1 mol/L NaOH.

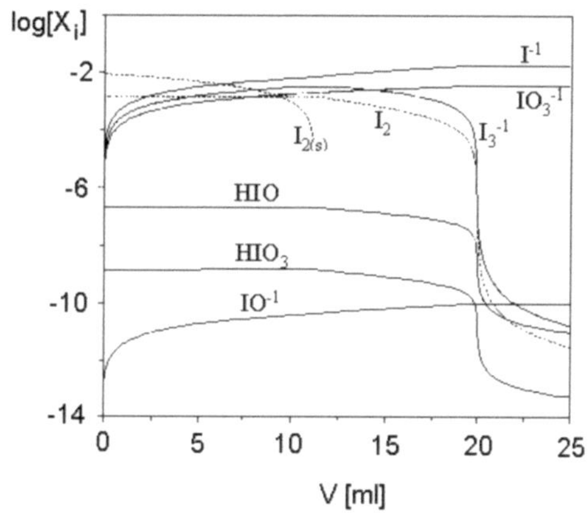

Fig. 7. The speciation curves plotted for I_2 + NaOH system.

9.2.3 Titration of KIO_3+KI+H_2SO_4 with $Na_2S_2O_3$

The pH changes can result from addition of a reagent that - apparently - does not appear, at first sight, acid-base properties. Rather unexpectedly, at first sight, $Na_2S_2O_3$ solution acts on the acidified (H_2SO_4) solution of KIO_3 (or KIO_3 + KI) as a strong base (like NaOH) see Fig. 8A,B (Michałowski, et al., 1996; Michałowski, et al., 2005). This reaction, known also from qualitative chemical analysis, can be derived from the related speciation plots as

$$IO_3^{-1} + 6S_2O_3^{-2} + 3H_2O = I^{-1} + 3S_4O_6^{-2} + 6OH^{-1}$$

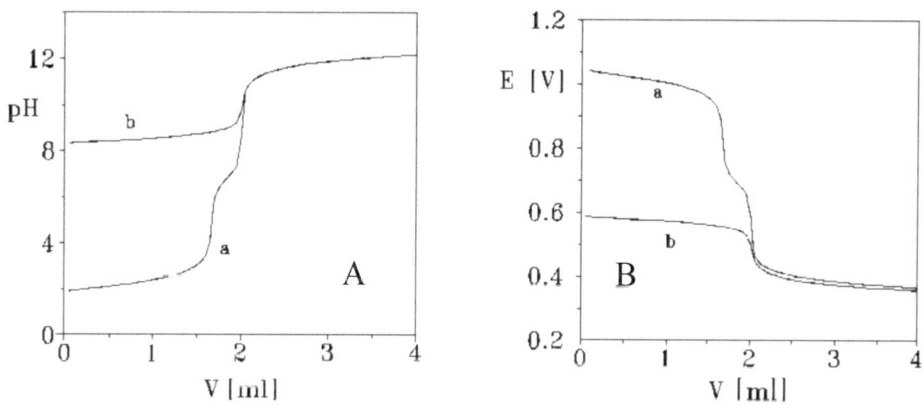

Fig. 8. Theoretical (A) pH vs. V, (B) E vs. V relationships for titration of V_0 = 100 mL of KIO_3 (0.05 mol/L) + KI (C_I mol/L) + H_2SO_4 (0.01 mol/L) as D with $Na_2S_2O_3$ (0.1 mol/L) as T, plotted at C_I = 0.1 mol/L (curve a) and C_I = 0 (curve b).

9.2.4 Titration of $FeSO_4$ + H_2SO_4 with $KMnO_4$

The plots related to the system where V_0 = 100 mL of $FeSO_4$ (C_0 = 0.01 mol/L) + H_2SO_4 (C_a = 1.0 mol/L) is titrated with V mL of C = 0.02 mol/L $KMnO_4$ are presented in Fig. 9. It was assumed there that the complexes $MnSO_4^{+1}$ and $Mn(SO_4)_2^{-1}$ are not formed in the system; i.e. $\gamma_1 = \gamma_2 = 0$ in Eq. (8) and in the related concentration balances for Fe, Mn and S.

Fig. 9A indicates the effect resulting from complexation of Fe^{+3} and Fe^{+2} by SO_4^{-2} ions; the course of titration curve a differs significantly from the curve b, where complexes $FeSO_4$, $FeSO_4^{+1}$, $Fe(SO_4)_2^{-1}$ and $MnSO_4$ were omitted in the related balances. The pH change in this system (Fig. 9B) results mainly from consumption of protons in reaction $MnO_4^{-1} + 8H^{+1} + 5e^{-1} = Mn^{+2} + 4H_2O$. Namely, MnO_4^{-1} acts also in acid-base reaction, in multiplied extent when compared with a strong base action, like "octopus" (Michałowski, et al., 2005). Greater pH changes in this system are protected by presence of great excess of H_2SO_4 that acts as buffering agent and acts against formation of solid **MnO_2** in reaction $MnO_4^{-1} + 4H^{+1} + 3e^{-1} =$ **MnO_2** $+ 2H_2O$. The species X_i are indicated at the corresponding dynamic speciation curves plotted in Figures 9C,D.

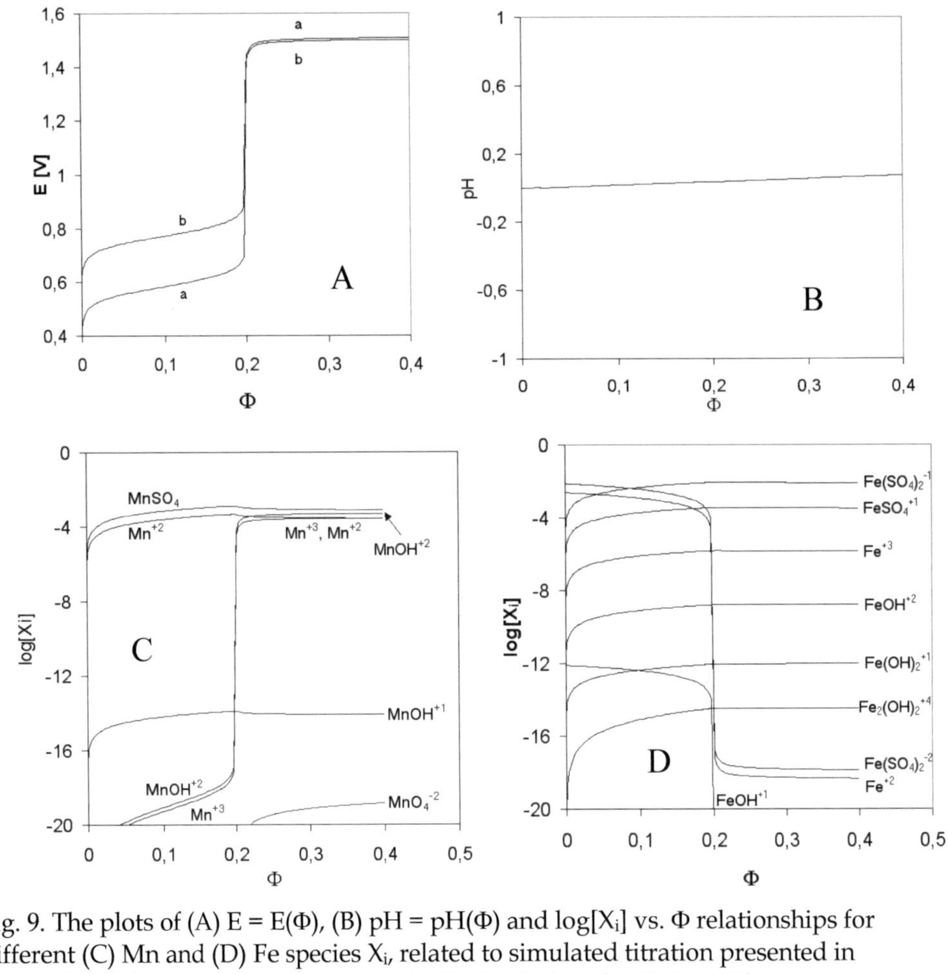

Fig. 9. The plots of (A) $E = E(\Phi)$, (B) $pH = pH(\Phi)$ and $\log[X_i]$ vs. Φ relationships for different (C) Mn and (D) Fe species X_i, related to simulated titration presented in section 9.2.4. (Michałowski and Lesiak, 1994b; Michałowski, 2001, 2010)

9.2.5 Titration of KIO_3+HCl+H_2SeO_3(+$HgCl_2$)with ascorbic acid

In common redox titrations, two or more elements, represented by different species, can participate redox equilibria. An interesting/spectacular example is the titration of V_0 mL of

D containing KIO_3 (C_0 = 0.01mol/L) + HCl (C_a = 0.02 mol/L) + H_2SeO_3 (C_{Se} = 0.02 mol/L) + $HgCl_2$ (C_{Hg} mol/L) with V mL of C mol/L ascorbic acid ($C_6H_8O_6$) as T, considered e.g., in (Michałowski and Lesiak, 1994b; Michałowski, 2001, 2010). From Fig. 10A,B we see that the presence of $HgCl_2$ in D transforms the curve a into curve b.

Moreover, Fig. 10b provides (rarely met) example, where pH of the D+T system passes through maximum; such a case was stated first time in (Michałowski and Lesiak, 1994b). The extreme pH values of the curves a and b in Fig. 10B correspond to the points of maximal drop on the curves a and b in Fig.10A. The non-monotonic shapes of pH vs. Φ relationships were also stated e.g., for D+T systems with VSO_4 in acidic (H_2SO_4) media titrated with $KMnO_4$ or $K_2Cr_2O_7$ (Michałowski and Lesiak, 1994b), KI titrated with chlorine water (Michalowski, et al., 1996).

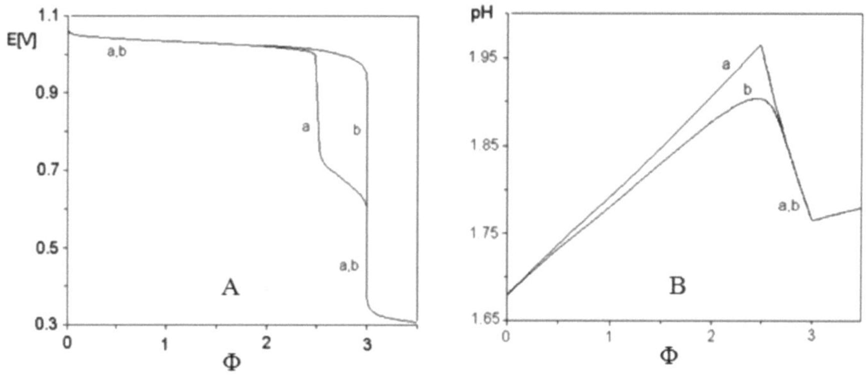

Fig. 10. The plots of: (A) E = E(Φ) and (B) pH = pH(Φ) relationships for D+T system specified in section 9.2.5, referred to absence (curve a) and presence (C_{Hg} = 0.07 mol/L, curve b) of $HgCl_2$ in D.

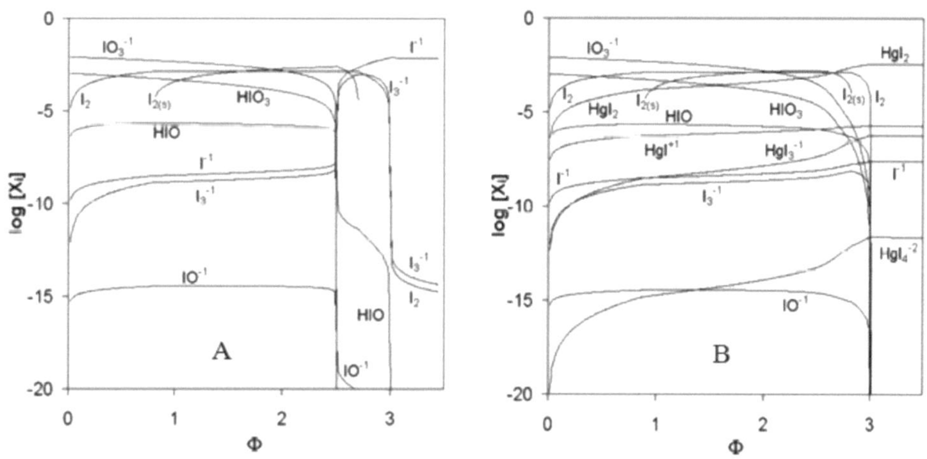

Fig. 11. The plots of speciation curves for different iodine species at C_0 = 0.01, C_a = 0.02, C_{Se} = 0.02, and C_{Hg} = 0 (in Fig. A) or C_{Hg} = 0.07 (in Fig. B); $\mathbf{I}_{2(s)}$ and I_2 – solid and soluble iodine species.

The speciation curves for iodine species in this system are presented in Fig. 11A,B. Among others, on this basis one can state that the growth in pH on the curve a in Fig. 11B within $\Phi \in$ <0, 2.5> can be explained by the set of reactions:

$$2IO_3^{-1}+5C_6H_8O_6+2H^{+1}=\mathbf{I_2}+5C_6H_6O_6+6H_2O$$

$$2IO_3^{-1}+5C_6H_8O_6+2H^{+1}=I_2+5C_6H_6O_6+6H_2O$$

$$2IO_3^{-1}+5C_6H_8O_6+2H^{+1}+I^{-1}=I_3^{-1}+5C_6H_6O_6+6H_2O$$

where protons are consumed. This inference results from the fact that within this Φ-interval a growth in concentration of I_2, $\mathbf{I_2}$ i I_3^{-1}, and decrease in concentration of IO_3^{-1} occur; in this respect, the main components are considered.

10. GATES as a tool for description of multi-step procedure and validation of physicochemical data

This section provides the detailed description of the complex procedure referred to iodometric determination of cupric ions. According to the procedure applied in this method, acidic (H_2SO_4) solution of $CuSO_4$ is neutralized first with NH_3 solution until the blue colour of the solution, resulting from presence of $Cu(NH_3)_i^{+2}$ species, is attained. Then acetic acid is added in excess, to secure pH ca. 3.5. The resulting solution is treated with an excess of KI, forming the precipitate of **CuI**:

$$2Cu^{+2}+4I^{-1}=2\mathbf{CuI}+\mathbf{I_2};2Cu^{+2}+4I^{-1}=2\mathbf{CuI}+I_2;2Cu^{+2}+5I^{-1}=2\mathbf{CuI}+I_3^{-1}$$

At a due excess of KI, $\mathbf{I_2}$ is not formed. The mixture (D) thus obtained is titrated with sodium thiosulphate solution as T:

$$I_2+2S_2O_3^{-2}=2I^{-1}+S_4O_6^{-2};I_3^{-1}+2S_2O_3^{-2}=3I^{-1}+S_4O_6^{-2}$$

Let us assume that V_0 = 100 ml of the solution containing $CuSO_4$ (C_0 = 0.01 mol/L), H_2SO_4 (C_a = 0.1 mol/L), NH_3 (C_N = 0.25 mol/L) and CH_3COOH (C_{Ac} = 0.75 mol/L), be treated with V_1 = 5.8 mL of C_I = 2.0 mol/L KI and then titrated with V ml of C = 0.1 mol/L $Na_2S_2O_3$.
On the first stage (Fig.12), we apply the following balances, $F_i = F_i(\mathbf{x}(V)) = 0$ (c^o – current concentration of **CuI**):

$$F_1=c^o+[Cu^{+1}]+[CuNH_3^{+1}]+[Cu(NH_3)_2^{+1}]+[CuI_2^{-1}]+[Cu^{+2}]+[CuOH^{+1}]+[Cu(OH)_2]+ [Cu(OH)_3^{-1}]+[Cu(OH)_4^{-2}]+[CuSO_4]+[CuIO_3^{+1}]+[CuNH_3^{+2}]+[Cu(NH_3)_2^{+2}]+ [Cu(NH_3)_3^{+2}]+[Cu(NH_3)_4^{+2}]+[CuCH_3COO^{+1}]+[Cu(CH_3COO)_2]-C_0V_0/(V_0+V)=0 \quad (21)$$

$$F_2=c^o+[I^{-1}]+2([I_2]+\alpha\cdot[\mathbf{I_2}])+3[I_3^{-1}]+[HIO]+[IO^{-1}]+[HIO_3]+[IO_3^{-1}]+ [H_5IO_6]+[H_4IO_6^{-1}]+[H_3IO_6^{-2}]+2[CuI_2^{-1}]+[CuIO_3^{+1}]-C_IV/(V_0+V)=0 \quad (22)$$

$$F_3=[HSO_4^{-1}]+[SO_4^{-2}]+[CuSO_4]-(C_0+C_a)V_0/(V_0+V)=0 \quad (23)$$

$$F_4=[NH_4^{+1}]+[NH_3]+[CuNH_3^{+1}]+2[Cu(NH_3)_2^{+1}]+[CuNH_3^{+2}]+2[Cu(NH_3)_2^{+2}]+ 3[Cu(NH_3)_3^{+2}]+4[Cu(NH_3)_4^{+2}]-C_NV_0/(V_0+V)=0 \quad (24)$$

$$F_5=[CH_3COOH]+[CH_3COO^{-1}]+[CuCH_3COO^{+1}]+2[Cu(CH_3COO)_2]-C_{Ac}V_0/(V_0+V)=0 \quad (25)$$

$$F_6=[H^{+1}]-[OH^{-1}]+[Cu^{+1}]-[CuI_2^{-1}]+2[Cu^{+2}]+[CuOH^{+1}]-[Cu(OH)_3^{-1}]-2[Cu(OH)_4^{-2}]+[CuIO_3^{+1}]-[I^{-1}]-[I_3^{-1}]-[IO^{-1}]-[IO_3^{-1}]-[H_4IO_6^{-1}]-2[H_3IO_6^{-2}]-[HSO_4^{-1}]-2[SO_4^{-2}]+[CuNH_3^{+1}]+[Cu(NH_3)_2^{+1}]+2[CuNH_3^{+2}]+2[Cu(NH_3)_2^{+2}]+2[Cu(NH_3)_3^{+2}]+2[Cu(NH_3)_4^{+2}]+[CuCH_3COO^{+1}]+C_IV/(V_0+V)-[CH_3COO^{-1}]+[NH_4^{+1}]=0 \quad (26)$$

$$F_7=(Z_1-1+Z_2+1)c^o+(Z_1-1)([Cu^{+1}]+[CuNH_3^{+1}]+[Cu(NH_3)_2^{+1}])+(Z_1-1+2(Z_2+1))[CuI_2^{-1}]+(Z_1-2)([Cu^{+2}]+[CuOH^{+1}]+[Cu(OH)_2]+[Cu(OH)_3^{-1}]+[Cu(OH)_4^{-2}]+[CuSO_4]+[CuNH_3^{+2}]+[Cu(NH_3)_2^{+2}]+[Cu(NH_3)_3^{+2}]+[Cu(NH_3)_4^{+2}]+[CuCH_3COO^{+1}]+[Cu(CH_3COO)_2])+(Z_1-2+Z_2-5)[CuIO_3^{+1}](Z_2+1)[I^{-1}]+(3Z_2+1)[I_3^{-1}]+2Z_2([I_2]+\alpha\cdot[\mathbf{I_2}])+(Z_2-1)([HIO]+[IO^{-1}])+(Z_2-5)([HIO_3]+[IO_3^{-1}])+(Z_2-7)([H_5IO_6]+[H_4IO_6^{-1}]+[H_3IO_6^{-2}])-((Z_1-2)C_0V_0+(Z_2+1)C_IV)/(V_0+V)=0 \quad (27)$$

where Z_1 = 29 for Cu, Z_2 = 53 for I. At high excess of I^{-1}, solid $\mathbf{I_2}$ is not formed, $\alpha = 0$ in (22) and (27).

Concentrations of different species in (22) - (27) are involved in the relations (A = 1/S, Eq. (12)):

$$\begin{aligned}
&[NH_4^{+1}] = 10^{9.35}\cdot[H^{+1}][NH_3],\\
&[CH_3COOH] = 10^{4.65}\cdot[H^{+1}][CH_3COO^{-1}],\\
&[CuOH^{+1}] = 10^{7}\cdot[Cu^{+2}][OH^{-1}],\\
&[Cu(OH)_2] = 10^{13.68}\cdot[Cu^{+2}][OH^{-1}]^2,\\
&[Cu(OH)_3^{-1}] = 10^{17}\cdot[Cu^{+2}][OH^{-1}]^3,\\
&[Cu(OH)_4^{-2}] = 10^{18.5}\cdot[Cu^{+2}][OH^{-1}]^4,\\
&[CuSO_4] = 10^{2.36}\cdot[Cu^{+2}][SO_4^{-2}],\\
&[CuIO_3^{+1}] = 10^{0.82}\cdot[Cu^{+2}][IO_3^{-1}],\\
&[CuI_2^{-1}] = 10^{8.85}\cdot[Cu^{+1}][I^{-1}]^2,\\
&[CuNH_3^{+2}] = 10^{3.39}\cdot[Cu^{+2}][NH_3],\\
&[Cu(NH_3)_2^{+2}] = 10^{7.33}\cdot[Cu^{+2}][NH_3]^2,\\
&[Cu(NH_3)_3^{+2}] = 10^{10.06}\cdot[Cu^{+2}][NH_3]^3,\\
&[Cu(NH_3)_4^{+2}] = 10^{12.03}\cdot[Cu^{+2}][NH_3]^4,\\
&[CuNH_3^{+1}] = 10^{5.93}\cdot[Cu^{+1}][NH_3],\\
&[Cu(NH_3)_2^{+1}] = 10^{10.86}\cdot[Cu^{+1}][NH_3]^2,\\
&[CuCH_3COO^{+1}] = 10^{2.24}\cdot[Cu^{+2}][CH_3COO^{-1}],\\
&[Cu(CH_3COO)_2] = 10^{3.3}\cdot[Cu^{+2}][CH_3COO^{-1}]^2,\\
&[I_2] = [I^{-1}]^2\cdot 10^{2A(E-0.62)},\\
&[I_3^{-1}] = [I^{-1}]^3\cdot 10^{2A(E-0.545)},\\
&[IO^{-1}] = [I^{-1}]\cdot 10^{2A(E-0.49)+2pH-28},\\
&[IO_3^{-1}] = [I^{-1}]\cdot 10^{6A(E-1.08)+6pH},\\
&[HIO] = 10^{10.6}\cdot[H^{+1}][IO^{-1}],\\
&[HIO_3] = 10^{0.79}\cdot[H^{+1}][IO_3^{-1}],\\
&[H_5IO_6] = [I^{-1}]\cdot 10^{8A(E-1.26)+7pH},\\
&[H_4IO_6^{-1}] = 10^{pH-3.3}\cdot[H_5IO_6],\\
&[H_3IO_6^{-2}] = [I^{-1}]\cdot 10^{8A(E-0.37)+9pH-126},\\
&[Cu^{+2}] = [Cu^{+1}]\cdot 10^{A(E-0.153)}
\end{aligned} \quad (28)$$

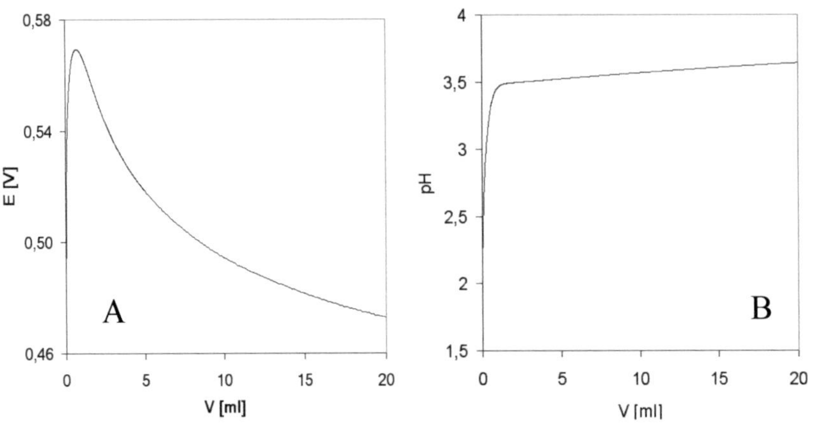

Fig. 12. The (A) E vs. V and (B) pH vs. V relationships during addition of 2.0 mol/L KI into $CuSO_4 + NH_3 + HAc$ system, plotted at $pK_{so} = 11.96$.

$$[Cu^{+1}][I^{-1}] = K_{so} \tag{29}$$

On the second stage, we take: $V = V_1$, $V_0' = V_0 + V_1 = 25 + 5.8 = 30.8$ mL, and apply the balances:

$$\begin{gathered}F_1=c^o+[Cu^{+1}]+[CuNH_3^{+1}]+[Cu(NH_3)_2^{+1}]+[CuI_2^{-1}]+[Cu^{+2}]+[CuOH^{+1}]+\\ [Cu(OH)_2]+[Cu(OH)_3^{-1}]+[Cu(OH)_4^{-2}]+[CuSO_4]+[CuIO_3^{+1}]+[CuNH_3^{+2}]+\\ [Cu(NH_3)_2^{+2}]+[Cu(NH_3)_3^{+2}]+[Cu(NH_3)_4^{+2}]+[CuCH_3COO^{+1}]+[Cu(CH_3COO)_2]+\\ [CuS_2O_3^{-1}]+[Cu(S_2O_3)_2^{-3}]+[Cu(S_2O_3)_3^{-5}]-C_0V_0/(V_0'+V)=0\end{gathered} \tag{30}$$

$$\begin{gathered}F_2=c^o+[I^{-1}]+2([I_2]+\alpha\cdot[\mathbf{I_2}])+3[I_3^{-1}]+[HIO]+[IO^{-1}]+\\ [HIO_3]+[IO_3^{-1}]+[H_5IO_6]+[H_4IO_6^{-1}]+[H_3IO_6^{-2}]+\\ 2[CuI_2^{-1}]+[CuIO_3^{+1}]-C_IV_1/(V_0'+V)=0\end{gathered} \tag{31}$$

$$F_3=[HSO_4^{-1}]+[SO_4^{-2}]+[CuSO_4]-(C_0+C_a)V_0/(V_0'+V)=0 \tag{32}$$

$$\begin{gathered}F_4=[NH_4^{+1}]+[NH_3]+[CuNH_3^{+1}]+2[Cu(NH_3)_2^{+1}]+\\ [CuNH_3^{+2}]+2[Cu(NH_3)_2^{+2}]+3[Cu(NH_3)_3^{+2}]+\\ 4[Cu(NH_3)_4^{+2}]-C_NV_0/(V_0'+V)=0\end{gathered} \tag{33}$$

$$F_5=[CH_3COOH]+[CH_3COO^{-1}]+[CuCH_3COO^{+1}]+2[Cu(CH_3COO)_2]-C_{Ac}V_0/(V_0'+V)=0 \tag{34}$$

$$\begin{gathered}F_6=[H_2S_2O_3]+[HS_2O_3^{-1}]+[S_2O_3^{-2}]+2[S_4O_6^{-2}]+[CuS_2O_3^{-1}]+\\ 2[Cu(S_2O_3)_2^{-3}]+3[Cu(S_2O_3)_3^{-5}]-CV/(V_0'+V)=0\end{gathered} \tag{35}$$

$$\begin{gathered}F_7=[H^{+1}]-[OH^{-1}]+[Cu^{+1}]-[CuI_2^{-1}]+2[Cu^{+2}]+[CuOH^{+1}]-[Cu(OH)_3^{-1}]-\\ 2[Cu(OH)_4^{-2}]+[CuIO_3^{+1}]-[I^{-1}]-[I_3^{-1}]-[IO^{-1}]-[IO_3^{-1}]-[H_4IO_6^{-1}]-2[H_3IO_6^{-2}]-\\ [HSO_4^{-1}]-2[SO_4^{-2}]+[CuNH_3^{+1}]+[Cu(NH_3)_2^{+1}]+2[CuNH_3^{+2}]+2[Cu(NH_3)_2^{+2}]+\\ 2[Cu(NH_3)_3^{+2}]+2[Cu(NH_3)_4^{+2}]+[CuCH_3COO^{+1}]+C_IV_1/(V_0'+V)-\\ [CH_3COO^{-1}]+[NH_4^{+1}]+2CV/(V_0'+V)-[HS_2O_3^{-1}]-2[S_2O_3^{-2}]-\\ 2[S_4O_6^{-2}]-[CuS_2O_3^{-1}]-3[Cu(S_2O_3)_2^{-3}]-5[Cu(S_2O_3)_3^{-5}]=0\end{gathered} \tag{36}$$

$$\begin{gathered}
F_8=(Z_1-1+Z_2+1)c^o+(Z_1-1)([CuNH_3^{+1}]+[Cu(NH_3)_2^{+1}])+(Z_1-1+2(Z_2+1))[CuI_2^{-1}]+\\
(Z_1-2)([Cu^{+2}]+[CuOH^{+1}]+[Cu(OH)_2]+[Cu(OH)_3^{-1}]+[Cu(OH)_4^{-2}]\\
+[CuSO_4]+[CuNH_3^{+2}]+[Cu(NH_3)_2^{+2}]+[Cu(NH_3)_3^{+2}]+[Cu(NH_3)_4^{+2}]+\\
[CuCH_3COO^{+1}]+[Cu(CH_3COO)_2])+(Z_1-2+Z_2-5)[CuIO_3^{+1}]+(Z_2+1)[I^{-1}]+\\
(3Z_2+1)[I_3^{-1}]+2Z_2([I_2]+\alpha\cdot[\mathbf{I_2}])+(Z_2-1)([HIO]+[IO^{-1}])+(Z_2-5)([HIO_3]+[IO_3^{-1}])+\\
(Z_2-7)([H_5IO_6]+[H_4IO_6^{-1}]+[H_3IO_6^{-2}])+2(Z_3-2)([H_2S_2O_3]+[HS_2O_3^{-1}]+\\
[S_2O_3^{-2}])+4(Z_3-2.5)[S_4O_6^{-2}]+(Z_1-1+2(Z_3-2))[CuS_2O_3^{-1}]+\\
(Z_1-1+4(Z_3-2))[Cu(S_2O_3)_2^{-3}]+(Z_1-1+6(Z_3-2))[Cu(S_2O_3)_3^{-5}]-\\
((Z_1-2)C_0V_0+(Z_2+1)C_IV_1+2(Z_3-2)CV/(V_0'+V)=0
\end{gathered} \tag{37}$$

where $Z_3 = 16$ for S. The additional relationships are as follows:

$$\begin{gathered}
[H_2S_2O_3]=10^{2.32}\cdot[H^{+1}]^2[S_2O_3^{-2}],\\
[HS_2O_3^{-1}]=10^{1.72}\cdot[H^{+1}][S_2O_3^{-2}],\\
[CuS_2O_3^{-1}]=10^{10.3}\cdot[Cu^{+1}][S_2O_3^{-2}],\\
[Cu(S_2O_3)_2^{-3}]=10^{12.2}\cdot[Cu^{+1}][S_2O_3^{-2}]^2,\\
[Cu(S_2O_3)_3^{-5}]=10^{13.8}\cdot[Cu^{+1}][S_2O_3^{-2}]^3,\\
[S_4O_6^{-2}]=[S_2O_3^{-2}]^2\cdot 10^{2A(E-0.09)}
\end{gathered} \tag{38}$$

To perform the calculation, one should choose first the set of independent (fundamental) variables. On the first stage, one can choose the variables: $\mathbf{x} = \mathbf{x}(V) = (x_1,\ldots,x_7)$, where $x_i = x_i(V)$, involved in the relations:

$$\begin{gathered}
x_1=pH,\ x_2=E, x_3=-\log[I^{-1}],\ x_4=-\log c^o,\\
x_5=-\log[SO_4^{-2}],\ x_6=-\log[NH_4^{+1}],\ x_7=-\log[CH_3COO^{-1}]
\end{gathered} \tag{39}$$

On the second stage, this set should be supplemented by the new variable $x_8 = -\log[S_4O_6^{-2}]$, i.e. $\mathbf{x} = (x_1,\ldots,x_8)$.

From calculations it results that addition of KI solution (first stage) causes first a growth followed by a drop in potential value (Fig.12A). It is accompanied by a growth in pH-value (Fig.12B). On the stage of $Na_2S_2O_3$ titration, potential E drops significantly at the vicinity of $\Phi = 1$ (Fig.13A). It is accompanied by a slight growth in pH-value (Fig.13B). Fig.13A

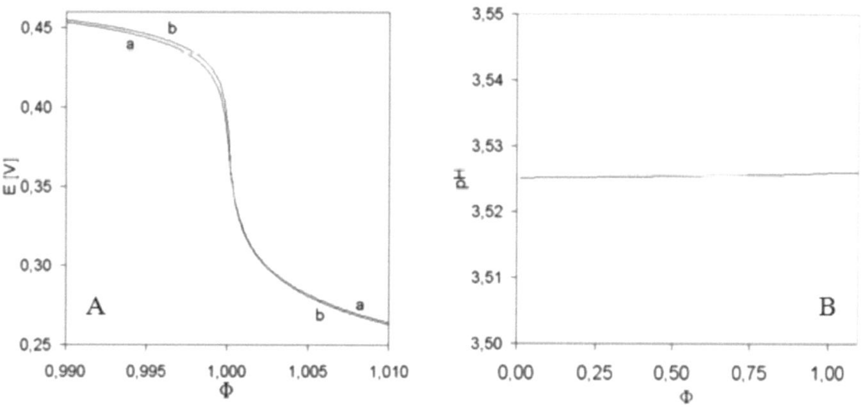

Fig. 13. The (A) E vs. Φ relationships plotted in close vicinity of $\Phi = 1$ at pK_{so} for **CuI** equal (a) 11.96, (b) 12.6 and (b); (B) pH vs. Φ relationship plotted at $pK_{so} = 11.96$.

indicates also a small difference between the plots of the related titration curves, calculated for two pK_{so} values: 11.96 and 12.6, found in literature. The speciation curves for some species on the stage of titration with $Na_2S_2O_3$ solution, are evidenced in Fig.14. One should be noticed that sulphate and thiosulfate species do not enter the same (elemental) balance, see Eqs. (32) and (35); the thiosulfate species are not oxidised by sulphate, i.e. the synproportionation reaction does not occur.

11. Other possibilities offered by GATES in area of redox systems

Potentiometric titration is a useful/sensitive method that enables, in context with the simulated data obtained according to GATES, to indicate different forbidden paths of chemical reactions. Simply, the shapes of $E = E(\Phi)$ and $pH = pH(\Phi)$ functions differ substantially at different assumptions presupposed in this respect. In order to confirm the metastable state according to GATES, one should omit all possible products forbidden by reaction barrier(s) in simulated calculations. Otherwise, one can release some reaction paths and check "what would happen" after inclusion of some species as the products obtained after virtual crossing the related reaction barriers. Such species are included into the balances and involved in the related equilibrium constants. This way one can also explain some phenomena observed during the titration or even … correct experimental data. Mere errors or inadvertences made in experimental titrations and on the step of graphical presentation of the results, can be indicated this way.

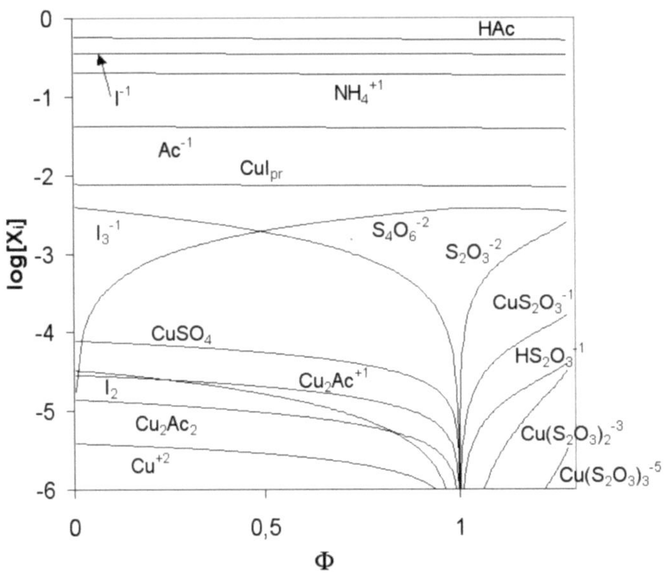

Fig. 14. The speciation curves plotted for titration of $CuSO_4 + NH_3 + HAc + KI$ with $Na_2S_2O_3$; $pK_{so} = 11.96$ for **CuI**; HAc = CH_3COOH.

11.1 GATES as a tool for correction/explanation of experimental data

The effect of $HgCl_2$ on the shape of titration curves $E = E(\Phi)$, referred to the system 9.2.5, was indicated in Fig. 10A. The shapes of those curves are in accordance with ones obtained experimentally. Namely, the curve in Fig. 15A is similar to the curve a in Fig. 10A, and the curve in Fig. 15B is similar to the curve b in Fig. 10A.

One can also notice some differences, however. First, the experimental data (potential E values, (1)) obtained in the system with calomel reference electrode were erroneously recalculated (2) when referred to normal hydrogen electrode (NHE scale) (Erdey, et al., 1951/2); simply, the potential of the calomel electrode was subtracted from (not added to) the experimental E-values. These errors were corrected in (Erdey and Svehla, 1973). The theoretical curves in Fig. 10A fall abruptly in the immediate vicinity of V = 0. Namely, E = 1.152 V at V = 0 for the curves a and b; at V = 0.01 mL, E equals 1.072 V for A and 1.068 V for B (in NHE scale). In this context one should be noted that the second experimental points in Figs. 15A,B, far distant from V = 0, are connected by a rounded line. One can also explain diffused indications in E values, registered in the middle part of the titration curve in Fig. 15A. After comparison with the speciation curves plotted in Figs. 11A,B, one can judge that these fluctuations can be accounted for kinetics of the solid iodine ($\mathbf{I_{2(s)}}$) precipitation/dissolution phenomena.

11.2 Testing the reaction paths

Referring again to the system 9.2.5, one can release some reaction paths, particularly the ones involved with oxidation of Se(IV)-species and reduction of Hg(II)-species. The paths are released by setting β = 1 or/and γ = 1 in Eq. (9), in charge balance and in concentration balances for Se and Hg. Inspection of the plots presented in Figures 16 and 17, and comparison with the plots in Fig. 10A,B leads to conclusion, that $\beta = \gamma = 0$ in the related balances, i.e. oxidation of Se(IV) and reduction of Hg(II) do not occur during the titration.

11.3 Validation of equilibrium data

Equilibrium data involved with electrolytic systems refer, among others, to stability constants of complexes and solubility products of precipitates. It results from the fact that the equilibrium data values attainable in literature are scattered or unknown.

Some doubts arise when some equilibrium data are unknown on the stage of collection of equilibrium data (Fig. 1). One can also check up the effect involved with omission of some types of complexes.

For example, the curve b plotted in Fig. 9A refers to omission of sulphate complexes in the related balances, referred to the system 9.2.4. The comparison of the corresponding plots provides some doubts related to the oversimplified approach applied frequently in literature. In this system, there were some doubts referred to possible *a priori* complexes of $Mn(SO_4)_i^{+3-2i}$ type; the related stability constants are unknown in literature. To check it, the calculations were made at different stability constants values, K_{3i}, pre-assumed for this purpose, $[Mn(SO_4)_i^{+3-2i}] = K_{3i}[Mn^{+3}][SO_4^{-2}]^i$. From Fig. 18 we see that, at higher K_{3i} values (comparable to ones related to $Fe(SO_4)_i^{+3-2i}$ complexes), the new inflection points appears at Φ = 0. 25 and disappears at lower K_{3i} values assumed in the simulating procedure. Comparing the simulated curves with one obtained experimentally, one can conclude that the complexes $Mn(SO_4)_i^{+3-2i}$ do not exist at all or their stability constants are small. Curves a and b in Fig. 13A illustrate the effect of discrepancy between different equilibrium constant values, here: solubility product for **CuI**.

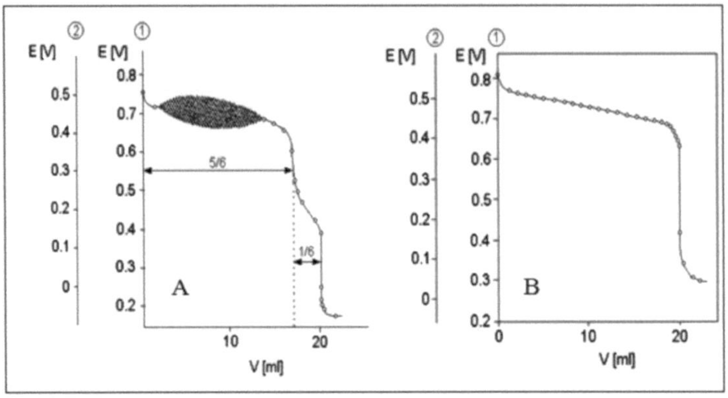

Fig. 15. The experimental titration curves copied from (Erdey, et al., 1951/2).

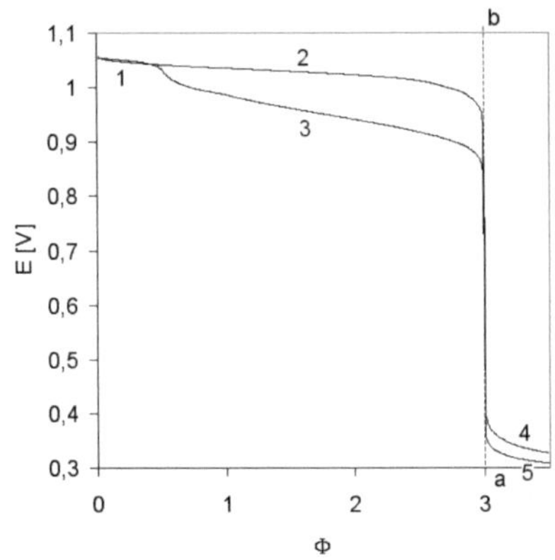

Fig. 16. The E vs. Φ relationships plotted under assumption that (*i*) $\beta = \gamma = 0$ – curve 125 ; (*ii*) $\beta = 1, \gamma = 0$ – curve 124; (*iii*) $\beta = 0, \gamma = 1$ – curve 135; (*iv*) $\beta = \gamma = 1$ – curve 134; $C_0 = 0.01$, $C_a = 0.02$, $C_{Se} = 0.02$, $C_{Hg} = 0.07$, $C = 0.1$ [mol/L].

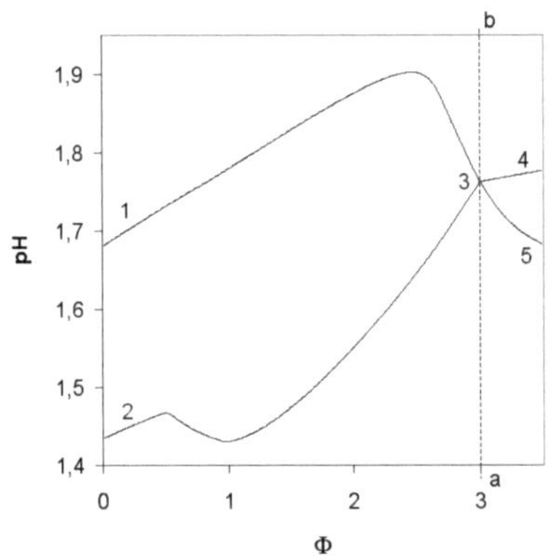

Fig. 17. The pH vs. Φ relationships plotted for the system in section 5.2.2 under assumption that (*i*) $\beta = \gamma = 0$ – curve 134 ; (*ii*) $\beta = 1, \gamma = 0$ – curve 135; (*iii*) $\beta = 0, \gamma = 1$ – curve 234; (*iv*) $\beta = \gamma = 1$ – curve 235; $C_0 = 0.01$, $C_a = 0.02$, $C_{Se} = 0.02$, $C_{Hg} = 0.07$, $C = 0.1$ [mol/L].

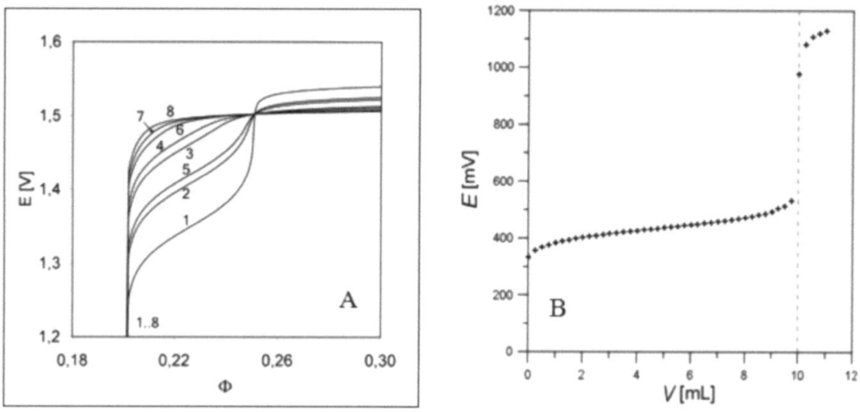

Fig. 18. (A) Fragments of hypothetical titration curves plotted for different pairs of stability constants (K_1, K_2) of the sulphate complexes $Mn(SO_4)_i^{+3-2i}$: 1 - (10^4, 10^7), 2 - (10^3, 10^6), 3 - ($10^{2.5}$, 10^5), 4 - (10^2, 10^4), 5 - (10^4, 0), 6 - (10^3, 0), 7 - (10^2, 0), 8 - (0, 0) and (B) the titration curve obtained experimentally; $FeSO_4$ (C_0 = 0.01 mol/L) + H_2SO_4 (C_a = 0.1 mol/L) as D titrated with C = 0.02 mol/L $KMnO_4$ as T (Michałowski and Lesiak, 1994b; Michałowski, 2010).

12. Resolution of non-equilibrium two-phase electrolytic batch systems with struvite

Some salts are not the equilibrium solid phases and transform into another solid phases when introduced into pure water or aqueous solution of a strong acid, or a strong base, and/or CO_2. Such instability characterizes, among others, some ternary salts, such as struvite, $\mathbf{MgNH_4PO_4}$ (Michałowski and Pietrzyk, 2006) or dolomite, $\mathbf{MgCa(CO_3)_2}$ (Michałowski and al., 2009). Resolution of such systems is realizable within GATES, with use of iterative computer programs, such as MATLAB.
For the study of struvite + aqueous solution system, let us apply the following notations: pC_0 = $-\log C_0$; pC_{CO2} =- $\log C_{CO2}$, pC_b = $-\log C_b$; pr1 = $MgNH_4PO_4$, pr2 = $Mg_3(PO_4)_2$, pr3 = $MgHPO_4$, pr4 = $Mg(OH)_2$, pr5 = $MgCO_3$; pri - precipitate of i-th kind (i = 1,...,5) with molar concentration [pri]; ppri = - log[pri]; K_{soi} - solubility product for pri (i=1,...,5).
The instability of struvite in aqueous media can be confirmed in computer simulations, done with use of iterative computer program MATLAB, realized within GATES. The approach to this non-redox system is based on charge and concentration balances, together with expressions for equilibrium constants, involving all physicochemical knowledge on the system in question, collected in (Michałowski and Pietrzyk, 2006). In some instances, the dissolution process consists of several steps, where different solid phases are formed.

12.1 Formulation of the system

The behavior of this system can be followed on the basis of formulation referred to the system where pure **pr1** is introduced into aqueous solution containing dissolved CO_2 (C_{CO2} mol/L) + KOH (C_b mol/l) + HCl (C_a); initial (t = 0) concentration of **pr1** in the system equals C_0 mol/L. Taking ppr1 = -log[**pr1**] as the steering variable, and denoting $\mathbf{x} = (x_1,\ldots,x_5)$ at $C_{CO2} > 0$, we write the balances $F_i(\mathbf{x}(ppr1)) = 0$ formulated as follows:

$$F_1=[\mathbf{pr1}]+3[\mathbf{pr2}]+[\mathbf{pr3}]+[\mathbf{pr4}]+[Mg^{+2}]+[MgOH^{+1}]+[MgH_2PO_4^{+1}]+[MgHPO_4]+[MgPO_4^{-1}]+[MgNH_3^{+2}]+[Mg(NH_3)_2^{+2}]+[Mg(NH_3)_3^{+2}]+[MgHCO_3^{+1}]+[MgCO_3]-C_0=0 \quad (40)$$

$$F_2=[\mathbf{pr1}]+[NH_4^{+1}]+[NH_3]+[MgNH_3^{+2}]+2[Mg(NH_3)_2^{+2}]+3[Mg(NH_3)_3^{+2}]-C_0=0 \quad (41)$$

$$F_3=[\mathbf{pr1}]+2[\mathbf{pr2}]+[\mathbf{pr3}]+[H_3PO_4]+[H_2PO_4^{-1}]+[HPO_4^{-2}]+[PO_4^{-3}]+[MgH_2PO_4^{+1}]+[MgHPO_4]+[MgPO_4^{-1}]-C_0=0 \quad (42)$$

$$F_4=[H^{+1}]-[OH^{-1}]+\Delta+[NH_4^{+1}]+2[Mg^{+2}]+[MgOH^{+1}]-[HCO_3^{-1}]-2[CO_3^{-2}]+[MgH_2PO_4^{+1}]-[MgPO_4^{-1}]+[MgHCO_3^{+1}]+2[MgNH_3^{+2}]+2[Mg(NH_3)_2^{+2}]+2[Mg(NH_3)_3^{+2}]-[H_2PO_4^{-1}]-2[HPO_4^{-2}]-3[PO_4^{-3}]=0 \quad (43)$$

$$F_5=[H_2CO_3]+[HCO_3^{-1}]+[CO_3^{-2}]+[MgHCO_3^{+1}]+[MgCO_3]-C_{CO2}=0 \quad (44)$$

where (in Eq. 43)

$$\Delta = C_b - C_a \quad (45)$$

On defined stage of pr1 dissolution, concentrations of some (or all) solid phases assumed zero value. To check it, the q_i values:

$$q_1=[Mg^{+2}]\cdot[NH_4^{+1}]\cdot[PO_4^{-3}]/K_{so1};\ q_2=[Mg^{+2}]^3\cdot[PO_4^{-3}]^2/K_{so2};\ q_3=[Mg^{+2}]\cdot[HPO_4^{-2}]/K_{so3};\ q_4=[Mg^{+2}]\cdot[OH^{-1}]^2/K_{so4};\ q_5=[Mg^{+2}]\cdot[CO_3^{-2}]/K_{so5} \quad (46)$$

for different potentially precipitable species pri (i=1,...,5) were 'peered' in computer program applied for this purpose.
Concentration of **$MgCO_3$**, i.e. [**pr5**], has not been included in the concentration balances (40) and (44) specified above. Simply, from the preliminary calculations it was stated that, at any case considered below, **pr5** does not exist as the equilibrium solid phase.
At the start for calculations, the fundamental variables were chosen, namely:

$$x_1=pMg=-\log[Mg^{+2}],\ x_2=pNH_3=-\log[NH_3],\ x_3=pHPO_4=-\log[HPO_4^{-2}],\ x_4=pH,\ x_5=pHCO_3=-\log[HCO_3^{-1}] \quad (47)$$

At $C_{CO2} = 0$ ($pC_{CO2} = \infty$), Eq. (44) does not enter in the set of balances and four fundamental variables, $\mathbf{x} = (x_1,\ldots,x_4)$, are applied

$$x_1=pMg=-\log[Mg^{+2}],x_2=pNH_3=-\log[NH_3],x_3=pHPO_4=-\log[HPO_4^{-2}],x_4=pH \quad (48)$$

and the sum of squares

$$SS = \sum_{i=1}^{n} [F_i(\mathbf{x}, ppr1)]^2 \quad (49)$$

is taken as the minimized (zeroed) function; n=5 at $C_{CO2} > 0$ and n=4 at $C_{CO2} = 0$.
At further steps of **pr1** dissolution in defined medium, the variable ppri = -log[**pri**], related to concentration [**pri**] of the precipitate **pri** formed in the system, was introduced against the old variable (e.g., pMg), when the solubility product K_{soi} for the precipitate **pri** was attained; some changes in the algorithm were also made. Decision on introducing the new variable has been done on the basis of 'peering' the $\log q_i$ values (Eq.(46)). This way, one can confirm that the solid species **pri** is (or is not) formed in the system, i.e. $\log q_i = 0$ or $\log q_i < 0$.

Generally, the calculation procedure and graphical presentation was similar to one described in the paper (Michałowski and Pietrzyk, 2006). It concerns particular species and values for the solubility or dissolution (s, mol/L) of **pr1**, expressed by the formula

$$s=[Mg^{+2}]+[MgOH^{+1}]+[MgH_2PO_4^{+1}]+[MgHPO_4]+[MgPO_4^{-1}]+ [MgNH_3^{+2}]+[Mg(NH_3)_2^{+2}]+[Mg(NH_3)_3^{+2}] \quad (50)$$

at $C_{CO2} = 0$, or

$$s' = s + [MgHCO_3^{+1}] + [MgCO_3] \quad (51)$$

at $C_{CO2} > 0$.

12.2 The struvite dissolution – graphical presentation

The results of calculations, presented graphically in Figs. 19 - 21, are referred to two concentrations C_0 [mol/L] of pr1: pC_0 = 3 and 2, when introduced it (t = 0) into aqueous solution of CO_2 (C_{CO2} mol/L) + KOH (C_b mol/L), C_a = 0. Particular cases: C_{CO2} = 0 and C_b = 0, were also considered.

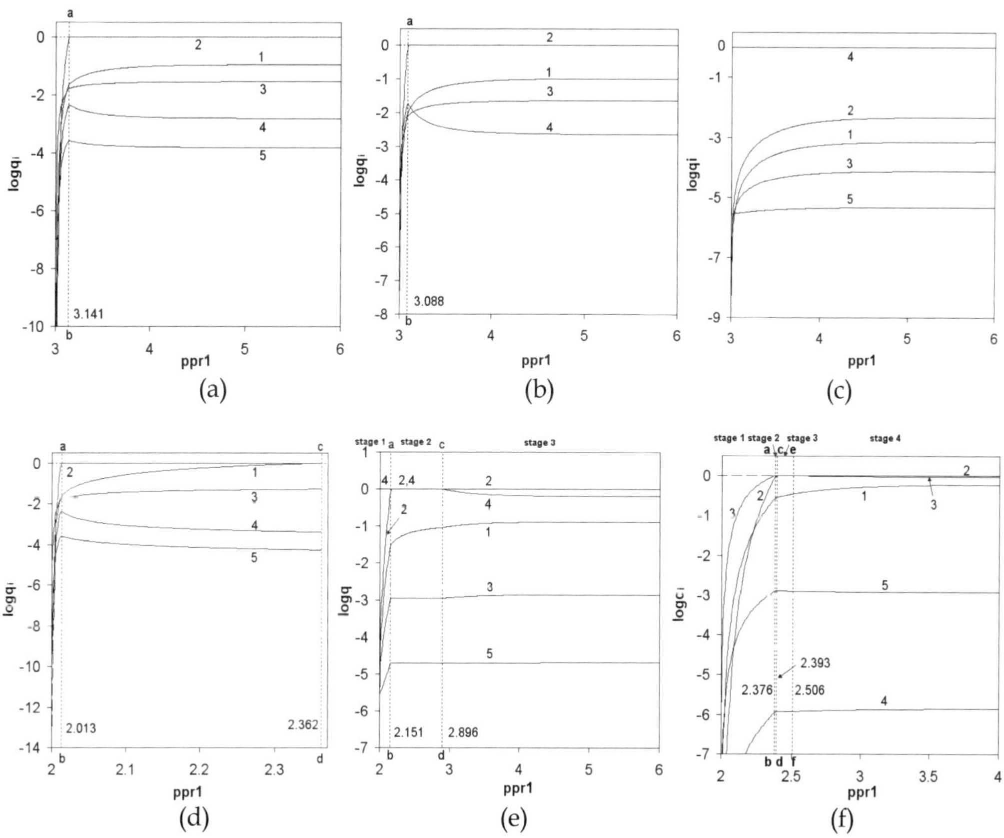

Fig. 19. The $\log q_i$ vs. ppr1 relationships for different pri (i = 1, ... ,5), at different sets of (pC_0, pC_{CO2}, pC_b) values: (a) (3, 4, ∞); (b) (3, ∞, ∞); (c) (3, 4, 2); (d) (2, 4, ∞); (e) (2, 4, 2); (f) (2, 2, ∞).

In further parts of this chapter, two values: $C_b = 0$ and $C_b = 10^{-2}$ [mol/L] for KOH concentration will be considered. The calculations will be done for different concentrations of CO_2, expressed by pC_{CO2} values, equal 2, 3, 4, 5 and ∞.

The results obtained provide the following conclusions.

At $pC_0 = 3$, $pC_{CO2} = 4$ and $pC_b = \infty$, the solubility product K_{so2} for **pr2** is attained at ppr1 = 3.141 (Fig. 19a), and then **pr2** is precipitated

$$3\mathbf{pr1} = \mathbf{pr2} + HPO_4^{-2} + NH_3 \tag{52}$$

This process lasts, up to total depletion of **pr1** (Fig.20a), i.e. the solubility product for **pr1** is not attained ($q_1 < 1$). The pH vs. **ppr1** relationship is presented in Fig. 21a. Before K_{so2} for **pr2** is attained, the values: [**pr2**] = [**pr3**] = [**pr4**] = 0 were assumed in Eqs. (40) and (42). Then, after K_{so2} attained, [**pr2**] is introduced into (40) and (42), as the new variable. The related speciation curves are plotted in Fig.20a. The plots in Figs. 19a, 20a and 21a can be compared with ones (Figs. 19b, 20b, 21b), related to $pC_0 = 3$, $pC_{CO2} = \infty$ and $pC_b = \infty$ (i.e. $C_{CO2}=C_b=0$). The course of speciation curves (Figs. 20a,20b) testifies on account of the validity of the reaction notation (52), that involves the predominating species in the system.

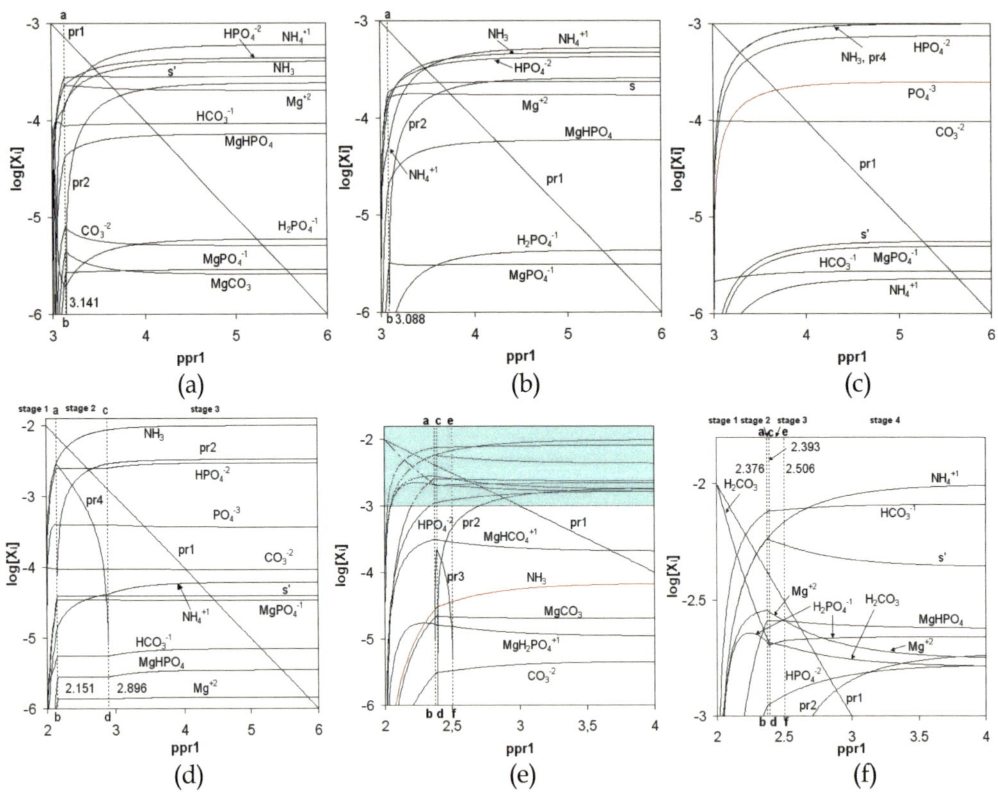

Fig. 20. The log[X_i] vs. ppr1 relationships for indicated components X_i at different sets of (pC_0, pC_{CO2}, pC_b) values: (a) (3, 4, ∞); (b) (3, ∞, ∞); (c) (3, 4, 2); (d) (2, 4, 2); (e) (2, 2, ∞); (f) (2, 2, ∞) (detailed part of Fig. e).

At $pC_0 = 3$, $pC_{CO2} = 4$ and $pC_b = 2$, i.e. for the case of **pr1** dissolution in alkaline media ($C_b >> C_{CO2}$), the **pr4** precipitates

$$\mathbf{pr1} + 2OH^{-1} = \mathbf{pr4} + NH_3 + HPO_4^{-2} \tag{53}$$

nearly from the very start of **pr1** dissolution, ppr1 = 3.000102 (Fig.19c,20c). The transformation of **pr1** into **pr4** lasts up to the total **pr1** depletion.

At $pC_0 = 2$, $pC_{CO2} = 4$ and $pC_b = \infty$, the solubility product for **pr2** is attained at ppr1 = 2.013 (Fig. 19d) and **pr2** precipitates according to reaction (52) up to ppr1 = 2.362, where the solubility product for **pr1** is crossed and the dissolution process is terminated. At equilibrium, the solid phase consists of the two non-dissolved species **pr2** + **pr1**. The pH vs. ppr1 relationship is presented in Fig. 21c.

At $pC_0 = 2$, $pC_{CO2} = 4$ and $pC_b = 2$, the process is more complicated and consists on three stages (Fig.19e). On the stage 1, **pr4** precipitates first (Eq. 53), nearly from the very start of **pr1** dissolution, up to ppr1 = 2.151, where K_{so2} for **pr2** is attained. Within the stage 2, the solution is saturated toward **pr2** and **pr4**. On this stage, the reaction, expressed by the notation

$$2\mathbf{pr1} + \mathbf{pr4} = \mathbf{pr2} + 2NH_3 + 2H_2O \tag{54}$$

occurs up to total depletion of **pr4** (at ppr1 = 2.896), see Fig.20d. On the stage 3, the reaction

$$3\mathbf{pr1} + 2OH^{-1} = \mathbf{pr2} + 3NH_3 + HPO_4^{-2} + 2H_2O \tag{55}$$

occurs up to total depletion of **pr1**, i.e. solubility product (K_{so1}) for **pr1** is not crossed. The pH changes, occurring during this process, are presented in Fig. 21d.

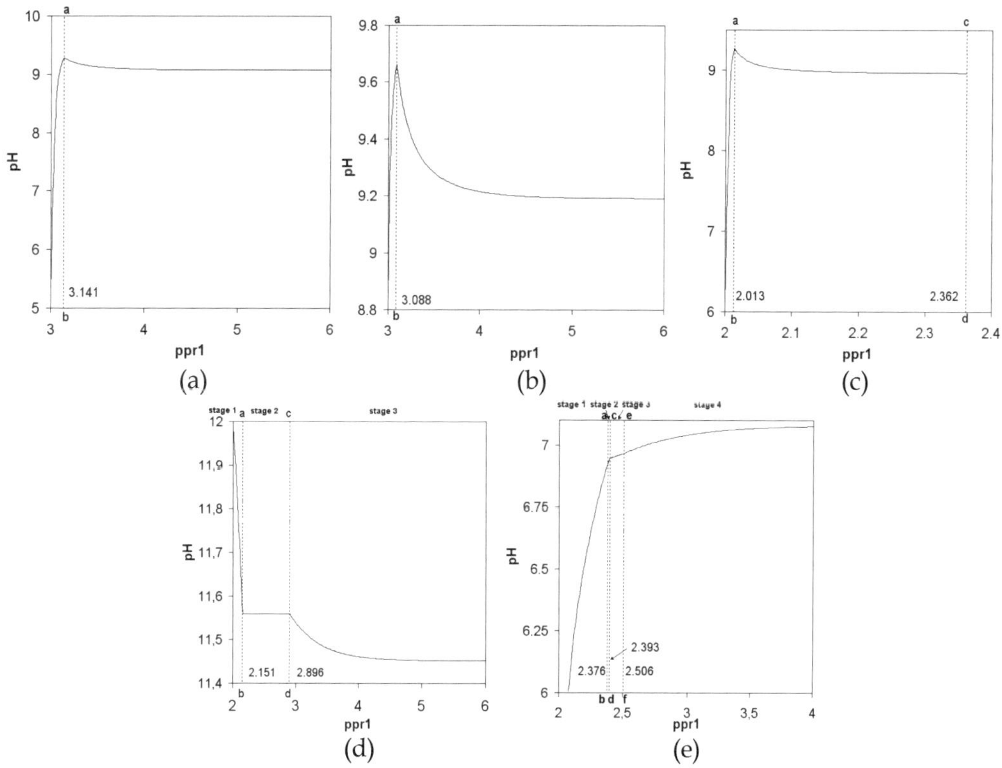

Fig. 21. The pH vs. ppr1 relationships plotted at different sets of (pC_0, pC_{CO2}, pC_b) values: (a) (3, 4, ∞); (b) (3, ∞, ∞); (c) (2, 4, ∞); (d) (2, 4, 2); (e) (2, 2, ∞).

At $pC_0 = 2$, $pC_{CO2} = 2$ and $pC_b = \infty$, after the solubility product for **pr3** attained (line ab at ppr1 = 2.376), **pr3** is the equilibrium solid phase up to ppr1 = 2.393 (line cd), where the solubility product for **pr2** is attained, see Fig.19f. For ppr1 $\in$ < 2.393, 2.506 >, two equilibrium solid phases (**pr2** and **pr3**) exist in the system. Then, at ppr1 = 2.506, **pr3** is totally depleted (Fig.20e,2f), and then **pr1** is totally transformed into **pr2**. On particular steps, the following, predominating reactions occur:

$$\mathbf{pr1} + 2H_2CO_3 = Mg^{+2} + NH_4^{+1} + H_2PO_4^{-1} + 2HCO_3^{-1} \quad (56)$$

$$\mathbf{pr1} + H_2CO_3 = \mathbf{pr3} + NH_4^{+1} + HCO_3^{-1} \quad (57)$$

$$\mathbf{pr1} + 2\mathbf{pr3} = \mathbf{pr2} + NH_4^{+1} + H_2PO_4^{-1} \quad (58)$$

$$3\mathbf{pr1} + 2H_2CO_3 = \mathbf{pr2} + 3NH_4^{+1} + H_2PO_4^{-1} + 2HCO_3^{-1} \quad (59)$$

At ppr1 > 2.506, only **pr2** is the equilibrium solid phase. The pH vs. ppr1 relationship is presented in Fig. 21e.
All the reaction equations specified above involve predominating species of the related systems. All them were formulated on the basis of the related speciation plots (Figs. 20a–20f) and confronted with the related plots of pH vs. ppr1 relationships. Particularly, OH^{-1} ions participate the reactions (53) and (55) as substrates and then pH of the solution decreases during the dissolution process on the stages 1 and 3 (see Fig. 21d). On the stage 2, we have pH $\cong$ constant (see Eq. 58 and Fig. 21d). A growth in concentration of NH_3 and HPO_4^{-2} is also reflected in the reactions (53) – (55) notations.

12.3 Composition of the solid phase when equimolar quantities of reagents are mixed

In this section, the solid products obtained after mixing equimolar solutions of $MgCl_2$ and $NH_4H_2PO_4$ are considered at $C_{CO2} = 0$, i.e. in absence of CO_2. The concentrations are then equal C mol/L for magnesium, nitrogen and phosphorus ($C_{Mg} = C_N = C_P = C$). It will be stated below that the solid phase composition is also affected by the C value.

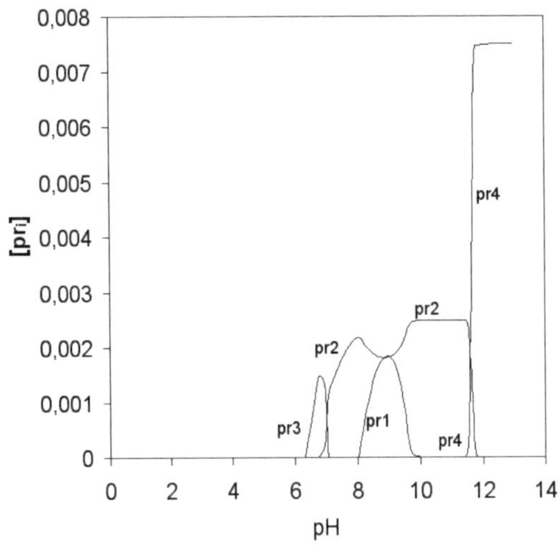

Fig. 22. The **[pri]** vs pH plots at C = 0.0075 mol/L.

The relations between concentrations of different precipitates were calculated at pK_{so1}=12.6, pK_{so2}=24.38 and different C-values (0.0075, 0.02 and 0.06) assumed and presented quantitatively in Figs. 22-24. In all instances, the values: pK_{so3} = 5.5, pK_{so4} = 10.74 and all other physicochemical data cited in [1] were assumed; **pr5** is not precipitated at any instances considered in this system. Particularly, at C = 0.0075 it is seen that concentrations of **pr1** and **pr2** are comparable at pH ca 9.

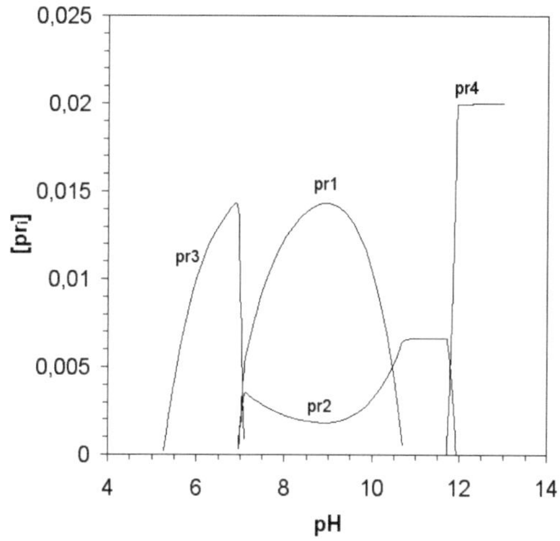

Fig. 23. The **[pri]** vs pH plots at C = 0.02 mol/L.

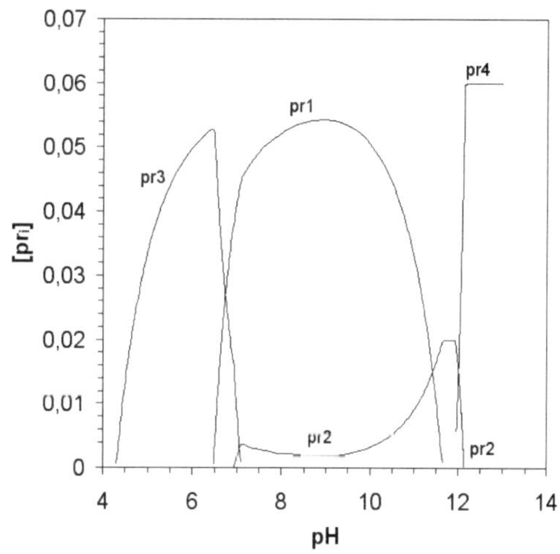

Fig. 24. The [pri] vs pH plots at C = 0.06 mol/L.

The equilibrium constants values quoted in literature for particular species formed in the system in question are divergent. It refers, among others, to different values for pK_{so1} and pK_{so2} quoted in literature. The calculations were done on the following way.

When the solubility product (K_{soi}) for a particular precipitate (**pri**) has been crossed, the concentration **[pri]** was involved in the related balances. At any case, the pH values (pH ≤ 13) were related to the systems with the equilibrium solid phase(s) involved. To omit the concentration of the points referred to different Δ-values, only a part of them were plotted in the related figures (Fig. 25ab,c). Except for the data specified in Fig. 25c, where **pr1** exists as the sole solid phase within pH ca 7 - 9, irrespectively on the C-value assumed on the ordinate. In other instances, **pr1** is accompanied by **pr2**.

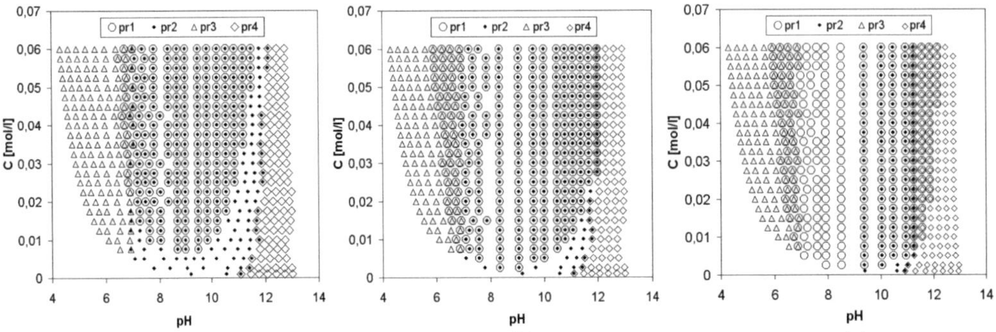

(a) (b) (c)

Fig. 25. The regions for indicated precipitates in (pH, C) area, calculated at different literature data for (pK_{so1} , pK_{so2}) pair: (a) (12.6, 24.38); (b) (13.15, 24.38); (c) 13.15, 23.1); pK_{sp3} = 5.5, pK_{so4} = 10.74 and other equilibrium data as ones quoted in [1].

13. A reference to kinetics in batch systems

GATES can be considered as the most general thermodynamic approach to electrolytic systems. However, one can find some reference of GATES to kinetic systems, and oscillating reactions in particular (Michałowski et al., 1996). The Belousov-Zhabotinsky (BZ) and the Bray-Liebhafsky (BL) systems, where temporal oscillations take place in continuously stirred batch reactors, are well-known examples there. Their oscillating behavior is not sufficiently known till now, as yet. The assumption of a perfect, vigorous stirring (with a stirrer or inert gas) under isothermal conditions enables the transport (diffusion) phenomena to be omitted in mathematical description of the process in question. One of the BZ oscillating systems is based on oxidation of organic components containing active methylene ($-CH_2-$) group (e.g., malonic or citric acid) with BrO_3^{-1} ions, in presence of cerium Ce^{+4}/Ce^{+3} pair, in acidic (H_2SO_4) media.

To elucidate the kinetics of oscillation, exhibited by changes in potential and/or absorbance of the system, some mathematical models were applied. For example, the model known as Oregonator was usually applied for description of BZ reaction in homogeneous, perfectly mixed batch systems. Although a number of papers appear each year in chemical periodicals, an expected turning-point in generalizing approach has not set in, however (Györgyi and Field, 1992).

The oscillating reactions can proceed at constant volume and constant total concentrations of all components consisting the system (solution). It enables the related balances involved in the system to be applied. Note that radical species can also be involved within GATES, compare with Eq. (5).

All oscillating reactions known hitherto are based on electron-transfer phenomena. As a particular case, a system containing a constant, defined number of reagents mixed together, can be considered. Thus, s+2 balances and their time derivatives, written in general forms (Michałowski et al., 1996):

$$\sum_j \alpha_{ij} \cdot [X_j^{z_j}] - \gamma_i = 0 \tag{60}$$

$$\sum_j \alpha_{ij} \cdot \frac{d[X_j^{z_j}]}{dt} = 0 \tag{61}$$

(i = 1,…,s+2) are valid. Eqs. (60) and (61) form a set of 2(s+2) linearly independent equations (60), completed by linearly independent relations between concentrations of some species. All primary, intermediate and final products originated from organic substance (e.g., malonic acid) should be involved in (60) and (61), also as complexes with other ions. A due set of parameters, of both thermodynamic (e.g., standard potentials, stability constants of complexes, dissociation constants) and kinetic (rate constants) nature, are involved in there. In closed systems, with diathermal walls securing isothermal course of reactions, equations (60) and (61) are considered as (independent on time) constraints put on concentrations and rated of reactions in the system.
The time-derivatives in Eq. (61) can be expressed as follows

$$\frac{d[X_j^{z_j}]}{dt} = \sum_u k_{ju} \cdot f_u(x) - \sum_v k_{jv} \cdot f_v(x) \tag{62}$$

where k_{jw} – rate constants, w = u, v, $k_{jw} \geq 0$, $f_u(x)$, $f_v(x)$ – functions involving rationally selected concentrations $[X_l]$. Some species entering the balances (60), e.g., $[Na^{+1}]$ introduced by sodium bromate in BZ system, do not participate the oscillation reactions and their concentrations remain unchanged, e.g., $d[Na^{+1}]/dt = 0$.
The set of independent variables should be then formulated. For example, bromine species can be expressed by relations similar to (16), obtained on the basis of mass action law, and formulae (12). The choice of independent variables is conditioned by appropriate measuring devices applied; e.g., $[Br^{-1}]$ is measured with ion-selective bromine electrode, potential E – with platinum indicator electrode, pH – with glass electrode – all inserted with a reference electrode, in perfectly mixed cell (reactor).
Concentrations of some components cannot be directly measured with a specific, indicator electrode. In such instances, other analytical techniques must be put in work; e.g., Ce(IV) species absorb light and this property can be exploited for analytical purposes. Absorbance A, measured at wavelength λ, can be expressed by equation

$$A = \sum_j \omega_j \cdot [X_j^{z_j}] \tag{63}$$

involving the species in defined λ-range; $\omega_j = \omega_j(\lambda)$ are the coefficients defined as products of molar absorptivities, $\varepsilon_j = \varepsilon_j(\lambda)$, and the path length (l) of light in cuvette, $\omega_j = \varepsilon_j \cdot l$. It enables any system of this kind to be resolved.
The measuring cell applied for determination of kinetic parameters should provide the possibility of simultaneous measurements of different parameters *in situ*, at different

moments of time t. The parameters considered can be found in iterative manner, through fitting the above equations to experimental data registered at different t values. Resolution of the equations and discrimination of the model may provide the temporal relationships, $y_j = y_j(t)$, namely: $[X_j] = f_j(t)$, E = E(t), pH = pH(t), A = A(t). The relationships can be presented graphically, in 2D and 3D space.
The rudimentary formulation of balances (60) and (61) requires, among others, a deep knowledge of intermediate species formed during gradual oxidation of the organic substance (considered as the paliwo of this reaction). The experience is also needed to distinguish between the processes proceeding instantly (where equilibrium constants are only involved) and ones of kinetic nature, where rate constants are also applied.
Some limitations are caused by nature of the species formed; e.g., a limited solubility of CO_2 in BZ or O_2 in BL has to be taken into account (Gyorgyi et al., 1992).

14. Conclusions

The computer simulation realized within GATES with use of iterative computer programs, e.g., MATLAB, provides quite a new quality in knowledge gaining. It enables to follow the details of the process, registered with use of measurable quantities, such as pH and/or potential E. When referred to redox systems, it enables to gain incomparably better knowledge (Michałowski, 2010) than one offered hitherto by the well-known Pourbaix diagrams. GATES enables to avoid the necessity of quantitative inferences based on fragile/rachitic chemical reaction notation, involving only some of the species existing in the system. From the GATES viewpoint, the 'stoichiometry' can be perceived only as a mnemonic term. In calculations, the metastable state is realised by omission of potential products in the related balances, whereas 'opening' a reaction pathway in metastable state is based on insertion of possible (from equilibrium viewpoint) products in the related balances. One can also test the interference effects, of different kind.
Concentrations of the species in redox systems cover frequently much wider range of values than in non-redox systems. For example, the concentrations of oxidized forms of chloride in the system 9.2.5 are negligibly small in comparison with $[Cl^{-1}]$; concentration of Cl_2 (the oxidized chlorine species of the highest concentration) is smaller than 10^{-14} mol/L. The concentrations of heptavalent iodine specie are lower than 10^{-20} mol/L in this system (Michałowski and Lesiak, 1994b). However, this information is not attainable *a priori*, i.e. before starting for calculations. Consideration of the generalized model before prior knowledge on the relative contents of different species, is the great advantage of GATES. The course of the plots referred to different species enables to distinguish between the main and accompanying reactions, see e.g., Figs. 6 and 7.
Some details inherent in two-phase systems cannot be tracked experimentally, with use of physicochemical or analytical instrumentation known hitherto. For example, any electrode introduced into two-phase system is the extraneous body acts as a centre of crystallisation in two-phase systems and disturbs e.g., nucleation processes occurred in such systems. Moreover, the indications of a measuring system lag behind the processes that, additionally, are based on the assumption that the process occurs uniformly within the whole system tested. The mixing device applied for this purpose is another kind of extraneous body, affecting similarly as the electrodes. Then the simulation of the dynamic processes according to GATES with use of the iterative computer program, e.g., MATLAB, involving all attainable (and pre-selected) physicochemical knowledge appears then to be the one and

only way to track them efficiently. It refers both to batch and dynamic systems, whose speciation can be followed this way.

Application of the simulating procedure (optimization *a priori*) enabled to apply some essential modifications and significant improvements of in the models applied for physicochemical and analytical needs Michałowski et al., 2008; Michałowski et al., 2011; Ponikvar et al., 2008).

According to author's experience, the main difficulties in the right description of redox systems arise on the line of junction between thermodynamics and kinetics; this line is not precisely defined in many metastable systems. One should notice that involving some species or a group of species in the balances is tantamount with 'overthrowing' the potential barrier for a reaction that is effective from thermodynamic viewpoint, but does not proceed with respect to the kinetics involved. All the inferences are based on firm, mathematical (algebraic) foundations, not on an extremely 'fragile' chemical notation principle that is only a faint imitation of a true, algebraic notation. The approach proposed allows to understand far better all physicochemical phenomena occurring in the system in question and improve some methods of analysis. All the facts testify very well about the potency of simulated calculations made, according to GATES, on the basis of all attainable physicochemical knowledge. Testing the complex redox and non-redox systems with use of iterative computer programs deserves wider popularisation among physico-chemists and chemists–analysts.

The generalised approach to electrolytic systems (GATES), with the generalized electron balance (GEB) concept included, is the most general theory related to thermodynamic description of equilibrium and metastable electrolytic systems, of any degree of complexity. Within GATES, all attainable/preselected physicochemical knowledge can be involved. GATES is related to non-redox and redox (batch and dynamic) systems. The GEB, results from elemental balances for H and O. Within GATES, stoichiometry is the derivative concept only.

All electrolytic systems can be reconstructed on the basis of three fundamental laws obligatory in GATES: (1) law of charge conservation, (2) conservation of elements, (3) law of mass action. Other laws known in chemistry originate from these laws. Summarizing, the GATES can be perceived as the introductory step for theory of everything (TOE) in chemistry of electrolytic systems.

15. References

Erdey, L., Bodor, E., Buzas,H., (1951/52), *Fresenius' Zeitschrift für Analytische Chemie*, 134 22-, ISSN: 0016-1152.

Erdey, L., Svehla, G., Ascorbinometric Titrations, Akadémiai Kiadó, Budapest 1973.

Györgyi, L., Field, R.J. (1992), A three-variable model of deterministic chaos in the Belousov–Zhabotinsky reaction, *Nature* Vol. 355, (27 February), pp. 808-810; ISSN : 0028-0836

Gyorgyi, L., Field, R.J., Noszticzius, Z., McCormic, W.D., Swinney, H.L., (1992), Confirmation of high flow; rate chaos in the Belousov- Zhabotinsky reaction, *Journal of Physical Chemistry*, Vol. 96, Issue 3, pp. 1228-1233; ISSN 0022-3654.

Michałowski, T., (1994), Calculation of pH and potential E for bromine aqueous solution, *Journal of Chemical Education*, Vol. 71, Issue 7, pp. 560-562, ISSN: 0021-9584

Michałowski, T., Lesiak, A., (1994a). Acid-base titration curves In disproportionating redox systems, *Journal of Chemical Education*, Vol. 71, Issue 8, pp. 632-636, ISSN: 0021-9584.

Michałowski, T., Lesiak, A., (1994b). Formulation of generalized equations for redox titration curves, *Chemia Analityczna (Warsaw)*, Vol. 39, pp. 623-637, ISSN: 0009-2223.

Michalowski, T, Wajda, N., Janecki, D.,(1996), An unified quantitative approach to electrolytic systems, *Chemia Analityczna (Warsaw)*, Vol. 41, Issue 4, pp. 667-685, ISSN: 0009-2223.

Michałowski, T. (2001), *Calculations in Analytical Chemistry with Elements of Computer Programming* (in Polish), ISBN: 83-7242-173-0, Cracow University of Technology, Cracow, Poland; ISBN: 83-7242-173-0.

Michalowski, T., Rymanowski, M., Pietrzyk, A., (2005), Nontypical Brønsted Acids and Bases, *Journal of Chemical Education*, Vol. 82, Issue 3, pp. 470-472, ISSN: 0021-9584.

Michałowski, T.., Pietrzyk, A., (2006), A thermodynamic study of struvite+water system, *Talanta*, 68 (2006) 594-601; ISSN 0039-9140.

Michałowski, T., Kupiec, K., Rymanowski, M. (2008), Numerical analysis of the Gran methods, *Analytica Chimica Acta*, Vol. 606, Issue 2, (January 14), pp. 172-183. ISSN: 0003-2670.

Michałowski,T., Borzęcka, M., Toporek, M., Wybraniec, S., Maciukiewicz, P., Pietrzyk, A., (2009) Quasistatic Processes in Non-Equilibrium Two-Phase Systems with Ternary Salts: II. Dolomite + Aqueous Media, *Chem. Anal. (Warsaw)* 54, 1203-1217

Michałowski, T. (2010). The Generalized Approach to Electrolytic Systems. I. Physicochemical and Analytical Implications, *Critical Reviews in Analytical Chemistry*, Vol. 40, Issue 1, (January, 2010) pp. 2-16, ISSN: 1040-8347

Michałowski, T., Pietrzyk A., Ponikvar-Svet, M., Rymanowski M. (2010), The Generalized Approach to Electrolytic Systems: II. The Generalized Equivalent Mass (GEM) Concept, *Critical Reviews in Analytical Chemistry*, Vol. 40, Issue 1 (January, 2010), pp. 17–29, ISSN: 1040-8347.

Michałowski, T., Pilarski, B., Ponikvar-Svet, M., Asuero, A.G., Kukwa, A., Młodzianowski, J., (2011), New methods applicable for calibration of indicator electrodes, *Talanta*, Vol. 83, Issue 5, pp. 1530-1537; ISSN 0039-9140.

Ponikvar, M., Michałowski, T., Kupiec, K., Wybraniec, S., Rymanowski, M. (2008), Experimental verification of the modified Gran methods applicable to redox systems, *Analytica Chimica Acta*, Vol. 628, Issue 2 (3 November), pp. 181-189 ISSN: 0003-2670.

2

From Discrete to Continuous Gene Regulation Models – A Tutorial Using the Odefy Toolbox

Jan Krumsiek[1,2], Dominik M. Wittmann[1,3] and Fabian J. Theis[1,3]
[1]*Institute of Bioinformatics and Systems Biology, Helmholtz Zentrum München*
[2]*Center of Life and Food Sciences, Technische Universität München*
[3]*Department of Mathematics, Technische Universität München*
Germany

1. Introduction

Vital functions of living organisms, such as immune responses or the metabolism, are controlled by complex regulatory networks. These networks comprise, amongst others, regulatory genes called transcription factors and cascades of information-processing proteins such as enzymes. The ultimate goal of the increasingly popular systems biology approach is to set-up extensive computer models that closely reflect the real-life behavior of these biological networks (Kitano, 2002; Werner, 2007). With a reasonable in silico implementation at hand, novel predictions, e.g. about the effect of gene mutations, can be generated by the computer.

The two basic modes of regulation we concentrate on here, are inhibition and activation between two factors. Figure 1A visualizes the relation between the concentrations of e.g. two transcription factors, which are linked by an activation (left-hand figure) or inhibition (right-hand figure). Figure 1B shows a network of interacting activations and inhibitions as it might be found in living cells. While a single regulatory interaction can easily be understood, the complex wiring of several interactions, even for a medium-scale model as depicted here, renders the manual investigation of the system's dynamics unfeasible. For further information on the concepts of regulation, we refer biologically interested readers to Alon (2006).

Classical computational modeling approaches attempt to describe biochemical reaction networks as systems of ordinary differential equations (ODEs) (Klipp et al., 2005; Tyson et al., 2002). This requires detailed knowledge about the molecular mechanisms in order to implement precise kinetic rate laws for each biochemical reaction. However, for many biological systems, and especially gene-regulatory networks, only qualitative information about interactions, like "A inhibits B", is available. A well-established workaround for this lack of information is the application of discrete modeling approaches. In Boolean methodology we abstract from actual molecule quantities and assign each player in the system the state on or off (e.g. active or inactive). Despite their simplicity, Boolean models have been shown to provide valuable information about the general dynamics and capabilities of the underlying system (Albert & Othmer, 2003; Fauré et al., 2006; Samaga et al., 2009).

To bridge the gap between discrete and fully quantitative models, we developed Odefy, a MATLAB- and Octave-compatible toolbox for the automated transformation of Boolean

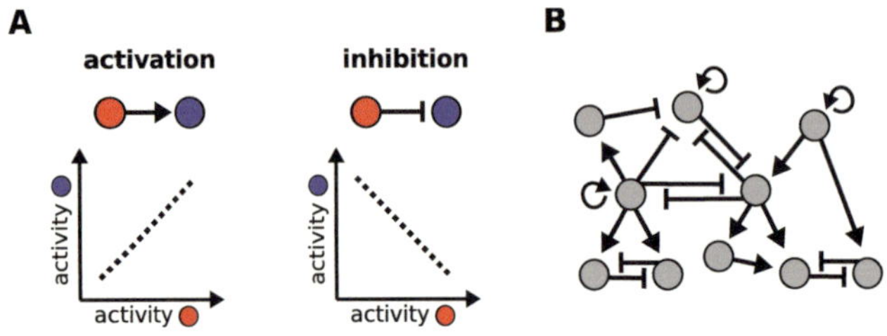

Fig. 1. **A** Two basic modes of regulation, e.g. between two genes and their proteins. If the regulatory factor (red) constitutes an activatory influence towards another factor (blue), it will increase the activity of the blue factor, whereby the magnitude of this activation is dependent on the expression of the red factor itself. Inhibition acts analogously, but the expression of both factors is anti-correlated. **B** Regulatory interactions are part of complex gene-regulatory networks which can be analyzed only by means of computational tools.

models into systems of ODEs (Krumsiek et al., 2010; Wittmann et al., 2009a). Odefy implements a canonical way of transforming Boolean into continuous models, where the use of multivariate polynomial interpolation allows transformation of logic operations into a system of ODEs. Furthermore, we optionally apply sigmoidal Hill functions to get reasonable approximations of real gene regulation dynamics. The Odefy software provides convenient access to different model sources, the conversion process itself and various analysis and export methods. After generating the ODEs, the user can easily adjust model parameters and perform time-course simulations using Odefy's graphical user interface. The ODE systems can be exported to MATLAB script files for further usage in MATLAB programs, to ODE script files for the R computing platform, to the SBML format, or to the well-established MATLAB Systems Biology Toolbox (Schmidt & Jirstrand, 2006). Due to the nice mathematical properties of the produced ODEs and the integration with state-of-the-art modeling tools, a variety of analysis methods can be immediately applied to the models generated by Odefy, including bifurcation analysis, parameter estimation, parameter sensitivity analysis, and the like.
This chapter is organized as follows. First, we will review the theoretical background of the Odefy method by introducing Boolean models, the interpolation process and Hill functions as a generalization of Michaelis-Menten kinetics. Next, the general structure of the Odefy toolbox as well as details about model representation and input formats are discussed. In the major part of this chapter, we will guide the reader through four sample applications of our toolbox, which include both regular Boolean modeling as well as Odefy-converted ODE models, see Table 1 for a detailed overview. The Odefy toolbox can be freely downloaded from `http://hmgu.de/cmb/odefy`. All codes and additional files used in the examples throughout this chapter are located at `http://hmgu.de/cmb/odefymaterials`.

2. Mathematical backgrounds

In the following, we provide a brief introduction to Boolean models in general, and the automatic conversion of Boolean models into continuous systems of ordinary differential equations. For more detailed information on these topics, we refer the reader to the papers Krumsiek et al. (2010); Thomas (1991); Wittmann et al. (2009a).

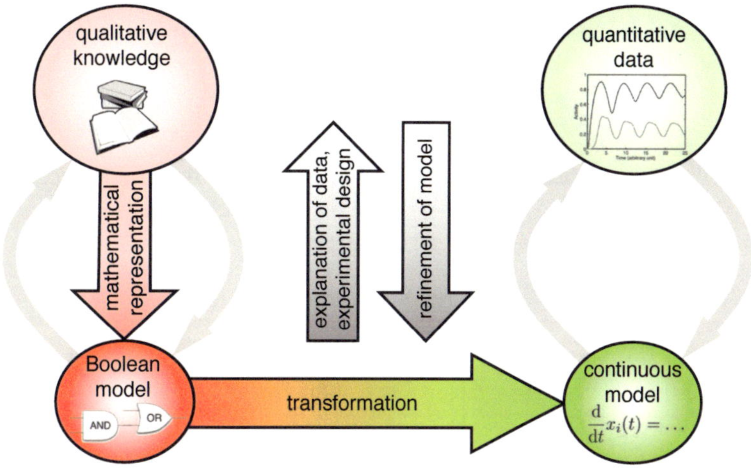

Fig. 2. Qualitative knowledge of regulatory interactions can readily be transformed into Boolean models. The models are then automatically converted to a continuous ODE model by our approach, making them suitable for quantitative analysis and comparison to real data. Figure taken from Wittmann et al. (2009a)

Section	Biological system	Odefy techniques
4	Toy example	the graphical user interface, the toolbox's main functionalities, definition of Boolean models in the yEd graph editor, adjustment of initial values and parameters, Boolean and ODE time-course simulations
5	The genetic toggle switch	advanced model input, advanced functionalities from the MATLAB command line, generating the Boolean state-transition graph, finding Boolean steady-states, phase-plane visualizations
6	Differentiation of mid- and hindbrain	automated model selection
7	Large-scale model of T-cells	export options, connecting Odefy to the SB toolbox, model to .mex compilation

Table 1. Overview of the biological systems and Odefy techniques explained in sections 4–6.

2.1 Boolean models

In a Boolean model, the actual concentration or activity of each factor is abstracted to be either 'on' or 'off', active or inactive, 1 or 0. In a system of N factors with discretized time, regulatory interactions can be described by a set of Boolean update rules that determine the value of each factor x_i at the next time step $t+1$, dependent on all factors in the current time step:

$$x_i(t+1) := B_i\left(x_{i1}(t), x_{i2}(t), \ldots, x_{iN_i}(t)\right) \in \{0,1\}\ , \quad i = 1,2,\ldots N\ .$$

Boolean update functions B_i could, for instance, be represented as multidimensional truth tables, containing an assignment of zero or one for each combination of input factors. A more convenient and intuitive way of representing Boolean update functions is the usage of symbolic equations with logical operators. For example,

$$A(t+1) = (B(t) \vee C(t)) \wedge \neg D(t)$$

represents a regulatory interaction where A will be 'on' in the next time step if and only if at least one of the activators B and C is present and the inhibitor D is absent. For simplicity, we leave out time dependencies in the Boolean equations:

$$A = (B \vee C) \wedge \neg D$$

Some exemplary evaluations for this equation: (i) if B=1,C=0,D=0 then A will be 1; (ii) likewise, if B=0,C=1,D=0 then A=1; (iii) if D=1, then A=0 regardless of the values of B and C.

When computing the follow-up state for the next time point $t+1$ from the current time point t, two principal updating schemes can be employed (cf. Fauré et al. (2006)). When following a *synchronous* updating policy, the states of all factors are updated at the same time. On the other hand, when performing *asynchronous* updating, the value of only one factor is changed during each time step. For the latter case, an update order for the players in the system is required. In Odefy, one can either provide a predefined update order (e.g. B, A, D, C) that will be followed, or one can let the toolbox randomly select a player at each new time step.

2.2 From Boolean models to ordinary differential equations

We now describe how to generate a system of ordinary differential equations (ODEs), given a set of Boolean update functions B_i. The main idea is to convert the above discrete model into a continuous ODE model, where each species x_i is allowed to take values $x_i \in [0,1]$, and its temporal development is described by the ordinary differential equation

$$\dot{\overline{x}}_i = \frac{1}{\tau_i}\left(\overline{B}_i\left(\overline{x}_{i1}, \overline{x}_{i2}, \ldots, \overline{x}_{iN_i}\right) - \overline{x}_i\right) .$$

The right-hand side of this equation consists of two parts, an activation function $\overline{B}_i$ describing the production of species x_i and a first-order decay term. An additional parameter τ_i is introduced to the system, which can be understood as the life-time of species x_i. $\overline{B}_i$ can be considered a continuous homologue of the Boolean update function. The key point is how it can be obtained from B_i in a computationally efficient manner. We present here three concrete approaches of extending a Boolean function to the continuous interval [0,1]. The basis of all three transformation methods are the so-called *BooleCubes*:

$$\overline{B}^{\mathrm{I}}\left(\overline{x}_1, \overline{x}_2, \ldots, \overline{x}_N\right) := \sum_{x_1=0}^{1} \sum_{x_2=0}^{1} \cdots \sum_{x_N=0}^{1} \left[B(x_1, x_2, \ldots, x_N) \cdot \prod_{i=1}^{N} \left(x_i \overline{x}_i + (1-x_i)\left(1-\overline{x}_i\right)\right) \right]$$

which we obtain by multilinear interpolation of the Boolean function B, cf. Figure 3A. The functions $\overline{B}^{\mathrm{I}}$ are affine multilinear. Many molecular interactions, however, are known to show a switch-like behavior, which can be modeled using sigmoidal *Hill functions* $f(\overline{x}) = \overline{x}^n / (\overline{x}^n + k^n)$, see Figure 3B. Hill functions are a generalization of the well-known

Michaelis-Menten kinetics assuming multiple binding sites (Alon, 2006). The two parameters n and k have a direct biological meaning. The Hill coefficient n determines the slope of the curve and is a measure of the cooperativity of the interaction. The parameter k corresponds to the threshold in the Boolean model, above which one defines the state of a species as 'on'. Mathematically speaking, it is the value at which the activation is half maximal, i.e. equal to 0.5. If not otherwise specified, Odefy assumes the default parameters n=3, k=0.5 and τ=1 for all equations.

We now introduce a Hill function f_i with parameters (n_i, k_i) for every interaction and define a new continuous function

$$\overline{B}^{\mathrm{H}}\left(\overline{x}_1, \ldots, \overline{x}_N\right) := \overline{B}^{\mathrm{I}}\left(f_1\left(\overline{x}_1\right), \ldots, f_N\left(\overline{x}_N\right)\right),$$

which we call *HillCubes*, see Figure 3C. One can show that for sufficiently large Hill exponents n, there will be a steady state of the continuous system in the neighborhood of each Boolean steady state Wittmann et al. (2009a). In other words, the continuous model is capable of reproducing the Boolean steady states, but of course displays a much richer dynamical behavior.

Note that Hill functions never assume the value 1, but rather approach it asymptotically. Hence, the HillCubes are not perfect homologues of the Boolean update function B. If this is desired a simple solution is to normalize the Hill functions to the unit interval. This yields another continuous (perfect) homologue of the Boolean function B

$$\overline{B}^{\mathrm{Hn}}\left(\overline{x}_1, \ldots, \overline{x}_N\right) := \overline{B}^{\mathrm{I}}\left(\frac{f_1\left(\overline{x}_1\right)}{f_1\left(1\right)}, \ldots, \frac{f_N\left(\overline{x}_N\right)}{f_N\left(1\right)}\right),$$

which we call *normalized HillCube*, see Figure 3D.

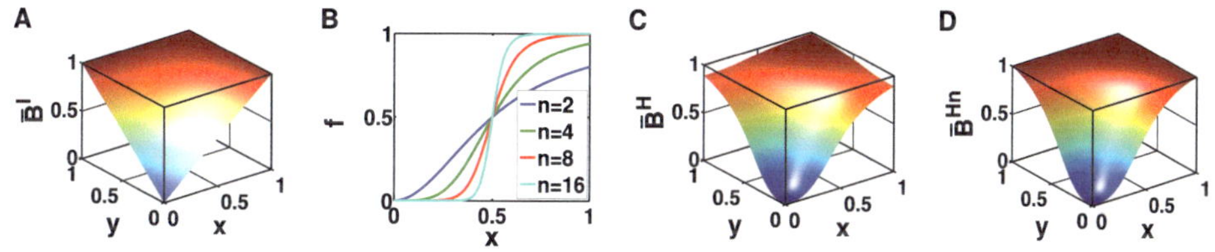

Fig. 3. **A** Multilinear interpolation of a two-variable OR gate (BooleCube) as the continuous homologues of Boolean functions. **B** Hill functions with Hill coefficients $n = 2, 4, 8, 16$ and $k = 0.5$ as continuous relaxation of a Boolean step function. **C** Composition of BooleCube from A with Hill functions (HillCube). **D** Normalized HillCube which actually assumes a value of 1 at the corners of the cube. Figure taken from Krumsiek et al. (2010).

3. The Odefy toolbox

This section explains how to start up the Odefy toolbox, and how Boolean models are represented as MATLAB structure variables. Note that the non-GUI functionality of Odefy is compatible with the freely available Octave toolbox[1]. After downloading and unpacking Odefy[2], we navigate to the respective directory in MATLAB and call

```
InitOdefy
```

which should display a startup message like this:

```
Odefy initialized
For detailed usage instructions type 'OdefyHelp'
or open /home/jan/work/odefy/doc/index.html in your webbrowser.
```

Odefy is now ready-to-use. The core object in the toolbox is a Boolean model which can be defined in various ways (Figure 4), two of which we will get to know in the example section 4. We will here discuss a small example, namely an incoherent feed-forward loop (Alon, 2006) defined by a set of Boolean equations:

```
model = ExpressionsToOdefy(...
    {'A=<>', 'B=A', 'C=A&&~B'});
```

In this model, A is defined as an input species without regulators (denoted by the <>), which never changes its current activity value. B is directly activated by A and will thus closely follow A's expression. Finally, C is activated by A and inhibited by B. Note the use of MATLAB Boolean operators in the Boolean expression. The equation reads "C will be active if A is active and B is not active". The command generates a MATLAB structure variable containing the Boolean model:

```
>> model

model =

    species: {'A'   'B'   'C'}
     tables: [1x3 struct]
       name: 'odefymodel'
```

The `tables` field contains the actual Boolean update functions encoded as multidimensional arrays, that is as hypercubes of edge length two:

```
>> model.tables(3).inspecies

ans =

     1     2

>> model.tables(3).truth

ans =

     0     0
     1     0
```

The third factor, C, has two input species 1 and 2, that is A and B. The four-element truth table precisely describes the above-mentioned "A and not B" logic defined in the symbolic Boolean equation. In order to update the state of a factor, Odefy looks up the corresponding value in the truth table, based on the current system state, and returns the new expression value.

With the defined Boolean model variable we can now access the full functionality of the toolbox, like simulations of the Boolean model and, of course, the conversion of Boolean

[1] http://www.gnu.org/software/octave/

[2] http://hmgu.de/cmb/odefy

models to ODE systems as described in section 2. The rest of this chapter provides various sample applications of the toolbox based on both Odefy's GUI dialogs and MATLAB command-line programming. For a complete reference of all Odefy features, we refer the reader to the Odefy online documentation at `http://hmgu.de/cmb/odefydocs`.

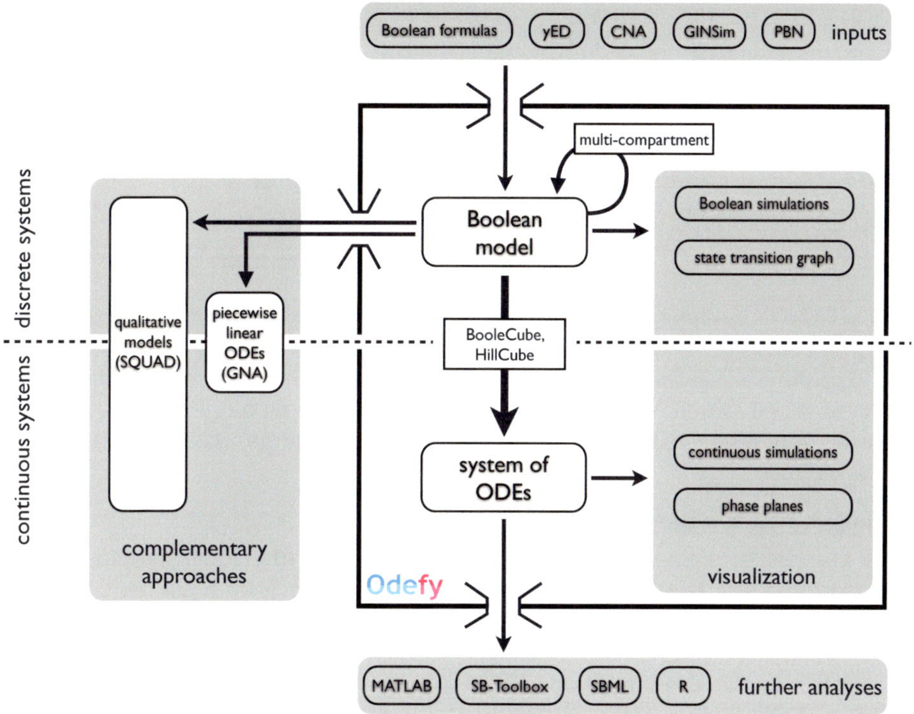

Fig. 4. General structure of the Odefy toolbox. Boolean models can be defined by various input formats. In this chapter, we will introduce both the usage of Boolean formulas and graphs created in the yEd graph editor. Once a Boolean model is created, the user can either concentrate on analyzing the Boolean model, or convert it to a system of ODEs and perform continuous analyses. The resulting models can be exported to several external formats. Figure taken from Krumsiek et al. (2010).

4. A toy example: First steps in Odefy

We will now familiarize the reader with the graphical user interface of the Odefy toolbox, which provides convenient access to the toolbox's main functionalities. In particular, we show how Boolean models can be defined in the yEd graph editor, how initial values and parameters can be adjusted and how Boolean and ODE time-course simulations are run. Note that the Boolean model employed here does not have a real biological background, but was rather constructed to contain important features of gene regulatory networks, like negative feedback, positive feedback, and different wirings of AND and OR logics.

A

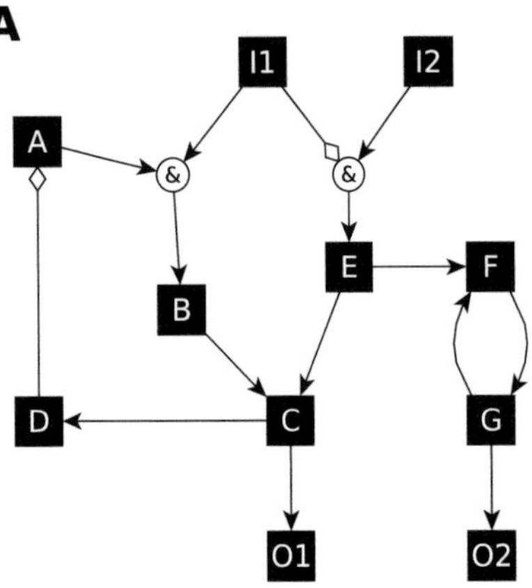

B

```
I1 = <>
I2 = <>
A = ~D
B = A && I1
C = B || E
D = C
E = ~I1 && I2
F = E || G
G = F
O2 = G
```

Fig. 5. Two ways of defining the same Boolean model. **A** Graphical representation of the regulatory interactions created in the yEd graph editor. Note the usage of "&" labeled nodes in order to create AND gates. Regular arrows represent activation whereas diamond head arrows stand for inhibition. **B** Boolean equations for the same model. We use <> to indicate input species with no regulators, and MATLAB Boolean operators `||`, `&&` and ~ to define the Boolean equations.

4.1 Definition of the Boolean model

The most convenient methods to define Boolean models in the Odefy toolbox are Boolean equations and the yEd graph editor[3]. A simple graph, where each node represents a factor of the system and each edge represents a regulatory interaction, is not sufficient to define a Boolean model, since we cannot distinguish between AND and OR gates of different inputs. Therefore, we adapted the intuitive hypergraph representation proposed by Klamt et al. (2006), as exemplarily demonstrated in Figure 5A. All incoming edges into a factor are interpreted as OR gates; for instance, C will be active when B or E is present. AND gates are created by using a special node labeled "&", e.g. E will be active when I2 is present and I1 is not present. We now load this model from a pre-created .graphml file which is contained in the Odefy materials download package. Ensure that Odefy is initialized first:

```
InitOdefy;
```

We can now call the `LoadModelFile` command, which automatically detects the underlying file format:

```
model = LoadModelFile('cnatoy.graphml');
```

As mentioned previously in this chapter, Boolean equations are a convenient alternative for constructing a Boolean model. While obviously the graphical depiction of the network is lost, Boolean equations can be rapidly setup and altered (Figure 5B). We can either load them from a text file containing one equation per line, or directly enter them into the MATLAB command line:

```
model = LoadModelFile('cnatoy.txt');
```

or

```
model = ExpressionsToOdefy({'I1 = <>', 'I2 = <>',
    'A = ~D', 'B = A && I1', ...
    'C = B || E', 'D = C', 'E = ~I1 && I2', 'F = E || G',
    'G = F', 'O2 = G'});
```

[3] http://www.yworks.com/en/products_yed_about.html

At this point, the `model` variable contains the full Boolean model depicted in Figure 5, stored as an Odefy-internal representation in a MATLAB structure.

4.2 Boolean simulation using the Odefy GUI

After defining the Boolean model within the Odefy toolbox, we now start analyzing the underlying system using Boolean simulations. We open the Odefy simulation GUI by entering:

```
Simulate(model);
```

A simulation window appears, in which we now setup a synchronous Boolean update policy, change some initial values and finally run the simulation (red arrows indicate required user actions):

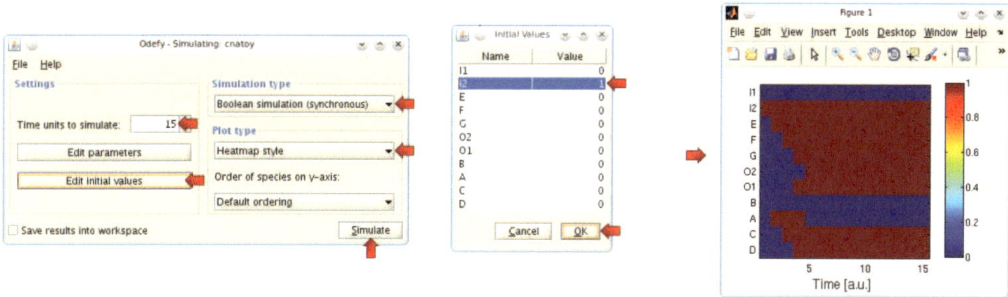

When the input species I2 is active while I1 is inactive, the signal can steadily propagate through the system due to the absent inhibition of E. All species, except for B and A, eventually reach an active steady state after a few simulation steps. A displays an interesting pulsing behavior induced by the negative regulation from C towards A. Initially, A is turned on since its inhibitor D is absent, but is then downregulated once the signal passes through the system. The system produces a substantially different behavior when both input species are active:

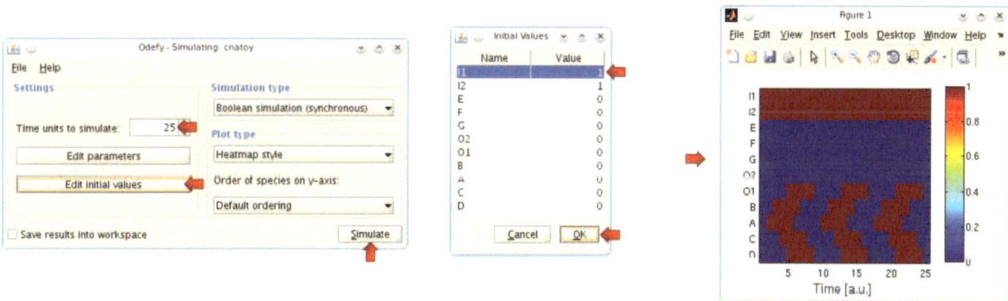

Interestingly, we now observe oscillations in the central part of the network, while the right-hand part with E, F, G and O2 stays deactivated. The oscillations are due to a negative feedback loop in the system along A, B, C and D. Negative feedback basically denotes a regulatory wiring where a player acts as its own inhibitor. In our setup, for example, A indirectly induces D via B and C, which in turn inhibits A. Our obtained results demonstrate that already a simple model can give rise to entirely different behaviors when certain parts of the system are activated or deactivated - here simulated via the initial values of the input species I1 and I2.

4.3 Continuous simulation

In the next steps we will learn how the automatic conversion of Boolean models to ODE systems allows us to quantitatively investigate the pulsing and oscillation effects observed in the Boolean simulation from the previous section. Again, we use the simulation GUI of Odefy, but this time we choose the normalized HillCube variant. In the GUI variant of Odefy, the conversion to an ODE system is automatically performed prior to the simulation.

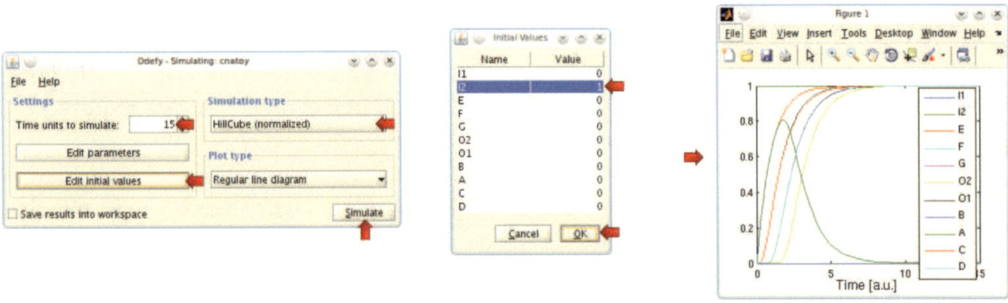

Note that the simulation runs with a set of default parameters for the regulatory interactions: n=3, k=0.5, tau=1. Similarly to the Boolean variant, we observe that all factors are successively activated except for A, which in the continuous version generates a smooth expression pulse lasting around 10 time steps. We also get quantitative insights now, since A does not go up to a full expression of 1.0, but reaches a maximum of only 0.8 before being deactivated. Next, we simulate the oscillatory scenario where both input species are present:

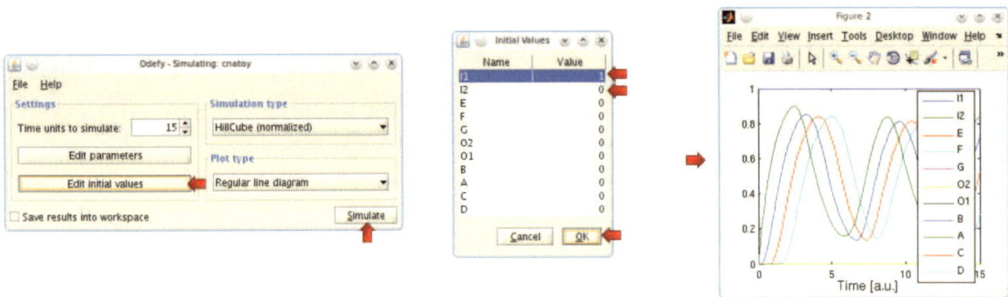

Again, the simulation trajectories show oscillations of the central model factors A, B, C, D and subsequently O1. Note that - in contrast to the Boolean version - the oscillations here display a specific frequency and amplitude. As will be seen in the next section, such quantitative features of the system are heavily dependent on the actual parameters chosen.

4.4 Adjusting the system parameters

As described at the beginning of this chapter, the ODE-converted version of our Boolean networks contain different parameters that control how strong and sensitive each regulatory interaction reacts, and how quick each species in the system responds to regulatory changes. In the following, we will exemplarily change some of the parameters in the oscillatory toy model scenario (the following GUI steps assume you already have performed the quantitative simulations from the previous sections):

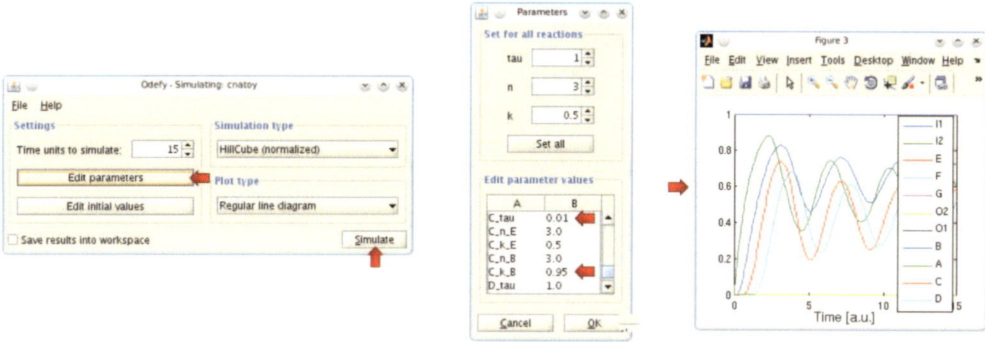

In this example, we changed two system parameters: (i) the tau parameter of C was set to a very small value, rendering C very responsive to regulatory changes, (ii) the k threshold parameter from B towards E is set to 0.95, and thus the activation of E by B is only constituted for very high values of B. The resulting simulation still shows the expected oscillatory behavior, but the amplitude, frequency and synchronicity of the recurring patterns are altered in comparison to the previous variants. This is an example for a behavior that could not have been investigated by using pure Boolean models alone, but actually required the incorporation of a quantitative modeling approach.

5. The genetic toggle switch: Advanced model input and analysis techniques

While the last section focused on achieving quick results using the Odefy graphical user interface, we now focus on actual MATLAB programming. This provides far more power and flexibility during analysis than the fixed set of options implemented in a GUI. Furthermore, we now focus on a real biological system, namely the mutual inhibition of two genes (Figure 6). Intuitively, only one of the two antagonistic factors can be fully active at any given time. This simple wiring thus provides an elegant way for a cell to robustly decide between two different states. Consequently, mutual inhibition is a frequently found regulatory motif in cell differentiation processes. For example, the differentiation of the erythroid and myeloid lineages in hematopoiesis, that is the production of blood cells in higher organisms, is governed by the two transcription factors PU.1 and GATA-1, which are known to repress each other's expression (Cantor & Orkin, 2001). Once the cell has decided to become an erythroid cell, the myeloid program is blocked, and vice versa.
The switch model will be implemented in MATLAB by specifying the regulatory logic between the two genes as sets of Boolean rules and subsequent automatic conversion into a set of ODEs. The resulting model state space is analyzed for the discrete as well as the continuous case (for the latter one we use the common phase-plane visualization technique). We particularly investigate how different parameters affect the multistationarity of the system, and whether the system obtains distinct behaviors when combining regulatory inputs either with an AND or an OR gate.

5.1 Model definition

We have already seen that defining a Boolean model from the MATLAB command line is straightforward, since we can directly enter Boolean equations into the code. We will generate

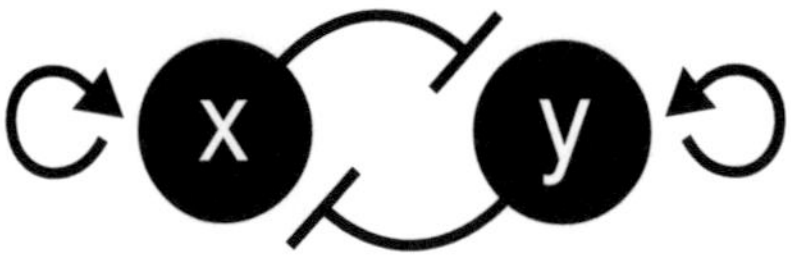

Fig. 6. Mutual inhibition and self-activation between two transcription factors.

two versions of the mutual switch model, one with an AND gate combining self-activation and the inhibition, and one with an OR gate:

```
switchAND = ExpressionsToOdefy({'x = x && ~y', 'y = y && ~x'});
switchOR  = ExpressionsToOdefy({'x = x || ~y', 'y = y || ~x'});
```

Similar to the GUI variant, we could also define the model in a file (yEd or Boolean expressions text file) and load the models from these files. While the definition directly within the code allows for rapid model alteration and prototypic analyses, the saving of the model in a file is the more convenient variant once model generation is finished.

5.2 Simulations from the command line

We want again to perform both Boolean and continuous simulations, but this time we control the entire computation from the MATLAB command line. First, we need to generate a simulation structure that holds all information required for the simulation, like initial states, simulation type and parameters (if applicable):

```
simstruct = CreateSimstruct(switchAND);
```

Within this simulation structure, we define a Boolean simulation for 5 time steps with asynchronous updating in random order (cf. section 2.1), starting from an initial value of x=1 and y=1:

```
simstruct.timeto = 5;
simstruct.type = 'boolrandom';
simstruct.initial = [1 1];
```

The actual simulation is now performed by calling the `OdefySimulation` function:

```
y = OdefySimulation(simstruct);
```

resulting, for example, in:

```
y =

     1     1     1     1     1
     1     0     0     0     0
```

While this result might not look to be very exciting, it actually reflects the main functionality of this regulatory network. The system falls into one of two follow-up states and stably stays within this state (→ a steady state). The player being expressed at the end of the simulation is randomly determined here, another simulation might result in this trajectory:

```
y =

     1     0     0     0     0
     1     1     1     1     1
```

Obviously, this very sharp switching is an effect of the Boolean discretization. For comparison, we will now create a continuous simulation of the same system:

```
simstruct.timeto = 10;
simstruct.type='hillcubenorm';
simstruct.initial = [0.6 0.4];
[t y] = OdefySimulation(simstruct);
```

We employed the normalized HillCube variant with 10 simulated time steps. Note that we could now use real-valued initial values instead of just 0 and 1. The simulated trajectory looks like this:

```
plot(t,y)
legend(switchAND.species);
xlabel('time');
ylabel('activity');
```

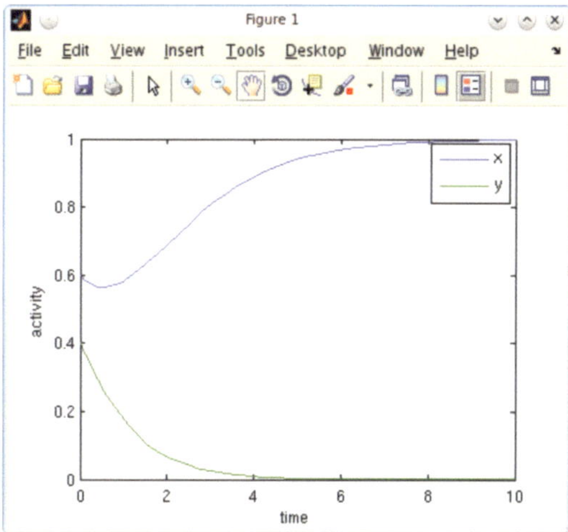

We observe a similar decision effect as for the Boolean variant, but this time in a fully quantitative fashion. Although both factors have similar activity values at the beginning of the simulation, the small excess of X is sufficient to drive the system to a steady state where X is present and Y is not. With reversed initial values, X would have gone to 0 and Y would have been fully expressed.

5.3 Exploring the Boolean state space

In the previous sections we learned how Boolean and continuous simulations of a regulatory model can be interpreted. However, it is important to understand that such simulations merely represents single trajectories through the space of possible spaces, and do not reflect the full capabilities of the system. Therefore, it is often desirable to calculate the full set of possible trajectories of the system, the so-called *state-transition graph* (STG) in the case of a discrete model. We will now learn how to calculate the Boolean steady states of a given model along with its STG using Odefy. The primary calculation consists of a single call:

```
[s g] = BooleanStates(switchAND);
```

The variable `s` now contains the set of steady states of this system where as the STG is represented a sparse matrix in g. Steady states are encoded as decimal representations of their Boolean counterparts and can be conveniently displayed using the `PrettyPrintStates` function:

```
>> PrettyPrintStates(switchAND,s)
x          0 1 0
y          0 0 1
3 states
```

We see that the system has three steady states which are intuitively explainable. If one of the factors is on, the activation of the respective other factor is prohibited, so the state is stable (second and third column). Furthermore, if no player is active then the system is dead, which also represents a stable state (first column). Instead of `PrettyPrintStates` you can also use the `StateMatrix` function which stores the same results in a matrix variable for further working steps:

```
>> m = StateMatrix(switchAND,s)

m =

     0     1     0
     0     0     1
```

The variable g contains the STG encoded as a sparse adjacency matrix of states, which can be readably displayed using the `PrettyPrintSTGraph` function:

```
>> PrettyPrintSTGraph(switchAND,g)
11 => 10
11 => 01
```

That is, from the state where both factors are active, either one of the two exclusive steady states can be reached. No further state transitions are possible in this system. If we repeat the procedure of `BooleanStates` calculation and printing of steady states and STG for the `switchOR` variant, we get the result displayed in Figure 7. Both variants are capable of switch-like decisions that end in a certain steady state. Whereas in the AND variant the 00 state is steady, the same holds true for the 11 state in the OR variant. At this point, we could compare these observations to results from a real biological system, that is evaluating whether the system switches from an activated or inactivated basal state, and thus select one of the two variants as "closer" to biological reality.

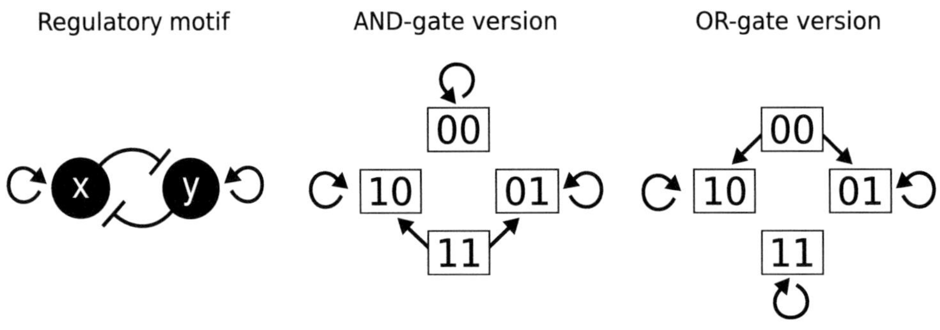

Fig. 7. State-transition graphs for the AND and OR variants of the mutual inhibition motif. Note that states without transitions going towards other states are the steady states of the system.

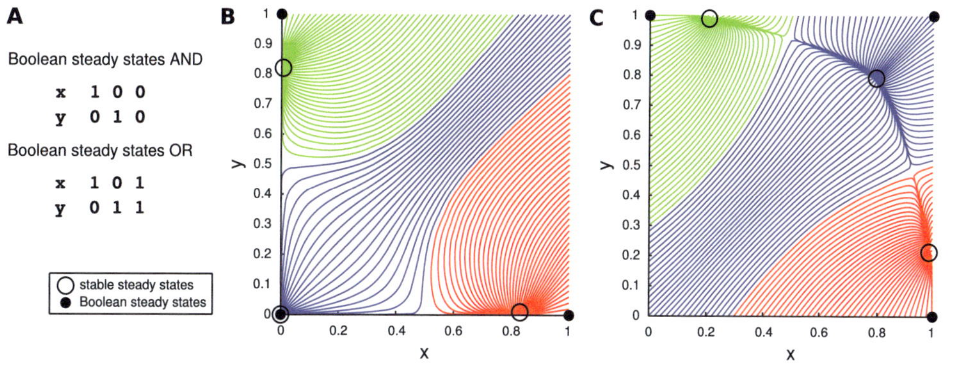

Fig. 8. **A** Boolean steady states of the OR and AND version of the mutual inhibitory switch model. **B,C** Phase planes visualizing the attractor landscapes of the AND and OR variants, respectively. The plots display trajectories of both dynamical systems from various initial concentrations. Trajectories with the same color fall into the same stable steady state. Both systems comprise three stable continuous steady states, each of which belongs to one Boolean steady state. Adapted from Krumsiek et al. (2010)

5.4 Exploring the continuous state space

Analogously to the Boolean state space described above, it is oftentimes desirable to investigate the behavior of the whole system for various internal states rather than concentrating on a single trajectory through the system. Since in the continuous case the system does not consist of a finite set of discrete states, we need a complementary approach to the state transition graphs introduced above. One possibility is the simulation of the continuous system from a variety of initial values and subsequent visualization in a two-dimensional phase plane (cf. Vries et al. (2006)):

```
simstruct = CreateSimstruct(switchAND);
figure;
OdefyPhasePlane(simstruct, 1, 0:0.1:1, 2, 0:0.1:1);
```

This code produces the phase plane plot displayed in Figure 8B. Depending on the initial values, the system falls into one of three stable steady states, where either one of the two factors is active while the other one is turned off, or where both players are inactive. Importantly, the three steady states are qualitatively identical to the three Boolean steady states (again shown in 8A). If we think of these trajectories as possible state trajectories in a living cell, this phase plane could describe for which expression levels of the two transcription factors the system will turn into either on of the two opposing differentiation lineages. Furthermore, by observing if in the third state real cells rather have both factors active or inactive, we could determine whether the AND or the OR variant is a more suitable model of the underlying system.

We now change the Hill exponent n in all regulatory functions from the standard value of 3 to 1, and recalculate the phase-plane for the OR version:

```
simstruct = CreateSimstruct(switchOR);
simstruct = SetParameters(simstruct, [], [], 'n', 1);
figure;
OdefyPhasePlane(simstruct, 1, 0:0.1:1, 2, 0:0.1:1);
```

producing the following phase plane plot:

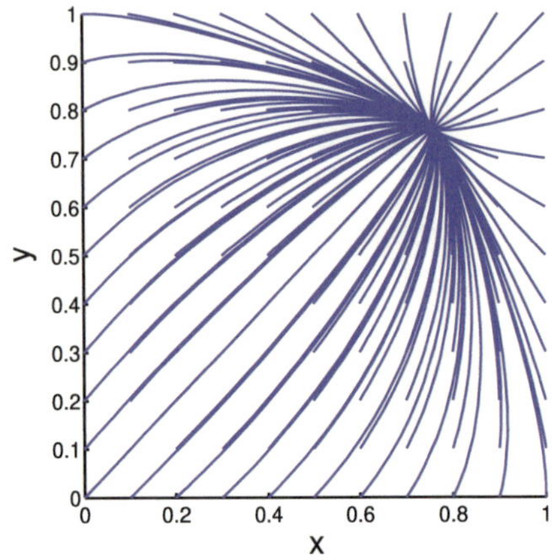

Interestingly, with this parameter configuration the system is not able to constitute a multistable behavior anymore. All trajectories fall into a single, central steady state with medium expression of both factors, regardless of the actual initial values of the simulation. This result is in line with findings from Glass & Kauffman (1973), who showed the requirement of cooperativity ($n \geq 2$) in order to generate multistationarity. Again, by comparing the system behavior with the real biological system we gain insights into the possibly correct parameter ranges. For our example here, since we assume stem cells to be able to obtain multistationarity, an n value below 2 seems rather unlikely.

5.5 Advanced command line usage: simulations using MATLAB's numerical ODE solvers

The continuous simulations shown above used Odefy's internal `OdefySimulation` function. However, in order to get full control of our ODE simulations the usage of MATLAB ODE .m files is desirable. We can generate such script files using the `SaveMatlabODE` function:

```
SaveMatlabODE(switchAND, 'myode.m', 'hillcubenorm');
rehash;
```

Note that `rehash` might be required so that the following code immediately finds the newly created function. The newly created file `myode.m` contains an ODE compatible with MATLAB's numerical solving functions. Next we set the initial values and change some parameters:

```
initial = zeros(2,1);
initial = SetInitialValue(initial, switchAND, 'x', 0.6);
initial = SetInitialValue(initial, switchAND, 'y', 0.4);

params = DefaultParameters(switchAND);
params = SetParameters(params,switchAND, [], [], 'n', 1);
```

The `SetInitialValue` and `SetParameters` function can not only work on a simulation structure, but can also be used to edit raw value and parameter matrices directly. Finally, we run the simulation by calling:

```
paramvec = ParameterVector(switchAND,params);
time = 10;
r = ode15s(@(t,y)myode(t,y,paramvec), [0 time], initial);
```

For further information on the result variable `r`, we refer the reader to the documentation of `ode15s`. Odefy's `Visualize` method facilitates plot generation by taking care of drawing and labeling:

```
Visualize(r.x,r.y,switchAND.species);
```

resulting in the following trajectories, which we have already analyzed several times throughout this example:

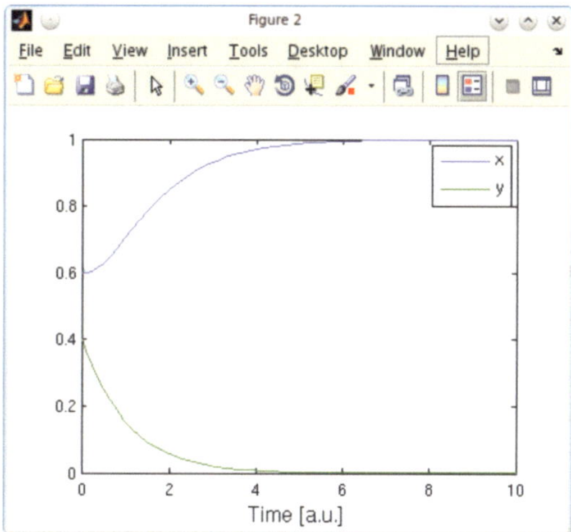

6. The differentiation of mid- and hindbrain: automatic model selection

A common problem in the modeling of biological systems is the existence of a plethora of possible models that could explain the observed behavior. Therefore, methods for the automatic evaluation of features on a whole series of models are often required. In our third example of dynamic modeling using Odefy we investigate a multicellular system from developmental biology. During vertebrate development, the differentiation of mid- and hindbrain is determined by several transcription and secreted factors, which are expressed in a well-defined spatial pattern (Prakash & Wurst, 2004), the mid-hindbrain boundary (MHB, see Figure 9, left). While transcription factors control the regulation of genes within the same cell, secreted factors are transported through the cell membrane in order to induce signaling cascades in surrounding cells. The gene expression pattern is again maintained by a tightly regulated regulatory network between the respective factors (Wittmann et al., 2009b). We will here focus on four major factors from the MHB system: the transcription factors Otx2 and Gbx2, as well as the secreted proteins Fgf8 and Wnt1.
From the technical point-of-view, we will learn how to create a whole ensemble of different regulatory models, and subsequently how to iterate over all models in order to check whether each regulatory wiring is capable of maintaining the sharp expression patterns at the MHB.

6.1 Modeling a multi-compartment system using Odefy

A substantial difference to the models we worked with in previous sections of this chapter is the presence of multiple, linearly arranged cells in the modeled biological system (recall Figure 9). Each of these cells contains the identical regulatory machinery which needs to be connected and replicated as visualized in Figure 10. Note that this regulatory wiring corresponds to the results published in Wittmann et al. (2009b); below we will discuss the existence of further compatible models. The transcription factors Otx2 and Gbx2 inhibit each other's expression and control the expression of the secreted factors Fgf8 and Wnt1. The latter

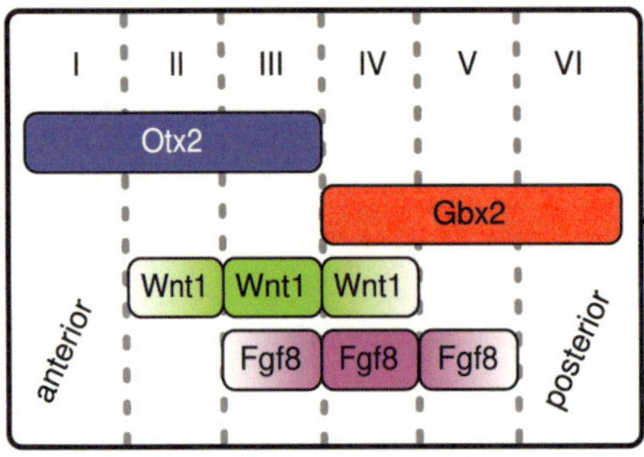

Expression	I	II	III	IV	V	VI
Otx2	1	1	1	0	0	0
Gbx2	0	0	0	1	1	1
Fgf8	0	0	0	1	0	0
Wnt1	0	0	1	0	0	0

Fig. 9. Expression patterns at the mid-hindbrain boundary. While the anterior part of the developing brain is dominated by Otx2 expression and Wnt1 signaling at the boundary, the posterior part shows Gbx2 expression and Fgf8 signaling. Note that in the left panel fading colors indicate secreted factors that do not translate into the discretized expression pattern on the right. Adapted from Krumsiek et al. (2010)

ones in turn enhance each others activity in the neighboring cells, simulating the secretion and diffusion of these proteins in the multicellular context. For our analysis, we will focus on only 6 "cells" – which could also represent a whole region during development at the MHB – linearly arranged next to each other.

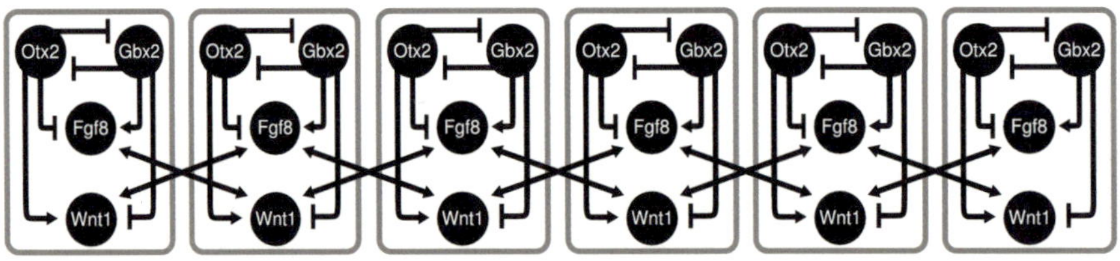

Fig. 10. Six-compartment model representing the different areas of the developing brain. Each unit contains the same regulatory network, neighboring cells are connected via the secreted protein Fgf8 and Wnt1.

In Odefy, we first need to define the core model, again using simple Boolean formulas for the representation of the regulatory wiring:

```
mhb = ExpressionsToOdefy({'Otx2=~Gbx2','Gbx2=~Otx2',...
    'Fgf8=~Otx2&&Gbx2&&Wnt1','Wnt1=~Gbx2&&Otx2&&Fgf8'});
```

Now, in order to automatically generate a connected six cell system, we make use of the Odefy `MultiModel` function:

```
multiMHB=MultiModel(mhb, [3 4], 6);
```

From the regulatory model `single` we generate 6 cells, whereas the third and fourth factors of the system are considered to be connected between neighboring cells. The variable `multiMHB` now contains the complete multi-cellular model comprising of a total of 24 factors:

```
multiMHB =

     tables: [1x24 struct]
       name: 'odefymodel_x_6'
    species: {24x1 cell}
```

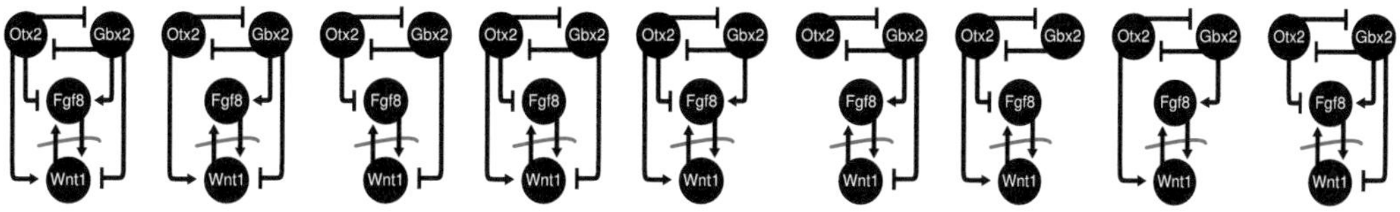

Fig. 11. All network variants known to give rise to a stable MHB boundary. For all networks we observe a mutual inhibition of Otx2 and Gbx2 and have antagonistic effects of these two factors on Fgf8 and Wnt1 expression. Moreover, we find that Fgf8 and Wnt1 require each other for their stable maintenance. Adapted from Krumsiek et al. (2010)

6.2 Automatic model selection procedure

In the following we will assemble a set over 100 distinct models between the four factors in our MHB system. We will have nine variants in total which indeed give rise to the correct behavior and are compatible to biological reality, and 100 randomly assembled networks which will obviously fail to produce a stable MHB. The following networks are the nine "positive" variants, cf. Krumsiek et al. (2010):

```
eqs = {};
eqs{end+1} = {'Otx2=~Gbx2','Gbx2=~Otx2','Fgf8=~Otx2&&Gbx2&&Wnt1',
    'Wnt1=~Gbx2&&Otx2&&Fgf8'};
eqs{end+1} = {'Otx2=~Gbx2','Gbx2=~Otx2','Fgf8=Gbx2&&Wnt1',
    'Wnt1=~Gbx2&&Otx2&&Fgf8'};
eqs{end+1} = {'Otx2=~Gbx2','Gbx2=~Otx2','Fgf8=~Otx2&&Gbx2&&Wnt1',
    'Wnt1=~Gbx2&&Fgf8'};
eqs{end+1} = {'Otx2=~Gbx2','Gbx2=~Otx2','Fgf8=~Otx2&&Wnt1',
    'Wnt1=~Gbx2&&Otx2&&Fgf8'};
eqs{end+1} = {'Otx2=~Gbx2','Gbx2=~Otx2','Fgf8=~Otx2&&Gbx2&&Wnt1',
    'Wnt1=Otx2&&Fgf8'};
eqs{end+1} = {'Otx2=~Gbx2','Gbx2=~Otx2','Fgf8=Gbx2&&Wnt1',
    'Wnt1=~Gbx2&&Fgf8'};
eqs{end+1} = {'Otx2=~Gbx2','Gbx2=~Otx2','Fgf8=~Otx2&&Wnt1',
    'Wnt1=Otx2&&Fgf8'};
eqs{end+1} = {'Otx2=~Gbx2','Gbx2=~Otx2','Fgf8=Gbx2&&Wnt1',
    'Wnt1=Otx2&&Fgf8'};
eqs{end+1} = {'Otx2=~Gbx2','Gbx2=~Otx2','Fgf8=~Otx2&&Wnt1',
    'Wnt1=~Gbx2&&Fgf8'};
```

The initial network we discussed in Figure 10 is the first one in this list, while all other networks represent subsets of the first one (Figure 11). Note that for now we only create single-compartment variants, the `MultiModel` function comes into play later on. Next, we need to generate actual Boolean models from these equations:

```
models={};
for i=1:numel(eqs)
    models{i} = ExpressionsToOdefy(eqs{i});
end
```

Next, we add a thousand randomly generated networks by using the `GraphToOdefy` function. This function takes the adjacency matrix of a regulatory network, interpreting 1 as activatory, -1 as inhibitory and 0 as no influence, and automatically generates an Odefy model structure:

```
for i=1:100
    models{end+1} =  GraphToOdefy(randi(3,4,4)-2);
end
```

The expression `randi(3,4,4)-2` creates a 4x4 matrix of values between -1 and 1. Note that if not explicitly specified, Odefy employs a standard logic to combine multiple inputs, where a player will be active whenever at least one activator and no inhibitors are present. Our `models` cell array now contains a total of 109 Boolean models, each of which we will test for its capability to create the MHB expression pattern. The general idea is to first convert each model to a multicompartment variant, and then let an ODE simulation run from the known stable MHB expression pattern in order to check whether the system departs from this required state. First, we need to define an initial state corresponding to the stable expression pattern from Figure 9:

```
init = [0 0 1 0 0 0 0 0 0 0 0 0 0 0 0 0 0 0 0 0 0 0 0 0 0 0 0 0 0 0 0 0 0
    0 1 1 0 0 0 0];
```

Next, we iterate over all networks and perform the actual testing:

```
for i=1:numel(models)
    multi = MultiModel(models{i}, [3 4], 6);
    simstruct = CreateSimstruct(multi);
    simstruct.initial = knownstate;
    simstruct.type = 'hillcubenorm';
    [t,y] = OdefySimulation(simstruct, 0);
    if all(y(end,:)>0.5 == knownstate)
        fprintf('Valid: Model %d\n', i);
    end
end
```

Note the usage of `CreateSimstruct` and `OdefySimulation` to create a continuous ODE simulation of the converted Boolean model, as previously described in this chapter. The final validation statement `if all(y(end,:)>0.5 == knownstate)` determines whether each player still fits to the known MHB expression state, considering each player above a value of 0.5 to be active. Be aware that the execution of the model selection code might take a few minutes, depending on your machine. Since it is very unlikely that any of the randomly generated models is actually capable of obtaining the desired behavior, the final command line result should look like this:

```
Valid: Model 1
Valid: Model 2
Valid: Model 3
Valid: Model 4
Valid: Model 5
Valid: Model 6
Valid: Model 7
Valid: Model 8
Valid: Model 9
```

Taken together, we demonstrated how to automatically test for a specific feature in a set of models. For illustration purposes and in order to actually get a positive result here, we added a set of models known to give rise to the desired behavior.

7. A large-scale model of T-cell signaling: connecting Odefy to the SB toolbox

In our final example we focus on a model of T-cell activation processes, which play a pivotal role in the immune system. The model employed here has been previously described in the literature and consists of 40 factors and 55 pairwise regulatory interactions (Wittmann et al., 2009a). We will demonstrate how to convert the Boolean model to its ODE version and export the result to the popular MATLAB Systems Biology toolbox[4]. From within this toolbox we can then conveniently perform simulations, steady state analysis as well as parameter sensitivity analysis. Furthermore, we will see how the compilation of an SB toolbox model to a .mex file MATLAB function dramatically increases the simulation speed of ODE systems.

7.1 The model

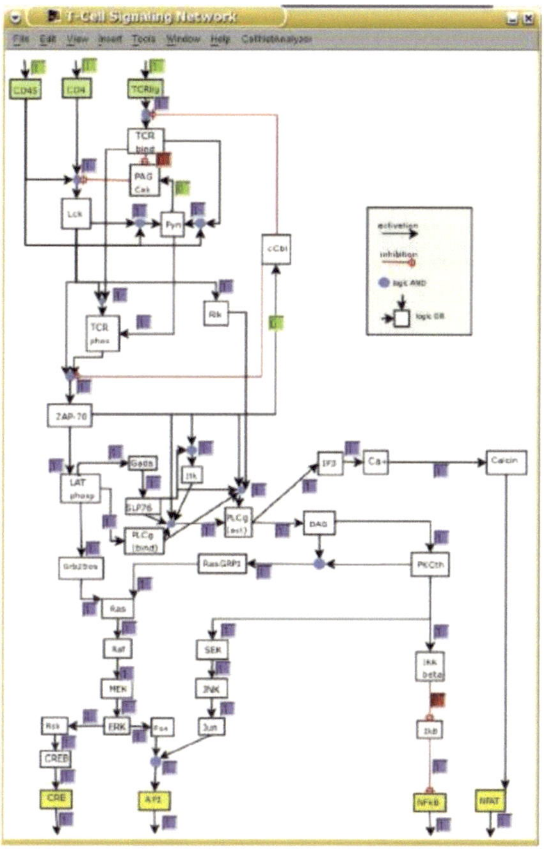

Fig. 12. Logical model of T-cell activation. The model contains a total of 40 factors and 49 regulatory interactions, with three input species - resembling T-cell receptors - and four output species - the activated transcription factors. Screenshot from CellNetAnalyzer (Klamt et al., 2006)

T-cells are part of the lymphoid immune system in higher eukaryotes. When foreign antigens, like bacterial cell surface markers, bind to certain receptors these cells, signaling cascades are triggered within the T-cell triggering the expression of several transcription factors in the nucleus. Ultimately, this leads to the initiation of a specific immune response aimed at eliminating the targeted foreign antigens (Klamt et al., 2006). The logical structure of the T-cell signaling model is shown in Figure 12. There are three inputs to the system: the T-cell receptor TCR, the coreceptor CD4 and an input for CD45; as well as four outputs:

[4] http://www.sbtoolbox2.org/

the transcription factors CRE, AP1, NFkB and NFAT. In total, the model comprises of 40 factors with 49 regulatory interactions. We will not provide a list of all Boolean formulas in this system here. The model can either be downloaded from the Odefy materials page[5], or obtained along with the CellNetAnalyzer toolbox[6]. In the following, we assume the Odefy model variable `tcell` to be existent in the current MATLAB workspace:

```
>> load tcell.mat
>> tcell

tcell =

    species: {1x40 cell}
     tables: [1x40 struct]
       name: 'Tcellsmall'
```

7.2 Exporting the ODE version to SB toolbox

At this point we require a working copy of the SBTOOLBOX2 package which can be freely obtained from the web[7]. We translate the Boolean T-cell model into its HillCube ODE counterpart and convert the resulting differential equation system into an SB toolbox internal representation:

```
sbmodel = CreateSBToolboxModel(tcell, 'hillcube', 1)
```

The third argument indicates whether to directly create an `SBmodel` object, or whether to generate an internal MATLAB structure representation of the model. Both variants should be compatible with the other SB toolbox functions. The result should now look like this:

```
SBmodel
        =======
        Name: Tcellsmall
        Number States:                    40
        Number Variables:                 0
        Number Parameters:                147
        Number Reactions:                 0
        Number Functions:                 0
```

We successfully created a HillCube ODE version of the Boolean T-cell model in SB toolbox. This allows us to make use of the full functionality of this toolbox, like regular simulations and steady state calculations for example:

```
init=zeros(numel(tcell.species),1);
init(strcmp(SBstates(sbmodel),'tcr'))=1;
init(strcmp(SBstates(sbmodel),'cd4'))=1;
init(strcmp(SBstates(sbmodel),'cd45'))=1;
sbmodel = SBinitialconditions(sbmodel,init);

SBsimulate(sbmodel);
ss=SBsteadystate(sbmodel);
```

We first set the initial values of the input factors TCR, CD4 and CD45 to 1 and then call the `SBsteadystate` function. The `ss` vector now contains steady states for all 40 factors in the system given the current initial states and parameters. `SBsimulate` will open the interactive simulation dialog of SB toolbox:

---

[5] http://hmgu.de/cmb/odefymaterials

[6] http://www.mpi-magdeburg.mpg.de/projects/cna/cna.html

[7] http://www.sbtoolbox2.org/

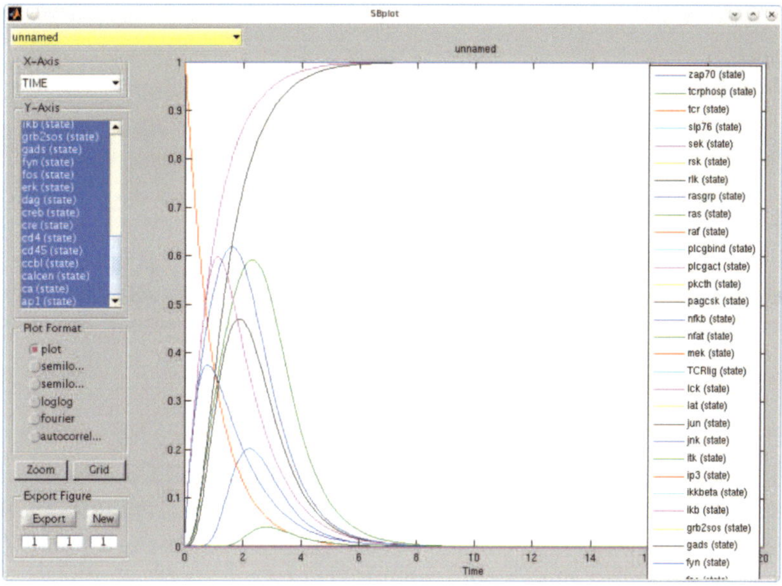

In addition to these simple functionalities we could also have achieved with the Odefy toolbox, we could now apply advanced dynamic model analysis techniques implemented in the SB toolbox. This includes, amongst others, local and global parameter sensitivity analysis (Zhang et al., 2010), bifurcation analysis (Waldherr et al., 2007) and parameter fitting methods (Lai et al., 2009).

7.3 Compiling the model to .mex format – fast model simulations

As our final example of connecting Odefy with the SB Toolbox, we will compile the T-cell model into the MATLAB .mex format. For this purpose we also need a copy of the SBPD Toolbox[8] in addition to the regulatory SB Toolbox. The compilation is performed in a single function call as follows:

```
SBPDmakeMEXmodel(sbmodel);
```

which will create a file called `Tcellsmall.mexa64` (the file extension might differ depending on the operating system and architecture) in the current working directory. Since the compiled SB toolbox functions employ a special numeric ODE integrator optimized for compiled models, the compiled version outperforms the regular simulation by far. To verify this, we let the system run from the initial state defined above and measure the elapsed time for the calculation:

```
tic;
for i=1:10
    r = SBsimulate(sbmodel,0:0.01:20);
end
toc;
```

yielding

```
Elapsed time is 13.585409 seconds.
```

on a Intel(R) Core(TM)2 Duo CPU P9700, 2.8 GHz. In contrast, the compiled model simulation is substantially faster:

[8] can also be obtained from `http://www.sbtoolbox2.org/`

```
tic;
for i=1:10
    r=Tcellsmall(0:0.01:20, init);
end
toc;
```

producing

```
Elapsed time is 0.100033 seconds.
```

That is, for the T-cell model the compiled version runs approximately 140 times faster than a regular simulation employing MATLAB built-in numerical ODE solvers. This feature can be particularly useful when a large number of simulations is required, e.g. for parameter optimization by fitting the simulated curves to measured experimental data.

8. Conclusion

In this tutorial we learned how to use the Odefy toolbox to model and analyze molecular biological systems. Boolean models can be readily constructed from qualitative literature information, but obviously have severe limitations due to the abstraction of activity values to zero and one. We presented an automatic approach to convert Boolean models into systems of ordinary differential equations. Using the Odefy toolbox, we worked through various hands-on examples explaining the creation of Boolean models, the automatic conversion to systems of ODEs and several analysis approaches for the resulting models. In particular, we explained the concepts of steady states (i.e. states that do not change over time), update policies, state spaces, phase planes and systems parameters. Furthermore, we worked with several real biological systems involved in stem cell differentiation, immune system response and embryonal tissue formation. The Odefy toolbox is regularly maintained, open-source and free of charge. Therefore it is a good starting point in the analysis of ODE-converted Boolean models as it can be easily extended and adjusted to specific needs, as well as connected to popular analysis tools like the Systems Biology Toolbox.

9. References

Albert, R. & Othmer, H. G. (2003). The topology of the regulatory interactions predicts the expression pattern of the segment polarity genes in drosophila melanogaster., *J Theor Biol* 223(1): 1–18.

Alon, U. (2006). *An Introduction to Systems Biology: Design Principles of Biological Circuits (Chapman & Hall/Crc Mathematical and Computational Biology Series)*, Chapman & Hall/CRC.

Cantor, A. B. & Orkin, S. H. (2001). Hematopoietic development: a balancing act., *Curr Opin Genet Dev* 11(5): 513–519.
URL: *http://www.ncbi.nlm.nih.gov/pubmed/11532392*

Fauré, A., Naldi, A., Chaouiya, C. & Thieffry, D. (2006). Dynamical analysis of a generic boolean model for the control of the mammalian cell cycle., *Bioinformatics* 22(14): e124–e131.
URL: *http://bioinformatics.oxfordjournals.org/cgi/content/short/22/14/e124*

Glass, L. & Kauffman, S. A. (1973). The logical analysis of continuous, non-linear biochemical control networks., *J Theor Biol* 39(1): 103–129.

Kitano, H. (2002). Systems biology: a brief overview., *Science* 295(5560): 1662–1664.
URL: *http://dx.doi.org/10.1126/science.1069492*

Klamt, S., Saez-Rodriguez, J., Lindquist, J. A., Simeoni, L. & Gilles, E. D. (2006). A methodology for the structural and functional analysis of signaling and regulatory networks., *BMC Bioinformatics* 7: 56.
URL: *http://dx.doi.org/10.1186/1471-2105-7-56*

Klipp, E., Herwig, R., Kowald, A., Wierling, C. & Lehrach, H. (2005). *Systems Biology in Practice: Concepts, Implementation and Application*, 1 edn, Wiley-VCH.
URL: *http://www.amazon.com/exec/obidos/redirect?tag=citeulike07-20&path=ASIN/3527310789*

Krumsiek, J., Pölsterl, S., Wittmann, D. M. & Theis, F. J. (2010). Odefy–from discrete to continuous models., *BMC Bioinformatics* 11: 233.
URL: *http://dx.doi.org/10.1186/1471-2105-11-233*

Lai, X., Nikolov, S., Wolkenhauer, O. & Vera, J. (2009). A multi-level model accounting for the effects of jak2-stat5 signal modulation in erythropoiesis., *Comput Biol Chem* 33(4): 312–324.
URL: *http://dx.doi.org/10.1016/j.compbiolchem.2009.07.003*

Prakash, N. & Wurst, W. (2004). Specification of midbrain territory., *Cell Tissue Res* 318(1): 5–14.
URL: *http://dx.doi.org/10.1007/s00441-004-0955-x*

Samaga, R., Saez-Rodriguez, J., Alexopoulos, L. G., Sorger, P. K. & Klamt, S. (2009). The logic of egfr/erbb signaling: theoretical properties and analysis of high-throughput data., *PLoS Comput Biol* 5(8): e1000438.
URL: *http://dx.doi.org/10.1371/journal.pcbi.1000438*

Schmidt, H. & Jirstrand, M. (2006). Systems biology toolbox for matlab: a computational platform for research in systems biology., *Bioinformatics* 22(4): 514–515.
URL: *http://dx.doi.org/10.1093/bioinformatics/bti799*

Thomas, R. (1991). Regulatory networks seen as asynchronous automata: A logical description, *Journal of Theoretical Biology* 153(1): 1 – 23.

Tyson, J. J., Csikasz-Nagy, A. & Novak, B. (2002). The dynamics of cell cycle regulation., *Bioessays* 24(12): 1095–1109.
URL: *http://dx.doi.org/10.1002/bies.10191*

Vries, G. d., Hillen, T., Lewis, M. & Schõnfisch, B. (2006). *A Course in Mathematical Biology: Quantitative Modeling with Mathematical and Computational (Monographs on Mathematical Modeling and Computation)*, SIAM.

Waldherr, S., Eissing, T., Chaves, M. & Allgöwer, F. (2007). Bistability preserving model reduction in apoptosis, *10th IFAC Comp. Appl. in Biotechn*, pp. 327–332.
URL: *http://arxiv.org/abs/q-bio/0702011*

Werner, E. (2007). All systems go, *Nature* 446(7135): 493–494.
URL: *http://www.nature.com/nature/journal/v446/n7135/full/446493a.html*

Wittmann, D. M., Blöchl, F., Trümbach, D., Wurst, W., Prakash, N. & Theis, F. J. (2009). Spatial analysis of expression patterns predicts genetic interactions at the mid-hindbrain boundary., *PLoS Comput Biol* 5(11): e1000569.
URL: *http://dx.doi.org/10.1371/journal.pcbi.1000569*

Wittmann, D. M., Krumsiek, J., Saez-Rodriguez, J., Lauffenburger, D. A., Klamt, S. & Theis, F. J. (2009). Transforming boolean models to continuous models: methodology and application to t-cell receptor signaling., *BMC Syst Biol* 3: 98.
URL: *http://dx.doi.org/10.1186/1752-0509-3-98*

Zhang, T., Wu, M., Chen, Q. & Sun, Z. (2010). Investigation into the regulation mechanisms of trail apoptosis pathway by mathematical modeling, *Acta Biochimica et Biophysica Sinica* 42(2): 98–108.
URL: *http://abbs.oxfordjournals.org/content/42/2/98.abstract*

3

Systematic Interpretation of High-Throughput Biological Data

Kurt Fellenberg
Ruhr-Universität Bochum
Germany

1. Introduction

MATLAB has evolved from the command-line-based ``MATrix LABoratory" into a fully-featured programming environment. But is it really practical for implementing a larger software package? Also if it is intended to run on servers and if Unix is preferred as a server operation system? What if there are more problem-related statistical methods available in R? Positive answers to these and more questions are shown in example discussing the ``Multi-Conditional Hybridization Processing System" (M-CHiPS). Here, as well, the name is not entirely descriptive because apart from the classical microarray hybridizations it takes data from e.g. antibody array incubations as well as methylation or quantitative tandem mass spectrometry data by now. The system was implemented predominantly in MATLAB. It currently contains more than 13,000 hybridizations, incubations, gels, runs etc. comprising all common microarray transcriptomics platforms but also genomic chip data, chip-based methylation data, 2D-DIGE gels, antibody arrays (both single and dual-channel), and TMT 6-plex MS/MS data. Apart from tumor biopsies, it contains also data about model organisms, e.g. *Trypansosoma brucei*, *Candida albicans*, and *Aspergillus fumigates*, to date 11 organisms in total.

While data stemming from e. g. Microarray and Mass Spectrometry platforms need very different preprocessing steps prior to data interpretation, the result can generally be regarded as a table with its columns representing some biological conditions, e.g. various genotypes, growth conditions or tumor stages, just to give some examples. Also, in most cases, each row roughly represents a "gene", more precisely standing for its DNA sequence, methylation status, RNA transcript abundance, or protein level. Thus, quantitative data stemming from different platforms and representing the status of either the transcriptome, methylome or the proteome can be collected in the very same format (database structure, MATLAB variables). Also, the same set of algorithms can be applied for analysis and visualization.

However, the patterns comprised by these large genes × conditions data tables cannot be understood without additional information. The behaviours of some ten thousands of genes need to be explained by Gene Ontology terms or transcription factor binding sites. And often hundreds of samples need to be related to represented genotypes, growth conditions or disease states in order to interpret these data. In addition to the signal intensities, M-CHiPS records information about the protocols involved (to track down systematic errors), sample biology and clinical data. Risk parameters such as alcohol consumption and smoking habit are stored along with e.g. tumor stage and grade, cytogenetical aberrations, and lymphnode invasion, just to provide few examples. These additional data can be of arbitrary level of detail, depending on the field of research. For tumor biopsies, recently 119 such clinical factors plus 155 technical factors are accounted for, just to give one example. All these data are acquired and stored in a statistically accessible format and integrated into exploratory data analysis. Thus, the expression patterns are related to (and interpreted by means of) the biological and/or clinical data.

Thus the presented approach integrates heterogenous data. But not only are the data heterogenous. The high-throughput data as well as the additional information are stored in a data warehouse currently providing an analysis platform for more than 80 participants (www.m-chips.org) of different opinions about how they want to analyze their data. In subsection 4.2.3, the chapter will contrast providing a large multitude of possible algorithms to choose from to common view and use as a communication platform and user friendliness in general. As a platform for scientists written by scientists, it equally serves the interests of the programmers to code their methods quickly in the programming language that best suits their needs (4.2.4). Apart from MATLAB, M-CHiPS uses R, C, Perl, Java, and SQL providing the best environment for fast implementation of each task. The chapter discusses further advantages of such heterogeneity, such as combining the wealth of microarray statistics available in R and Bioconductor, with systems biology tools prevalently coded in MATLAB (4.1.4). It also discusses problems such as difficult installation and distribution as well as possible solutions (distribution as virtual machines, 4.2.4).

The last part of the chapter (section 5) is dedicated to what can be learned from such biological high-throughput data by inferring gene regulatory networks.

2. High-throughput biological data

Bioinformatics is a relatively new field. It started out with the need for interpreting accumulating amounts of sequence data. Thus the analysis of gene and/or protein sequences is what one may call ``classical'' bioinformatics. While sequence analysis still provides ample opportunity for scientific research, it is nowadays only one out of many bioinformatics subfields. Structure prediction attempts to delineate three-dimensional structures of proteins from their sequences. Microscopic and other biological or clinical (i.e. computer tomographical) images are used to model cellular or physiological processes. And quantitative, so called ``omics'' data record the status of many to all genes of an organism in one measurement. The status of a gene can be measured on different regulatory levels, corresponding to different processes involved in gene expression. While **genomics** refers to the abundance and the sequence of all genes, **epigenomics** data record e.g. the genes' degree of methylation (determining if a gene can be transcribed or not). Transcription of a gene means copying its information (stored as DNA sequence in the nucleus of the cell) into a data medium (much like a DVD or other media) that can leave the cell nucleus. This medium transports the information into the surrounding cytoplasm (where the hereby encoded protein is produced). It is called "messenger RNA" or "transcript". Transcript levels are reflected by (quantitative) **transcriptomics** data. Presence of the transcript is a prerequisite for producing the encoded protein in a process called translation. However, regulatory mechanisms governing this process as well as different decay rates both for different transcripts and for different proteins interfere with a direct proportional relationship of transcript and protein levels in most cases. Protein levels (i.e. the actual results of gene expression) are recorded by **proteomics** data. Each of these "omics" types characterizes a certain level of gene expression. There are more kinds of "omics" data, e.g. **metabolomics** data recording the status of the metabolites, small molecules that are intermediates of the biochemical reactions that make up the metabolism. However, the following examples will be restricted to gene expression, for simplicity.

All of the above-mentioned levels of gene expression have been monitored already prior to the advent of high-throughput measuring techniques. The traditional way of study, e.g. by southern blot (genomics), northern blot (transcriptomics), or western blot (proteomics), is limited in the number of genes that can be recorded in one measurement, however. High-throughput techniques aim at multiplexing the assay, amplifying the number of genes measured in parallel by a factor of thousand or more, thus to assess the entire genome, methylome, transcriptome, or proteome of the organism under study. While such data bear great potential, e.g. for understanding the biological system as a whole, large numbers of simultaneously measured genes also introduce problems. Forty gene signals provided by traditional assays can be taken at face value as they are read out by eye (without requiring a computer). In contrast, 40,000 rows of recent quantitative data tables need careful statistical evaluation before being interpreted by machine learning techniques. Large numbers of e. g. transcription profiles necessitate statistical evaluation because any such profile may occur by chance within such a large data table.

Further, even disregarding all genes that do not show reproducible change throughout a set of biological conditions under study, computer-based interpretation (machine learning) is simply necessary, because the number of profiles showing significant change (mostly several hundreds to thousands) is still too large for visual inspection.

3. Computational requirements

With the necessity for computational data analysis, the question arises which type of computing power is needed. In contrast to e.g. sequence analysis, high-throughput data analysis does not need large amounts of processor time. Instead of parallelizing and batch-queuing, analysis proceeds interactively, tightly regulated, i.e. visually controlled, interpreted, and repeatedly parametrized by the user. However, high-throughput data analysis cannot always be performed on any desktop computer either, because it requires considerable amounts of RAM (at least for large datasets). Thus, although high-throughput data analysis may not require high-performance computing (in terms of "number crunching"), it is still best run on servers.

Using a server, its memory can be shared among many users logging in to it on demand. As detailed later, this kind of analysis can furthermore do with access to a database (4.3), webservice (4.2.1), and large numbers of different installed packages and libraries (4.1.3). Many of these software packages are open source and sometimes tricky to install. Apart from having at hand large chunks of RAM, the user is spared to perform tricky installations and updates as well as database administration. Webservers, database servers, and calculation servers sporting large numbers of heterogeneous, in part open-source packages and libraries are traditionally run on Unix operation systems. While in former times a lack of stability simply rendered Windows out of the question, it is still common belief among systems administrators that Unix maintenance is slightly less laborious. Also, I personally prefer Unix inter-process communication. Further it appears desirable to compile MATLAB code such that many users can use it on the server at the same time without running short of

licenses. Both licensed MATLAB and MATLAB compiler are available for both Windows and Unix. However, there are differences in graphics performance.
In 1998, MATLAB was still being developed in/for Unix. But times have changed. Graphics windows building up fast in Windows were appearing comparably slow when run under Unix ever since, suggesting that it is now being developed in/for Windows and merely ported to Unix. Performance was still bearable, however, until graphical user interface (GUI) such as menus, sliders, buttons etc. coded in C were entirely replaced by Java code. The Java versions are unbearably slow, particularly when accessed via secure shell (SSH) on a server from a client. For me that posed a serious problem. Being dependent on a Unix server solution for above reasons, I was seriously tempted to switch back to older MATLAB versions for the sole reason of perfect GUI performance. Also, I did not seem to be the only one having this problem. Comments on this I found on the internet tended to reflect some colleagues' anger to such extend that they cannot be cited here for reason of bad language. As older versions of MATLAB do not work for systems biology and other recent toolboxes, version downgrade was not an option. It therefore appeared that I had no choice other than to dispense with Unix / ssh. But what to do when client-side calculation is not possible for lack of memory? When switching to Windows is not intended?
A workaround presented itself with the development of data compression (plus caching and reduction of round trip time) for X connections designed for slow network connections. NX (http://www.nomachine.com) transports graphical data via the ssh port 22 with such high velocities that it nearly compensates for the poor Unix-server MATLAB-GUI performance. It was originally developed and the recent version is sold by the company Nomachine. There is also an open-source version maintained by Berlios (which unfortunately didn't work for all M-CHiPS functions in 2007). Needless to mention that I do hope that the Java GUI will be revisited by the Mathworks developing team in the future. But via NX, server-side Linux MATLAB graphics is useable. A further advantage of NX is that the free client is most easily set up on OSX or Windows running on the vast majority of lab clients as well as on the personal laptop of the average biologist. In this way, users can interact as if M-CHiPS were just another Windows program installed on their machine, but without tedious installation. Further, NX shows equally satisfying performance on clients old and new, having large or small memory, via connections fast and slow, i.e. even from home via DSL.

4. Data diversity and integration

Abovementioned configuration allows to provide MATLAB functions as well as other code to multiple users, e.g. within a department, core facility, company, or world-wide. As described, life scientists can use this service without having to bother with hardware administration, database administration, update or even installation. For these reasons, software as a service (SAAS) is a popular and also commercially successful way e.g. to deliver microarray analysis algorithms to the user. However, different users have different demands. The differences can roughly be categorized into being related to different technical platforms used for data acquisition (such as microarrays or mass spectrometry), related to different fields of research (plants or human cancer), or preference of certain machine learning methods.

4.1 Technical platforms

There is a multitude of different high-throughput techniques for acquiring "omics" data. As explained in section 2, following examples focus on the different regulatory levels of gene expression. In order to provide an outline of the technical development, microarray platforms are discussed in more detail.

4.1.1 Microarrays

Biological high-throughput quantification started out in the 1990s with the advent of cDNA microarrays. Originally, in comparison to recent arrays very large nylon membranes were hybridized with radioactively labelled transcripts. Within shortest time, microarrays became popular. Although (and possibly because few people were actually aware of this at that time) data quality was abysmally poor. The flexibility of the nylon membrane as well as first-version imaging programs intolerant of deviations from the spotting grid caused a considerable share of spots being affiliated to the wrong genes. Also, although radioactivity actually shows a superior (wider) linear range of measured intensities when compared to the recently used fluorescent dyes, it provided only for a single channel. Thus each difference in the amount of spotted cDNA, for example due to a differing concentration of the spotted liquid as caused by a newly made PCR for spotting a new array batch, directly affected the signal intensities. This heavily distorted observed transcription patterns. Nowadays, self-made microarrays are small glass slides (no flexibility, miniaturization increases the signal-to-noise ratio), hybridized with two colors (channels) simultaneously. The colors refer to two different biological conditions labelled with two different fluorescent dyes. RNA abundances under the two conditions under study compete for binding sites at the same spot. Ratios (e.g. red divided by green) reflecting this competition are less dependent on the absolute number of binding sites (i.e. the amount of spotted cDNA) than the absolute signal intensities of only one channel. While even modern self-made chips still suffer from other systematic errors, e.g. related to the difference between individual pins used for spotting or related to the spatial distribution throughout the chip surface, commercially available microarrays mostly do not show any of these problems any more. Furthermore, modern commercial arrays show lower noise levels in comparison to recent self-made arrays (and these in turn in comparison to previous versions of self-made arrays), thus increasing reproducibility.

But even more beneficial than the substantial increase in data quality since 1998 is the increase in the variety of what can be measured. While at first microarrays were used only for recording transcript (mRNA) abundance, all levels of regulation mentioned in section 2 nowadays can be measured with microarrays. **Genomic** microarrays can be used to assess DNA sequences, for example to monitor hotspots of HIV genome mutation enabling the virus to evade patients' immune systems (Gonzalez et al., 2004; Schanne et al., 2008). **Epigenomic** microarrays that assess the methylation status of so-called CpG islands in or near promoters (regulatory sequences) of genes are used e.g. to study epigenetic changes in cancer. **Transcriptomic** (mRNA detecting) microarrays are still heavily used, the trend going from self-made arrays (cDNA spotted on glass support) to commercial platforms comprising photo-chemically on-chip synthesized oligomeres (Affimetrix), oligomeres applied to the chip surface by ink jet technology (Agilent), or first immobilized on tiny beads that in turn are randomly dispersed over the chip surface (Illumina), just to provide a few examples. Recently, the role of transcriptomic microarrays is gradually taken over by so-called next generation sequencing. Here, mRNA molecules (after being reversely transcribed into cDNA molecules) are sequenced. Instances of occurrence of each sequence are counted, providing a score for mRNA abundance in the cell. While sequencing as such is a long-established technique, throughput and feasibility necessary for transcriptomics use

by ordinary laboratories has been achieved only few years ago. Nevertheless, this technique may well supersede transcriptomic microarrays in the near future. **Proteomic** microarrays are used to assess abundances of the ultimate products of gene expression, the proteins. To this end, molecules able to specifically bind a certain protein, so-called antibodies, are immobilized on the microarray. Incubating such a chip with a mixture of proteins from a biological sample labelled with a fluorescent dye, each protein binds to its antibody. Its abundance (concentration) will be proportional to the detected fluorescent signal.
Unfortunately, the affinities of antibodies to their proteins differ considerably from antibody to antibody. These differences are even more severe than the differences in the amount of spotted cDNA abovementioned for transcriptomic cDNA microarrays. Thus the absolute signals can not be taken at face value. However, as for the transcriptomic cDNA arrays, a possible solution is to incubate with two different samples, each labelled with a different color (fluorescent dye). The ratio of the two signal intensities (e.g. a protein being two-fold upregulated in cancer as compared to normal tissue) for each protein will be largely independent of the antibody affinities. More than two conditions (dyes) can be measured simultaneously, each resulting in a so-called "channel" of the measurement.

4.1.2 Other platforms

The general categorization into single-channel and multi-channel data also applies to other technical platforms. There are, for example, both single-channel and multi-channel quantitative mass spectrometry and 2D-gel data. Using 2D-gels, a complex mixture of proteins extracted from a given sample is separated first by charge (first dimension), thereafter by mass (second dimension). In contrast to the microarray technique, the separation is not achieved by each protein binding to its specific antibody immobilized on the chip at a certain location. Instead, proteins are separated by running through the gel in an electric field, their velocity depending on their specific charge, and their size. As for microarrays, the separation results in each protein being located at a different x-y-coordinate, thus providing a distinct signal. A gel can be loaded with a protein mixture from only one biological condition, quantifying the proteins e.g. by measuring the staining intensity of a silver staining, resulting in single-channel data. For multi-channel data, protein mixtures stemming from different biological conditions are labelled with different fluorescent dyes, one color for each biological condition. Thus, after running the gel, at the specific x-y-location of a certain protein each color refers to the abundance of that protein under a certain condition. Unlike with microarrays, there is no competition for binding sites at a certain location among protein molecules of different color. Nevertheless, data of different channels are not completely independent.
In general, regardless of the technique, separate channels acquired by the same measurement (i.e. hybridization, incubation, gel, run, ...) share the systematic errors of this particular measurement and thus tend show a certain degree of dependency. They should therefore not be handled in the same way as single-channel data, where each "channel" stems from a separate measurement. Data representation (database structure, MATLAB variables, etc.) and algorithms need to be designed accordingly. Fortunately, independent of the particular platform, the acquired data are always either single- or multi-channel data. In the latter case, different channels stemming from the same measurement show a certain degree of dependency. This is also true for all technical platforms.
As a last example of this incomplete list of quantitative high-throughput techniques assessing biological samples, I will briefly mention a technique that, albeit long

established for small molecules, only recently unfolded its potential for high-throughput quantitative proteomics. Mass spectrometry assesses the mass-to-charge ratio of ions. To this end, proteins are first digested into smaller pieces (peptides) by enzymes (e.g. trypsine), then separated (e.g. by liquid chromatography) before being ionized. Ionization can be carried out e.g. by a laser beam from a crystalline matrix (matrix-assisted laser desorption/ionization, abbreviated MALDI) or by dispersion into an aerosol from a liquid (eletrospray ionization, ESI). Movement of these ions in an electric field (in high vacuum) is observed in order to determine their mass-to-charge ratio. This can be achieved simply by measuring the time an ion needs to travel from one end of an evacuated tube to the other (time of flight, TOF), or by other means (e.g. Quadrupole, Orbitrap). The detection works via induced charge when the ion hits a surface (at the destination end of the flight-tube in case of TOF) or e.g. via an AC image current induced as oscillating ions pass nearby (Orbitrap).

Unlike e.g. for antibody microarray data where each protein can be identified through its location on the array, for mass spectrometry the quantification must be accompanied by a complex identification procedure. To this end, ions of a particular mass-to-charge ratio are fragmented by collision with inert gas molecules (mostly nitrogen or argon). The fragments are then subjected to a second round of mass spectrometry assessment (tandem mass spectrometry or MS/MS). The resulting MS2 spectrum contains enough information to identify the unfragmented peptide ion, in a second step eventually enabling to deduce the original protein. Like other techniques, quantitative mass spectrometry can be used to execute single-channel measurements (label-free) or to produce multi-channel data, measuring several biological conditions (up to 6 e.g. via TMT labelling) at the same time.

4.1.3 Data integration

Above examples illustrate that the input into any comprehensive software solution is highly diverse. For cDNA microarrays alone several so called imaging software packages exist (e.g. Genepix, Bioimage, AIS and Xdigitize) that convert the pixel intensities of the scanned microarray image into one signal intensity per gene. Also, specialized software is available for the equivalent task in case of 2D-gels (e.g. Decider) and for protein identification in case of mass spectrometry (Mascot, Sequest), just to name few examples. Thus, the first step necessarily means to parse different formats for import. Furthermore, different platforms require different preprocessing steps which deal with platform-specific systematic errors. While local background subtraction may alleviate local spatial bias in different areas of a microarray, mass spectrometry spectra may require isotope correction and other measures specific for mass spectrometry. Any comprehensive software solution necessarily needs to provide a considerable number of specialized algorithms in order to parse and preprocess each type of data.

On the positive side, there are also certain preprocessing steps required for all platforms alike. Normalization of multiplicative and/or additive offsets between different biological conditions is generally required, since pipetting errors or different label incorporation rates affect the overall signal intensities obtained for each biological sample. Also, more than half of the genes of higher organisms tend to be not expressed to a measurable amount in a typical multi-conditional experiment (with the exception of studying embryonic development). Thus, for each dataset, regardless of the technique it is acquired by, genes whose signal intensities remain below the detection limit throughout all biological conditions under study can (and should) be filtered out. Regarding the fold-changes (ratios with a certain biological reference condition in the denominator) instead of absolute signal intensities is common practice for microarray and other high-throughput data. A gene switching from a signal of 0.001 (e.g. in normal tissue) to 0.002 (in cancer) would be otherwise interpreted as being two-fold upregulated, although meaningful signals may start only in the range of 10^3.

Further, measurements need to be performed repeatedly in order to assess the reproducibility of a signal. Repetitions are cost- and labor-intensive. There have been many attempts to compute a p-value from one single measurement alone, more than ten years ago for microarray measurements as well as recently in the mass spectrometry field (Zhang et al., 2006). However, distributions of gene abundance signals tend to vary, e.g. with signal intensity. For each one-measurement statistical tests I know of, a quantile-quantile plot revealed that its distribution assumption does not hold. Thus these tests do not at all yield proper p-values. While this is inconvenient for the wet-lab life scientist, it simplifies data integration for the bioinformatician. For few, i.e. in the range of three to four repetitions, the significance of gene signals can be tested e.g. using the limma package (by Gordon Smyth; for reference see Smyth, 2005), which is based on a very reasonable distribution assumption. This method, albeit originally developed for microarray data, seems to work properly for mass spectrometry data, as well. If there are six or more repeatedly performed measurements per condition (there usually are not), permutation tests such as the Significance Analysis of Microarray Data (SAM; Tusher, 2001) should be used. The latter can do without any distribution assumption, extracting the distribution from the data (by randomly permutating the measurements many times). Thus, there is no reason not to use it e.g. also for mass spectrometry data. At the very moment, six repetitions represent considerable costs here. However, this may become feasible in the future.

Thus, data integration can be achieved by a limited set of platform-specific preprocessing steps before data are collected into a genes × measurements matrix variable. The last step of preprocessing, the normalization, can be applied to data stemming from any platform in the same manner. There are different normalization algorithms such as loglinear normalization (Beißbarth, 2000), locally weighted scatterplot smoothing (LOWESS; Cleveland, 1979), quantile normalization (Bolstad, 2003), or variance stabilization (Huber, 2002) that can be applied under different circumstances (e.g. variance stabilization when differing variances for low and high signal intensities pose a problem). However, the choice depends less on the particular platform, but on particularities of the data and in part on personal preference (which will be discussed in detail in 4.2.3). The way a normalization is iterated to produce directly comparable numbers throughout all measurements of a multiconditional experiment depends on the data being single- or multichannel. In the latter case each non-control channel is fitted to the local control channel of the same measurement (hybridization, incubation, run, ...). In the former case (single channel), each measurement is fitted to the median of the repeatedly performed measurements of the control condition. Either single- or multi-channel data will be obtained from any technical platform. Thus, one of the two above ways to iterate normalization methods will be applicable – in combination with any of the above normalization methods, regardless of which technical platform the data stem from.

The resulting normalized data can universally be stored in another genes × measurements matrix of the same size. Thereafter, single genes are filtered out that show low signals throughout the conditions under study, or insignificant (e.g. irreproducible) change. Sometimes it pays off to discard a single (outlying) measurement instead of too many genes. In each case, the filtering process results in yet another genes × measurements matrix, but one of considerably reduced size, this time. Thus, preprocessing results stemming from a plethora of different technical platforms are stored in a common format.

4.1.4 Coding requirements

Above examples illustrate the demands placed on any comprehensive software solution. It needs to provide a multitude of both platform-specific and ubiquitously applicable algorithms. For any larger collection of interacting functions, one should think about ways to intelligently structure such code in order to properly develop a larger software package. Aspects range from re-using code, object oriented programming, and providing to the users a quick (one-click, automated) way of reporting bugs, to implementing a quickly adaptable menu structure, and using a concurrent version system.

In addition to simply being large, such a collection of algorithms tends to be under constant development. Better versions of already comprised algorithms will appear, new functions will need to be added regularly. Without extensive manpower, satisfactory maintenance of the system is only feasible when original source code (delivered along with the published method) can be plugged. Unfortunately, the vast majority of abovementioned algorithms for parsing data from different microarray platforms, preprocessing, and statistics is written in R. The programming environment R (http://www.r-project.org), an open-source version of S+, is the „natural habitat" of the statistician. In contrast to Matlab it provides tailored data types facilitating the handling of factors and levels, and more than one type of for missing values (NaN), to provide only two examples. For microarray and other high-throughput biological data, there is a comprehensive open-source R toolbox called Bioconductor (www.bioconductor.org), providing a collection of recently 460 R packages written and maintained by scientists all over the world, free to use. Several collegues (bioinformaticians) who were programming in Matlab in the 1980s switched to R for one or the other of above advantages since then.

However, Bioconductor can be regarded a platform made by bioinformaticians for bioinformaticians. Command-line style invocation and parametrization tends to „unhinge" many biologists who prefer clearly laid out menus, buttons and sliders, interactive graphics, in short a program that can be entirely operated by mouse click. Graphical user interfaces (GUI) as well as interactive graphs (e.g. returning x and y coordinates upon mouse click into the figure), although by now possible also in R, are the traditional domain of Matlab. In my opinion, implementation of both is considerably easier and thus faster than in R even to date. Moreover, in the field of systems biology (the science of modeling, simulating, and predicting the interplay of genes as a whole) the trend appears to be vice versa, with more tools being coded in Matlab than in R. In order to combine systems biology as well as fast implementation of user-friendly GUI and interactive graphs of Matlab with the statistical treasure trove readily available in R, both environments need to be interfaced. This can be achieved e.g. by the R.matlab-package maintained by Henrik Bengtsson (http://cran.r-project.org/web/packages/R.matlab). Entirely written in R, it provides (amongst other options for establishing a connection) two functions converting variables dumped into a matlab workspace (.mat) file into an R workspace and vice versa. The slight performance disadvantage of writing to and reading from hard disk is more than compensated for by perfect safety and reliability (no memory manipulation, no segmentation faults).

Furthermore, the interface is most easy to use (invoking one function for reading, one for writing) and appears to convert Matlab variables of each class (at least all classes we tested, incl. e.g. structs) into the best corresponding R data type. In order to plug algorithms written in R in a multi-user scenario, M-CHiPS dumps only the required variables into a .mat file located in the /tmp folder, its filename comprising the user name (so to prevent collision with other users' actions). Then an R shell is invoked by Unix command that reads the variables, invokes the R function to perform, and stores the result in another .mat file. For seamless inter-process communication via hard disk, it is advisable to await complete writing of a file by the other process (e.g. by using a different result filename for the R to Matlab direction and waiting for the R process to delete the first file as a signal that it finished writing the second one). As both processes run on the same machine (meaning the same hard drive buffer), this procedure is reasonably fast. The time needed for transporting the data to and from R is negligible in comparision to the runtime of any R code that was interfaced to M-CHiPS, as long as only the required variables are transferred instead of transferring the whole workspace.

4.2 Machine learning methods

As shown above, preprocessing of biological high-throughput quantifications generally starts with parsing the particular format of an input file. The imported data sometimes have to undergo platform-specific preprocessing steps, always followed by normalization and filtering. The preprocessing ends with a data table of reduced size, rows representing genes, columns representing measurements. Normalization has taken care of systematic differences among measurements (caused e.g. by differing label incorporation rates) rendering all numbers in the data table directly comparable. The data are now ready for "high-level analysis" (as opposed to preprocessing).

4.2.1 Common workspace organization

From before normalization and onwards, the data are also kept in common format, regardless of the acquisition platform. Thus, high-level analysis can take place on a commonly structured workspace. The M-CHiPS workspace documentation (http://mchips.org/workspace.html) provides an example of how such a workspace may look like. Fig. 1 shows the format of selected variables. Variable names are provided in blue color. Variable prim shows the typical genes × measurements matrix format, while stain and multichannel are vectors keeping track of which measurement belongs to which biological condition and to which hybridization (incubation, gel, or MS run), respectively. The names are related to the first task they were introduced for, i. e. color-coding (staining) graphical objects according to the biological conditions they belong to, and affiliating the different channels to multi-channel hybridizations, respectively. The name "prim" is explained later. Variables ngen and nexp are both scalars holding the numbers of genes and measurements (1998 referred to as "experiments" before the latter term was transferred to the multi-conditional dataset as a whole), respectively. The variable prim records the data before normalization. Normalized data and ratios are stored in separate variables. At the risk of occupying too much memory, keeping both the raw data and normalized intensities is necessary because analysis is an iterative procedure rather than following a fixed workflow. Both ratios and absolute intensities (as well as ranks) may be subjected to analysis algorithms in any temporal order. Even the raw data may be needed at a later stage, e. g. if the resulting plots reveal saturation effects. In this case, data will be re-filtered for saturation which is best detected by assessing the raw data.

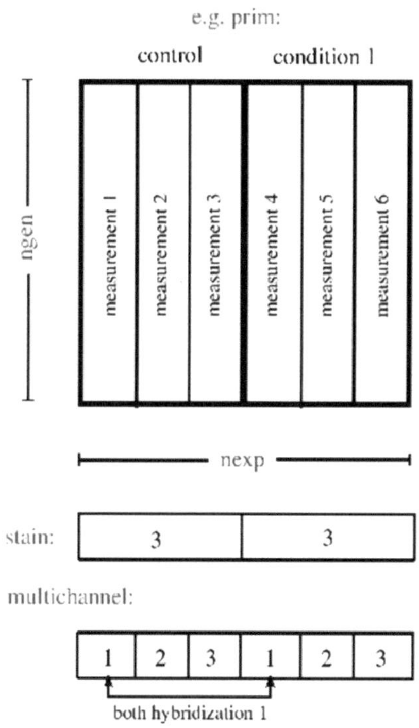

Fig. 1. Selected variable formats, variable names are shown in blue.

Because filtering can be repeated with different parameters at any time, rows representing genes that have been filtered out cannot be removed from the variables, either. Index variable "geneorder" holds the row numbers of the genes that "survived" the current filtering, in a sequence determined by a current sorting criterion. Other indexes record which genes (or measurements) have been selected by the user. Tab. 1 provides an exemplary list of variables, sorted by content and format.

The name "prim" stands for the primary of e.g. two spot sets on a microarray that may result from spotting each gene in duplicate. Thus, the purpose of prim (and secu) is to separately hold each single set of signals (available for all genes) that stems from the same channel or from the same single-channel measurement. Such sets stemming from the same channel share the same measuring procedure including sampling, labelling, as well as hybridization, incubation, or the like, thus being highly dependent. As a result, they cannot serve as independent repetitions for statistical tests (i.e. they ought to be averaged beforehand). Nevertheless, for the M-CHiPS workspace, such sets are kept separate because they can provide an "atomic" unit of variance in plots whose axes are dimensionless. A lack of units is typical for the entire field. Raw data are acquired by e.g. scanners or mass detectors in arbitrary machine units. Already at the stage of data acquisition, these machine units tend to be incomparable to those of data produced by other machines. Later on during data analysis, the signal intensities are often converted into ratios or distance measures for which the unit cancels out. In such cases, the difference between primary and secondary spots on an array stands for the minimal distance beyond which biological differences cannot be resolved even after optimizing the wet-lab protocol. Simply put, whenever a difference between two conditions is not considerably larger than this minimal distance, the conditions cannot be distinguished by the technique.

- Data
    - ngen x nexp data matrices:
        - prim - raw data (primary spot set)
        - secu - raw data (secondary spot set)
        - fitprim - normalized absolute (or estimated) intensities (primary spot set)
        - fitsecu - normalized absolute (or estimated) intensities (secondary spot set)
        - flatprim - normalized (linear) ratios (primary spot set)
        - flatsecu - normalized (linear) ratios (secondary spot set)
        - there are distances and ranks, as well
        - gen (containing the spot numbers) as well as experim (containing the measurement IDs) are in the same format for easy handling)
    - ngen x ncon (quality-) matrices:
        - pvalue - two-class pvalues
        - fpvalue - multi-class (i.e. only one per gene, but same size for compatibility)
        - minmaxseparation - min/max separation (Beißbarth, 2000)
        - stddevseparation – standard deviation separation (Beißbarth, 2000)
    - data annotation:
        - ginfo - gene annotations
        - anno - experiment annotations
- Metadata
        - family - array family (chip type)
        - experim - measurement IDs, multichannel - hybridizations
        - backgroundsubtraction
        - normalization
        - pvalues
        - filtermode1, filtermodebytimepoints1, filtermode2, filtermodebytimepoints2, filtermode3, filtermodebytimepoints3 - filter constraints
        - geneorder - filter result: index of filtered genes (sorted by sortmode)
        - ca.meta - correspondence analysis (input, type, ...)

Table 1. Incomplete workspace list, variable names are shown in blue

In addition to gene × measurement data matrices, Tab. 1 lists matrices comprising only as many columns as there are biological conditions (comprising quality scores such as p-values) as well as differently structured variables holding gene and experiment annotations that will be discussed below (4.3.1). Last but not least, all analysis steps – including the selection of raw data, all preprocessing steps as well as "high-level analyses" are recorded along with their parametrization. Thus, the entire analysis procedure is comprehensively documented by metadata in order to be able to reproduce the result. Metadata are also listed in the header of result reports that can be shared via internet by mouse click. Result reports are protected by passwords that are made available to collaborators. To date, they can consist of a shortlist of user-selected genes with signal intensities and ratios color-coded according to statistical significance (HTML), or of a complete list of raw signals plus nearly all computed values (tab delimited spreadsheet), or of MATLAB figures amended with explanatory text (HTML).

4.2.2 Machine learning

The MATLAB figures depicted in such result reports are generally produced by machine learning techniques. Machine learning can be divided into supervised and unsupervised learning. Supervised learning, also called classification, takes as input a grouping of objects of a so-called "training set". Such a training set may e.g. consist of tumor samples for which the exact tumor type (class) is known. The method learns properties within the data (e.g. affiliated to the expression profiles of certain genes) that can serve to discriminate these classes. Any such property (e.g. high expression of a certain gene) should be homogenously present within a certain class, but absent in at least one other class, so to distinguish the two classes. The entirety of learned properties is called a "classifier". The classifier can be used to sort a new cancer sample of yet unknown class affiliation into the correct class. While this is practised with data acquired from tailor-made cancer microarrays in order to provide physicians with additional information for their decisions on cancer therapy, its use is largely restricted to the clinics or any other area of application providing established and clear-cut classes to affiliate to.

Basic research often lacks such established classes or any other prior knowledge about the acquired data. At first, new hypothesis need to be generated by a more exploratory approach. Unsupervised learning does not need any group affiliations beforehand. Solely on the basis of the data, unsupervised machine learning methods extract clusters of objects whose quantified signals behave similar within the cluster but different in comparison to objects of a different cluster. Naming all unsupervised methods already being applied to the analysis of biological high-throughput data is beyond the scope of this chapter. It would result in an outline of applied statistics. Additionally, a few methods have been newly developed specifically for microarray data. Interestingly, the first clustering method applied to microarray data by Eisen and co-workers (Eisen, 1998), hierarchical clustering, is still most widely used. Because each following method had to be proven superior in one or the other aspect in order to get published, this appears tantamount e.g. to using Windows 3.1.

The one aspect all unsupervised methods have in common is that a scoring for similar (or dissimilar) behaviour has to be defined beforehand. While some algorithms are traditionally run on one particular so-called "distance measure", others operate on a wide variety of distance measures. In principle, each algorithm can be adapted to run on each distance measure. This is just not supported by each piece of software and might require altering the original source code.

4.2.3 User preferences and user-friendliness

User preferences are diverse, with each user preferring a particular method she or he is used to. Having seen many different data sets visualized by one and the same preferred method, a user is able to assess data quality as well as predominant variances and coherences with one quick glance. Being used to a method, interpretation of the produced plots takes only a minimum of time. Also, the hypothesis generated hereby tend to prove correct the more often, the more plots of the kind the user has studied. Thus, an experienced user will prefer her or his particular method for good reason. In other words, lack of one particular method represents a good reason for not using a software. Therefore, all commercial as well as the vast majority of academic packages aim at implementing the entire set of unsupervised methods as comprehensively as possible. Abovementioned common organization of workspace variables facilitates plugging of a new method. Interfacing to R commonly enables to do so even without translating the code.

But is "the more" always "the better"? Obviously, more methods increase chances to find one's preferred method. However, this applies only to the experienced user. For users new to the field, an overwhelming number of possibilities represents more of a curse rather than being an asset. For hierarchical clustering alone, they need to choose between various distance measures (Euklidean, Mahalanobis, City Block, X^2, Correlation, ...), in combination with either single or complete or average linkage. Above six distance measures multiplied with three different ways to update the distance table upon merging two clusters result in 18 possibilities to parametrize only one method. Each way recognizes different properties of the data, and will thus visualize different patterns. Thus, the 18 different parametrizations will produce 18 different results. Multiplied by a considerable number of different methods, the user will be faced with an overwhelming number of different results, not knowing which to select for further investigation. Making such an unpleasant situation even worse, analysis of biological high-throughput data holds in stock a number of pitfalls to the inexperienced. To pick one from the examples already provided, Euclidean distance, albeit simple and commonly known (representing the "every-day distance" computed by Pythagoras), and therefore often listed as first item of pull-down menus, is by no means suitable for clustering absolute signal intensities in a biological context. Here, it is useful to sort e.g. a transcription factor whose abundance regulates the expression of a set of target genes into the same cluster as its targets. Biological conditions in which the transcription factor is highly abundant will show high abundance also for the target genes, and vice versa. However, while the transcription factor shares the expression behaviour (shape of curve) with its targets, its absolute expression level (amplitude of curve) will be much lower. Therefore, Euklidean distance will affiliate transcription factor and targets into different clusters (of low and high expression, regardless of relative trends). Other distance measures such as the correlation distance (computed as one minus the correlation coefficient) will cluster together similarly shaped (i.e. correlating) expression profiles regardless of the absolute level of expression and are therefore more useful for biological research.

In order to grant usability also to the inexperienced, a variety of measures can be taken. Different options, either for choosing one of many possible algorithms for a certain task, or for parametrizing it, should be always accompanied by one default suggestion which works reasonably well for most types of data. Sharing a common method among different users also facilitates communication among collaborating scientists. Data and results can be shared without explaining the process from the former to the latter. Along the same lines, abovementioned automated web distribution of result reports facilitates using the system as a communication platform.

It goes without saying that usability of a software package is further enhanced by a clear menu structure guiding the user to the methods provided for a certain task with one default method clearly tagged. However, there are also more complex tasks for which providing one default workflow is insufficient. "Experience" e.g. of how a proper signal intensity threshold can be estimated and applied in order to filter out inactive genes or which reproducibility measure makes sense for a certain number of repetitions (see 4.1.3) can be handed on from the programmer to the user in form of a wizard. In M-CHiPS, the filter wizard, after assessing the data, selects from the multitude of possible measures (here filters as well as filter parameters) a subset that, according to more than thirteen years of filtering high-throughput data, appears most suitable for these data. However, since unexpected situations may occur with any new dataset, this is only a starting point. The results should be critically supervised by the user. Starting from this "initial guess", the user also needs to adapt the parameters iteratively in order to optimize filtering results. To this end, the wizard presents the suggested filters in a temporal sequence best suited for visual supervision of their outcome. It also provides guidance with respect to the parametrization by briefly (in few words) hinting at what to look at and by asking simple questions. Much like preferring mouse click over command line operation, users tend to achieve their goal (e.g. proper filtering) much faster by using a wizard than by reading the manual.

4.2.4 Programmers' preferences and ease of implementation

Providing such user friendly features (in particular wizards) costs considerable time. In contrast to commercial enterprises, implementing a user friendly system in an academic setting appears an ambitious goal. Packages coded by scientists for scientists (such as Bioconductor) tend to focus on command line interfaces and manuals (here "vignettes") instead of featuring mouse-clicks and wizards.

On the positive side, MATLAB provides the opportunity to code graphical objects very quickly. Figures are important for the user to visually supervise the analysis process. In M-CHiPS, normalization of each measurement can be evaluated by looking at a scatter plot of the measurement versus the control it is to be fitted to. As the human eye is able to detect patterns in fractions of seconds, artefacts such as saturation effects (data points concentrated into a line orthogonal to a particular axis as if "shifted by a snowplough") will not escape the user, even within the short timeframe the figures need to build up. The normalization performance is represented by a regression line or curve (depending on linear or log scale and on the normalization method). If the regression line leaves the center of the cloud of data points, the user will revisit the plot in order to decide on using a different normalization method, using a saturation filter, or discarding this particular measurement for poor quality.

In MATLAB, such figures can also be easily interacted with by mouse click, e.g. for selecting a cluster of genes by clicking a fence around it that is closed by hitting the middle mouse button. Furthermore, the M-CHiPS workspace holds variables for storing the status of such selections (see http://mchips.org/workspace.html, at the end of the paragraph headed "Genes"). Each newly coded figure displaying genes can be quickly endowed with gene tags by adding one command. Thus MATLAB provides the opportunity for user-friendliness and swift coding at the same time.

As already discussed, implementation time for many statistical algorithms can be saved by interfacing to R. Much like a user prefers certain methods, a programmer will save considerable time in programming environments she or he is used to. This applies not only to MATLAB and R. Personally, I am used to coding tasks requiring regular expressions in Perl, simply because in former times this was not possible in MATLAB. While nowadays comfortable handling of regular expressions is available both in MATLAB and R, I still prefer to use Perl for regular expressions. As discussed below (4.3), other tasks are best implemented on database level, by using SQL. Thus, interfacing to other languages not only provides the opportunity to plug already implemented code. It also eases new implementations by meeting programmers' preferences as well as by providing the "ideal" environment for each particular task.

As one would expect, using MATLAB, R, C, Perl, Java, and SQL within one system also causes problems. Sloppy programming of interfaces (e.g. accessing memory not properly allocated) may result in fatal errors (segmentation faults). Object oriented programming may increase safety and avoid bugs within one language. Nowadays, this is possible for all of the above languages except SQL. But how to send objects and events back and forth through an interface? For M-CHiPS, it proved a successful strategy to keep any interface as simple as possible. The database interface transports only a limited number of data types, resulting in short mex files. Type casting can be done within either MATLAB or SQL. Also, the heterogeneity of factors and levels associated to different fields of research (as discussed in the next chapter) is handled already at database level instead of implementing a large and error prone middleware. Data are transported to and from Perl simply via Unix pipe. Wherever possible, already implemented and tested interfaces where used, such as Perl DBI (http://dbi.perl.org) for accessing the database from Perl. This module is also independent of the database management system (DBMS) used. Using query syntax common to all SQL dialects, in particular refraining from object-relational extensions which tend to be DBMS specific, allows to switch e.g. from PostgreSQL to Oracle without breaking code.

Thus, either using well-established or simple and clear-cut own implementations, problems caused by interfaces are minimal. However, for seamless interaction of the components, such a heterogeneous system requires many modules, libraries, and packages. Installation represents a considerable workload in and of itself, interfering with distributing the system. With the advent of server virtualization, however, all components can be distributed as a whole. Such a virtual machine can be regarded a "computer within a computer". It comprises the system including all necessary modules, libraries, and packages plus the operation system in a tested configuration. Further, it will run (with few exceptions) on any hardware and, thanks to extensive standardization, on (almost) any host operation system.

4.3 Fields of research

Differences related to different technical platforms used for data acquisition (such as microarrays or mass spectrometry), as well as user preferences of different machine learning methods result in the need to add and maintain a large set of algorithms, a task best coped with by interfacing to R and other languages. However, in addition to using different platforms to acquire their data, users will work on different types of samples stemming from highly diverse biological contexts. In the following I will put forward the thesis that computer-aided interpretation of data from different fields of research with one and the same software package is best coped with by interfacing to a database.

4.3.1 Data interpretation

As already mentioned (4.2), analysis of data stemming from new research is necessarily exploratory. In many cases, few hypothesis exist. Thus, the first task of data analysis is to generate hypotheses that can stand verification by subsequent statistical tests. To this end, M-CHiPS provides an unsupervised method that is most exploratory and easy to parametrize as a common view. Correspondence analysis (Fellenberg, 2001) is regularly used by most M-CHiPS users. Belonging to the subclass of planar projection (also called ordination) methods, it shows how discrete (or fuzzy) cluster borders are. Much like principal components analysis, objects will be neighbours in the projection plot, whose quantified signals behave similar. However, unlike principal component analysis, it is able to visualize more than one kind of objects at the same time, also displaying the correspondence (interrelation) between objects of different kind. At this stage, only two kinds of objects exist, genes and measurements.

A typical data matrix comprises three or more repeatedly performed measurements (as columns) for each biological condition, with two to at most a few hundred conditions. In stark contrast, the numbers of genes typically range from minimum hundreds to mostly several ten thousands, also resulting in large numbers of genes within each observed cluster. In order to interpret the data, it is necessary to characterize such a gene cluster in terms of one or more descriptive traits. Because a list of hundreds of genes along with their names and traits is too large for visual inspection, extracting descriptive traits has better be done by automatic means. A trait is the more descriptive for a chosen cluster, the more common it is to all (or at least a large share of) cluster members, and the fewer its occurrences outside the cluster (hence to discriminate the cluster from other clusters). Apart from simply comparing the overall frequency of each trait to its frequency in a particular user-selected cluster (Fellenberg, 2003), the traits can e.g. also be visualized by correspondence analysis. To this end, characteristic traits are filtered (from the vast majority of uninformative ones) and displayed as centroids in the middle of the cluster of genes they apply to (Busold, 2005).

For any statistics simple or sophisticated the instances of occurrence for any given trait must be countable by a computer. For genes, among other sources, the gene ontology (GO) initiative (http://geneontology.org) provides a controlled vocabulary of terms annotating gene products in a computer-readable format. The terms are subcategorized from general to special traits by "is a" and "part of" relations that form the edges of a directed acyclic graph. The same set of terms (ordered by the same graph) is applicable to the genes of every organism under study, a priceless bonus for data integration.

4.3.2 Differences between yeast, plants, and human cancer

The value of any trait set universally applicable to all fields of research can be best appreciated by regarding traits for which this is not the case. While any gene either shows phospholipid-translocating ATPase activity (GO:0004012) or not, growth conditions may be characterized by temperature, additive concentrations, and other variables of continuous range. Also, a biological sample can be processed by a wide variety of different wet-lab protocols prior to data acquisition and preprocessing. Each step may influence the observed patterns by contributing specific systematic errors. Thus, representing these steps within the sample annotations can serve to track down artefacts. Even more complex than the description of wet-lab protocols (but also more interesting) is the description of the samples. Their composition ranges from only one cell type and heterogeneous mixtures to complete organs and organisms. Organisms, genotypes, phenotypes, disease stages, clinical data, or culture conditions may need to be accounted for. Biological contexts under study by means of high-throughput quantification are highly diverse. Traits annotating culture conditions for yeast are not applicable to plants growing in a green house. Soil type and circadian light rythms are irrelevant to cancer research. There are initiatives to describe all fields of research into one ontology (MAGE-OM; Brazma, 2003). However, the complexity of the controlled vocabulary is overwhelming. Most terms are not applicable to a particular field of research, while terms important to describe novel aspects of a new biological context are often missing. Often it is not known a priori if a particular trait is relevant for the biological context under study or not. Omitting it bears the risk of overlooking something important.

As for the genes, lists of hundreds of samples along with their specific traits are too large for visual inspection. Thus, the global players driving the observed expression patterns of the samples need to be extracted from a large number of irrelevant traits computationally. M-CHiPS organizes these traits in a database tailored for computational analysis (data warehouse; Fellenberg, 2002). The database structure is flexible enough to provide for each field of research a tailor-made arbitrarily structured trait set comprising both enumeration type variables and those of continuous range. It also accounts for rapid growths of each trait set with new kinds of experiments. These very different trait sets (currently 13, see http://mchips.de#annos) are presented to the analysis algorithms in a unified way such that all fields of research can be operated by the same algorithms. As already mentioned, the heterogeneity of the sets is already encapsulated on database level (granted US patent US7650343) such that no middleware is required and the database interface can be kept small and simple.

As for the genes and samples, or for genes and samples and gene traits, correspondence analysis can visualize correspondence between genes and samples and sample traits at the same time. Like the gene traits, sample traits are represented as centroids of the samples they apply to. Prior to visualization, however, any continuous value ranges must be discretized into bins of highest possible correlation to the expression data. Furthermore, the filtering approach (selecting relevant traits) is a different one. However, the main principle difference to interpreting genes by means of gene traits is that sample traits only become necessary for computer-aided interpretation of large numbers of samples. For two or three conditions under study, an analyst can keep track of all differences without using a computer. In this case, one correspondence analysis plot is able to capture the total variance (information content, inertia) between all conditions. The typical use case for sample traits is more a dataset comprising hundreds of samples, e.g. stemming from cancer biopsies. Here, a single plot can only account for the predominant variations, at the risk overlooking minor (but possibly interesting) changes. Since pathological classification is not always reliable and (more importantly) because unexpected groupings could be concealed by imposing known classes, the variance cannot be reduced in this way. However, the total variance can be systematically dissected into pieces sequentially visualized by separate correspondence analysis plots. Thus, no important detail can escape the analyst's attention (Fellenberg, 2006).

5. Systems biology

Systematic interpretation, as described above, means to systematically screen the entire information content of a data matrix step by step for exploratory research (as opposed to verifying a hypothesis or just trying out things). It should be carefully discriminated from data interpretation at systems level, which stands for a different approach. Here, the focus lies on the interplay of genes. A gene may be regulated by one or more other genes or by its own abundance (auto regulation), or it may regulate one or more other genes. For some genes, all three events may even take place at the same time. A gene regulatory network, albeit complex, is by no means chaotic. Several so-called network motives (e.g. feed-forward

loops) could be identified to occur significantly more often in biological networks than at random (Alon, 2007). Network fluxes are rigorously controlled, resources carefully spent only where needed (e.g. as an investment into swift reaction times). Much like traffic lights, key switches tightly coordinate the temporal order of important events, e.g. for cell division. Reverse engineering gene regulatory networks stands for reconstructing such networks from data. Each dependency (e.g. gene A represses gene B) must be estimated from the traces it leaves in data (signals for B decrease when signals for A increase). Therefore, data obtained from controlled system perturbations (removing one or more particular genes at a time, e.g. by so-called "RNA Inference") are most valuable for reverse engineering, followed by time course data. Temporally unrelated biological conditions (e. g. cancer biopsies, each representing an end point of possibly different courses of disease progression) are less informative, but reverse engineering is still possible (Basso, 2005). Traditionally, reverse engineering is carried out with few selected genes, only. One cannot expect to elucidate the dependencies of some ten thousand genes on the basis of only dozens of observations (measurements). Once again, data integration is vital. Since large datasets are rare, it pays off to merge several smaller datasets in order to delineate robust networks for considerable numbers of genes. This is even possible across different technical platforms by adapting the differing scales (Culhane, 2003).
However, many datasets that would be interesting to merge have been recorded for different species, posing the additional problem to affiliate genes across species. Orthology relations (affiliating genes of one species to another) can be one-to-one, one-to-many, or even many-to-many. Furthermore, evolution events so-called sub- or neofunctionalization may assign new functions to certain genes. This results in that some genes of the same (or a very similar) sequence carry out "different jobs" in different species and should thus not be affiliated for merging datasets. In March 2010, we published a method capable of merging datasets across species on the basis of the expression data alone. The algorithm is tailor-made for reverse engineering of gene regulatory networks, converging on the optimal number of nodes for network inference. It could be shown that the networks inferred from cross-species merges are superior to the ones obtained from the single datasets alone in terms of both sensitivity, specificity, accuracy, and the number of comprised network motifs. Not being restricted to two datasets, it offers the opportunity to merge arbitrary numbers of datasets in order to reliably infer large common gene regulatory networks across species (Moghaddas Gholami, 2010).

6. Conclusion

Unlike only a few decades ago, nowadays biology is a quantitative science. With the advent of systems biology, it is now at the verge of formalizing properties of living systems, modelling systems behaviour, and reliable predictions. Exploiting the already large number of high-throughput biological datasets will considerably contribute to this end. Interpretation of high-throughput biological data is facilitated by integration of heterogeneous data. Differences result from different technical platforms for data acquisition, highly diverse fields of research, and different species. A multitude of algorithms is needed for integration, causing the additional problems of different user preferences (of methods) and programmer preferences (of languages). This poses the question if a larger software package can be developed in a user-friendly manner in an academic setting at all, and if MATLAB is the right programming language for this task in particular.

The M-CHiPS project provides prove of principle that a larger software system can be developed and maintained in an academic setting. It is user-friendly, received grant money for development of a commercially distributable prototype and was awarded a price from a business plan award. It comprises many novel approaches. Its database structure has been patented (granted US patent). Analysis algorithms operating the database, implemented and constantly amended over the years by a small team of scientists, have been thoroughly tested by more than 80 users (also scientists). Being a server-based solution (SAAS), it frees the user from installation, update, database administration, or any maintenance. M-CHiPS is predominantly coded in MATLAB.
Its MATLAB code is compiled, running without a MATLAB license for any number of users. R, Bioconductor, Perl, C (database interface as mex files), SQL, as well as all the required Linux libraries are installed such that they seamlessly work together. The installation (which would otherwise represent considerable work) is being available as a whole in form of virtual machines. For flexible allocation of computing resources, web server, file server and database server are separate. It is e.g. possible to run three calculation servers on different machines together with the same database server, or also to run all services on one and the same machine. As PostgreSQL is quickly installed and because different versions of backend and client are uncritical as long as the difference is not too large, it is a good compromise to put database server as well as file server "bare metal" while using the calculation server and the database server as virtual machines.
Experienced administrators will have no difficulties also setting up an Apache web server and installing the packages needed for database acess of the Perl/CGI scripts. However, in our experience performance decrease by virtualization is negligible, both for web and calculation services. In stark contrast to e.g. sequence analysis and protein identification in mass spectrometry, the interactive process of high-throughput quantification hardly provides any perceivable delay, anyway. Therefore, installing web and in particular calculation servers directly on a machine is certainly not worth the effort. Packed into virtual machines, the advantage of having at hand various programming languages for swiftly amending the package does not interfere with its distribution. Combining the wealth of high-throughput biological data statistics prevalently available in R with systems biology tools in MATLAB as well as Perl, Java, SQL and other languages, it satisfies the needs of users and programmers alike and can thus serve as a communications platform both for sharing data and algorithms.

7. Acknowledgement

I am indepted to Martin Vingron, Tim Beißbarth, Christian Busold, Dieter Finkenzeller, Liang Chunguang, Meju Kaipparettu, Radhika Upadhyayula, Amit Agarwal, Mahesh Visvanathan, Corinna Schmitt, and Amin Mohaddas Gholami for contributing with code, further to Martin Vingron, Benedikt Brors, Jürgen Dippon, and Stefan Winter for contributing with ideas.
I wish to thank Jörg Hoheisel, Nicole Hauser, Judith Boer, Marcel Scheideler, Susanne Grahlmann, Frank Diehl, Verena Aign, Andrea Bauer, Helene Tournu, Arno Meijer, Luis Lombardia, Manuel Beccera, Andy Hayes, Albert Neutzner, Nikolaus Schlaich, Tamara Korica, Boris Beckmann, Melanie Bey, Claudia Hartmann, Diana Stjepandic, Kerstin Hasenpusch-Theil, Marcus Frohme, Britta Koch, Marc Hild, Fabian Kruse, Marc Valls, Julia Klopp, Olaf Witt, Kerstin Böhm, Christian Weinel, José Pérez-Ortín, Matthias Nees, Arnaud

Lagorce, Melanie Bier, Sonja Bastuck, Gaelle Dubois, Yana Syagailo, Jan Wiemer, Wladislaw Kusnezow, Patrick Kuery, Daniel Wenzler, Andrea Busch, Sarah Marsal Barril, Rainer Schuler, Benjamin Altenhein, Angela Becker, Li Zheng, Stefanie Brems, Rocio Alba, Bo Xu, Duc van Luu, Iana Siagailo, Martina Brachold, Klaudia Kuranda, Enrico Ragni, Viola Denninger, Martin Brenndoerfer, Stephane Boeuf, Karoliina Pelttari, Eric Steck, Michaela Burkhardt, Michaela Schanne, Prachiti Narvekar, Sandra Bloethner, Anja Boos, Sven Christian, Yi-Ping Lin, Christoph Schröder, Linda Ottoboni, Frank Holtrup, Mahmoud Youns, Rafael Queiroz, Rosa Hernandez-Barbado, Daniela Albrecht, Neeme Tönisson, Raphael Martinez, Christopher Lößner, Florian Haas, Li Lu, Sheng-Jia Zhang, Jorge Soza-Ried, Corinna Wagner, Fiona Pachl, and Zhixiang Wu for contributing with data and testing.
I am thankful to the NGFN program of the German Federal Ministry of Education and Research as well as to the Department of Plant Physiology of the Ruhr University in Bochum for funding. Support for the development of the software platform M-CHiPS was provided by the Helmholtz Association.

8. References

Alon, U. (2007). Network motifs: theory and experimental. *Nature Reviews Genetics*, Vol.8, No.6, (June 2007), pp. 450-461, ISSN 1471-0056

Basso, K.; Margolin, A. A.; Stolovitzky, G.; Klein, U.; Dalla-Favera, R.; & Califano, A. (2005). Reverse engineering of regulatory networks in human B cells. *Nature Genetics*, Vol.37, (March 2005), pp. 382-390, ISSN 1061-4036

Beißbarth, T.; Fellenberg, K.; Brors, B.; Arribas-Prat, R.; Boer, J. M.; Hauser, N. C.; Scheideler, M.; Hoheisel, J. D.; Schuetz, G.; Poustka, A.; & Vingron, M. (2000). Processing and quality control of DNA array hybridization data. *Bioinformatics*, Vol.16, No.11, (June 2000), pp. 1014-1022, ISSN 1367-4803

Bolstad, B. M.; Irizarry, R. A.; Anstrand, M.; & Speed, T. P. (2003). A comparison of normalization methods for high density oligonucleotide array data based on variance and bias. *Bioinformatics*, Vol.19, No.2, (January 2003), pp. 185-193, ISSN 1367-4803

Brazma, A.; Parkinson, H.; Sarkans, U.; Shojatalab, M; Vilo, J.; Abeygunawardena, N.; Holloway, E.; Kapushesky, M.; Kemmeren, P.; Garcia Lara, G.; Oezcimen, A.; Rocca-Serra, P.; & Sansone, S. (2003). ArrayExpress—a public repository for microarray gene expression data at the EBI. *Nucleic Acids Research*, Vol.31, No.1, (January 2003), pp. 68-71, ISSN 0305-1048

Busold, C. H.; Winter, S.; Hauser, N.; Bauer, A.; Dippon, J.; Hoheisel, J. D.; & Fellenberg, K. (2005). Integration of GO annotations in Correspondence Analysis: facilitating the interpretation of microarray data.. *Bioinformatics*, Vol.21, No.10, (March 2005), pp. 2424-2429, ISSN 1367-4803

Cleveland, W. S. (1979). Robust Locally Weighted Regression and Smoothing Scatterplots. *Journal of the American Statistical Association*, Vol.74, No.368, (December 1979), pp. 829-836, ISSN 0003-2638

Culhane, A. C.; Perrière, G.; & Higgins, D. G. (2003). Cross-platform comparison and visualisation of gene expression data using co-inertia analysis. *BMC Bioinformatics*, Vol.4, (November 2003), pp. 59ff, ISSN 1471-2105

Eisen, M. B.; Spellman, P. T.; Brown, P. O.; & Botstein, D. (1998). Cluster analysis and display of genome-wide expression. *Proceedings of the National Academy of Sciences,* Vol.95, No.25, (December 1998), pp. 14863-14868, ISSN 0027-8424

Fellenberg, K.; Hauser, N. C.; Brors, B.; Neutzner, A.; Hoheisel, J. D.; & Vingron, M. (2001). Correspondence Analysis Applied to Microarray Data. *Proceedings of the National Academy of Sciences,* Vol.98, No.19, (September 2001), pp. 10781-10786, ISSN 0027-8424

Fellenberg, K.; Hauser, N. C.; Brors, B.; Hoheisel, J. D.; & Vingron, M. (2002). Microarray data warehouse allowing for inclusion of experiment annotations in statistical analysis. *Bioinformatics,* Vol.18, No.3, (March 2002), pp. 423-433, ISSN 1367-4803

Fellenberg, K. ; Vingron, M. ; Hauser, N. C. ; & Hoheisel, J. D. (2003). Correspondence analysis with microarray data, In: *Perspectives in Gene Expression,* K. Appasani, (Ed.), 307-343, Eaton Publishing, ISBN 978-1881299165, Westboro, MA

Fellenberg, K.; Busold, C. H.; Witt, O.; Bauer, A.; Beckmann, B.; Hauser, N. C.; Frohme, M; Winter, S.; Dippon, J.; & Hoheisel, J. D. (2006). Systematic interpretation of microarray data using experiment annotations. *BMC Genomics,* Vol.7, (December 2006), pp. 319ff, ISSN 1471-2164

Gonzalez, R.; Masquelier, B.; Fleury, H.; Lacroix, B.; Troesch, A.; Vernet, G. & Telles, J. N. (2004). Detection of Human Immunodeficiency Virus Type 1 Antiretroviral Resistance Mutations by High-Density DNA Probe Arrays. *Journal of Clinical Microbiology,* Vol.42, No.7, (July 2004), pp. 2907-2912, ISSN 0095-1137

Huber, W.; von Heydebreck, A.; Sültmann, H.; Poustka, A.; & Vingron, M. (2002). Variance stabilization applied to microarray data calibration and to the quantification of differential expression. *Bioinformatics,* Vol.18, Suppl. 1, (March 2002), pp. S96-104, ISSN 1367-4803

Moghaddas Gholami, A. & Fellenberg, K. (2010). Cross-species common regulatory network inference without requirement for prior gene affiliation. *Bioinformatics,* Vol.26, No. 8, (March 2010), pp. 1082-1090, ISSN 1367-4803

Schanné, M.; Bodem, J. ; Gerhold-Ay, A.; Jacob, A.; Fellenberg, K.; Kräusslich, H.G.; & Hoheisel, J. D. (2008). Genotypic resistance testing in HIV by arrayed primer extension. *Analytical and Bioanalytical Chemistry,* Vol.391, No.5, (July 2008), pp. 1661-1669, ISSN 1618-2642

Smyth, G. K. (2005). limma: Linear Models for Microarray Data, In: *Bioinformatics and Computationtional Biology Solutions Using R and Bioconductor,* R. Gentleman, V. J. Carey, W. Huber, R. A. Irizarry, & S. Dudoit, (Eds.), 397-420, Springer, ISBN ISBN 978-0-387-25146-2, New York

Tusher, V. G.; Tibshirani, R., & Chu, G. (2001). Significance analysis of microarrays applied to the ionizing radiation. *Proceedings of the National Academy of Sciences,* Vol.98, No.9, (April 2001), pp. 5116-5121, ISSN 0027-8424

Zhang, B.; VerBerkmoes, N. C.; Langston, M. A.; Uberbacher, E.; Hettich, R. L., Samatova, N.F. (2006). Detecting differential and correlated protein expression in label-free shotgun. *Journal of Proteome Research,* Vol.5, No.11, (November 2006), pp. 2909-2918, ISSN 1535-3893

4

Hysteresis Voltage Control of DVR Based on Unipolar PWM

Hadi Ezoji[1], Abdol Reza Sheikhaleslami[2], Masood Shahverdi[3], Arash Ghatresamani[4] and Mohamad Hosein Alborzi[3]
[1]Islamic Azad University-Nowshahr Branch, Shahid Karimi ST, Nowshahr,
[2]Electrical & Computer Engineering Department, Babol University of Technology, Babol,
[3]Mapna Electrical and Control Engineering, Karaj,
[4]Islamshahr-sayad shirazi Ave.-Islamshahr Islamic Azad University,
Iran

1. Introduction

Power quality problems like voltage sag, voltage swell and harmonic are major concern of the industrial and commercial electrical consumers due to enormous loss in terms of time and money. This is due to the Advent of a large numbers of sophisticated electrical and electronic equipment, such as computers, programmable logic controllers, variable speed drives, and so forth. The use of these equipments often requires power supplies of very high quality.

Some special equipment is sensitive to voltage disturbances, especially if these take up to several periods, the circuit does not work. Therefore, these adverse effects of voltage changes necessitate the existence of effective mitigating devices. There are various solutions to these problems. One of the most effective solutions is the installation of a dynamic voltage restorer (DVR).

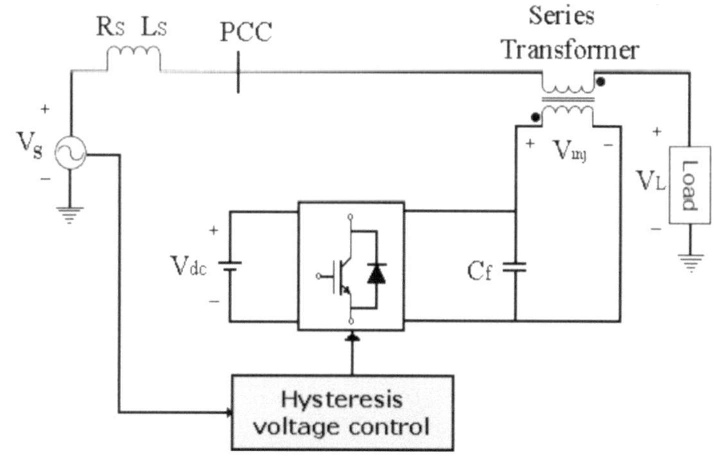

Fig. 1. Schematic diagram of a typical DVR.

DVR is the one of the custom power devices, which has excellent dynamic capabilities. It is well suited to protect sensitive loads from short duration voltage sag or swell. DVR is basically a controlled voltage source installed between the supply and a sensitive load. It injects a voltage on the system in order to compensate any disturbance affecting the load voltage. Basic operating principle of a DVR as shown in Fig. 1.
Voltage sag/swell that occurs more frequently than any other power quality phenomenon is known as the most important power quality problems in the power distribution systems.
Voltage sag is defined as a sudden reduction of supply voltage down 90% to 10% of nominal. According to the standard, a typical duration of sag is from 10 ms to 1 minute. On the other hand, Voltage swell is defined as a sudden increasing of supply voltage up 110% to 180% in rms voltage at the network fundamental frequency with duration from 10 ms to 1 minute.
Voltage sag/swell often caused by faults such as single line-to-ground fault, double line-to-ground fault on the power distribution system or due to starting of large induction motors or energizing a large capacitor bank. Voltage sag/swell can interrupt or lead to malfunction of any electric equipment which is sensitive to voltage variations.
IEEE 519-1992 and IEEE 1159-1995 describe the Voltage sags /swells as shown in Fig.2.

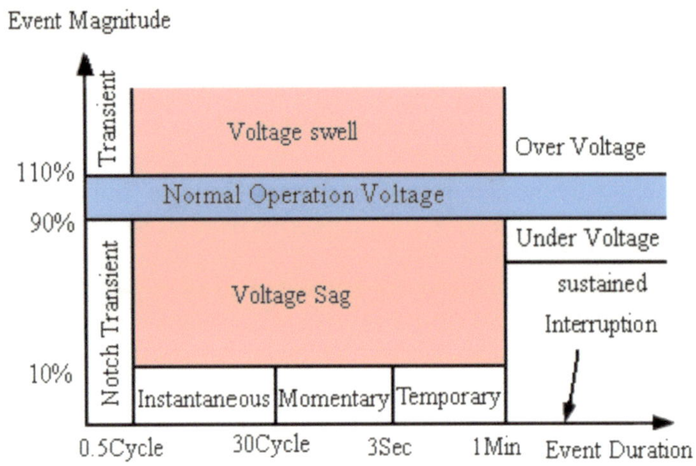

Fig. 2. Voltage Reduction Standard of IEEE Std. 1159-1995.

2. DVR power circuit

The power circuit of the DVR is shown in Fig.1. The DVR consists of mainly a three-phase Voltage-Sourced Converter (VSC), a coupling transformer, passive filter and a control system to regulate the output voltage of VSC:

2.1 Voltage source converter (VSC)

A voltage-source converter is a power electronic device, which can generate a sinusoidal voltage with any required magnitude, frequency and phase angle. This converter injects a dynamically controlled voltage in series with the supply voltage through three single-phase transformers to correct the load voltage. It consists of Insulated Gate Bipolar Transistors (IGBT) as switches. The switching pulses of the IGBT are the output from the hysteresis voltage controller.

2.2 Coupling transformer

Basic function is to step up and electrical isolation the ac low voltage supplied by the VSC to the required voltage. In this study single-phase injection transformer is used. For three phases DVR, three single phase injection transformers can be used.

2.3 A Passive filter

A Passive filter consists of a capacitor that is placed at the high voltage side of coupling transformer. This filter rejects the switching harmonic components from the injected voltage.

2.4 Control system

The aim of the control scheme is to maintain a balanced and constant load voltage at the nominal value under system disturbances. In this chapter, control system is based on hysteresis voltage control.

3. Conventional control strategies

Several control techniques have been proposed for voltage sag compensation such as pre-sag method, in-phase method and minimal energy control.

3.1 Pre-sag compensation technique

In this compensation technique, the DVR supplies the difference between the sagged and pre-sag voltage and restores the voltage magnitude and the phase angle to the nominal pre sag condition.

The main defect of this technique is it requires a higher capacity energy storage device. Fig.3 (a) shows the phasor diagram for the pre-sag control strategy.

In this diagram, $V_{pre\text{-}sag}$ and V_{Sag} are voltage at the point of common coupling (PCC), respectively before and during the sag. In this case V_{DVR} is the voltage injected by the DVR, which can be obtained as:

$$|V_{inj}| = |V_{pre\text{-}sag}| - |V_{Sag}| \tag{1}$$

$$\theta_{inj} = \tan^{-1}\left(\frac{V_{pre\text{-}sag}\sin(\theta_{pre\text{-}sag})}{V_{pre\text{-}sag}\cos(\theta_{pre\text{-}sag}) - V_{Sag}\cos(\theta_{Sag})}\right) \tag{2}$$

3.2 In-phase compensation technique

In this technique, only the voltage magnitude is compensated. V_{DVR} is in-phase with the left hand side voltage of DVR. This method minimizes the voltage injected by the DVR, unlike in the pre-sag compensation. Fig.3 (b) shows phase diagram for the in-phase compensation technique

$$V_{DVR} = V_{inj}$$

$$|V_{inj}| = |V_{pre\text{-}sag}| - |V_{Sag}| \tag{3}$$

$$\angle V_{inj} = \theta_{inj} = \theta_S$$

3.3 Energy optimization technique

Pre-sag compensation and in-phase compensation must inject active power to loads almost all the time. Due to the limit of energy storage capacity of DC link, the DVR restoration time and performance are confined in these methods. The fundamental idea of energy optimization method is to make injection active power zero. In order to minimize the use of real power the voltages are injected at 90° phase angle to the supply current. Fig.3 (c) shows a phasor diagram to describe the Energy optimization Control method.
The selection of one of these strategies influences the design of the parameters of DVR. In this chapter, the control strategy adopted is Pre-sag compensation to maintain load voltage to pre-fault value.

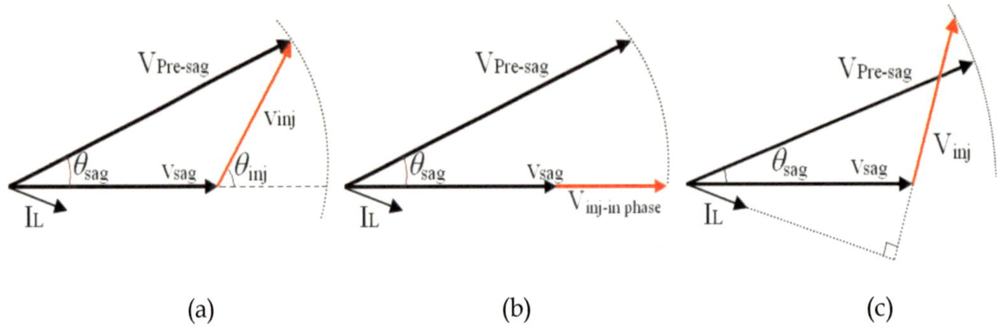

Fig. 3. Conventional control strategies. (a) Pre-sag compensation technique, (b) In-phase compensation technique, (c) Energy optimized compensation technique.

This chapter presents a hysteresis voltage control technique based on unipolar PWM to improve the quality of output voltage. The hysteresis voltage control of DVR has not been studied in our knowledge. The proposed method is validated through modeling in MATLAB SIMULINK.
This is chapter organized as follows: in next section, the power circuit of DVR is described briefly. Then we introduce conventional strategies for control. In next section, we state about control of the DVR and present our method to this end. Finally, experimental results are presented.

4. Control of the DVR

4.1 Detection of sag / swell in the supply voltage

The main stages of the control system of a DVR are as follows: detection of the start and finish of the sag, voltage reference generation, injection voltage generation, and protection of the system.
In Ref [9], several detection techniques have been analyzed and compared. In this chapter, monitoring of V_d and V_q is used to return the magnitude and phase load voltage to the magnitude and phase reference load voltage. The control system is presented in Fig. 4.
The three-phase supply voltage is connected to a transformation block that convert to rotating frame (d q) with using a software based Phase - Lock Loop (PLL). Three-phase voltage is transformed by using Park transform, from a-b-c to o-d-q frame:

$$\begin{bmatrix} v_d \\ v_q \\ v_o \end{bmatrix} = p \begin{bmatrix} v_a \\ v_b \\ v_c \end{bmatrix} \quad (2)$$

$$p = \sqrt{\frac{2}{3}} \begin{bmatrix} \cos(\theta) & \cos(\theta - \frac{2\pi}{3}) & \cos(\theta - \frac{4\pi}{3}) \\ \sin(\theta) & \sin(\theta - \frac{2\pi}{3}) & \sin(\theta - \frac{4\pi}{3}) \\ \frac{1}{\sqrt{2}} & \frac{1}{\sqrt{2}} & \frac{1}{\sqrt{2}} \end{bmatrix} \quad (3)$$

$$\theta = \theta_0 - \int_0^t \omega t \, dt$$

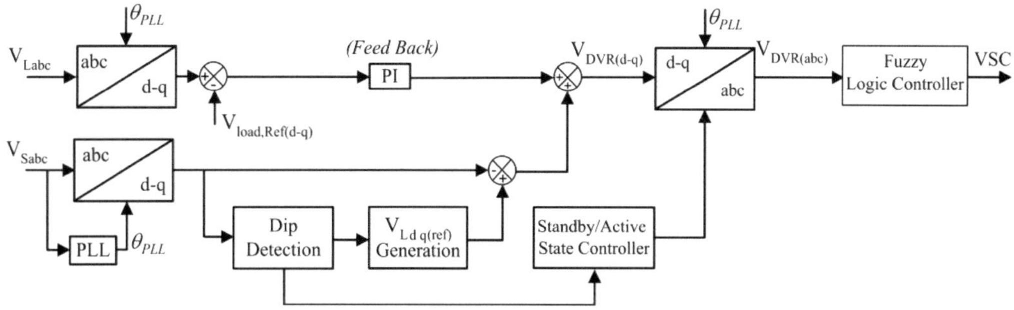

Fig. 4. Control structure of DVR

If voltage sag/swell occurs, the detection block generates the reference load voltage. The sag detection strategy is based on Root Means Square (rms) for the error vector which can be used for symmetrical and non symmetrical sags with any associated phase jump. Load voltage feedback is also added, and it is implemented in the odq frame to minimize any steady state error in the fundamental component.

The injected voltage is also generated according to difference between the reference load voltage and supply voltage and it is applied to the VSC to produce the preferred voltage using hysteresis voltage control.

4.2 Hysteresis voltage control

In this chapter, Hysteresis Band Voltage control is used to control load voltage and determine switching signals for inverter switches.

There are bands above and under the reference voltage. If the difference between the reference and inverter voltage reaches to the upper (lower) limit, the voltage is forced to decrease (increase) as shown in Fig.4.

In this method, the following relation is applied Where *HB* and f_c are Hysteresis band and switching frequency, respectively.

$$T_1 + T_2 = T_c = 1/f_c \quad (5)$$

Fig.5 shows a single phase diagram of a full bridge inverter that is connected in series with a sensitive load. The inverter can be controlled in unipolar or bipolar PWM methods.

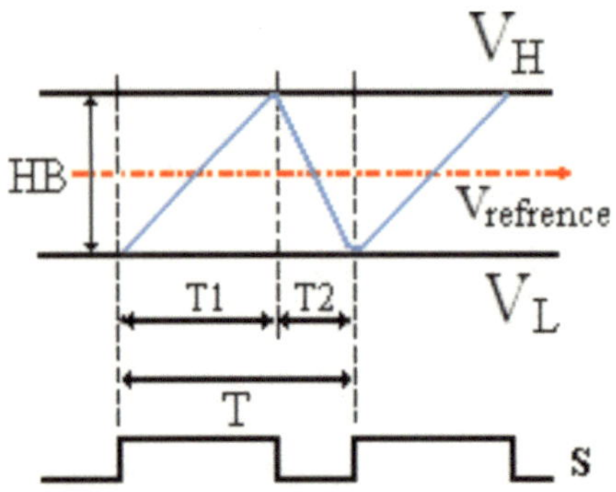

Fig. 5. Hysteresis band voltage control.

The HB that has inverse proportional relation with switching frequency is defined as the difference between V_H and V_L ($HB=V_H-V_L$) [19-20].
In present chapter, for pulse switching generation for DVR, random hysteresis voltage control is analyzed. The biopolar modulation is base of this analyze.
In bipolar switching scheme, as shown in Fig.6, there are two bands and the controller turns on and turns off the switch pairs (S_1, S_3 or S_2, S_4) at the same time to generate $+V_{dc}$ or -Vdc at the output of inverter.

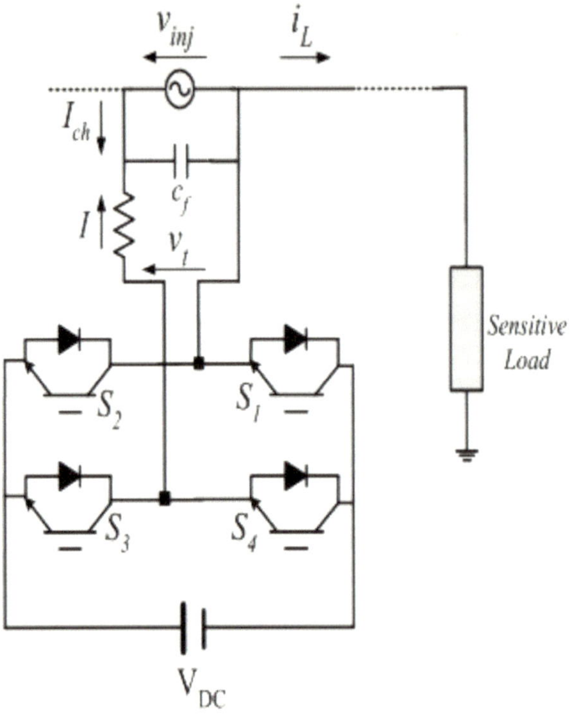

Fig. 6. Single phase full bridge inverter

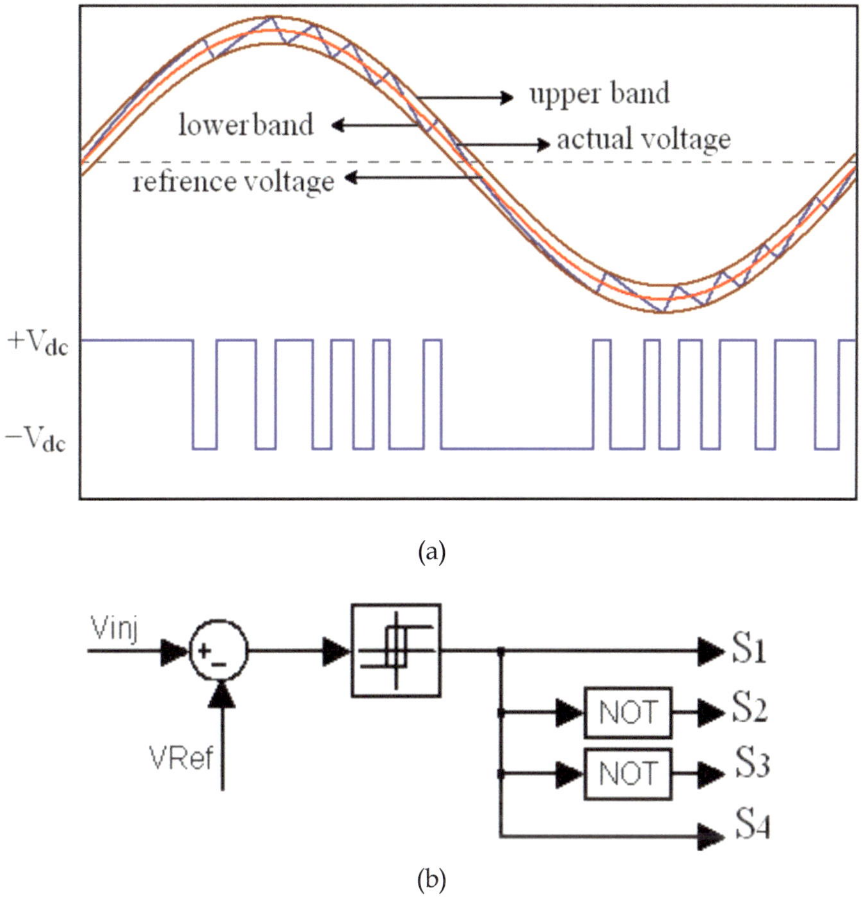

Fig. 6. Bipolar hysteresis voltage control (a) out put voltage with lower and higher bands (b) switching signals.

5. Proposed method

We are now in position to introduce our proposed method named Hysteresis voltage control based on unipolar switching Technique as shown in Fig 7.

In the unipolar modulation, four voltage bands are used to achieve proper switching states to control the load voltage.

The first upper and lower bands (HB_1) are used when the output current is changed between ($+V_{dc}$ & 0) or ($-V_{dc}$ or 0) and the second upper and lower bands (HB_2) are used to change the current level Fig 7(a).

There are four switching states for switches (S_1, S_2) and (S_3, S_4) as shown in Fig.7(b) As a result, three levels are generated $+V_{dc}$, $-V_{dc}$ or 0 at the output of inverter. In comparison with other PWM methods, the hysteresis voltage control has a variable switching frequency, very fast response and simple operation [13].

The switching functions of both B and C phases are determined similarly using corresponding reference and measured voltage band (HB) [13].

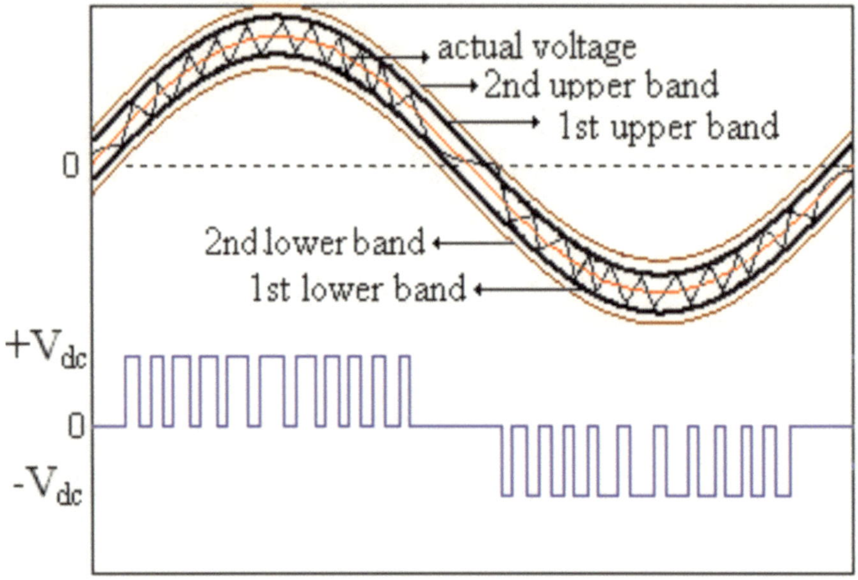

(a)

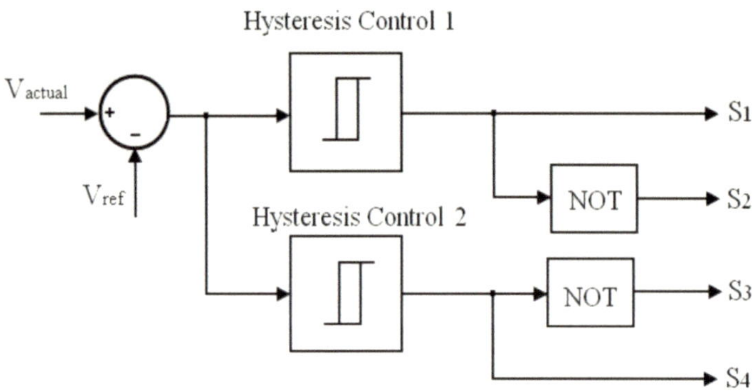

(b)

Fig. 7. Unipolar hysteresis voltage control (a) out put voltage with lower and higher bands (b) switching signals

6. Simulation results

The proposed method is validated by simulation results of MATLAB. Simulation parameters are shown in table 1. DVR with unioplar voltage control is applied to compensate load voltage. In order to demonstrate the performance of the DVR using unioplar switchin technique to control, a Simulink diagram is proposed as shown in Fig.8.

To have a fair comparison, in this simulation it has been considered same situation as mentioned in Ref [12].

Parameter	Value
Supply voltage (V_{L-L})	415V
V_{dc} ,C_F	120V, 500uF
Series Transformer(V_{Ph-Ph})	96V / 240V
Z_{Trans}	0.004 + *j* 0.008
R_{Load}, L_{Load}	31.84 Ω, 0.139 *H*

Table 1. Case study parameters

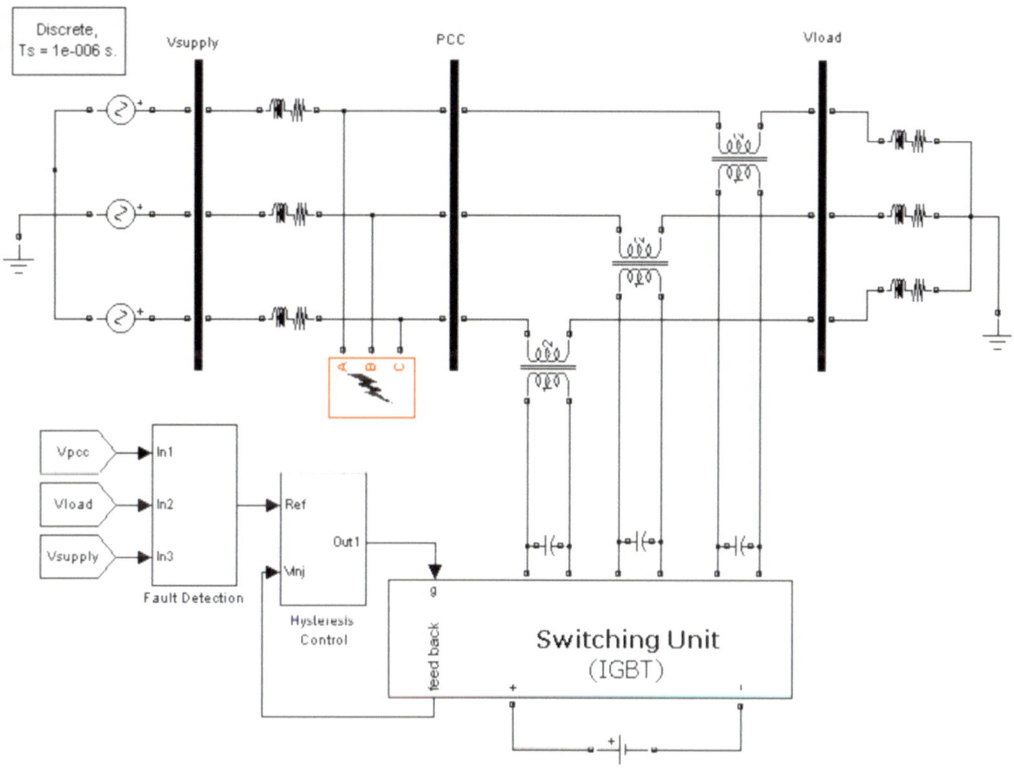

Fig. 8. Simulation model of DVR in MATLAB.

A. Voltage sags

In the first case, we assume that there is a 30% three-phase voltage sag with +30 phase jump in phase-a in supply voltage that is initiated at 0.1s and it is kept until 1.8 s. The results for HB_1=0.005 and HB_2=0.007 are shown in Fig .9.

Fig .9 (b) and (c) show the series of voltage components injected by the DVR and compensated load voltage, respectively.

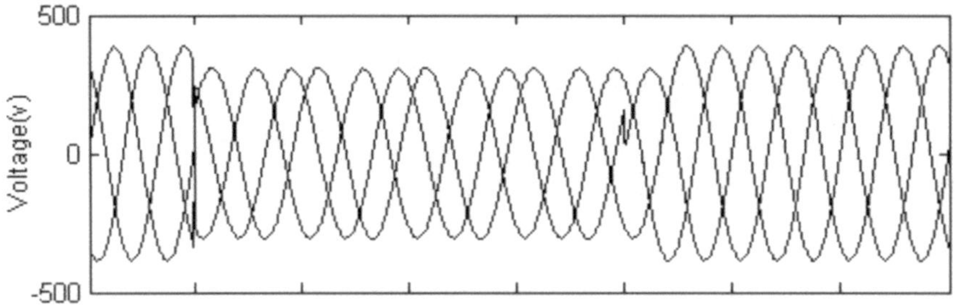

(a) Supply voltages.

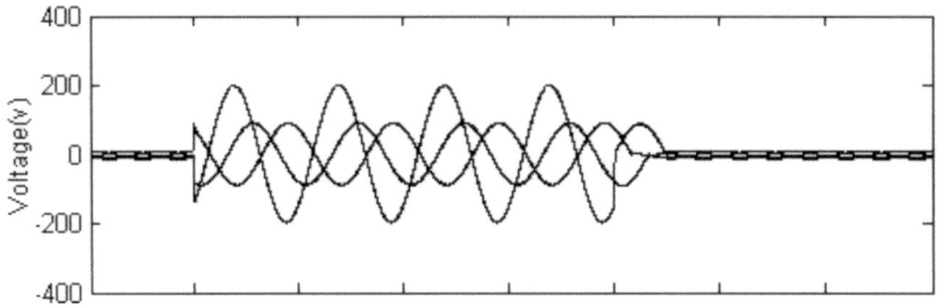

(b) Injected voltage.

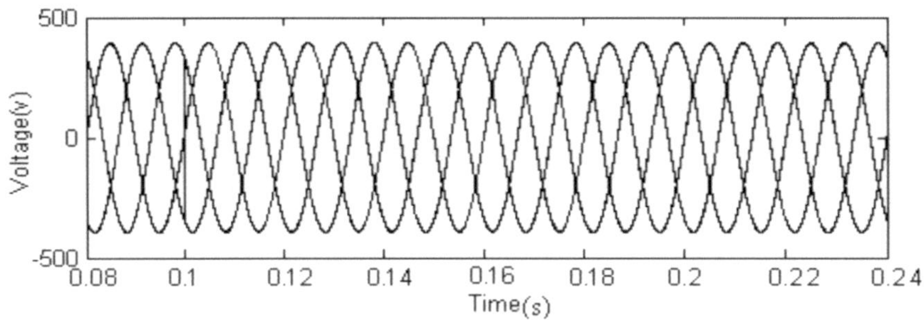

(c) Load voltage, V_L.

Fig. 9. Simulation result of DVR response to a balance voltage sag (HB1=0.005, HB2=0.007).

B. Voltage swell

In the second case, performance of DVR for a voltage swell condition is investigated. Here, a voltage swell with 30% three-phase voltage swell with +30 phase jump in phase-a starts at 0.1s and ends at 1.8 s is considered. The injected voltage that is produced by DVR in order to correct the load voltage and the load voltage for HB_1=0.005 and HB_2=0.007 are shown in Fig. 10(b) and (c), respectively.

To evaluate the quality of the load voltage during the operation of DVR, Total Harmonic Distortion (THD) is calculated with various HB.

Table 1 shows the obtained results for each HB_1 and HB_2.

Table 2 summarizes the THD values for the constant HB_1 and various HB_2.

For further study on the control scheme performance, the results obtained in Table 2, 3 is plotted in Fig. 11 and Fig.12.

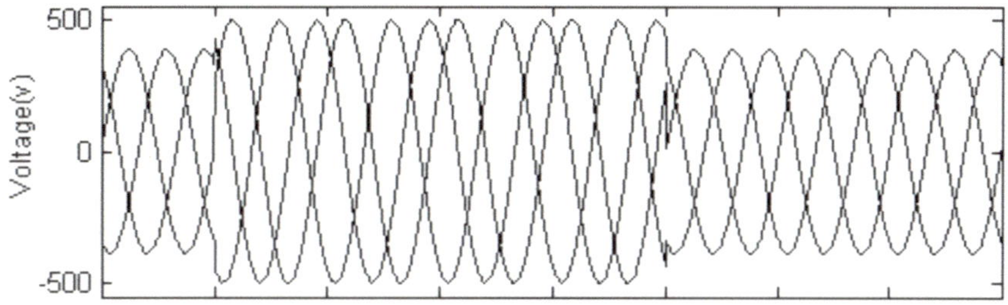

(a) Supply voltages.

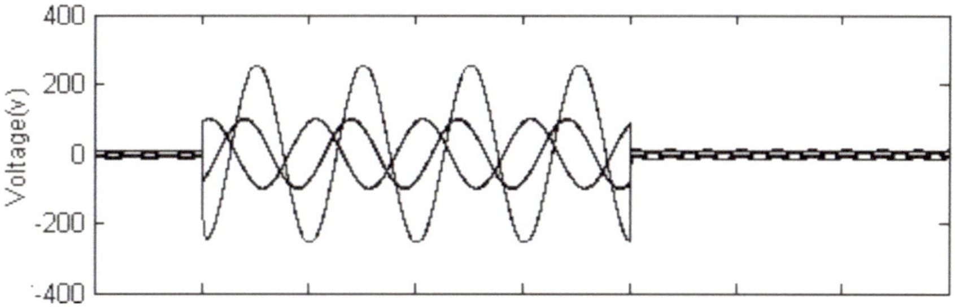

(b) Injected voltage, V_{DVR}.

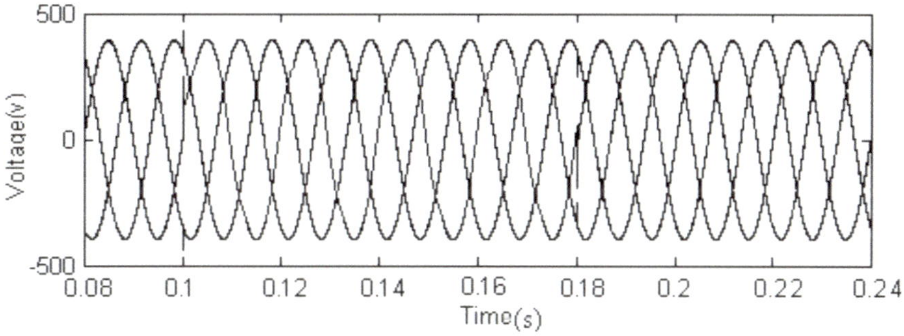

(c) Lad voltage, V_L.

Fig. 10. Simulation result of DVR response to a Balance voltage Swell (HB_1=0.005, HB_2=0.007).

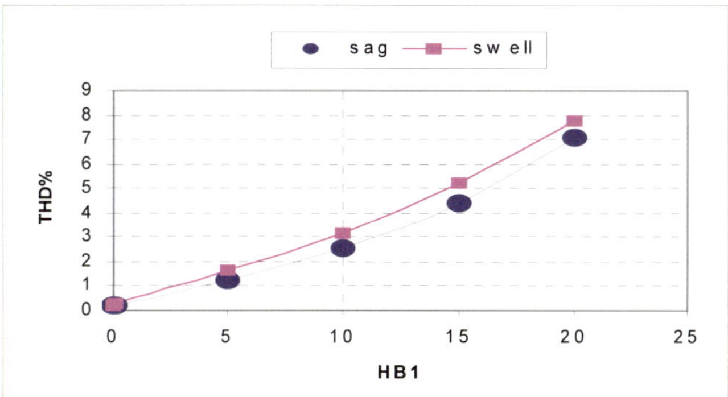

Fig. 11. Increase of THD with various HB_1 and HB_2.

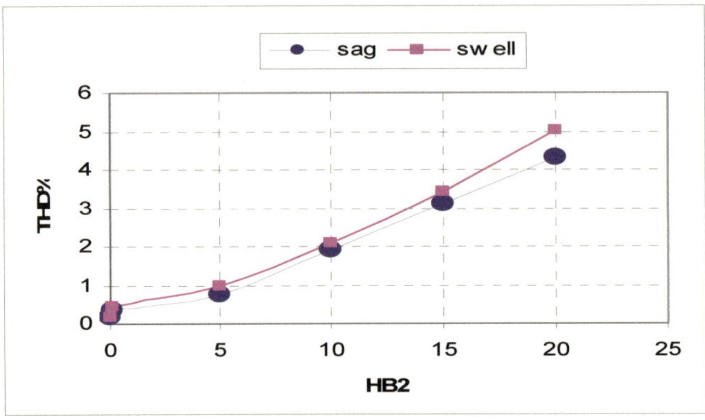

Fig. 12. Increase of THD with constant HB_1 and various HB_2.

Hysteresis Band		THD (%)	
HB_1	HB_2	Sag	swell
0.005	0.007	0.187	0.199
0.1	0.12	0.213	0.243
5	7	1.251	1.623
10	12	2.564	3.157
15	17	4.387	5.217
20	22	7.06	7.74

Table 2. THD for Load voltage for various values of HB1 and HB2.

Hysteresis Band		THD (%)	
HB_1	HB_2	Sag	swell
0.005	0.007	0.187	0.199
0.005	0.1	0.34	045
0.005	5	0.75	0.98
0.005	10	1.91	2.13
0.005	15	3.23	3.42
0.005	20	4.35	5.01

Table 3. THD for Load voltage for the constant values HB1 and various values HB2 for 30% voltage sag and swell.

As it can be seen, with growth of the $HB_1$and HB_2, THD of the load voltage correspondingly raises but the effect of increasing the HB on THD of the load voltage under voltage swell is more than THD of the voltage sag. It is obvious that the THD value varies when ever HB_1 and HB_2 value vary or when HB_1 is contented and HB_2 value varies. But THD of the load voltage under the voltage swell is greater than the voltage sag case. Therefore HB value has to be selected based on the voltage sag test.

With comparison of the obtained results in this chapter and Ref [12] in the voltage sag case, it can be observed that calculated THD in unipolar control is lower than bipolar control. In the other word, quality voltage in unipolar control is more than bipolar control. Fig 13.

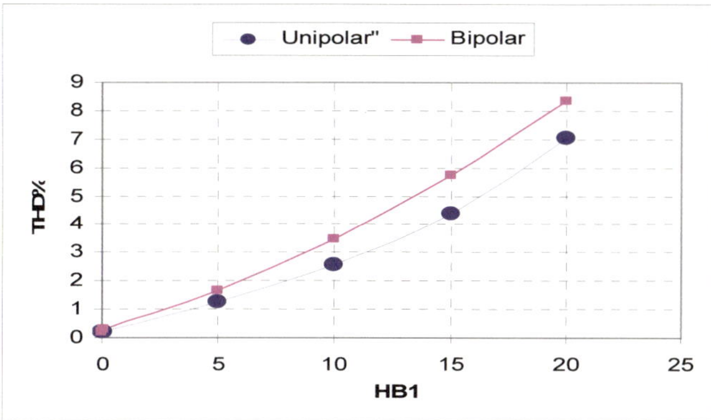

Fig. 13. Comparison of the in unipolar control and bipolar control.

This chapter introduces a hysteresis voltage control technique based on unipolar Pulse Width Modulation (PWM) For Dynamic Voltage Restorer to improve the quality of load voltage. The validity of recommended method is testified by results of the simulation in MATLAB SIMULINK.

To evaluate the quality of the load voltage during the operation of DVR, THD is calculated. The simulation result shows that increasing the HB, in swell condition THD of the load voltage is more than this THD amount in sag condition. The HB value can be found through the voltage sag test procedure by try and error.

8. References

[1] P. Boonchiam, and N. Mithulananthan."Dynamic Control Strategy in Medium Voltage DVR for Mitigating Voltage Sags/Swells" 2006 *International Conference on Power System Technology.*

[2] M.R. Banaei, S.H. Hosseini, S. Khanmohamadi a and G.B. Gharehpetian "Verification of a new energy control strategy for dynamic voltage restorer by simulation". *Elsevier,* Received 17 March 2004accepted 7 March 2005 Available online 29 April 2005. pp. 113-125.

[3] Paisan Boonchiaml Promsak Apiratikull and Nadarajah Mithulananthan2. "Detailed Analysis of Load Voltage Compensation for Dynamic Voltage Restorers" Record of the 2006 *IEEE Conference.*

[4] Kasuni Perera, Daniel Salomonsson, Arulampalam Atputharajah and Sanath Alahakoon. "Automated Control Technique for a Single Phase Dynamic Voltage Restorer" pp 63-68.Conference *ICIA,* 2006 IEEE.

[5] M.A. Hannan, and A. Mohamed, "Modeling and analysis of a 24-pulse dynamic voltage restorer in a distribution system" Research and Development, pp. 192-195. 2002. SCOReD 2002, *student conference* on16-17 July 2002.

[6] Christoph Meyer, Christoph Romaus, Rik W. De Doncker. "Optimized Control Strategy for a Medium-Voltage DVR" pp1887-1993. Record of the 2005 *IEEE Conference.*

[7] John Godsk Nielsen, Frede Blaabjerg and Ned Mohan "Control Strategies for Dynamic Voltage Restorer Compensating Voltage Sags with Phase Jump". Record of the 2005 *IEEE Conference*. pp.1267-1273.

[8] H. Kim. " Minimal energy control for a dynamic voltage restorer" *in: Proceedings of PCC Conference, IEEE* 2002, vol. 2, Osaka (JP), pp. 428–433.

[9] Chris Fitzer, Mike Barnes, and Peter Green." Voltage Sag Detection Technique for a Dynamic Voltage Restorer" *IEEE Transactions on industry applications*, VOL. 40, NO. 1, january/february 2004. pp.203-212.

[10] John Godsk Nielsen, Michael Newman, Hans Nielsen, and Frede Blaabjerg." Control and Testing of a Dynamic Voltage Restorer (DVR) at Medium Voltage Level" pp.806-813. *IEEE Transactions on power electronics* VOL. 19, NO. 3, MAY 2004.

[11] Bharat Singh Rajpurohit and Sri Niwas Singh." Performance Evaluation of Current Control Algorithms Used for Active Power Filters". pp.2570-2575. EUROCON 2007 *The International Conference on "Computer as a Tool"* Warsaw, September 9-12.

[12] Fawzi AL Jowder. " Modeling and Simulation of Dynamic Vltage Restorer (DVR) Based on Hysteresis Vltage Control". pp.1726-1731. The 33rd Annual Conference of the *IEEE Industrial Electronics Society (IECON)* Nov. 5-8, 2007, Taipei, Taiwan..

[13] Firuz Zare and Alireza Nami."A New Random Current Control Technique for a Single-Phase Inverter with Bipolar and Unipolar Modulations. pp.149-156. *Record of the IEEE* 2007.

5

Modeling & Simulation of Hysteresis Current Controlled Inverters Using MATLAB

Ahmad Albanna
Mississippi State University
General Motors Corporation
United States of America

1. Introduction

Hysteresis inverters are used in many low and medium voltage utility applications when the inverter line current is required to track a sinusoidal reference within a specified error margin. Line harmonic generation from those inverters depends principally on the particular switching pattern applied to the valves. The switching pattern of hysteresis inverters is produced through line current feedback and it is not pre-determined unlike the case, for instance, of Sinusoidal Pulse-Width Modulation (SPWM) where the inverter switching function is independent of the instantaneous line current and the inverter harmonics can be obtained from the switching function harmonics.

This chapter derives closed-form analytical approximations of the harmonic output of single-phase half-bridge inverter employing fixed or variable band hysteresis current control. The chapter is organized as follows: the harmonic output of the fixed-band hysteresis current control is derived in Section 2, followed by similar derivations of the harmonic output of the variable-band hysteresis controller in Section 3. The developed models are validated in Section 4 through performing different simulations studies and comparing results obtained from the models to those computed from MATLAB/Simulink. The chapter is summarized and concluded in section 5.

2. Fixed-band hysteresis control

2.1 System description

Fig.1 shows a single-phase neutral-point inverter. For simplicity, we assume that the dc voltage supplied by the DG source is divided into two constant and balanced dc sources, as in the figure, each of value V_c. The RL element on the ac side represents the combined line and transformer inductance and losses. The ac source v_{sa} represents the system voltage seen at the inverter terminals. The inverter line current i_a, in Fig.1, tracks a sinusoidal reference $i_a^* = \sqrt{2}I_a^* \sin(\omega_1 t + \phi)$ through the action of the relay band and the error current $e_a(t) = i_a^* - i_a$. In Fig.2, the fundamental frequency voltage at the inverter ac terminals when the line current equals the reference current is the reference voltage, $v_a^* = \sqrt{2}V_a^* \sin(\omega_1 t + \theta)$. Fig.2 compares the reference voltage to the instantaneous inverter voltage resulting from the action of the hysteresis loop.

$$R\cdot e_a + L\frac{d}{dt}(e_a) = v_a^* - v_a$$

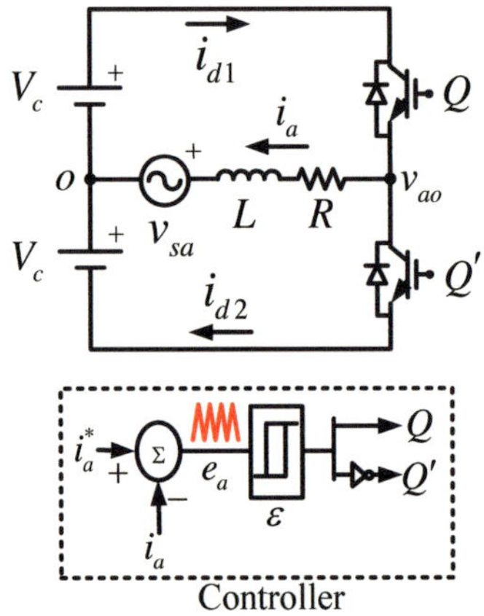

Fig. 1. Single-phase half-bridge inverter with fixed-band hysteresis control.

Referring to Fig.2, when valve Q is turned on, the inverter voltage is $v_a = V_c > v_a^*$; this forces the line current i_a to slope upward until the lower limit of the relay band is reached at $e_a(t) = -\varepsilon$. At that moment, the relay switches on Q' and the inverter voltage becomes $v_a = -V_c < v_a^*$, forcing the line current to reverse downward until the upper limit of the relay band is reached at $e_a(t) = \varepsilon$.

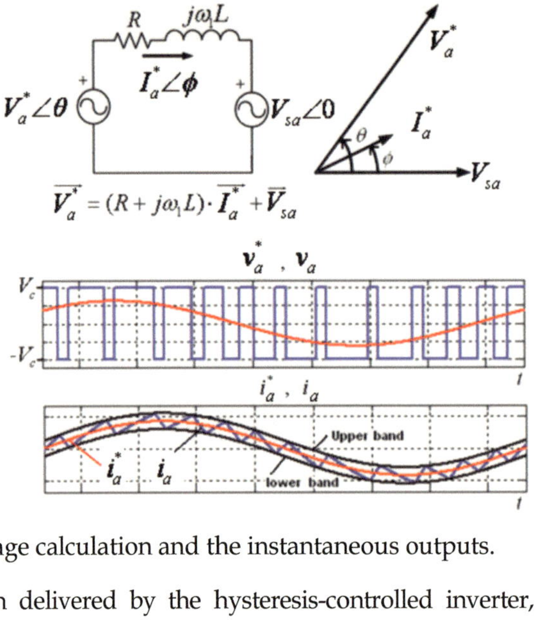

Fig. 2. Reference voltage calculation and the instantaneous outputs.

The bang-bang action delivered by the hysteresis-controlled inverter, therefore, drives the instantaneous line current to track the reference within the relay band $(-\varepsilon, \varepsilon)$. With reference to Fig.3 and Fig.4, the action of the hysteresis inverter described above produces an error current waveform $e_a(t)$ close to a triangular pulse-train with modulating duty cycle and frequency.

2.2 Error current mathematical description

The approach described in this section closely approximates the error current produced by the fixed-band hysteresis action, by a frequency-modulated triangular signal whose time-varying characteristics are computed from the system and controller parameters. Subsequently, the harmonic spectrum of the error current is derived by calculating the Fourier transform of the complex envelope of frequency modulated signal.

Results in the literature derived the instantaneous frequency of the triangular error current $f_{ia}(t)$ in terms of the system parameters ($R=0$). Using these results and referring to Fig.3 (Albanna & Hatziadoniu, 2009, 2010):

$$t_1 = \frac{2\varepsilon L}{V_c\left[1+M\sin\left(\omega_1 t+\theta\right)\right]},\ t_2 = \frac{2\varepsilon L}{V_c\left[1-M\cdot\sin\left(\omega_1 t+\theta\right)\right]}, \tag{1}$$

and therefore:

$$f_{ia}(t) = \frac{1}{T} = f_c + \frac{V_c M^2}{8\varepsilon L}\cdot\cos\left(2\omega_1 t+2\theta\right) \tag{2}$$

where the average switching (carrier) frequency f_c is given by

$$f_c = \frac{V_c}{4\varepsilon L}\cdot\left[1-\frac{M^2}{2}\right], \tag{3}$$

and M is the amplitude modulation index of the inverter expressed in terms of the peak reference voltage and the dc voltage as:

$$M = \frac{\sqrt{2}\,V_a^*}{V_c}. \tag{4}$$

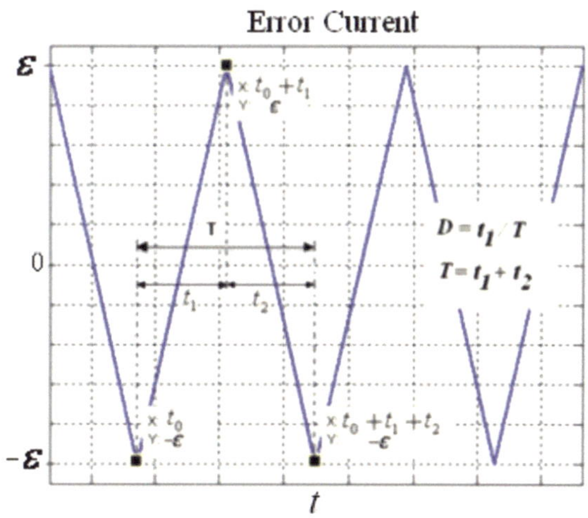

Fig. 3. Detail of $e_a(t)$.

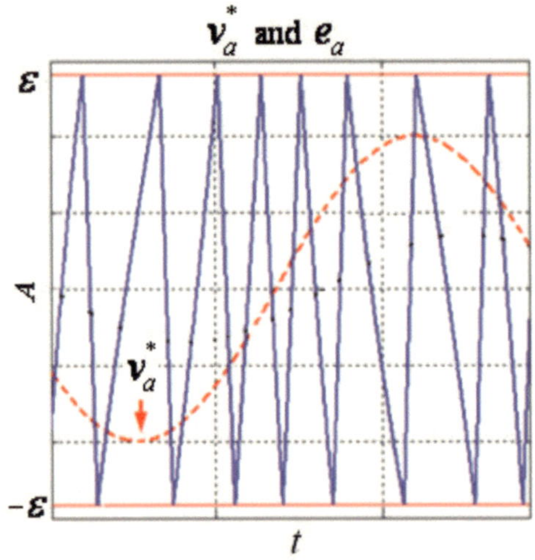

Fig. 4. Effect of v_a^* on the error current duty cycle.

Examining (2), the instantaneous frequency $f_{ia}(t)$ of the error current $e_a(t)$ consists of the carrier frequency f_c and a modulating part that explicitly determines the bandwidth of the error current spectrum, as it will be shown later in this chapter. Notice that the modulating frequency is twice the fundamental frequency, that is, $2f_1$.

Now, with the help of Fig.3, we define the instantaneous duty cycle of the error current $D(t)$ as the ratio of the rising edge time t_1 to the instantaneous period T. Noting that $D(t) = t_1 \cdot f_{ia}(t)$, we obtain after using (1), (2) and manipulating,

$$D(t) = 0.5 - 0.5 \cdot M \cdot \sin(\omega_1 t + \theta). \tag{5}$$

Implicit into (3) is the reference voltage v_a^*. The relation between the instantaneous duty cycle and the reference voltage can be demonstrated in Fig.4: the duty cycle reaches its maximum value at the minimum of v_a^*; it becomes 0.5 (symmetric form) at the zero of v_a^*; and it reaches its minimum value (tilt in the opposite direction) at the crest of v_a^*. Next, we will express $e_a(t)$ by the Fourier series of a triangular pulse-train having an instantaneous duty cycle $D(t)$ and an instantaneous frequency $f_{ia}(t)$:

$$e_a(t) = \sum_{n=1}^{\infty} \frac{-2\varepsilon}{\pi^2} \cdot \frac{(-1)^n}{n^2} \cdot \frac{\sin[n\pi(1-D(t))]}{D(t)[1-D(t)]} \cdot \sin\left(2\pi n \int_0^t f_{ia}(\tau)\,d\tau\right). \tag{6}$$

As the Fourier series of the triangular signal converges rapidly, the error current spectrum is approximated using the first term of the series in (6). Therefore truncating (6) to $n=1$ and using (2) yields

$$e_a(t) \approx \frac{2\varepsilon}{\pi^2} \cdot \frac{\sin[\pi D(t)]}{D(t)[1-D(t)]} \cdot \sin(\omega_c t + \beta \sin(2\omega_1 t + 2\theta) - \varphi), \tag{7}$$

where $\varphi = \beta \sin(2\theta)$. The frequency modulation index

$$\beta = \frac{V_c M^2}{8\varepsilon L} \cdot \frac{1}{2f_1} \tag{8}$$

determines the frequency bandwidth

$$BW = 4(\beta + 1) f_1 \tag{9}$$

that contains 98% of the spectral energy of the modulated sinusoid in (7). To simplify (7) further, we use the following convenient approximation (see Appendix-A for the derivation): Given that, $0 \le D(t) \le 1$, then

$$\frac{\sin[\pi D(t)]}{D(t)[1 - D(t)]} \approx (4 - \pi) \cdot \sin[\pi D(t)] + \pi . \tag{10}$$

Therefore (7) becomes,

$$e_a(t) \approx \frac{2\varepsilon}{\pi^2} \cdot [\pi + (4 - \pi)\sin(\pi D(t))] \cdot \sin(\omega_c t + \beta \sin(2\omega_1 t + 2\theta) - \varphi) . \tag{11}$$

Substituting $D(t)$ from (5) into (11) and manipulating, we obtain

$$e_a(t) \approx \frac{2\varepsilon}{\pi^2} \cdot \left(\pi + (4 - \pi)\cos\left(\frac{\pi M}{2} \sin(\omega_1 t + \theta) \right) \right) \cdot \sin(\omega_c t + \beta \sin(2\omega_1 t + 2\theta) - \varphi) \tag{12}$$

Next, the cosine term in (12) is simplified by using the infinite product identity and truncating to the first term. That is,

$$\cos(x) = \prod_{n-1}^{\infty} \left(1 - \frac{x^2}{\pi^2 (n - 0.5)^2} \right) \approx 1 - \frac{4x^2}{\pi^2} , \tag{13}$$

Substituting (13) into (12) and manipulating, the error current approximation becomes:

$$e_a(t) \approx \underbrace{[(8 - k) + k\cos(2\omega_1 t + 2\theta)]}_{e_1(t)} \cdot \underbrace{\left[\frac{\varepsilon}{\pi^2} \cdot \sin(\omega_c t + \beta \sin(2\omega_1 t + 2\theta) - \varphi) \right]}_{e_2(t)} , \tag{14}$$

where $k = (4 - \pi)M^2$. The harmonic spectrum $E_a(f)$ of the error current is the convolution of the spectra of the product terms $e_1(t)$ and $e_2(t)$ in (14). Therefore,

$$E_a(f) = \left[(8 - k)\delta(f) + \frac{k}{2} e^{j2\theta} \delta(f - 2f_1) + \frac{k}{2} e^{-j2\theta} \delta(f + 2f_1) \right] \otimes E_2(f) , \tag{15}$$

where $\otimes$ denotes convolution. In order to calculate $E_2(f)$, we rewrite $e_2(t)$ as

$$e_2(t) = \frac{\varepsilon}{j2\pi^2} \left(e^{j\omega_c t} \cdot e^{-j\varphi} \cdot e^{j\beta \sin(2\omega_1 t + 2\theta)} - e^{-j\omega_c t} \cdot e^{j\varphi} \cdot e^{-j\beta \sin(2\omega_1 t + 2\theta)} \right) . \tag{16}$$

The positive frequency half of the spectrum $E_2(f)$ is therefore given by

$$E_2(f) = \frac{\varepsilon}{j2\pi^2} \sum_{n=-\infty}^{\infty} J_n(\beta) \cdot e^{j(2n\theta-\varphi)} \cdot \delta_{(f_c+2nf_1)}, \tag{17}$$

where $\delta_x = \delta(f-x)$ is the Dirac function, and J_n is the Bessel function of the first kind and order n. Substituting (17) into (15), and convoluting, we obtain:

$$E_a(f) = \frac{\varepsilon}{j2\pi^2} \sum_{n=-\infty}^{\infty} \left(\frac{k}{2}[J_{n-1}(\beta) + J_{n+1}(\beta)] + (8-k)J_n(\beta) \right) \cdot e^{j(2n\theta-\varphi)} \cdot \delta_{(f_c+2nf_1)}. \tag{18}$$

Using the recurrence relation of the Bessel functions,

$$J_{n+1}(\beta) + J_{n-1}(\beta) = \frac{2n}{\beta} J_n(\beta), \tag{19}$$

the positive half of the error current spectrum takes the final form:

$$E_a(f) = \sum_{n=-\infty}^{n=\infty} E_n \, e^{j(2n\theta-\varphi)} \cdot \delta_{(f_c-2nf_1)}, \tag{20}$$

where,

$$E_n = \frac{\varepsilon}{j2\pi^2} \left(\frac{kn}{\beta} - k + 8 \right) J_n(\beta). \tag{21}$$

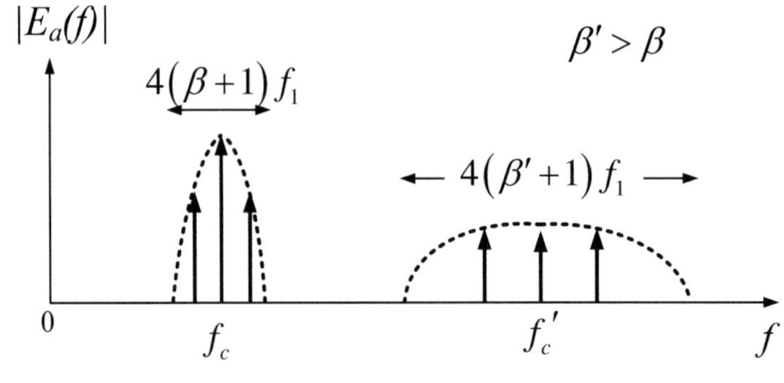

Fig. 5. Effect of changing β on the harmonic spectrum.

The calculation of the non-characteristic harmonic currents using (20) is easily executed numerically as it only manipulates a single array of Bessel functions. The spectral energy is distributed symmetrically around the carrier frequency f_c with spectrum bands stepped apart by $2f_1$. Fig.5 shows the harmonic spectrum of the error current as a function of the frequency modulation index β. If the operating conditions of the inverter forces β to increase to β', then the spectral energy shifts to higher carrier frequency f_c'. Additionally, as the average spectral energy is independent of β and depends on the error bandwidth ε, the spectral energy spreads over wider range of frequencies, $4(\beta'+1)f_1$, with an overall decrease in the band magnitudes to attain the average spectral energy at a constant level as shown in Fig.5. The Total Harmonic Distortion (THD) of the line current is independent of β and is directly proportional to the relay bandwidth ε.

2.3 Model approximation

The harmonic model derived in the previous section describes the exact spectral characteristics of the error current by including the duty cycle $D(t)$ to facilitate the effect of the reference voltage v_a^* on the error current amplitude and tilting. Moreover, the consideration of $D(t)$ in (6) predicts the amplitude of the error current precisely, which in turn, would result in accurate computation of the spectrum bands magnitudes according to (20). The model can be further simplified to serve the same functionality in without significant loss of numerical accuracy. As the instantaneous frequency of the error current, given by (2), is independent of $D(t)$, the spectral characteristics such as f_c and BW are also independent of D and therefore, setting $D(t)$ to its average value 0.5 will slightly affect the magnitude of the spectrum bands according to (7). Subsequently, the error current harmonic spectrum simplifies to

$$E_a(f)=\frac{4\varepsilon}{j\pi^2}\sum_{n=-\infty}^{n=\infty} J_n(\beta)\cdot e^{j(2n\theta-\varphi)}\cdot \delta_{(f_c-2nf_1)}, \tag{22}$$

where the carrier (average) frequency f_c is given by (3), the frequency modulation index β is given by (8). The 3 dB frequency bandwidth BW that contains 98% of the spectral energy is given by (9).

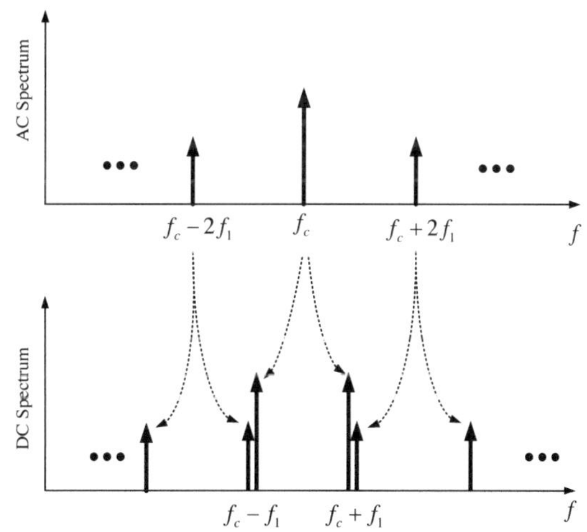

Fig. 6. AC harmonics transfer to the inverter dc side.

2.4 Dc current harmonics

The hysteresis switching action transfers the ac harmonic currents into the inverter dc side through the demodulation process of the inverter. As the switching function is not defined

for hysteresis inverters, the harmonic currents transfer can be modeled through balancing the instantaneous input dc and output ac power equations.
With reference to Fig.1, and assuming a small relay bandwidth (i.e. $i_a^* \approx i_a$), the application of Kirchhoff Current Law (KCL) at node a gives:

$$i_{d1} = i_a^* + i_{d2}. \tag{23}$$

The power balance equation over the switching period when Q' is on is given by:

$$i_{d2} = \frac{1}{V_c} \cdot v_a(t) \cdot i_a(t). \tag{24}$$

Using the instantaneous output voltage

$$v_a = v_a^* - L \cdot \left(\frac{d}{dt} e_a \right) \tag{25}$$

in (24), the dc current i_{d1} will have the form:

$$i_{d1}(t) = \frac{v_a^* \cdot i_a^*}{V_c} + i_a^* - \frac{L}{V_c} \cdot i_a^* \cdot \left(\frac{d}{dt} e_a \right), \tag{26}$$

where $\dot{x}$ is the derivative of x with respect to time. Using the product-to-sum trigonometric identity and simplifying yields:

$$i_{d1}(t) = \frac{\sqrt{2} M I_a^*}{2} \cos(\theta - \phi) + i_a^* - \frac{\sqrt{2} M I_a^*}{2} \cos(2\omega_1 t + \theta + \phi) - \frac{L}{V_c} \dot{e}_a \cdot i_a^*. \tag{27}$$

The positive half of the dc current spectrum is thus computed from the application of the Fourier transform and convolution properties on (27), resulting in

$$I_{d1}(f) = I_0 \cdot \delta_0 + I_1 \cdot \delta_{f_1} + I_2 \cdot \delta_{2f_1} + f \cdot I_h \cdot \left(E_a(f + f_1) - E_a(f - f_1) \right), \tag{28}$$

where $E_a(f)$ is the error current spectrum given by (22). The average, fundamental, and harmonic components of the dc current spectrum are respectively given by

$$\begin{aligned} I_0 &= \frac{\sqrt{2}}{2} \cdot M \cdot I_a^* \cdot \cos(\theta - \phi), \\ I_1 &= \frac{\sqrt{2}}{j2} \cdot I_a^* \cdot e^{j\phi}, \quad I_2 = \frac{\sqrt{2}}{4} \cdot M \cdot I_a^* \cdot e^{j(\theta - \phi)}, \text{ and} \\ I_h &= \frac{\sqrt{2}\pi}{V_c} \cdot L \cdot I_a^*. \end{aligned} \tag{29}$$

Each spectrum band of the ac harmonic current creates two spectrum bands in the dc side due to the convolution process implicitly applied in (28). For instance, the magnitude of the ac spectrum band at f_c is first scaled by f_c according to (28) then it is shifted by $\pm f_1$ to create the two dc bands pinned at $f_c \pm f_1$ as shown in Fig.6. Consequently, every two successive bands in the ac spectrum create one corresponding dc spectrum band that is located half the frequency distance between the two ac bands.

2.5 Harmonic generation under distorted system voltages

The harmonic performance of the hysteresis inverter in Fig.7 under distorted dc and ac system voltages is analyzed. The presence of background harmonics in the ac and dc voltages will affect the instantaneous frequency of the inverter according to (30) as

$$f'_{ia}(t) = \frac{V_c}{4\varepsilon L} \cdot \left[1 - \left(\frac{v_a^*}{V_c} + \frac{v_h}{V_c} - \frac{v_k}{V_c} \right)^2 \right]. \qquad (30)$$

where the dc distortion v_k, and the distortion of the ac system voltage, v_h, are given as:

$$\begin{aligned} v_k &= \sqrt{2} V_k \sin\left(k\omega_1 t + \gamma_k\right) \\ v_h &= \sqrt{2} V_h \sin\left(h\omega_1 t + \gamma_h\right) \end{aligned} . \qquad (31)$$

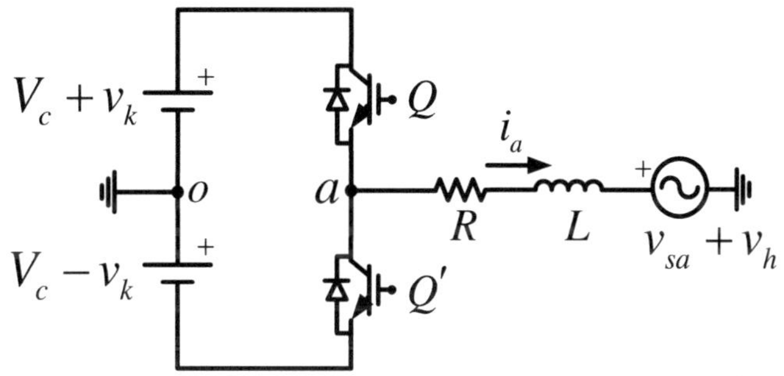

Fig. 7. Hysteresis inverter operating with distorted system voltages.

Notice that in (31), k and h need not be integers. Substituting (31) in (30) and assuming small distortion magnitudes, the instantaneous frequency of the error current e_u simplifies to:

$$f'_{ia}(t) = f_{ia}(t) - \Delta f_{ac}(t) + \Delta f_{dc}(t), \qquad (32)$$

where $f_{ia}(t)$ is given by (2) and

$$\begin{aligned} \Delta f_{ac}(t) &= \frac{V_c}{4\varepsilon L} \cdot M \cdot M_h \cdot \left[\cos\left([h-1]\omega_1 t + \gamma_h - \theta\right) - \cos\left([h+1]\omega_1 t + \gamma_h + \theta\right) \right], \\ \Delta f_{dc}(t) &= \frac{V_c}{4\varepsilon L} \cdot M \cdot M_k \cdot \left[\cos\left([k-1]\omega_1 t + \gamma_k - \theta\right) - \cos\left([k+1]\omega_1 t + \gamma_k + \theta\right) \right], \end{aligned} \qquad (33)$$

are the frequency noise terms due to the system background distortions. The amplitude modulation indices of the ac and dc harmonic distortions are given by :

$$M_h = \frac{\sqrt{2}V_h}{V_c}, \text{ and } M_k = \frac{\sqrt{2}V_k}{V_c}. \tag{34}$$

Integrating (32), the error current $e_a(t)$ is thus approximated by the frequency-modulated sinusoid:

$$e_a'(t) = \frac{8\varepsilon}{\pi^2}\sin\left[\omega_c t + \beta\sin(2\omega_1 t + 2\theta) - \varphi + \psi_{ac} + \psi_{dc}\right]. \tag{35}$$

In (35): the carrier frequency f_c is given by (3); the frequency modulation index β is given by (3); $\varphi = \beta\sin(2\theta)$; and

$$\begin{aligned} \psi_{ac} &= \beta_h^+ \sin([h+1]\omega_1 t + \gamma_h + \theta) - \beta_h^- \sin([h-1]\omega_1 t + \gamma_h - \theta) + \varphi_{ac}, \\ \psi_{dc} &= \beta_k^- \sin([k-1]\omega_1 t + \gamma_k - \theta) - \beta_k^+ \sin([k+1]\omega_1 t + \gamma_k + \theta) + \varphi_{dc}. \end{aligned} \tag{36}$$

where $\varphi_{ac} = \beta_h^- \sin(\gamma_h - \theta) - \beta_h^+ \sin(\gamma_h + \theta)$,and $\varphi_{dc} = \beta_k^+ \sin(\gamma_k + \theta) - \beta_h^- \sin(\gamma_k - \theta)$. The corresponding ac and dc frequency modulation indices are given by

$$\begin{aligned} \beta_h^+ &= \frac{V_c}{4\varepsilon L}\cdot M\cdot M_h\cdot\frac{1}{(h+1)\cdot f_1}; \quad \beta_h^- = \frac{V_c}{4\varepsilon L}\cdot M\cdot M_h\cdot\frac{1}{(h-1)\cdot f_1}; \\ \beta_k^+ &= \frac{V_c}{4\varepsilon L}\cdot M\cdot M_k\cdot\frac{1}{(k+1)\cdot f_1}; \quad \beta_k^- = \frac{V_c}{4\varepsilon L}\cdot M\cdot M_k\cdot\frac{1}{(k-1)\cdot f_1}. \end{aligned} \tag{37}$$

Applying the Fourier transform and convolution properties on (35), the positive half of the frequency spectrum $E_a'(f)$ simplifies to:

$$E_a'(f) = E_a(f) \otimes \Im_{ach}(f) \otimes \Im_{dck}(f), \tag{38}$$

Where $E_a(f)$ is given by (22) and

$$\begin{aligned} \Im_{ach} &= e^{j\varphi_{ac}}\left(\sum_{n=-\infty}^{\infty} J_n(\beta_h^+)\cdot e^{jn(\gamma_h+\theta)}\cdot\delta_{(h+1)nf_1}\right)\otimes\left(\sum_{n=-\infty}^{\infty} J_n(\beta_h^-)\cdot e^{-jn(\gamma_h-\theta)}\cdot\delta_{-(h-1)nf_1}\right), \\ \Im_{dck} &= e^{j\varphi_{ac}}\left(\sum_{n=-\infty}^{\infty} J_n(\beta_k^+)\cdot e^{-jn(\gamma_k+\theta)}\cdot\delta_{-(k+1)nf_1}\right)\otimes\left(\sum_{n=-\infty}^{\infty} J_n(\beta_k^-)\cdot e^{jn(\gamma_k-\theta)}\cdot\delta_{(k-1)nf_1}\right), \end{aligned} \tag{39}$$

are the ac and dc modulating spectra. Generally, for any H number of ac voltage distortions and K number of dc distortions, (40) is applied first to calculate the total ac and dc modulating spectra, then (38) is used to compute the error current harmonic spectrum.

$$\begin{aligned} \Im_{acH}(f) &= \bigotimes_H \Im_{ach}, \\ \Im_{dcK}(f) &= \bigotimes_K \Im_{dck}. \end{aligned} \tag{40}$$

3. Variable-band hysteresis control

3.1 Error current mathematical description

The harmonic line generation of the half-bridge inverter of Fig.1 under the variable-band hysteresis current control is derived. The constant switching frequency of the error current in (2), i.e. $f_{ia}(t) = f_o$, is achieved by limiting the amplitude of the error current to stay within the variable band [54, 55]:

$$\varepsilon_a(t) = \varepsilon_o\left[1 - 0.5M^2 + 0.5M^2\cos(2\omega_1 t + 2\theta)\right], \tag{41}$$

where the maximum value of the modulating relay bandwidth is

$$\varepsilon_o = \frac{V_c}{4Lf_o}, \tag{42}$$

and f_o is the target switching frequency. Subsequently, the error current is approximated by the amplitude-modulated sinusoid of frequency f_o as:

$$e_a(t) = \frac{8}{\pi^2}\cdot\varepsilon_a(t)\cdot\sin(2\pi f_o t) \tag{43}$$

Substituting (41) in (43) and then applying the Fourier transform, the positive half of the frequency spectrum of $E_a(f)$ is:

$$E_a(f) = \frac{4\varepsilon_o}{j\pi^2}\left[\left(1 - \frac{M^2}{2}\right)\delta_{f_o} + \frac{M^2}{4}\left(e^{-j2\theta}\delta_{(f_o-2f_1)} + e^{j2\theta}\delta_{(f_o+2f_1)}\right)\right]. \tag{44}$$

The error current spectrum in (44) consists of a center band at the switching frequency f_o and two side bands located at $f_o \pm 2f_1$. The frequency bandwidth that contains the spectral energy of (44) is simply $4f_1$.

3.2 Dc current harmonics

The approach developed in 2.2.4 also applies to compute the dc current harmonic spectrum when the variable-band hysteresis control. The positive half of the dc current harmonic spectrum is computed by substituting (44) in (28).

3.3 Harmonic generation under distorted system voltages

The presence of background harmonics in the ac and dc voltages, given in (31) will affect the instantaneous frequency of the inverter according to (30). Subsequently, to achieve the constant switching frequency f_o, the modulating error band in (41) will also contain the corresponding distortions terms as

$$\varepsilon_a(t) = \varepsilon_a^o(t) - \varepsilon_a^{ac}(t) + \varepsilon_a^{dc}(t), \tag{45}$$

where $\varepsilon_a^o(t)$ is the error under zero background distortion given by (41), and

$$\varepsilon_a^{ac}(t) = 2\varepsilon_o M M_h \sin\left(h\omega_1 t + \gamma_h\right)\sin\left(\omega_1 t + \theta\right),$$
$$\varepsilon_a^{dc}(t) = 2\varepsilon_o M M_k \sin\left(k\omega_1 t + \gamma_k\right)\sin\left(\omega_1 t + \theta\right), \tag{46}$$

where M_h and M_k define the modulation index of the ac and dc background distortion terms respectively as (34).

The new terms introduced by the background distortion appear as amplitude modulations in (45). The error current $e_a'(t)$ is then expressed as:

$$e_a'(t) = \frac{8}{\pi^2}\left[\varepsilon_a^o(t) - \varepsilon_a^{ac}(t) + \varepsilon_a^{dc}(t)\right]\sin\left(2\pi f_o t\right). \tag{47}$$

The harmonic spectrum of the error current $E_a'(f)$ simplifies to

$$E_a'(t) = E_a(f) - E_a^{ac}(f) + E_a^{dc}(f), \tag{48}$$

where $E_a(f)$ is the zero-background-distortion error as in (44), and the new terms due to background distortion:

$$E_a^{ac} = \frac{2MM_h\varepsilon_o}{j\pi^2}\cdot\Big[e^{j(\gamma_h-\theta)}\cdot\delta_{f_o+(h-1)f_1} + e^{-j(\gamma_h-\theta)}\cdot\delta_{f_o-(h-1)f_1} - e^{j(\gamma_h+\theta)}\delta_{f_o+(h+1)f_1} - e^{-j(\gamma_h+\theta)}\cdot\delta_{f_o-(h+1)f_1}\Big],$$
$$E_a^{dc} = \frac{2MM_k\varepsilon_o}{j\pi^2}\cdot\Big[e^{j(\gamma_k-\theta)}\cdot\delta_{f_o+(k-1)f_1} + e^{-j(\gamma_k-\theta)}\cdot\delta_{f_o-(k-1)f_1} - e^{j(\gamma_k+\theta)}\cdot\delta_{f_o+(k+1)f_1} - e^{-j(\gamma_k+\theta)}\cdot\delta_{f_o-(k+1)f_1}\Big]. \tag{49}$$

Examining (49), the presence of the harmonic distortions in the system tends to scatter the spectrum over lower frequencies, more specifically, to $f_o - (h+1)f_1$, for $h > k$ or to $f_o - (k+1)f_1$ for $k > h$.

4. Simulation

The harmonic performance of the half-bridge inverter under the fixed- and variable-band hysteresis control is analyzed. Results computed from the developed models are compared to those obtained from time-domain simulations using MATLAB/Simulink. Multiple simulation studies are conducted to study the harmonic response of the inverter under line and control parameter variations. The grid-connected inverter of Fig.1 is simulated in Simulink using: $V_c = 400\,V$, $V_{sa} = 120\ V_{rms}$, $f_1 = 60\,Hz$, $R = 1.88\,\Omega$, and $L = 20\,mH$. In order to limit the THD of the line current to 10%, the line current tracks the sinusoidal reference $i_a^* = \sqrt{2}\cdot 15\cdot\sin\left(\omega_1 t\right)\,A$ within the maximum relay bandwidth of $\varepsilon = \varepsilon_o = 2.82\,A$.

4.1 Fixed-band hysteresis current control

The ac outputs of the half-bridge inverter under the fixed-band hysteresis current control are shown in Fig.8. the fundamental component v_a^* of the bipolar output voltage v_a has a peak value of 263.7 V. the inverter line current i_a tracks the sinusoidal reference within an absolute error margin ε. The error current resulting from the fixed-band hysteresis action resembles a frequency-modulate triangular signal of constant amplitude. The implicit relation between the error current duty cycle and the reference voltage v_a^* is clearly seen in Fig.8. The symmetric duty cycle, i.e. $D = 0.5$, happens whenever the reference voltage approaches a zero crossing.

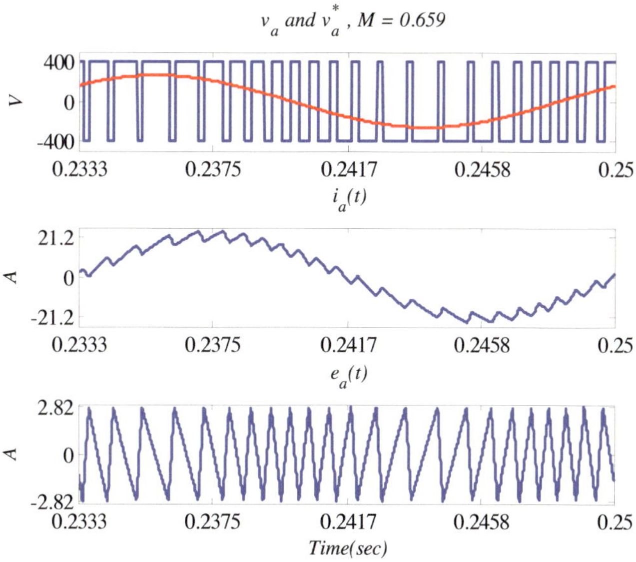

Fig. 8. Inverter ac outputs under fixed-band hysteresis control.

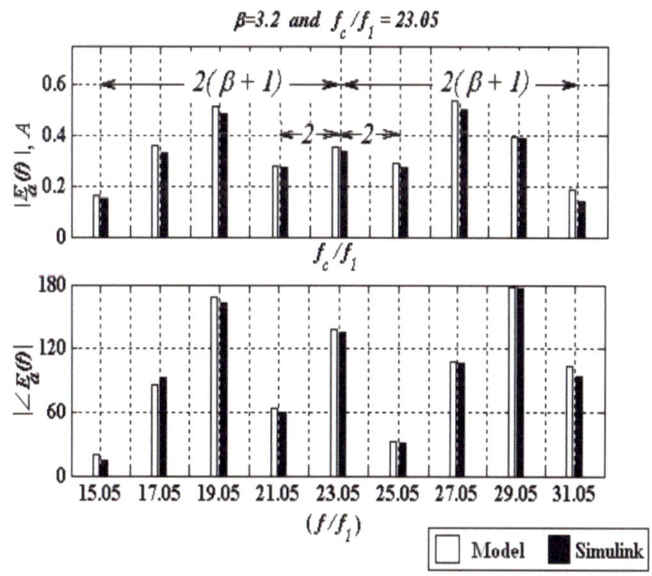

Fig. 9. Simulation results obtained from the developed model and Simulink.

The harmonic parameters of the model are computed the system and controller parameters as follows: substituting the reference voltage in (4) results in an amplitude modulation index of $M = 0.659$; from (3), the carrier frequency is $f_c = 23.05 f_1 = 1383\,Hz$; and from (8), the frequency modulation index is $\beta = 3.2$ 3.2. Fig.9 compares the harmonic spectrum of the error current $E_a(f)$ computed from (20) to that obtained from the Fourier analysis of the time-domain simulation results using Simulink. The figure shows a good agreement between the two spectra in terms of frequency order, magnitude and angle.

The spectrum bands are concentrated around the order of the carrier frequency and are stepped apart by two fundamental frequency orders $2f_1$ as shown in Fig.9. With reference to (9) and Fig.9, it is shown that 98% of the spectrum power is laying in the bandwidth $BW = 4(\beta + 1) f_1 \approx 16 f_1$. Therefore, the spectrum bands outside this range contribute insignificantly to the total spectrum power and thus can be truncated from the spectrum for easier numerical applications.

To study the effect of line parameter variations on the harmonic performance of the inverter, the DG source voltage is decreased to have the dc voltage $V_c = 350\ V$, then the harmonic spectrum is recomputed using the model and compared to the results obtained from Simulink. Decreasing V_c will increase M and β according to (4) and (8) respectively, but will decrease f_c according to (3).

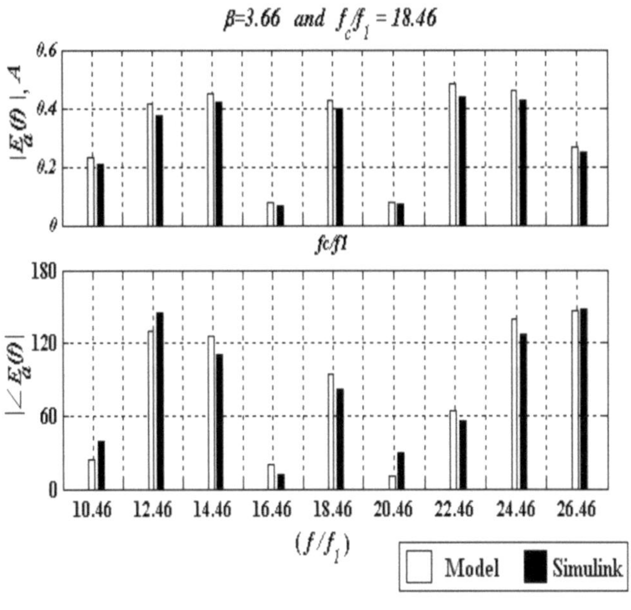

Fig. 10. $E_a(f)$ | when V_c is decreased to 350V.

With reference to the results shown in Fig.10, the harmonic spectrum $E_a(f)$ will shift to the lower frequency order of, approximately, 18, and will span a wider range, as β is greater. The frequency bandwidth has slightly increased to $18 f_1$ from the previous value of $16 f_1$ due to the slight increase in $\beta = 3.2$ to $\beta = 3.66$.

The total spectral energy of the error current depends on the relay bandwidth ε and it is independent of β . As β increases the spectrum energy redistributes such that the bands closer to f_c decrease in magnitude and those that are farther from f_c increase as shown in Fig.10. The Total Harmonic Distortion (THD) of the line current thus will not be affected by changing V_c .

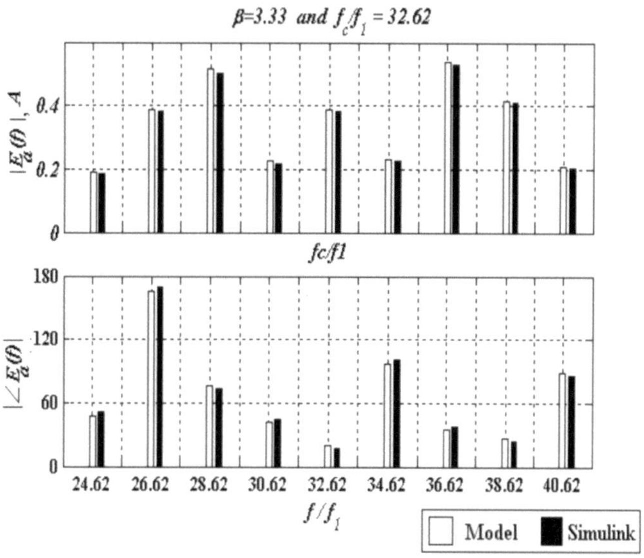

Fig. 11. $|E_a(f)|$ when the system inductance is decreased by 25%.

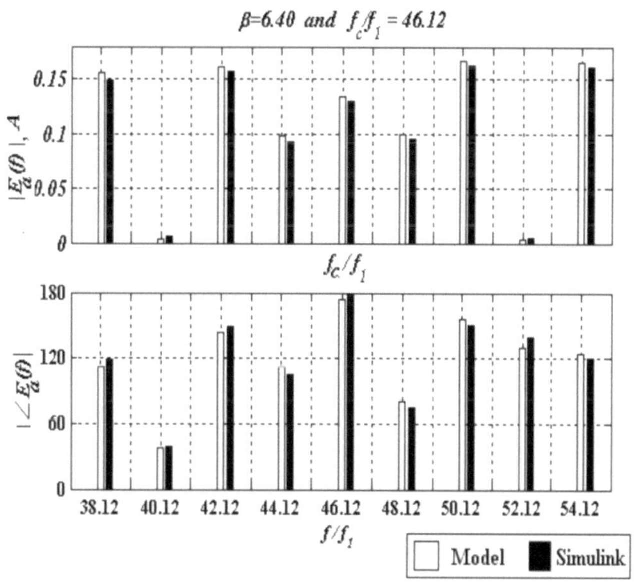

Fig. 12. Results from reducing ε by 50%.

Next, the system and control parameters are set to their original values and the inductance is decreased by 25% to $L = 15\,mH$. The results are shown in Fig.11. Lower inductance results in higher switching frequency according to (3) and higher β according to (8). The harmonic spectrum $E_a(f)$ shifts to higher frequencies as f_c is increasing, and the spectrum spans a wider range as β is increasing. The amplitude modulation index M and D are affected by the system inductance variation since the inverter reference voltage v_a^* depends on system inductance L.

The width of the relay band is reduced by half while maintaining the rest of the parameters at their base values. As (4) indicates, M is independent of ε and thus it remains unchanged from its value of 0.659. Referring to Fig.12, as the error band is reduced by half, the carrier frequency doubles and the harmonic spectrum $E_a(f)$ will be concentrated around, approximately, the order of 46. The frequency modulation index β doubles and thus the spectrum spreads over a wider frequency range overall decreasing in magnitude, as seen in Fig.12. Under these conditions, the THD of the line current will decrease to approximately 5% as the spectral energy of the spectrum is proportional to the relay bandwidth ε.

To study the harmonic performance of the inverter under distorted system voltages, the system and control parameters are set to the original values and the 11th order voltage oscillator $v_{11}(t) = 15 \cdot \sin(11 \cdot \omega_1 t)\ V$ is included in the source voltage v_s to simulate a distorted ac network voltage. The simulation is run for 30 fundamental periods to ensure solution transients are vanishing, and the last fundamental period of the inverter ac outputs are shown in Fig.13.

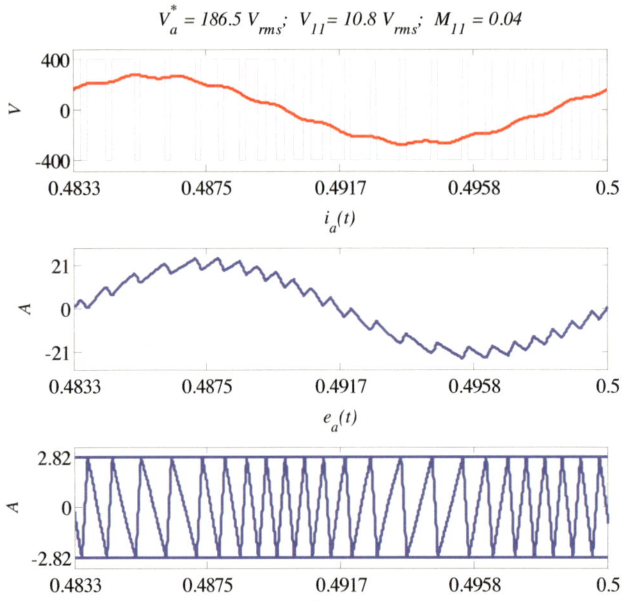

Fig. 13. Effect of injecting the 11th ac harmonic voltage on the inverter ac outputs.

Comparing Fig.8 and Fig.13, the reference voltage is distorted due to the presence of the 11th voltage oscillator in the source. The output voltage of the inverter is still bipolar, i.e. $v_a = \pm 400\,V$. Fig. 14 compares the instantaneous frequency of the error current under sinusoidal ac voltage f_{ia} to that under the distorted ac system voltage f'_{ia}.

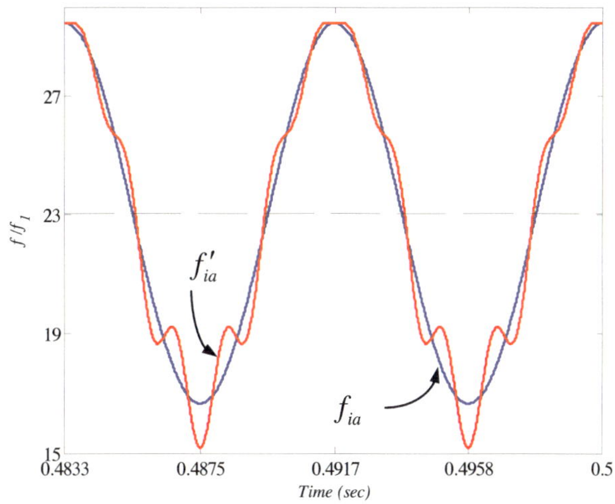

Fig. 14. Instantaneous frequency of $e_a(t)$ when v_s is distorted.

According to (32), the carrier frequency $f_c = 23.05 f_1$ is constant and independent of the distortion terms. The amplitude modulation index $M_{11} = 0.038$ is computed from (34), subsequently, the harmonic parameters $\beta_{11}^{+} = 0.062$ and $\beta_{11}^{-} = 0.074$ are computed from (37).

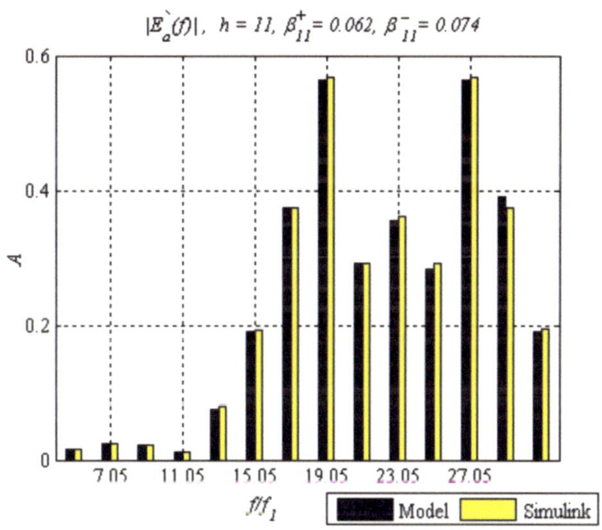

Fig. 15. Error spectrum when v_{sa} contains the 11th oscillator voltage.

Fig.15 compares the harmonic spectrum $E'_a(f)$ obtained from (38) to that computed from the Fourier analysis of Simulink outputs with very good agreement in terms of frequency order and magnitude. The spectral energy is centered on the carrier frequency $f_c = 23.05 f_1$ with spectrum bands are stepped apart by $2f_1$. The frequency bandwidth increases due to the distortion terms, and as Fig.15 shows, the spectrum bands leaks to as low of a frequency order as 5. Notice that the THD of the line current did not change as the controller bandwidth did not change.

Similar analysis is performed to study the harmonic performance of the inverter when the dc voltage contains the distortion $v_8(t) = 28.2 \cdot \sin(8\omega_1 t)\ V$. The inverter instantaneous outputs obtained from Simulink are shown in Fig.16. Notice that the voltage v_a is still bipolar but distorted.

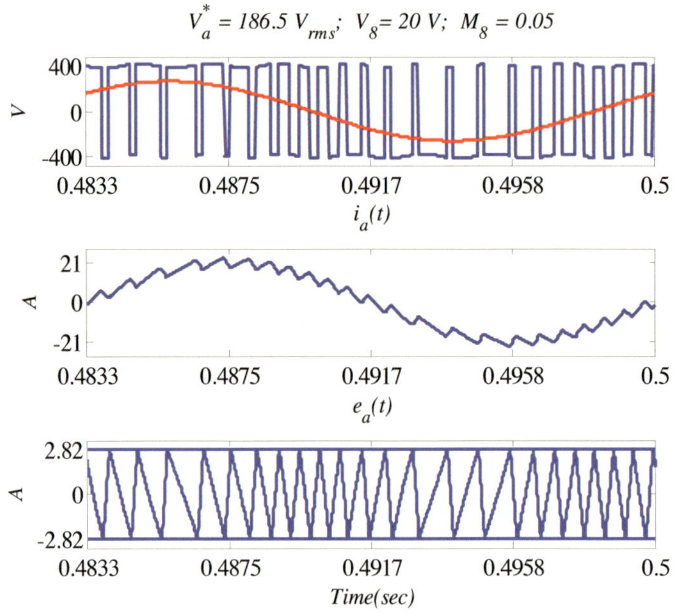

Fig. 16. Effect of injecting the 8th dc harmonic voltage on the inverter ac outputs.

The dc distortions impose additional noise component on the instantaneous frequency, see Fig.17, and subsequently, according to (38) the harmonic spectrum is drifting to lower order harmonics as shown in Fig.18.

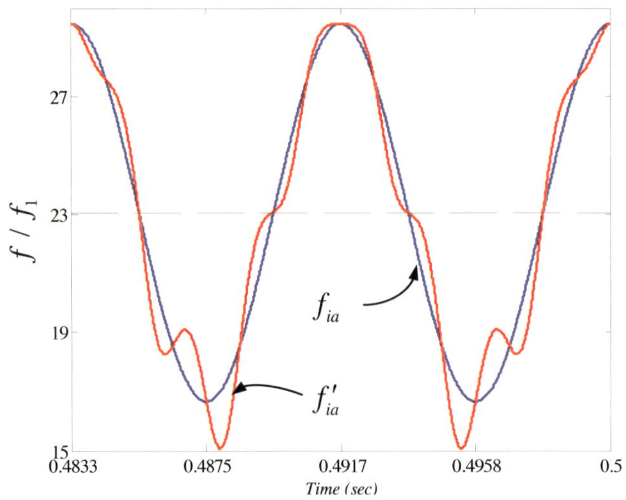

Fig. 17. Frequency of $e_a(t)$ when the input dc is distorted.

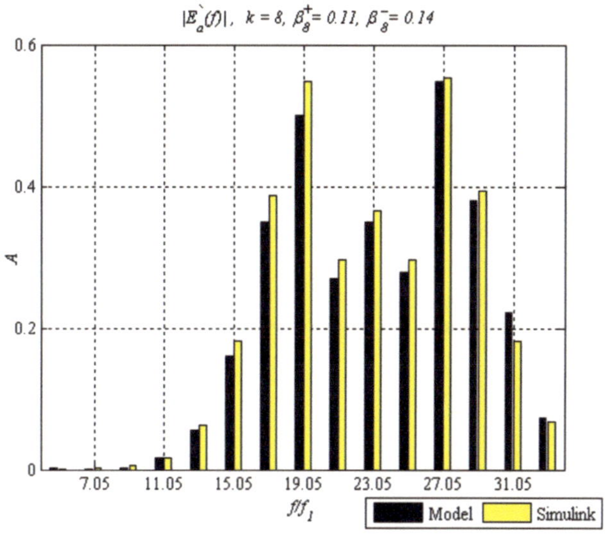

Fig. 18. Error spectrum when the 8th dc background distortion exists.

4.2 Variable-band hysteresis control

The harmonic performance of the same half-bridge inverter used in section 2.4.1 is analyzed when the variable-band hysteresis current control is employed. Similar harmonic studies to those in the previous section are performed to compute the spectral characteristics of the inverter harmonic outputs using the developed models in section 2.3 and compare them with results obtained from time-domain simulations using Simulink.

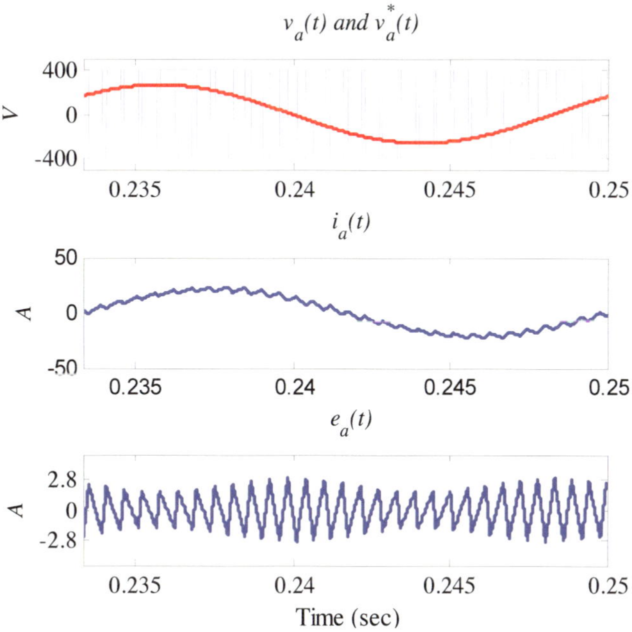

Fig. 19. Instantaneous outputs of the variable-band hysteresis control.

The instantaneous line outputs of the single-phase inverter operating under variable hysteresis control are shown in Fig.19. With the maximum relay band ε_o is set to 2.82, the error current $e_a(t)$ resulting from the variable-band control is an amplitude-modulated triangular signal of carrier frequency f_o. Regardless of the adopted switching pattern, the reference voltage is $v_a^* = 263.7 \cdot \sin\left(\omega_1 t + 37^\circ\right) V$ and hence, $M = 0.659$. From (42), the average frequency is $f_o = 29.4 f_1$. Fig.20 compares the spectrum $E_a(f)$ computed from (44) to that computed from the harmonic analysis of time-domain simulation of the inverter using Simulink. The figure shows a good agreement between the two spectra in terms of frequency order and magnitude. The center band is located at $f_o = 29.4 \cdot f_1$ and the side bands are stepped by $2f_1$ as shown in Fig.20. The spectral energy of $E_a(f)$ is distributed over the frequency range $27.4f_1$ to $31.4f_1$ (i.e. $BW = 4 \cdot f_1$).

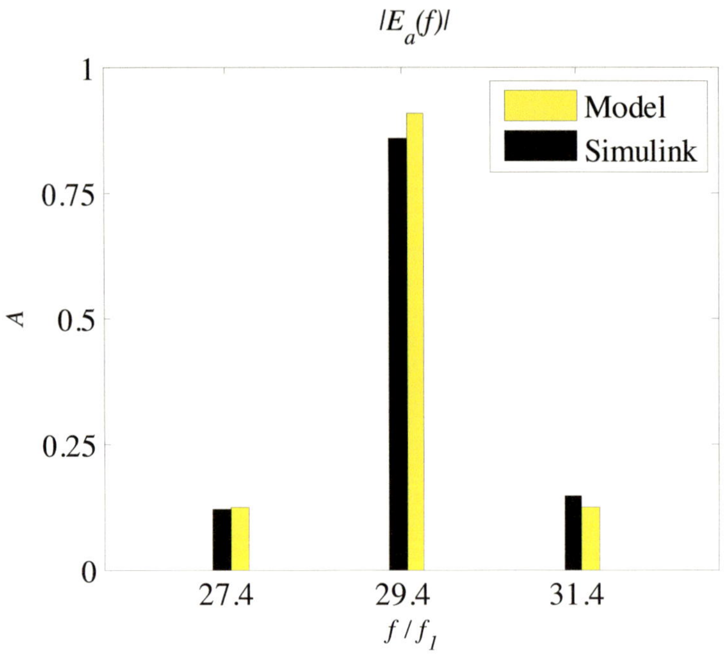

Fig. 20. Comparing model results to Simulink.

The dc voltage V_c was decreased to $350V$ while all other parameters remain unchanged from Study 1. Decreasing V_c will decrease f_o according to (42).
The new values are shown in Fig.21. Consequently, the spectrum $E_a(f)$ will shift to the lower frequency order of, approximately, 25.7, while spanning over the constant bandwidth of $4f_1$. The spectral magnitudes of $E_a(f)$ depend on the relay bandwidth ε_o and M; therefore, with fixing ε_o and decreasing V_c, according to (44), the center band magnitude decreases as M is increasing. While the magnitudes of the side bands are directly proportional to M, their magnitudes will increase. This is clear from comparing the harmonic in Fig.21 to that of Fig.20. Similar to the fixed-band control, the Total Harmonic Distortion (THD) of the line current is independent of V_c.

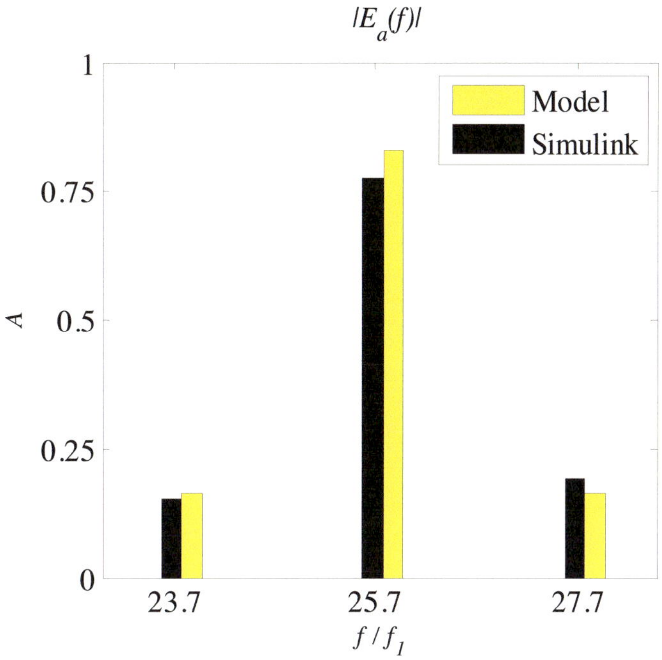

Fig. 21. Error spectra when $V_c = 350\,V$.

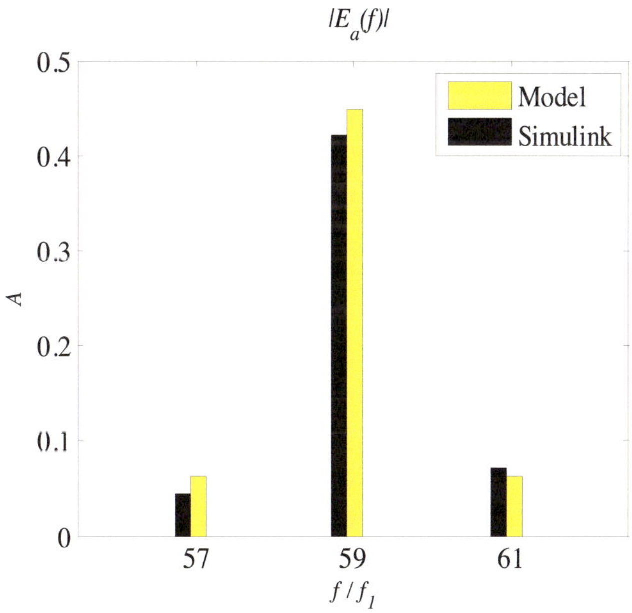

Fig. 22. Error spectra when relay bandwidth is halved.

when ε_o is halved, the carrier frequency f_o doubles and the harmonic spectrum $E_a(f)$ will be concentrated around, approximately, the order of 59. The THD of the line current will

decrease to as low as 5% since ε_o decreases. This is demonstrated when comparing the harmonic spectra of Fig.22 and Fig.20.
The value of the inductance is decreased to $L = 15\,mH$. The results are shown in Fig.23.

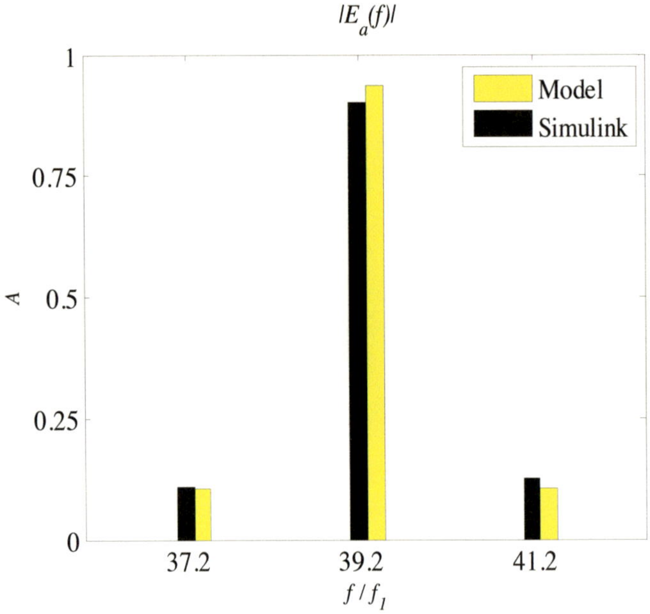

Fig. 23. Inverter harmonic response to 25% reduction in *L*.

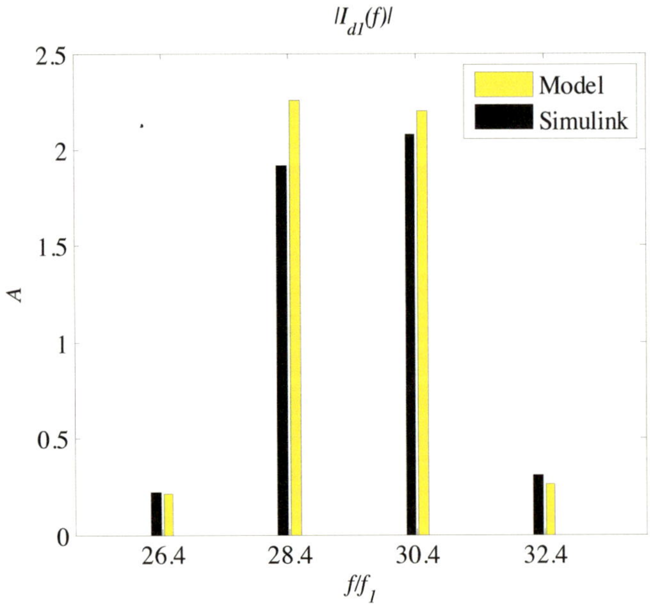

Fig. 24. DC current harmonics under variable-band control.

Lower inductance results in higher switching frequency. The harmonic spectrum $E_a(f)$ shifts to higher frequencies as f_o is increasing to $39.2f_1$. As M is directly proportional to the system inductance, M decreases and therefore, the magnitude of the center band slightly increases while the side bands decrease in magnitude as shown in Fig.23. The dc current harmonics are computed from substituting (44) in (28). The resulting spectra are shown in Fig.24 with good agreement in terms of frequency orders and magnitudes.

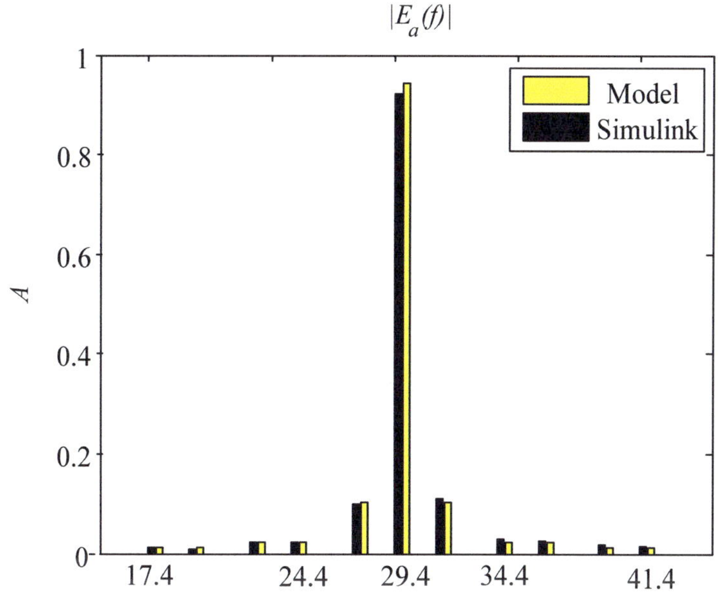

Fig. 25. Error current under distorted dc and ac system voltages.

The harmonic performance of the inverter under distorted system voltages is studied by simulating the system with the distorted 8th order dc voltage $v_8(t) = 28.2 \cdot \sin(8\omega_1 t)\ V$ and the 11th order ac voltage $v_{11}(t) = 15 \cdot \sin(11 \cdot \omega_1 t)\ V$. Results obtained from model using (48) and (49) are compared to those computed from Simulink in Fig.25, the model predicts the frequency distribution of the dc current harmonics and accurately predicts their magnitudes.

4.3 Comparison and discussion

The spectral characteristics of the line current under the fixed- and variable-band hysteresis control are compared in this section. For identical system configurations and controller settings, i.e. $\varepsilon = \varepsilon_o$, the analytical relation between f_c and f_o is stated in terms of the amplitude modulation index M as: $f_c = \left(1 - 0.5M^2\right) \cdot f_o$. The inverter operates at higher switching frequency when it employs the variable-band hysteresis control. In addition, from a harmonic perspective, the frequency bandwidth of $E_a(f)$ in the variable-band control mode is constant ($4f_1$) and independent of the system and controller parameters; unlike the fixed-band controller where the bandwidth BW depends implicitly on the system and controller parameters through the frequency modulation index β.

The THD of the line current is directly proportional to relay bandwidth. For similar controllers setting $\varepsilon = \varepsilon_0$, the THD is constant as the average spectral energy of the line current is constant. In fixed- and variable-band modes, the variation of system parameters shifts the spectral energy of $E_a(f)$ to higher or lower frequency orders (depending on the carrier frequency), while simultaneously redistributing the spectral energy over the frequency bandwidth BW. The spectral energy of the error current is independent of system parameters; and hence, the THD of the line current is constant for different system settings.

5. Conclusion

A closed-form numerically efficient approximation for the error current harmonic spectrum of single-phase two-level inverters employing either fixed- or variable-band hysteresis current control is derived. The models are based on the amplitude and frequency modulation theorems.

The instantaneous frequency of the inverter is first derived. Then it is used to closely approximate the error current by a modulated sinusoid. The error current harmonic spectrum is basically the Fourier transform of error current complex envelop. In the case of the fixed-band control, the spectrum reduces to a series of Bessel functions of the first kind whose argument is implicitly expressed in terms of the system and controller parameters, where as in the variable-band mode, the spectrum reduces to a 3-element array.

The spectral characteristics such as the carrier frequency and frequency bandwidth are derived analytically and related to line parameters; it is a development useful in inverter-network harmonic interactions. Unlike time-domain simulators, the developed models provide fast numerical solution of the harmonic spectrum as they only involve numerical computation of single arrays. Simulation results agree closely with the developed frequency-domain models in terms of frequency order, magnitude and angle.

In addition to the single-phase two-level inverter, the proposed approximations apply also to the harmonic output of certain three-phase two-level inverters where independent phase control is applicable, such as the neutral point inverter, and the full-bridge inverter in bipolar operation.

6. Future directions of research

The models detailed in this chapter can be extended in a number of ways, both in terms of improving the proposed models as well as in the application of the models in other PWM applications.

The developed models neglected the dynamics of the Phase-Locked Loop (PLL) and assumed that the inverter line current tracks a pure sinusoidal reference current. Possible extensions of the models include the effect of the harmonic current propagation through the ac network and the deterioration of the terminal voltage at the interface level and its effect on the reference current generation. As the PLL synchronizes the reference current with the terminal voltage, the propagation of harmonic currents might affect the detection of the zeros-crossings of the terminal voltage resulting in generating a distorted reference current. The hysteresis controller consequently will force the line current to track a non-sinusoidal reference which, in turn, modifies the harmonic output of the inverter.

The implementation of an LC filter at the inverter ac terminals could trigger a parallel-resonance which tends to amplify the harmonic voltages and currents in the ac network

leading, in some cases, to potential harmonic instabilities. The improvement of the developed models to include the effect the filter capacitance on the harmonic performance of the inverter is an interesting improvement.
Reviews of the developed models show that hysteresis current controlled inverters can have a 'switching function' notation similar to those inherit with the Sinusoidal PWM inverters. The switching function is based on the error current characteristics which implicitly depend on the system and controller parameters. Such development will enable the various time- and frequency-domain algorithms developed for the harmonic assessment of linear PWM inverters to be applied to hysteresis controlled inverters.
Harmonic load flow studies of systems incorporating inverters with hysteresis current control can be formulated based on the developed models. The iterative solution of the harmonic load flow shall incorporate the harmonic magnitudes and angles obtained from the developed models for a faster convergence to the steady state solution.

7. Appendix - A

Function $f(x)=\dfrac{\sin(\pi x)}{x(1-x)}$, $x\in[0,\,1]$ satisfies $\lim\limits_{x\to 0} f(x)=\lim\limits_{x\to 1} f(x)=\pi$, is continuous, convex and has even symmetry in $[0,\,1]$. The approximation of $f(x)$ in $[0,\,1]$, $\bar{f}(x)=A\cdot\sin(\pi x)+\pi$,

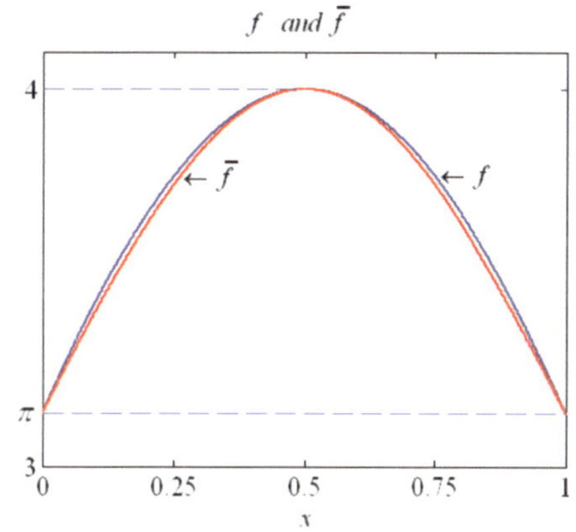

Fig. A1. Approximation of $f(x)=\dfrac{\sin(\pi x)}{x(1-x)}$ by $\bar{f}(x)=(4-\pi)\cdot\sin(\pi x)+\pi$.

satisfies the same properties in $[0,\,1]$. Subsequently, constant A is calculated such that the square error over the interval $[0,\,1]$ $\Delta f^2=\int_0^1\left(f(x)-\bar{f}(x)\right)^2 dx$ is minimized. Substituting the expressions of $f(x)$ and $\bar{f}(x)$ into the mean-squared-error Δf^2 and evaluating the integrals numerically yields a function of the parameter A, as $\Delta f^2(A)=0.5A^2-0.858A+0.3833$. Therefore, the value of A that minimizes Δf^2 is $A=0.858$ or $A=4-\pi$. Functions $f(x)$ and $\bar{f}(x)$ are shown in Fig. A1.

8. References

Albanna, A. & Hatziadoniu, C. J. (2009). Harmonic Analysis of Hysteresis Controlled Grid-Connected Inverters, *proceedings of the Power Systems Conference and Exposition*, Seattle, WA, March, 2009.

Albanna, A. & Hatziadoniu, C. J. (2009). Harmonic Modeling of Single-Phase Three-Level Hysteresis Inverters, *proceedings of the North American Power Symposium*, Starkville, Mississippi, October, 2009

Albanna, A. & Hatziadoniu, C. J. (2009). Harmonic Modeling of Three-Phase Neutral-Point Inverters, *proceedings of the North American Power Symposium*, Starkville, Mississippi, October, 2009

Albanna, A. & Hatziadoniu, C. J. (2010). Harmonic Modeling and Analysis of Multiple Residential Photo-Voltaic Generators, *proceedings of the Power and Energy Conference at Illinois*, Urbana-Champaign, Illinois, February 2010

Albanna, A. & Hatziadoniu, C. J. (2010). Harmonic Modeling of Hysteresis Inverters in Frequency Domain", *IEEE Transactions on Power Electronics*, May 2010

6

84 Pulse Converter, Design and Simulations with Matlab

Antonio Valderrábano González[1],
Juan Manuel Ramirez[2] and Francisco Beltrán Carbajal[3]
[1]*Universidad Politécnica de la Zona Metropolitana de Guadalajara,*
[2]*Cinvestav, Unidad Guadalajara,*
[3]*Universidad Autónoma Metropolitana, Plantel Azcapotzalco, Departamento de Energía*
México

1. Introduction

Flexible Alternating Current Transmission System (FACTS) devices have been proposed for fast dynamic control of voltage, impedance, and phase angle in high-voltage AC lines. The application of this technology has opened new and better opportunities for an appropriate transmission and distribution control. The efforts performed all over the world to improve the power quality have originated several power conditioners, which by themselves contribute to power degradation due to switching of the semiconductor devices, and harmonic effects generated in the converters. Thus, big elements have been used as filters, pursuing to have appropriate power quality with low extra noise. Because of that, this technology has not been probed in stringent applications such as hospitals or airports, which are two of the environments to consider. The series and shunt power systems compensation are used with the purpose of improving the operating conditions; respect to the voltage, the compensation has the purpose of handling reactive power to maintain bus voltages close to their nominal values, reduce line currents, and reduce system losses. The voltage magnitude in some buses may be controlled through sophisticated and versatile devices such as the StatCom, which is the smaller and most cost effective FACTS device in many applications (Hingorani, 2007), and is a power reactive source (Acha et al., 2004; Song & Johns, 1999). By regulation of the StatCom's output voltage magnitude, the reactive power exchanged between the StatCom and the transmission system can be controlled (CIGRE, 1998; Davalos, 2003; El-Moursi & Sharaf, 2005; Hingorani & Gyugyi, 2000;Wang, 2000).

This Chapter describes how the assembling of a Voltage Source Converter (VSC) that meets the IEEE Std. 519-1992 (IEEE Recommended Practices and Requirements for Harmonic Control in Electrical Power Systems) is performed, and emphasizes its development through Matlab simulations. The low Total Harmonic Distortion (THD) that this VSC produces allows this power conditioner to be considered for its use on stringent applications or in the reactive power compensation and the power quality improvement. The reinjection principle used, makes this proposal to be considered as an affordable solution to the sinusoidal synthesization due to the reduced number of switches needed. The reinjection transformer is one of the most important elements in this configuration, and it can have a wide turn ratio's variation without leading out the special application standards.

The conventional PI controllers applied to maintain the output voltage of the StatCom around nominal conditions exhibit poor performance under severe disturbances, where the error signal jumps with big steps in magnitude. The strategy followed in this research, employs the error and error's variation to break down the control action into smaller sections that can be selected according to simple rules. Simulation results evidence the proposal's suitability validating each part of the device.

2. 84-pulses StatCom

The StatCom is a power electronic-based Synchronous Voltage Generator (SVG) able to provide fast and continuous capacitive and inductive reactive power supply. It generates a three-phase voltage, synchronized with the transmission voltage, from a DC energy source, and it is connected to the Electrical Power System (EPS) by a coupling transformer. The regulation on the magnitude of the StatCom's output voltage, gives rise to the reactive power exchange between the StatCom and the transmission system. The StatCom's basic structure illustrated on Fig. 1 consists of a step-down transformer, a three-phase voltage source converter (VSC), and a DC capacitor (CIGRE, 1998; Davalos, 2003; El-Moursi & Sharaf, 2005; Norouzi & Shard, 2003; Song & Johns, 1999).

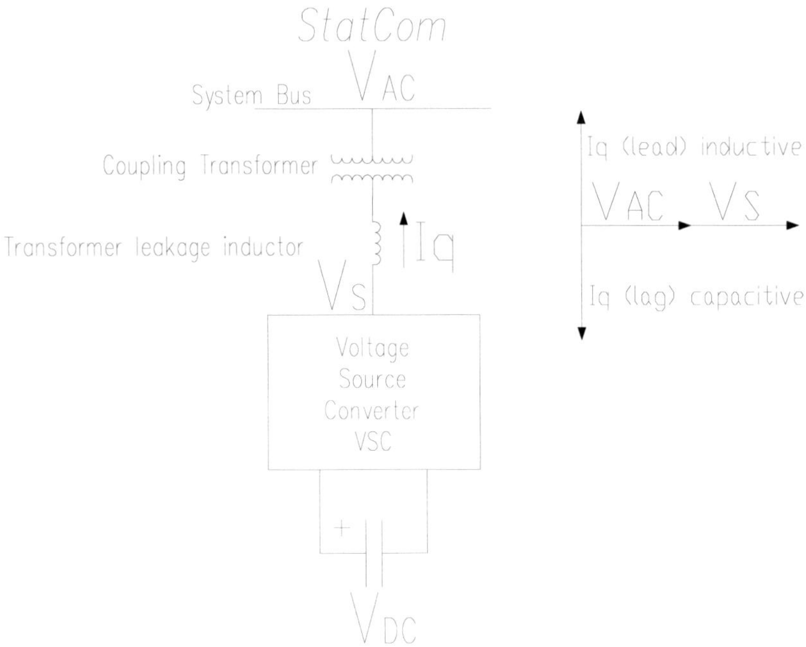

Fig. 1. StatCom's Basic Structure

This chapter is focused on the internal structure of the proposed VSC to get a low THD output voltage. Likewise, the main aspects to connect the StatCom to the grid are reviewed.

2.1 Reinjection configuration

There are three main strategies to build a Voltage Source Converter (VSC): (i) the multipulse; (ii) the multilevel; (iii) and the pulse width modulation (PWM) (Pan & Zhang,

2007; Liu et al., 2004). In the *multipulse* strategy, the period of the signal is broken down into equal sized parts in relation to the pulse number. The switches are triggered once per cycle at the fundamental frequency, and the amplitude on each pulse is controlled mainly by the output magnetic stage. The more pulses produces the less output Total Harmonic Distortion (THD). In the *multilevel* strategy, the DC source has to be broken down into parts of equal amplitude (x), given rise to a 2x-1 levels signal. Switches commute once per cycle at the fundamental frequency. The THD depends on the amount of DC sources or divisions available in the DC link. On the other hand, the PWM technique uses fast commutations to reach a low THD. The faster commutations are, the lower THD. However, it is limited due to the commutation speed of the switches and requires always an output filter coupled to the grid. This research deals with a combination of the first two strategies with emphasis on the use of multipulse configuration in order to reach the minimum total harmonic distortion.

There is a difference on the twelve-pulse converter used in this work, respect to the standard twelve-pulse converter. The DC source is not common to both six-pulse modules. In this proposition, a positive multipulse signal between the main terminals of the first six-pulse converter and another positive multipulse signal with opposite phase between the main terminals of the second six-pulse converter are connected. In order to have a neutral point, the negative of the first converter is connected to the positive of the second converter, as presented on Fig. 2.

Each branch in the six-pulse converters must generate electrical signals with 120° of displacement between them; the upper switch is conducting while the lower one is open and vice versa (180° voltage source operation) (Krause et al., 2002).

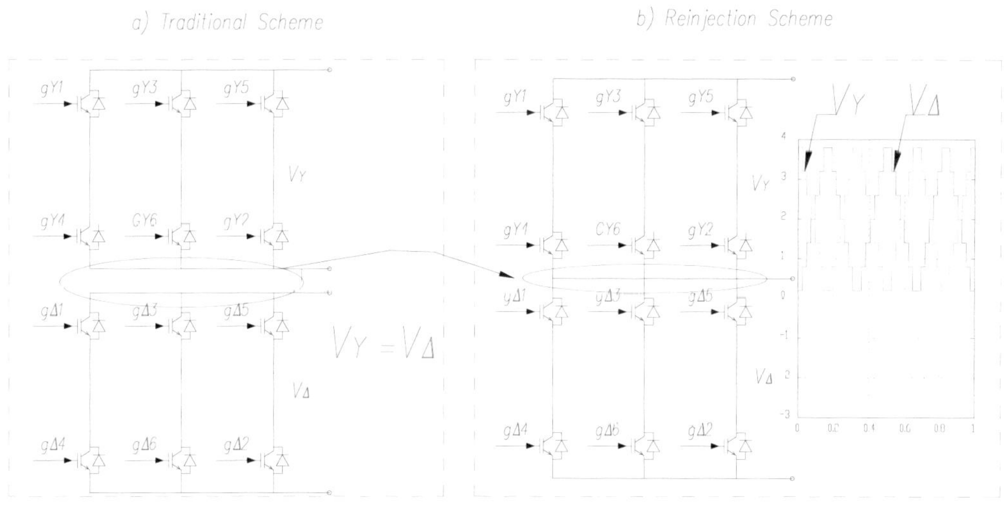

Fig. 2. (a) 12-pulse Traditional Scheme, (b) 12-pulse Reinjection Scheme fed by a 7 level converter.

A 30° displacement in the firing sequence of both converters must be considered. Transformer's turn ratios are 1:1 and 1: $\sqrt{3}$ on the YY and YΔ transformers, respectively. In order to operate the VSC in special applications such as airports or hospitals, on this chapter, an 84 level voltage signal is proposed, generated through a 7 level auxiliary circuit operating as a re-injection scheme. The auxiliary circuit is common to the three phases, reducing the number of extra components. The topology to provide the pulse multiplication is detailed in (Pan & Zhang, 2007; Liu et al., 2003, 2004a, 2004b; Han et al., 2005; Voraphonpiput & Chatratana, 2004), and illustrated in Fig. 3.

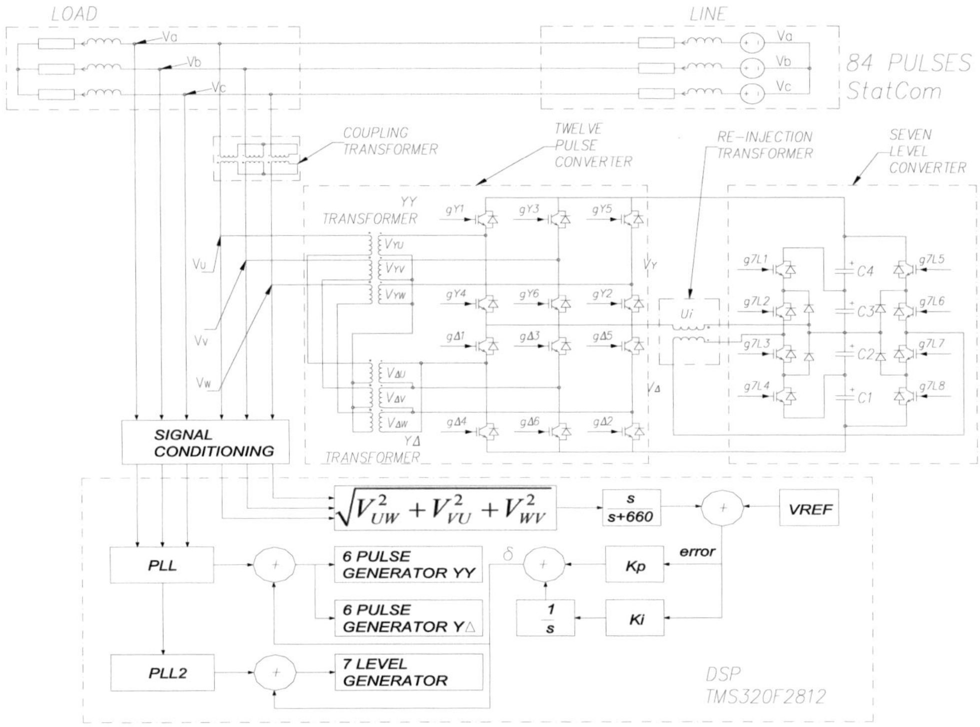

Fig. 3. 84-pulse StatCom structure

2.2 Total harmonic distortion

In order to apply the seven level inverter output voltage to feed the standard twelve-pulse converter, special care should be paid to not inject negative voltage into V_Y or V_Δ; notice the inclusion of the injection transformer between both arrays. Thus, input voltages in the six-pulse converter may be regulated by adjusting the injection voltage U_i by:

$$V_Y = V_{DC} + U_i \tag{1}$$

$$V_\Delta = V_{DC} - U_i \tag{2}$$

The injection voltage is determined by the seven level inverter switching pattern and the injection transformer turns ratio. When voltages V_Y and V_Δ are used as inputs to the six-pulse converters, a cleaner VSC output voltage comes about. Fig. 4 exhibits the strategy to generate V_{YU} and $V_{\Delta U}$ as the interaction of the seven level output and the corresponding six-pulse signals. These signals have been obtained from an electrical simulation developed in PLECS®, within Matlab /Simulink environment.

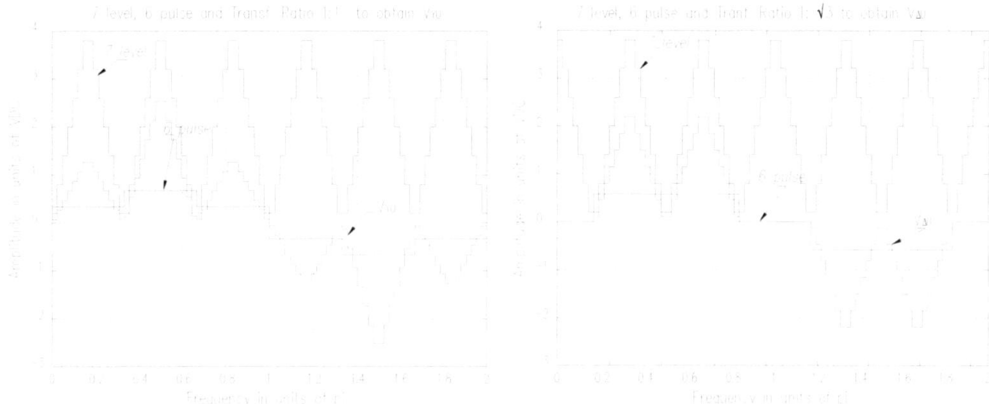

Fig. 4. Mixing seven level, six-pulse signals, and transformer ratios to attain V_{YU} and $V_{\Delta U}$.

Through the 1:1 ratio in the YY TRANSFORMER, and $1:\sqrt{3}$ for the $Y\Delta$ TRANSFORMER, adding their corresponding output signals, the 84-pulses line-to-neutral signal VU emerges, with the harmonic spectrum in Fig. 5 (linear scale) and in Fig. 6 (logarithmic scale).

Fig. 5. 84-pulses line-to-neutral output voltage and harmonic content (linear scale)

Fig. 6. 84-pulses line-to-neutral output voltage and harmonic content (logarithmic scale)

The StatCom's phase voltage VU is an odd symmetric signal, so that the Fourier's even terms become zero. Thus,

$$V_U(t) = \sum_{n=1}^{\infty} V_{U_{2n-1}} \sin\left((2n-1)\omega t\right) \tag{3}$$

$$V_{U_{2n-1}} = \frac{4V}{3\pi(2n-1)}\left(A_{2n-1} + aB_{2n-1}\right) \tag{4}$$

$$A_{2n-1} = 2 + 2\cos\left(\frac{1}{3}\pi(2n-1)\right) + 2\sqrt{3}\cos\left(\frac{1}{6}\pi(2n-1)\right) \tag{5}$$

$$B_{2n-1} = \sum_{i=0}^{20} Coeff_i \cos\left(\frac{i}{42}\pi(2n-1)\right) \tag{6}$$

$$Coeff = \left\{\begin{array}{ccccccc} -3, & 1, & 1, & 1, & 1, & 1, & 1,\ldots \\ -3\sqrt{3}, & \sqrt{3}-1, & \sqrt{3}-1, & \sqrt{3}-1, & \sqrt{3}-1, & \sqrt{3}-1, & \sqrt{3}-1,\ldots \\ -3, & -\sqrt{3}+2, & -\sqrt{3}+2, & -\sqrt{3}+2, & -\sqrt{3}+2, & -\sqrt{3}+2, & -\sqrt{3}+2 \end{array}\right\} \tag{7}$$

being a the re-injection transformer's turns ratio.

The 84-pulse signal value (VU) depends on the injection transformer turns ratio a, which is determined in order to minimize the THD, defined by (Pan et al., 2007, IEEE Std. 519-1992)

$$THD_{VU} = \sqrt{\frac{\sum_{n=2}^{\infty} V_{Un}^2}{V_{U1}^2}} \tag{8}$$

The minimization of THD yields the parameter a. In this research such calculation has been carried out in Matlab with n = 7200, and increments Δa = 0.0001. With these parameters, the minimum THD becomes 2.358% with $a = 0.5609$, value employed on the previous figures.

The distortion limits according to the IEEE Std. 519 indicate that the allowed THD in voltage is 10% in dedicated systems, 5% in general systems, and 3% for special applications as hospitals and airports .

Table 1 presents the minimum THD in the output voltage produced with several multipulse configurations. The THD produced through this proposition allows its use even in applications with stringent quality requirements; it exhibits less dependence to variations on the transformer's turns ratio a, which can have variations until ±12.5% to get a maximum THD lower than 3%. This means that a strict reinjection transformer's turn ratio is not needed to get a THD within a stringent condition. Fig. 7. illustrates the dependence of the THD with respect to variations in the re-injection transformer's turn ratio a. All these values had been obtained using Matlab.

2.3 StatCom's arrangement

Connecting the improved VSC to the system for reactive compensation requires several points to be taken into account. This section deals with such details using Fig. 3 as the main scheme, including a coupling transformer 13.8 kV : 13.8 kV, and considering the transmission line parameters presented on Table 2, at 75°C.

Number of pulses	THD (%)
12	15.22
24	7.38
48	3.8
60	3.159
84	2.358

Table 1. Minimum THD produced through the multipulse VSC

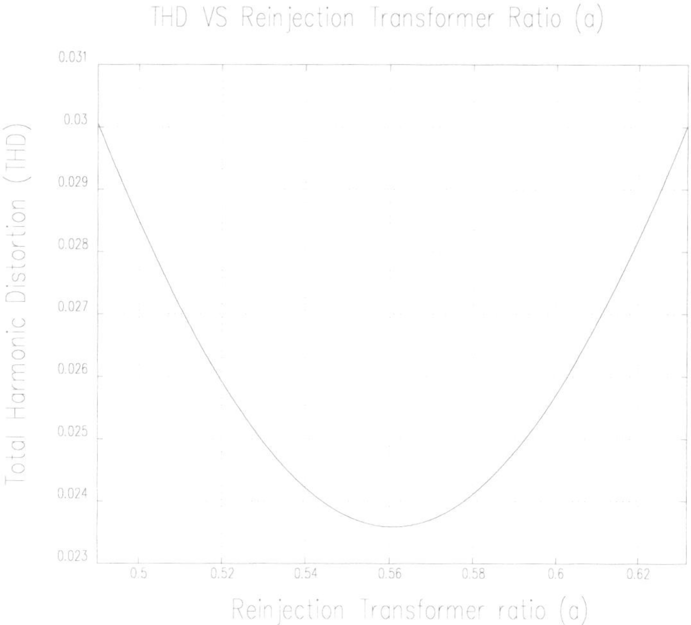

Fig. 7. Dependence of the THD with respect to the reinjection transformer's turn ratio

Parameter	Value
Conductor code name	Grosbeak Aluminum Conductor Composite Core (ACCC)
Voltage rating (peak)	13.8kV
Resistance	0.0839 Ω/ km
Inductive Reactance	0.2574 Ω / km
Line length	50km
Load Resistance	202.5 Ω
Load Inductive Reactance	0.6H

Table 2. Transmission Line parameters used.

If we pursue to eliminate the active power exchange between the StatCom and the system, taking into consideration the reactive power compensation, the DC voltage sources are replaced by capacitors.
Secondly, it must be ensured that the StatCom's frequency and phase angle are equal to the system ones; these parameters will be obtained by using a novel synchronizing arrangement able to detect instantaneously the phase angle. The seven level inverter must switch at six times the frequency of the six-pulse converters to ensure phase and frequency.
The digital signal processor (DSP)-control implementation must take the voltage levels needed for the ADC (analog/digital converter) to detect the signals with appropriate precision, and must refresh the output data before to take new samples in order to be considered real time. It is also needed to provide isolation from the power stage.

2.3.1 Synchronization of signals

The Phase-Locked-Loop (PLL) is the synchronizing circuit responsible for the determination of the system's frequency and phase-angle of the fundamental positive sequence voltage of the controlled AC bus(Aredes, & Santos Jr., 2000). The PLL utilizes the Stationary Reference Frame in order to reduce computational costs, and helps to improve the system's dynamic performance (Cho & Song, 2001). Digital PLL is an algorithm able to detect the fundamental component of the phase-voltages, synchronizing the output signal to the frequency and phase of the input one. This algorithm does not require a zero crossing detection routine for the input voltage or the generation of internal reference signals for the input current (Mussa & Mohr, 2004). The PLL strategy used employs a correction value determined by the signs of α and β, which is added to a $-\tan^{-1}\left(\frac{\alpha}{\beta}\right)$ function, Fig. 8.

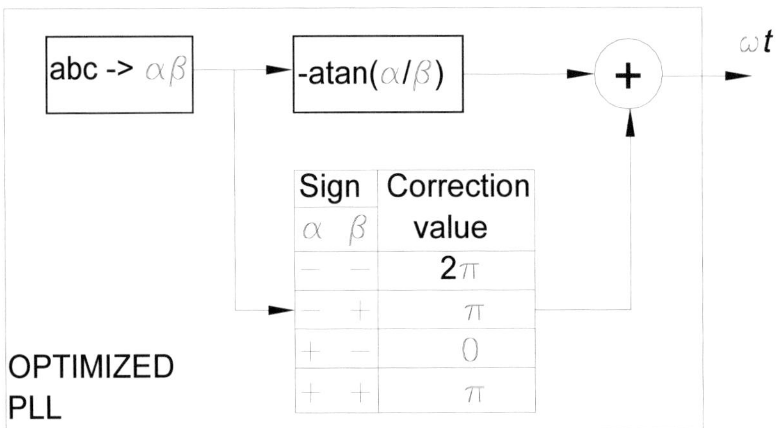

Fig. 8. PLL Strategy

This block synchronizes the PLL's zero output with respect to the startup of the α signal, when the β signal presents its minimum value, Fig. 9.

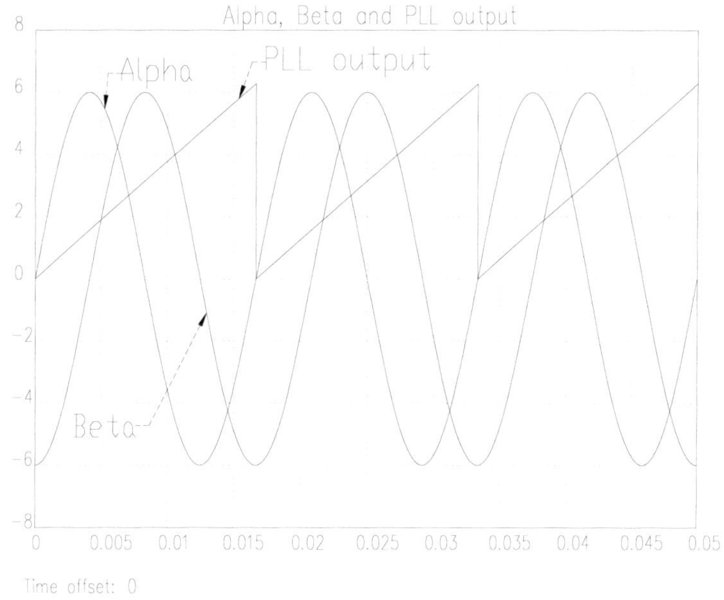

Fig. 9. $\alpha, \beta,$ and PLL-output

2.3.2 Firing sequence

The second block is the six-pulse generator, which is responsible to generate the pulse sequence to fire the three-phase IGBT array. It consists of an array of six-pulse spaced 60° each other. In this block, the IGBT will operate at full 180° for the *on* period and 180° for the *off* period. Any disturbance in the frequency will be captured by the synchronizing block, preventing errors. The falling border in the synchronizing block output signal is added to a series of six 60° spaced signals that would be sent to the opto-coupler block gate, which will feed each six-pulse converter. The off sequence turns out in a similar way but waiting 180° to keep the same duration on and off in each IGBT, Fig. 10.

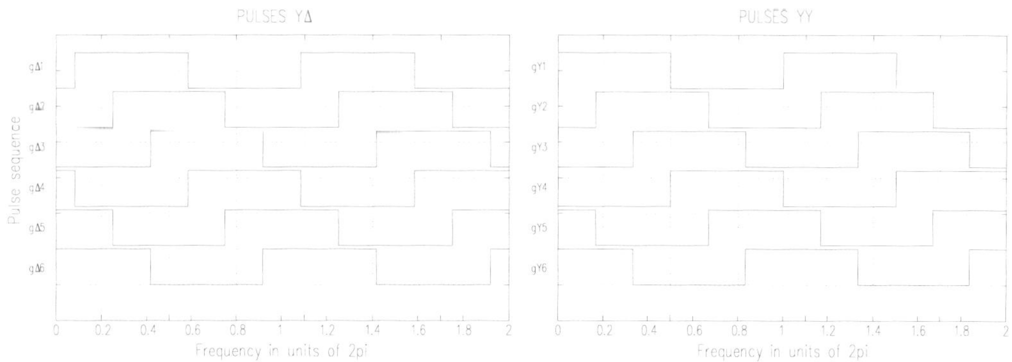

Fig. 10. Firing sequence for the six-pulses modules

2.3.3 Seven level generator

In order to produce the pulse sequence needed to generate the seven level inverter, six times the frequency of the six-pulse generator should be ensured beginning at the same time. This is achieved by monitoring the falling border in the novel PLL output signal, and using it along with the modulus operator with the $\pi/3$ argument. This signal will be the period for the seven level generator, which will modify its state each $\pi/42$ rad. Fig. 11 depicts the asymmetric pulse sequence for such seven level inverter, along with the seven level voltage for a complete sinusoidal cycle and a $\pi/3$ zoom-in, in order to observe the detailed pulse signals.

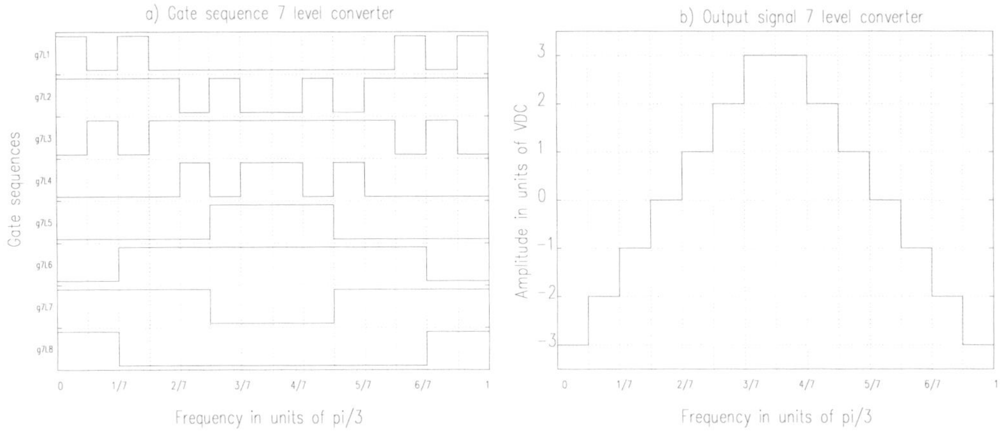

Fig. 11. Seven level gate signals

2.3.4 Angle's control circuit

The reactive power exchange between the AC system and the compensator is controlled by varying the fundamental component magnitude of the inverter voltage, above and below the AC system level. The compensator control is achieved by small variations in the semiconductor devices' switching angle, so that the fundamental component of the voltage generated by the inverter is forced to lag or lead the AC system voltage by a few degrees. This causes active power to flow into or out of the inverter, modifying the value of the DC capacitor voltage, and consequently the magnitude of the inverter terminal voltage, and the resultant reactive power (Davalos, 2003). The angle's control block diagram is described in (Cho & Song, 2001) for a PI controller, and depicted in Fig. 12. The inputs are the line-to-line voltages of the controlled AC bus prior to the coupling transformer. The reference voltage VREF is chosen as the RMS value for a pure sinusoidal three phase signal, which is $\sqrt{1.5}$ times the peak of the line voltage. This value is compared to the filtered RMS StatCom voltage output (VRMS) multiplied by the coupling transformer's turn ratio; it may contain an oscillating component. The output signal δ corresponds to the displacement angle of the generated multipulse voltage, with respect to the controlled AC bus voltage (primary voltage of the converter transformer). The low-pass-filter (LPF) is tuned to remove the characteristic harmonic content in the multipulse configuration; for the twelve-pulse it begins with the 11th harmonic. The PI controller has a limiting factor by dividing the error signal by the reference voltage VREF in order to have the δ signal with a maximum value of -1 when the StatCom output is equal to zero. In the following chapter special attention is paid to the fuzzy segmented PI controller.

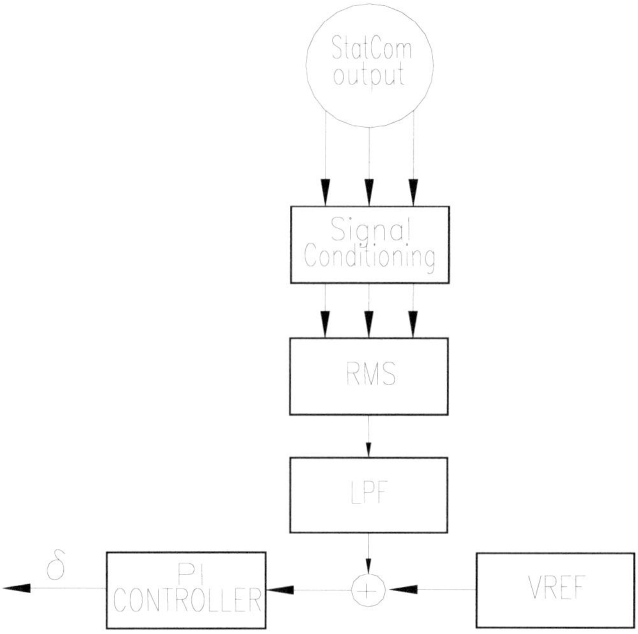

Fig. 12. StatCom's power angle control

3. Control strategy

Conventional PI or PID regulators have been applied to control the StatCom's output voltage around nominal conditions or subject to disturb like voltage unbalance (Hochgraf & Lasseter, 1998; Blazic & Papic, 2006; Li et al., 2007; Cavaliere et al., 2002). Such controllers may exhibit poor performance under other disturbances, where the error signal jumps with big steps in magnitude. In this research, it is desireable to find a controller that can deal with most of the problems detailed in (Seymour & Horsley, 2005). The strategy followed employs the error and error's variation to break down the control action in smaller sections that can be selected according to simple rules.

3.1 Segmented PI controller

The complete system presented on Fig. 2 was tested in Matlab under several disturbances using a PI controller tunned for steady state operation. Special attention was paid to measure the error and estimate the error's increment when the disturbances were applied. It was verified that a motor startup is a quite demanding situation to test the StatCom's performance, so it was used to define the membership function limits. For simplicity on the controller design, crisp membership functions were used to describe seven linguistic variables similarly to the fuzzy set notation as follows:

Linguistic Variable	Meaning
NB	negative big
NM	negative medium
NS	negative small
Z	Zero
PS	positive small
PM	positive medium
PB	positive big

Table 3. Linguistic variables used.

Fig. 13 a) displays the error signal, which varies from -1 to +1, and Fig. 13 b) displays the variation on the error signal. This variation was estimated using Matlab ode23t solver with variable step. The error *(e)* and its variation *(de)* are represented by lowercase as the independent variables; they are continuous values. The uppercase represents the fuzzy set obtained by selecting the indicated membership functions limits.

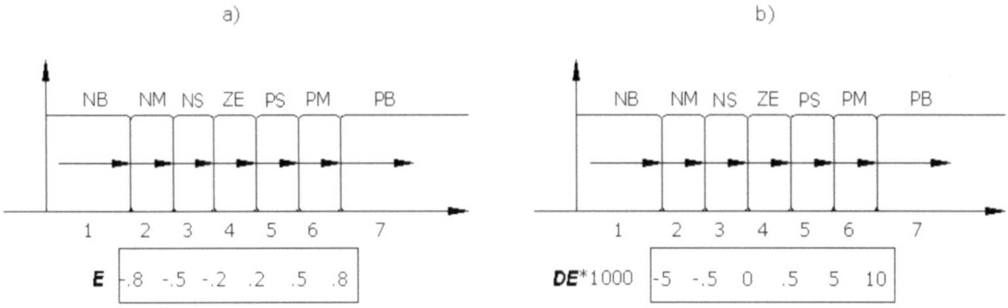

$$E = \begin{cases} NB & -\infty < e \leq -.8 \\ NM & -.8 < e \leq -.5 \\ NS & -.5 < e \leq -.2 \\ ZE & -.2 < e \leq .2 \\ PS & .2 < e \leq .5 \\ PM & .5 < e \leq .8 \\ PB & .8 < e \leq \infty \end{cases} \qquad DE*1000 = \begin{cases} NB & -\infty < de \leq -5 \\ NM & -5 < de \leq -.5 \\ NS & -.5 < de \leq 0 \\ ZE & 0 < de \leq .5 \\ PS & .5 < de \leq 5 \\ PM & 5 < de \leq 10 \\ PB & 10 < de \leq \infty \end{cases}$$

Fig. 13. Membership functions

Fuzzy control rules are usually obtained empirically. This chapter uses the rules presented in (Pal & Mudi, 2008) to define the zones of the segmented PI illustrated on Table 4.

E \ DE	NB	NM	NS	ZE	PS	PM	PB
NB	1	1	1	2	3	3	4
NM	1	2	2	2	3	4	5
NS	1	2	3	3	4	5	6
ZE	1	2	3	4	5	6	7
PS	2	3	4	5	5	6	7
PM	3	4	5	6	6	6	7
PB	4	5	6	7	7	7	7

Table 4. Control rules

The strategy to tune the segmented PI zones is summarized in the following steps.

1. Tune up a conventional PI at steady state. The proportional and integral gains obtained were: $K_P = 0.5411$, and $K_I = 20.3718$. Such values were used on the segmented PI controller as the starting point, preserving the same gain values in the seven zones. Thus, firstly the conventional PI and the segmented PI controllers are equivalent.
2. Taking into account that capacitors are used in the DC link in order to the system operates as StatCom, initially without charge, the maximum error is -1. It is convenient to adjust the gains' value zone 1 due to it corresponds to the biggest negative error and the biggest negative error's variation. To adjust the values of this zone, we must maintain K_P as low as possible to keep the system stable. Then, reduce K_I to the value that allows less oscillation in the segmented PI sections.
3. After this step, zone 1 would have the values for the biggest negative error and error's variation, and the other zones the original steady state values.
4. Starting up an induction motor when the capacitors are fully charged is considered one of the most demanding situations and is used for adjusting the remaining zones. To tune the gains of segment 2, use the value of K_P as low as possible to keep the system stable. Then, reduce K_I to the value that allows less oscillation in the zones presented on the right and low corner of Fig. 17.
5. Repeat step 3 for sections 3, 5, 6, and 7 in sequence. This will bring up to the segmented PI, Table 5. After tuning up the seven zones, the output will be between zones 3 and 4 on steady state.

It is important to note that using a different disturbance, the values would vary slightly, but this was the most demanding condition.

Fuzzy Rule	Kp	Ki
1	0.5252	5.0929
2	0.5411	38.9929
3	0.5570	40.7436
4	0.5729	40.7436
5	0.5570	20.3718
6	0.4933	20.3718
7	0.3183	40.7436

Table 5. Gain values of the segmented PI

3.2 Simulation results

The StatCom model and the segmented PI controller with the values obtained from the previous section were simulated in Matlab/Simulink, using Piece-wise Linear Electrical Circuit Simulation (PLECS). PLECS was used because it is a fast simulation toolbox for electrical circuits within the Simulink environment specially designed for power electronics systems. It is also a powerful tool for any combined simulation of electrical circuits and controls (http://www.plexim.com, 2010) . The PLL-block feeds the two six-pulse generators at the fundamental frequency and it is used to bring forth the seven level pulses at six times the fundamental frequency to have them synchronized to the system and configured as the 84-pulse StatCom. The δ signal calculated from the segmented PI controller is utilized to lag or lead the StatCom voltage with respect to the system. While the phase-angle lags the bus voltage ($\delta < 0$), energy is flowing to the DC capacitor, charging it and doing the StatCom draws capacitive current. Contrarily, inductive current is drawn while ($\delta > 0$) (Aredes & Santos Jr., 2000). The figures 14 to 16 illustrate the system behavior when short-duration root-mean-square (rms) problems (IEEE Std 1159, 2009) are presented.

A Sag or dip is a reduction of AC voltage at a given frequency lasting from 0.5 cycles to 30 cycles and magnitudes between 0.1 to 0.9 pu, it is usually caused by system faults, and is often the result of switching on loads with heavy startup currents (Seymour & Horsley, 2005; IEEE Std 1159, 2009). Fig. 14 exhibits the system behavior when a Sag of 6 cycles and 0.3 pu appears on the system. Using a conventional PI controlled StatCom the error has several oscillations as presented in Fig. 14a; Fig. 14b is the error when a segmented PI controlled StatCom is employed. The smoother and faster behavior of this new controller

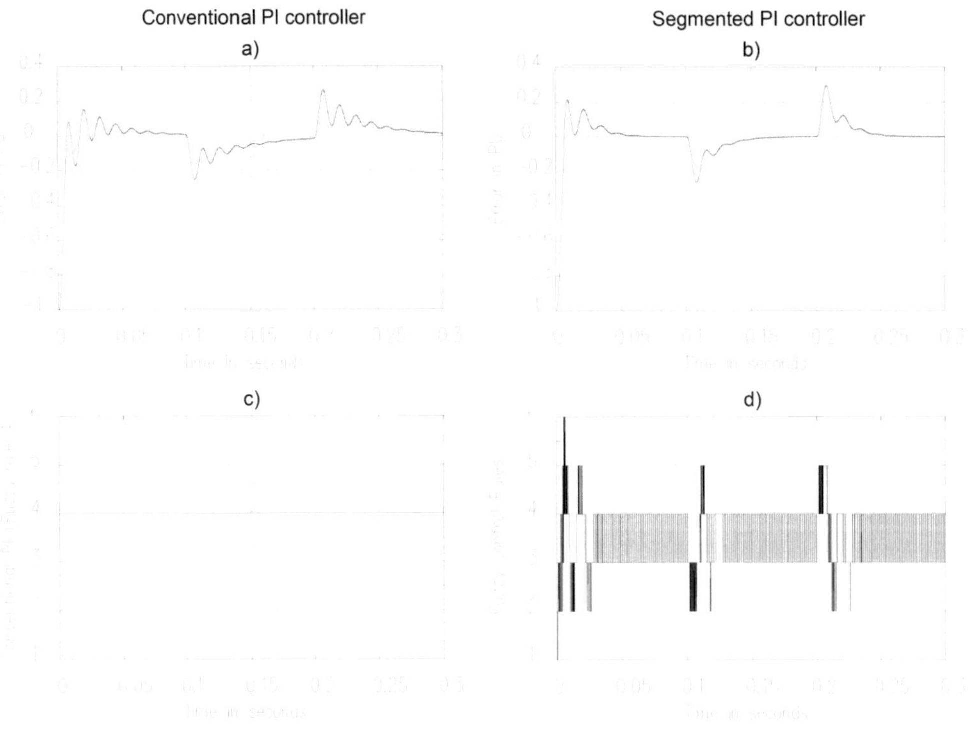

Fig. 14. Sag 0.3 PU

becomes visible. Figs. 14c-d are included to illustrate the rules corresponding to each error and error's increment. Rules 3 and 4 on Table 5 indicate that integral gains are the same for both regions, and proportional gains vary slightly, so, having the segmented PI controller switching among these two zones would bring the system to a good performance. The conventional PI controller used the original values and this is presented as rule number 4, which was the starting point for calculating the segmented PI gains.
Contrarily to a Sag, a Swell represents an increase in the AC voltage, lasting from 0.5 cycles to 30 cycles and magnitudes between 1.1 to 1.8 pu. Swells commonly arise due to high-impedance neutral connections, sudden (especially large) load reductions, and a single-phase fault on a three-phase system (Seymour & Horsley, 2005; IEEE Std 1159, 2009). Fig 15 illustrates the system under a swell of 6 cycles and 0.3 pu. It can be noticed that Fig 15a presents more oscillation than Fig. 15b. Also the steady state is reached faster using the segmented PI controlled StatCom. Again, Figs. 15c-d are included to illustrate the rules corresponding to each error and the error's increment, using original values in rule number 4 for the conventional PI controller, and switching between rules 3 and 4 for the segmented PI controller, which is the behavior needed.

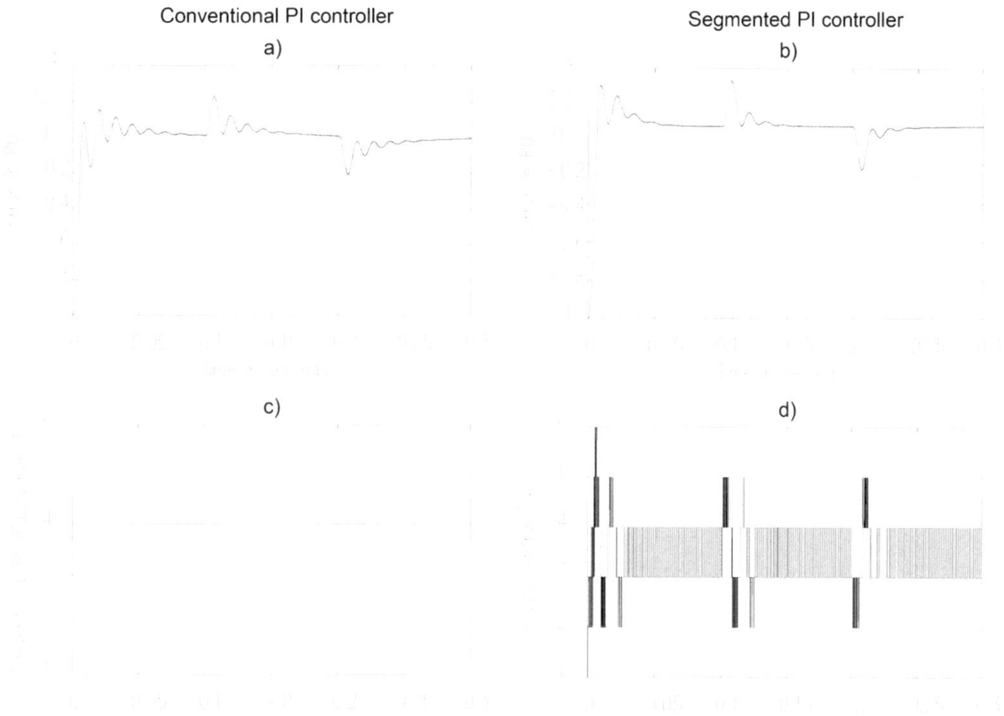

Fig. 15. Swell 0.3 PU

An interruption is one of the most demanding problems presented at the source nodes, and occurs when the supply voltage or load current decreases to less than 0.1 pu for a period of time not exceeding 1 min. Interruptions can be the result of power system faults, equipment or control failures. An interruption, whether it is instantaneous, momentary, temporary, or sustained, can cause disruption, damage, and downtime, from the home user up to the industrial user, and it can cause equipment damage, ruination of product, as well as the cost associated with downtime, cleanup, and restart (Seymour & Horsley, 2005; IEEE Std 1159, 2009). Fig 16 illustrates the controllers' error behavior after a 3 cycles three-phase fault at the load bus. The error is defined as the difference between the measured voltage and the reference voltage; the greatest error becomes -1 while the fault is on, but, once this one is released, the error is bigger than 1 pu with a conventional PI, Fig. 16a. In contrast, the segmented PI presents an error around 0.4 pu, Fig. 16b. Notice the oscillations in the conventional PI response of Fig 16a last about .1 sec. which correspond to 6 complete cycles to reach steady-state values, while these oscillations are smoothed with the use of the segmented controller, having stable values in about .05 sec. Figs. 16c-d are included to illustrate rule number 4 for the conventional PI controller, and the rules of the segmented PI, respectively. Once again, switching between rules 3 and 4 are found on the steady-state conditions for this kind of failure as expected.

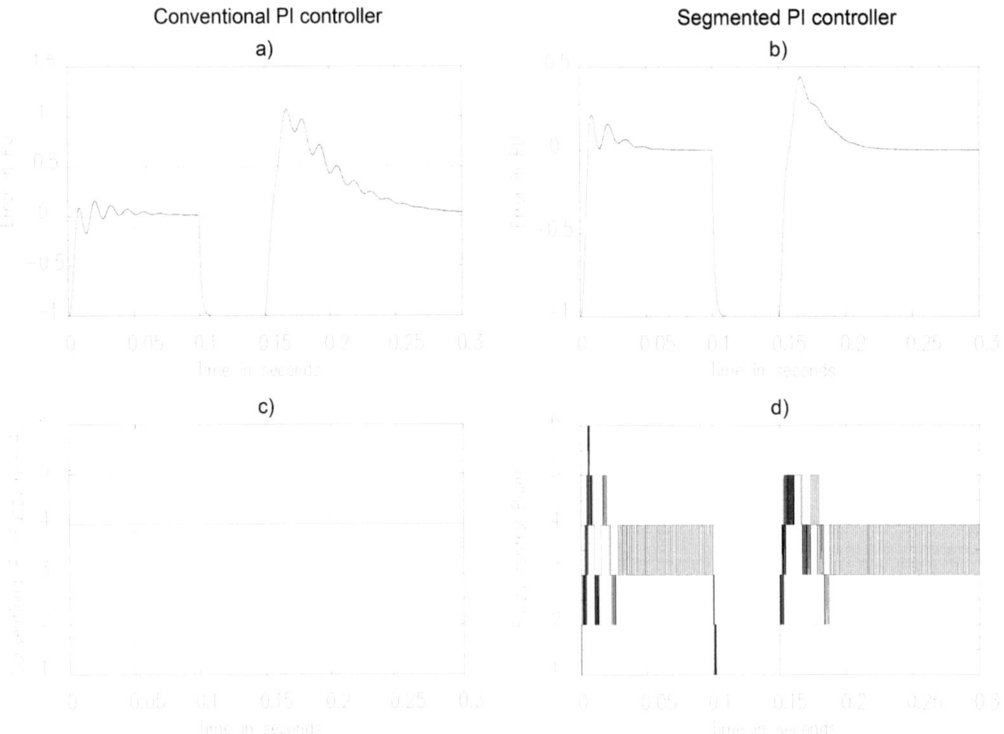

Fig. 16. Three-Phase Failure

Oscillatory transients and voltage fluctuation commonly arise when a motor is connected. At this point, a sudden change in the steady-state condition of a signal's voltage, current, or both is performed and a series of random changes in magnitude and frequency is presented. pthe error when a motor load is started.
The parameters of the induction motor are the ones of table 6:

Motor parameter	Value
Nominal Power	2250HP (2300V)
Rs	0.029 Ohms
Lls	0.0006 Henries
Rr	.022 Ohms
Llr	0.0006 Henries
Lm	0.0346 Henries
J	6.5107 Joules

Table 6. Motor parameters used on motor startup simulation

The error for the conventional PI has several big oscillations, Fig. 17a, while the segmented one exhibits very fast response to reach the steady state, and minimum oscillation, Fig. 17b. Figs. 17 c-d are also included to illustrate the rule number 4 (conventional PI controller), and the rules of the segmented PI, respectively.

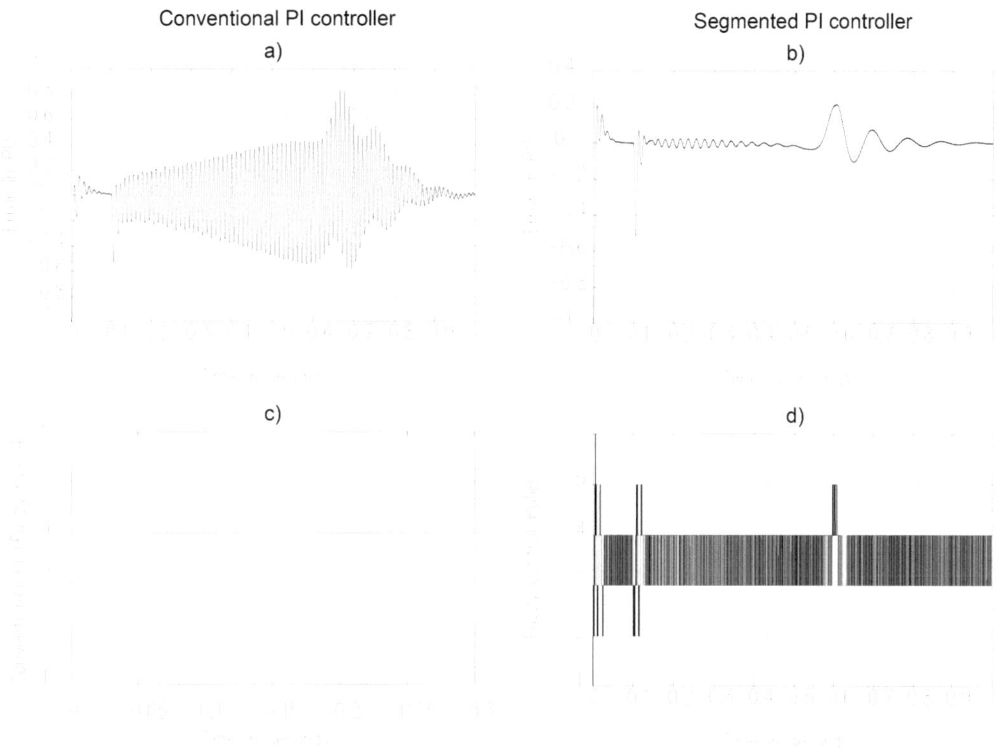

Fig. 17. Motor Start up

With these simulations it is demonstrated that when the system is stressed, the segmented PI controller exhibits a quite appropriate response.

4. Conclusion

This chapter presents a study about one of the most used VSC-based FACTS devices: the StatCom.

A novel strategy to generate higher pulse number by combining one twelve-pulse converter with a seven level converter, in order to attain the overall 84-pulses VSC performance with the corresponding high quality voltage wave, has been presented. The associated seven level converter is built through the combination of two three level topologies with asymmetric gate pattern inverters. The explanation of the control stages is described.

Through simulations, the suitability of the proposal is demonstrated. The reinjection principle, mainly applicable with Total Harmonic Distortion reduction purposes, has been demonstrated utilizing the harmonics' calculation. With this low THD, the inverter is able to be used in special applications. The proposition allows savings in the total amount of employed switches along with a small quantity of capacitors to prevent problems of unbalancing.

The segmented PI controller introduced, gives a fast and appropriate response when used for connecting the StatCom to the system on common but stressful situations. Two of the most common failures on the system have been addressed (Sag and Swell) having performance similar to conventional PI controllers. Three phase failure releases are some of the biggest problems to solve due to high peaks received on the loads; this problem is significantly reduced with the use of segmented PI controller. Induction motor startup is one of the most demanding situations for the power system, and the use of a segmented PI controller had demonstrated a very fast response to bring the motor to steady-state condition.

5. References

ABB Power Systems AB, "ABB STATCOM For flexibility in power systems", Västerås, A02-0165E

Acha, E., Fuerte-Esquivel, C. R., Ambriz, H., Angeles, C.: *FACTS. Modelling and Simulation in Power Networks*. (John Wiley and Sons, LTD, 2004.)

Aredes, M., Santos Jr., G.: "A Robust Control for Multipulse StatComs," Proceedings of IPEC 2000, Vol. 4, pp. 2163 - 2168, Tokyo, 2000.

Blazic, B.; Papic, I.; "Improved D-StatCom control for operation with unbalanced currents and voltages", IEEE Transactions on Power Delivery, Volume: 21 , Issue: 1 2006 , pp 225 - 233

Cavaliere, C.A.C.; Watanabe, E.H.; Aredes, M.; "Multi-pulse STATCOM operation under unbalanced voltages ",IEEE Power Engineering Society Winter Meeting, 2002. Volume: 1, 2002 , pp 567 - 572

CIGRE, "Static Synchronous Compensator", working group 14.19, September 1998.

Davalos-Marin, R.: 'Detailed Analysis of a multi-pulse StatCom', Cinvestav - Internal Report. May 2003, http://www.dispositivosfacts.com.mx/dir_tesis_doc.html

El-Moursi, M. S.; Sharaf, A. M. "Novel Controllers for the 48-Pulse VSC StatCom and SSSC for Voltage Regulation and Reactive Power Compensation", IEEE Transactions on Power Systems, Vol. 20, No. 4, November 2005, pp. 1985-1997

Han, B., Choo, W., Choi, J., Park, Y., Cho, Y.: "New Configuration of 36-Pulse Voltage source Converter Using Pulse-Interleaving Circuit", Proceedings of the Eight International Conference on Electrical Machines and Systems 2005, September 27-29, 2005

Hingorani, N.G.; , "FACTS Technology - State of the Art, Current Challenges and the Future Prospects," Power Engineering Society General Meeting, 2007. IEEE , vol., no., pp.1-4, 24-28 June 2007

Hingorani, N. G., and Gyugyi, L.: 'Understanding FACTS,' (IEEE Press 2000).

Hochgraf, C.; Lasseter, R.H.: "Statcom controls for operation with unbalanced voltages", IEEE Transactions on Power Delivery, Volume: 13 , Issue: 2, 1998 , pp 538 - 544

IEEE Std 519-1992: IEEE Recommended Practices and Requirements for Harmonic Control in Electrical Power Systems, 1992.

Jin-Ho Cho, Eui-Ho Song, "Stationary Reference Frame-Based Simple Active Power Filter with Voltage Regulation", Industrial Electronics, 2001. Proceedings. ISIE 2001. IEEE International Symposium on, Vol. 3, June 2001, pp. 2044-2048

Krause, P. C., Wasynczuk, O., and Sud, S. D.: 'Analysis of Electric Machinery an Drive Systems, Second Edition,' (IEEE Series on Power Engineering, pp. 487, 2002)

Kuang Li; Jinjun Liu; Zhaoan Wang; Biao Wei; "Strategies and Operating Point Optimization of STATCOM Control for Voltage Unbalance Mitigation in Three-Phase Three-Wire Systems ", IEEE Transactions on Power Delivery, Volume: 22 , Issue: 1, 2007 , pp 413 - 422

Liu, Y. H., Arrillaga, J., Watson, N. R.: "A New STATCOM Configuration Using Multi-Level DC Voltage Reinjection for High Power Application", IEEE Transactions on Power Delivery, Vol. 19, No. 4, October 2004, pp. 1828-1834.

Liu, Y. H.; Perera, L. B.; Arrillaga J. and Watson, N. R. "Harmonic Reduction in the Double Bridge Parallel Converter by Multi-Level DC-Voltage Reinjection", 2004 Intenational Conference on Power System Technology POWERCON 2004, 21-24 November 2004

Liu, Y. H.; Watson, N. R.; Arrillaga, J. "A New Concept for the Control of the Harmonic Content of Voltage Source Converters", The Fifth International Conference on Power Electronics and Drive Systems, 2003, 17-20 Nov. 2003, pp. 793- 798 Vol.1

Norouzi, Amir H.; Shard, A.M. "A Novel Control Scheme for the STATCOM Stability Enhancement", 2003 IEEE PES Transmission and Distribution Conference and Exposition, Sept. 2003

Pal, A. K., Mudi, R. K." Self-Tuning Fuzzy PI Controller and its Application to HVAC Systems", International Journal of Computational Cognition, vol.6, no.1, March 2008, pages 25-30.

Pan, W., Xu, Z., Zhang, J.: "Novel configuration of 60-pulse voltage source converter for StatCom application," International Journal of Emerging Electric Power Systems, Vol 8, Issue 5, 2007, Article 7.

Piece-wise Linear Electrical Circuit Simulation, User Manual Version 3.0, http://www.plexim.com, accessed on February 2010

Samir Ahmad Mussa, Hari Bruno Mohr, "Three-phase Digital PLL for Synchronizing on Three-Phase/Switch/Level Boost Rectifier by DSP", 35th Annual IEEE Power Electronics Specialists Conference Aachen, Germany, 2004, pp. 3659-366

Seymour, Joseph; Horsley,Terry; "The Seven Types of Power Problems", White paper # 18, APC Legendary Reliability, 2005 American Power Conversion

Song, Yong Hua; Johns, Allan T. "Flexible AC transmission systems FACTS", IEE Power and Energy Series 30, 1999.

Voraphonpiput, N.; Chatratana, S. "Analysis of Quasi 24-Pulse StatCom Operation and Control Using ATP-EMTP", TENCON 2004. 2004 IEEE Region 10 Conference, Nov. 2004 Vol. 3, pp. 359- 362

Wang, H. F.: *Applications of damping torque analysis to StatCom control,* Electrical Power and Energy Systems, Vol. 22, 2000, pp. 197-204.

7

Available Transfer Capability Calculation

Mojgan Hojabri and Hashim Hizam
Universiti Putra Malaysia
Malaysia

1. Introduction

The maximum power that can be transferred from one area to another area is called transfer capability. In 1996, North American Electric Reliability Council (NERC) established a framework for Available Transfer Capability (ATC) definition and evaluation. According to the NERC definition, ATC is the transfer capability remaining between two points above and beyond already committed uses (NERC, 1996). The ATC value between two points is given as:

$$ATC = TTC - TRM - CBM - ETC \tag{1.1}$$

Where TTC is total transfer capability, TRM is transmission reliability margin, CBM is capacity benefit margin and ETC is existing transmission commitment including customer services between the same two points. In power marketing, the interconnected power system may comprise many areas corresponding to utilities. The operation of the system is reported to an Independent System Operator (ISO). The ISO may receive all demands of energy. All of energy demands may be accepted if they are less than ATC between two areas. ATC must also be calculated by ISO in real time for all the areas under its territory. Evaluating the risk of violation of the transfer capability, because of the random events such as random failures of power system equipments, is an important point that must be considered to compute the probability that transfer capability will not exceed the required value.

In 1992 the Federal Energy Regulatory Commission (FERC), after gathering the industrial comments, published a series of issues an electrical marketing. The orders No. 888 (NERC, 1996) and No 889 (FERC, 1996) are two famous issues of FERC which were presented in 1996. These orders provided key guidelines to energy market players for better competition in the US power market. FERC order 888 mandated the separation of electrical services and marketing functions to determine the standard price of energy for a better customer choice. FERC order 889 mandated the information of Available Transfer Capability (ATC) and Total Transfer Capability (TTC) of power utilities must be posted on the Open Access Same-time Information System (OASIS) (FERC, 1996). FERC order 2000 built upon the ISO concept by encouraging smaller transmission companies to join together into RTOs (Regional Transmission Organizations). Order 888, 889 and 2000 have included a lot of major milestones that have caused different kind of electrical market structures and business practices in US. ATC was explained by the FERC as the measure of remaining in the physical transmission network over committed uses. TTC is also

determined as the total power that can be sent in a reliable way. The aim of ATC and TTC calculation and posting them to OASIS is to enhance the open access transmission system by making a market signal of the capability of a transmission system to deliver electrical energy.
North American Electric Reliability Council (NERC) proposed a numerical approximation of the ATC in 1995 and 1996 (NERC, 1995; NERC, 1996) According to the NERC definition, ATC is the difference between TTC and the sum of the Transmission Reliability Margin (TRM), Capability Benefit Margin (CBM), and the Existing Transmission Commitments (ETC). The real power transfer at the first security violation excluding existing transmission commitments is the total TTC. TRM is defined as the amount of the transmission transfer capability necessary to ensure that the interconnected network is secure under a reasonable range of uncertainties in system conditions. CBM is determined as the amount of TTC reserved by Load Serving Entities (LSE) to certify for power generating from transfer lines by considering generation reliability (NERC, 1996).

1.1 Available transfer capability

According to the NERC definition in Equation 1.1, utilities would have to determine adequately their ATCs to ensure that system reliability is maintained while serving a wide range of transmission transactions. ATC must be calculated, updated and reported continuously to LSE in normal and contingency situation. The ATC calculation must be covered all below principles (Sauer & Grijalva, 1999):

1. Provide the logical and reliable indication of transfer capability.
2. Identification time-variant conditions, synchronous power transfers, and parallel flows.
3. Considering the dependence on points of injection / extraction.
4. Considering regional coordination.
5. Covering the NERC and other organizational system reliability criteria and guides.
6. Coordinate reasonable uncertainties in transmission system conditions and provide flexibility

Usually determination of transfer capability and other related margins has been coordinated by the North American Electric Reliability Council. Operating studies commonly seek to determine limitations due to the following types of problems (Merryl, 1998).

1. Thermal overloads Limitation
2. Voltage stability Limitation
3. Voltage limitation
4. Power generated Limitation
5. Reactive power generated Limitation
6. Load Power Limitation

Based on market demands, ATC is computed hourly, daily or monthly. In ATC calculations, definite factors such as contingencies that would represent most serious disturbances, unit commitment, accuracy of load forecast and distribution, system topology and configuration, and maintenance scheduling should be taken into account. System control devices such as voltage regulators and reactive power control devices also have a direct impact on ATC values. The literatures on ATC calculation can be divided into deterministic and probabilistic methods. Deterministic ATC calculation methods, determine ATC for definite time and certain environment. Straight forward implement, easy and fast are most important beneficial of using these methods. However these methods could not consider system uncertainties. The uncertainty is one of the important natures of the power system behavior to determine the ATC. In the regulated environment, weather factors, load forecast and fault of generators, lines and transformers have most effects on ATC estimation for planning system. Moreover they are increased since the uncertainty in bid acceptance procedures, customer response to prices and control of interruptible loads (Sakis Meliopoulos, Wook Kang, & Cokkinides, 2000). These uncertainties must be quantified for the next few hours by ISO in real time. Therefore, probabilistic ATC calculation methods must be used to cover this problem.

1.1.1 Review of previous works on deterministic methods

Previous researches can give comprehensive information during the operational planning stage which is off-line executed shortly before the real-time operation, while the latter may provide timely relevant data to on-line operational performance. For on-line calculation, i.e. in an operation environment where ATC values are posted on a short-term (usually one to several hours or even shorter) basis, calculation of ATC may be performed for most limiting constraints. The methods of on line ATC calculation are based on deterministic model, and they may be solved by several methods, such as: DC Power Flow (DCPF), Power Transfer Distribution Factor (PTDF), Generation Shifting Factor (GSF), Repeated Power Flow (RPF), and Line Outage Distribution Factor (LODF), Continuation Power Flow (CPF), and Optimal Power Flow (OPF) methods.

DC Power Flow has been widely used to calculate thermal limit with great speed. However DC power flow cannot deal with other limiting factors. Distribution factors based on DC or AC power flow methods were proposed for calculating ATC in (Flueck, Chiang, & Shah, 1996; Ilic, Yoon, & Dept, 1997; Gisin, B.S, M.V., & Mitsche, 1999; Li & Liu, 2002; Venkatesh, R, & Prasad, 2004; Ghawghawe, Thakre, & L, 2006). Because of the relative ease, coupled with the mild computational burden involved in computing these factors, they have found widespread application in the industry (Hamoud, 2000). Power Transfer Distribution Factor (PTDF) using DC power flow and AC power flow are derived to calculate ATC. In DCPTDF method (Wood, 1996), DC load flow i.e. a linear model, is considered. These methods are fast but they are not accurate. ACPTDF was used by (Kumar, Srivastava, & Singh, 2004) for determination of ATC of a practical system. It considers the determination of power transfer distribution factors, computed at a base case load flow using sensitivity properties of Newton Raphson Load Flow (NRLF) Jacobean. Line Outage Distribution Factor (LODF) describes the power flow change due to the outage of other branch. LODF can be obtained directly by DC power flow equation. It describes the branch power flow changes due to the power increase between the sending subsystem and receiving subsystem. In other words, it describes the power ratio of the monitored branch power changes with respect to the power change of the study transfer after single branch is outage. Therefore, LODF is valid for the network topology after single branch is outage. To compute the first contingency incremental transfer capability the LODF and PTDF was combined by (Yang & Brent, 2001).

NEMMCO in Australia power market performs its constraint management and construct its constraint thermal equations by means of Generation Shift Factor (GSF). In terms of ISO-NE, it uses GSF and other linear distribution factors in a variety of planning and operating analyses, including the determination of available transfer capability (ATC). The merits of these linear distribution factors lie in their fast and simple algorithms compared to traditional Newton-Raphson (N-R) load flow. Continuation Power Flow (CPF) is implemented by (Shaaban, Ni, & Wu, 2000; Hur, Kim, B,H, & Son, 2001). They incorporate the effects of reactive power flows, voltage limits and voltage collapse, and the traditional thermal loading effect. It can trace the power flow solution curve, starting at a base load, leading to the steady state voltage stability limit or the critical maximum loading point of the system. It overcomes the singularity of the Jacobian matrix close to the critical point. However, to increase a certain power transfer, CPF uses a common loading factor for a specific cluster of generator(s) and load(s), which might lead to a conservative TTC value since the optimal distribution of generation or loading is ignored. Besides, the implementation of CPF involves parameterization, predictor, corrector and step-size control, which are complicated. Since CPF increases the loading factor along certain directions without considering control effects, it may give conservative transfer capability results (Ou & Singh, 2002). However the Optimal Power Flow (OPF) method can symmetrically handle the operational problems but since the approximation is used the accuracy of this calculation is low. It also causes convergence problems due to a huge number of variable and equations for large scale electric power systems. Optimal power flow with transient stability constraints was proposed by (Tuglie, Dicorato, Scala, & Scarpellini, 2000; Chen, Tada, & Okamoto, 2001) where the differential equations are used to define the domain. The security constrained OPF method (Hur, Park, K, & Kim, 2003; Shaaban M. , Li, Yan, Ni, & Wu, 2003; Gao, Zhou, M, & Li, 2006), has also been used to solve the Steady-State Security Constrained (SSSC) ATC problem. However, the correct representation of security constraints (and even more so if post-contingency actions are to be taken into account) may cause a great increase of orders of magnitudes in problem size. OPF methods might be the most promising one for calculating TTC and should be given more considerable attention (Dai, McCalley, & Vittal, 2000; Diao, Mohamed, & Ni, 2000; Yue, Junji, & Takeshi, 2003). Up till now, the OPF based techniques for TTC calculation are very slow and cannot be applied online yet. Therefore, developing a quick and accurate method for TTC calculation, which can effectively consider various likely contingencies and stability constraints, is still a technical challenge. Repeated Power Flow method (RPF) (Gao, Morison, & Kundur, 1996; Ou & Singh, 2003) repeatedly solves conventional power flow equations at a succession of points along the specified transfer directions while CPF solves a set of augmented power flow equations to obtain the solution curve passing through the nose point without encountering the numerical difficulty of ill-conditioning. Compared to any OPF method, RPF can provide P-V and V-Q curves for voltage stability studied. Moreover adjustment method of control variables in RPF is relatively easy. Compared to the CPF method, the implementation of RPF method is much easier and the time for convergence time is less (Gravener, Nwankpa, & Yeoh, 1999).

The comparison of the performance of deterministic methods is listed in Table 1.1. This table shows the steady state constraints which are considered for deterministic ATC computation methods. Based on this table, DC power flow has been widely used to calculate deterministic ATC by thermal limit. However DC power flow cannot deal with other limiting factors. In PTDF, LODF and GSF methods, only thermal limitation could be taken into account too. However RPF, CPF and OPF could calculate the deterministic ATC with thermal, voltage and stability limitations. Therefore, the computation accuracy of these RPF, CPF and OPF are better than the DCPF, PTDF, LODF and GSF.

Method	Constraints Considered		
	Thermal	Voltage	Stability
DCPF	Yes	No	No
PTDF	Yes	No	No
LODF	Yes	No	No
GSF	Yes	No	No
RPF	Yes	Yes	Yes
CPF	Yes	Yes	Yes
OPF	Yes	Yes	Yes

Table 1.1. Performance Comparisons of Deterministic ATC Methods

1.2 Review of Krylov subspace methods

A Krylov subspace methods is one of the most important classes of iterative methods for solving linear algebraic systems, which are spanned by the initial residual and by vectors formed by repeated multiplication of the initial residual by the system matrix (Jorg Liesen, 2004). The Krylov subspace methods have been developed and perfected since early 1980's for the iterative solution of the linear problem $Ax = b$ for large, sparse and nonsymmetric A-matrices. The approach is to minimize the residual r in the formulation of $r = b - Ax$ (Kulkarnil, Pai, & Sauer, 2001). Because these methods form a basis, it is clear that this method converges in N iterations when N is the matrix size. With more powerful computers and better methods it is possible to solve larger and more complex problem for the application ranging from quantum chromo dynamics to air control problems (Simoncini & Szyld, 2007). Krylov subspace methods known as iterative methods among the "Top 10" algorithmic ideas of the 20th century for solving linear systems (Ciprara, 2000). This is due to the capability of Krylov subspace to be built using only a function that computes the multiplication of the system matrix and a vector. Hence, the system matrix itself will not be formed or sorted explicitly and it is suited for application in large and sparse linear systems (Jorg Liesen, 2004).

1.3 Krylov subspace method applications in power system

Recently, a set of Krylov subspace-based, reduced order modeling techniques have been introduced for the efficient simulation of large linear systems. These algorithms, which include the Pad´e via Lanczos (PVL) (Feldmann & Freund, 1995), Arnoldi (Silveira, Kamon, & White, 1995), and congruence transformation (Kerns, Wemple, & Yang, 1995) processes, produce more accurate and higher order approximations compared to Automatic Waveform Evaluation (AWE) and its derivatives. Despite their superior performance to moment matching techniques, applications of Krylov subspace techniques have been limited to lumped RLC circuits (Mustafa & Andreas, 1997). Preconditioned Krylov subspace iterative methods to perform fast DC and transient simulations for large-scale linear circuits with an emphasis on power delivery circuits was proposed by (Tsung Hao & Charlie, 2001). Their method has been shown to be faster than traditional iterative methods without preconditioning. To take advantage of the fast convergence of these methods, the Nodal Analysis is proven to be feasible for general RLC circuits and the system matrix for transient simulation is indeed Symmetric Positive Definite (SPD), which is long believed not feasible.

Krylov subspace was used by (Adam, 1996) method as iterative method, for the practical solution of the load flow problem. The approach developed was called the Kylov Subspace Power Flow (KSPF).
A continuation power flow method was presented by (Hiroyuki Mori, 2007) with the linear and nonlinear predictor based Newton-GMRES method to reduce computational time of the conventional hybrid method. This method used the preconditioned iterative method to solve the sets of linear equations in the N-R corrector. The conventional methods used the direct methods such as the LU factorization. However, they are not efficient for a large-scaled sparse matrix because of the occurrence of the fill-in elements. On the other hand, the iterative methods are also more efficient if the condition number of the coefficient matrix in better. They employed generalized minimum residual (GMRES) method that is one of the Krylov subspace methods for solving a set of linear equations with a non symmetrical coefficient matrix. Their result shows, Newton GMRES method has a good performance on the convergence characteristics in comparison with other iterative methods and is suitable for the continuation power flow method.

2. ATC computation

2.1 Introduction

Transfer capability of a transmission system is a measure of unutilized capability of the system at a given time and depends on a number of factors such as the system generation dispatch, system load level, load distribution in network, power transfer between areas and the limit imposed on the transmission network due to thermal, voltage and stability considerations (Gnanadass, Manivannan, & Palanivelu, 2003). In other words, ATC is a measure of the megawatt capability of the system over and above already committed uses.

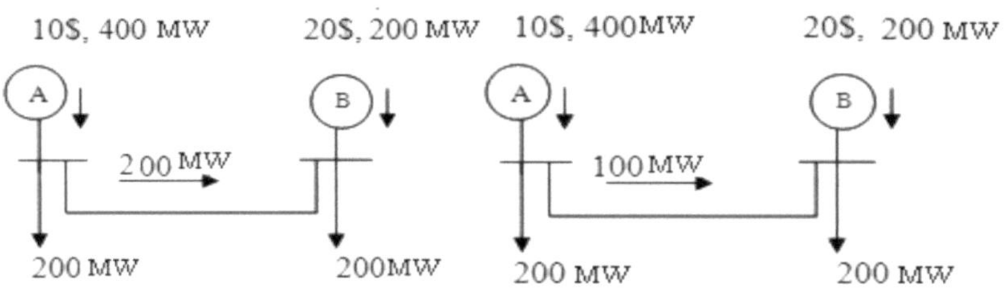

(a) Without Transfer Limitation (b) With Transfer Limitation

Fig. 2.1. Power Transfer Capability between Two Buses

To illustrate the available transfer capability, a simple example of Figure 2.1 is used which shows a two bus system connected by a transfer line. Each zone has a 200 MW constant load. Bus A has a 400 MW generator with an incremental cost of $10/MWh. Bus B has a 200 MW generator with an incremental cost of $20/MWh (Assuming both generators bid their incremental costs). If there is no transfer limit as shown in Figure 2.1(a), all 400 MW of load will be bought from generator A at $10/MWh, at a cost of $4000/h. With 100MW transfer limitation (Figure 2.1(b)), then 300 MW will be bought from A at $10/MWh and the remaining 100 MWh must be bought from generator B at $20/MWh, a total cost of $5000/h. Congestion has created a market inefficiency about 25%, even without strategic behavior by the generators. It has also created unlimited market power for generator B. B can also increase its bid as much as it wants, because the loads must still buy 100 MW from it. Generator B's market power would be limited if there was an additional generator in zone B with a higher incremental cost, or if the loads had nonzero price elasticity and reduced their energy purchase as prices increased. In the real power system, cases of both limited and unlimited market power due to congestion can occur. Unlimited market power is probably not tolerable.

In another example of ATC calculation, Figure 2.2 shows two area systems. Where P_{gi} and P_{gj} are power generated in sending and receiving area. And P_{li} and P_{lj} are power utilized in sending and receiving area. In this case, ATC from sending area i to the receiving area j, are determined at a certain state by Equation (2.1)

$$ATC_{ij} = \left(\sum P_{gi} - \sum P_{li}\right) - \left(\sum P_{gj} - \sum P_{lj}\right) \quad (2.1)$$

Where $\sum P_{gi}$ and $\sum P_{gj}$ are total power generated in the sending and receiving area. And $\sum P_{li}$ and $\sum P_{lj}$ are the total power utilized in the sending and receiving area. By applying a linear optimization method and considering ATC limitations, deterministic ATC can be determined. The block diagram of the general concept of deterministic is shown in Figure 2.3. These computational steps will be described in the following sections.

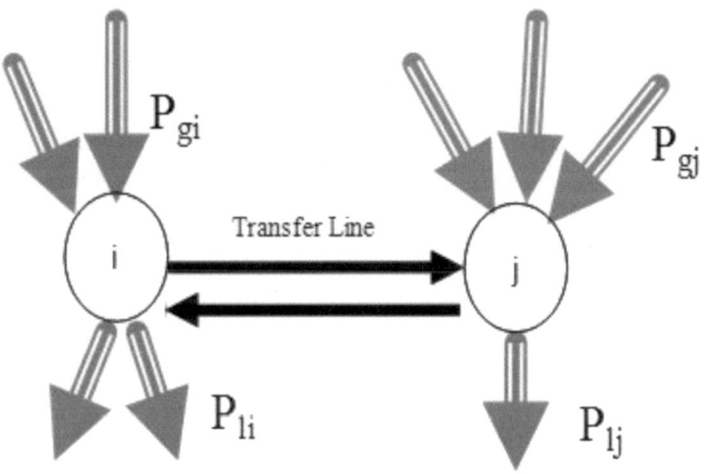

Fig. 2.2. Power Transfer between Two Areas

In this research, Equation (2.1) is employed to determine the ATC between two areas. Therefore, the ATC could be calculated for multilateral situation. The impact of other lines, generators and loads on power transfer could be taken into account. Then the ATC computation will be more realistic. Another benefit of this method is by using linear programming, which makes the ATC computations simple. Moreover the nonlinear behavior of ATC equations are considered by using one of the best iteration methods called Krylov subspace method. Critical line outage impact with time varying load for each bus is used directly to provide probability feature of the ATC. Therefore mean, standard deviation, skewness and kortusis are calculated and analyzed to explain the ATC for system planning.

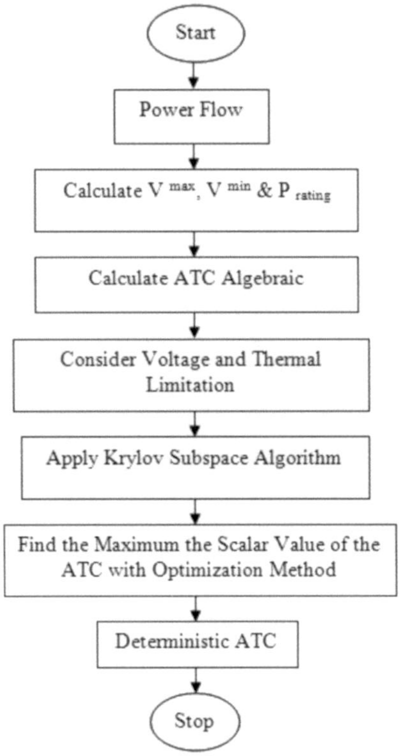

Fig. 2.3. The General Concept of the Proposed Algorithm for Deterministic ATC

2.2 Deterministic ATC determination

2.2.1 Algebraic calculations

In this section, ${dP_{line}}/{dp_{ij}}$ and ${d|V|}/{dp_{ij}}$ are determined by using algebraic calculations, where ${dP_{line}}/{dp_{ij}}$ and ${d|V|}/{dp_{ij}}$ are line flow power sensitivity factor and voltage magnitude sensitivity factor, and these give:

$$\left({dP_{line}}/{dP_{ij}} \right) = \mathrm{diag}(B_{line})L(E_{11} + E_{12}PF) \tag{2.2}$$

$$\left({d|V|}/{dP_{ij}} \right) = (E_{21} + E_{22}PF) \tag{2.3}$$

Where diag(B_{line}) represents a diagonal matrix whose elements are B_{line} (for each transmission line), L is the incident matrix, PF is the power factor, and E_{11}, E_{12}, E_{21} and E_{22} are the sub matrixes of inverse Jacobian matrix. This can be achieved by steps below (Hadi, 2002):

1. Define load flow equation by considering inverse Jacobian Equation (2.4) where inverse Jacobian sub matrixes are calculated from Equation (2.5).
2. Replace ΔQ in Equation (2. 4) with Equation (2. 8) to set $({}^{d|V|}/_{dp_{ij}})$.
3. Use Equations (2. 6) and (2. 7) to set $\Delta\delta = \frac{\Delta P_{line}}{LB_{line}}$
4. Obtain $({}^{dP_{line}}/_{dp_{ij}})$ from Equations (2. 4), (2. 8) and step 3.

$$\begin{bmatrix} \frac{\Delta\delta}{\Delta|V|} \end{bmatrix} = [J]^{-1} \begin{bmatrix} \frac{\Delta P}{\Delta Q} \end{bmatrix} \tag{2.4}$$

$$[J]^{-1} = \begin{bmatrix} E_{11} & E_{12} \\ E_{21} & E_{22} \end{bmatrix} \tag{2.5}$$

$$\Delta dP_{line} = (\Delta\delta_{i\_}\Delta\delta_j)\, B_{line} \tag{2.6}$$

$$\Delta\acute{\delta} = (\Delta\delta_i - \Delta\delta_j) = L. \tag{2.7}$$

$$\Delta Q = PF.\Delta \tag{2.8}$$

Note: L is the incident matrix by (number of branch) * (number of lines) size and include 0, 1 and -1 to display direction of power transferred.

Due to nonlinear behavior of power systems, linear approximation $({}^{dP_{line}}/_{dp_{ij}})$ and $({}^{d|V|}/_{dp_{ij}})$ can yield errors in the value of the ATC. In order to get a more precise ATC, an efficient iterative approach must be used. One of the most powerful tools for solving large and sparse systems of linear algebraic equations is a class of iterative methods called Krylov subspace methods. These iterative methods will be described comprehensively in Section 3.2.3. The significant advantages are low memory requirements and good approximation properties. To determine the ATC value for multilateral transactions the sum of ATC in Equation (2.9) must be considered,

$$\textstyle\sum_k ATC_{ij} \quad , k = 1,2,3 \tag{2.9}$$

Where k is the total number of transactions.

2.2.2 Linear Programming (LP)

Linear Programming (LP) is a mathematical method for finding a way to achieve the best result in a given mathematical model for some requirements represented as linear equations. Linear programming is a technique to optimize the linear objective function, with linear equality and linear inequality constraints. Given a polytope and a real-valued affine function defined on this polytope, where this function has the smallest (or largest) value if such point exists, a Linear Programming method with search through the polytope vertices will find a point. A linear programming method will find a point on the polytope where this function has the smallest (or largest) value if such point exists, by searching through the polytope vertices. Linear Programming is a problem that can be expressed in canonical form (Erling D, 2001):

$$\text{Maximize: } C^T x$$

$$\text{Subject to: } Ax \leq b$$

Where x represents the vector of variables to be determined, c and b are known vectors of coefficients and A is a known matrix of coefficients. The $C^T x$ is an objective function that requires to be maximized or minimized. The equation $Ax \leq b$ is the constraint which specifies a convex polytope over which the objective function is to be optimized. Linear Programming can be applied to various fields of study. It is used most extensively in business, economics and engineering problems. In Matlab programming, optimization toolbox is presented to solve a linear programming problem as:

$$min_x f_x^T \text{ such that } A.x \leq b$$

$$A_{eq}.x = b_{eq}$$

$$l_b \leq x \leq u_b$$

Where f, x, b_{eq}, l_b *and* u_b are matrices.

Example 1: Find the minimum of $f(x_1, x_2, x_3, x_4) = -3x_1 - 6x_2 - 8x_3 - 9x_4$ with $11x_1 - 5x_2 + 3x_3 + 2x_4 \leq 30, 2x_1 + 15x_2 + 3x_3 + 6x_4 \leq 12, 3x_1 + 8x_2 + 7x_3 + 4x_4 \leq 15$ *and* $9x_1 + 5x_2 + x_3 + 4x_4 \leq 30$ inequalies when $0 \leq x_1, x_2, x_3, x_4$.

To solve this problem, first enter the coefficients and next call a linear programming routine as new M-file:

$$f = [-3; -6, -8, -9];$$

$$A = \begin{bmatrix} 11 & -5 & 3 & 2 \\ 2 & 15 & 3 & 6 \\ 3 & 8 & 7 & 3 \\ 9 & 5 & 1 & 4 \end{bmatrix};$$

$$b = [30;\ 12;\ 15;\ 30];$$

$$lb = zeros(4,1);$$

$$[x] = linprog(f, A, b, [\ \ ], [\ \ ], lb)$$

The solution x will be appeared in command windows as:

$$x = \begin{matrix} 0.0000 \\ 0.0000 \\ 1.6364 \\ 1.1818 \end{matrix}$$

As previous noted, ATC can be defined by linear optimization. By considering ATC calculation of Equation (2.1), the objective function for the calculation of ATC is formulated as (Gnanadass & Ajjarapu, 2008):

$$f = \min\left(\left(\sum P_{gj} - \sum P_{lj}\right) - \left(\sum P_{gi} - \sum P_{li}\right)\right) \tag{2.10}$$

The objective function measures the power exchange between the sending and receiving areas. The constraints involved include,

a. Equality power balance constraint. Mathematically, each bilateral transaction between the sending and receiving bus i must satisfy the power balance relationship.

$$P_{gi} = P_{lj} \tag{2.11}$$

For multilateral transactions, this equation is extended to:

$$\sum_i P_{gi}^k = \sum_j P_{lj}^k \quad , k = 1,2,3 \ldots \tag{2.12}$$

Where k is the total number of transactions.

b. Inequality constraints on real power generation and utilization of both the sending and receiving area.

$$P_{gi}^{base} \le P_{gi} \le P_{gi}^{max} \tag{2.13}$$

$$P_{lj}^{base} \le P_{lj} \le P_{lj}^{max} \tag{2.14}$$

Where P_{gi}^{base} and P_{lj}^{base} are the values of the real power generation and utilization of load flow in the sending and receiving areas, P_{gi}^{max} and P_{lj}^{max} are the maximum of real power generation and utilization in the sending and receiving areas.

c. Inequality constraints on power rating and voltage limitations.

With use of algebraic equations based load flow, margins for ATC calculation from bus i to bus j are represented in Equations (2.15 and 2.16) and Equations (2.18 and 2.19). For thermal limitations the equations are,

$$ATC_{ij}\left(\frac{dP_{line}}{dp_{ij}}\right) + P_{line} \le P_{max} \tag{2.15}$$

$$-P_{max} \le ATC_{ij}\left(\frac{dP_{line}}{dp_{ij}}\right) + P_{line} \tag{2.16}$$

Where P_{max} is determined as P_{rating} in Equation (2.17).

$$P_{max} = P_{rating} = \frac{|V_i||V_j|}{X_{ij}} \tag{2.17}$$

Where V_i and V_j are bus voltage of the sending and receiving areas. And X_{ij} is the reactance between bus i and bus j. For voltage limitations,

$$ATC_{ij}\left(\frac{d|V|}{dp_{ij}}\right) + |V| \le |V|_{max} \tag{2.18}$$

$$|V|_{min} \le ATC_{ij}\left(\frac{d|V|}{dp_{ij}}\right) + |V| \tag{2.19}$$

Where ${dP_{line}}/{dp_{ij}}$ and ${d|V|}/{dp_{ij}}$ are calculated from Equations (2.2 and 2.3). Note:

Reactive power (q) constraints must be considered as active power constraints in equations 2.11-2.14.

2.2.3 Krylov subspace methods for ATC calculations

Krylov subspace methods form the most important class of iterative solution method. Approximation for the iterative solution of the linear problem $Ax = b$ for large, sparse and nonsymmetrical A-matrices, started more than 30 years ago (Adam, 1996). The approach was to minimize the residual r in the formulation $r = b - Ax$. This led to techniques like, Biconjugate Gradients (BiCG), Biconjugate Gradients Stabilized (BICBSTAB), Conjugate Gradients Squared (CGS), Generalized Minimal Residual (GMRES), Least Square (LSQR), Minimal Residual (MINRES), Quasi-Minimal Residual (QMR) and Symmetric LQ (SYMMLQ).

The solution strategy will depend on the nature of the problem to be solved which can be best characterized by the spectrum (the totality of the eigenvalues) of the system matrix A. The best and fastest convergence is obtained, in descending order, for A being:

a. symmetrical (all eigenvalues are real) and definite,
b. symmetric indefinite,
c. nonsymmetrical (complex eigenvalues may exist in conjugate pairs) and definite real, and
d. nonsymmetrical general

However MINRES, CG and SYMMLQ can solve symmetrical and indefinite linear system whereas BICGSTAB, LSQR, QMR and GMRES are more suitable to handle nonsymmetrical and definite linear problems (Ioannis K, 2007). In order to solve the algebraic programming problem mentioned in Section 2.2.1 and the necessity to use an iterative method, Krylov subspace methods are added to the ATC computations. Therefore the ATC margins equations can be represented in the general form:

$$f(x) = 0 \tag{2.20}$$

Where x represents ATC_{ij} vector form (number of branches) from Equations (2.15 and 2.16) and also ATC_{ij} vector form (number of buses) of Equations (2.18 and 2.19). With iteration step k, Equation (2.20) gives the residual r_k.

$$r_k = f(x_k) \tag{2.21}$$

And the linearized form is:

$$r_k = b - Ax_k \tag{2.22}$$

Where A represents diag(${dP_{line}}/{dp_{ij}}$) or diag(${d|V|}/{dp_{ij}}$) in diagonal matrix form (number of branches) x (number of branches) or (number of buses) x (number of buses), and b gives $P_{rating} - P_{line}$ or $-P_{rating} - P_{line}$ in vector form (number of branches) and $|V|_{max} - |V|$ or $|V| - |V|_{min}$ in vector form (number of buses) while the Equations (2.15, 2.16, 2.18 and 2.19) can be rewritten as in Equations (2.23- 2.26). In this case, the nature of A is nonsymmetrical and definite. However, all of the Krylov subspace methods can be used for ATC computation but BICGSTAB, LSQR, QMR and GMRES are more suitable to handle this case.

$$ATC_{ij} = \frac{-P_{rating} - P_{line}}{(dP_{line}/dp_{ij})} \quad (2.23)$$

$$ATC_{ij} = \frac{|V|_{max} - |V|}{(dV/dp_{ij})} \quad (2.24)$$

$$ATC_{ij} = \frac{-P_{rating} - P_{line}}{(dP_{line}/dp_{ij})} \quad (2.25)$$

$$ATC_{ij} = \frac{|V|_{min} - |V|}{(dV/dp_{ij})} \quad (2.26)$$

Generalized Minimal Residual (GMRES) method flowchart is presented in Figure 2.5 as an example of Krylov subspace methods for solving linear equations iteratively. It starts with an initial guess value of x_0 and a known vector b and A matrix obtained from the load flow. A function then calculates the Ax_0 using $\mathrm{diag}(dP_{line}/dp_{ij})$ or $\mathrm{diag}(d|V|/dp_{ij})$. The GMRES subroutine then starts to iteratively minimize the residual $r_k = b - Ax_k$. The program is then run in a loop up to some tolerance or until the maximum iteration is reached. At each step, when a new r is determined, it updates the value of x and asks the user to provide the Ax_k using the updated value.

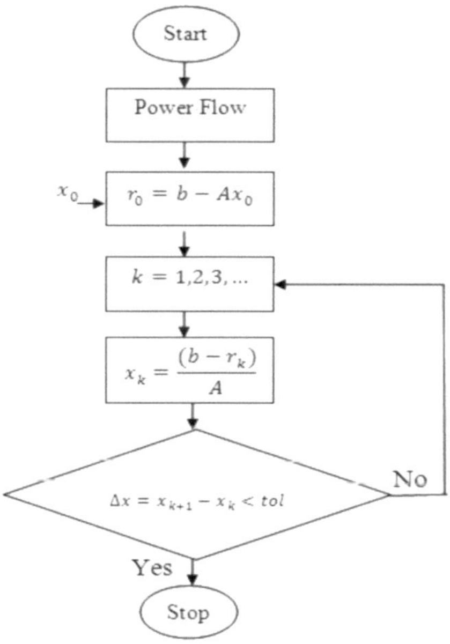

Fig. 2.5. Flowchart for GMRES Algorithm

In Matlab programming GMRES must be defined as $[x] = gmres(A, b, restart, tol, maxit, M1, M2, X_0)$. This function attempts to solve the system of linear equations $A * x = b\ for\ x$. Then n by n coefficient matrix A must be square and should be large and sparse. Then column vector b must have length n. A can be a function handle afun such that afun(x) returns $A * x$. If GMRES converges, a message to that effect is displayed. If GMRES fails to converge after the maximum number of iterations or halts for any reason, a warning message is printed displaying the relative residual $norm(b - A * x)/norm(b)$ and the iteration number at which the method stopped or failed. GMRES restarts the method in every inner iteration. The maximum number of outer iterations is $\min({}^{n}/_{restart}, n)$. If restart is n or [ ], then GMRES does not restart and the maximum number of total iterations is $\min(n, 10)$. In GMRES function," tol" specifies the tolerance of the method. If "tol" is [ ], then GMRES uses the default, $1e - 6$. "maxit specifies the maximum number of outer iteration, i.e., the total number of iteration does not exceed restart*maxit. If maxit is [ ] then GMRES uses the default, $\min({}^{n}/_{restart}, 10)$. If restart is n or [ ], then the maximum number of total iterations is maxit (instead of restart*maxit). "M1" and "M2" or M=M1*M2 are preconditioned and effectively solve the system $inv(M) * A * x = inv(M) * b\ for\ x$. If M is [ ] then GMRES applies no preconditioned. M can be a function handle $mfun$ such that $mfun(x)$ returns $(M\backslash x)$. Finally, x_0 specifies the first initial guess. If x_0 is [ ], then GMRES uses the default, an all zero vector.

3. Result and discussion

In this section, illustrations of ATC calculations are presented. For this purpose the IEEE 30 and IEEE 118 (Kish, 1995) bus system are used. In the first the residual, CPU time and the deterministic ATC are obtained based on Krylov subspace methods and explained for IEEE 30 and IEEE 118 bus system. Finally the deterministic ATC results of IEEE 30 bus system are compared with other methods. The deterministic ATC calculation is a significant part of the probabilistic ATC calculation process. Therefore, it is important that the deterministic ATC formulation is done precisely. For the first step, the deterministic ATC equations shown in Section 2.2 are used for IEEE 30 and IEEE 118 bus system to find the deterministic ATC.

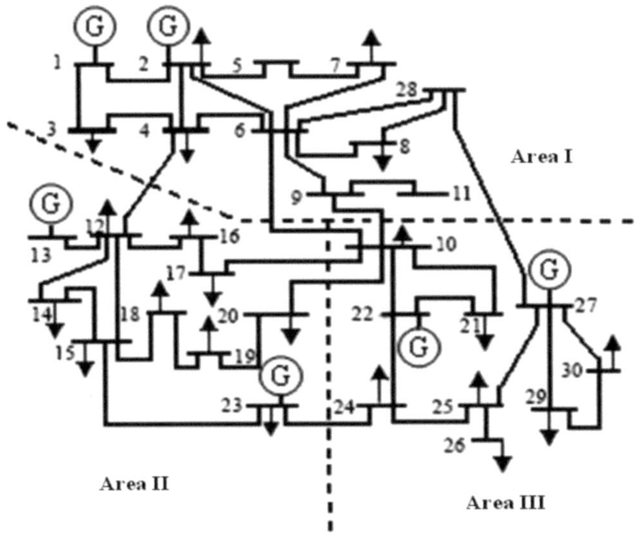

Fig. 3.1. IEEE 30 Bus System

IEEE 30 bus system (Figure 3.1) comprises of 6 generators, 20 load buses and 41 lines, and IEEE 118 bus system (Figure 3.3) has 118 buses, 186 branches and 91 loads. All computations in this study were performed on 2.2 GHz RAM, 1G RAM and 160 hard disk computers. Because of the nonlinear behavior of load flow equations, the use of iterative methods need to be used for the ATC linear algebraic equations. One of the most powerful tools for solving large and sparse systems of linear algebraic equations is a class of iterative methods called Krylov subspace methods. The significant advantages of Krylov subspace methods are low memory requirements and good approximation properties. Eight Krylov subspace methods are mentioned in Section 2.2.3. All of these methods are defined in MATLAB software and could be used as iteration method for deterministic ATC calculation.

The CPU time is achieved by calculating the time taken for deterministic ATC computation by using Krylov subspace methods for IEEE 30 and IEEE 118 bus systems using MATLAB programming. The CPU time results are shown in Figure 3.2. In Figure 3.2, the CPU time for eight Krylov methods mentioned in Section 2.2.3 are presented. Based on this result, the CPU times of ATC computation for IEEE 30 bus system range from $0.75 - 0.82$ seconds. The CPU times result for IEEE 118 bus system is between $10.18 - 10.39$ seconds.

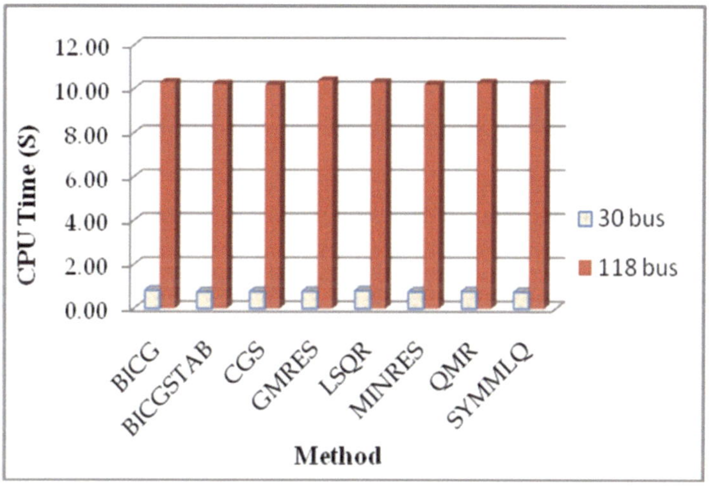

Fig. 3.2. CPU Time Comparison of Krylov Subspace Methods for Deterministic ATC (IEEE 30 and 118 bus system)

The computation of residual is done in MATLAB programming for each of Krylov subspace methods. The residual r_k is defined in Equation (2.21). A sample result in MATLAB is shown in Figure 3.5 using LSQR and SYMMLQ for IEEE 30 bus system. The number of iteration and residual of the deterministic ATC computation are shown in this figure. Figure 3.4 presents the residual value of the ATC computations by applying each of Krylov subspace methods for IEEE 30 and 118 bus system. One of the most important findings of Figure 4.4 is the result obtained from the LSQR, which achieved a residual around 1.01×10^{-10} and 5.3×10^{-10} for IEEE 30 and 118 bus system respectively. According to this figure, it indicates that the residual of LSQR is very different from others. CGS in both system and BICGSTAB in IEEE 118 bus system have highest residual. However other results are in the same range of around 1.8×10^{-8}. Other performance of Krylov subspace methods like number of iteration are shown Tables 3.1 and 3.2.

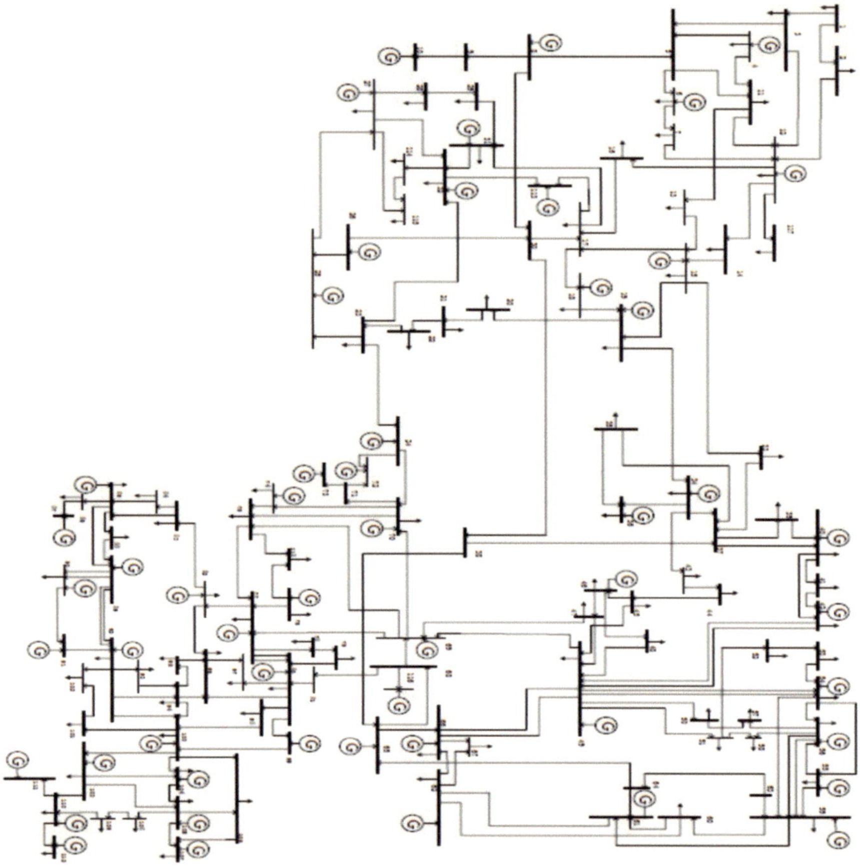

Fig. 3.3. IEEE 118 Bus System

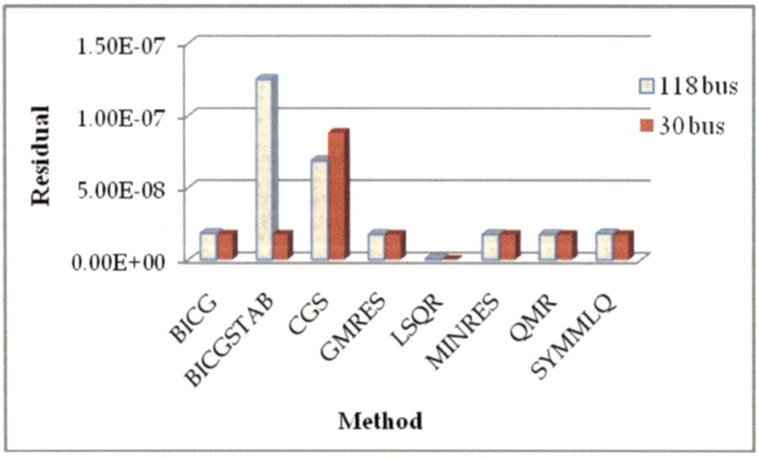

Fig. 3.4. Residual Comparison of Krylov Subspace Methods for Deterministic ATC (IEEE 30 and 118 bus system)

```
3926  lsqr converged at iteration 8 to a solution with relative residual 3.9e-013
3927  lsqr converged at iteration 13 to a solution with relative residual 1.8e-011
3928  lsqr converged at iteration 7 to a solution with relative residual 6.9e-011
3929  lsqr converged at iteration 6 to a solution with relative residual 5.6e-013
3930  lsqr converged at iteration 7 to a solution with relative residual 2.2e-011
3931  lsqr converged at iteration 7 to a solution with relative residual 1.3e-009
3932  lsqr converged at iteration 4 to a solution with relative residual 7.3e-017
3933  lsqr converged at iteration 2 to a solution with relative residual 1.7e-016
3934  lsqr converged at iteration 2 to a solution with relative residual 9.6e-016
3935  lsqr converged at iteration 2 to a solution with relative residual 2.9e-016
3936  lsqr converged at iteration 2 to a solution with relative residual 1.3e-016
3937  lsqr converged at iteration 2 to a solution with relative residual 4.9e-016
3938  lsqr converged at iteration 2 to a solution with relative residual 2.6e-016
3939  lsqr converged at iteration 2 to a solution with relative residual 8.4e-018

4597  symmlq converged at iteration 7 to a solution with relative residual 4.5e-016
4598  symmlq converged at iteration 10 to a solution with relative residual 2.5e-007
4599  symmlq converged at iteration 6 to a solution with relative residual 1.5e-014
4600  symmlq converged at iteration 5 to a solution with relative residual 9.4e-016
4601  symmlq converged at iteration 6 to a solution with relative residual 2.7e-014
4602  symmlq converged at iteration 6 to a solution with relative residual 1.7e-014
4603  symmlq converged at iteration 3 to a solution with relative residual 1.3e-016
4604  symmlq converged at iteration 1 to a solution with relative residual 3.1e-016
4605  symmlq converged at iteration 1 to a solution with relative residual 1.8e-016
4606  symmlq converged at iteration 1 to a solution with relative residual 5.7e-016
4607  symmlq converged at iteration 1 to a solution with relative residual 0
4608  symmlq converged at iteration 1 to a solution with relative residual 3.5e-016
4609  symmlq converged at iteration 1 to a solution with relative residual 3.1e-016
4610  symmlq converged at iteration 1 to a solution with relative residual 2.2e-016
```

Fig. 3.5. Matlab Programming Results for LSQR and SYMMLQ Methods (IEEE 30 bus system)

Linear optimization mentioned in Section 2.2.2 is applied to the deterministic ATC calculation with all the constraints considered. The important constraints for calculating ATC are voltage and thermal rating. In these calculations the minimum and the maximum voltage are considered between 0.94 -1.04 of the base voltage for all the bus voltages. The thermal limitation is determined from Equations (2.15 and 2.16) of Section 2.2.2. In this computation, it was assumed that the voltage stability is always above the thermal and voltage constraints and reactive power demands at each load buses are constant.

Deterministic ATC results are represented in Tables 3.1 and 3.2 for IEEE 30 and IEEE 118 bus system. Each of these systems have 3 transaction paths as shown in Figures 3.1 and 3.6, the first one is between area 1 and area 2 (called T1), the second one is between area 1 and area 3 (called T2) and last one is between area 2 and area 3 (called T3). Residual, number of iteration and CPU time results are shown in columns 2, 3 and 4 of Tables 3.1 and 3.2 for IEEE 30 and 118 bus system. According to the results of ATC for T1, T2 and T3 in columns 5, 6 and 7 of these tables, the amount of the ATC of IEEE 30 bus system, is the same for all Krylov subspace methods which are 106.814, 102.925 and 48.03 MW for three transaction paths. The difference between the residuals in IEEE 118 bus system appears in the amount of ATC especially for T2 in Table 3.2. By comparing the performance results of Krylov subspace methods in Tables 3.1 and 3.2, it seems the result of LSQR is more appropriate to be used for ATC computations because of the low residual. This is related to generate the conjugate vectors ω_i from the orthogonal vectors v_i via an orthogonal transformation in LSQR algorithm. LSQR is also more reliable in variance circumstance than the other Krylov subspace methods (Christopher & Michael, 1982).

Krylov Subspace Methods	Residual	Iteration Number	CPU Time (S)	Deterministic ATC(MW)		
				T1	T2	T3
BICG	1.79E-08	5	0.82	106.814	102.925	48.030
BICGSTAB	1.79E-08	4	0.75	106.814	102.925	48.030
CGS	8.84E-08	4	0.76	106.814	102.925	48.030
GMRES	1.79E-08	5	0.78	106.814	102.925	48.030
LSQR	1.01E-10	5	0.81	106.814	102.925	48.030
MINRES	1.79E-08	4	0.76	106.814	102.925	48.030
QMR	1.79E-08	5	0.78	106.814	102.925	48.030
SYMMLQ	1.79E-08	4	0.75	106.814	102.925	48.030

Table 3.1. Performance of Krylov Subspace Methods on Deterministic ATC for IEEE 30 Bus System

Krylov Subspace Methods	Residual	Iteration Number	CPU Time (S)	Deterministic ATC(MW)		
				T1	T2	T3
BICG	1.83E-08	5	10.30	426.214	408.882	773.551
BICGSTAB	1.25E-07	4	10.22	426.214	143.846	773.532
CGS	6.89E-08	4	10.18	426.214	408.849	773.532
GMRES	1.77E-08	5	10.39	426.214	408.886	773.551
LSQR	5.38E-10	5	10.29	426.214	408.882	773.551
MINRES	1.77E-08	4	10.20	426.214	397.986	773.551
QMR	1.77E-08	5	10.28	426.214	408.882	773.551
SYMMLQ	1.83E-08	4	10.24	426.214	409.066	773.551

Table 3.2. Performance of Krylov Subspace Methods on Deterministic ATC for IEEE 118 Bus System

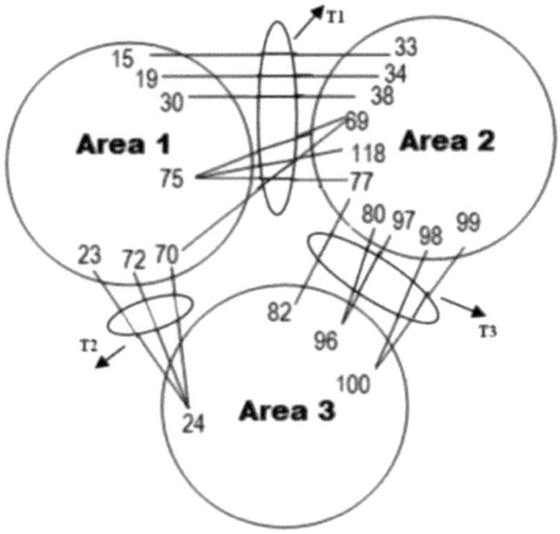

Fig. 3.6. Transaction Lines between Areas - IEEE 118 Bus System

4. Conclusion

The major contribution from this chapter is the application of the Krylov subspace methods to improve the ATC algebraic computations by using linear calculations for nonlinear nature of power system by Matlab programming. Eight Krylov subspace methods were used for ATC calculation and tested on IEEE 30 bus and IEEE 118 bus systems. The CPU time and residual were measured and compared to select the most appropriate method for ATC computation. Residual is an important parameter of Krylov subspace methods which help the algorithm to accurately determine the correct value to enable the corrector to reach the correct point. In these Krylov subspace techniques, there are no matrix factorizations and only space matrix-vector multiplication or evaluation of residual is used. This is the main contributing factor for its efficiency which is very significant for large systems. Deterministic ATC results for all Krylov subspace were done and their results comparison indicated that the amount of ATC for IEEE 30 bus system did not show significant change. For IEEE 118 bus system, because of the difference in residuals, different ATC were obtained. Unlike the other ATC algebraic computation methods, Krylov Algebraic Method (KAM) determined ATC for multilateral transactions. For this, the effects of lines, generators and loads were considered for ATC computation.

5. References

Adam, S. (1996). Fundamental Concepts of a Krylov Subspace Power Flow Methodology. *IEEE Transactions on Power Systems* , *11* (3), 1528 - 1537.

Chen, L., Tada, Y., & Okamoto, H. (2001). Optimal Operation Solutions of Power Systems with Transient Stability Constraints. *IEEE Transactions on Circuits and Systems* , *48* (3), 327-339.

Christopher, C., & Michael, A. (1982). LSQR: An Algorithm for Sparse Linear Equations and Sparse Least Squares. *ACM Transactions on Mathematical Software* , *8* (1), 43-71.

Ciprara, B. (2000). The Best of The 20th Century: editors Name Top 10 Algorithm. *Society for Industrial and Applied Mathematics (SIAM)* , *33* (4), 1.

Dai, Y., McCalley, J. D., & Vittal, V. (2000). Simplification Expansion and Enhancement of Direct Interior Point Algorithm for Power System Maximum Load Ability. *IEEE Transactions on Power Systems*, *15* (3), 1014 - 1021 .

Diao, Q., Mohamed, S., & Ni, Y. (2000). Inter-area Total Transfer Capability Calculation Using Sequential Quadratic Programming Method in Power Market. *Automation of Electric Power Systems*, *24* (24), 5-8.

Erling D, A. (2001). *Linear optimization: Theory, Methods, and Extensions.* EKA Consulting APS.

Feldmann, P., & Freund, R. W. (1995). Efficient Linear Circuit Analysis by Pad´e Approximation Via the Lancsoz Process. *IEEE Transactions on Computer-Aided Design*, *14* (5), 639–649.

FERC. (1996). *Open Access Same-Time Information System and Standards of Conduct.* Federal Energy Regulatory Commission.

Flueck, A. J., Chiang, H. D., & Shah, K. S. (1996). Investigation the Installed Real Power Transfer Capability of a Large Scale Power System Under a Proposed Multiarea Interchange Schedule Using CPFLOW. *IEEE Transaction on Power Systems* , *11* (2), 883 – 889.

Gao, B., Morison, G., & Kundur, P. (1996). Towards the Development of a Systematic Approach for Voltage Stability Assessment of Large-Scale Power Systems. *IEEE Transactions on Power Systems*, *11* (3), 1314 - 1324.

Gao, Zhou, Y., M, & Li, G. (2006). Sequential Monte Carlo Simulation Based Available Transfer Capability Calculation. *International Conference on Power System Technology*, (pp. 1-6). Chongqing .

Ghawghawe, Thakre, N., & L, K. (2006). Application of Power Flow Sensitivity Analysis and PTDF for Determination of ATC. *IEEE International Conference on Power Electronics, Drives and Energy Systems.* New Delhi.

Gisin, B.S, O., M.V., & Mitsche, J. (1999). Practical Methods for Transfer Limit Analysis in the Power Industry Deregulated Environment. *Power Industry Computer Applications*, (pp. 261-266). Santa clara CA.

Gnanadass, R., & Ajjarapu, V. (2008). Assessment of Dynamic Available Transfer Capability using FDR PSO Algorithm. *Elektrika Journal of Electrical Engineering* , *10* (1), 20-25.

Gnanadass, R., Manivannan, K., & Palanivelu, T. (2003). Assessment of Available Transfer Capability for Practical Power Systems with Margins. *Conference on Convergent Technologies for Asia-Pacific Region*, *1*, pp. 445 - 449.

Gravener, M., Nwankpa, H. C., & Yeoh, T. (1999). ATC Computational Issues. *International Conference on Power System*, (pp. 1-6). Hawaii.

Hadi, S. (2002). *Power Systems Analysis, Second Edition.* McGraw-Hill.

Hamoud, G. (2000). Feasibility Assessment of Simultaneous Bilateral Transactions in a Deregulated Environment. *IEEE Transaction on Power System* , *15* (1), 22–26.

Hiroyuki Mori, a. K. (2007). Continuation Newton-GMRES Power Flow with Linear and Nonlinear Predictors. *Large Engineering Systems Conference on Power Systems*, (pp. 171 - 175).

Hur, D. P., Kim, J. K., B,H, & Son, K. M. (2001). *Security Constrained Optimal Power Flow for the Evaluation of Transmission Capability on Electric Power System.* Vancouver: Power Engineering Society Summer Meeting.

Hur, Park, D., K, J., & Kim, B. H. (2003). Application of Distributed Optimal Power Flow to Power System Security Assessment. *Electrical Power Components System*, *31* (1), 71-80.

Ilic, M., Yoon, Y., & Dept, A. (1997). Available Transmission Capacity (ATC) and Its Value Under Open Access. *IEEE Transaction on Power Systems*, *12* (2), 636 - 645.

Ioannis K, A. (2007). *Computational Theory of Iterative Methods* (Vol. 15). Elsevier.

Jorg Liesen, P. T. (2004). Convergence Analysis of Krylov Subspace Methods. *GAMM-Mitteilungen*, *27* (2), 153-173.

Kerns, K. J., Wemple, I. L., & Yang, A. T. (1995). Stable and Efficient Reduction of Substrate Model Networks Using Congruence Transforms. *IEEE/ACM International Conference on Computer-Aided Design*, (pp. 207–214).

Kish, L. (1995). *Survey Sampling*. New York: John Wiley & Sons.

Kulkarnil, A. y., Pai, M. A., & Sauer, P. W. (2001). Iterative Solver Techniques in Fast Dynamic Calculations of Power Systems. *International Journal of Electrical Power & Energy Systems*, *23* (3), 237-244.

Kumar, A., Srivastava, S. C., & Singh, S. N. (2004). Available Transfer Capability (ATC) Determination in a Competitive Electricity Market Using AC Distribution Factors. *Electric Power Components and Systems*, *32* (9), 927-939.

Li, C., & Liu, C. (2002). A New Algorithm for Available Transfer Capability Computation. *International Journal of Electric Power Energy System*, *24* (2), 159–66.

Merryl, H. (1998). *Probabilistic Available Capacity*. IEEE PES Winter Meeting.

Mustafa, C., & Andreas, C. C. (1997). Simulation of Multiconductor Transmission Lines Using Krylov Subspace Order-Reduction Techniques. *IEEE Transactions on Computer-Aided Design and Systems*, *16* (5), 485–496.

NERC, R. (1995). *Available Transfer Capability Definitions and Determinations*. North American Electric Reliability Council.

NERC, R. (1996). *Available Transfer Capability Definitions and Determinations*. North American Electric Reliability Council.

NERC, R. (1996). *Promoting Utility Competition Through Open Aces, Non-Discriminatory Transmission Service by Public Utilities: Recovery of Standard Cost by Public Utilities and Transmission Utilities*. Federal Energy Regulatory Commission.

Ou, Y., & Singh, C. (2002). Assessment of Available Transfer Capability and Margins. *IEEE Transaction on Power Systems*, *17* (2), 463–468.

Ou, Y., & Singh, C. (2003). Calculation of Risk and Statistical Indices Associated with Available Transfer : Generation, Transmission and Distribution. *IEE Proceedings, 50*, pp. 239 - 244. College Station, TX, USA.

Sakis Meliopoulos, A. P., Wook Kang, S., & Cokkinides, G. (2000). Probabilistic Transfer Capability Assessment in a Deregulated Environment. *IEEE Proc.International Conference on System Sciences*. Hawaii.

Sauer, P., & Grijalva, S. (1999). Error Analysis in Electric Power System Available Transfer Capability Computation. *Decision Support Systems*, *24* (3-4), 321-330.

Shaaban, M., Li, W., Yan, Z., Ni, Y., & Wu, F. (2003). Calculation of Total Transfer Capability Incorporating the Effect of Reactive Power. *Electric Power Systems Research*, *64* (3), 181-188.

Shaaban, M., Ni, Y., & Wu, F. (2000). Transfer Capability Computations in Deregulated Power Systems. *International Conference on System Sciences*, (pp. 1-5). Hawaii.

Silveira, L. M., Kamon, M., & White, J. (1995). Efficient Reduced-Order Modeling of Frequency-Dependent Coupling Inductances Associated with 3-D Interconnect Structures. *IEEE Design Automation Conference, 19*, pp. 376–380.

Simoncini, V., & Szyld, D. (2007). Recent Computational Developments in Krylov Subspace Methods for Linear Systems. *Numerical Linear Algebra Application , 14*, 1-59.

Tsung Hao, C., & Charlie, C. P. (2001). Efficient Large-Scale Power Grid Analysis Based on Preconditioned Krylov-Subspace Iterative Methods. *Conference on Design Automation*, (pp. 559-562). Las Vegas,Nevada, USA.

Tuglie, E. D., Dicorato, M., Scala, M. L., & Scarpellini, P. (2000). A Static Optimization Approach to Access Dynamic Available Transfer Capability. *IEEE Tranactions on Power Systems , 15* (3), 1069–1076.

Venkatesh, P., R, G., & Prasad, P. (2004). Available Transfer Capability Determination Using Power Distribution Factors. *Journal of Emerging Electric Power Systems , 1* (2), Article 1009.

Wood, A. (1996). *Power Generation Operation and Control.* New York: Willey.

Yang, L., & Brent, r. (2001). The Improved Conjugate Gradient Squared (ICGS) Method on Parallel Distributed Memory Artitectures. *Workshop Proceedings of the International Conference on Parallel Processing (ICPP-HPSECA01).* Valencia, Spain.

Yue, Y., Junji, K., & Takeshi, N. (2003). A Solution of Dynamic Available Transfer Capability by means of Stability Constrained Optimal Power Flow. *IEEE Bologna Power Tech,* (p. 8). Bologna.

8

Multiuser Systems Implementations in Fading Environments

Ioana Marcu, Simona Halunga, Octavian Fratu and Dragos Vizireanu
POLITEHNICA University of Bucharest,
Electronics, Telecommunications and Information Theory Faculty
Romania

1. Introduction

The theory of multiuser detection technique has been developed during the 90s [Verdu, 1998], but its application gained a high potential especially for large mobile networks when the base station has to demodulate the signals coming from all mobile users [Verdu, 1998; Sakrison, 1966].

The performances of multiuser detection systems are affected mostly by the multiple access interference, but also by the type of channel involved and the impairments it might introduce. Therefore, important roles for improving the detection processes are played by the type of noise and interferences affecting the signals transmitted by different users. Selection of spreading codes to differentiate the users plays an important role in the system performances and in the capacity of the system [Halunga & Vizireanu, 2009]. There are important conclusions when the signals of the users are not perfectly orthogonal and/or when they have unequal amplitude [Kadous& Sayeed, 2002], [Halunga & Vizireanu, 2010].

In a wireless mobile communication system, the transmitted signal is affected by multipath phenomenon, which causes fluctuations in the received signal's amplitude, phase and angle of arrival, giving rise to the multipath fading. Small-scale fading is called Rayleigh fading if there are multiple reflective paths that are large in number and there is no line-of-sight component. The small-scale fading envelope is described by a Rician probability density function [Verdu, 1998], [Marcu, 2007].

Recent research [Halunga & Vizireanu, 2010] led us to several conclusions related to the performances of multiuser detectors in different conditions. These conditions include variation of amplitudes, selective choice of (non) orthogonal spreading sequences and analysis of coding/decoding techniques used for recovering the original signals the users transmit. It is very important to mention that the noise on the channel has been considered in all previous simulations as AWGN (Additive White Gaussian Noise).

This chapter implies analysis of multiuser detection systems in the presence of Rayleigh and Rician fading with Doppler shift superimposed over the AWGN noise. The goal of our research is to illustrate the performances of different multiuser detectors such as conventional detector and MMSE (Minimum Mean-Square Error) synchronous linear detectors in the presence of selective fading. The evaluation criterion for multiuser systems performances is BER (Bit Error Rate) depending on SNR (Signal to Noise Ratio). Several conclusions will be withdrawn based on multiple simulations.

2. Multiuser detection systems

Multiuser detection systems implement different algorithms to demodulate one or more digital signals in the presence of multiuser interference. The need for such techniques arises notably in wireless communication channels, in which either intentional non-orthogonal signaling (e.g., CDMA - Code Division Multiple Access) or non-ideal channel effects (e.g., multipath) lead to received signals from multiple users that are not orthogonal to one another [MTU EE5560].

The influence of multiple access interference (MAI) is critical at the receiver end, whether this is the mobile or base station. In CDMA system a tight power control system prevents more powerful users to affect the performances of less powerful ones. In order to reduce the negative effects of near-far problem or any kind of impairments [Halunga S., 2009] several error-correcting codes can be used. Usually the mathematical formulas for defining multiple-access noise are complicated and can be implemented in a very complex structure, and certainly much less randomness than white Gaussian background noise. By exploiting that structure, multi-user detection can increase spectral efficiency, receiver sensitivity, and the number of users the system can sustain [Verdu, 2000].

Several types of multiuser detectors will be analyzed in different transmission/reception environment and they include conventional detector and MMSE multiuser detector.

2.1 Conventional multiuser detector

The conventional matched-filter detector, the optimal structure for single user scenario [Verdu, 1998], is the simplest linear multiuser detector. By correlating with a signal that takes into account the structure of the multiple access interference, it is possible to obtain a rather dramatic improvement of the bit-error rate of the conventional detector [Poor, 1997], but the complexity of the receiver increases significantly.

The detector consists of a bank of matched filters and the decision at the receiver end is undertaken, based on the sign of the signal from the output of filters.

The block diagram of the conventional detector is shown in fig. 1. [Verdu, 1998], [Halunga, 2010]

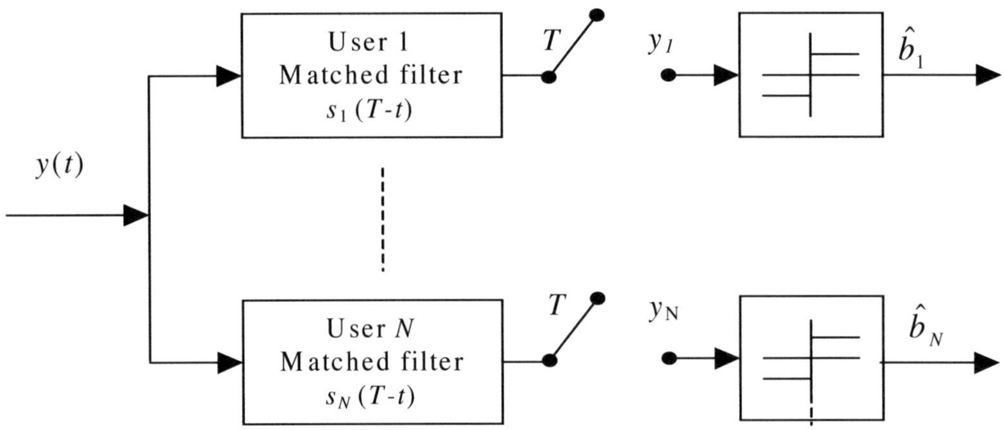

Fig. 1. General architecture of conventional multiuser detector

The outputs of matched filters can be written in matrix representation as

$$Y=RAb+N \tag{1}$$

- $\mathbf{Y}=[y_1, y_2, \dots y_N]^T$: column vector with the outputs of the matched filters;
- R: cross-correlation matrix containing correlation coefficients (ex.: ρ_{kj} represent the correlation coefficient between signal of the user k and signal of the user j);
- $\mathbf{A}=diag\{A_1, A_2, \dots A_N\}$: diagonal matrix of the amplitudes of the received bits;
- $\mathbf{b}=[b_1, b_2, \dots b_N]^T$: column vector with bits received from all users;
- $\mathbf{N}=[n_1, n_2, \dots n_N]^T$: sampled noise vector.

The estimated bit, after the threshold comparison, is

$$\hat{b}_k = \operatorname{sgn}(y_k) = \operatorname{sgn}\left(A_k b_k + \sum_{j \neq k} A_j b_j \rho_{kj} + n_k \right) \tag{2}$$

The random error is thus influenced by the noise samples n_k, correlated with the spreading codes, and by the interference from the other users [Halunga, 2009].

2.2 MMSE multiuser detector

It is shown that MMSE detector, when compared with other detection schemes has the advantage that an explicit knowledge of interference parameters is not required, since filter parameters can be adapted to achieve the MMSE solution. [Khairnar, 2005]

In MMSE detection schemes, the filter represents a trade-off between noise amplification and interference suppression. [Bohnke, 2003]

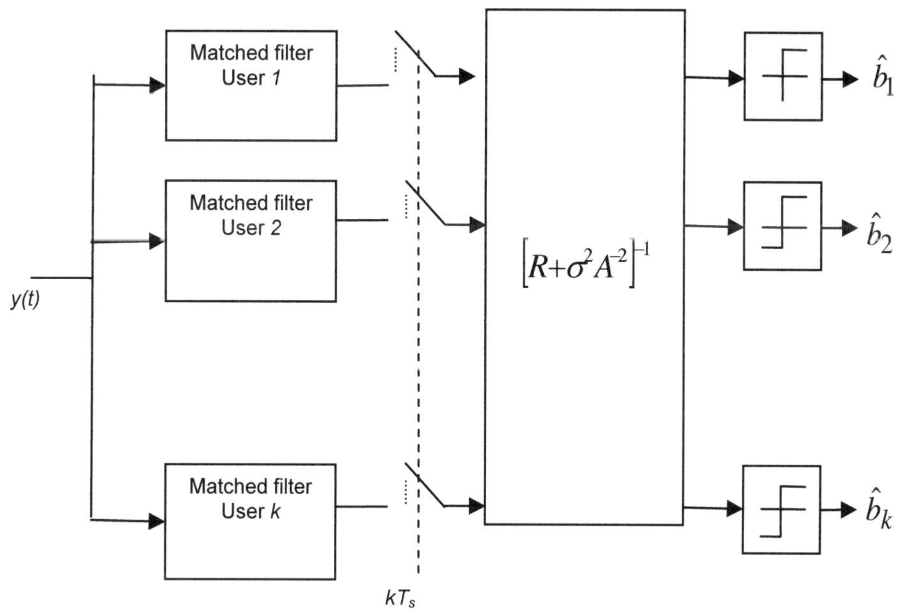

Fig. 2. MMSE multiuser detector

The principle of MMSE detector consists of minimization between bits corresponding to every user and the output of matched filters. The solution is represented by a linear mathematical transformation that depends on the correlation degree between users' signals, amplitude of the signals and on the noise on the channel. In addition to the conventional multiuser scheme, the blocks containing this transformation is placed after the matched filter output and before the sign block [Verdu, 1998], [Halunga, 2010].
This linear transformation can be expressed as:

$$\left[R+\sigma^2 A^{-2}\right]^{-1} \tag{3}$$

After finding this value, one can estimate for every k user the transmitted data by extracting the correponding column for each of them. This way the decision on the transmitted bit from every k user is: [Verdu, 1998]

$$\hat{b}_k = \operatorname{sgn}\left(\frac{1}{A_k}\left(\left[R+\sigma^2 A^{-2}\right]^{-1} y\right)_k\right) = \operatorname{sgn}\left(\left(\left[R+\sigma^2 A^{-2}\right] y\right)_k\right) \tag{4}$$

where every parameter is detailed in Eq. (1) and σ^2 is the variance of the noise.

3. Fading concepts

In mobile communication systems, the channel is distorted by fading and multipath propagation and the BER is affected in the same manner. Based on the distance over which a mobile moves, there are two different types of fading effects: large-scale fading and small-scale fading [Sklar, 1997]. It has been taken in consideration the small-scale fading which refers to the dramatic changes in signal amplitude and phase as a result of a spatial positioning between a receiver and a transmitter.
Rayleigh fading is a statistical model for the effect of a propagation environment on a radio signal, such as that used in wireless devices. [Li, 2009] The probability density function (pdf) is:

$$p(w_0) = \begin{cases} \dfrac{w_0}{\sigma^2}\exp\left[-\dfrac{w_0^2}{2\sigma^2}\right] & for\ w_0 \geq 0 \\ 0 & elsewhere \end{cases} \tag{5}$$

where w_0 is the envelope amplitude of the received signal and σ^2 is the pre-detection mean power of the multipath signal.
The Rayleigh faded component is sometimes called the random or scatter or diffuse component. The Rayleigh pdf results from having no mirrored component of the signal; thus, for a single link it represents the pdf associated with the worst case of fading per mean received signal power. [Rahnema, 2008].
When a dominant non-fading signal component is present, the small-scale fading envelope is described by a Rician fading. As the amplitude of the specular component approaches zero, the Rician pdf approaches a Rayleigh pdf, expressed as:

$$p(w_0) = \begin{cases} \dfrac{w_0}{\sigma^2}\exp\left[-\dfrac{\left(w_0^{\,2}+A^2\right)}{2\sigma^2}\right] I_0\left(\dfrac{w_0 A}{\sigma^2}\right) & for\ w_0 \geq 0, A \geq 0 \\ 0 & elsewhere \end{cases} \tag{6}$$

where σ^2 is the average power of the multipath signal and A is the amplitude of the specular component.
The Rician distribution is often described in terms of a parameter K defined as the ratio of the power in the non-fading signal component to the power in multipath signal. Also the Rician probability density function approaches Rayleigh pdf as K tends to zero. [Goldsmith, 2005]

$$K = \frac{A^2}{2\sigma^2} \tag{7}$$

4. Simulation results

All simulations were performed in Matlab environment. Our analysis started from the results obtained with multiuser detectors in synchronous CDMA system. In addition we introduced a small-scale fading on the communication channel. This fading component was added to the already existing AWGN and we observed its influence on the overall performances of multiple access system.
The communication channel is used by two users transmitting signals simultaneously.
For both conventional and MMSE detectors the received signals that will be processed by the matched filters are:

$$y\_rec = A_k b_k + \sum_{j \neq k} A_j b_j \rho_{kj} + n_k + Mat\_fading \tag{8}$$

where b_j are the transmitted bits; ρ_{kj} represents the correlation coefficient between user's j signal and user's k signal; n_k is the AWGN and *Mat_fading* represents the matrix containing values of Rayleigh/Rician fading superimposed on AWGN.
Fading parameters have been created in Matlab environment and for both Rayleigh and for Rician fading there were defined: the sample time of the input signal and the maximum Doppler shift.
Simulations include analysis of equal/non-equal amplitudes for signals and the vectors for amplitudes are:

$$A = [3 \;\; 3] \; (V) \tag{9}$$

$$A = [1.5 \;\; 4] \; (V) \tag{10}$$

Since correlation between users' signals lead to multiple access interference, we studied the influence of this parameter in presence of AWGN and fading. In order to create the CDMA system we have used orthogonal/non-orthogonal spreading sequences. We have combined their effect with the effects of imperfect balance of the users' signals powers.
The normalized orthogonal/non-orthogonal spreading sequences are given in Eq. (11), (12):

$$\begin{aligned} S_1 &= [1 \;\; 1 \;\; 1 \; \text{-}1 \;\; 1 \;\; 1 \;\; 1 \; \text{-}1] / \sqrt{8} \\ S_2 &= [1 \;\; 1 \;\; 1 \; \text{-}1 \; \text{-}1 \; \text{-}1 \; \text{-}1 \;\; 1] / \sqrt{8} \end{aligned} \tag{11}$$

$$\begin{aligned} S_1 &= [1 \; \text{-}1 \; \text{-}1 \;\; 1 \;\; 1 \; \text{-}1 \;\; 1 \; \text{-}1] / \sqrt{8} \\ S_2 &= [1 \; \text{-}1 \;\; 1 \; \text{-}1 \; \text{-}1 \;\; 1 \; \text{-}1 \;\; 1] / \sqrt{8} \end{aligned} \tag{12}$$

The significances of the symbols on figures in this chapter are:
M1 - multiuser detector for user 1
M2 - multiuser detector for user 2
M1 Rayleigh/Rician - multiuser detector for user 1 in presence of Rayleigh/Rician fading phenomenon
M2 Rayleigh/Rician - multiuser detector for user 2 in presence of Rayleigh/Rician fading phenomenon
All figures presented in this chapter include analysis of equal/unequal amplitudes of the signals, different correlation degrees between users' signals and the influence of fading over the global performances of the CDMA system.

4.1 Conventional multiuser detector

4.1.1 Signals with equal powers; Correlation coefficient=0

This simulation includes usage of amplitudes in Eq. (9) and orthogonal spreading sequences in (11). The results are illustrated in Fig.3.

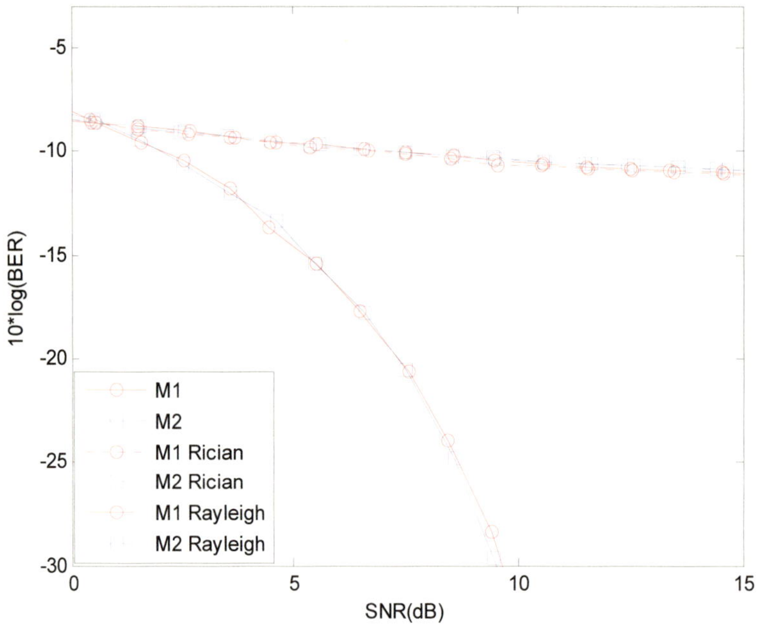

Fig. 3. Performances of conventional detector using signals with equal amplitudes, orthogonal spreading sequences, in the presence of Rayleigh/Rician fading

From Fig. 3 several observations can be made:

- Conventional multiuser detector leads to good performances when the noise on the joint channel is AWGN. The curve for BER values decreases faster reaching -32,4 dB for SNR=10 dB. When signal's level is the same as the AWGN level, the performance is still acceptable since BER is approx. -8,5 dB and it is important to mention that AWGN does not influence the performances for both users.
- If Rayleigh/Rician fading is added over the already existing AWGN, the performances are very poor and the values for BER stay almost constant at -8dB for small SNR values

and decrease slow reaching -11 dB for large SNR values. This way it can be said that the performances of this communication system are significantly influenced by fading presence superimposed on the AWGN.

- The importance of dominant component existing in Rician fading is not relevant in this case because the differences in BER values for both type of fading are very small.
- From BER values point of view it is obvious that the presence of fading is critically affecting the performances, but when fading is not added on AWGN, BER decreases with almost 38 dB as SNR varies from 0 to 15 dB.

In order to support the conclusions presented above, Table 1 illustrates the performances of the system in all three cases.

SNR (dB)	Multiuser Rayleigh BER (dB)	Multiuser Rician BER (dB)	Multiuser Detector BER (dB)
0	-8,65	-8,65	-8,49
5	-9,64	-9,64	-13,88
10	-10,42	-10,42	-32,4
15	-11	-11	-46

Table 1. BER values for equal/orthogonal case for conventional detector

4.1.2 Signals with equal powers; Correlation coefficient=0.5

This simulation includes usage of amplitudes in Eq. (9) and non-orthogonal spreading sequences in (12). Results are illustrated in Fig.4.

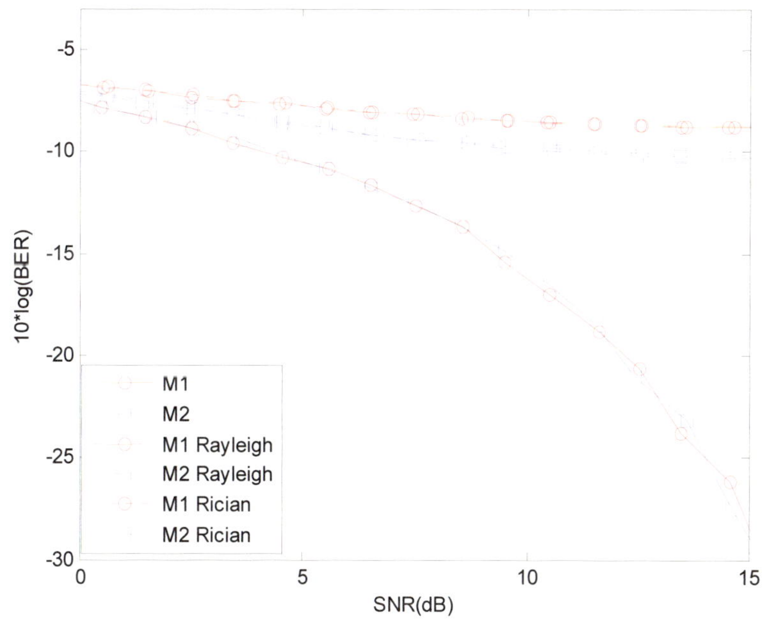

Fig. 4. Performances of conventional detector using signals with equal amplitudes, non-orthogonal spreading sequences, in the presence of Rayleigh/Rician fading

- From Fig.4 we can see that if the signals are correlated, the performances are deteriorated significantly; still the effect is not obvious in the case in which the channel is affected by AWGN only;
- Addition of Rayleigh or Rice fading decrease the BER results even more than in the previous case;
- With respect to the case studied in 4.1.1., the decrease **induced** by the fading in the correlated-users case is not very large (less than 2 dB on average);
- It appears also a small difference between the two users (around 1,5 dB).
- Yet BER values are not decreasing as much as in the previous case, and this can be interpreted as the influence of cross-correlation. For SNR=0 dB in presence of fading BER≈ -8dB represents a satisfactory performance.

A more conclusive analysis is given in Table 2.

SNR (dB)	Multiuser Rayleigh BER (dB)		Multiuser Rician BER (dB)		Multiuser Detector BER (dB)
	User1	User2	User1	User2	
0	-7,25	-7,3	-7,25	-7,3	-7,82
5	-7,8	-8,82	-7,8	-8,82	-10,53
10	-8,53	-9,83	-8,53	-9,83	-16,55
15	-8,8	-10,28	-8,8	-10,28	-28

Table 2. BER values for equal/non-orthogonal case for conventional detector

4.1.3 Signals with non-equal powers; Correlation coefficient=0

This simulation includes usage of amplitudes values from Eq. (10) and non-orthogonal spreading sequences in (11). The results are illustrated in Fig.5.

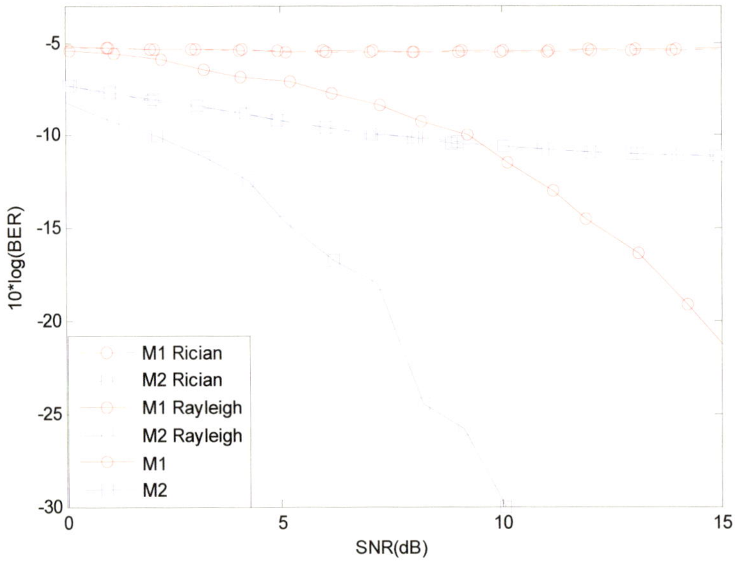

Fig. 5. Performances of conventional detector using signals with unequal amplitudes, orthogonal spreading sequences, in the presence of Rayleigh/Rician fading

Analysis of Fig. 5 provides the following conclusions:

- Regardless the communication conditions, the performances of conventional detector are notable just in the case of AWGN and only for the user with the highest power of the signal. All performances are influenced by the imperfect balance of the signals' powers and by the presence of Rayleigh/Rician fading.
- An important difference between the performances obtained for the two users can be seen only for simple conventional detector in the case of AWGN channel. This way for lower SNRs there is a difference in BER value of 8-11 dB between the performances of both users and it increases up to almost 28 dB for SNR=15dB.
- The second user, with the smallest amplitude of signal, has very poor performances: it barely achieves -6dB and decreases very slowly, for the simple conventional detector, up to -21dB for SNR=15dB which, at this point, represents a good performance.
- When Rayleigh / Rice fading is added over the AWGN, the performances of both users deteriorates dramatically, due to the inter-correlation induced by the fading and Doppler shift. The BER performances stay almost constant with SNR.
- When the signal power increase, when fading is present, the performances are not significantly improved with respect to the low power signal. The gain is about 6dB for both Rayleigh and Rician fading for large SNRs values.

From these results it is obvious that performances of simple conventional detector can be improved only with use of more powerful averaging, interpolation or equalization algorithms in order to decrease the BER as SNR increase.

SNR (dB)	Multiuser Rayleigh BER (dB)		Multiuser Rician BER (dB)		Multiuser Detector BER (dB)	
	User1	User2	User1	User2	User1	User2
0	-5,11	-7,34	-5,11	-7,34	-5,43	-8,38
5	-5,42	-9,32	-5,42	-9,32	-6,94	-14,69
10	-5,43	-10,59	-5,43	-10,59	-11,32	-30
15	-5,25	-11,15	-5,25	-11,15	-21	-48,12

Table 3. BER values for non-equal/orthogonal case for conventional detector

4.2 MMSE multiuser detector

4.2.1 Signals with equal powers; Correlation coefficient=0

Fig. 6 illustrates the results as BER vs. SNR in the case of MMSE multiuser detector when the users' signals have the same power given in Eq. (9) and the spreading sequences used are orthogonal (11).

Observing Fig. 6 several conclusion can be highlighted:

- The presence of Rayleigh/Rician fading channel affects significantly the performances of MMSE multiuser detector. Even when the communication is achieved in an ideal environment (equal powers of signals and orthogonal spreading codes), this type of detector does not manage to reduce the effect of fading and therefore BER values are poor, regardless the SNR values.

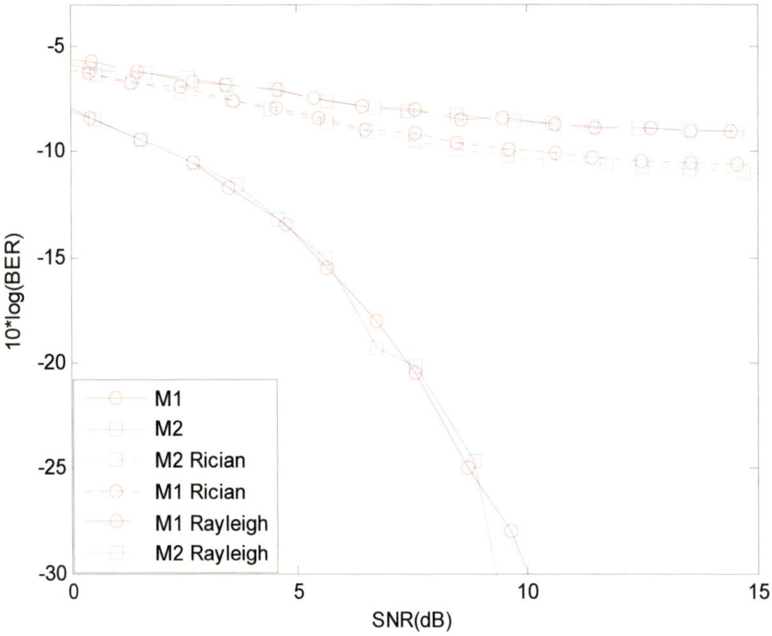

Fig. 6. Performances of MMSE detector using signals with equal amplitudes, orthogonal spreading sequences, in the presence of Rayleigh/Rician fading

- A gain of 5,6 dB can be observed for SNR between (0-15) dB in the case of Rician fading, but for Rayleigh fading the increase is 1,5 dB less than in the Rician case. For a better supervision of fading effects under these conditions one solution might be the significant increase of SNR values.
- Simple MMSE detector leads to BER=-8dB for SNR=0dB which represents a good performance of the system. The performance of simple conventional detector illustrated a BER equals also -8dB when the transmission/reception of signals was achieved in identical conditions. This is the result of MMSE detector taking into account the multiple access interference which obviously affects the performances of the system.
- In general, the results obtained with the MMSE detector are closed to the performances achieved with the conventional detector when fading is not superimposed over the AWGN channel.

Table 5 summarizes several BER values gathered from Fig.6.

SNR (dB)	Multiuser Rayleigh BER (dB)	Multiuser Rician BER (dB)	Multiuser Detector BER (dB)
0	-5	-5	-8
5	-7,37	-8,2	-13,89
10	-8,65	-10,14	-28,12
15	-9,05	-10,6	-45

Table 5. BER values for non-equal/orthogonal case for MMSE detector

4.2.2 Signals with equal powers; Correlation coefficient=0.5

The simulation conditions are: same power for signals in Eq. (9) and non-orthogonal spreading sequences in (12). Fig. 7 illustrates the behaviour of simple MMSE detector in presence of AWGN channel and in presence of Rayleigh/Rician fading channel.

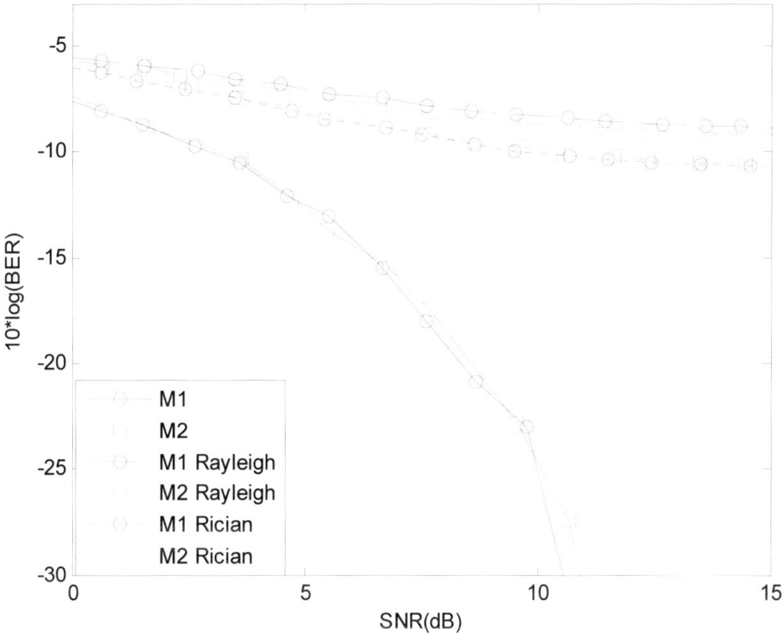

Fig. 7. Performances of MMSE detector using signals with equal amplitudes, non-orthogonal spreading sequences, in the presence of Rayleigh/Rician fading

Based on Fig.7 it can be stated:

- The influence of correlation coefficient does not affect the performances of simple MMSE detector as much as the performances of the conventional one, since both users lead to similar performances. BER values are similar to the ones obtained in the ideal case with a difference of 1dB for SNR=15dB.
- By comparison, if Rayleigh/Rician fading occurs, the performances are improved in the case of Rician fading. As SNR values increase, BER values for Rayleigh fading tend to remain constant and distant from the values achieved with Rician fading.
- In the case of Rayleigh fading the performances are degrading and, in effect, the influence of correlation between users' signals and fading superimposed on AWGN represent critical parameters for this CDMA communication system when MMSE multiuser detectors are involved.

- Under conditions of non-orthogonality between signals and Rician fading, the system can lead to acceptable BER values but only for large SNR values.

Table 6 comes as support for the conclusions extracted from Fig. 7.

SNR (dB)	Multiuser Rayleigh BER (dB)	Multiuser Rician BER (dB)	Multiuser Detector BER (dB)
0	-6,11	-6,11	-7,64
5	-6,81	-7,83	-12,83
10	-8,21	-9,76	-23,01
15	-9,2	-10,73	-50

Table 6. BER values for equal/non-orthogonal case for MMSE detector

4.2.3 Signals with non-equal powers; Correlation coefficient=0

Simulation assumed that users have signal with different powers (determined by the amplitudes in Eq (9)) and signals are not correlated (spreading sequences given in Eq. (10)).

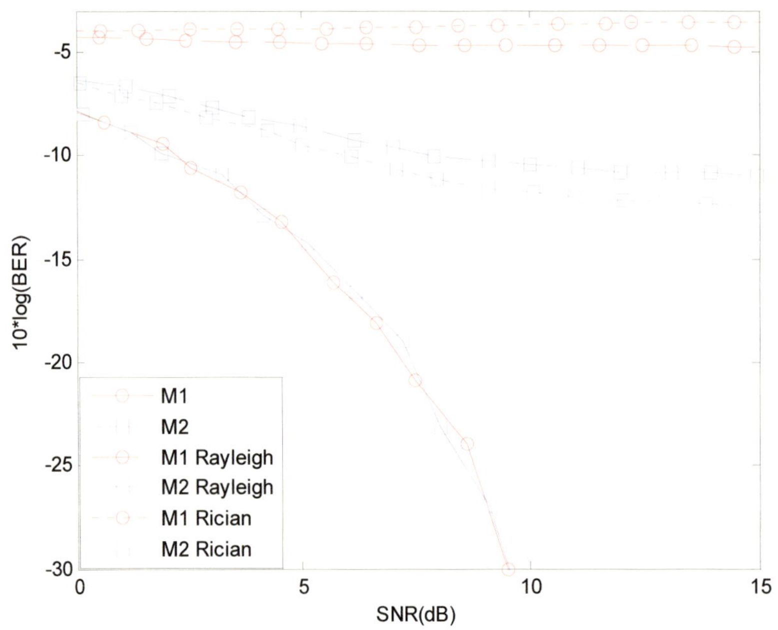

Fig. 8. Performances of MMSE detector using signals with unequal amplitudes, orthogonal spreading sequences, in the presence of Rayleigh/Rician fading

Discussion on Fig. 8 leads to the following conclusions:

- The performances of the simple MMSE multiuser detector are improved in this case, being comparable to performances obtained in the ideal case. For SNR=5dB, it can be achieved a BER approx. -14 dB. This proves that MMSE detector, in an AWGN channel, can overcome the deficiency of imperfect ballast signals.
- For the low-power user, the performances degrade as SNR increase when fading is added over the AWGN. It appears that BER remains constant at about -4,5 dB for larger SNRs.
- Acceptable values for BER can be obtained in the case of Rician fading for the high-power user. It can be seen that BER values decrease constantly for all SNR interval studied. For SNR=15 dB, BER equals -12,41 dB but still far from the performance achieved with simple MMSE detector (BER≈-44dB for the same SNR value).
- In the presence of fading added over the AWGN, MMSE detector cannot reduce the effect of non-equal powers of signals and, in conclusion, the behaviour of the system, for each user, is completely different. Good performances are achieved for the user with the highest power of the signal.
- As an advantage, if the channel is described only by AWGN, MMSE detector can reduce/almost eliminate the theoretical disadvantage introduces by imperfect balanced amplitudes of signals. Both users illustrate the same behaviour for all SNR values.

Table 7 consists of values of BER for every user in all studied cases presented in Fig.8.

SNR (dB)	Multiuser Rayleigh BER (dB)		Multiuser Rician BER (dB)		Multiuser Detector BER (dB)
	User1	User2	User1	User2	User1-2
0	-4,3	-6,55	-4	-6,55	-8
5	-4,58	-8,55	-3,93	-9,48	-14,23
10	-4,73	-10,47	-3,73	-11,76	-33,98
15	-4,76	-10,99	-3,6	-12,41	-43,64

Table 7. BER values for non-equal/orthogonal case for MMSE detector

The final section "Conclusion" summarizes the conclusions deduced from all simulation results and enumerated in Chapter 4.

5. Conclusion

The analysis of multiuser detection technique is still under research because of the changes appearing in the communication environment. Phenomenon such as fading may occur due to propagation of the signals on multiple paths between transmitter and receiver or may appear when the signals are shadowing from obstacles from the propagation paths (affecting the wave propagation). Both conventional and MMSE multiuser detector's performances are significantly affected by the fading phenomenon.

- In the case of conventional detector, the best BER values are achieved in the case of perfect orthogonality of signals and when all users have the same amplitude of the signal. This way BER can reach -14 dB for SNR=5dB and the curve of BER values decreases very fast as SNR increases.
- When fading is added to the AWGN on the channel, conventional detector cannot eliminate this disadvantage and therefore BER values tends to remain constant. The performances are very poor whether we analyse Rayleigh or Rician fading and BER goes around -8dB for all SNR values.
- In the case of conventional multiuser detector, the effect of imperfect balanced signals is important and it represents a critical parameter that affects the performances of the system. This way the user with low-power signal may not achieve its communication due to the fact that he cannot cross a BER value equal to -8dB and can reach -11 dB for large SNR values. Instead, the user with high-power signal achieves rapidly very good values of BER. For SNR=15dB it achieves BER approx. -13 dB.
- By comparison with performances of conventional detector, the MMSE multiuser detector is not capable to compensate almost any disadvantage and its performances are poor. Though it is obvious from Fig. 7 and Fig. 8 that MMSE detector manages to illustrate the same behaviour for both user regardless the conditions, the values for BER are still small.
- In the case of MMSE detector the worst performances are achieved when Rayleigh/Rician fading occurs. This observation is available in the case of imperfect ballast powers of the signal. Evidently, this type of detector cannot be used in presence of fading when the powers of the signals are small. Even for the user with high power signal the values for BER are not very good but the decrease of its values is constant and therefore this detector might be applied for systems in which the powers of the signals are increased.
- MMSE detector behaves well in the case of correlation between users' signals and the values of BER start from -8dB for SNR=0 dB and reach -50dB for SNR=15dB.
- In conclusion, regardless the type of studied multiuser detector the global performances are affected when fading is superimposed over the AWGN. In addition to this critical component is the effect of imperfect ballast powers of the signals. Conventional detector succeeds in compensating in a certain measure this disadvantage but for MMSE detector the performances are seriously affected. This detector might be used only in systems with high-power users. This way the best performances are achieved with conventional detector.
- The overall analysis led to the conclusion that the best performances can be achieved in presence of AWGN. If fading phenomenon occurs, better performances of the systems have been obtained in the presence of Rician fading instead of Rayleigh fading especially when high-power user is involved.
- Our future work will include integration of Rayleigh/Rician fading in optimal detector and, for all three types of detectors, a coding/decoding technique such as convolutional or turbo will be applied in order to increase the performances of these systems.

6. Acknowledgment

This research activity was supported by UEFISCU Romania under the grant PN-II ID-1695 / No.635 / 2009 and by NATO's Public Diplomacy Division in the framework of "Science for Peace" through the SfP-982469 "Reconfigurable Interoperability of Wireless Communications Systems (RIWCoS)" project.

7. References

Verdu S. (1998). *Multiser Detection*, 1st ed. Cambridge University Press, 1998

Sakrison D. J. (1966). *Stochastic approximation: A recursive method for solving regression problems*, Advances in Communication Systems, no. 2, pp. 51-106, 1966

Halunga S., Vizireanu D.N. (2009). "Performance evaluation for conventional and MMSE multiuser detection algorithms in imperfect reception conditions", Digital Signal Processing, Elsevier, ISSN: 1051-2004, p 166-168, 2009

Sayeed A.M., Kadous T.A. (2002). *Equivalence of Linear MMSE Detection in DS-CDMA and MC-CDMA Systems over Time and Frequency Selective Channels*, EURASIP Journal on Advances in Signal Processing, Vol. 2002,Issue: 12 Pages, record No.: 1335-1354

Halunga S., Vizireanu D.N, Fratu O. (2010)„Imperfect cross-correlation and amplitude balance effects on conventional multiuser decoder with turbo encoding", Digital Signal Processing, 2010, Elsevier, ISSN: 1051-2004, p. 191-200 (ISI Web of Knowledge) (2010)

Marcu I., Halunga S., Fratu O., Constantin I. (2007)., *Turbocoding Performances with and without Fading*, ECAI 2007 - International Conference - Second Edition, Electronics, Computers and Artificial Intelligence, 29th - 30th June, 2007, Piteşti MTU EE5560: *Multiuser Detection*, CRN #13888; Section: 0A, Spring 2005

Halunga S., Marcu I., Fratu O., Marghescu I. (2009). *Orthogonality, amplitude and number of users efects on conventional multiuser detection using turbo decoding*, EUROCON 2009, 18-23 May 2009, Sankt Petersburg, Rusia, pp. 2000-2004

Verdú S (2000). *Wireless Bandwidth in the Making*, IEEE Communications Magazine, pp.53-58, ISBN 0163-6804, July 2000

Poor V (1997). *Probability of Error in MMSE Multiuser Detection*, IEEE Transactions On Information Theory, vol. 43, no. 3, pp.858-871, May 1997

Khairnar K., Nema S. (2005). *Comparison of Multi-User Detectors of DS-CDMA System*, World Academy of Science, Engineering and Technology 10, pp. 193-195

Bohnke R., Wubben D., Kuhn V., Kammeyer K-D. (2003). *Reduced complexity MMSE detection for BLAST architectures*, IEEE Global Telecommunications Conference, 2003. GLOBECOM '03, vol.4, pp. 2258 - 2262, ISBN: 0-7803-7974-8, 1-5 Dec. 2003

Sklar B. (1997). *Rayleigh Fading Channels in Mobile Digital Communication Systems*, Part I: Characterization," IEEE Commun. Mag., vol. 35, no. 9, Sept. 1997, pp. 136–46

Li, G., Fan, P., Letaief, K.B. (2009). *Rayleigh fading networks: a cross-layer way*, IEEE Transactions on Communications, vol. 57, pp. 520 – 529, ISSN: 0090-6778, 2009

Rahnema M. (2008). *UMTS Network Planning, Optimization, and Inter-Operation with GSM*, Wiley Publishing House, N-13: 978-0470823019, 320 pp, 2007

Goldsmith A.(2005). *Wireless Communications*, Cambridge University Press, ISBN 978-0-521-83716-3, 672 pp., 2005

9

System-Level Simulations Investigating the System-on-Chip Implementation of 60-GHz Transceivers for Wireless Uncompressed HD Video Communications

Domenico Pepe[1] and Domenico Zito[1,2]
[1]*Tyndall National Institute*
[2]*Dept. of Electrical and Electronic Engineering, University College Cork, Cork, Ireland*

1. Introduction

In 2001, the Federal Communications Commission (FCC) allocated an unlicensed 7-GHz wide band in the radio-frequency (RF) spectrum from 57 to 64 GHz for wireless communications (FCC, 2001). This is the widest portion of radio-frequency spectrum ever allocated in an exclusive way for wireless unlicensed applications, allowing multi-gigabit-per-second wireless communications. Other countries worldwide have allocated the 60-GHz band for unlicensed wireless communications (Japan (Ministry of Internal Affairs and Communications [MIC]), 2008), Australia (Australian Communications and Media Authority [ACMA], 2005), Korea (Ministry of Information Communication of Korea, 2006), Europe (ETSI, 2006)), allowing in principle a universal compatibility for the systems operating in that band. Fig. 1 shows the 60-GHz frequency band allocations in USA, Canada, Japan, Australia, Korea and Europe.
Another reason that makes the 60-GHz band very attractive is the coverage range, which is limited to about 10m caused by the dramatic attenuation in the signal propagation. This is due primarily to the high path loss at 60GHz, and moreover the peak of resonance of the oxygen molecule, allowing several Wireless Personal Area Networks (WPANs) to operate closely without interfering. Moreover, at the millimetre-waves (mm-waves) it is easier to implement very directional antennas, thus allowing the implementations of highly directional communication links. Line-Of-Sight (LOS) communication may help in alleviating the design challenges of the wireless transceiver.
One of the most promising applications that will benefit of the huge amount of bandwidth available in the 60-GHz range is the uncompressed High-Definition (HD) video communication (Singh, et al., 2008). The reasons that make attractive the uncompressed video streaming are that compression and decompression (codec) in transmitter and receiver, respectively, exhibit some drawbacks such as latency which can not be tolerated in real time applications (e.g. videogames), degradation in the video quality, and compatibility issues between devices that use different codec techniques. The HD video signal has a resolution of

1920×1080 pixels, with each pixel described by three colour components of 8 bits (24 bits per pixel) and a frame rate of 60Hz. Thus, a data rate of about 3 Gb/s is required for the transmission of the sole video data, without considering audio data and control signals.

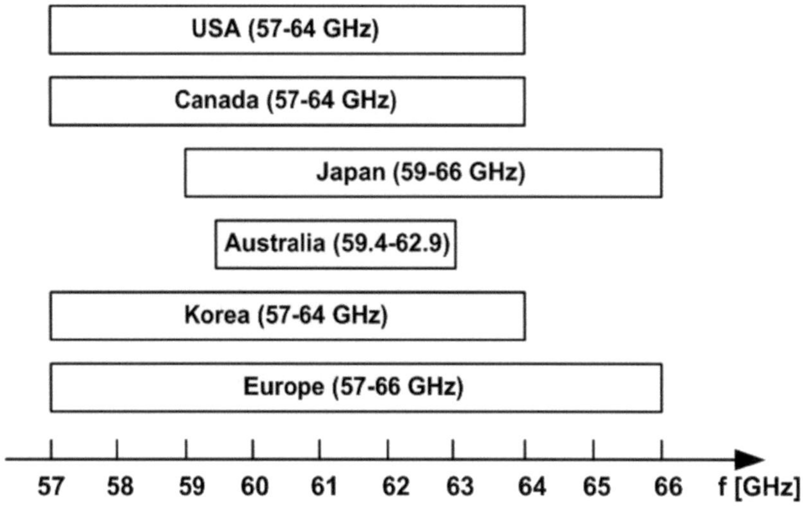

Fig. 1. Worldwide allocations of 60-GHz unlicensed bands

Even though III-V technologies such as Gallium Arsenide (GaAs) allow the implementation of faster active devices, Complementary Metal-Oxide-Semiconductor (CMOS) technology is the best choice for low cost and high volume market applications. The recent advances in silicon technologies allow us to implement integrated transceivers operating at the millimetre-waves, enabling the realization of a new class of mass-market devices for very high data rate communications (Niknejad, 2007). Some 60-GHz building blocks and entire transceivers have been already published (Terry Yao, et al., 2006; Marcu, et al., 2009). In spite of these encouraging results in the integration, there is a lack of the literature on system-level study, which could allow us to get an insight into the implications of the building-blocks specifications and technology potential and limitations about the overall wireless system-on-chip implementation. Such a study could contribute to fulfil this lack of the literature and identify more in detail the circuit- and system-level design challenges, as dealt preliminarly in (Pepe&Zito, 2010a; Pepe&Zito, 2010b).

This Chapter reports a system-level study of a 60-GHz wireless system for uncompressed HD video communications, carried out by means of MATLAB®. In particular, the study is addressed to explore the implementation of 60-GHz transceivers in nano-scale CMOS technology. The implementation in MATLAB® of a model of the high data rate physical layer based on the specification released by the consortium WirelessHD® (WirelessHD, 2009) will be discussed. The system simulations of the bit error rate (BER) are carried out in order to derive the requirements of the 60-GHz transceiver building blocks. This study takes into consideration the performance achievable by using a 65nm CMOS technology. This study includes also system simulations which consider some primary non-idealities of RF transceivers, as the Power Amplifier (PA) non-linearity, Local Oscillator (LO) Phase Noise (PN) and receiver Noise Figure (NF). In Section 2, the standard WirelessHD® is described in short. In Section 3, the system simulations of the High data Rate Physical layer (HRP) of the 60-GHz system for uncompressed HD video communications by using MATLAB® are described and some results are reported. Moreover, the specifications of the building-blocks are derived. In Section 4, the results of system simulations obtained by taking into account transceiver non-idealities are shown. In Section 5, the conclusions are drawn.

2. Introduction to WirelessHD® specifications

Several international standard organizations and associations of industrial partners are working to define the specifications for millimetre-wave systems operating in the 60-GHz band (IEEE 802.15.3c, 2009; Wireless Gigabit Alliance; WirelessHD). The WirelessHD consortium is an industry-led effort aimed at defining a worldwide standard specification for the next-generation wireless digital network interfaces for consumer electronics and personal computing products. The WirelessHD specifications have been planned and optimized for wireless display connectivity, achieving in its first generation implementation high-speed rates up to 4Gb/s at 10 meters for the consumer electronics, based on the 60-GHz millimetre-wave frequency band. A summary of the specifications required for the High data Rate Physical (HRP) layer is shown in Table 1 (WirelessHD, 2009).
WirelessHD® defines a wireless protocol that enables consumer devices to create a Wireless Video Area Network (WVAN) with the possibility of streaming uncompressed HD video data, at a typical maximum range of 10m. WVANs consist of one Coordinator and zero or more Stations (see Fig. 2). Typically the Coordinator is the sink of the video stream transmitted by the Stations, for example a video display, while the Station can be a source and/or sink of data. The Coordinator and the Stations communicate through a HRP, while the Stations can communicate between each other by means of a Low data Rate Physical layer (LRP). The HRP supports multi-Gb/s throughput at distance of 10m through adaptive antenna technology. The HRP is very directional and can only be used for unidirectional casting. The LRP supports lower data rates and has a omni-directional coverage. A summary of the specifications defined for the HRP layer are shown in Table 1 (WirelessHD, 2009).

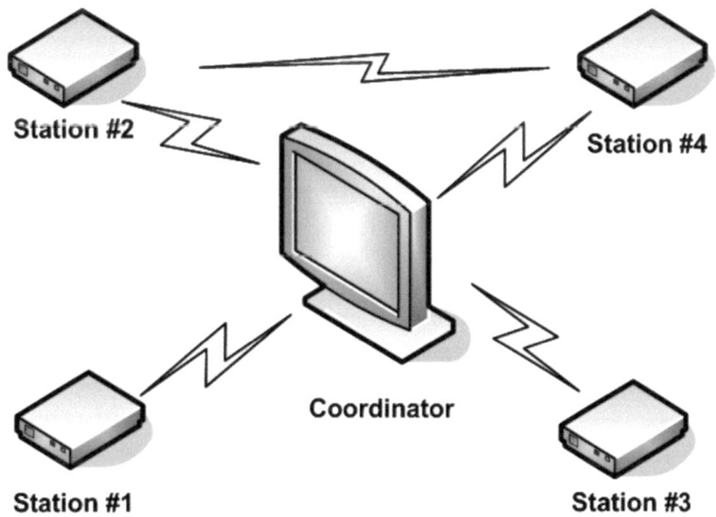

Fig. 2. Scheme of a possible WVAN

Parameter	Value
Bandwidth	1.76 GHz
Reference sampling rate	2.538 GS/s
Number of subcarriers	512
Guard interval	64/ Reference sampling rate
Symbol duration	FFT period+Guard interval
Number of data subcarriers	336
Number of DC subcarriers	3
Number of pilots	16
Number of null subcarriers	157
Modulation	QPSK,16QAM-OFDM
Outer block code	RS(216/224)
Inner code	1/3,2/3(EEP), 4/5+4/7(UEP)
Operating range	10m
BER	$<4x10^{-11}$

Table 1. Summary of the 60-GHz WirelessHD® HRP Specifications

The 57-66GHz band has been divided in four channels for the HRP, of which not all are available everywhere, i.e. depending on the regulatory restrictions of the different countries. A BER of 4×10^{-11} (quasi error-free) at an operating range of 10m is required in order to have a pixel error ratio less than 10^{-9} for 24 bit color. This is achieved by using a concatenated channel code made by an outer Reed-Solomon (216/224) block code and an inner convolutional code, (4/5) and (4/7) for the least significant bits and the most significant bits respectively (Unequal Error Protection, UEP). This is due to the fact that in video communication, unlike data communication, the bits are not equally important: the most significant bits have more impact on the video quality (Singh, et al. 2008), thus the most significant bits are coded with a more robust code.

3. High data rate layer system simulations by MATLAB®

For integrated circuits characterized by a low or moderate complexity, the traditional design approach is bottom-up. Here, the building blocks are designed individually and then co-integrated and verified all together. This approach, while still useful for small systems, exhibits several drawbacks if applied also to large designs. In fact, large designs could require very long simulation time and considerable hardware (since the system is described at transistor level). Moreover, in large designs, the greatest impact on performance and functionality is found at the architectural level more than at the circuit level. Therefore, to address the design of modern integrated circuits characterized by complex architectures and consisting of mixed analog and digital subsystems, a top-down design approach is needed to overcome the limitations of the bottom-up design strategy (Kundert, 2003). In a top-down approach, the architecture is defined by means of block diagrams, so that it could be simulated and optimized by using a system simulator such as MATLAB®. From these system-level simulations, the specifications of the single blocks can be derived accurately. The circuits are designed individually to meet such specifications, and finally the circuits are co-integrated into a single chip. Last, the chip performance are verified and compared with the original requirements.

In Subsection 3.1 the HRP layer based on the 60-GHz WirelessHD communication standard and its modelling in MATLAB® are described. In Subsection 3.2, the results of BER simulations of such system are shown and the specifications of the building blocks for the RF transceiver at 60-GHz are derived.

3.1 HRP transceiver in MATLAB®: description and implementation

In order to evaluate the feasibility and the performance required by the 60-GHz wireless transceivers, system simulations of a high data rate physical layer can be carried out within MATLAB®. The block diagram of the 60-GHz physical layer implemented in MATLAB® is shown in Fig. 3.

After that the uncompressed HD video source data have been processed by the Media Access Control (MAC) layer, an error protection is added to them. The input stream is coded by means of a concatenated channel code made by an outer code (216/224, Reed-Solomon) and an inner code (4/5, 4/7 convolutional). This error protection scheme is fairly robust: in case of Digital Video Broadcasting-Satellite (DVB-S) standard systems described a block diagram similar to that shown in Fig. 3, it can provide a quasi-error free BER of 10^{-10} - 10^{-11} with non-corrected error rates of 10^{-2} (DVB-S; Fisher, 2008). Interleavers are added in order to protect the transmission against burst errors. MATLAB® provides built-in functions for error-control coding and interleaving. Reed-Solomon codes are based on the principle of linear algebra and they protect a block of data with an error protection.

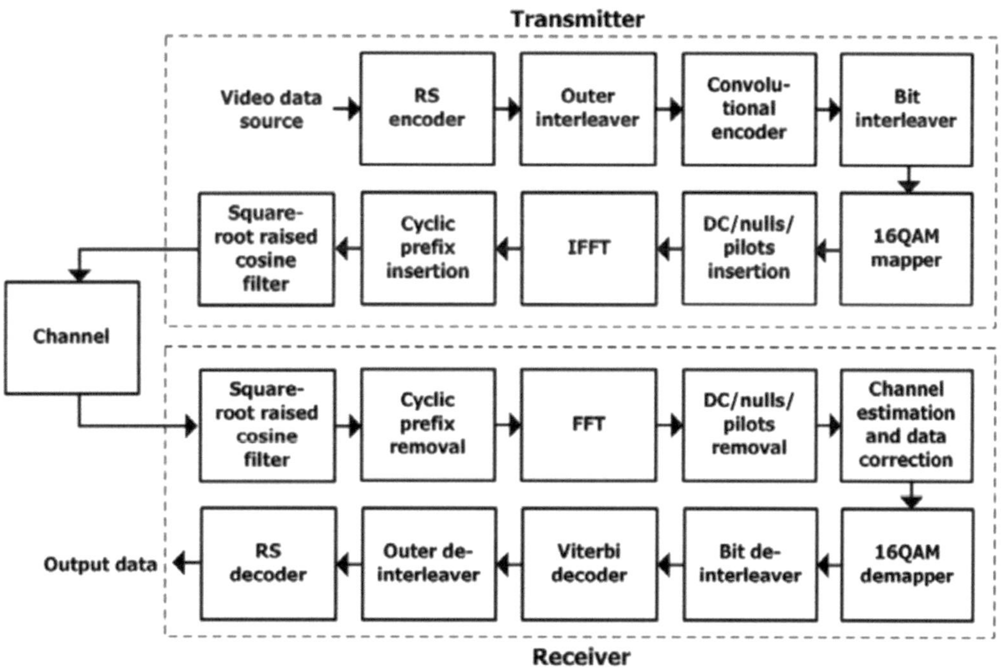

Fig. 3. Block diagram of the 60-GHz WirelessHD HRP model implemented in MATLAB

Reed-Solomon encoder and decoder can be created with the functions `rsenc` and `rsdec` respectively:

```
% RS encoder
RScode=rsenc(msg, nRS, kRS);
...
% RS decoder
decoded = rsdec(rxcode,nRS,kRS);
```

where `msg` is the input string of symbols to be encoded, `nRS` and `kRS` are the length of the encoded and original symbols, 224 and 216, respectively. Interleaving and de-interleaving are easily performed by means of the functions `randintrlv` and `randdeintrlv`.

The convolutional encoder uses a constrain length equal to 7, mother code rate 1/3, generator polynomial g0=133oct, g1=171oct, g2= 165oct (IEEE, 2009). The standard require eight parallel convolutional encoders, in which the first four encoders for the first outer Reed-Solomon coding branch and the last four encoders for the second outer Reed-Solomon coding branch. In Equal Error Protection (EEP) mode all the eight encoders shall use the same inner code rate. In the UEP mode, the top four encoders shall use rate 4/7 convolutional codes, while the bottom four encoders shall use rate 4/5 convolutional codes. In order to ease the simulations, the EEP mode has been considered, with a punctured code rate of 2/3 (obtained by the mother code 1/3). Convolutional encoded data is punctured in order to make the desired code rate using the puncturing pattern [1 1 1 0 0 0]. The code implemented in MATLAB® is shown hereinafter.

```
% Convolutional encoding
trellis=poly2trellis(7,[133 171 165]);
punctcode=convenc(outerbits, trellis, [1 1 1 0 0 0]);
...
% Convolutional decoding
decodedmsg=vitdec(rxmsg, trellis, tblen, 'trunc', 'hard',
[1 1 1 0 0 0]);
```

`poly2trellis` is a function that converts the convolutional code polynomials to a trellis description. That is used by the function `convenc, that` encodes the binary vector `outerbits` using the convolutional encoder whose MATLAB trellis structure is `trellis`, applying the punctured pattern [1 1 1 0 0 0]. On the decoder side, the function `vitdec` decodes the vector `rxmsg` using the Viterbi algorithm.

After the coding operation, the data are modulated. A data rate of 3.807Gb/s is achieved by employing a 16 Quadrature Amplitude Modulation (QAM) - Orthogonal Frequency-Division Multiplexing (OFDM) modulation (WirelessHD, 2009). The bits are grouped in

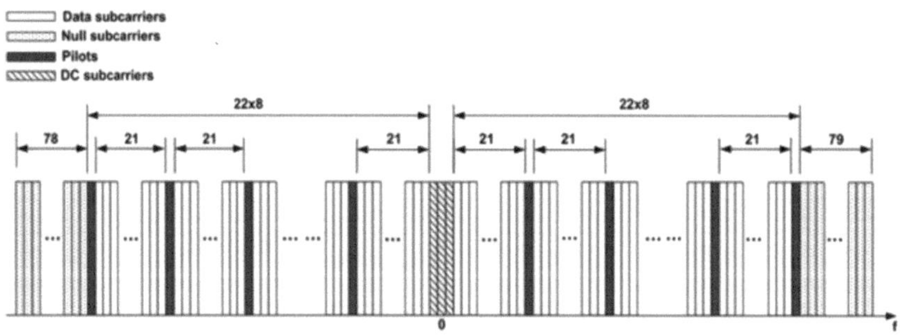

Fig. 4. OFDM symbol in the frequency domain (with the specific choice of pilots, dc and nulls subcarriers)

symbols of four bits each, having values between 0 and 2^4-1=15. These data are sent to the symbol mapper, which maps the input bits into 16QAM Gray-coded symbols. The 16QAM mapper and demapper can be implemented by means of the functions `qammod` and `qamdemod` available in MATLAB®. The output data of the symbol mapper are then parallelized, and pilots, dc and null tones are added up. The pilot tones are used for frame detection, carrier frequency offset estimation and channel estimation (Chiu, et al., 2000). Typically the central subcarriers are not used since they correspond to a dc component in baseband. The outer subcarriers are usually unused for data transmission in order to allow a low-pass filtering with a larger transition band after the digital to analog converter (Olsson & Johansonn, 2005). The HRP subcarriers in a OFDM symbols could be allocated as shown in Fig. 4.
An Inverse Fast Fourier Transform (IFFT) operation (size 512) is then applied to the resulting stream in order to have OFDM symbols in which each subcarrier is modulated by the 16QAM symbols provided by the mapper, dc, nulls and pilots. In order to improve the immunity to inter-symbol interferences, a cyclic prefix consisting of the last 64 samples of the symbol is inserted at the beginning of the OFDM symbol itself. A section of code of the modulator and cyclic prefix insertion is reported hereinafter.

```
% 16QAM modulation
16qammod=qammod(4bitsymbols, 16, 0, 'gray');
modreshaped=reshape(16qammod, 336, mappedmsglenght/336).';
% dc, nulls, pilots insertion
ofdmsymbolf=[zeros(mappedmsglenght/336,78)
    pilot*ones(mappedmsglenght/336,1)
            modreshaped(:,[1:21]) ...
...
% OFDM modulation
 ofdmsymbolt=ifft(ofdmsymbolf.').';
% cyclix prefix insertion
 ofdmsymbolt=[ofdmsymbolt (:,[449:512]) ofdmsymbolt];
```

The data stream is shaped by means of a square-root raised cosine filter and then transmitted.
As for the receiver, after that the down-conversion and filtering have been performed, the cyclic prefix is removed from the OFDM symbol, and the Fast Fourier Transform (FFT) operation is carried out on the received stream. Since the output of the dc mapper is sensitive to the amplitude of the input symbols, a block for channel estimation and gain correction has been implemented in MATLAB®. For each OFDM symbol received, the channel response C(k) is estimated extracting the amplitude received pilot values and dividing them by the expected values as follows:

$$C(k)=\frac{P_{RX}(k)}{P(k)} \tag{1}$$

where k is the pilot index, $P_{RX}(k)$ are the amplitude of received pilot values and P(k) the amplitude of the expected pilots. Then the data subcarriers are multiplied by the inverse of the coefficient C(k) of the nearest pilot tone.
System simulations have been performed by considering an Additive White Gaussian Noise (AWGN) channel. The BER simulations of the system shown in Fig. 3 have been carried out. In particular, an input string of about 6,000,000 bits has been used as source for the 60-GHz

system, limited by the hardware capabilities of our workstation. The curves of the BER at the input of the baseband receiver, before and after the concatenated channel coded blocks, are shown in Fig. 5.

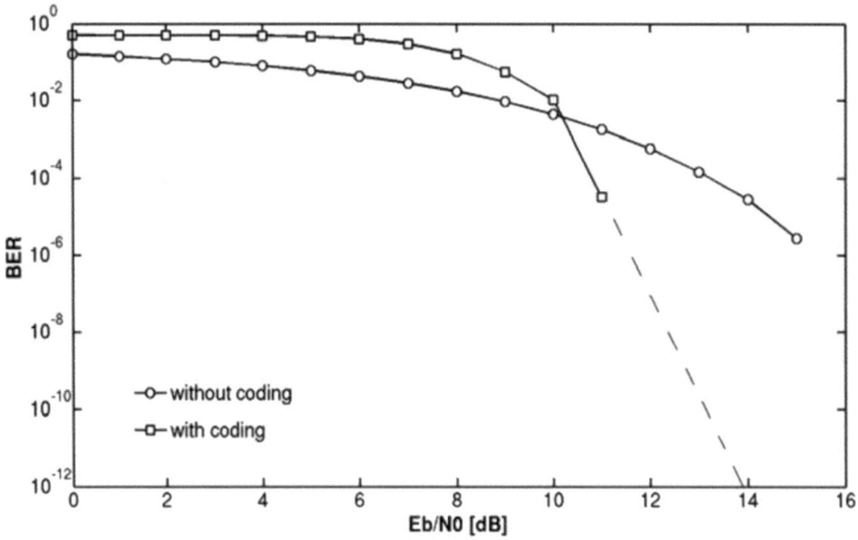

Fig. 5. BER with and without concatenated channel coding. The dashed line is a linear extrapolation of the BER curve obtained by means of simulations of the system of Fig. 3

By extending linearly the last part of the curve of the BER (that is a worsening condition with respect to the real case), we obtain a BER of 4×10^{-11} for a energy per bit to noise power spectral density ratio (Eb/N0) lower than 14 dB, which corresponds to a signal-to-noise ratio (SNR) of 16.74 dB, as calculated from the formula

$$SNR|_{dB} = Eb/N0|_{dB} + 10\times Log_{10}k + 10\times Log_{10}\left(\frac{dsc}{nFFT}\right) + 10\times Log_{10}\left(\frac{nFFT}{nFFT+CP}\right) + \\ +10\times Log_{10}\left(\frac{kRS}{nRS}\right) + 10\times Log_{10}\left(\frac{kCon}{nCon}\right) \quad (2)$$

where $k=Log_2(M)$ and M is the size of the modulation (16 in this case), dsc is the number of data subcarriers (336), nFFT the FFT size (512), CP is the guard interval (64), kRS/nRS is the Reed-Solomon coding rate (216/224) and kCon/nCon is the convolutional coding rate (2/3).

3.2 HRP transceiver in MATLAB®: simulation results and system specifications

From the system simulations described in Section 3 we can see that a SNR of 16.74 dB allows the achievement of a quasi-error free BER of 4×10^{-11}. A SNR of 23 dB has been considered to have 6 dB of margin at least. The receiver sensitivity is equal to

$$S_{RX}|_{dB} = k_B T|_{dB} + 10\times Log_{10}(B) + SNR|_{dB} + NF|_{dB} \quad (3)$$

where k_B is the Boltzmann constant (1.23×10^{-23}[W/K]), T is the antenna temperature (290K), B the occupied bandwidth (2GHz) and NF the receiver noise figure. In order to have a

receiver sensitivity of at least -50 dBm (Karaoguz, 2009), NF is required to be lower than 8 dB. This value is achievable in latest CMOS processes, e.g. 65nm.
In this study, we consider direct-conversion transceivers (homodyne, see Fig. 6) since in principle they allow the highest level of integration.

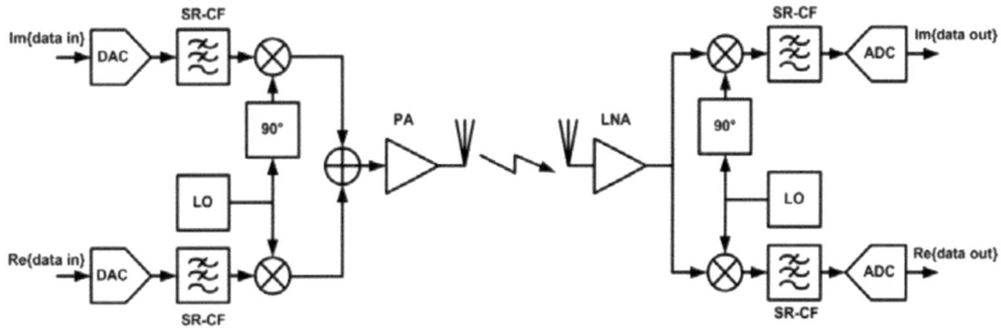

Fig. 6. Block diagram of a homodyne transceiver

Therefore, by taking into account the capabilities of the 65nm CMOS technology at 60 GHz, if we consider the achievable performance for a Low Noise Amplifier (LNA) such as a gain of 15 dB and noise figure of 6 dB (Terry Yao, et al., 2007; Huang, et al., 2009; Zito, et al., 2007)) and for the mixer, such as a gain of -2dB and noise figure of 15 dB (Zhang, et al., 2009)), the resulting noise figure of the LNA-Mixer cascade equals to 6.5 dB.
At 60 GHz the path loss is very high. At 10m (this is the operating range required by the standard WirelessHD®) the free-space path loss amounts to

$$PL\Big|_{dB} = \left(\frac{4\pi df}{c}\right)^2\Bigg|_{dB} = 88dB \tag{4}$$

where d is the operating range (10m), f is the carrier frequency (60 GHz) and c is the speed of light in air (3×10^8).
Thus, it results that the power delivered by the power amplifier has to be quite high in order to provide a signal with adequate power at the receiver antenna. The typical antenna gain is expected to be 10 to 20 dBi (Karaoguz, 2009). If we consider an antenna gain of 10 dB (both in transmission and reception) and NF of 7 dB, then the output power delivered by the PA has to be 14 dBm, at least, in order to achieve an operating range of 10m. This is a high value for the CMOS implementation of the PA. Recently, examples of PAs with 1-dB compression point higher than 14 dBm have been reported in literature (Law, et al., 2010; Jen, et al., 2009). In spite of this, the PA has to be also highly linear, since OFDM modulation is characterized by a very high peak-to-average power ratio (the back-off amounts approximately to 10dB).

4. Transceiver non-idealities

The performance of radio-frequency transceivers are usually described by means of deterministic quantities such as gain, noise, linearity, bandwidth. On the other hand, digital baseband circuitry performance are described in terms of statistic quantities, such as the BER. In order to fill the gap between digital and RF circuits, models running in both the environments are needed. Radio-frequency behavioural models allow us to introduce radio-frequency non-linearity and simulate their effects in the overall system comprehensive of the digital baseband part (Kundert, 2003; Chen, 2006). Behavioural models of the building blocks of the RF transceiver can be developed within MATLAB® and inserted into the overall system model description in order to evaluate how the transceiver non-linearities affect the performance of the system.

4.1 Power amplifier non-linearity effects

Since OFDM modulation presents a very high peak-to-average power ratio, the effect of PA non-linearity can not be neglected in system simulations.
The output voltage (v_{out}) of a memory-less non-linear amplifier can be expressed by:

$$v_{out}(t)=a_1 v_{in}(t)+a_2 v_{in}^2(t)+a_3 v_{in}^3(t)+... \tag{5}$$

where v_{in} is the input voltage.
By applying a sinusoidal input voltage at frequency ω_0 ($v_{in} = V_0\cos(\omega_0 t)$) the output can be expressed as follows:

$$v_{out}(t)=\frac{a_2 V_0^2}{2}+\left(a_1 V_0+\frac{3a_3 V_0^3}{4}\right)\cos(\omega_0 t)+\frac{a_2 V_0^2}{2}\cos(2\omega_0 t)+\frac{a_3 V_0^3}{4}\cos(3\omega_0 t)+... \tag{6}$$

If we consider the fundamental harmonic only, the Input-referred 1-dB Compression Point (ICP1dB) can be calculated from the formula

$$20\log(a_1 V_{i1dB})\text{-1dB}=20\log(a_1 v_i+\frac{3}{4}a_3 v_i^3) \tag{7}$$

where V_{i1dB} is the voltage ICP1dB.
The third-order polynomial model above of the PA can be implemented in MATLAB® in order to include the non-linear effects of the gain compression of power amplifier in system simulations. By exploiting Equation (7), the MATLAB® code of the PA can be written as follows:

```
PA_ICP1dB_dBm=PA_OCP1dB_dBm-PA_gain_dB+1;
PA_IV1dB_dB=PA_ICP1dB_dBm-30; % dBm to dB
PA_IV1dB=10.^(PA_IV1dB_dB/20) % dB to linear
PA_Vgain=10.^(PA_gain_dB/20);
PAout=ofdmsymbolt.*PA_Vgain-
        (ofdmsymbolt.^3).*(0.11.*PA_Vgain.*(1/(PA_IV1dB.^2)));
```

where `PA_gain_dB` and `PA_Vgain` are the PA gain (dB and linear voltage gain) set to obtain the desired average transmitted output power (i.e., 15 dBm in this study), and `PA_OCP1dB_dBm` is the Output-referred 1-dB Compression Point (OCP1dB) of the PA. The input-output characteristic of a PA, with 15-dB gain and 20-dBm OCP1dB, is shown in Fig. 7.
Fig. 8 reports the results of BER simulations for an average transmitted power of 15 dBm for several values of OCP1dB. Note that BER performance are practically unaffected for OCP1dB 10dB higher than the average transmitted power. The BER is still acceptable for OCP1dB 5dB higher than the average transmitted power, whereas for an OCP1dB equal to the average transmitted power the BER is impaired significantly.

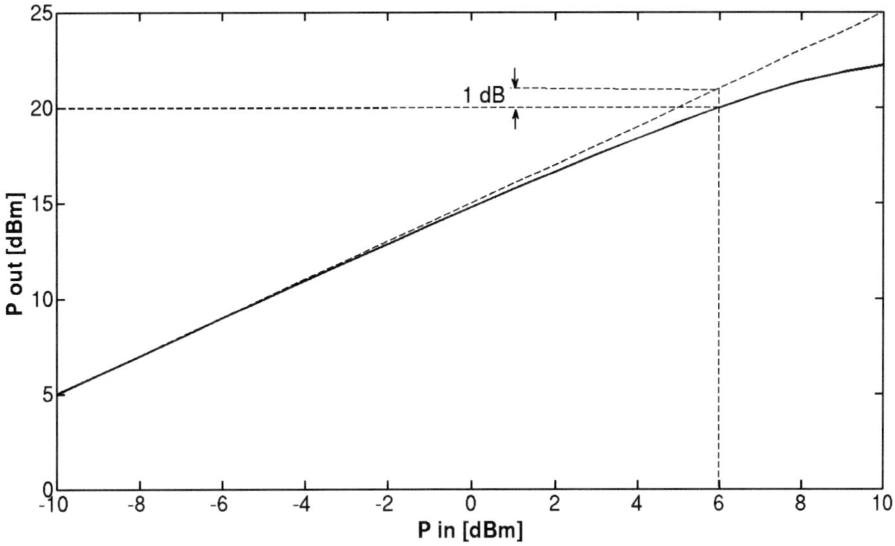

Fig. 7. Input-output characteristic of a power amplifier

These system simulations have been carried out by simulating the overall system comprehensive of the Forward Error Correction (FEC) blocks (i.e., Reed-Solomon and convolutional coding). In order to make faster simulations, BER system simulations without FEC can be performed, and then the coding gain can be applied later (i.e. from simulation results shown in Fig. we can see that for Eb/N0=14dB the BER drops from $\approx 5*10^{-4}$ without FEC to $\approx 10^{-12}$ with FEC).

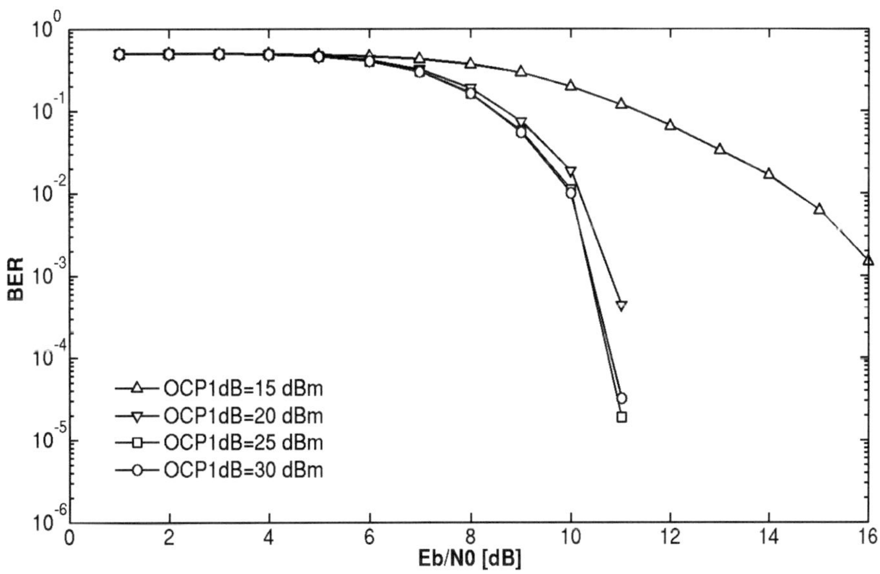

Fig. 8. BER versus Eb/N0 for several values of the output referred 1-dB compression point of the power amplifier, for an average transmitted power of of 15 dBm

4.2 Local oscillator phase noise effects

A simple model of the local oscillator phase noise can be implemented in MATLAB® in order to investigate how the phase noise affects the performance of the entire system. In order to do that, a time domain phase noise generator model has to be implemented. In this case study the Power Spectral Density (PSD) of the phase noise is modelled with a Lorentzian shape. The Lorentzian spectrum is constant at low frequencies and rolls off with a first order slope after the corner frequency (Chen, 2006). The phase noise is generated by filtering a White Gaussian Noise (WGN) through a digital filter. The power of the WGN (P_{WGN}) can be expressed as follows:

$$P_{WGN}[dB]=P_{PHASE}\big|_{dB}+PN\big|_{dB}+10\times\log(f_s)+10\times\log\left(\frac{1MHz}{f_p}\right) \tag{8}$$

where P_{PHASE} is equal to π^2, PN is the Phase Noise, f_s is the sampling frequency and f_p the corner frequency of the Lorentzian spectrum. This noise is by a first order low pass digital filter with corner frequency equal to f_p (MATLAB® code reported hereinafter).

```
% white gaussian noise
noise=wgn(m, n, Pwgn,'dBW');
% filtering
b=[1 1];
a=[(1+fs/(pi*fp)) (1-fs/(pi*fp))];
pnoise=filter(b,a,noise_wgn);
```

The normalized PSD of the LO voltage noise for f_s=100MHz and f_p=10kHz is shown in Fig. 9.

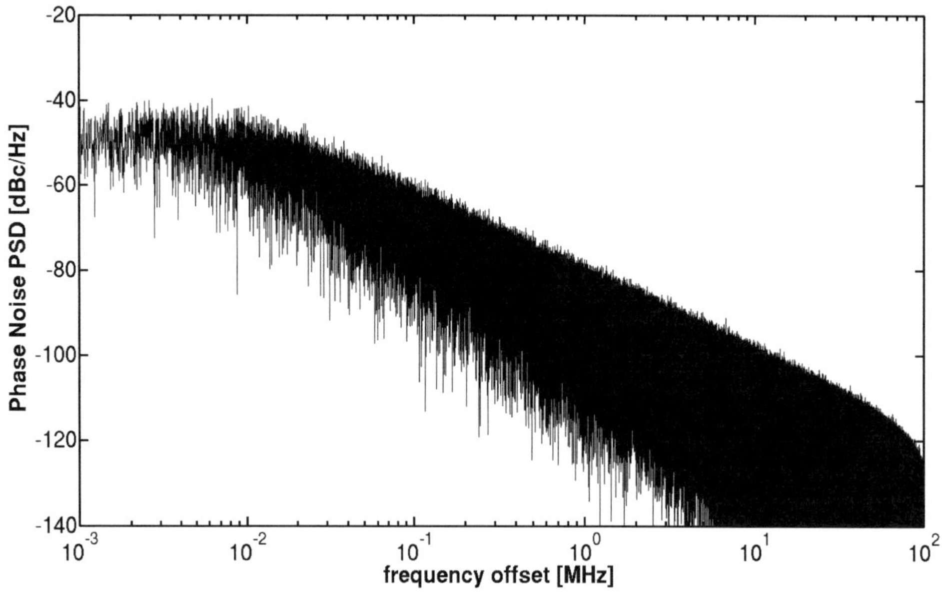

Fig. 9. PSD of the phase noise modeled in MATLAB®

In the system simulations the phase noise has been added to both the LOs of the transmitter and receiver. The BER performance for several value of LO phase noise are shown in Fig. 10. It can be noted how this system is very sensitive to the phase noise and that acceptable results are obtained only for PN lower than -100dBc/Hz.

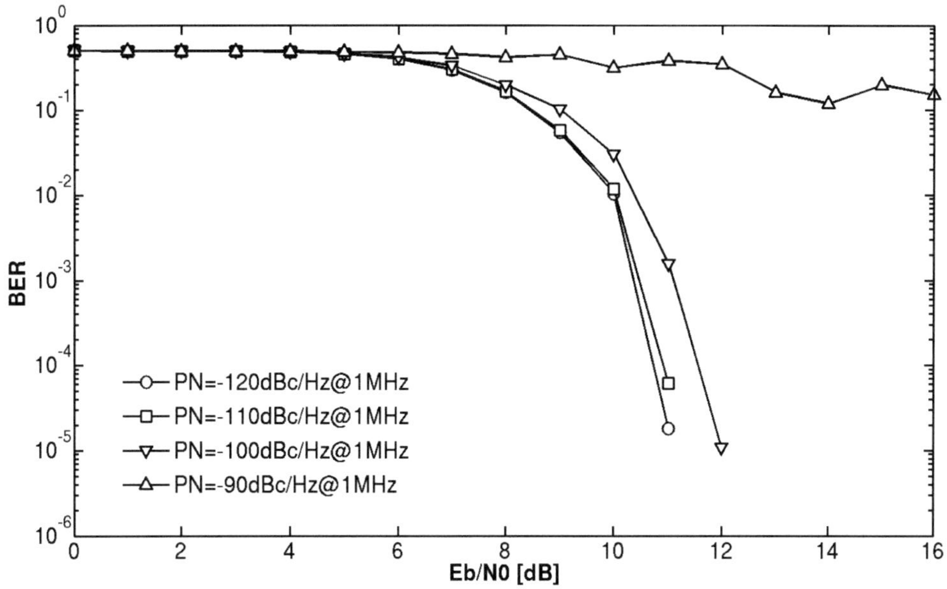

Fig. 10. BER versus Eb/N0 for several values of PN

4.3 System simulations by taking into account transceivers non-idealities

System simulations have been carried out considering an average transmitted power of 15 dBm, PA OCP1dB equal to 20 dBm, LO phase noise equal to -100dBc/Hz and noise figure of the receiver chain (i.e. LNA and mixer) equal to 7 dB, for AWGN and fading channels (Rician and Rayleigh). The results in terms of BER versus transmitter-receiver distance are shown in Fig. 11.

Acceptable performance are obtained also in case of fading channels. This is due to the channel coding, the adaptive filter at the receiver and the modulation scheme (OFDM) that is fairly robust in presence of fading channels.

It is worth mentioning that the specifications calculated in Subsection 4.1 are related to a transceiver with single-transmitter and single-receiver. In practice, the overall transceiver could be implemented on silicon by exploiting multiple transceivers connected to an array of highly directional antennas (Gilbert, et al., 2008; Doan, et al., 2004). This way, not only the antenna beam-form can be steered in order to improve the link between transmitter and receiver, but also the specifications of transmitters and receivers will be more relaxed, since the power delivered will be N times greater than that delivered by a unit element and the receiver noise figure will be reduced of $10\times Log_{10}N$ dB, where N is the number of transceivers in parallel.

Note that an increase in the number of elements of the array leads to higher power consumption of the overall communication system, thus a trade-off between performance and power consumption has to be taken into account for the optimal design of the wireless transceiver.

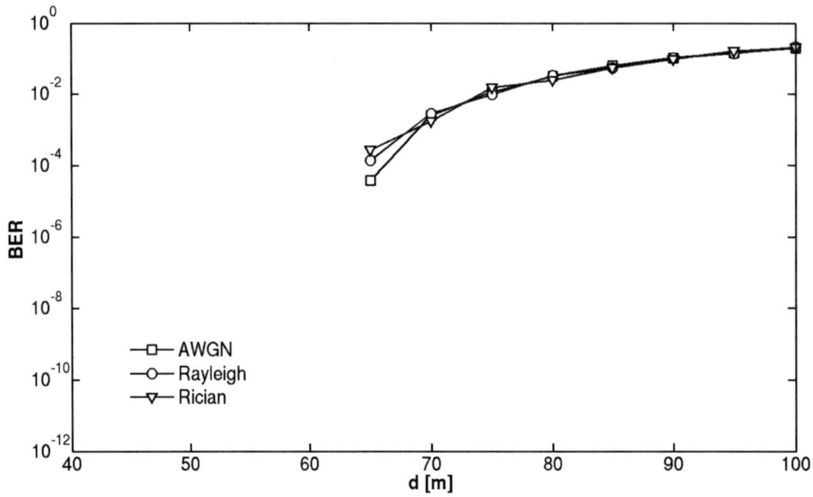

Fig. 11. BER versus distance for AWGN, Rayleigh and Rician channels

5. Conclusion

In 2001, the FCC allocated an unlicensed 7-GHz band in the 60GHz radio frequency range for wireless communications. This band is the widest portion of radio-frequency spectrum ever allocated for wireless applications, allowing multi-gigabit-per-second wireless communications. One of the most promising applications, that will benefit of such a huge amount of bandwidth, is the uncompressed HD video streaming. In this Chapter, a 60-GHz system for the emerging wireless uncompressed video communication has been studied and the possibility of realizing transceivers integrated in CMOS technology has been investigated. To address the design of modern integrated circuits, that can have complex architectures and made by mixed analog and digital subsystems as this one, a top-down design approach is needed. The architecture of the chip can be defined as a block diagram, and simulated and optimized using MATLAB® as a system simulator. A model of the high data rate physical layer, based on the specifications released by the consortium WirelessHD®, has been implemented in MATLAB® and system simulations have been carried out. These simulations allowed us to investigate the feasibility of the wireless transceiver in CMOS technology and to derive the preliminary specifications of its building blocks for a System-on-Chip implementation. The impact of transceiver non-idealities, such as PA non-linearity, LO phase noise, LNA and mixer noise on the BER have been investigated through system simulations made within MATLAB®. This study confirms the opportunity offered by MATLAB® as system-level CAD tool for the design, simulation and optimization of very complex system-on-chip, including analog, mixed-signals and digital integrated circuits, such as CMOS 60-GHz transceivers for emerging high-speed wireless applications.

6. Acknowledgment

This work has been supported in part by Science Foundation Ireland (SFI) under Grant 08/IN.1/I854 and Irish Research Council for Science, Engineering and Technology (IRCSET) under Grant R13485.

7. References

Australian Communications and Media Authority, (2005), Radiocommunications (Low Interference Potential Devices) Class License Variation 2005 (no. 1)

Chen, J.E. (May 2006). Modeling RF Systems, Available from http://www.designers-guide.org/Modeling/modeling-rf-systems.pdf

Chiu, Y. ; Markovic, D.; Tang, H. ; Zhang, N. (December 2000). OFDM receiver design, Final Report 12/12/2000, University of California Berkeley

Doan, C.H. ; Emami, S. ; Sobel, D.A. ; Niknejad, A.M. ; Brodersen, R.W. (2004). Design considerations for 60 GHz CMOS radios, *IEEE Communication Magazine*, Vol. 42, No. 12, (December 2004), pp. 132-140, ISSN 0163-6804

DVB-S Standard in a nut shell, Available from http://www.complextoreal.com/dvbs.htm

ETSI DTR/ERM-RM-049, (2006). Electromagnetic compatibility and Radio spectrum Matters (ERM); System Reference Document; Technical Characteristics of Multiple Gigabit Wireless Systems in the 60 GHz Range

Federal Communications Commission, (2001). Code of Federal Regulation, title 47 Telecommunication, Chapter 1, part 15.255

Fisher, W. (2008). *Digital Video and Audio Broadcasting Technology: A Practical Engineering Guide*, Springer, ISBN 978-3-540-76358-1, Germany

Gilbert, J.M. ; Doan, C. H. ; Emami, S. ; Shung, C.B. (2008). A 4-Gbps Uncompressed Wireless HD A/V Transceiver Chipset, *IEEE Micro*, Vol. 28, No. 2, (March-April 2008), pp. 56-64, ISSN 0272-1732

Huang, B.-J. ; Lin, K.-Y. ; Wang, H. (2009), Millimeter-Wave Low Power and Miniature CMOS Multicascode Low-Noise Amplifiers with Noise Reduction Topology, *IEEE Transactions on Microwave Theory and Techniques*, Vol. 52, No. 12, (December 2009), pp. 3049-3059, ISSN 0018-9480

IEEE, (October 2009). Part 15.3: Wireless Medium Access Control (MAC) and Physical Layer (PHY) Specifications for High Rate Wireless Personal Area Networks (WPANs)

IEEE 802.15 WPAN Task Group 3c (TG3c) Millimeter Wave Alternative PHY, Available from http://ieee802.org/15/pub/TG3c.html

Jen, Y.-N. ; Tsai, J.–H. ; Huang, T.-W. ; Wang, H. (2009). Design and analysis of a 55-71 GHz compact and broadband distributed active transformer power amplifier in 90-nm CMOS process, *IEEE Transaction on Microwave Techinques and Theory*, Vol. 57, No. 7, (July 2009), pp. 1637-1646, ISSN 0018-9480

Karaoguz J., (September 2009). IEEE 802.11-09-0960-00-00ad, Wireless HD Specification and Coexistance Capabilities, Available from: https://mentor.ieee.org/802.11/dcn/09/11-09-0960-00-00ad-wirelesshd-coexistence.ppt

Kundert, K. (February 2003). Principles of Top-Down Mixed-Signal Design, Available from http://www.designers-guide.org/Design/tdd-principles.pdf

Law, C.Y. & Pham, A.-V. (2010). A high-gain 60GHz power amplifier with 20dBm output power in 90nm CMOS, *Digest of Technical Papers of IEEE International Solid-State Circuits Conference*, pp. 426–427, ISSN 0193-6530, San Francisco, California, USA, February 7-11, 2010

Marcu, C.; Chowdhury, D.; Thakkar, C.; Jung-Dong Park; Ling-Kai Kong; Tabesh, M.; Yanjie Wang; Afshar, B.; Gupta, A.; Arbabian, A.; Gambini, S.; Zamani, R.; Alon, E.;

Niknejad, A.M. (2009). A 90 nm CMOS low-power 60GHz transceiver with integrated baseband circuitry, *IEEE Journal of Solid-State Circuits,* Vol.44 , No.12, (December 2009), pp. 3434-3447, ISSN 0018-9200

Ministry of Information Communication of Korea, (2006). Frequency Allocation Comment of 60 GHz band

Ministry of Internal Affairs and Communications, (2008). Frequency Assignment Plan, Available from: http://www.tele.soumu.go.jp/e/adm/freq/search/share/plan.htm

Niknejad, A. (2007). 0-60 GHz in Four Years: 60 GHz RF in Digital CMOS, *IEEE Solid-State Circuits Newsletter*, Vol.12, No.2, (Spring 2007), pp. 5-9, ISSN 1098-4232

Ollson, M. & Johansson, H. (2005). OFDM Carrier Frequency Offset Estimation Using Null Subcarriers, *10th International OFDM Workshop*, Hamburg, Germany, August 30-September 1, 2005

Pepe, D. & Zito, D. (2010a). 60-GHz CMOS Transceivers for Uncompressed Wireless HD Video Communication, *Proceedings of the Royal Irish Academy Committee for Communications and Radio Science, Research Colloquium on Wireless as an Enabling Technology: Innovation for a Critical infrastructure,* pp. 115-117, ISBN:978-1-904890-3, Dublin, Ireland, April 21-22, 2010

Pepe, D. & Zito, D. (2010b). 60-GHz transceivers for wireless HD uncompressed video communication in nano-era CMOS technology, *Proceedings of 15th IEEE Mediterranean Electrotechnical Conference*, pp. 1237 – 1240, ISBN 978-1-4244-5793-9, La Valletta, Malta, April 26-28, 2010

Singh, H.; Jisung, O. ; Changyeul, K. ; Xiangping, Q. ; Huai-Rong, S. ; Chiu, N. (2008). A 60 GHz wireless network for enabling uncompressed video communication, *IEEE Communications Magazine,* Vol.46, No.12, (December 2008), pp. 71-78, ISSN 0163-6804

Terry Yao; Gordon M. Q.; Tang K.K.W.; Yau K.H.K.; Ming-Ta Yang; Schvan P.; Voinigescu S. P. (2007). Algorithmic Design of CMOS LNAs and PAs for 60-GHz Radio, *IEEE Journal of Solid-State Circuits*, Vol. 42, No. 5, (May 2007), pp. 1044–1057, ISSN 0018-9200

Wireless Gigabit Alliance, Available from http://wirelessgigabitalliance.org/

WirelessHD, Available from http://www.wirelesshd.org/

WirelessHD (August 2009). WirelessHD Specification Overview, Available from http://www.wirelesshd.org/pdfs/WirelessHD-Specification-Overview-v1%200%204%20Aug09.pdf

Zhang, N. ; Xu, H. ; Wu, H.-T. ; O, K.K. (2009). W-Band Active Down-Conversion Mixer in Bulk CMOS, *IEEE Microwave and Wireless Components Letters,* Vol. 19, No. 2, (February 2009), pp. 98-100, ISSN 0018-9200

Zito, D.; Pepe, D.; Neri, B.; Taris, T.; Begueret, J.-B.; Deval, Y.; Belot, D. (2007). A Novel LNA Topology with Transformer-based Input Integrated Matching and its 60-GHz Millimeter-wave CMOS 65-nm Design, *Proceedings of IEEE International Conference on Electronics, Circuits and Systems,* pp. 1340-1343, ISBN 978-1-4244-1377-5, Marrakesh, Morocco, December 11-14, 2007

10

Low-Noise, Low-Sensitivity Active-RC Allpole Filters Using MATLAB Optimization

Dražen Jurišić
University of Zagreb, Faculty of Electrical Engineering and Computing, Zagreb, Croatia

1. Introduction

The application of Matlab, combining its symbolic and numeric calculation capabilities, to calculate noise and sensitivity properties of allpole active-RC filters is shown. Transfer function coefficients calculations, as well as plotting of amplitude-frequency and phase-frequency characteristics (Bode plots) have been performed using Matlab. Thus, using Matlab a comparison of different design strategies of active-RC filters is done. It is shown that active-RC filters can be designed to have low sensitivity to passive components and at the same time possess low output thermal noise. The classical methods were used to determine output noise of the filters. It was found that low-sensitivity filters with minimum noise have reduced resistance levels, low Q-factors, low-noise operational amplifiers (opamps) and use impedance tapering design. The design procedure of low-noise and low-sensitivity, positive- and negative-feedback, second- and third-order low-pass (LP), high-pass (HP) and band-pass (BP) allpole filters, using impedance tapering, is presented. The optimum designs, regarding both performances of most useful filter sections are summarized (as a cookbook programmed in Matlab) and demonstrated on examples. The relationship between the low sensitivity and low output noise, that are the most important performance of active-RC filters, is investigated, and optimum designs that reduce both performances are presented.

A considerable improvement in sensitivity of single-amplifier active-RC allpole filters to passive circuit components is achieved using the design technique called 'impedance tapering' (Moschytz, 1999), and as shown in (Jurisic et al., 2010a) at the same time they will have low output thermal noise. The improvement in noise and sensitivity comes free of charge, in that it requires simply the selection of appropriate component values. Preliminary results of the investigation of the relation between low sensitivity and low thermal noise performances using impedance tapering on the numeric basis using Matlab have been presented in (Jurisic & Moschytz, 2000; Jurisic, 2002).

For LP filters of second- and third-order the complete analytical proofs for noise properties of the desensitized filters are given in (Jurisic et al., 2010a). By means of classical methods as in (Jurisic et al., 2010a) closed-form expressions are derived in (Jurisic et al., 2010c), providing insight into noise characteristics of the LP, HP and BP active-RC filters using different designs. LP, HP and BP, low-sensitivity and low-noise filter sections using positive and negative feedback, that have been considered in (Jurisic et al., 2010c) are presented here. These filters are of low power because they use only one opamp per circuit. The design of optimal second- and third-order sections referred to as 'Biquads' and 'Bitriplets', regarding low passive and active sensitivities has been summarized in the table form as a cookbook in (Jurisic et al., 2010b). For common filter types, such as Butterworth and Chebyshev, design tables with normalized component values for designing single-amplifier LP filters up to the sixth-order with low passive sensitivity to component tolerances have been presented in (Jurisic et al., 2008). The filter sections considered in (Jurisic et al., 2010c) and repeated here have been recommended in (Moschytz & Horn, 1981; Jurisic et al., 2010b) as high-quality filter sections. It was shown in (Jurisic & Moschytz, 2000; Jurisic, 2002; Jurisic et al., 2008, 2010a, 2010b, 2010c), that both noise and sensitivity are directly proportional to the pole Q's and, therefore, to the pass band ripple specified by the filter requirements. The smaller the required ripple, the lower the pole Q's. Besides, it is wise to keep the filter order n as low as the specifications will permit, because the lower the filter order, the lower the pole Q's. Also, it was shown that positive-feedback filter blocks are useful for the realization of the LP and HP filters (belonging to class 4, according to the classification in (Moschytz & Horn, 1981), the representatives are SAK: Sallen and Key filters). Filters with negative feedback (class 3 SAB: Single-amplifier Biquad) are better for the BP filters, where the BP-C Biquad is preferable because it has lower noise than BP-R. A summary of figures and equations that investigate sensitivity and noise performance of active RC filters, and have been calculated in (Jurisic & Moschytz, 2000; Jurisic, 2002; Jurisic et al., 2008, 2010a, 2010b, 2010c), by Matlab, will be presented here. Numeric and symbolic routines that were used in those calculations are shown here in details.

In Section 2 a brief review of noise and sensitivity is given and the most important equations are defined. These equations will be used by Matlab in Section 3 to analyze a second-order LP filter as representative example. In Section 4 the results of analysis using Matlab of the LP, HP and BP sections of second- and third-order filters are summarized. Those results were obtained with the same Matlab algorithms as in Section 3 for the second-order LP filter, and are presented in the form of optimum-design procedures. The chapter ends with the conclusion in Section 5.

2. A brief review of noise and sensitivity of active-RC filters

2.1 Output noise and dynamic range

Thermal (or Johnson) noise is a result of random fluctuations of voltages or currents that seriously limit the processing of signals by analog circuits. Because this noise is caused by random motion of free charges and is proportional to temperature, it is referred to as thermal noise (Jurisic et al., 2010a).

The most important sources of noise in active-RC filters are resistors and opamps. For the purpose of noise analysis, appropriate noise models for resistors and opamps must be used. Resistors are represented by the well-known Nyquist voltage or current noise models shown in Figure 1(a) and (b), consisting of noiseless resistors and noise sources whose values are defined by the squared noise voltage density within the narrow frequency band Δf, i.e.,

$$e_{nR}^2(f) = 4kTR\,, \tag{1}$$

or the squared noise current density given by

$$i_{nR}^2(f) = 4kT / R\,, \tag{2}$$

where $k = 1.38 \cdot 10^{-23}$ [J/K] is Boltzmann's constant, T is the absolute temperature of a conductor in Kelvin [K]. All examples are calculated for 22°C (T=295K), i.e., room temperature.

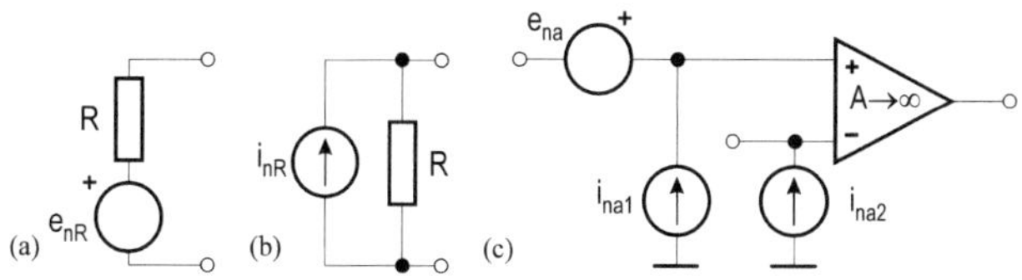

Fig. 1. (a) Voltage noise model of a resistor. (b) Current noise model of a resistor. (c) An opamp noise model.

The noise defined by (1) and (2) has a constant spectrum over the frequency band, and is referred to as 'white noise'. The squared noise spectral density in (1) has the dimension [V^2/Hz], unless written $e_{nR}^2(\omega) = (2kT / \pi)R$; in which case it has the dimension [V^2/rad/s]. The dimension of the spectrum in (2) is [A^2/Hz], unless written $i_{nR}^2(\omega) = 2kT / (\pi R)$; in which case it has the dimension [A^2/rad/s]. The noise in real capacitors is also of thermal origin and is negligible.

The noise in opams is caused by the built-in semiconductors and resistors. The equivalent schematic of a noisy opamp is shown in Figure 1(c), i.e., a noiseless opamp combined with voltage and current noise sources. For the TL081/TI (Texas instruments) FET input opamp, typical values found in the data-sheets are $e_{na}(f)$=17nV/√Hz and $i_{na1}(f) \approx i_{na2}(f)$=0.01pA/√Hz. These values are considered constant within the frequency interval up to about 50 kHz and have been used in the noise analysis here.

The noise is additive and the spectral power density of the noise voltage at the output terminal is obtained by adding the contributions from each source. Thus, the squared output noise spectral density, derived from all the noise sources and their corresponding *noise transfer functions*, is given by (Schaumann et al., 1990):

$$e_{no}^2(\omega) = \sum_{k=1}^{m} \left|T_{i,k}(j\omega)\right|^2 (i_{nR,a})_k^2 + \sum_{l=1}^{n} \left|T_{v,l}(j\omega)\right|^2 (e_{nR,a})_l^2 , \quad (3)$$

where $T_{i,k}(j\omega)$ is the transfer impedance, i.e. the ratio of the output voltage and input current of the kth current noise source $(i_n)_k$, and $T_{v,l}(j\omega)$ is the corresponding voltage transfer function, i.e. the ratio of the output voltage and the input voltage of the lth voltage noise source $(e_n)_l$.

The total output noise power is obtained by the integration of the mean-square noise spectral density $e^2_{no}(\omega)$ in (3) over the total frequency band from 0 to ∞; thus:

$$\left(E_{no}\right)_{rms}^2 = \int_0^{\infty} e_{no}^2(\omega) d\omega . \quad (4)$$

The *dynamic range* is defined by:

$$D_R = 20\log \frac{\left(V_{so\ rms}\right)_{\max}}{\left(E_{no}\right)_{rms}} \quad [\text{dB}] , \quad (5)$$

where $\left(V_{so\ rms}\right)_{\max}$ represents the maximum undistorted rms voltage at the output, and the denominator is the *noise floor* defined by the square root of (4). $\left(V_{so\ rms}\right)_{\max}$ is determined by the opamp slew rate, power supply voltage, and the corresponding THD factor of the filter. In our examples we use a $10V_{pp}$ signal which yields

$$\left(V_{so\ rms}\right)_{\max}=5/\sqrt{2}\ [\mathrm{V}]. \tag{6}$$

2.2 Sensitivity to passive component variations

Sensitivity analysis provides information on network changes caused by small deviations of passive component values. Given the network function $F(s, x_1,\ldots, x_N)$, where s is a complex variable and x_k (k=1 ,..., N) are real parameters of the filter, the relative deviation of F, $\Delta F/F$, due to the relative deviations $\Delta x_k/x_k$ (k=1 ,..., N) is given to the first approximation by:

$$\frac{\Delta F}{F}\cong S_{x_k}^{F}\cdot\frac{\Delta x_k}{x_k}, \tag{7}$$

where $S_{x_k}^{F}$ represents the relative sensitivity of the function F to variations of a single parameter (component) x_k, namely:

$$S_{x_k}^{F}=\frac{x_k}{F}\frac{dF}{dx_k}. \tag{8}$$

If several components deviate from the nominal value, a criterion for assessing the deviation of the function F due to the change of several parameters must be used. With $\Delta x_k/x_k$ considered to be an independent random variable with zero mean and identical standard deviation σ_x, the squared standard deviation σ^2_F of the relative change $\Delta F/F$ is given by:

$$\sigma_F^2=\sigma_x^2\sum_{k=1}^{N}\left[S_{x_k}^{|F(j\omega)|}\right]^2. \tag{9}$$

σ_F is therefore dependent on the component sensitivities $S_{x_k}^{F}$, but also on the number of passive components N. The more components the circuit has, the larger the sensitivity. Equation (9) defines multi-parametric measure of sensitivity (Schoeffler, 1964; Laker & Gaussi, 1975; Schaumann et al., 1990).

In the following Section, all Matlab calculations regarding noise and sensitivity performance will be demonstrated on the second-order LP filter circuit with positive feedback (class-4 or Sallen and Key). All Matlab commands and variables will appear in the text using `Courier New` font.

3. Application to second-order LP filter

3.1 Calculating transfer function coefficients and parameters using 'symbolic toolbox' in Matlab

Consider the second-order low-pass active-RC allpole filter circuit (Biquad) shown in Figure 2(a). This circuit belongs to the positive feedback or class-4 (Sallen and Key) filters

(Moschytz & Horn, 1981). In Figure 2(b) there is a simplified version of the same circuit with the voltage-controlled voltage source (VCVS) having voltage gain β. For an ideal opamp in the non-inverting mode it is given by

$$\beta = 1 + R_F / R_G \,. \tag{10}$$

Note that the voltage gain β of the class-4 circuit is positive and larger than or equal to unity. Voltage transfer function for the filters in Figure 2 expressed in terms of the coefficients a_i (i=0, 1, 2) is given by

$$T(s) = \frac{V_{out}}{V_g} = \frac{N(s)}{D(s)} = K \cdot \frac{a_0}{s^2 + a_1 s + a_0}\,, \tag{11a}$$

and in terms of the pole frequency ω_p, the pole Q, q_p and the gain factor K by:

$$T(s) = \frac{V_{out}}{V_g} = K \cdot \frac{\omega_p^2}{s^2 + \dfrac{\omega_p}{q_p} s + \omega_p^2}\,, \tag{11b}$$

where

$$\begin{aligned} a_0 &= \omega_p^2 = \frac{1}{R_1 R_2 C_1 C_2}\,, \\ a_1 &= \frac{\omega_p}{q_p} = \frac{R_1(C_1 + C_2) + R_2 C_2 - \beta R_1 C_1}{R_1 R_2 C_1 C_2}\,, \\ q_p &= \frac{\sqrt{R_1 R_2 C_1 C_2}}{R_1(C_1 + C_2) + R_2 C_2 - \beta R_1 C_1}\,, \\ K &= \beta. \end{aligned} \tag{11c}$$

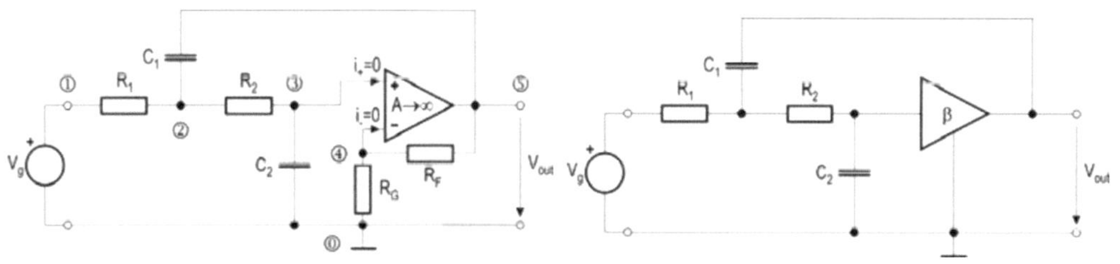

(a) (b)

Fig. 2. Second-order Sallen and Key LP active-*RC* filter. (a) With ideal opamp having feedback resistors R_F and R_G, and nodes for transfer-function calculus. (b) Simplified circuit with the gain element replaced by VCVS β.

To calculate the voltage transfer function $T(s)=V_{out}(s)/V_g(s)$ of the Biquad in Figure 2(a), consider the following system of nodal equations (note that the last equation represents the opamp):

$$
\begin{aligned}
&(1) \quad V_1 = V_g \\
&(2) \quad -V_1\frac{1}{R_1} + V_2\left(\frac{1}{R_1} + \frac{1}{R_2} + sC_1\right) - V_3\frac{1}{R_2} - V_5 sC_1 = 0 \\
&(3) \quad -V_2\frac{1}{R_2} + V_3\left(\frac{1}{R_2} + sC_2\right) = 0 \\
&(4) \quad V_3\left(\frac{1}{R_F} + \frac{1}{R_G}\right) - V_5\frac{1}{R_F} = 0 \\
&(5) \quad A\cdot(V_3 - V_5) = V_5 = V_{out}, A \to \infty, i_+ = 0, i_- = 0.
\end{aligned}
\tag{12}
$$

The system of Equations (12) can be solved using 'Symbolic toolbox' in Matlab. The following Matlab code solves the system of equations:

i. Matlab command `syms` defines symbolic variables in Matlab's workspace:

```
syms A R1 R2 C1 C2 RF RG s Vg V1 V2 V3 V4 V5;
```

ii. Matlab command `solve` is used to solve analytically above system of five Equations (12) for the five voltages V_1 to V_5 as unknowns. The unknowns are defined in the last row of command `solve`. Note that all variables used in `solve` are defined as symbolic.

```
CircuitEquations=solve(...
    'V1=Vg',...
    '-V1*1/R1 + V2*(1/R1+1/R2+s*C1)-V3*1/R2 - V5*s*C1=0',...
    '-V2*1/R2 + V3*(1/R2+s*C2)=0',...
    'V4*(1/RG+1/RF)-V5/RF=0',...
    '(V3-V4)*A =V5',...
    'V1','V2','V3','V4','V5');
```

iii. Once all variables are known simple symbolic division of V_5/V_1 yields the desired transfer function (limit value for $A\to\infty$ has to be applied, as well):

```
Tofs=CircuitEquations.V5/CircuitEquations.V1;
Tofsa=limit(Tofs,A,Inf);
```

Another way of presentation polynomials is by collecting all coefficients that multiply 's':

```
Tofsc=collect(Tofsa,s);
```

iv. Transfer function coefficients and parameters readily follow.
To obtain coefficients, it is useful to separate numerator and denominator using the following command:

```
[numTa,denTa]=numden(Tofsa);
syms a2 a1 a0 wp qp k;
denLP2=coeffs(denTa,s)/RG;
numLP2=coeffs(numTa,s)/RG;
```

Now coefficients follow

```
a0=denLP2(1)/denLP2(3);
a1=denLP2(2)/denLP2(3);
a2=denLP2(3)/denLP2(3);
```

And parameters

```
k=numLP2;
wp=sqrt(a0);
qp=wp/a1;
```

Typing command `whos` we obtain the following answer about variables in Matlab workspace:

```
>> whos
  Name                   Size                     Bytes  Class

  A                      1x1                        126  sym object
  C1                     1x1                        128  sym object
  C2                     1x1                        128  sym object
  CircuitEquations       1x1                       2828  struct array
  Tofs                   1x1                        496  sym object
  Tofsa                  1x1                        252  sym object
  Tofsc                  1x1                        248  sym object
  R1                     1x1                        128  sym object
  R2                     1x1                        128  sym object
  RF                     1x1                        128  sym object
  RG                     1x1                        128  sym object
  V1                     1x1                        128  sym object
  V2                     1x1                        128  sym object
  V3                     1x1                        128  sym object
  V4                     1x1                        128  sym object
  V5                     1x1                        128  sym object
  Vg                     1x1                        128  sym object
  a0                     1x1                        150  sym object
  a1                     1x1                        210  sym object
  a2                     1x1                        126  sym object
  denTa                  1x1                        232  sym object
  denLP2                 1x3                        330  sym object
  k                      1x1                        144  sym object
  numTa                  1x1                        134  sym object
  numLP2                 1x1                        144  sym object
  qp                     1x1                        254  sym object
  s                      1x1                        126  sym object
  wp                     1x1                        166  sym object

Grand total is 1436 elements using 7502 bytes
```

It can be seen that all variables that are defined and calculated so far are of *symbolic* type.
We can now check the values of the variables. For example we are interested in voltage transfer function `Tofsa`. Matlab gives the following answer, when we invoke the variable:

```
>> Tofsa

Tofsa =

(RF+RG)/(s*C2*R2*RG+R2*s^2*C1*R1*C2*RG-s*C1*R1*RF+RG+R1*s*C2*RG)
```

The command `pretty` presents the results in a more beautiful way.

```
>> pretty(Tofsa)

                              RF + RG
 --------------------------------------------------------------
                    2
 s C2 R2 RG + R2 s  C1 R1 C2 RG - s C1 R1 RF + RG + R1 s C2 RG
```

Or we could invoke variable `Tofsc` (see above that `Tofsc` is the same as `Tofsa`, but with collected coefficients that multiply powers of 's').

```
>> pretty(Tofsc)

                          RF + RG
 ------------------------------------------------------------
     2
 R2 s  C1 R1 C2 RG + (C2 R2 RG - C1 R1 RF + R1 C2 RG) s + RG
```

Other variables follow using `pretty` command.

```
>> pretty(a0)

                   1
              -----------
              R2 C1 R1 C2
>> pretty(a1)

         C2 R2 RG - C1 R1 RF + R1 C2 RG
         ------------------------------
                RG R2 C1 R1 C2

>> pretty(a2)

                   1
>> pretty(wp)

             /     1     \1/2
             |-----------|
             \R2 C1 R1 C2/
>> pretty(qp)

         /     1     \1/2
         |-----------|    RG R2 C1 R1 C2
         \R2 C1 R1 C2/
         --------------------------------
         C2 R2 RG - C1 R1 RF + R1 C2 RG
>> pretty(k)

                RF + RG
                -------
                  RG
```

Next, according to simplified circuit in Figure 2(b) having the replacement of the gain element by β defined in (10), we can substitute values for R_F and R_G using the command subs and obtain simpler results [in the following example we perform substitution $R_F \rightarrow R_G(\beta-1)$]. New symbolic variable is beta

```
>> syms beta
>> a1=subs(a1,RF,'(beta-1)*RG');
>> pretty(a1)

                    C2 R2 RG - C1 R1 (beta - 1) RG + R1 C2 RG
                    -----------------------------------------
                                 RG R2 C1 R1 C2
```

Note that we have obtained R_G both in the numerator and denominator, and it can be abbreviated. To simplify equations it is possible to use several Matlab commands for *simplifications*. For example, to rewrite the coefficient a_1 in several other forms, we can use commands for simplification, such as:

```
>> pretty(simple(a1))

                              1       beta       1        1
                            ----- - ----- + ----- + -----
                            C1 R1   R2 C2   R2 C2   R2 C1
>> pretty(simplify(a1))

                          -C2 R2 + C1 R1 beta - C1 R1 - R1 C2
                        - -----------------------------------
                                      R2 C1 R1 C2
```

The final form of the coefficient a_1 is the simplest one, and is the same as in (11c) above. Using the same Matlab procedures as presented above, we have calculated all coefficients and parameters of the different filters' transfer functions in this Chapter.

If we want to calculate the numerical values of coefficients a_i (i=0, 1, 2) when component values are given, we simply use subs command. First we define the (e.g. normalized) numerical values of components in the Matlab's workspace, and then we invoke subs:

```
>> R1=1;R2=1;C1=0.5;C2=2;
>> a0val=subs(a0)

a0val =

     1
>> whos a0 a0val
  Name          Size                      Bytes  Class

  a0            1x1                         150  sym object
  a0val         1x1                           8  double array

Grand total is 15 elements using 158 bytes
```

Note that the new variable a0val is of the double type and has numerical value equal to 1, whereas the symbolic variable a0 did not change its type. Numerical variables are of type double.

3.2 Drawing amplitude- and phase-frequency characteristics of transfer function using symbolic and numeric calculations in Matlab

Suppose we now want to plot Bode diagram of the transfer function, e.g. of the `Tofsa`, using the *symbolic* solutions already available (see above). We present the usage of the Matlab in *numeric* way, as well. Suppose we already have symbolic values in the Workspace such as:

```
>> pretty(Tofsa)
                                   RF + RG
   -------------------------------------------------------------
                                                               2
   RG - C1 R1 RF s + C2 R1 RG s + C2 R2 RG s + C1 C2 R1 R2 RG s
```

Define set of element values (normalized):

```
>> R1=1;R2=1;C1=1;C2=1;RG=1;RF=1.8;
```

Now the variables representing elements R_1, R_2, C_1, C_2, R_G, and R_F changed in the workspace to `double` and have values; they become numeric. Substitute those elements into transfer function `Tofsa` using the command `subs`.

```
>> Tofsa1=subs(Tofsa);
>> pretty(Tofsa1)
         14
   ----------------
     / 2    s     \
   5 | s  + - + 1 |
     \      5     /
```

Note that in new transfer function `Tofsa1` an independent variable is *symbolic* variable `s`. To calculate the amplitude-frequency characteristic, i.e., the magnitude of the filter's voltage transfer function we first have to define frequency range of ω, as a vector of discrete values in `wd`, make substitution $s=j\omega$ into $T(s)$ (in Matlab represented by `Tofsa1`) to obtain $T(j\omega)$, and finally calculate absolute value of the magnitude in dB by $\alpha(\omega)=20 \log |T(j\omega)|$. The phase-frequency characteristic is $\varphi(\omega)=\arg T(j\omega)$ and is calculated using `atan2()`. This can be performed in following sequence of commands:

```
wd = logspace(-1,1,200);
ad1 = subs(Tofsa1,s,i*wd);
Alphad=20*log10(abs(ad1));
semilogx(wd, Alphad, 'g-');
axis([wd(1) wd(end) -40 30]);
title('Amplitude Characteristic');
legend('Circuit 1 (normalized)');
xlabel('Frequency /rad/s');ylabel('Magnitude / dB');
grid;

Phid=180/pi*atan2(imag(ad1),real(ad1));
semilogx(wd, Phid, 'g-');
axis([wd(1) wd(end) -180 0]);
title('Phase Characteristic');
legend('Circuit 1 (normalized)');
xlabel('Frequency /rad/s');ylabel('Phase / deg');
grid;
```

Commands are self-explanatory. The amplitude- and phase-frequency characteristics thus obtained are shown in Figure 3. Note that we have generated vectors of values `wd`, `Alphad` and `Phid` to be plotted in logarithmic scale by the command `semilogx` (instead, we could have used command `plot` to generate linear axis).
The next example defines new set of second-order LP filter element values (those are obtained when above normalized elements are denormalized to the frequency $\omega_0=2\pi\cdot 86\cdot 10^3$ rad/s and impedance R_0=37kΩ; see in (Jurisic et al., 2008) how):

```
>> R1=37e3;R2=37e3;C1=50e-12;C2=50e-12;RG=1e4;RF=1.8e4;
```

Those element values were calculated starting from transfer function parameters ω_p= $2\pi\cdot 86\cdot 10^3$ rad/s and q_p=5 and are represented as example 1) non-tapered filter (ρ=1, and r=1) (see Equation (18) and Table 3 in Section 4 below). We refer to those values as 'Circuit 1'.

```
>> Tofsa2=subs(Tofsa);
>> pretty(Tofsa2)

                                        28000
 ------------------------------------------------------------------------------------
                                                2
   800318296602402496323046008438980478515625 s        4473025532574128109375 s
 ---------------------------------------------------- + ------------------------ + 10000
 23384026197294446691258957323460528314494920687616   1208925819614629174706176
```

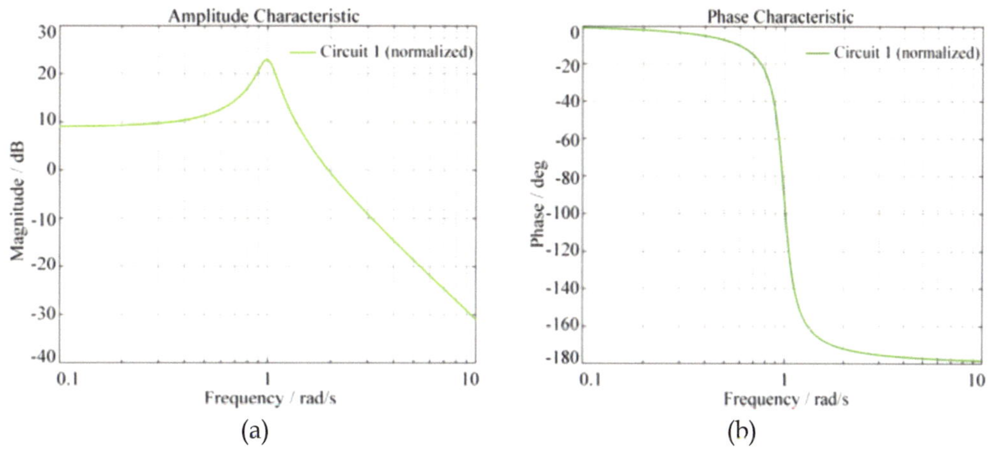

Fig. 3. Transfer-function (a) magnitude and (b) phase for Circuit 1 (normalized).

It is seen that the denormalized-transfer-function presentation in symbolic way is not very useful. It is possible rather to use numeric and vector presentation of the `Tofsa2`. First we have to separate numerator and denominator of `Tofsa2` by typing:

```
>> [num2, den2]=numden(Tofsa2);
```

then we have to convert obtained symbolic data of `num2` and `den2` into vectors `n2` and `d2`:

```
>> n2=sym2poly(num2)
n2 =
  6.5475e+053

>> d2=sym2poly(den2)
d2 =
  1.0e+053 *

    0.0000    0.0000    2.3384
```

and finally use command `tf` to write transfer function which uses vectors with numeric values:

```
>> tf(n2,d2)

 Transfer function:
              6.548e053
---------------------------------------
8.003e041 s^2 + 8.652e046 s + 2.338e053
```

If we divide numerator and denominator by the coefficient of s^2 in the denominator, i.e., `d2(1)`, we have a more appropriate form:

```
>> tf(n2/d2(1),d2/d2(1))

 Transfer function:
         8.181e011
----------------------------
s^2 + 1.081e005 s + 2.922e011
```

Obviously, the use of Matlab (numeric) vectors provides a more compact and useful representation of the denormalized transfer function.
Finally, note that when several (N) filter sections are connected in a cascade, the overall transfer function of that cascade can be very simply calculated by symbolic multiplication of sections' transfer functions $T_i(s)$ (i=1, ..., N), i.e. `T=T1*...*TN`, if $T_i(s)$ are defined in a symbolic way. On the other hand, if numerator and denominator polynomials of $T_i(s)$ are defined numerically (i.e. in a vector form), a more complicated procedure of multiplying vectors using (convolution) command `conv` should be used.

3.3 Calculating noise transfer function using symbolic calculations in Matlab
Using the noise models for the resistors and opamps from Figure 1, we obtain noise spot sources shown in Figure 4(a).

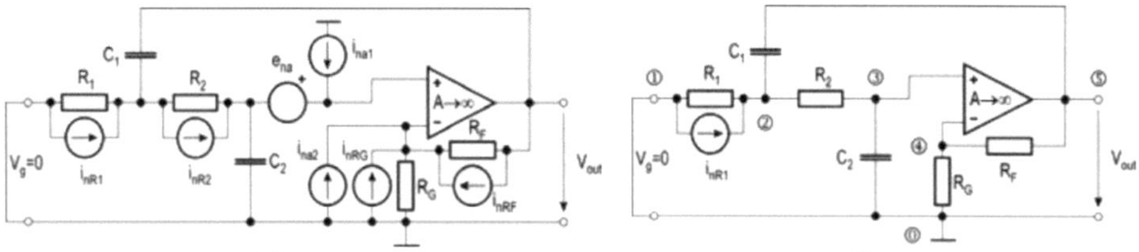

Fig. 4. (a) Noise sources for second-order LP filter. (b) Noise transfer function for contribution of R_1.

The *noise transfer functions* as in (3) $T_x(s)=V_{out}/N_x$ from each equivalent voltage or current noise source to the output of the filter in Figure 4(a) has to be evaluated.
As a first example we find the contribution of noise produced by resistor R_1 at the filter's output. We have to calculate the transfer resistance $T_{i,R1}(s)=V_{out}(s)/I_{nR1}(s)$. According to Figure 4(b) we write the following system of nodal equations:

$$\begin{array}{ll}
(1) & V_1 = 0 \\
(2) & -V_1\dfrac{1}{R_1} + V_2\left(\dfrac{1}{R_1}+\dfrac{1}{R_2}+sC_1\right) - V_3\dfrac{1}{R_2} - V_5 sC_1 = I_{nR1} \\
(3) & -V_2\dfrac{1}{R_2} + V_3\left(\dfrac{1}{R_2}+sC_2\right) = 0 \\
(4) & V_4\left(\dfrac{1}{R_F}+\dfrac{1}{R_G}\right) - V_5\dfrac{1}{R_F} = 0 \\
(5) & A\cdot\left(V_3 - V_4\right) = V_5
\end{array} \tag{13}$$

The system of Equations (13) can be solved using Matlab Symbolic toolbox in the same way as the system of Equations (12) presented above. The following Matlab code solves the system of Equations (13):

```
CircuitEquations=solve(...
    'V1=0',...
    '-V1*1/R1 + V2*(1/R1+1/R2+s*C1)-V3*1/R2 - V5*s*C1=InR1',...
    '-V2*1/R2 + V3*(1/R2+s*C2)=0',...
    'V4*(1/RG+1/RF)-V5/RF=0',...
    '(V3-V4)*A =V5',...
    'V1','V2','V3','V4','V5');
IR1ofs=CircuitEquations.V5/InR1;
IR1ofsa=limit(IR1ofs,A,Inf);
[numIR1a,denIR1a]=numden(IR1ofsa);
syms a2 a1 a0 b0
denIR1=coeffs(denIR1a,s)/RG;
numIR1=coeffs(numIR1a,s)/RG;
%Coefficients of the transfer function
a0=denIR1(1)/denIR1(3);
a1=denIR1(2)/denIR1(3);
a2=denIR1(3)/denIR1(3);
b0=numIR1/denIR1(3);
```

In Matlab workspace we can check the value of each coefficient calculated by above program, simply, by typing the corresponding variable. For example, we present the value of the coefficient b_0 in the numerator by typing:

```
>> pretty(b0)

  --     RF + RG     --
  |   -----------    |
  -- C1 C2 R2 RG --
```

The coefficients a_0, a_1 and a_2 are the same as those of the voltage transfer function calculated in Section 3.1 above, which means that two transfer functions have the same denominator, i.e., $D(s)$. Thus, the only useful data is the coefficient b_0. The transfer resistance $T_{i,R1}(s)$ is obtained.

The *noise transfer functions* of all noise spot sources in Figure 4(a) have been calculated and presented in Table 1 in the same way as $T_{i,R1}(s)$ above. We use current sources in the resistor noise model. N_x is either the voltage or current noise source of the element denoted by x.

3.4 Drawing output noise spectral density of active-RC filters using numeric calculations in Matlab

Noise transfer functions for second-order LP filter, generated using Matlab in Section 3.3, are shown in Table 1. We can retype them and use Matlab in only *numerical* mode to calculate noise spectral density curves at the output, that are defined as a square root of (3). Define set of element values (Circuit 1)

```
>> R1=37e3;R2=37e3;C1=50e-12;C2=50e-12;RG=1e4;RF=1.8e4;
```

N_x	$T_x(s)$
V_g	$\beta\dfrac{1}{R_1R_2C_1C_2}\Big/D(s)$
$i_{nR1}, i_{nR11}, i_{nR12}$	$\beta\dfrac{1}{R_2C_1C_2}\Big/D(s)$
i_{nR2}	$\beta\left[\dfrac{1}{C_2}s+\dfrac{1}{R_1C_1C_2}\right]\Big/D(s)$
i_{na1}	$\beta\left[\dfrac{1}{C_2}s+\dfrac{1}{R_1C_1C_2}+\dfrac{1}{R_2C_1C_2}\right]\Big/D(s)$
$i_{na2}, i_{nRG}, i_{nRF}, e_{na}^*$	$-R_F\left[s^2+\dfrac{R_2C_2+R_1C_2+R_1C_1}{R_1R_2C_1C_2}s+\dfrac{1}{R_1R_2C_1C_2}\right]\Big/D(s)$
	$D(s)=s^2+\dfrac{R_2C_2+R_1C_2+R_1C_1(1-\beta)}{R_1R_2C_1C_2}s+\dfrac{1}{R_1R_2C_1C_2}$

Table 1. Noise transfer functions for second-order LP filter (*e_{na} has β instead $-R_F$).

We draw the curve:

```
%   FREQUENCY RANGE
    Nfreq=200;
    Fstart=1e4; %Hz
    Fstop=1e6; %Hz
    fd =logspace(log10(Fstart),log10(Fstop),Nfreq);
    %   NOISE SOURCES at temperature T=295K (22 deg C)
    IR1=sqrt(4*1.38e-23*295/R1);
    IR2=sqrt(4*1.38e-23*295/R2);
    IRF=sqrt(4*1.38e-23*295/RF);
    IRG=sqrt(4*1.38e-23*295/RG);
    EP=17e-9;
    IP=0.01e-12;
    IM=0.01E-12;
```

```
    %   TRANSFER FUNCTIONS OF EVERY NOISE SOURCE
    D=1/(R1*R2*C1*C2) - (fd*2*pi).^2 + ...
i*(fd*2*pi)*(1/(R1*C1)+1/(R2*C1)-RF/(R2*C2*RG));
    H=(1/(R1*R2*C1*C2)*(1+RF/RG))./D;
    numerator=(1/(R1*R2*C1*C2)*(1+RF/RG))*conj(D);
    phase=atan(imag(numerator)./real(numerator));
    TR1=(1/(R2*C1*C2)*(1+RF/RG))./D;
    TR2=((1+RF/RG)*(1/(R1*C1*C2)+i*(fd*2*pi)*1/C2))./D;
    TIP=((1+RF/RG)*(1/(R1*C1*C2)+1/(R2*C1*C2)+i*(fd*2*pi)*1/C2))./D;
    TIM=-RF*(1/(R1*R2*C1*C2)-(fd*2*pi).^2 + ...
i*(fd*2*pi)*(1/(R1*C1)+1/(R2*C1)+1/(R2*C2)))./D;
    TRG=TIM;
    TRF=TIM;
    TEP=(1+RF/RG)*(1/(R1*R2*C1*C2)-...

(fd*2*pi).^2+i*(fd*2*pi)*(1/(R1*C1)+1/(R2*C1)+1/(R2*C2)))./D;


    %   SQUARES OF TRANS. FUNCTIONS
    TR1A =(abs(TR1)).^2;
    TR2A =(abs(TR2)).^2;
    TIPA =(abs(TIP)).^2;
    TIMA =(abs(TIM)).^2;
    TRGA =TIMA;
    TRFA =TIMA;
    TEPA =(abs(TEP)).^2;

    %   SPECTRAL DENSITY OF EVERY NOISE SOURCE
    UR1 =TR1A*IR1^2;
    UR2 =TR2A*IR2^2;
    UIP =TIPA*IP^2;
    UIM =TIMA*IM^2;
    UEP =TEPA*EP^2;
    URG =TRGA*IRG^2;
    URF =TRFA*IRF^2;

    %   OVERALL SPECTRAL DENSITY PLOT
    U2=sqrt(UR1+UR2+UIP+UIM+URF+UEP+URG);
    semilogx(fd,U2,'k-');
    titletext=sprintf('Output Noise');title(titletext);
    xlabel('Frequency / kHz');
    ylabel('Noise Spectral Density / \muV/\surdHz');
    axis ([fd(1) fd(Nfreq) 0 3e-6]); grid;

    %   Numerical integration of Total Noise Power at the Output (RMS)
    Eno = sqrt(sum(U22(1:Nfreq))/(Nfreq-1)*(fd(Nfreq)-fd(1)));
```

To draw the second curve, apply the following method. Define the second set of element values, that are represented as example 4) ideally tapered filter (ρ=4, and r=4), (see Equation (18) and Table 3 in Section 4 below). We refer to those values as 'Circuit 2'.

```
>> R1=23.1e3;R2=92.4e3;C1=80e-12;C2=20e-12;RG=1e4;RF=1.05e4;
>> hold on;
>> redo all above equations; use 'r--' for the second curve shape
>> hold off;
>> legend('Circuit 1', 'Circuit 2');
```

Output noise spectral density is shown in Figure 5.
Furthermore, two values of rms voltages E_{no} (representing total noise power at the output or *the noise floor*) as defined by the square root of (4), have been calculated as a result of

numerical integration in Matlab code given above, and they are as follows: E_{no1}=176.0 μV (Circuit 1 or example #1 in Table 3) and E_{no2}=127.7 μV (Circuit 2 or example #4 in Table 3). They are shown in the last column of Table 3, in Section 4.
For all filter examples the rms total output noise E_{no} was calculated numerically using Matlab and presented in the last column of Tables.
To plot output noise spectral density and calculate total output noise voltage it was easy to retype the noise transfer function expressions from Table 1 in Matlab code. In the following Section 3.5 it is shown that retyping of long expressions is sometimes unacceptable (e.g. to calculate the sensitivity). Then we have another option to use Matlab in *symbolic* mode.

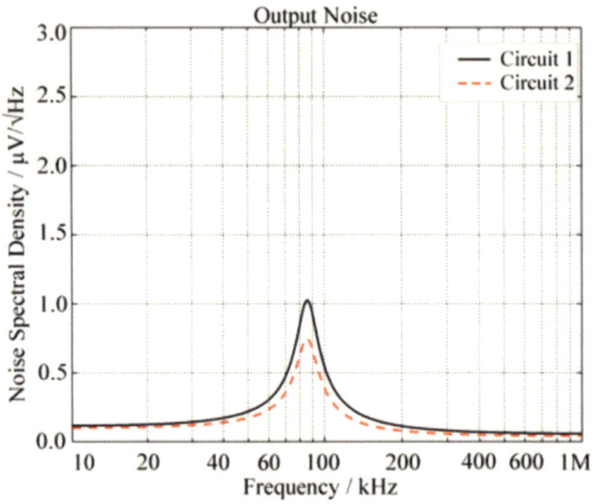

Fig. 5. Output noise spectral density of Circuit 1 and Circuit 2 (denormalized).

3.5 Sensitivity characteristic of active-RC filter using both symbolic and numeric calculations in Matlab

To efficiently calculate multi-parametric sensitivity in (9), we use a mixture of symbolic and numeric capabilities of Matlab.
Suppose F in (7)-(9) is our transfer function $T(s)=N(s)/D(s)$ defined by (11), where x_k are elements R_1, R_2, C_1, C_2, R_F and R_G. We will use previous *symbolic* results of transfer functions numerator `numLP2` and denominator `denLP2`, and Matlab operation of symbolic differentiation `diff` to produce relative sensitivity in (8). To calculate the transfer function sensitivity as defined by (8) we will also apply the following rule:

$$S_{x_k}^{|T(j\omega)|} = S_{x_k}^{|N(j\omega)|} - S_{x_k}^{|D(j\omega)|}. \tag{14}$$

To construct (14), we proceed as follows. The following code reveal numerator and denominator as function of components. (Division of both numerator and denominator by R_G is just to have nicer presentation.) First we make the substitution $s=j\omega$ into $N(s)$ and $D(s)$. Then we have to produce absolute values of $N(j\omega)$ and $D(j\omega)$. In the subsequent step we perform symbolic differentiation using Matlab command `diff` or the operator `D`.

```
>> den=simplify(denTa/RG);
>> pretty(den)

                                      2   C1 R1 RF s
  C2 R1 s + C2 R2 s + C1 C2 R1 R2 s  - ---------- + 1
                                              RG

>> denofw = subs(den,s,i*wd)

denofw =

C2*R2*wd*i - C1*C2*R1*R2*wd^2 + 1 - (C1*R1*RF*wd*i)/RG + C2*R1*wd*i
```

(To calculate all components and frequency values as real variables we have to retype real and imaginary parts of `denofw`.)

```
>> syms wd;
>> redenofw= - C1*C2*R1*R2*wd^2 + 1;
>> imdenofw= C2*R2*wd - (C1*R1*RF*wd)/RG + C2*R1*wd;

>> absden=sqrt(redenofw^2+imdenofw^2);
>> pretty(absden)
  / /                      C1 R1 RF wd \2                   2     2 \1/2
  | | C2 R1 wd + C2 R2 wd - ----------- |  + (C1 C2 R1 R2 wd  - 1)  |
  \ \                          RG      /                           /

>> SDR1=diff(absden,R1)*R1/absden;
>> pretty(SDR1)

   /   /         C1 RF wd \ /                       C1 R1 RF wd \              2                 2      \
R1 | 2 | C2 wd - -------- | | C2 R1 wd + C2 R2 wd - ----------- | + 2 C1 C2 R2 wd  (C1 C2 R1 R2 wd  - 1) |
   \   \            RG    / \                          RG       /                                       /
---------------------------------------------------------------------------------------------------------
                   / /                      C1 R1 RF wd \2                  2     2 \
                 2 | | C2 R1 wd + C2 R2 wd - ----------- |  + (C1 C2 R1 R2 wd  - 1)  |
                   \ \                          RG      /                          /
```

The same calculus (with simpler results) can be done for the numerator:

```
>> num=simplify(numTa/RG);
>> pretty(num)

  RF
     + 1
  RG
>> numofw = subs(num,s,i*wd)

numofw =

RF/RG + 1

>> renumofw= RF/RG + 1;
>> imnumofw= 0;

>> absnum=sqrt(renumofw^2+imnumofw^2);
```

```
>> pretty(absnum)

   / / RF     \2 \1/2
   | | -- + 1 |   |
   \ \ RG     /   /

>> SNR1=diff(absnum,R1)*R1/absnum;
>> pretty(SNR1)

   0
```

Sensitivity of the numerator to R_1 is zero. We have obviously obtained too long result to be analyzed by observation. We continue to form sensitivities to all remaining components in symbolic form.

```
>> SDR2=diff(absden,R2)*R2/absden;
>> SDC1=diff(absden,C1)*C1/absden;
>> SDC2=diff(absden,C2)*C2/absden;
>> SDRF=diff(absden,RF)*RF/absden;
>> SDRG=diff(absden,RG)*RG/absden;

>> SNR2=diff(absnum,R2)*R2/absnum;
>> SNC1=diff(absnum,C1)*C1/absnum;
>> SNC2=diff(absnum,C2)*C2/absnum;
>> SNRF=diff(absnum,RF)*RF/absnum;
>> SNRG=diff(absnum,RG)*RG/absnum;
```

By application of rule (14), we form sensitivities to each component, whose squares we finally have to sum, and form (9).

```
>>SCH=(SNR1-SDR1)^2+(SNR2-SDR2)^2+(SNC1-SDC1)^2+(SNC2-SDC2)^2+...
(SNRF-SDRF)^2+(SNRG-SDRG)^2;
```

The resulting analytical form of multi-parametric sensitivity is as follows:

```
>> SigmaAlpha=sqrt(SCH)*0.01*8.68588964;
```

The multiplication by 0.01 defines the standard deviation of all passive elements σ_x in (9) to be 1%. The multiplication by 8.68588965 converts the standard deviation σ_F in (9) into decibels.

When typing `SigmaAlpha` in Matlab's workspace, a very large symbolic expression is obtained. We do not present it here (it is not recommended to try!). Because it is too large neither is it useful for an analytical investigation, nor can it be retyped, nor presented in table form. Instead we will substitute in this large analytical expression for `SigmaAlpha` *component values* and draw it *numerically*. This has more sense.

Define first set of element values (Circuit 1 with equal capacitors and equal resistors):

```
>> R1=37e3;R2=37e3;C1=50e-12;C2=50e-12;RG=1e4;RF=1.8e4;
```

By equating to values, elements changed in the workspace to `double` and they have become numeric. Substitute those elements into `SigmaAlpha`.

```
>> Schoefler1=subs(SigmaAlpha);
```

Note that in new variable `Schoefler1` independent variable is symbolic `wd`. To calculate its magnitude, we have to define first the frequency range of ω, as a vector of discrete values in `wd`. When the frequency in Hz is defined, we have to multiply it by 2π. The frequency assumed ranges from 10kHz to 1MHz.

```
>> fd = logspace(4,6,200);
>> wd = 2*pi*fd;
>> Sch1 = subs(Schoefler1,wd);
>> semilogx(fd, Sch1, 'g-.');
>> title('Multi-Parametric Sensitivity');
>> xlabel('Frequency / kHz'); ylabel('\sigma_{\alpha} / dB');
>> legend('Circuit 1');
>> axis([fd(1) fd(end) 0 2.5])
>> grid;
```

This is all needed to plot the sensitivity curve of Circuit 1.
To add the second example, we set the element values of Circuit 2 in the Matlab workspace:

```
>> R1=23.1e3;R2=92.4e3;C1=80e-12;C2=20e-12;RG=1e4;RF=1.05e4;
```

Then we substitute symbolic elements (components) in the `SigmaAlpha` with the numeric values of components in the workspace to obtain new numeric vales for sensitivity

```
>> Schoefler2=subs(SigmaAlpha);
>> Sch2 = subs(Schoefler2,wd);
```

Finally, to draw both curves we type

```
>> semilogx(fd, Sch1, 'k-', fd, Sch2, 'r--');
>> title('Multi-Parametric Sensitivity');
>> xlabel('Frequency / kHz'); ylabel('\sigma_{\alpha} / dB');
>> legend('Circuit 1', 'Circuit 2');
>> axis([fd(1) fd(end) 0 2.5])
>> grid;
```

Sensitivity curves of Circuit 1 and Circuit 2 are shown in Figure 6. Recall that both circuits realize the same transfer-function magnitude which is shown in Figure 3(a) above. Note that only several lines of Matlab instructions have to be repeated, and none of large analytical expressions have to be retyped.
In the following Chapter 4, we will use Matlab routines presented so far to construct examples of different filter designs. According to the results obtained from noise and sensitivity analyses we prove the optimum design.

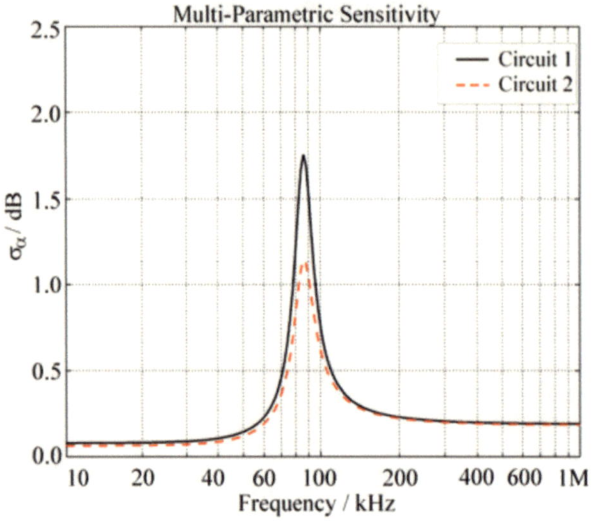

Fig. 6. Standard deviation of magnitudes of Circuit 1 and Circuit 2 (sensitivity).

4. Application to second- and third-order LP, BP, and HP filters

4.1 Second-order Biquads

Consider the second-order Biquads that realize LP, HP and BP transfer functions, shown in Figure 7. Those are the Biquads that are recommended as high-quality building blocks; see (Moschytz & Horn, 1981; Jurisic et al., 2010b, 2010c). In (Moschytz & Horn, 1981) only the design procedure for min. GSP is given (and by that providing the minimum *active* sensitivity design). On the basis of component ratios in the passive, frequency-dependent feedback network of the Biquads in Figure 7, defined by:

$$\rho = C_1 / C_2, r = R_2 / R_1, \tag{15}$$

the detailed step-by-step design of those filters, in the form of cookbook, for optimum *passive* and *active* sensitivities as well as low noise is considered in (Jurisic et al., 2010b, 2010c). The optimum design is presented in Table 1 in (Jurisic et al., 2010c) and is programmed using Matlab.

Note that the Biquads in Figure 7 shown vertically are related by the complementary transformation, whereas those shown horizontally are RC-CR duals of each other. Thus, complementary circuits are LP (class-4: positive feedback) and BP-C (class-3: negative feedback), as well as HP (class-4) and BP-R (class-3). In class-4 case there is β, whereas in class-3 there is $\overline{\beta}$, that are related by:

$$1/\beta + 1/\overline{\beta} = 1. \tag{16}$$

Dual Biquads in Figure 7 are LP and HP (class-4), as well as BP-C and BP-R (class-3); they belong to the same class.

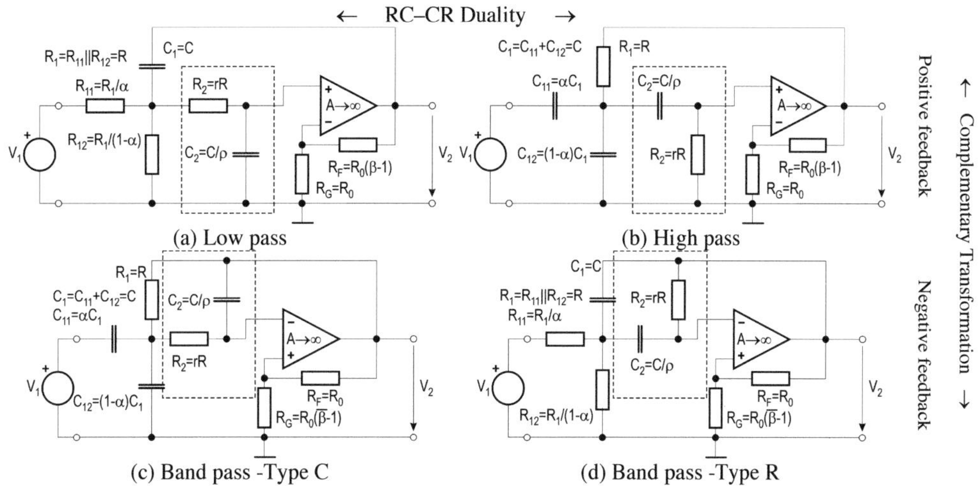

Fig. 7. Second-order LP, HP and BP active-*RC* filters with impedance scaling factors *r* and *ρ*.

Voltage transfer functions for all the filters shown in Figure 7 in terms of the pole frequency ω_p, the pole Q, q_p and the gain factor *K*, are defined by:

$$T(s)=\frac{V_2}{V_1}=\frac{N(s)}{D(s)}=K\cdot\frac{n(s)}{s^2+\dfrac{\omega_p}{q_p}s+\omega_p^2}, \tag{17a}$$

where numerators $n(s)$ are given by:

$$n_{HP}(s)=s^2,\quad n_{BP}(s)=\omega_p\cdot s,\quad n_{LP}(s)=\omega_p^2. \tag{17b}$$

Parameters ω_p, q_p and *K*, as functions of filter components, are given in Table 2. They are calculated using Matlab procedures presented in Section 3.1. Referring to Figure 7, the voltage attenuation factor α ($0<\alpha\leq 1$), which decouples gains *K* and β, see (Moschytz, 1999), is defined by the voltage divider at the input of the filter circuits. Note that all filters in Figure 7 have the same expressions for ω_p, and that the expressions for pole Q, q_p are identical only for complementary circuits. This is the reason why complementary circuits have *identical* sensitivity properties and share the same optimum design, see (Jurisic et al., 2010c).

(a) LP and (c) BP-C	(b) HP and (d) BP-R
$\omega_p=\dfrac{1}{\sqrt{R_1R_2C_1C_2}}$, $q_p=\dfrac{\sqrt{R_1R_2C_1C_2}}{R_1(C_1+C_2)+R_2C_2-\beta R_1C_1}$, $K=\alpha\beta$ for LP and $K=\alpha\bar{\beta}q_p\sqrt{R_1C_1/(R_2C_2)}$ for BP-C.	$\omega_p=\dfrac{1}{\sqrt{R_1R_2C_1C_2}}$, $q_p=\dfrac{\sqrt{R_1R_2C_1C_2}}{(R_1+R_2)C_2+R_1C_1-\beta R_2C_2}$, $K=\alpha\beta$ for HP and $K=\alpha\bar{\beta}q_p\sqrt{R_2C_2/(R_1C_1)}$ for BP-R.

Table 2. Transfer function parameters of second-order active-RC filters in Figure 7.

No.	Filter\Design Parameter	r	ρ	$\hat{q}$	β	C_1	C_2	C_{TOT}	R_1	R_2	R_{TOT}	E_{no}
1	Non Tapered	1	1	0.333	2.8	50	50	100	37	37	74	176.0
2	Capacitively Tapered	1	4	0.333	1.4	80	20	100	46.3	46.3	92.5	102.5
3	Resistively Tapered	4	1	0.333	5.6	50	50	100	18.5	74	92.5	360.9
4	Ideally Tapered	4	4	0.444	2.05	80	20	100	23.1	92.5	115.6	127.7
5	Cap-Taper and min. GSP	1.85	4	0.397	1.58	80	20	100	34.02	62.9	96.94	103.9

Table 3. Component values and rms output noise E_{no} of design examples of second-order LP and BP-C filters as in Figure 7(a) and (c) with $\omega_p=2\pi\cdot 86$krad/s and $q_p=5$ (resistors in [kΩ], capacitors in [pF], noise in [μV]).

No.	Filter\Design Parameter	r	ρ	$\hat{q}$	β	C_1	C_2	C_{TOT}	R_1	R_2	R_{TOT}	E_{no}
1	Non Tapered	1	1	0.333	2.8	50	50	100	37	37	74	201.6
2	Capacitively Tapered	1	4	0.333	5.6	80	20	100	46.3	46.3	92.5	460.1
3	Resistively Tapered	4	1	0.333	1.4	50	50	100	18.5	74	92.5	96.73
4	Ideally Tapered	4	4	0.444	2.05	80	20	100	23.1	92.5	115.6	137.0
5	Res-Taper and min. GSP	4	1.85	0.397	1.58	65	35	100	19.4	77.6	97.0	100.3

Table 4. Component values and rms output noise E_{no} of design examples of second-order HP and BP-R filters as in Figure 7(b) and (d) with $\omega_p=2\pi\cdot 86$krad/s and $q_p=5$ (resistors in [kΩ], capacitors in [pF], noise in [μV]).

On the other hand, two 'dual' circuits will have *dual* sensitivities and dual optimum designs. Dual means that the roles of resistor ratios are interchanged by the corresponding capacitor ratios, and vice versa.

It is shown in (Jurisic et al., 2010c) that complementary Biquads have *identical* noise transfer functions and, therefore, the same output noise.

An optimization of both sensitivity *and* noise performance is possible by varying the general impedance tapering factors (15) of the resistors and capacitors in the passive-RC network of the filters in Figure 7, see (Moschytz, 1999; Jurisic et al., 2010b). By increasing $r>1$ and/or $\rho>1$, the R_2 and C_2 impedances are increased. High-impedance sections are surrounded by dashed rectangles in Figure 7.

For illustration, let us consider the following practical design example as one in (Moschytz, 1999):

$$\omega_p = 2\pi \cdot 86 \text{ kHz}; \quad q_p = 5; \quad C_{TOT} = 100 \text{ pF}. \tag{18}$$

As is shown in (Moschytz, 1999), there are various ways of impedance tapering a circuit. By application of various impedance scaling factors in (15), the resulting component values of the different types of tapered LP (and BP-C) circuits are listed in Table 3, and the components of HP (and BP-R) filters are listed in Table 4. The corresponding transfer function magnitudes are shown in Figure 8 using Matlab (see Section 3.2). In order to compare the different circuits with regard to their noise performance, the total capacitance for each is held constant, i.e. C_{TOT}=100pF.

A multi-parametric sensitivity analysis was performed using Matlab (see Section 3.5) on the filter examples in Tables 3 and 4 with the resistor and capacitor values assumed to be uncorrelated random variables, with zero-mean and 1% standard deviation. The standard

deviation $\sigma_\alpha(\omega)$[dB] of the variation of the logarithmic gain $\Delta\alpha=8.68588\cdot\Delta|T(\omega)|/|T(\omega)|$ [dB] was calculated, with respect to all passive components, and plotted for the cases in Tables 3 and 4 in Figure 9. There exist four different plots for all four Biquads in Figure 7.
In Figures 9(a) and (c) it is shown that the LP and BP-C filters no. 2, i.e. the capacitively-tapered filters with equal resistors (ρ=4 and r=1) have the minimum sensitivity to passive component variations (Moschytz, 1999). The next best result is obtained with filter no. 5, i.e. the capacitively-tapered filter with minimum Gain-Sensitivity-Product (GSP).
It is shown in Figure 9(b) and (d) that the HP and BP-R filters no. 3, i.e. the resistively tapered filters with equal resistors (having component values in the third row in Table 4) have the minimum sensitivity to passive component variations. The next best result is the 'optimum' design no. 5.
To conclude, the sensitivity curves in Figure 9 confirm that complementary Biquads have identical optimum design, whereas dual Biquads have dual optimum designs. All complementary and dual Biquads in Figure 7 have *identical* sensitivity figure of merit (all corresponding Schoeffler sensitivity curves in Figure 9 are equally high).

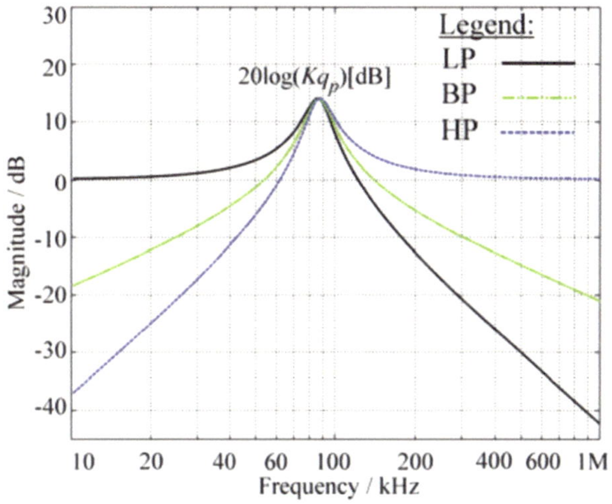

Fig. 8. Transfer function magnitudes of LP, HP and BP second-order filter examples [with (18) and K=1].

The output noise spectral density e_{no} defined by square roof of (3) has been calculated using Matlab (see Sections 3.3 and 3.4) and for these filters is shown in Figure 10. Note that there are only two figures; one for both the (complementary) LP and BP-C filters, i.e. Figure 10(a), because they have identical noise properties, and the other for HP and BP-R filters, i.e. Figure 10(b). The total rms output noise voltage E_{no} defined by square root of (4) are presented in the last columns of Tables 3 and 4 (Jurisic et al., 2010c).
Considering the noise spectral density in Figure 10(a) and the E_{no} column in Table 3, we conclude that the LP and BP-C filters, with the lowest output noise and maximum dynamic range, are again filters no. 2. The second best results are obtained with filters no. 5, and these results are the same as those for minimum sensitivity shown above (see Figures 9a and c).

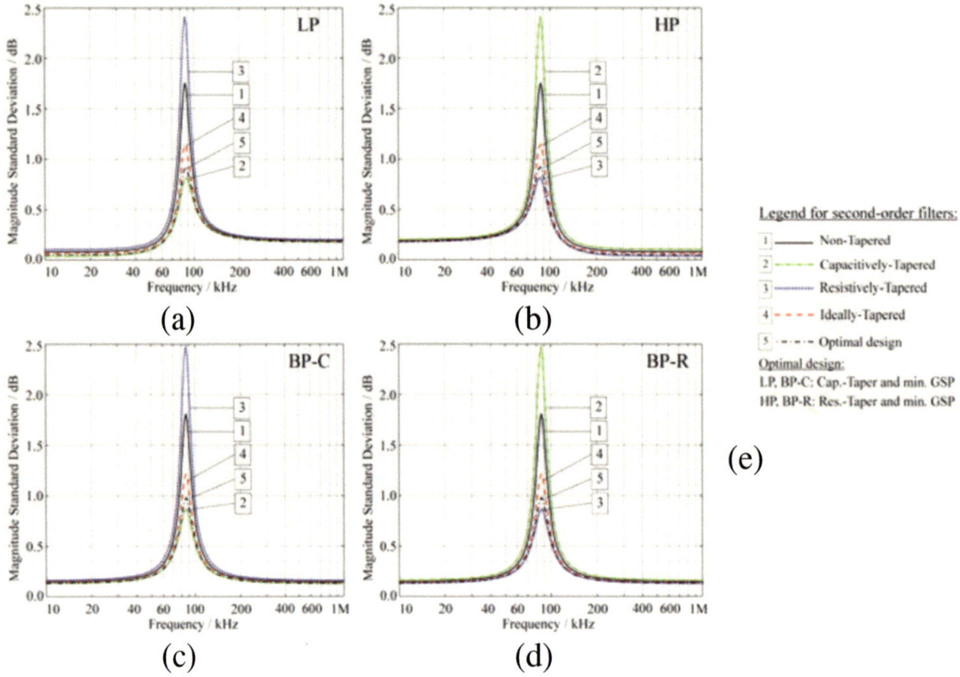

Fig. 9. Schoeffler sensitivities of second-order (a) LP, (c)BP-C filter examples in Table 3 and (b) HP, (d) BP-R filter examples given in Table 4. (e) Legend.

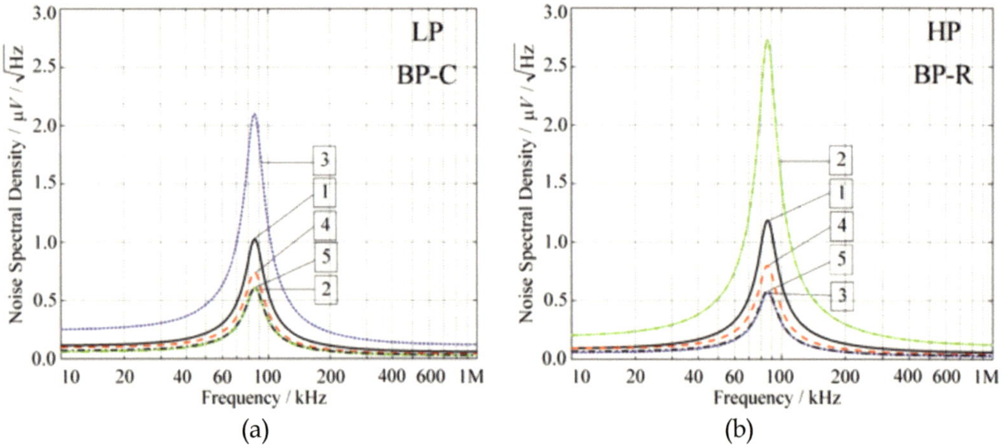

Fig. 10. Output noise spectral densities of second-order (a) LP/BP-C and (b) HP/BP-R filter examples given in Tables 3 and 4.

Analysis of the results in Figure 10(b) and the E_{no} column in Table 4 leads to conclusion that designs no. 3 and no. 5 of the HP and BP-R filters have best noise performance, as well as minimum sensitivity (see Figures 9b and d).

The noise analysis above confirms that complementary circuits have *identical* noise properties and, on the other hand, those related by the RC–CR duality have *different* noise properties. Thus, there is a difference between LP and its dual counterpart HP filter in an output noise value. From inspection of Figure 10 it results that the noise of the HP filter is larger than that of the LP filter, for all design examples.

Consequently, we propose to use the LP and BP-C Biquads in Figure 7(a) and (c) as recommended second-order active filter building blocks, because they have better noise figure-of-merit, and the HP Biquad in Figure 7(b) as a second-order active filter building block for high-pass filters, if low noise and sensitivity properties are wanted. Unfortunately, it is unavoidable, that HP realizations will have a little bit worse noise performance.

4.2 Third-order Bitriplets

The extension to third-order filter sections follows precisely the same principles as those above. Unlike with second-order filters, third-order filters cannot be ideally tapered; instead only capacitive or resistive tapering is possible (Moschytz, 1999).

Let us consider the third-order filter sections (Bitriplets) that realize LP and HP transfer functions, shown in Figure 11. Optimum design of those filters for low *passive and active* sensitivities, as well as *low noise*, is given in (Jurisic et al., 2010b, 2010c). The optimum design is presented in Table 6 in (Jurisic et al., 2010c) and is programmed using Matlab. In (Jurisic et al., 2010a, 2010c), the detailed noise analysis on the analytical basis is given for the third-order LP and the (dual) HP circuits in Figure 11. Both sensitivity and noise analysis are performed using Matlab routines in Section 3.

Voltage transfer functions for the filters in Figure 11 are given by:

$$T(s)=\frac{V_2}{V_1}=K\cdot\frac{n(s)}{s^3+a_2s^2+a_1s+a_0}=K\cdot\frac{n(s)}{(s+\gamma)\left(s^2+\frac{\omega_p}{q_p}s+\omega_p^2\right)} \tag{19a}$$

where numerators $n(s)$ are given by:

$$n_{HP}(s)=s^3,\ n_{LP}(s)=a_0=\gamma\omega_p^2\,. \tag{19b}$$

Coefficients a_i (i=0, 1, 2), and gain K as functions of filter components are given in Table 5.

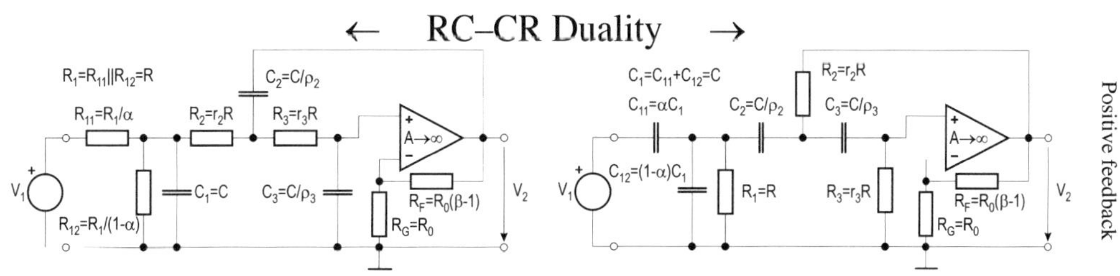

(a) Low pass (b) High pass

Fig. 11. Third-order LP and HP active-*RC* filters with impedance scaling factors r_i and ρ_i (i=2, 3).

Coefficient	(a) LP
$a_0 = \gamma\omega_p^2$	$\left(R_1R_2R_3C_1C_2C_3\right)^{-1}$
$a_1 = \omega_p^2 + \frac{\gamma\omega_p}{q_p}$	$\frac{R_1C_1 + (R_1 + R_2 + R_3)C_3 + (1-\beta)C_2(R_1 + R_2)}{R_1R_2R_3C_1C_2C_3}$
$a_2 = \gamma + \frac{\omega_p}{q_p}$	$\frac{R_1R_2C_1C_3 + R_1R_3C_3(C_1 + C_2) + R_2R_3C_2C_3 + (1-\beta)R_1R_2C_1C_2}{R_1R_2R_3C_1C_2C_3}$
K	$\alpha\beta$
Coefficient	(b) HP
a_0	$\left(R_1R_2R_3C_1C_2C_3\right)^{-1}$
a_1	$\frac{R_1(C_1 + C_2) + R_2(C_2 + C_3) + R_3C_3(1-\beta)}{R_1R_2R_3C_1C_2C_3}$
a_2	$\frac{R_1R_2C_1(C_2 + C_3) + R_2C_2C_3(R_1 + R_3) + R_1R_3C_3(C_1 + C_2)(1-\beta)}{R_1R_2R_3C_1C_2C_3}$
K	$\alpha\beta$

Table 5. Transfer function coefficients of third-order active-*RC* filters with positive feedback in Figure 11.

An optimization of both sensitivity *and* noise performance is possible by varying the general impedance scaling factors of the resistors and capacitors in the passive network of the filters in Figure 11, see (Moschytz, 1999):

$$R_1 = R,\ R_2 = r_2R,\ R_3 = r_3R,\ C_1 = C,\ C_2 = C/\rho_2,\ C_3 = C/\rho_3. \tag{20}$$

The quantity referred to as 'design frequency' is defined by $\omega_0=1/(RC)$ (Moschytz, 1999).
The third-order LP and HP filters with the minimum sensitivity to component tolerances as well as the lowest output noise and maximum dynamic range are the circuits designed in the optimum way as presented in Table 6 in (Jurisic et al., 2010c). The LP filter circuit was designed by capacitive impedance tapering with $\rho_2=\rho$, $\rho_3=\rho^2$; $\rho>1$ and ω_0 chosen to provide $r_2\approx r_3$. In the case of the third-order HP filter, the optimum design is dual: circuit has to be designed by resistive impedance tapering with $r_2=r$, $r_3=r^2$; $r>1$ and ω_0 chosen to provide $\rho_2\approx\rho_3$. Thus, the minimum-noise and minimum-sensitivity designs coincide.
Comparing the output noise of two third-order dual circuits we see again that HP filter has *larger* noise than LP filter, although their sensitivities are *identical*, see (Jurisic et al., 2010c).

5. Conclusion

In this paper the application of Matlab analysis of active-RC filters performed regarding noise and sensitivity to component tolerances performance is demonstrated. All Matlab routines used in the analysis are presented. It is shown in (Jurisic et al., 2010c) and repeated here that LP, BP and HP allpole active-RC filters of second- and third-order that are designed in (Jurisic et al., 2010b) for minimum sensitivity to component tolerances, are also superior in terms of low output thermal noise when compared with standard designs. The filters are of low power because they use only one opamp.

What is shown here is that the second-order, allpole, single-amplifier LP/HP filters with positive feedback, designed using capacitive/resistive impedance tapering in order to minimize sensitivity to component tolerances, also posses the minimum output thermal noise. The second-order BP-C filter with negative feedback is recommended filter block when the low noise is required. The same is shown for low-sensitivity, third-order, LP and HP filters of the same topology. Using low-noise opamps and metal-film small-valued resistors together with the proposed design method, low-sensitivity *and* low-noise filters result simultaneously. The mechanism by which the sensitivity to component tolerances of the LP, HP and BP allpole active-RC filters is reduced, also efficiently reduces the total noise at the filter output. Designs are presented in the form of optimum design tables programmed in Matlab [see Tables 1 and 6 in (Jurisic et al., 2010c)].

All curves are constructed by the presented Matlab code, and all calculations have been performed using Matlab.

6. References

Jurišić, D., & Moschytz, G. S. (2000). Low Noise Active-RC Low-, High- and Band-pass Allpole Filters Using Impedance Tapering. *Proceedings of MEleCon 2000*, Lemesos, Cyprus, (May 29-31, 2000.), pp. 591–594

Jurišić, D. (April 17th, 2002). *Active RC Filter Design Using Impedance Tapering*. Zagreb, Croatia: Ph. D. Thesis, University of Zagreb, April 2002.

Jurišić, D., Moschytz, G. S., & Mijat, N. (2008). Low-Sensitivity, Single-Amplifier, Active-RC Allpole Filters Using Tables. *Automatika*, Vol. 49, No. 3-4, (Nov. 2008), pp. 159–173, ISSN 0005-1144, Available from http://hrcak.srce.hr/automatika

Jurišić, D., Moschytz, G. S., & Mijat, N. (2010). Low-Noise, Low-Sensitivity, Active-RC Allpole Filters Using Impedance Tapering. *International Journal of Circuit Theory and Applications*, doi: 10.1002/cta.740, ISSN 0098-9886

Jurišić, D., Moschytz, G. S., & Mijat, N. (2010). Low-Sensitivity Active-RC Allpole Filters Using Optimized Biquads. *Automatika*, Vol. 51, No. 1, (Mar. 2010), pp. 55–70, ISSN 0005-1144, Available from http://hrcak.srce.hr/automatika

Jurišić, D., Moschytz, G. S., & Mijat, N. (2010). Low-Noise Active-RC Allpole Filters Using Optimized Biquads. *Automatika*, Vol. 51, No. 4, (Dec. 2010), pp. 361-373, ISSN 0005-1144, Available from http://hrcak.srce.hr/automatika

Laker, K. R., & Ghausi, M. S. (1975). Statistical Multiparameter Sensitivity—A Valuable Measure for CAD. *Proceedings of ISCAS 1975*, April 1975., pp. 333–336.

Moschytz, G. S., & Horn, P. (1981). *Active Filter Design Handbook*. John Wiley and Sons, ISBN 978-0471278504, Chichester, UK.: 1981, (IBM Progr. Disk: ISBN 0471-915 43 2)

Moschytz, G. S. (1999). Low-Sensitivity, Low-Power, Active-RC Allpole Filters Using Impedance Tapering. *IEEE Trans. on Circuits and Systems – Part II*, Vol. CAS-46, No. 8, (Aug 1999), pp. 1009–1026, ISSN 1057-7130

Schaumann, R., Ghausi, M. S., & Laker, K. R. (1990) *Design of Analog Filters, Passive, Active RC, and Switched Capacitor*, Prentice Hall, ISBN 978-0132002882, New Jersey 1990

Schoeffler, J. D. (1964). The Synthesis of Minimum Sensitivity Networks. *IEEE Trans. on Circuits Theory*, Vol. 11, No. 2, (June. 1964), pp. 271–276, ISSN 0018-9324

11

On Design of CIC Decimators

Gordana Jovanovic Dolecek and Javier Diaz-Carmona
Institute INAOE Puebla, Institute ITC Celaya
Mexico

1. Introduction

The process of changing sampling rate of a signal is called sampling rate conversion (SRC). Systems that employ multiple sampling rates in the processing of digital signals are called multirate digital signal processing systems.

Multirate systems have different applications, such as efficient filtering, subband coding, audio and video signals, analog/digital conversion, software defined radio and communications, among others (Jovanovic Dolecek, 2002).

The reduction of a sampling rate is called decimation and consists of two stages: filtering and downsampling. If signal is not properly bandlimited the overlapping of the repeated replicas of the original spectrum occurs. This effect is called aliasing and may destroy the useful information of the decimated signal. That is why we need filtering to avoid this unwanted effect.

The most simple decimation filter is comb filter which does not require multipliers. One efficient implementation of this filter is called CIC (Cascaded-Integrator-Comb) filter proposed by Hogenauer (Hogenauer, 1981). Because of the popularity of this structure many authors also call the comb filter as CIC filter. In this chapter we will use term CIC filter. Due to its simplicity, the CIC filter is usually used in the first stage of decimation. However, the filter exhibits a high passband droop and a low attenuation in so called folding bands (bands around the zeros of CIC filter), which can be not acceptable in different applications. During last several years the improvement of the CIC filter characteristics attracted many researchers. Different methods have been proposed to improve the characteristics of the CIC filters, keeping its simplicity.

In this chapter we present different proposed methods to improve CIC magnitude characteristics illustrated with examples and MATLAB programs.

The rest of the chapter is organized in the following way. Next Section describes the CIC filter. Section 3 introduces the methods for the CIC passband improvement followed by the Section 4 which presents the methods for the CIC stopband improvement. The methods for both, the CIC passband and stopband improvements are described in Section 5.

2. CIC filter

CIC (Cascaded-Integrator-Comb) filter (Hogenauer, 1981) is widely used as the decimation filter due to its simplicity; it requires no multiplication or coefficient storage but rather only additions/subtractions. This filter consists of two main sections, cascaded integrators and combs, separated by a down-sampler, as shown in Fig. 1.

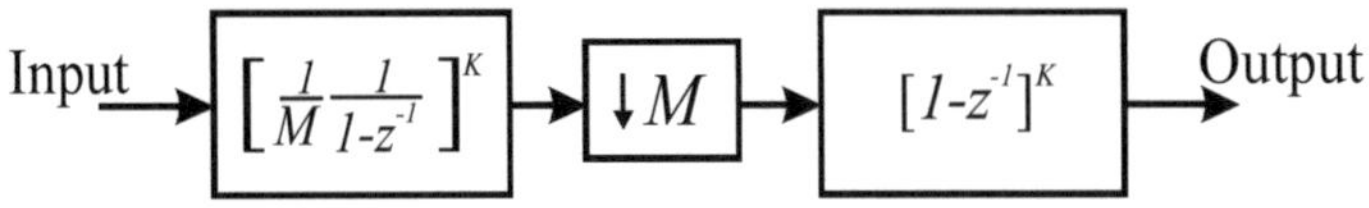

Fig. 1. CIC filter.

The transfer function of the resulting decimation filter, also known as a RRS (recursive running sum) or comb filter is given by

$$H_{comb}(z)=\left[\frac{1}{M}\left(\frac{1-z^{-M}}{1-z^{-1}}\right)\right]^K, \quad (1)$$

where M is the decimation factor, and K is the number of the stages. The transfer function in (1) will be also referred to as the comb filter. The integrator section works at the higher input data rate thereby resulting in higher chip area and higher power dissipation for this section. In order to resolve this problem the non-recursive structure of Eq. (1) can be used (Aboushady et al., 2001), (Gao at al., 2000),

$$H(z)=\left[\frac{1}{M}\right]^K\left[1+z^{-1}+z^{-2}+\ldots+z^{-(M-1)}\right]^K. \quad (2)$$

Implementing $H(z)$ of Eq. (2) in a polyphase form, the filtering at the high input rate can be moved to the lower rate. In this chapter we do not discuss the CIC implementation issues.

2.1 Magnitude characteristic

The magnitude characteristic of the comb decimator must satisfy two requirements:

- To have a low droop in the frequency band defined by the passband frequency ω_p in order to preserve the signal after decimation.
- To have a high attenuations in so called folding bands, i. e. the bands around of the zeros of the comb filter,

$$\left[\frac{2\pi i}{M}-\omega_p;\frac{2\pi i}{M}+\omega_p\right], \text{ for } i=\begin{cases}1,\ldots,M/2 & for \quad M\ even\\ 1,\ldots,(M-1)/2 & for \quad M\ odd\end{cases} \quad (3)$$

We define the passband frequency as the frequency where the worst case of passband droop occurs, (Kwentus, Willson, 1997),

$$\omega_p=\frac{\pi}{MR}, \quad (4)$$

where R is the decimation stage that follows the CIC decimation stage, and that is usually much less than M.

The magnitude response of the comb filter exhibits a linear-phase, lowpass characteristic which can be expressed as

$$\left|H_{comb}(e^{j\omega})\right|=\left|\frac{1}{M}\frac{\sin(\omega M/2)}{\sin(\omega/2)}\right|^K. \quad (5)$$

Figure 2.a shows the magnitude characteristics in dB for M=8 and the values of K=1, 3, and 5.

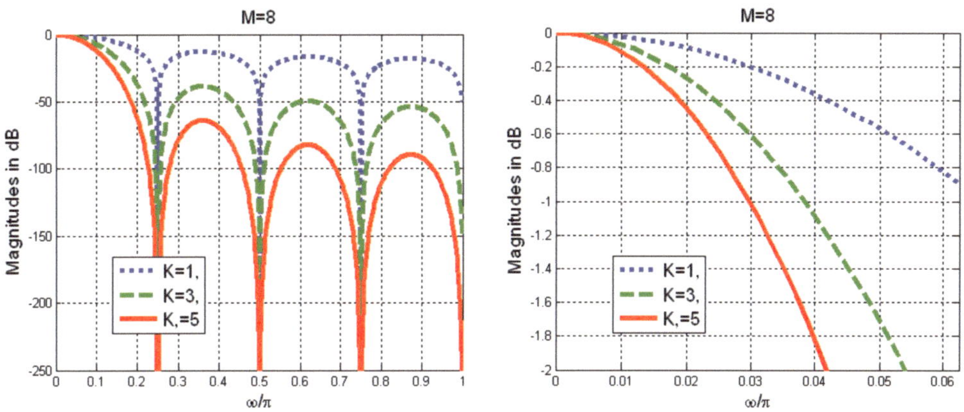

a. Overall magnitude responses. b. Passband zooms.

Fig. 2. Magnitude responses of comb filters.

Note that the attenuations in the folding bands are increased by increasing the numbers of stages. However, an increasing in the number of stages results in the increasing of the passband droop as shown in Fig. 2.b. In the continuation we will consider different methods to improve the comb magnitude characteristics keeping its simplicity.

3. Methods for the passband improvement

The motivation behind the compensation methods is to appropriately modify the original CIC characteristic in the desired passband such that the compensator filter has as low complexity as possible. Different methods have been proposed to compensate for the CIC passband droop. We classify the methods as the methods for the narrowband compensation (R>2), and the methods for the wideband compensation (R=2). Methods specified in (Fernandez-Vazquez & Jovanovic Dolecek, 2009, 2011), (Kim et al. 2006) employ optimization techniques, whereby the resulting compensation filters require multipliers. The method described in (Yeung & Chan, 2004) suggests the multiplierless design of a second order compensation filter where the filter coefficients are expressed as a sum of power of two (SOPOT) and are computed using the random search algorithm. The simple multiplierless compensator with only one parameter, which depends on the number of the stages K of the CIC filter, is proposed in (Jovanovic Dolecek & Mitra, 2008). This filter provides a good compensation in a narrow passband. The wide-band compensators have been recently proposed in (Jovanovic Dolecek, 2009), and (Jovanovic Dolecek & Dolecek, 2010).

We define the following desirable CIC compensator properties:

- The proposed filter should work at a low sampling rate;
- Multiplierless design and a second order at low rate;
- Simple design i.e., that it is not necessary redesign the filter for new values of M and K;
- That the compensation filter practically does not depends on the decimation factor M. This is a very desirable characteristic because the compensator remains the same across different values of M, provided that the value of K stays the same.

3.1 Narrowband CIC compensation

We describe here the compensation filter (Jovanovic Dolecek & Mitra, 2008) because this filter satisfies all the properties mentioned previously.
Consider a filter with the magnitude response

$$\left|G(e^{j\omega})\right| = \left|1 + 2^{-b}\sin^2(\omega M/2)\right|, \tag{6}$$

where b is a integer parameter.
Using the well known relation

$$\sin^2(\alpha) = (1 - \cos(2\alpha))/2, \tag{7}$$

the corresponding transfer function can be expressed as

$$G(z^M) = -2^{-(b+2)}\left[1 - (2^{b+2} + 2)z^{-M} + z^{-2M}\right]. \tag{8}$$

Denoting

$$A = -2^{-(b+2)}; B = -(2^{b+2} + 2), \tag{9}$$

we arrive at

$$G(z^M) = A\left[1 - Bz^{-M} + z^{-2M}\right]. \tag{10}$$

The compensator filter has the scaling factor A and a single coefficient B which requires only one adder. Additionally, the compensator can be implemented at a lower rate after the downsampling by M by making use of the multirate identity (Jovanovic Dolecek, 2002), becoming a second order filter,

$$G(z) = A\left[1 - Bz^{-1} + z^{-2}\right]. \tag{11}$$

In that way the filter does not depend on the decimation factor M but only on the number of the stages K which defines the parameter b in (9). Table 1 shows typical values for b at different values of K.

Parameter K	Parameter b, R=8
2	2
3	2
4	1
5	0
6	0

Table 1. Typical parameters b for different values of K.

The overall transfer function of the cascaded CIC and compensator is

$$H(z) = H_{comb}(z)G(z^M), \tag{12}$$

where $H_{comb}(z)$ and $G(z^M)$ are given in (1) and (10), respectively.

Example 1: We compensate the CIC filter with M=16 and K=5 . From Table 1 we have b=0. The passband characteristics of the compensator, along with that of the compensated CIC and the CIC filters, are shown in Fig.3.

3.2 Wideband CIC compensation

We turn now our attention to the wideband compensators satisfying the desirable characteristics previously mentioned.

In (Jovanovic Dolecek, 2009) a novel decimation filter

$$G(z^M) = G_c^{K_1}(z^M), \tag{13}$$

is proposed, where K_1 is the parameter that depends on the number of cascaded CIC filters K,

$$K_1 = \begin{cases} K & for \quad 1 < K \le 3 \\ K-1 & for \quad K > 3 \end{cases}, \tag{14}$$

and

$$G_c(z^M) = -2^{-4}[z^{-M} - (2^4+2)z^{-2M} + z^{-3M}]. \tag{15}$$

The coefficients of the filter (15) are obtained using the condition that the compensator magnitude characteristic has the value 1 for ω=0 and minimizing the squared error in the passband. Finally, the coefficients thus obtained are rounded using the rounding constant $r=2^{-6}$.

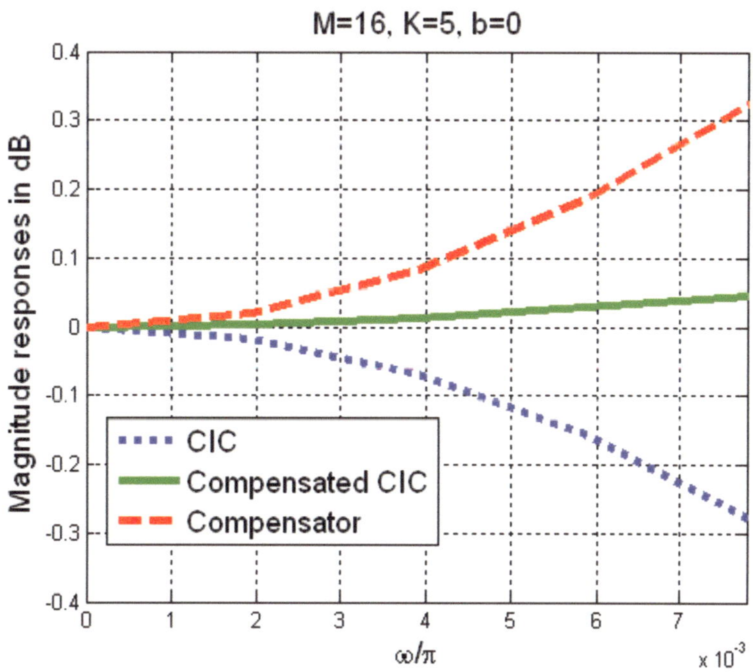

Fig. 3. Magnitude responses of CIC, Compensator and cascaded CIC-compensator.

The total number of additions depends on K, as given by

$$N_{add} = \begin{cases} 3K & for \quad K \leq 3 \\ 3K-3 & for \quad K > 3 \end{cases}. \tag{16}$$

This filter can be moved to a lower rate becoming

$$G(z) = -2^{-4}[z^{-1} - (2^4 + 2)z^{-2} + z^{-3}]. \tag{17}$$

The overall transfer function of the compensated CIC filter, obtained from (1) and (13)-(15) is as follows

$$H(z) = H_{comb}(z)G(z^M) = H_{comb}(z)G_c^{K_1}(z^M). \tag{18}$$

Note that the filter (17) does not depend on the decimation factor M. Additionally, the filter (17) has a very interesting property i.e. it does not depend on K and its structure remains the same for all values of K and M. However, the number of the cascaded compensators K_1 depends on the parameter K, as indicated in (14). The method is illustrated in the following example.

Example 2: In this example we compensate the CIC filter with M=20 and K=5. From (14) it follows that K_1=4. The magnitude responses of the compensated CIC, along with the responses of the compensator and CIC filters, are shown in Fig.4. From (16) the total number of adders in compensator 3K-3, equal 12.

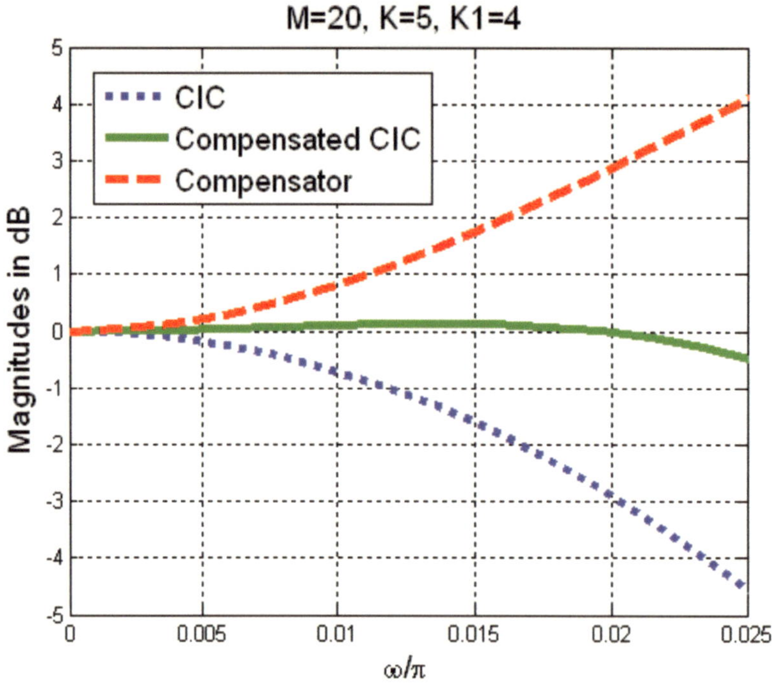

Fig. 4. Wideband compensation method (Jovanovic Dolecek, 2009).

Example 3: In this example we apply the compensator from (Jovanovic Dolecek, 2009) to the CIC filter with M=25 and K=2; in this case K_1=2. The required number of adders for the decimator is $3K$=6. Figure 5 shows the corresponding magnitude responses.
We will refer here the method from (Jovanovic Dolecek, 2009) as the Compensation method 1.
Another simple wideband multiplierless compensator has been proposed in (Jovanovic Dolecek & Dolecek, 2010). The goal put in it, was that the resulting passband deviation be less than 0.4 dB, and to decrease the number of adders comparing with the Compensation method 1.
To this end the following filter has been proposed,

$$H_c(z^M) = bz^{-M} + az^{-2M} + bz^{-3M}, \tag{19}$$

with the corresponding magnitude response

$$|H_c(\omega)| = |2b\cos(M\omega) + a|. \tag{20}$$

The coefficients a and b, obtained in (Jovanovic Dolecek & Dolecek, 2010), are as follows

$$b = 0.5\left[1 - \frac{\alpha M^K \sin^K(\pi/4M)}{\sin^K(\pi/4)}\right]. \tag{21}$$

$$a = 1 - \left[1 - \frac{\alpha M^K \sin^K(\pi/4M)}{\sin^K(\pi/4)}\right]. \tag{22}$$

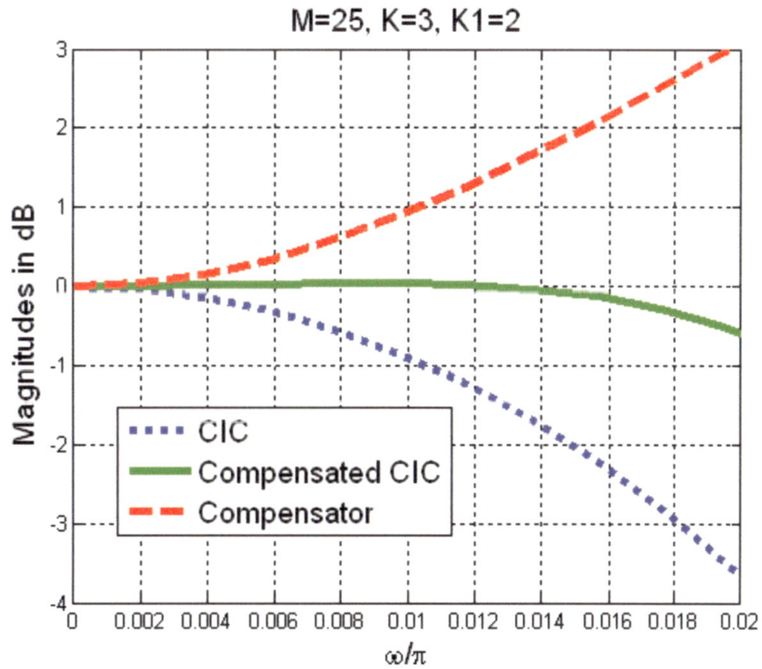

Fig. 5. Wideband CIC compensation using the Compensation method 1.

The initial value of the parameter a is 1 and the value is adjusted in order to satisfy

$$\max\{|1 - H_c(\omega)H(\omega)|\} = d_p \leq \delta_p$$
$$\omega \in [0, \omega_p]. \tag{23}$$

Let us indicate how the coefficients a and b depend on M for a given K. To this end, considering that for a small value of φ, $\sin(\varphi) \sim \varphi$, and knowing that M»1, we have

$$b \approx 0.5\left[1 - \frac{\alpha\pi^K}{4^K \sin^K(\pi/4)}\right]. \tag{24}$$

$$a \approx 1 - \left[1 - \frac{\alpha\pi^K}{4^K \sin^K(\pi/4)}\right]. \tag{25}$$

From (20), (24) and (25) it follows the desirable characteristic, that the compensator does not depend on the decimation factor M but only on the parameter K, is satisfied. Next, the coefficients (24) and (25) are rounded to the nearest integer, using the rounding constant $r=2^{-5}$, resulting in

$$H_p(z^M) = S[Bz^{-M} + Az^{-2M} + Bz^{-3M}], \tag{26}$$

where S is the scaling factor and A and B are integers, which can be implemented using only adders and shifts. Consequently the decimator (26) is also multiplierless.
We also note that the compensator can be moved to a lower rate using the multirate identity, (Jovanovic Dolecek, 2002), thereby becoming a second order filter,

$$H_p(z^M) = S[Bz^{-1} + Az^{-2} + Bz^{-3}]. \tag{27}$$

Table 2 shows the values for S, A and B for different values of K. The total number of additions and the corresponding passband deviations are also shown.

K	S	B	A	d_p[dB]	Number of additions
1	2^{-4}	-1	2^4+2^1	0.142	3
2	2^{-3}	-1	2^3+2^1	0.234	3
3	2^{-4}	$-2^{-2}-2^0$	$2^4+2^2+2^1$	0.297	5
4	2^{-2}	-1	2^2+2^1	0.342	3
5	2^{-4}	-2^2-2^0	$2^4+2^3+2^1$	0.377	5

Table 2. The design parameters.

We make the following observations:

- The maximum number of adders is 5.
- The passband deviation is less than δ_p =0.4dB.
- The smallest deviation is obtained for K = 1, (d_p=0.142dB), while the largest is for K = 5, (d_p=0.377dB).

The method is illustrated in the following examples.
Example 4: We compensate the CIC filter with M=32 and K=4. The values of B, A, and S, from Table 2, are -1, 2^2+2^1, and 2^{-2}, respectively. The magnitude responses are illustrated in Fig.6.

Example 5: We compare the methods (Jovanovic Dolecek, 2009) and (Jovanovic Dolecek & Dolecek, 2010) for M=16 and K=4 and 5. The result is shown in Fig. 7. For K=4 the methods (Jovanovic Dolecek, 2009) and (Jovanovic Dolecek & Dolecek, 2010) require 9 and 3 adders , respectively. For K=5 the method (Jovanovic Dolecek & Dolecek, 2010) requires 5 adders whereas the method (Jovanovic Dolecek, 2009) requires 12 adders.

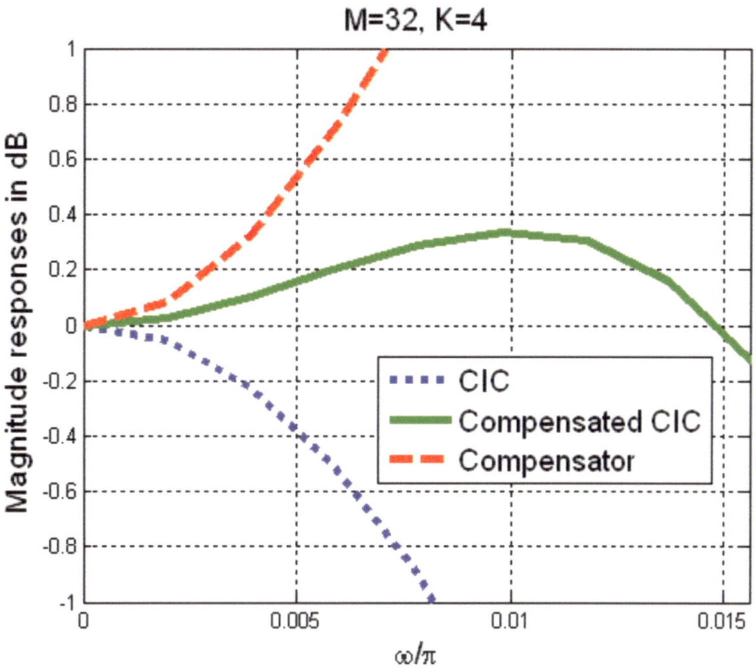

Fig. 6. Wideband CIC compensation using the method (Jovanovic Dolecek & Dolecek, 2010).

4. Methods for the stopband improvement

Presti, (Presti, 2000), introduced the CIC zero rotation and proposed the Rotated Sinc (RS) filter to increase the attenuations and widths in the folding bands. By applying a clockwise rotation of β radians to any zero of CIC filter, we obtain the following transfer function

$$H_u(z) = \frac{1}{M}\frac{1 - z^{-M}e^{j\beta M}}{1 - z^{-1}e^{j\beta}}. \tag{28}$$

An expression equivalent to (28) is obtained by applying the opposite rotation

$$H_d(z) = \frac{1}{M}\frac{1 - z^{-M}e^{-j\beta M}}{1 - z^{-1}e^{-j\beta}}. \tag{29}$$

These two filters have complex coefficients, but they can be cascaded, thus obtaining a filter $H_r(z)$ with real coefficients

$$H_r(z) = H_u(z)H_d(z) = \frac{1}{M^2}\frac{1 - 2\cos(\beta M)z^{-M} + z^{-2M}}{1 - 2\cos(\beta)z^{-1} + z^{-2}}. \tag{30}$$

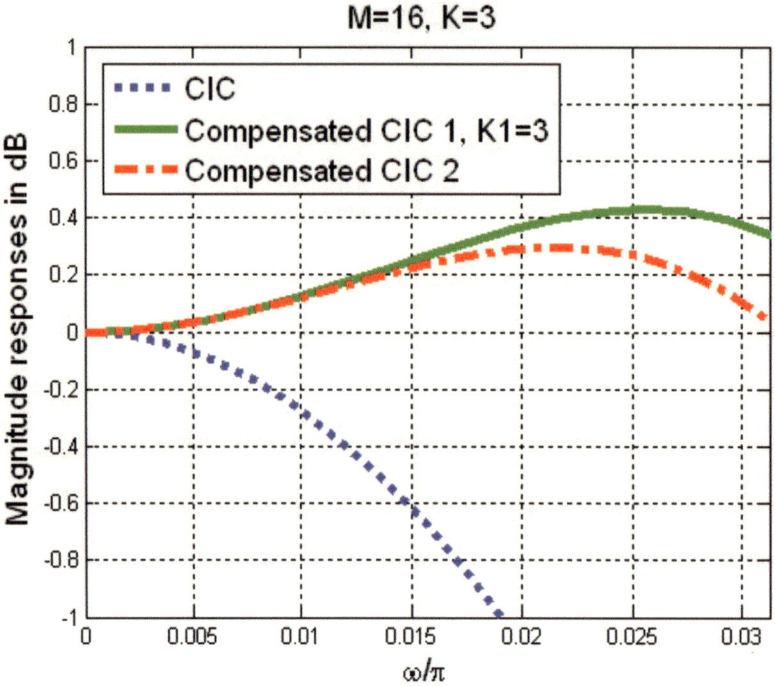

a. *K*=3.

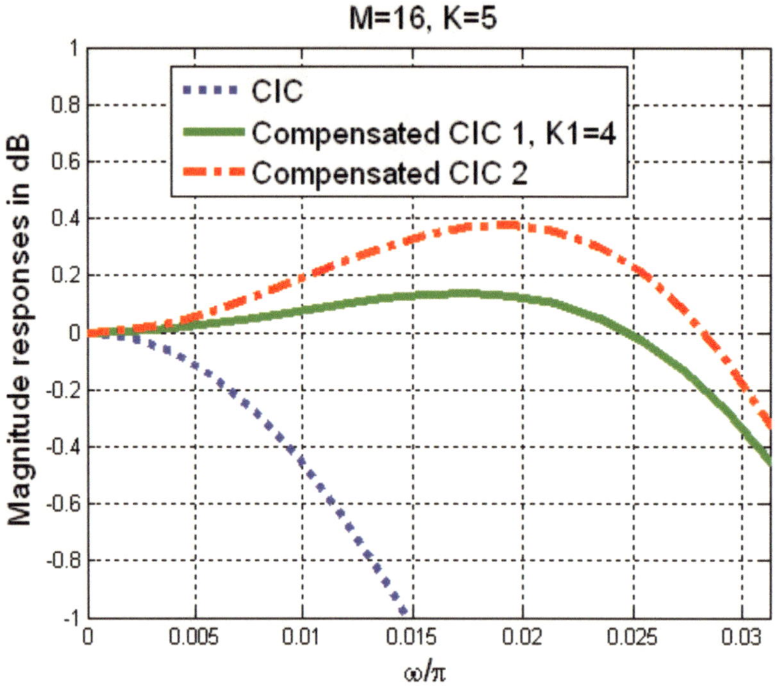

b. *K*=5.

Fig. 7. Comparisons of compensators.

The cascade of CIC filter and the filter (30) is reffered by Presti as RS filter, $H_R(z)$,

$$H_R(z) = H_{comb}(z)H_r(z)\,. \tag{31}$$

The magnitude response of this filter is given as

$$\left|H_R(e^{j\omega})\right| = \left|\frac{1}{M^3}\frac{\sin(\omega M/2)}{\sin(\omega/2)}\right|^K \left|\frac{\sin((\omega+\beta)M/2)}{\sin((\omega+\beta)/2)}\right|^K \left|\frac{\sin((\omega-\beta)M/2)}{\sin((\omega-\beta)/2)}\right|^K. \tag{32}$$

Example 6: Using the method Presti, we design the RS filter for M=16, K=1, and β=0.0184. The magnitude response is shown in Fig.8.

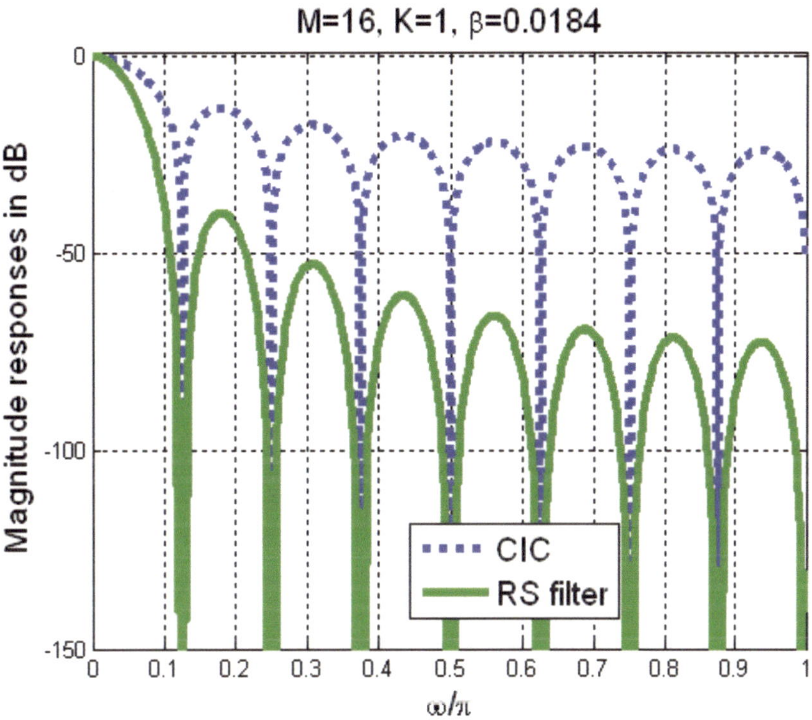

Fig. 8. Illustration of RS filter. (Presti, 2000).

Note that the folding band widths are wider and the attenuations are increased in comparison with the CIC filter. However, the passband droop is increased and additionally RS filter needs two multipliers, one working at high input rate. (See (30)).
In (Jovanovic Dolecek & Mitra, 2004) the modification of the Presti method has been proposed for the case if M can be represented as a product of two factors

$$M=M_1\,M_2. \tag{33}$$

The transfer function (1) can be rewritten as

$$H(z) = H_1^{K_1}(z)H_2^{K_2}(z^{M_1})\,. \tag{34}$$

where

$$H_1(z) = \frac{1}{M_1}\frac{1-z^{-M_1}}{1-z^{-1}}; \qquad H_2(z^{M_1}) = \frac{1}{M_2}\frac{1-z^{-M_1 M_2}}{1-z^{-M_1}}. \tag{35}$$

The filter $H_2(z)$ can be moved to a low rate which is M_2 time lesser than the high input rate. Additionally, the polyphase decomposition of the filter $H_1(z)$ move all filtering to a lower rate. The corresponding RS filter is modified in such way that it can also be moved to a lower rate.

$$H_{rm}(z) = H_{um}(z)H_{dm}(z) = \frac{1}{M_2^2}\frac{1-2\cos(\beta M)z^{-M}+z^{-2M}}{1-2\cos(\beta M_1)z^{-1}+z^{-2M_1}}. \tag{36}$$

The modified RS filter is

$$H_{Rm}(z) = H_{comb}(z)H_{rm}(z). \tag{37}$$

The corresponding magnitude response is

$$\left|H_{Rm}(e^{j\omega})\right| = \left|\frac{1}{M}\frac{\sin(\omega M/2)}{\sin(\omega/2)}\right|^K \left|\frac{\sin((\omega+\beta)M/2)}{M\sin((\omega+\beta)M_1/2)}\right| \left|\frac{\sin((\omega-\beta)M/2)}{M\sin((\omega-\beta)M_1/2)}\right|. \tag{38}$$

Next example compares the (38) with the RS filter.

Example 7: We use the same design parameters as in Example 6 taking K_1=3 and K_2=2 and M_1=M_2=4. The magnitude responses along with the zoom in the first folding band are shown in Fig. 9. Note that the attenuation in the all folding bands except the last one, are improved. Additionally, the filter $H_r(z)$ works at a lower rate.

The method in (Jovanovic Dolecek & Mitra, 2005a) includes the multistage structure and improves deteriorated passband. The generalized approach to the CIC zero-rotation, has been proposed in (Laddomada, 2007), where the generalized comb (GC) has been proposed. An economical class of droop-compensated GC filters has been proposed in (Jovanovic Dolecek & Laddomada, 2010).

Note the following:

- Folding bands are wider and with increased attenuations comparing with those of the corresponding comb filter.
- The RS filter needs two multipliers, one working at the high input rate.
- During the quantization of the coefficients in RS filter, the pole-zero cancellation can be lost resulting in instability.
- The most critical is the first folding band of a comb filter where the worst case aliasing occurs because it has less attenuation than other folding bands.

To this end in order to solve some of the above mentioned problems we propose to introduce the zero-rotation only in the first folding band yielding in the zero-rotation term (ZRT), (Jovanovic Dolecek, 2010a),

$$\begin{aligned} H_{ZR}(z) &= k(1-z^{-1}e^{-j\beta})(1-z^{-1}e^{j\beta}) \\ &= k(1-2\cos(\beta)z^{-1}+z^{-2}) \end{aligned} \tag{39}$$

where k is the normalizing constant introduced to ensure that the magnitude characteristic is equal to 1 at ω =0.

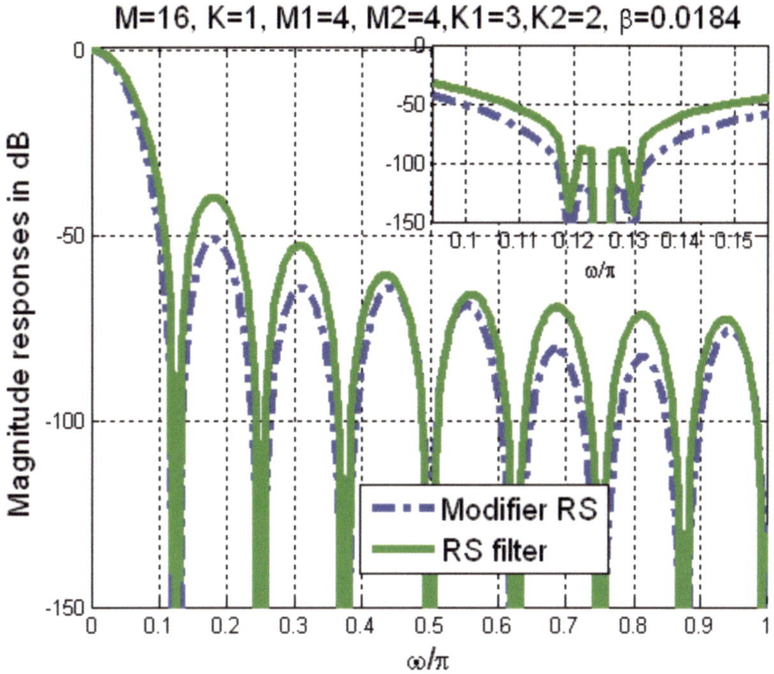

Fig. 9. Comparison of RS and modified RS filters.

Considering that *R* in (4) is equal to 2, the pass band is defined by the pass band cutoff frequency

$$\omega_p = \frac{\pi}{2M}. \tag{40}$$

The introduced zero must be in the first folding band, near the point where the worst case aliasing occurs, $2\pi/M-\omega_p$,

$$\beta = \frac{2\pi}{M} - \frac{\pi}{(\beta_0+2)M}, \tag{41}$$

where β_0 is the term which approaches slightly zero from the left end of the first folding band to the right position, within the first folding band. Typical value for β_0=0.99. The normalized constant *k* is,

$$k = \frac{1}{2-2\cos(\frac{2\pi}{M} - \frac{\pi}{(\beta_0+2)M})}. \tag{42}$$

Using (41) the cascade of the combs from (1) and the ZRT (39) is given as

$$H_{COMB,ZR} = \left[\frac{1}{M}\frac{1-z^{-M}}{1-z^{-1}}\right]^K \times k(1-2z^{-1}\cos(\frac{2\pi}{M} - \frac{\pi}{(\beta_0+2)M}) + z^{-2}). \tag{43}$$

The first folding band is wider than the CIC first folding band. However, the side lobes are increased and the pass band droop is also increased. To decrease attenuation in all other folding bands we propose to use cascade of the expanded cosine filters,

$$H_{COS}(z) = \prod_{k}\left[\frac{1}{2}(1+z^{-N_k})\right]^{K_k}, \tag{44}$$

resulting in

$$H_{COMB,ZR,COS}(z) = H_{COMB}(z)H_{ZR}(z)H_{COS}(z). \tag{45}$$

The method is illustrated in the following example.

Example 8: Let us consider CIC filter with M=12, K=5 and K=6. The expanded cosine filters are

$$H_{COS}(z) = \prod_{k=1}^{6}\left[\frac{1}{2}(1+z^{-N_k})\right]^{K_k}, N_k = k; K_1 = 2; K_k = 1, \quad for\ k = 2,...,6; \tag{46}$$

The magnitude responses along with the passband zoom are shown in Fig.10. Note that the first folding band is wider and that exhibits higher attenuation than the first folding bands of CIC filters for K=5 and 6. See (Jovanovic Dolecek, 2010a) for more details about the choice of design parameters and the multiplierless design.

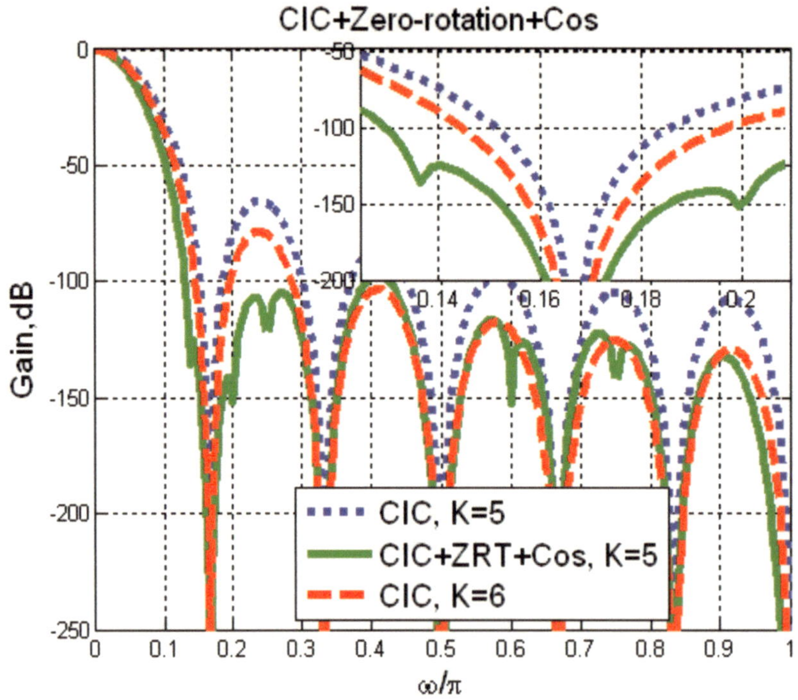

Fig. 10. Illustration of method (Jovanovic Dolecek, 2010a).

Another approach to improving the CIC stopband characteristic has been proposed in (Jovanovic Dolecek & Diaz-Carmona, 2005). The method is based on the cosine prefilters introduced in (Lian & Lim, 1993). Recently, the method based on the extended search of cyclotomic polynomials has been also proposed (Laddomada at al, 2011).

5. Methods for the passband and stopband improvement

In this section we consider some methods applied for the simultaneous improvement in the CIC passband and stopband. The pioneer work has been presented in (Kwentus & Willson, 1997), where the sharpening technique originally introduced by (Kaiser & Hamming, 1977) was applied. The sharpening technique uses the sharpening polynomials to improve the passband and the stopband characteristics of the symmetrical FIR (Finite impulse response) filter. Kwentus and Willson used the polynomial $H_{sh}=3H^2-2H^3$, where H is the CIC filter (1) and $K=K_1$. The corresponding magnitude response of the sharpened CIC filter is

$$\left|H_{shcomb}(e^{j\omega})\right| = \left|3\left(\frac{1}{M}\frac{\sin(\omega M/2)}{\sin(\omega/2)}\right)^{2K_1} - 2\left(\frac{1}{M}\frac{\sin(\omega M/2)}{\sin(\omega/2)}\right)^{3K_1}\right|. \tag{47}$$

The method is illustrated in the Example 9.

Example 9: The parameters of the CIC filter are M=16 and K=5 and K_1=3. Figure 11a shows the magnitude responses of the sharpened CIC filter and the CIC filter with K=5. Figure 11b shows the zooms in the passband and in the first folding band. Note that both the passband and the stopband are improved.

The main drawback of this method is that the sharpening is performed at high input rate. A method where the decimation is split into two stages, and the sharpening is performed only in the second stage considering that the decimation factor M is an even number, has been proposed in (Jovanovic Dolecek & Mitra, 2003). The method was generalized later for the case where the decimation factor M can be expressed as in (33). The first stage is the less simple CIC filter (M_1<M), which can be implemented either in recursive or non recursive form.

$$H_1(z) = \frac{1}{M_1}\frac{1-z^{-M_1}}{1-z^{-1}} = \sum_{i=0}^{M_1-1} z^{-i}. \tag{48}$$

In the second stage is the less complex CIC filter, (M_2<M)

$$H_2(z) = \frac{1}{M_2}\frac{1-z^{-M_2}}{1-z^{-1}}. \tag{49}$$

The overall transfer function is

$$H(z) = H_1^{K_1}(z) Sh\{H_2^{K_2}(z^{M_1})\}, \tag{50}$$

where Sh{.} means sharpening of {.}, and

$$K_1 \geq 2K_2. \tag{51}$$

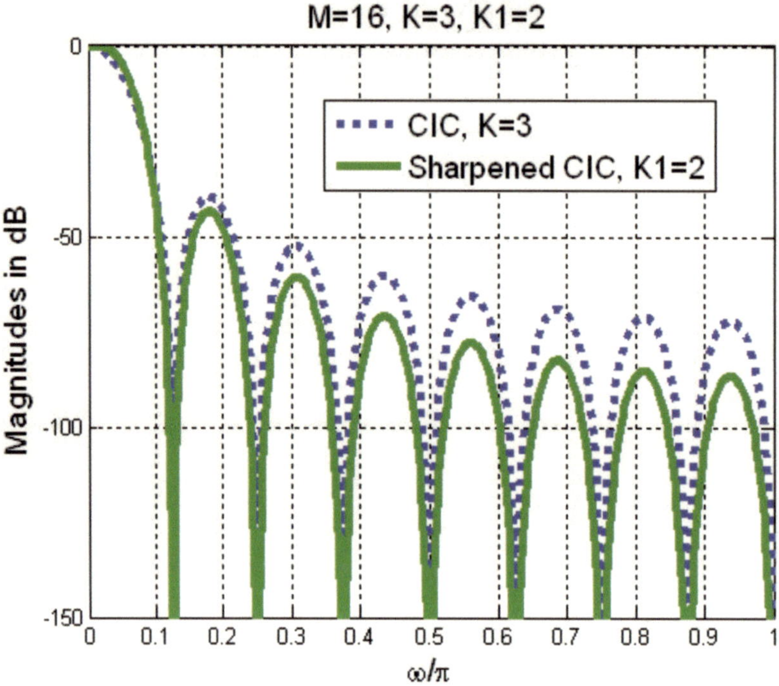

a. Overall magnitude responses.

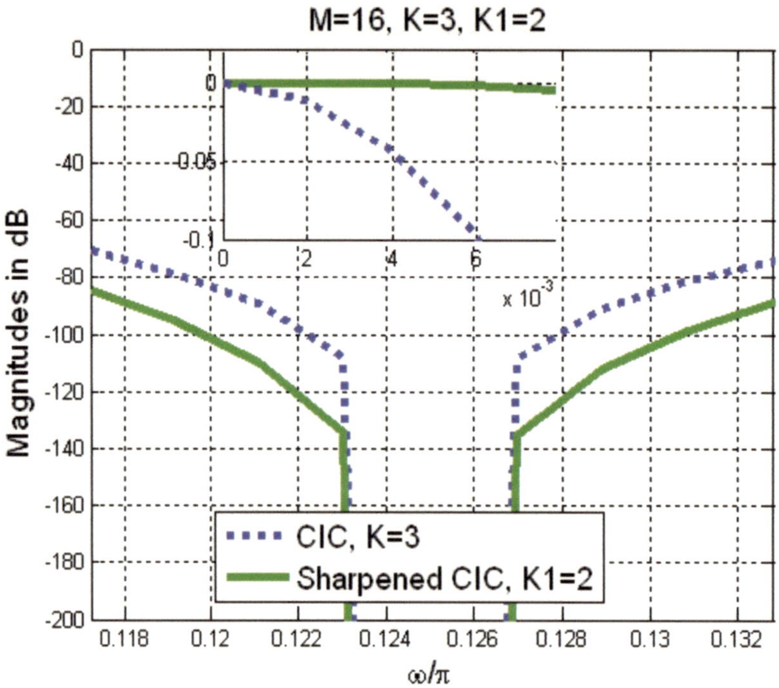

b. Passband and the first folding band zooms.

Fig. 11. Illustration of sharpening method.

The corresponding magnitude response is

$$\left|H(e^{j\omega})\right| = \left|\left(\frac{1}{M_1}\frac{\sin(\omega M_1/2)}{\sin(\omega/2)}\right)^{K_1}\left\{3\times\left(\frac{1}{M_2}\frac{\sin(\omega M/2)}{\sin(\omega M_1/2)}\right)^{2K_2} - 2\times\left(\frac{1}{M_2}\frac{\sin(\omega M/2)}{\sin(\omega M_1/2)}\right)^{3K_2}\right\}\right|. \quad (52)$$

Next examples (10) and (11) illustrate the method.

Example 10: Consider M=16 and M_1=M_2=4. The parameters K_1 and K_2 are respectively 5, and 2, and K=4. The magnitude responses and the pasband zoom are shown in Fig.12.

In the following example we compare the original sharpening method with the modified sharpening method (Jovanovic Dolecek & Mitra, 2005b).

Example 11. We compare the modified sharpening method with the original sharpening method, considering M=16 and K=4. In the modified sharpening M_1=M_2=4, K_1=5 and K_2=4. Figure 13 shows the magnitude responses and the corresponding passband zoom. Note that the original sharpening has better passband characteristic while the modified sharpening method has higher attenuations in the folding bands.

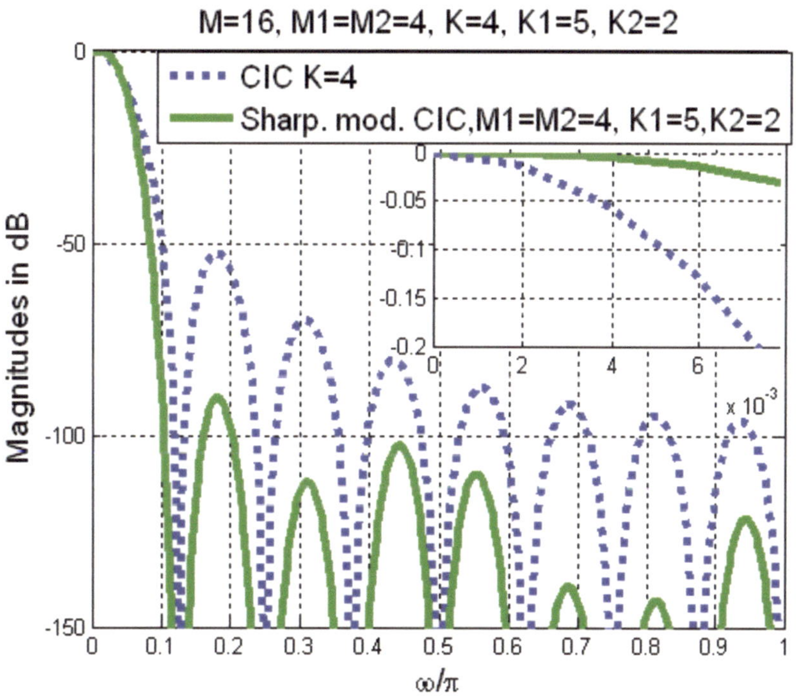

Fig. 12. Modified sharpening and CIC filters magnitude responses.

The number of authors presented different modifications of sharpening method, like (Jovanovic Dolecek, 2010b), (Laddomada & Mondin, 2004), (Jovanovic Dolecek & Harris, 2009). In (Jovanovic Dolecek & Mitra, 2010), the two-stage CIC filter with the compensator (10) has been proposed.

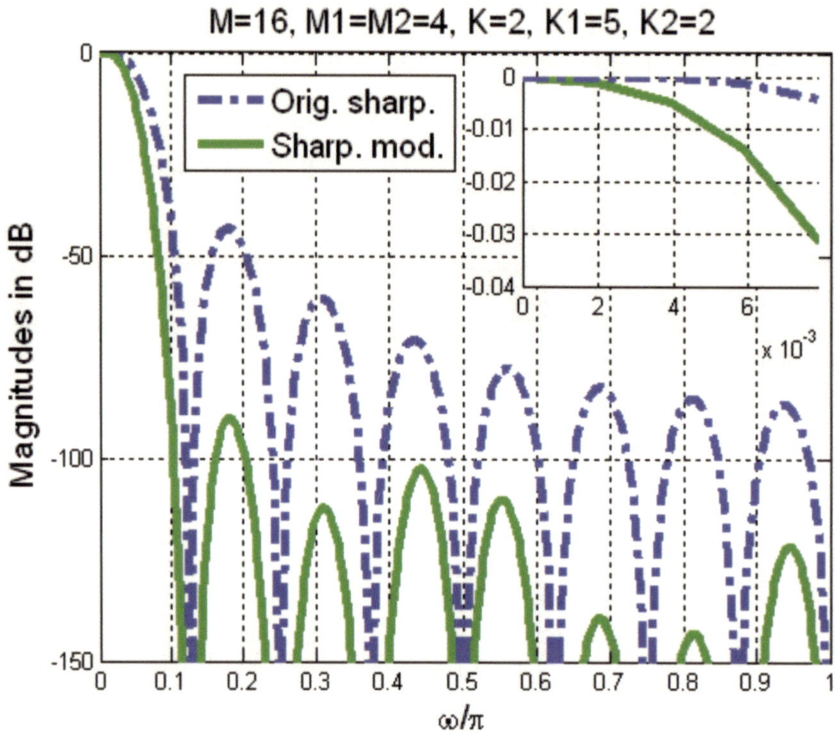

Fig. 13. Comparison of original and modified sharpening method.

The procedure of the design is given in the following steps:

1. For a given M choose the value M_1, in a such way that the factors M_1 and M_2 are close to each other in values, such that $M_1 \leq M_2$ to obtain the filters (48) and (49).
2. Choose the number of the stages K_1 and K_2 depending of the desired alias rejection (see Table 3 for tentative values).
3. For given K_1 and K_2, choose value of b according to Table 3.

Parameters (K_1, K_2)	A in dB	b
(2,2)	-46.5	2
(2,3)	-68.75	1
(3,4)	-92.25	1
(4,5)	-115	0
(4,6)	-139.34	0

Table 3. Parameters of design.

This method is illustrated in the following example.

Example 12: We consider the decimator with M =16 and at least 130 dB worst-case aliasing attenuation. We choose M_1=M_2=4. From Table 3 we get K_1=4, K_2=6 and b=0. The method is compared with the two-stage sharpening with K_1=4 and K_2=2 in Fig.14. Note that the two-stage compensated method has better characteristics.

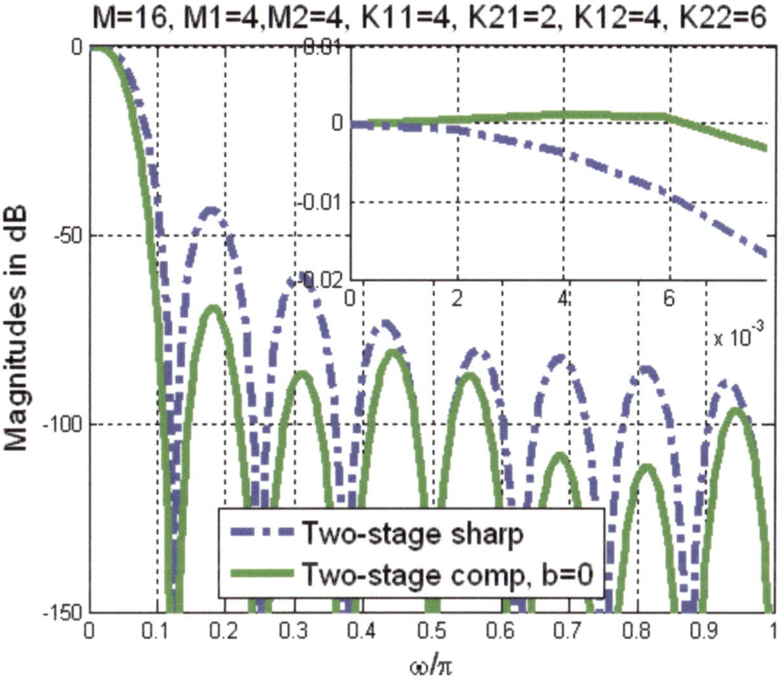

Fig. 14. Comparison of two-stage methods: sharpening and compensated.

6. Conclusion

This chapter presents different methods that have been proposed to improve the magnitude characteristics of the CIC decimator. Particularly, the methods are divided into 3 groups depending if the improvement is only in the passband, the stopband or in both i.e. passband and stopband. Only a few methods in each group are described and illustrated in examples. All examples are done in MATLAB and programs can be downloaded from the INAOE web page www-elec.inaoep.mx/paginas_personales/gordana.php.

The CIC filter implementation, which is another important issue concerning the CIC filter, was not considered in this chapter.

7. Acknowledgment

Authors thank to CONACYT and to the Institute INAOE for the support.

8. References

Aboushady, H. et al. (2001). Efficient Polyphase Decomposition of Comb Decimation Filters in Sigma Delta Analog-to Digital Converters, *IEEE Transactions on Circuits and Systems II*, Vol. 48, No. 10, (October 2001), pp. 898-905, ISSN 1057-7130.

Fernandez-Vazquez, A. & Jovanovic Dolecek, G. (2009). A General Method to design GCF Compensation Filter, *IEEE Transactions on Circuits and Systems II: Express Brief*, Vol. 56, No. 5, (May 2009), pp. 409-413, ISSN 1549-7747.

Fernandez-Vazquez, A. & Jovanovic Dolecek, G. (2011). An L_2 Design of GCF Compensation Filter, *Signal Processing*, (Elsevier), Vol. 91, No. 5, (May 2011), pp. 1143-1149, ISSN 0165-1684.

Gao, Y. et al. (2000). A Comparison Design of Comb Decimators for Sigma-Delta Analog-to Digital Converters, *Analog Integrated Circuits and Signal Processing*, Vol. 22, No. 1, (January 2000), pp. 51-60, ISSN 0925-1030.

Hogenauer, E. (1981). An Economical Class of Digital Filters for Decimation and Interpolation, *IEEE Transactions Acoustic, Speech and Signal Processing*, Vol. ASSP-29, (Apr.1981), pp. 155-162, ISSN 0096-3518.

Jovanovic Dolecek, G. (Editor), (2002). *Multirate Systems, Design and Applications*, Idea Group Publishing, ISBN 1-930708-30-0, Hershey, USA, 2002.

Jovanovic Dolecek, G. & Mitra, S. K. (2003). Efficient Sharpening of CIC Decimation Filter, Proceedings *2003 International Conference on Acoustics, Speech, and Signal Processing ICASSP 2003*, pp.VI.385-VI.388, ISBN 0-7803-7664-1, Hong Kong, China, April, 6-10, 2003.

Jovanovic Dolecek, G. & Mitra, S. K. (2004). Efficient Multistage Comb-Modifed Rotated Sinc (RS) decimator. Proceedings *XII European Signal Processing Conference EUSIPCO-2004*, pp. 1425-1428, ISBN 0-7803-7664-1, Vienna, Austria, September, 6-10, 2004.

Jovanovic Dolecek, G. & Mitra, S. K. (2005a). A New Multistage Comb-modified Rotated Sinc (RS) Decimator with Sharpened Magnitude Response, *IEICE Transactions on Information and Systems: Special Issue on Recent Advances in Circuits and Systems*, Vol. E88-D, No. 7, (July 2005),pp. 1331-1339, ISSN 105-0011.

Jovanovic Dolecek, G. & Mitra, S. K. (2005b). A New Two-Stage Sharpened Comb Decimator', *IEEE Transactions on Circuits and Systems-I: Regular papers*, Vol. 52, No. 7, (July 2005), pp. 1416-1420, ISSN 1057-7122.

Jovanovic Dolecek, Diaz-Carmona, J. (2005). A New Cascaded Modified CIC-Cosine Decimation, Proceedings *2005 IEEE International Symposium on Circuits and Systems, ISCAS 2005*, pp. 3733-3736, ISBN 0-7803-8835-6, Kobe, Japan, May 23-26, 2005.

Jovanovic Dolecek, G. & Mitra, S. K. (2008), Simple Method for Compensation of CIC Decimation Filter, *Electronics Letters*, Vol. 44, No. 19, (September 11, 2008), ISSN 0013-5194.

Jovanovic Dolecek, G. (2009). Simple Wideband CIC Compensator, *Electronics Letters*, Vol. 45, No. 24, (November 2009), pp. 1270-1272, ISSN 0013-5194.

Jovanovic Dolecek, G. & Harris, F. (2009). Design of Wideband Compensator Filter for a Digital IF Receiver", *Digital Signal Processing,* (Elsevier), Vol. 19, No. 5, (Sept, 2009) pp. 827-837, ISSN 1051-2004.

Jovanovic Dolecek, G. (2010a). Simplified Rotated SINC (RS) Filter for Sigma-Delta A/D Conversion, Proceedings of *International Conference on Green Circuits and Systems ICGCS 2010,* pp. 283-288, ISBN 978-1-4244-6877-5, Shangai, China, June, 21-23, 2010.

Jovanovic Dolecek, G. (2010 b). Low Power Sharpened Comb Decimation Filter, Proceedings of *International Conference on Green Circuits and Systems ICGCS 2010,* pp.226-229, ISBN 978-1-4244-6877-5, Shangai, China, June , 21-23, 2010.

Jovanovic Dolecek, G. & Dolecek, L. (2010). Novel Multiplierless Wide-Band CIC Compensator, Proceedings *2010 IEEE International Symposium on Circuits and Systems ISCAS 2010,* pp. 283-288, ISBN 978-1-4244-6877-5, Paris, France, May 30th-June 2nd, 2010.

Jovanovic Dolecek, G. & Laddomada, M. (2010). An Economical Class of Droop-Compensated Generalized Comb Filters: Analysis and Design, *IEEE Transactions on Circuits and Systems II: Express Brief,* Vol. 51, No. 4, (April 2010), pp. 275-279, ISSN 1549-7747.

Jovanovic Dolecek, G. & Mitra, S. K. (2010). *IET Signal Processing,* Vol. 4, No. 1, (March (2010), pp. 22-29. ISSN 1751-96-75.

Kaiser, F. & Hamming, R.W. (1977). Sharpening the Response of a Symmetric Nonrecursive Filter by Multiple Use of the Same Filter, *IEEE Transactions Acoustic, Speech and Signal Processing,* Vol. 25, No. 5, (October 1977), pp. 415-422, ISSN 0096-3518.

Kim, S., et al., (2006). Design of CIC Roll-off Compensation Filter in a W-CDMA Digital Receiver, *Digital Signal Processing, (Elsevier),* Vol. 16, No. 6, (November 2006), pp. 846-854, ISSN 1051-2004.

Kwentus A. &. Willson, Jr. A, (1997). Application of Filter Sharpening to Cascaded Integrator-Comb Decimation Filters, *IEEE Transactions on Signal Processing,* Vol. 45, No. 2, (February 1997), pp. 457-467, ISSN 1057-7122.

Laddomada, M. & Mondin, M. (2004). Decimation Schemes for Sigma-Delta A/D Converters Based on Kaiser and Hamming Sharpened Filters, *IEE Proceedings of Vision, Image and Signal Processing,* Vol. 151, No. 4, (August 2004), pp. 287-296, ISSN 1350-245X.

Laddomada, M. (2007). Generalized comb decimation filters for Sigma-Delta A/D converters: Analysis and design, *IEEE Transactions on Circuits and Systems-I: Regular papers,* Vol. 54, No. 5, (May 2007), pp. 994-1005, ISSN 1057-7122.

Laddomadda, M. Troncoso, D. & Jovanovic Dolecek, G. (2011). Design of Multiplierless Decimation Filters Using an Extended Search of Cyclotomic Polynomials, *IEEE Transactions on Circuits and Systems II: Express Brief,* (In press), ISSN 1549-7747.

Lian, J. & Lim, J.C. (1993). New Prefilter Structure for Designing FIR Filters, *Electronic Letters,* Vol. 93, No. 12, (May 1993), pp. 1034-1035, ISSN 0013-5194.

Presti, L. L. (2000). Efficient modified-sinc filters for sigma-delta A/D converters, *IEEE Transactions on Circuits and Systems-II: Analog and Digital Signal Processing*, Vol. 47, No. 11, (November 2000), pp. 1204-1213, ISSN 1057-7130.

Yeung, K. S. & Chan, S. C. (2004). The Design and Multiplier-less Realization of Software Radio Receivers with Reduced System Delay, *IEEE Transactions on Circuits and Systems-I: Regular papers*, Vol. 51, No. 12, (December 2004), pp. 2444-2459, ISSN 1057-7122.

12

Fractional Delay Digital Filters

Javier Diaz-Carmona and Gordana Jovanovic Dolecek
Institute ITC Celaya, Institute INAOE Puebla, Mexico

1. Introduction

The chapter goal is focused to introduce the concept of fractional delay filters (FDF), as well as a concise description of most of the existing design techniques. For this purpose, several illustrative examples are presented, where each design method is implemented by MATLAB programs.

A fractional delay filter is a filter of digital type having as main function to delay the processed input signal a fractional of the sampling period time. There are several applications where such signal delay value is required, examples of such systems are: timing adjustment in all-digital receivers (symbol synchronization), conversion between arbitrary sampling frequencies, echo cancellation, speech coding and synthesis, musical instruments modelling etc. (Laakson et al., 1996).

In order to achieve the fractional delay filter function, two main frequency-domain specifications must be met by the filter. The filter magnitude frequency response must have an all-pass behaviour in a wide frequency range, as well as its phase frequency response must be linear with a fixed fractional slope through the bandwidth.

Several FIR design methods have been reported during the last two decades. There are two main design approaches: time-domain and frequency-domain design methods. In first one, the fractional delay filter coefficients are easily obtained through classical mathematical interpolation formulas, but there is a small flexibility to meet frequency-domain specifications. On the other hand, the frequency-domain methods are based on frequency optimization process, and a more frequency specification control is available. One important result of frequency-domain methods is a highly efficient implementation structure called Farrow structure, which allows online fractional value update.

The chapter is organized as follows. Next section gives the formal definition of fractional delay filter. In the third section, some design methods are briefly described. Two efficient implementation structures for wideband fractional delay filter, as well as description of recently reported design methods for such structures, are illustrated in fourth section. MATLAB designed examples and concluding remarks are presented in fifth and sixth sections, respectively.

2. Fractional delay filter definition

The continuous-time output signal $y_a(t)$ of a general signal delay system is defined by:

$$y_a(t) = x(t - t_l), \tag{1}$$

where $x(t)$ is the continuous-time input signal and t_l the obtained time delay value. In a discrete-time system, the input-output relationship of a signal delay system is expressed as:

$$y(lT) = x(nT - DT), \tag{2}$$

where the delay value is given by DT, $y(lT)$ and $x(nT)$ are the discrete-time versions of output and input signals, respectively, and T is the sampling period time.
A signal delay value equal to a multiple of the sampling period, D as an integer N, can be easily implemented in a discrete-time system by memory elements storing the signal value for a time of NT:

$$y(lT) = x(nT - NT). \tag{3}$$

In this case, the signal delay value is limited to be only N time the sampling period, t_l=NT. For instance in telephone quality signals, with a sampling frequency of 8 KHz, only delays values multiple of 125µseconds are allowed.
Let us introduce the FDF function using time-domain signals sketched in Fig 1. The FDF output $y(lT)$, squared samples, is obtained a delay time t_l after input $x(n_l)$, with a delay value $\mu_l T$ given as a fraction of the sampling period time, $0<\mu_l<1$. As shown in Fig. 1, the fractional delay value μ_l may be variable; this way, it can be changed at any desired time.
The fundamental design problem of a FDF is to obtain the FDF unit impulse response $h_{FD}(n,\mu)$, in such a way that the obtained output value $y(lT)$ = $y_a(DT)$ be as close as possible to $y_a(t_l)$ for $0<\mu_l<1$. The simplified block diagram for a FDF is shown in Fig. 2, which output for a no causal FIR FDF filter is given by the discrete-time convolution:

$$y(lT) = \sum_{k=-N_{FD}/2}^{N_{FD}/2-1} x(n_l - k) h_{FD}(k, \mu_l), \tag{4}$$

where N_{FD} is the even length of the FDF. The system function $H(z)$ of the FDF can be expressed as:

$$H(z) = z^{-D}, \tag{5}$$

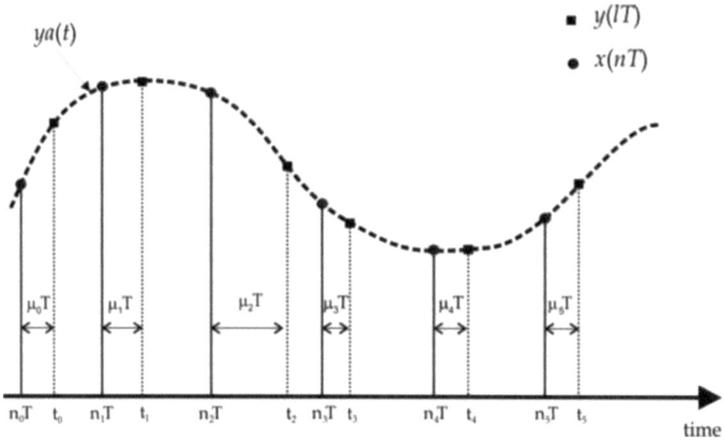

Fig. 1. FDF time-domain behaviour.

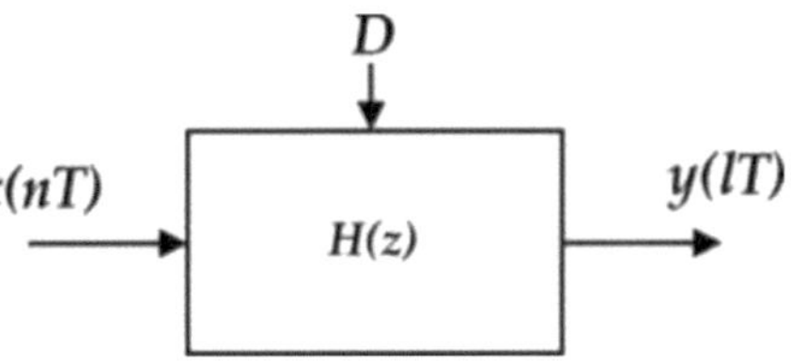

Fig. 2. Simplified block diagram for a FDF.

where the delay value is given as: $D = D_{fix}+\mu_l$, D_{fix} is a fixed delay value and μ_l is the desired fractional delay value. As a consequence, the ideal frequency response of a FDF $H_{id}(\omega,\mu_l)$ is:

$$H_{id}(\omega,\mu_l) = e^{-j(D_{fix}+\mu_l)\omega}. \tag{6}$$

Hence the ideal FDF frequency response has an all-band unity magnitude response:

$$|H_{id}(\omega,\mu_l)| = 1, \ |\omega| \le \pi, \tag{7}$$

and a linear frequency phase response with a constant phase delay given, respectively, by:

$$\theta_{id}(\omega,\mu_l) = -D\omega, \tag{8}$$

$$\tau_{pid}(\omega,\mu_l) = D. \tag{9}$$

The main goal of all existing FDF design methods, based on a frequency design approach, is to obtain the FDF filter coefficients through approximating this ideal frequency performance.

Applying inverse discrete Fourier transform to the ideal FDF frequency response, the ideal FDF filter unit impulse response $h_{id}(n,\mu)$ is obtained as:

$$h_{id}(n,\mu) = \frac{\sin\left[\pi(n-D)\right]}{\pi(n-D)} = \sin c(n-D). \tag{10}$$

Given a desired factional delay value, the FDF coefficients can be easily obtained with this infinite length delayed *sinc* function. Due to this infinite length, it is evident that an FIR FDF will be always an approximation to the ideal case.

As an illustrative example, the ideal FDF unit impulse responses for two delay values D= 3.0 (D_{fix}=3.0 and μ= 0) and D=3.65 (D_{fix}=3.0 and μ= 0.65) are shown in Fig. 3 and 4, respectively. The unit impulse responses were obtained using MATLAB function *sinc*. The FDF unit impulse responses are shown as solid lines, and the delayed sinc function as dot line. In the first case, only one three-sample delay is needed, which can be easily implemented with memory components as described above. However, the FDF unit impulse response for the second case has an infinite number of nonzero coefficients (IIR) and it is a no causal sequence, which makes it impractical for implementing in real-time applications.

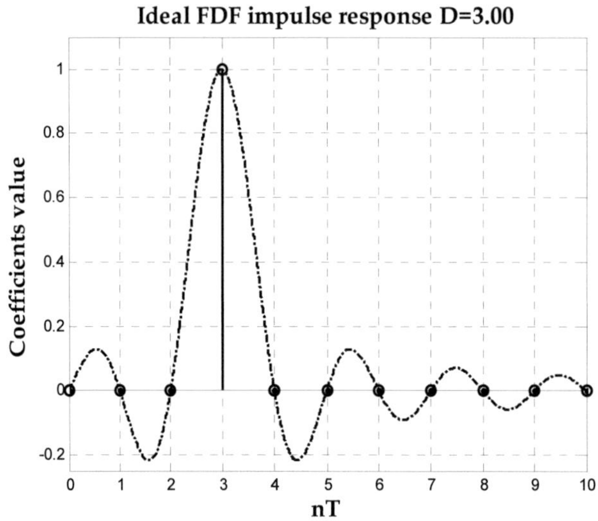

Fig. 3. Ideal FDF unit impulse response for D=3.0.

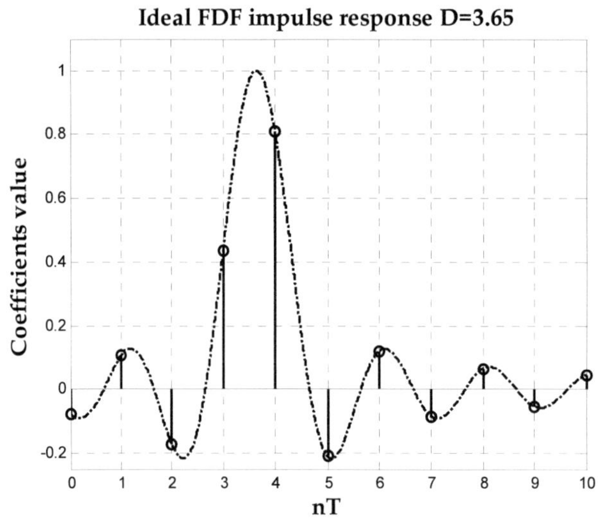

Fig. 4. Ideal FDF unit impulse response for D=3.65.

3. FDF Design methods

The existing design methods for FIR FDF use a large range of strategies to approximate as close as possible the ideal FDF unit impulse response $h_{id}(n,\mu)$. It is possible to highlight three main strategies:

- *Magnitude frequency response approximation:* The FDF unit impulse response is obtained such that its frequency magnitude response is as close as possible to the ideal FDF one, accordingly to some defined error criterion.

- *Interpolation design method:* The design approach is based on computing FDF coefficients through classical mathematical interpolation methods, such as Lagrange or B-spline. The design is a completely time-domain approach.
- *Hybrid analogue-digital model approach:* The FDF design is accomplished through the use of an analogue-digital model. The design methods using this strategy are based on a frequency-domain approach.

A concise description of each one of these strategies is presented in the following.

3.1 Magnitude frequency response approximation

The design method goal is to obtain the FDF unit impulse response $h_{FD}(n,\mu)$ based on comparing its magnitude frequency response with the ideal one. The frequency response of the designed FDF with even-length N_{FD} is given by:

$$H_{FD}(\omega,\mu)=\sum_{k=-N_{FD}/2+1}^{N_{FD}/2} h_{FD}(k,\mu)e^{-j\omega k}. \tag{11}$$

One of the criterions used for the magnitude frequency response comparison is the least squares magnitude error defined as:

$$e_2(\omega)=\frac{1}{\pi}\int_0^{\omega_p}\left|H_{DF}(\omega,\mu)-H_{id}(\omega,\mu)\right|^2 d\omega. \tag{12}$$

The error function $e_2(\omega)$ is minimized by truncating the ideal unit impulse response to N_{FD} samples, which can be interpreted as applying a delayed M-length window $w(\text{n})$ to the ideal IIR FDF unit impulse response:

$$h_{FD}(n,\mu)=h_{id}(n-D,\mu)\,w(n-D), \tag{13}$$

where $\omega(n)$ is equal to unity in the interval $0\leq n\leq N_{FD}-1$ and zero otherwise.
The windowing process on the ideal unit impulse response causes not-desired effects on the FDF frequency response, in particular the Gibbs phenomenon for rectangular window (Proakis & Manolakis, 1995).
In general, the performance of a FDF obtained by truncating the *sinc* function is usually not acceptable in practice. As a design example, the FDF frequency magnitude and phase responses for D=3.65, using a rectangular window with N_{FD}=50, are shown in Fig 5. We can see that the obtained FDF bandwidth is less than 0.9π and although the IIR *sinc* function has been truncated up to 50 taps, neither its frequency magnitude nor its phase response are constant.
The windowed unit impulse response $h_{FD}(n,\mu)$ has a low-pass frequency response, in this way it can be modified to approximate only a desired pass-band interval $(0,\alpha\pi)$ as follows:

$$h_{FD}(n,\mu)=\begin{cases}\alpha\,\mathrm{sin}\,c\left[\alpha(n-D)\right] & \text{for}\ \ 0\leq n\leq N_{FD}-1\\ 0 & \text{otherwise}\end{cases}. \tag{14}$$

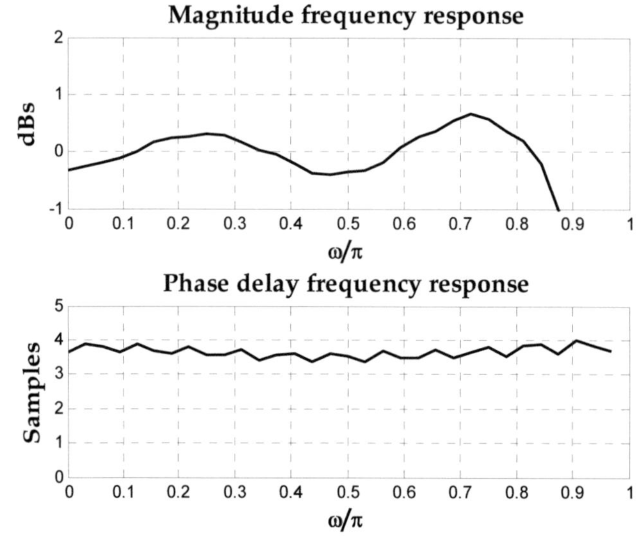

Fig. 5. FDF frequency response for D=3.65 with rectangular window, N_{FD}=50.

The magnitude and phase responses of a FDF with N_{FD}= 8 and α=0.5 are shown in Fig. 6, which were obtained using MATLAB. The phase delay range is from *D*=3.0 to 3.5 samples with an increment of 0.1. More constant phase delay responses and narrower bandwidth is achieved.

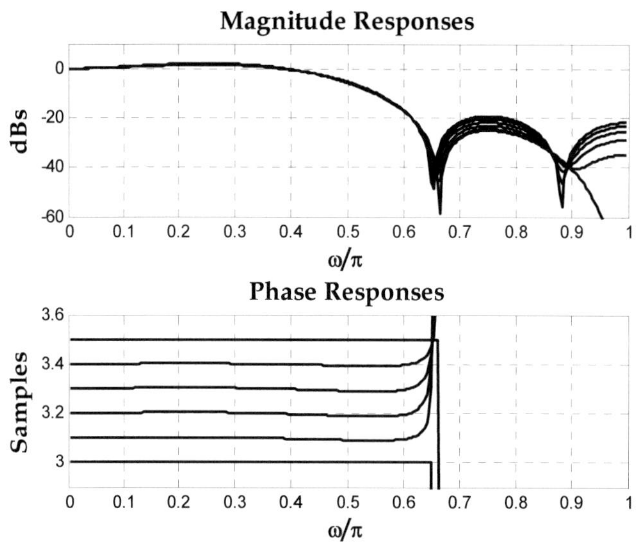

Fig. 6. FDF frequency responses using windowing method for *D*=3.0 to 3.5 with N_{FD} = 8 and α =0.5.

In principle, window-based design is fast and easy. However, in practical applications it is difficult to meet a desired magnitude and phase specifications by adjusting window parameters. In order to meet a variable fractional delay specification, a real-time coefficient

update method is required. This can be achieved storing the window values in memory and computing the values of the *sinc* function on line, but this would require large memory size for fine fractional delay resolution (Vesma, 1999).
The smallest least squares error can be achieved by defining its response only in a desired frequency band and by leaving the rest as a "don't care" band. This can be done using a frequency-domain weighting as follows (Laakson et al., 1996):

$$e_3(\omega) = \frac{1}{\pi}\int_0^{\omega_p} W(\omega)\left|H_{DF}(\omega,\mu) - H_{id}(\omega,\mu)\right|^2, \tag{15}$$

where ω_p is the desired pass-band frequency and $W(\omega)$ represents the weighting frequency function, which defines the corresponding weight to each band. In this way, the error is defined only in the FDF pass-band, hence the optimization process is applied in this particular frequency range.
In Fig. 7 are shown the FDF frequency responses designed with this method using $W(\omega)=1$, $N_{FD} = 8$ and $\alpha=0.5$. We can see a notable improvement in the resulting FDF bandwidth compared with the one obtained using the least square method, Fig. 6.
There is another design method based on the magnitude frequency response approach, which computes the FDF coefficients by minimizing the error function:

$$e_4(\omega) = \max_{0\le\omega\le\omega_p}\left|H_{FD}(\omega,\mu) - H_{id}(\omega,\mu)\right|. \tag{16}$$

The solution to this optimization problem is given by the minimax method proposed by (Oetken, 1979). The obtained FDF has an equiripple pass-band magnitude response. As an illustrative example, the frequency response of an FDF designed through this minimax method is shown in Fig. 8, where N_{FD}=20 and ω_p=0.9π.

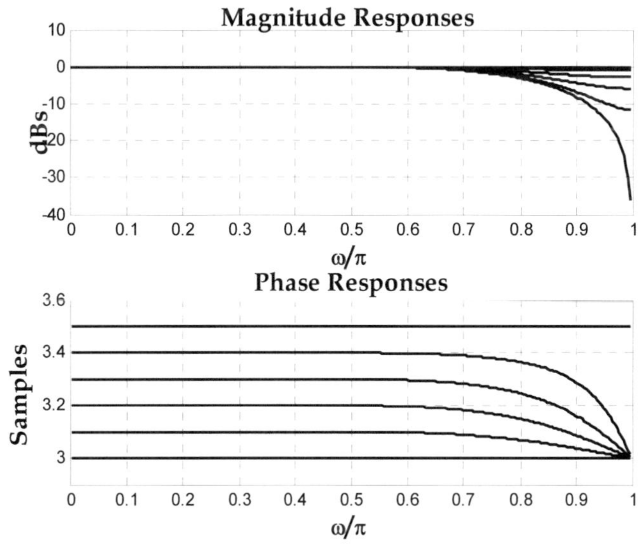

Fig. 7. FDF frequency responses using weighted least square method for D=3.0 to 3.5 with N_{FD} = 8 and α=0.5.

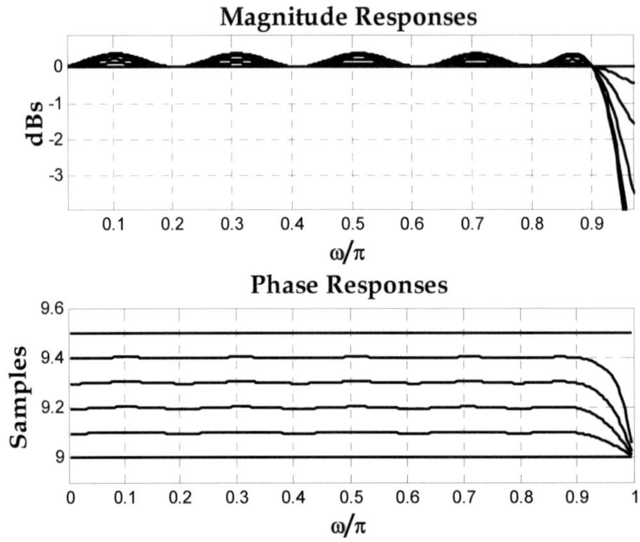

Fig. 8. FDF Frequency responses using minimax method for D=9.0 to 9.5 with N_{FD} = 20 and α =0.9.

3.2 Interpolation design approach

Instead of minimizing an error function, the FDF coefficients are computed from making the error function maximally-flat at ω=0. This means that the derivatives of an error function are equal to zero at this frequency point:

$$\left.\frac{\partial^n e_c(\omega)}{\partial \omega^n}\right|_{\omega=0} = 0, \quad n = 0,1,2,....N_{FD}-1, \tag{17}$$

the complex error function is defined as:

$$e_c(\omega) = H_{FD}(\omega, \mu_l) - H_{id}(\omega, \mu_l), \tag{18}$$

where $H_{FD}(\omega,\mu_l)$ is the designed FDF frequency response, and $H_{id}(\omega,\mu_l)$ is the ideal FDF frequency response, given by equation (6). The solution of this approximation is the classical Lagrange interpolation formula, where the FDF coefficients are computed with the closed form equation:

$$h_L(n) = \prod_{\substack{k=0 \\ k\neq n}}^{N_{FD}} \frac{D-k}{n-k} \quad n = 0,1,2,....N_{FD}, \tag{19}$$

where N_{FD} is the FDF length and the desired delay $D = \lfloor N_{FD}/2 \rfloor + \mu_l$. We can note that the filter length is the unique design parameter for this method.

The FDF frequency responses, designed with Lagrange interpolation, with a length of 10 are shown in Fig. 9. As expected, a flat magnitude response at low frequencies is presented; a narrow bandwidth is also obtained.

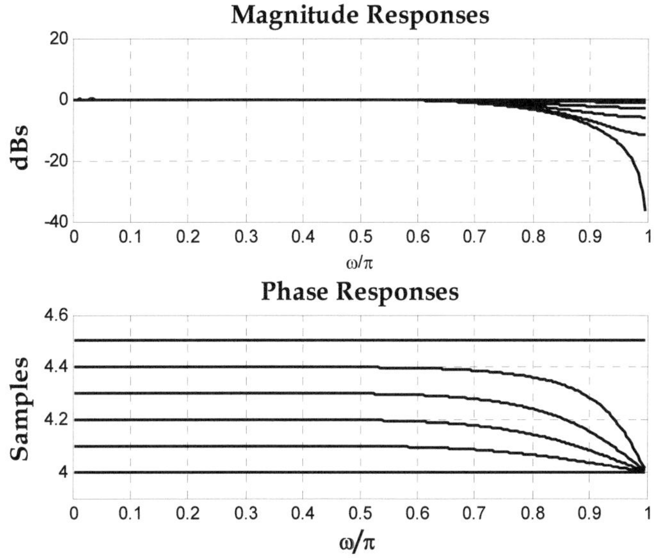

Fig. 9. FDF Frequency responses using Lagrange interpolation for D=4.0 to 4.5 with N_{FD} = 10.

The use of this design method has three main advantages (Laakson et al., 1994): 1) the ease to compute the FDF coefficients from one closed form equation, 2) the FDF magnitude frequency response at low frequencies is completely flat, 3) a FDF with polynomial-defined coefficients allows the use of an efficient implementation structure called Farrow structure, which will be described in section 3.3.

On the other hand, there are some disadvantages to be taken into account when a Lagrange interpolation is used in FDF design: 1) the achieved bandwidth is narrow, 2) the design is made in time-domain and then any frequency information of the processed signal is not taken into account; this is a big problem because the time-domain characteristics of the signals are not usually known, and what is known is their frequency band, 3) if the polynomial order is N_{FD}; then the FDF length will be N_{FD}, 4) since only one design parameter is used, the design control of FDF specifications in frequency-domain is limited.

The use of Lagrange interpolation for FDF design is proposed in (Ging-Shing & Che-Ho, 1990, 1992), where closed form equations are presented for coefficients computing of the desired FDF filter. A combination of a multirate structure and a Lagrange-designed FDF is described in (Murphy et al., 1994), where an improved bandwidth is achieved.

The interpolation design approach is not limited only to Lagrange interpolation; some design methods using spline and parabolic interpolations were reported in (Vesma, 1995) and (Erup et al., 1993), respectively.

3.3 Hybrid analogue-digital model approach

In this approach, the FDF design methods are based on the hybrid analogue-digital model proposed by (Ramstad, 1984), which is shown in Fig. 10. The fractional delay of the digital signal $x(n)$ is made in the analogue domain through a re-sampling process at the desired time delay t_l. Hence a digital to analogue converter is taken into account in the model, where a reconstruction analog filter $h_a(t)$ is used.

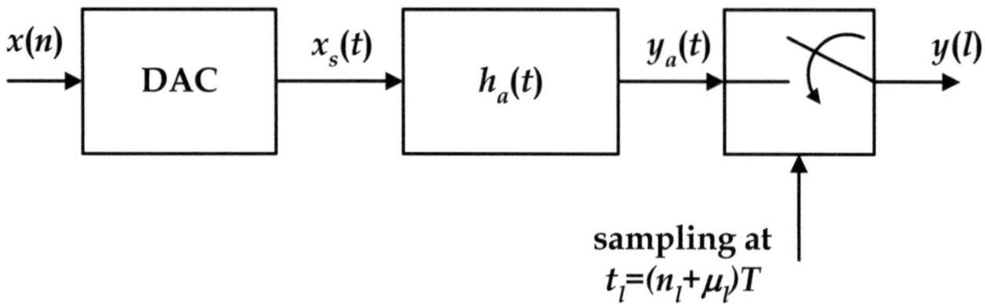

Fig. 10. Hybrid analogue-digital model.

An important result of this modelling is the relationship between the analogue reconstruction filer $h_a(t)$ and the discrete-time FDF unit impulse response $h_{FD}(n,\mu)$, which is given by:

$$h_{FD}(n,\mu) = h_a((n+\mu_l)T), \tag{20}$$

where n=-N_{FD}/2,-N_{FD}/2+1,...., N_{FD}/2-1, and T is the signal sampling frequency. The model output is obtained by the convolution expression:

$$y(l) = \sum_{k=0}^{N_{FD}-1} x(n_l - k + N_{FD}/2) h_a((k + \mu_l - N_{FD}/2)T). \tag{21}$$

This means that for a given desired fractional value, the FDF coefficients can be obtained from a designed continuous-time filter.
The design methods using this approach approximate the reconstruction filter $h_a(t)$ in each interval of length T by means of a polynomial-based interpolation as follows:

$$h_a((n+\mu_l)T) = \sum_{m=0}^{M} c_m(n)\mu_l^m, \tag{22}$$

for k=-N_{FD}/2,-N_{FD}/2+1,...., N_{FD}/2-1. The $c_m(k)$'s are the unknown polynomial coefficients and M is the polynomials order.
If equation (22) is substituted in equation (21), the resulted output signal can be expressed as:

$$y(l) = \sum_{m=0}^{M} v_m(n_l)\mu_l^m, \tag{23}$$

where:

$$v_m(n_l) = \sum_{k=0}^{N_{FD}-1} x(n_l - k + N_{FD}/2) c_m(k - N_{FD}/2), \tag{24}$$

are the output samples of the M+1 FIR filters with a system function:

$$C_m(z) = \sum_{k=0}^{N_{FD}-1} c_m(k - N_{FD}/2) z^{-k}. \tag{25}$$

The implementation of such polynomial-based approach results in the Farrow structure, (Farrow, 1988), sketched in Fig. 11. This implementation is a highly efficient structure composed of a parallel connection of $M+1$ fixed filters, having online fractional delay value update capability. This structure allows that the FDF design problem be focused to obtain each one of the fixed branch filters $c_m(k)$ and the FDF structure output is computed from the desired fractional delay given online μ_l.
The coefficients of each branch filter $C_m(z)$ are determined from the polynomial coefficients of the reconstruction filter impulse response $h_a(t)$. Two mainly polynomial-based interpolation filters are used: 1) conventional time-domain design such as Lagrange interpolation, 2) frequency-domain design such as minimax and least mean squares optimization.

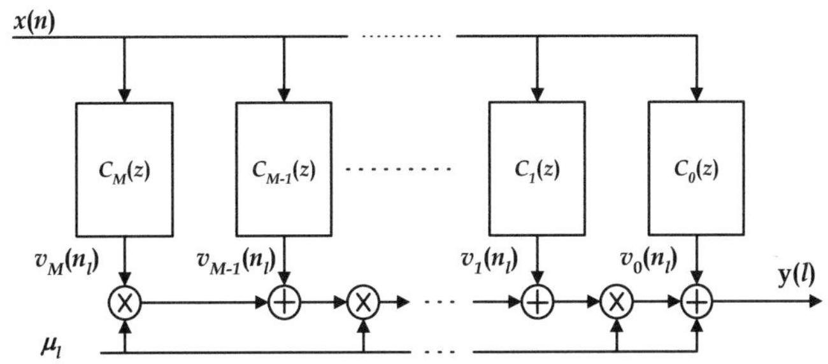

Fig. 11. Farrow structure.

As were pointed out previously, Lagrange interpolation has several disadvantages. A better polynomial approximation of the reconstruction filter is using a frequency-domain approach, which is achieved by optimizing the polynomial coefficients of the impulse response $h_a(t)$ directly in the frequency-domain. Some of the design methods are based on the optimization of the discrete-time filter $h_{FD}(n,\mu_l))$ and others on making the optimization of the reconstruction filter $h_a(t)$. Once that this filter is obtained, the Farrow structure branch filters $c_m(k)$ are related to $h_{FD}(n,m_l)$ using equations (20) and (22). One of main advantages of frequency-domain design methods is that they have at least three design parameters: filter length N_{FD}, interpolation order M, and pass-band frequency ω_p.
There are several methods using the frequency design method (Vesma, 1999). In (Farrow, 1988) a least-mean-squares optimization is proposed in such a way that the squared error between $H_{FD}(\omega,\mu_l)$ and the ideal response $H_{id}(\omega,\mu_l)$ is minimized for $0\leq\omega\leq\omega_p$ and for $0\leq\mu_l<1$. The design method reported in (Laakson et al., 1995) is based on optimizing $c_m(k)$ to minimize the squared error between $h_a(t)$ and the $h_{FD}(n,\mu_l)$ filters, which is designed through the magnitude frequency response approximation approach, see section 3.1. The design method introduced in (Vesma et al., 1998) is based on approximating the Farrow structure output samples $v_m(n_l)$ as an mth order differentiator; this is a Taylor series approximation of the input signal. In this sense, $C_m(\omega)$ approximates in a minimax or L_2 sense the ideal response of the mth order differentiator, denoted as $D_m(\omega)$, in the desired pass-band frequencies. In (Vesma & Saramaki, 1997) the designed FDF phase delay approximates the ideal phase delay value μ_l in a minimax sense for $0\leq\omega\leq\omega_p$ and for $0\leq\mu_l<1$ with the restriction that the maximum pass-band amplitude deviation from unity be smaller than the worst-case amplitude deviation, occurring when μ=0.5.

4. FDF Implementation structures

As were described in section 3.3, one of the most important results of the analogue-digital model in designing FDF filters is the highly efficient Farrow structure implementation, which was deduced from a piecewise approximation of the reconstruction filter through a polynomial based interpolation. The interpolation process is made as a frequency-domain optimization in most of the existing design methods.

An important design parameter is the FDF bandwidth. A wideband specification, meaning a pass-band frequency of 0.9π or wider, imposes a high polynomial order M as well as high branch filters length N_{FD}. The resulting number of products in the Farrow structure is given by $N_{FD}(M+1)+M$, hence in order to reduce the number of arithmetic operations per output sample in the Farrow structure, a reduction either in the polynomial order or in the FDF length is required.

Some design approaches for efficient implementation structures have been proposed to reduce the number of arithmetic operations in a wideband FDF. A modified Farrow structure, reported in (Vesma & Samaraki, 1996), is an extension of the polynomial based interpolation method. In (Johansson & Lowerborg, 2003), a frequency optimization technique is used a modified Farrow structure achieving a lower arithmetic complexity with different branch filters lengths. In (Yli-Kaakinen & Saramaki, 2006a, 2006a, 2007), multiplierless techniques were proposed for minimizing the number of arithmetic operations in the branch filters of the modified Farrow structure. A combination of a two-rate factor multirate structure and a time-domain designed FDF (Lagrange) was reported in (Murphy et al., 1994). The same approach is reported in (Hermanowicz, 2004), where symmetric Farrow structure branch filters are computed in time-domain with a symbolic approach. A combination of the two-rate factor multirate structure with a frequency-domain optimization process was firstly proposed in (Jovanovic-Docelek & Diaz-Carmona, 2002). In subsequence methods (Hermanowicz & Johansson, 2005) and (Johansson & Hermanowicz &, 2006), different optimization processes were applied to the same multirate structure. In (Hermanowicz & Johansson, 2005), a two stage FDF jointly optimized technique is applied. In (Johansson & Hermanowicz, 2006) a complexity reduction is achieved by using an approximately linear phase IIR filter instead of a linear phase FIR in the interpolation process.

Most of the recently reported FDF design methods are based on the modified Farrow structure as well as on the multirate Farrow structure. Such implementation structures are briefly described in the following.

4.1 Modified Farrow structure

The modified Farrow structure is obtained by approximating the reconstruction filter with the interpolation variable $2\mu_l$-1 instead of μ_l in equation (22):

$$h_a\left((n+\mu_l)T\right)=\sum_{m=0}^{M} c_m^{'}(k)\left(2\mu_l-1\right)^m , \tag{26}$$

for k=-N_{FD}/2,-N_{FD}/2+1,...., N_{FD}/2-1. The first four basis polynomials are shown in Fig. 12. The symmetry property $h_a(-t)$= h_a(t) is achieved by:

$$c_m^{'}(n)=(-1)^m c_m^{'}(-n-1) , \tag{27}$$

for $m = 0, 1, 2, \ldots, M$ and $n = 0, 1, \ldots, N_{FD}/2$. Using this condition, the number of unknowns is reduced to half.

The reconstruction filter $h_a(t)$ can be now approximated as follows:

$$h_a(t) = \sum_{n=0}^{N_{FD}/2} \sum_{m=0}^{M} c'_m(n) g(n,m,t), \tag{28}$$

where $c_m(n)$ are the unknown coefficients and $g(n,m,t)$'s are basis functions reported in (Vesma & Samaraki, 1996).

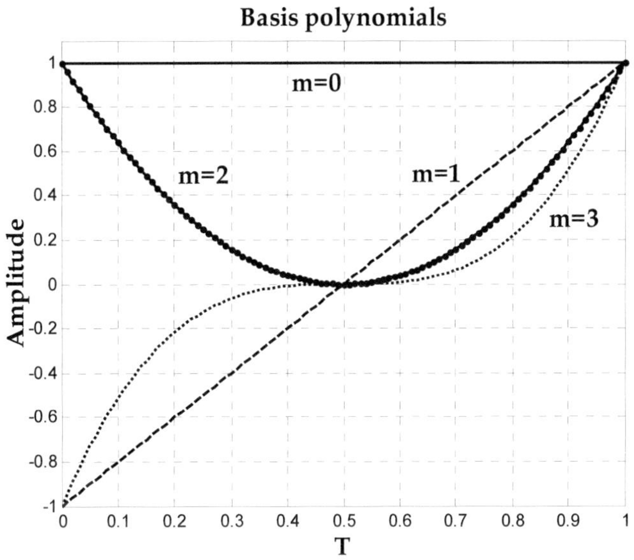

Fig. 12. Basis polynomials for modified Farrow structure for $0 < m \leq 3$.

The modified Farrow structure has the following properties: 1) polynomial coefficients $c_m(n)$ are symmetrical, according to equation (27); 2) The factional value μ_l is substituted by $2\mu_l - 1$, the resulting implementation of the modified Farrow structure is shown in Fig. 13; 3) the number of products per output sample is reduced from $N_{FD}(M+1)+M$ to $N_{FD}(M+1)/2+M$.

The frequency design method in (Vesma et al., 1998) is based on the following properties of the branch digital filters $C_m(z)$:

- The FIR filter $C_m(z)$, $0 \leq m \leq M$, in the original Farrow structure is the mth order Taylor approximation to the continuous-time interpolated input signal.
- In the modified Farrow structure, the FIR filters $C'_m(z)$ are linear phase type II filters when m is even and type IV when m is odd.

Each filter $C_m(z)$ approximates in magnitude the function $K_m w^m$, where K_m is a constant. The ideal frequency response of an mth order differentiator is $(j\omega)^m$, hence the ideal response of each $C_m(z)$ filter in the Farrow structure is an mth order differentiator.

In same way, it is possible to approximate the input signal through Taylor series in a modified Farrow structure for each $C'_m(z)$, (Vesma et al., 1998). The mth order differential approximation to the continuous-time interpolated input signal is done through the branch filter $C'_m(z)$, with a frequency response given as:

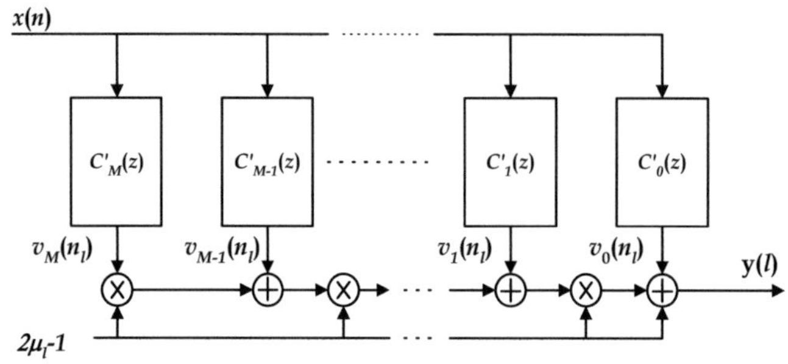

Fig. 13. Modified Farrow structure.

$$C'_m(\omega) = e^{j\omega(N_{FD}-1)/2}\frac{(-j\omega)^m}{2^m m!}. \tag{29}$$

The input design parameters are: the filter length N_{FD}, the polynomial order M, and the desired pass-band frequency ω_p.
The N_{FD} coefficients of the $M+1$ $C'_m(z)$ FIR filters are computed in such a way that the following error function is minimized in a least square sense through the frequency range $[0,\omega_p]$:

$$e_m(\omega) = \left|\sum_{n=o}^{N_{FD}/2-1}\left[c_m(N_{FD}/2-n)\right]\gamma(m,n,\omega) - D(m,\omega)\right|, \tag{30}$$

where:

$$D(m,\omega) = \frac{(-\omega)^m}{2^m m!},\quad \gamma(m,n,\omega) = 2\cos\left[(n+1/2)\omega\right],\ m\ \ even$$
$$\gamma(m,n,\omega) = 2\sin\left[(n+1/2)\omega\right],\ m\ \ odd \tag{31}$$

Hence the objective function is given as:

$$E_1 = \int_0^{\omega_p}\left[\sum_{n=0}^{N_{FD}/2-1} c_m(N_{FD}/2-1)\gamma(m,n,\omega) - D(m,\omega)\right]d\omega. \tag{32}$$

From this equation it can be observed that the design of a wide bandwidth FDF requires an extensive computing workload. For high fractional delay resolution FDF, high precise differentiator approximations are required; this imply high branch filters length, N_{FD}, and high polynomial order, M. Hence a FDF structure with high number of arithmetic operations per output sample is obtained.

4.2 Multirate Farrow structure

A two-rate-factor structure in (Murphy et al., 1994), is proposed for designing FDF in time-domain. The input signal bandwidth is reduced by increasing to a double sampling frequency value. In this way Lagrange interpolation is used in the filter coefficients computing, resulting in a wideband FDF.
The multirate structure, shown in Fig. 14, is composed of three stages. The first one is an upsampler and a half-band image suppressor $H_{HB}(z)$ for incrementing twice the input

sampling frequency. Second stage is the FDF $H_{DF}(z)$, which is designed in time-domain through Lagrange interpolation. Since the signal processing frequency of $H_{DF}(z)$ is twice the input sampling frequency, such filter can be designed to meet only half of the required bandwidth. Last stage deals with a downsampler for decreasing the sampling frequency to its original value. Notice that the fractional delay is doubled because the sampling frequency is twice. Such multirate structure can be implemented as the single-sampling-frequency structure shown in Fig. 15, where $H_0(z)$ and $H_1(z)$ are the first and second polyphase components of the half-band filter $H_{HB}(z)$, respectively. In the same way $H_{FD0}(z)$ and $H_{FD1}(z)$ are the polyphase components of the FDF $H_{FD}(z)$ (Murphy et al, 1994).
The resulting implementation structure for $H_{DF}(z)$ designed as a modified Farrow structure and after some structure reductions (Jovanovic-Dolecek & Diaz-Carmona, 2002) is shown in Fig. 16. The filters $C_{m,0}(z)$ and $C_{m,1}(z)$ are the first and second polyphase components of the branch filter $C_m(z)$, respectively.

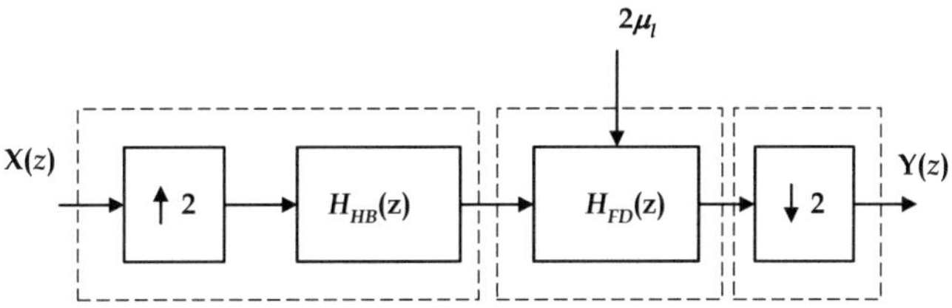

Fig. 14. FDF Multirate structure.

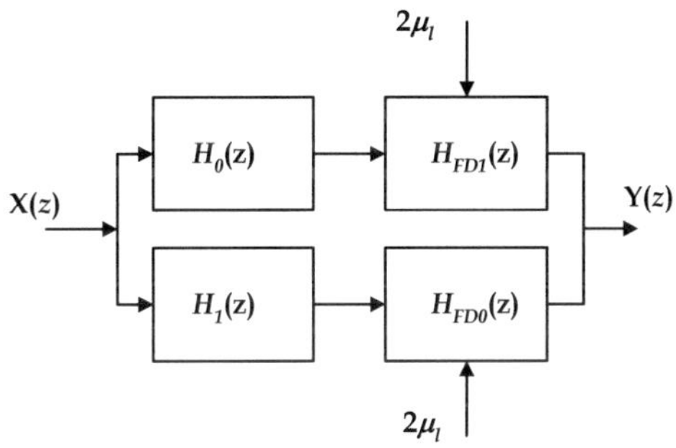

Fig. 15. Single-sampling-frequency structure.

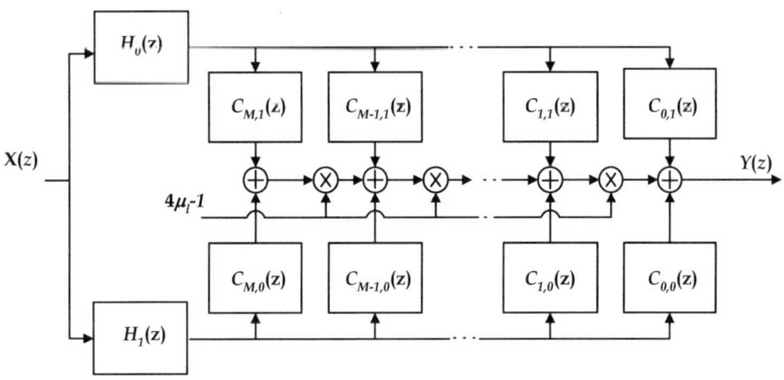

Fig. 16. Equivalent single-sampling-frequency structure.

The use of the obtained structure in combination with a frequency optimization method for computing the branch filters $C_m(z)$ coefficients was exploited in (Jovanovic-Dolecek & Diaz-Carmona, 2002). The approach is a least mean square approximation of each one of the mth differentiator of input signal, which is applied through the half of the desired pass-band. The resulting objective function, obtained this way from equation (32), is:

$$E_2 = \int_0^{\frac{\omega_p}{2}} \left[\sum_{n=0}^{N_{FD}/2-1} c_m \left(N_{FD}/2-1\right) \gamma\left(m,n,\omega\right) - D\left(m,\omega\right) \right] d\omega . \tag{33}$$

The decrease in the optimization frequency range allows an abrupt reduction in the coefficient computation time for wideband FDF, and this less severe condition allows a resulting structure with smaller length of filters $C_m(z)$.

The half-band $H_{HB}(z)$ filter plays a key role in the bandwidth and fractional delay resolution of the FDF filter. The higher stop-band attenuation of filter $H_{HB}(z)$, the higher resulting fractional delay resolution. Similarly, the narrower transition band of $H_{HB}(z)$ provides the wider resulting bandwidth.

In (Ramirez-Conejo, 2010) and (Ramirez-Conejo et al., 2010a), the branch filters coefficients $c_m(n)$ are obtained approximating each mth differentiator with the use of another frequency optimization method. The magnitude and phase frequency response errors are defined, for $0 \le w \le w_p$ and $0 \le \mu_l \le 1$, respectively as:

$$e_{mag}\left(\omega\right) = \left|H_{FD}\left(\omega\right)\right| - 1, \tag{34}$$

$$e_{pha}\left(\omega\right) = -\frac{\phi\left(\omega\right)}{\omega} - \left(D_{fix} + \mu_l\right), \tag{35}$$

where $H_{FD}(\omega)$ and $\phi(\omega)$ are, respectively, the frequency and phase responses of the FDF filter to be designed. In the same way, this method can also be extended for designing FDF with complex specifications, where the complex error used is given by equation (18).

The coefficients computing of the resulting FDF structure, shown in Fig. 16, is done through frequency optimization for global magnitude approximation to the ideal frequency response in a minimax sense. The objective function is defined as:

$$\Delta_m = \max_{0 \le \mu_l \le 1} \left[\max_{0 \le \omega \le \omega_p} \left| e_m\left(\omega\right) \right| \right]. \tag{36}$$

The objective function is minimized until a magnitude error specification δ_m is met. In order to meet both magnitude and phase errors, the global phase delay error is constrained to meet the phase delay restriction:

$$\Delta_p = \max_{0 \le \mu_l \le 1} \left[\max_{0 \le \omega \le \omega_p} \left| e_p\left(\omega\right) \right| \right] \le \delta_p , \tag{37}$$

where δ_p is the FDF phase delay error specification. The minimax optimization can de performed using the function *fminmax* available in the MATLAB Optimization Toolbox.
As is well known, the initial solution plays a key role in a minimax optimization process, (Johansson & Lowenborg, 2003), the proposed initial solution is the individual branch filters approximations to the mth differentiator in a least mean squares sense, accordingly to (Jovanovic-Delecek & Diaz-Carmona, 2002):

$$E_m = \int_0^{\omega_p/2} \left[e_m(\omega) \right]^2 d\omega \,. \tag{38}$$

The initial half-band filter $H_{HB}(z)$ to the frequency optimization process can be designed as a Doph-Chebyshev window or as an equirriple filter. The final hafband coefficients are obtained as a result of the optimization.
The fact of using the proposed optimization process allows the design of a wideband FDF structure with small arithmetic complexity. Examples of such designing are presented in section 5.
An implementation of this FDF design method is reported in (Ramirez-Conejo et al., 2010b), where the resulting structure, as one shown in Fig. 16, is implemented in a reconfigurable hardware platform.

5. FDF Design examples

The results obtained with FDF design methods described in (Diaz-Carmona et al., 2010) and (Ramirez-Conejo et al., 2010) are shown through three design examples, that were implemented in MATLAB.
Example 1:
The design example is based on the method described in (Diaz-Carmona et al., 2010). The desired FDF bandwidth is 0.9π, and a fractional delay resolution of 1/10000.
A half-band filter $H_{HB}(z)$ with 241 coefficients was used, which was designed with a Dolph-Chebyshev window, with a stop-band attenuation of 140 dBs. The design parameters are: M=12 and N_{FD}=10 with a resulting structure arithmetic of 202 products per output sample.
The frequency optimization is applied up to only ω_p=0.45π, causing a notably computing workload reduction, compared with an optimization on the whole desired bandwidth (Vesma et al., 1998). As a matter of comparison, the MATLAB computing time in a PC running at 2GHz for the optimization on half of the desired pass-band is 1.94 seconds and 110 seconds for the optimization on the whole pass-band. The first seven differentiator approximations for both cases are shown in Fig. 17 and Fig. 18.
The frequency responses of the resulted FDF from μ=0.008 to 0.01 samples for the half pass-band and for the whole pass-band optimization process, are shown in Fig. 19 and Fig. 20, respectively.
The use of the optimization process (Vesma et al., 1998) with design parameters of M=12 and N_{FD}=104 results in a total number of 688 products per output sample. Accordingly to the described example in (Zhao & Yu, 2006), using a weighted least squares design method, an implementation structure with N_{FD}=67 and M=7 is required to meet ω_p=0.9π, which results in arithmetic complexity of 543 products per output sample.

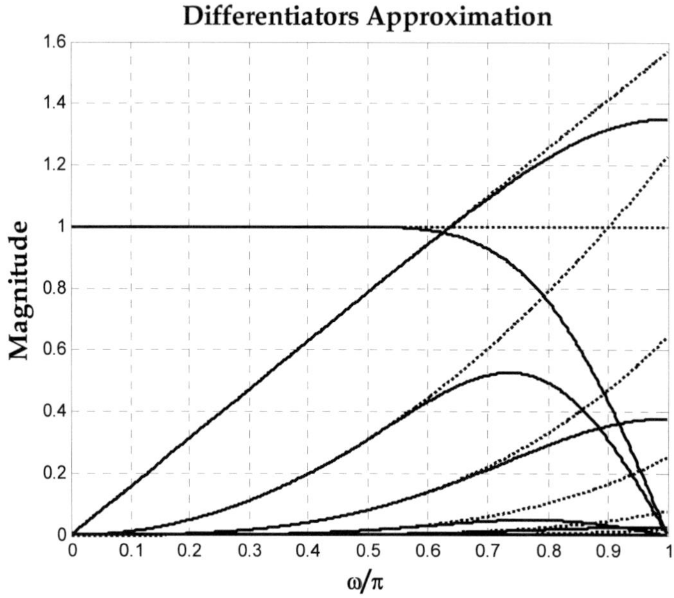

Fig. 17. Frequency responses of the first seven ideal differentiators (dotted line) and the obtained approximations (solid line) in $0 \le \omega \le 0.45\pi$ with $N_{FD}=10$ and $M=12$.

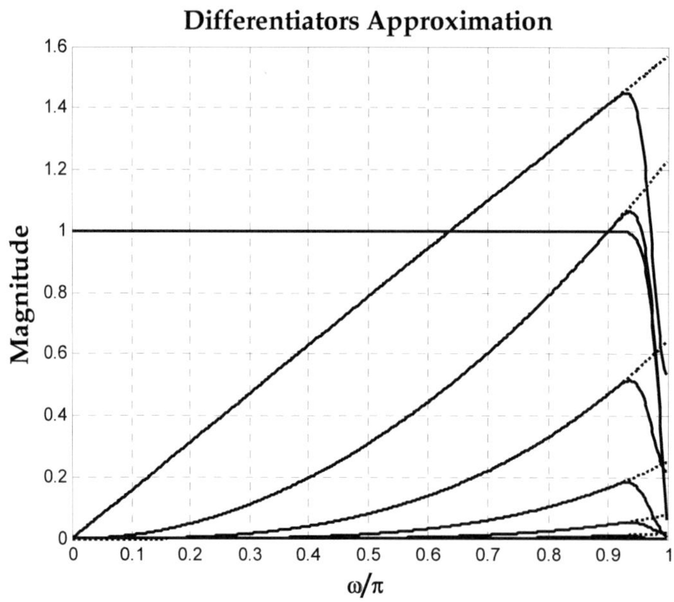

Fig. 18. First seven differentiator ideal frequency responses (dotted line) and obtained approximations (solid line) in $0 \le \omega \le 0.9\pi$ with $N_{FD}=104$ and $M=12$.

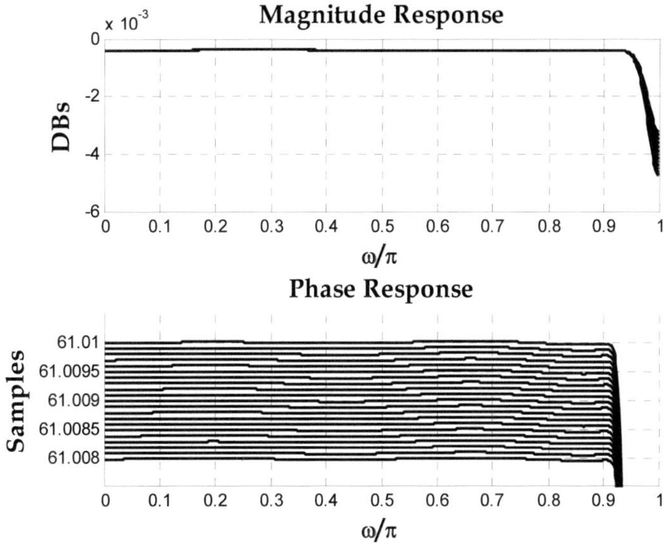

Fig. 19. FDF frequency responses using half band frequency optimization method for μ_l=0.0080 to 0.0100 with N_{FD} = 10 and M=12.

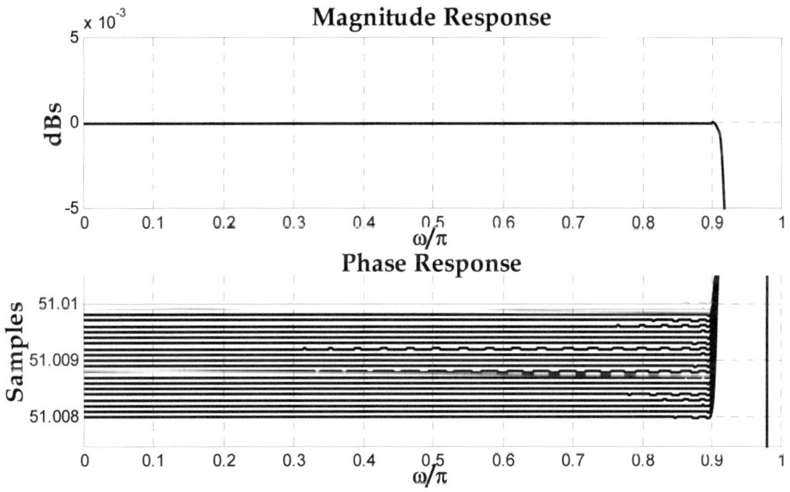

Fig. 20. FDF frequency responses, using all-bandwidth frequency optimization method for μ_l=0.0080 to 0.0100 with N_{FD}=104 and M=12.

In order to compare the frequency-domain approximation achieved by the described method with existing design methods results, the frequency-domain absolute error $e(\omega,\mu)$, the maximum absolute error e_{max}, and the root mean square error e_{rms} are defined, like in (Zhao & Yu, 2006), by:

$$e(\omega,\mu) = \left|H_{FD}(\omega,\mu) - H_{id}(\omega,\mu)\right|, \tag{39}$$

$$e_{\max} = \max\{e(\omega,\mu)\},\ 0 \le \omega \le \omega_p,\ 0 \le \mu \le 1, \quad (40)$$

$$e_{rms} = \left[\int_0^{\omega_p} \int_0^1 e^2(\omega,\mu)\, d\mu d\omega \right]^{1/2}. \quad (41)$$

The maximum absolute magnitude error and the root mean square error obtained are shown in Table 1, reported in (Diaz-Carmona et al., 2010), as well as the results reported by some design methods.

Method	e_{max}(dBs)	e_{rms}
(Tarczynski et al., 1997)	-100.0088	2.9107×10^{-6}
(Wu-Sheng, & Tian-Bo, 1999)	-100.7215	2.7706×10^{-6}
(Tian-Bo, 2001)	-99.9208	4.931×10^{-4}
(Zhao & Yu, 2006)	-99.3669	2.8119×10^{-6}
(Vesma et al., 1998)	-93.69	4.81×10^{-4}
(Diaz-Carmona et al., 2010)	-86.17	2.78×10^{-4}

Table 1. Magnitude frequency response error comparison.

Example 2:

The FDF is designed using the explained minimax optimization approach applied on the single-sampling-frequency structure, Fig. 16, according to (Ramirez et al., 2010a). The FDF specifications are: $\omega_p = 0.9\pi$, $\delta_m = 0.01$ and $\delta_p = 0.001$, the same ones as in the design example of (Yli-Kaakinen & Saramaki, 2006a). The given criterion is met with $N_{FD} = 7$ and $M = 4$ and a half-band filter length of 55. The overall structure requires *Prod* = 32 multipliers, *Add* = 47 adders, resulting in a $\Delta_m = 0.0094448$ and $\Delta_p = 0.00096649$. The magnitude and phase delay responses obtained for $\mu_l = 0$ to 0.5 with 0.1 delay increment are depicted in Fig. 21. The results obtained, and compared with those reported by other design methods, are shown in Table 2 . The design described requires less multipliers and adders than (Vesma & Saramaki, 1997), (Johansson, & Lowenborg, 2003), the same number of multipliers and nine less adders than (Yli-Kaakinen & Saramaki, 2006a), one more multiplier and three less adders than (Yli-Kaakinen & Saramaki, 2006b), and two more multipliers than (Yli-Kaakinen, & Saramaki, 2007).

Method	Arithmetic complexity					
	N_{FD}	*M*	*Prod*	*Add*	Δm	Δp
(Vesma & Saramaki, 1997)	26	4	69	91	0.006571	0.0006571
(Johansson, & Lowenborg, 2003)	28	5	57	72	0.005608	0.0005608
(Yli-Kaakinen & Saramaki, 2006a)	28	4	32	56	0.009069	0.0009069
(Yli-Kaakinen & Saramaki, 2006b)	28	4	31	50	0.009742	0.0009742
(Yli-Kaakinen & Saramaki, 2007)	28	4	30	-	0.009501	0.0009501
(Ramirez-Conejo et al.,2010)	7	4	32	47	0.0094448	0.0009664

- Not reported

Table 2. Arithmetic complexity results for example 2.

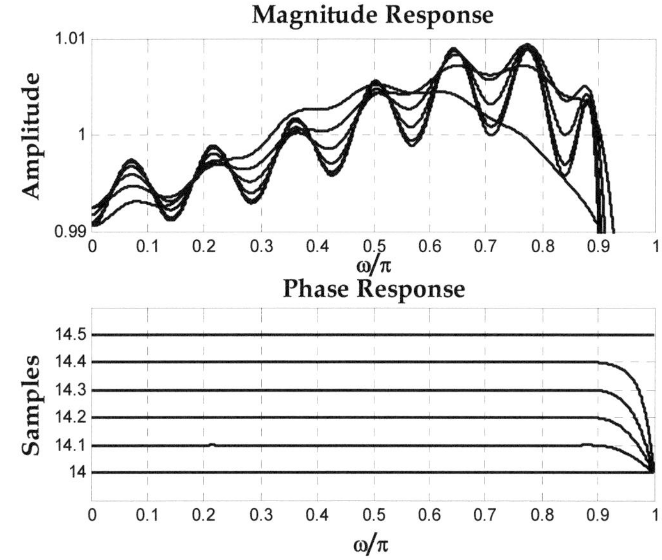

Fig. 21. FDF frequency responses, using minimax optimization approach in example 2.

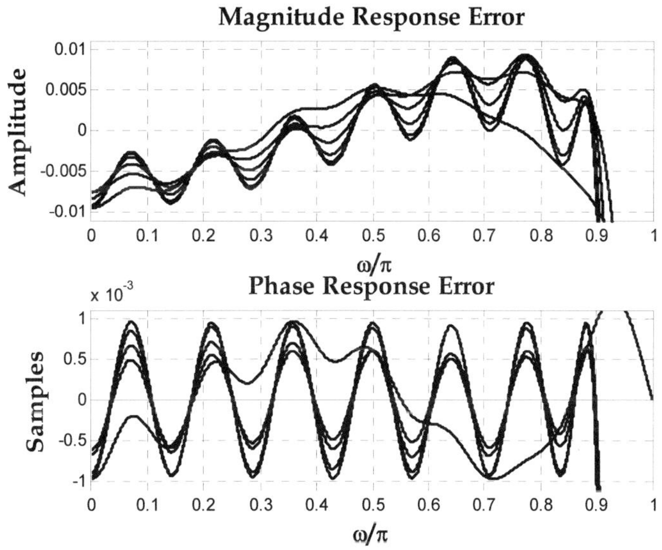

Fig. 22. FDF frequency response errors, using minimax optimization approach in example 2.

Example 3:

This example shows that the same minimax optimization approach can be extended for approximating a global complex error. For this purpose, the filter design example described in (Johansson & Lowenborg 2003) is used, which specifications are $\omega_p = 0.9\pi$, and maximum global complex error of $\delta c = 0.0042$. Such specifications are met with $N_{FD} = 7$ and $M = 4$ and a half-band filter length of 69. The overall structure requires $Prod = 35$ multipliers with a resulting maximum complex error $\Delta_c = 0.0036195$. The results obtained are compared in

Table 3 with the reported ones in existing methods. The described method requires less multipliers than (Johansson & Lowenborg 2003), (Hermanowicz, 2004) and case A of (Hermanowicz & Johansson, 2005). Reported multipliers of (Johansson & Hermanowicz, 2006) and case B of (Hermanowicz & Johansson, 2005) are less than the obtained with the presented design method. It should be pointed out that in (Johansson & Hermanowicz, 2006) an IIR half-band filter is used and in case B of (Hermanowicz & Johansson, 2005) and (Johansson & Hermanowicz, 2006) a switching technique between two multirate structures must be implemented. The resulted complex error magnitude is shown in Fig. 23 for fractional delay values from D =17.5 to 18.0 with 0.1 increment, magnitude response of the designed FDF is shown in Fig. 24 and errors of magnitude and phase frequency responses are presented in Fig 25.

Method	**Arithmetic complexity**		
	N_{FD}	M	*Prod*
(Johansson & Lowenborg 2003)	39	6	73
(Johansson & Lowenborg 2003)[a]	31	5	50
(Hermanowicz, 2004)	11	6	60(54)
(Hermanowicz & Johansson, 2005)	7	5	36
(Hermanowicz & Johansson, 2005)[b]	7	3	26
(Johansson & Hermanowicz, 2006)	-	6	32
(Johansson & Hermanowicz, 2006)[b]	-	3	22
(Ramirez-Conejo et al., 2010)	7	4	35

a. Minimax design with subfilters jointly optimized.

Table 3. Arithmetic complexity results for example 3.

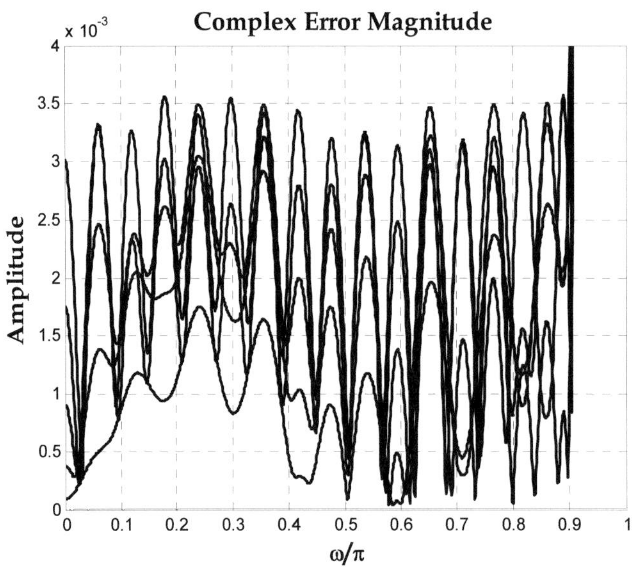

Fig. 23. FDF frequency complex error, using minimax optimization approach in example 3.

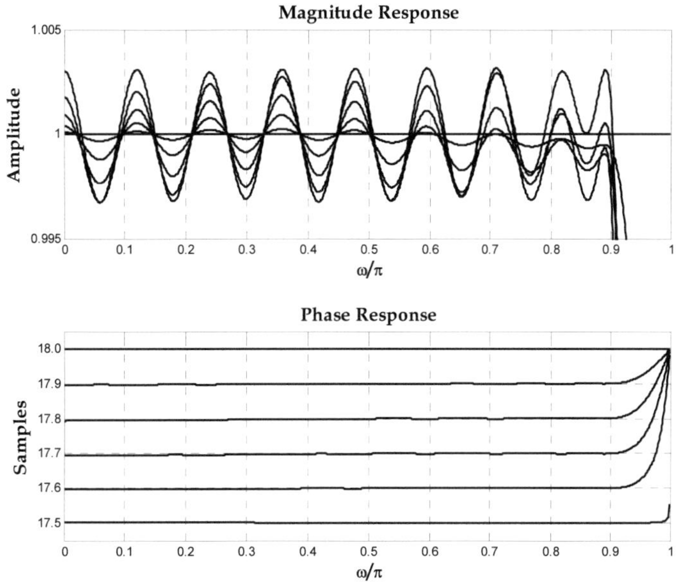

Fig. 24. FDF frequency response using minimax optimization approach in example 3.

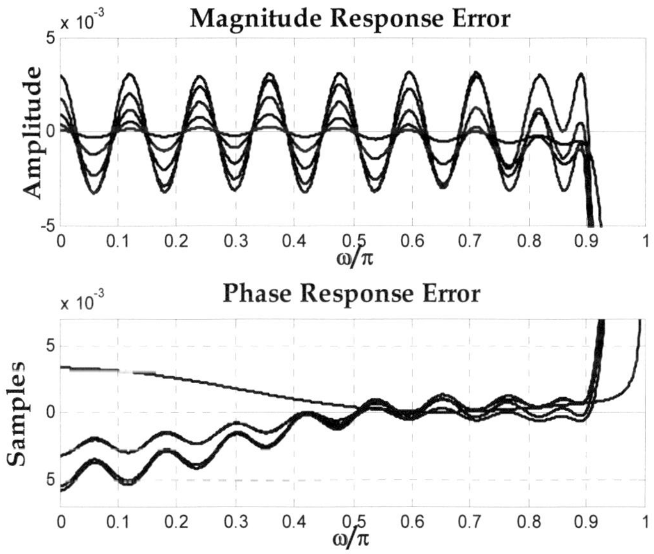

Fig. 25. FDF frequency response errors using minimax optimization approach in example 3.

6. Conclusion

The concept of fractional delay filter is introduced, as well as a general description of most of the existing design methods for FIR fractional delay filters is presented. Accordingly to the explained concepts and to the results of recently reported design methods, one of the most challenging approaches for designing fractional delay filters is the use of frequency-domain optimization methods. The use of MATLAB as a design and simulation platform is a very useful tool to achieve a fractional delay filter that meets best the required frequency specifications dictated by a particular application.

7. Acknowledgment

Authors would like to thank to the Technological Institute of Celaya at Guanajuato State, Mexico for the facilities in the project development, and CONACYT for the support.

8. References

Diaz-Carmona, J.; Jovanovic-Dolecek, G. & Ramirez-Agundis, A. (2010). Frequency-based optimization design for fractional delay FIR filters. *International Journal of Digital Multimedia Broadcasting,* Vol.2010, (January 2010), pp. 1-6, ISSN 1687-7578.

Erup, L.; Gardner, F. & Harris, F. (1993). Interpolation in digital modems-part II: implementation and performance. *IEEE Trans. on Communications,* Vol.41, (June 1993), pp. 998-1008.

Farrow, C. (1988). A continuously variable digital delay element, *Proceedings of IEEE Int. Symp. Circuits and Systems,* pp. 2641-2645, Espoo, Finland, June, 1988.

Gardner, F. (1993). Interpolation in digital modems-part I: fundamentals. *IEEE Trans. on Communications,* Vol.41, (March 1993), pp. 501-507.

Ging-Shing, L. & Che-Ho, W. (1992). A new variable fractional sample delay filter with nonlinear interpolation. *IEEE Trans. on Circuits Syst.,* Vol.39, (February 1992), pp. 123-126.

Ging-Shing, L. & Che-Ho, W. (1990). Programmable fractional sample delay filter with Lagrange interpolator. *Electronics Letters,* Vol.26, Issue19, (September 1990), pp. 1608-1610.

Hermanowicz, E. (2004). On designing a wideband fractional delay filter using the Farrow approach, *Proceedings of XII European Signal Processing Conference,* pp. 961-964, Vienna, Austria, September 6-10, 2004.

Hermanowicz, E. & Johansson, H. (2005). On designing minimax adjustable wideband fractional delay FIR filters using two-rate approach, *Proceedings of European Conference on Circuit Theory and Design,* pp. 473-440, Cork, Ireland, August 29-September 1, 2005.

Johansson, H. & Lowenborg, P. (2003). On the design of adjustable fractional delay FIR filters. *IEEE Trans. on Circuits and Syst.-II, Analog and Digital Signal Processing,* Vol.50, (April 2003), pp. 164-169.

Johansson, H. & Hermanowicz, E. (2006). Adjustable fractional delay filters utilizing the Farrow structure and multirate techniques, *Proceedings Sixth Int. Workshop Spectral Methods Multirate Signal Processing,*Florence, Italy, September 1-2, 2006.

Jovanovic-Dolecek, G. & Diaz-Carmona, J. (2002). One structure for fractional delay filter with small number of multipliers, *Electronics Letters,* Vol.18, Issue19, (September 2002), pp. 1083-1084.

Laakson, T.; Valimaki, V.; Karjalainen, M. & Laine, U. (1996). Splitting the unit delay. *IEEE Signal Processing Magazine,* Vol.13, No.1, (January 1996), pp. 30-60.

Murphy, N.; Krukowski A. & Kale I. (1994). Implementation of wideband integer and fractional delay element. *Electronics Letters,* Vol.30, Issue20, (September 1994), pp. 1654-1659.

Oetken, G. (1979). A new approach for the design of digital interpolation filters. *IEEE Trans. on Acoust., Speech, Signal Process.,* Vol.ASSP-27, (December 1979), pp. 637-643.

Proakis, J. & Manolakis, D. (1995). *Digital Signal Processing: Principles, Algorithms and Applications,* Prentice Hall, ISBN 978-0133737622, USA.

Ramirez-Conejo, G. (2010). *Diseño e implementación de filtros de retraso fraccionario,* Master in Science thesis, Technological Institute of Celaya, Celaya Mexico, (June, 2010).

Ramirez-Conejo, G.; Diaz-Carmona, J.; Delgado-Frias, J.; Jovanovic-Dolecek, G. & Prado-Olivarez, J. (2010a). Adjustable fractional delay FIR filters design using multirate and frequency optimization techniques, *Proceedings of Trigésima Convención de Centroamérica y Panáma del IEEE, CONCAPAN XXX,* San José, Costa Rica, November 17-18, 2010.

Ramirez-Conejo, G.; Diaz-Carmona, J.; Delgado-Frias, J.; Padilla-Medina, A. & Ramirez-Agundis, A. (2010b). FPGA implementation of adjustable wideband fractional delay FIR filters, *Proceedings International Conference On Reconfigurable Computing and FPGAs,* December 13-15, 2010.

Ramstad T. (1984). Digital methods for conversion between arbitrary sampling frequencies. *IEEE Trans. on Acoust. Speech, Signal Processing,* Vol.ASSP-32, (June 1984), pp. 577-591.

Tarczynski, A.; Cain, G.; Hermanovicz, E. & Rojewski, M. (1997). WLS design of variable frequency response FIR response, *Proceedings IEEE International Symp. On Circuits and Systems,* pp. 2244-2247, Hong Kong, June 9-12, 1997.

Tian-Bo, D. (2001). Discretization-free design of variable fractional-delay FIR filters. *IEEE Trans. On Circuits and Systems-II: Analog and Digital Signal Processing,* Vol.48, (June 2001), pp. 637-644.

Vesma, J. (1999). *Optimization Applications of Polynomial-Based Interpolation Filters,* PhD thesis, University of Technology, Tampere Finland, (May 1999), ISBN 952-15-0206-1.

Vesma, J. (1995). *Timing adjustment in digital receivers using interpolation,* Master in Science thesis, University of Technology, Tampere Finland, (November 1995).

Vesma, J. & Samaraki, T. (1996). Interpolation filters with arbitrary frequency response for all digital receivers, *Proceedings of IEEE Int. Sust. Circuits Syst.,* pp. 568-571, Georgia, USA, May 12-15, 1996.

Vesma, J.; Hamila, R.; Saramaki, T. & Renfors, M. (1998). Design of polynomial-based interpolation filters based on Taylor series, *Proceedings of IX European signal Processing Conference,* pp. 283-286, Rodhes, Greece, September 8-11, 1998.

Vesma, J. & Saramaki, T. (1997). Optimization and efficient implementation of FIR filters with adjustable fractional delay, *Proceedings IEEE Int. Symp. Circuits and Systems,* pp. 2256-2259, Hong Kong, June 9-12, 1997.

Wu-Sheng, L. & Tian-Bo, D. (1999). An improved weighted least-squares design for variable fractional delay FIR filters. *IEEE Trans. On Circuits and Systems-II: Analog and Digital Signal Processing,* Vol.46, (August 1999), pp. 1035-1049.

Yli-Kaakinen, J. & Saramaki, T. (2006a). Multiplication-free polynomial based FIR filters with an adjustable fractional delay. *Springer Circuits, syst., Signal Processing,* Vol.25, (April 2006), pp. 265-294.

Yli-Kaakinen, J. & Saramaki, T. (2006b). An efficient structure for FIR filters with an adjustable fractional delay, *Proceedings of Digital Signal Processing Applications,* pp. 617-623, Moscow, Russia, March 29-31, 2006.

Yli-Kaakinen, J. & Saramaki, T. (2007). A simplified structure for FIR filters with an adjustable fractional delay, *Proceedings of IEEE Int. Symp. Circuits and Systems,* pp. 3439-3442, New Orleans, USA, May 27-30, 2007.

Zhao, H. & Yu, J. (2006). A simple and efficient design of variable fractional delay FIR filters. *IEEE Trans. On Circuits and Systems-II: Express Brief,* Vol.53, (February 2006), pp. 157-160.

13

On Fractional-Order PID Design

Mohammad Reza Faieghi and Abbas Nemati
Department of Electrical Engineering,
Miyaneh Branch, Islamic Azad University,
Miyaneh,
Iran

1. Introduction

Fractional-order calculus is an area of mathematics that deals with derivatives and integrals from non-integer orders. In other words, it is a generalization of the traditional calculus that leads to similar concepts and tools, but with a much wider applicability. In the last two decades, fractional calculus has been rediscovered by scientists and engineers and applied in an increasing number of fields, namely in the area of control theory. The success of fractional-order controllers is unquestionable with a lot of success due to emerging of effective methods in differentiation and integration of non-integer order equations.

Fractional-order proportional-integral-derivative (FOPID) controllers have received a considerable attention in the last years both from academic and industrial point of view. In fact, in principle, they provide more flexibility in the controller design, with respect to the standard PID controllers,because they have five parameters to select (instead of three). However, this also implies that the tuning of the controller can be much more complex. In order to address this problem, different methods for the design of a FOPID controller have been proposed in the literature.

The concept of FOPID controllers was proposed by Podlubny in 1997 (Podlubny et al., 1997; Podlubny, 1999a). He also demonstrated the better response of this type of controller, in comparison with the classical PID controller, when used for the control of fractional order systems. A frequency domain approach by using FOPID controllers is also studied in (Vinagre et al., 2000). In (Monje et al., 2004), an optimization method is presented where the parameters of the FOPID are tuned such that predefined design specifications are satisfied. Ziegler-Nichols tuning rules for FOPID are reported in (Valerio & Costa, 2006). Further research activities are runnig in order to develop new tuning methods and investigate the applications of FOPIDs. In (Jesus & Machado, 2008) control of heat diffusion system via FOPID controllers are studied and different tuning methods are applied. Control of an irrigation canal using rule-based FOPID is given in (Domingues, 2010). In (Karimi et al., 2009) the authors applied an optimal FOPID tuned by Particle Swarm Optimzation (PSO) algorithm to control the Automatic Voltage Regulator (AVR) system. There are other papers published in the recent

years where the tuning of FOPID controller via PSO such as (Maiti et al., 2008) was investigated.
More recently, new tuning methods are proposed in (Padula & Visioli, 2010a). Robust FOPID design for First-Order Plus Dead-Time (FOPDT) models are reported in (Yeroglu et al., 2010). In (Charef & Fergani, 2010) a design method is reoported, using the impulse response. Set point weighting of FOPIDs are given in (Padula & Visioli, et al., 2010b). Besides, FOPIDs for integral processes in (Padula & Visioli, et al., 2010c), adaptive design for robot manipulators in (Delavari et al., 2010) and loop shaping design in (Tabatabaei & Haeri, 2010) are studied.
The aim of this chapter is to study some of the well-known tuning methods of FOPIDs proposed in the recent literature. In this chapter, design of FOPID controllers is presented via different approaches include optimization methods, Ziegler-Nichols tuning rules, and the Padula & Visioli method. In addition, several interesting illustrative examples are presented. Simulations have been carried out using MATLAB via Ninteger toolbox (Valerio & Costa, 2004). Thus, a brief introduction about the toolbox is given.
The rest of this chapter is organized as follows: In section 2, basic definitions of fractional calculus and its frequency domain approximation is presented. Section 3 introduces the Ninteger toolbox. Section 4 includes the basic concepts of FOPID controllers. Several design methods are presented in sections 5 to 8 and finally, concluding remarks are given in section 9.

2. Fractional calculus

In this section, basic definitions of fractional calculus as well as its approximation method is given.

2.1 Definitions

The differintegral operator, denoted by ${}_aD_t^q$, is a combined differentiation-integration operator commonly used in fractional calculus. This operator is a notation for taking both the fractional derivative and the fractional integral in a single expression and is defined by

$$ {}_aD_t^q = \begin{cases} \dfrac{d^q}{dt^q} & q > 0 \\ 1 & q = 0 \\ \int_a^t (d\tau)^{-q} & q < 0 \end{cases} \tag{1} $$

Where q is the fractional order which can be a complex number and a and t are the limits of the operation. There are some definitions for fractional derivatives. The commonly used definitions are Grunwald–Letnikov, Riemann–Liouville, and Caputo definitions (Podlubny, 1999b). The Grunwald–Letnikov definition is given by

$$ {}_aD_t^q f(t) = \frac{d^q f(t)}{d(t-a)^q} = \lim_{N\to\infty}\left[\frac{t-a}{N}\right]^{-q} \sum_{j=0}^{N-1} (-1)^j \binom{q}{j} f(t - j\left[\frac{t-a}{N}\right]) \tag{2} $$

The Riemann–Liouville definition is the simplest and easiest definition to use. This definition is given by

$$ {}_aD_t^q f(t) = \frac{d^q f(t)}{d(t-a)^q} = \frac{1}{\Gamma(n-q)} \frac{d^n}{dt^n} \int_0^t (t-\tau)^{n-q-1} f(\tau) d\tau \qquad (3) $$

where n is the first integer which is not less than q i.e. $n-1 \le q < n$ and Γ is the Gamma function.

$$ \Gamma(z) = \int_0^\infty t^{z-1} e^{-t} dt \qquad (4) $$

For functions $f(t)$ having n continuous derivatives for $t \ge 0$ where $n-1 \le q < n$, the Grunwald–Letnikov and the Riemann–Liouville definitions are equivalent. The Laplace transforms of the Riemann–Liouville fractional integral and derivative are given as follows:

$$ L\{{}_0D_t^q f(t)\} = s^q F(s) - \sum_{k=0}^{n-1} s^k \, {}_0D_t^{q-k-1} f(0) \qquad n-1 < q \le n \in N \qquad (5) $$

Unfortunately, the Riemann–Liouville fractional derivative appears unsuitable to be treated by the Laplace transform technique because it requires the knowledge of the non-integer order derivatives of the function at $t=0$. This problem does not exist in the Caputo definition that is sometimes referred as smooth fractional derivative in literature. This definition of derivative is defined by

$$ {}_aD_t^q f(t) = \begin{cases} \dfrac{1}{\Gamma(m-q)} \displaystyle\int_0^t \frac{f^{(m)}(\tau)}{(t-\tau)^{q+1-m}} d\tau & m-1 < q < m \\ \dfrac{d^m}{dt^m} f(t) & q = m \end{cases} \qquad (6) $$

where m is the first integer larger than q. It is found that the equations with Riemann-Liouville operators are equivalent to those with Caputo operators by homogeneous initial conditions assumption. The Laplace transform of the Caputo fractional derivative is

$$ L\{{}_0D_t^q f(t)\} = s^q F(s) - \sum_{k=0}^{n-1} s^{q-k-1} f^{(k)}(0) \qquad n-1 < q \le n \in N \qquad (7) $$

Contrary to the Laplace transform of the Riemann–Liouville fractional derivative, only integer order derivatives of function f are appeared in the Laplace transform of the Caputo fractional derivative. For zero initial conditions, Eq. (7) reduces to

$$ L\{{}_0D_t^q f(t)\} = s^q F(s) \qquad (8) $$

In the rest of this paper, the notation D^q, indicates the Caputo fractional derivative.

2.2 Approximation methods

The numerical simulation of a fractional differential equation is not simple as that of an ordinary differential equation. Since most of the fractional-order differential equations do not have exact analytic solutions, so approximation and numerical techniques must be used. Several analytical and numerical methods have been proposed to solve the fractional-order differential equations. The method which is considered in this chapter is based on the approximation of the fractional-order system behavior in the frequency domain. To simulate a fractional-order system by using the frequency domain approximations, the fractional order equations of the system is first considered in the frequency domain and then Laplace form of the fractional integral operator is replaced by its integer order approximation. Then the approximated equations in frequency domain are transformed back into the time domain. The resulted ordinary differential equations can be numerically solved by applying the well-known numerical methods.

One of the best-known approximations is due to Oustaloup and is given by (Oustaloup, 1991)

$$s^q = k\prod_{n=1}^{N}\frac{1+\dfrac{s}{\omega_{zn}}}{1+\dfrac{s}{\omega_{pn}}} \quad q>0 \tag{9}$$

The approximation is valid in the frequency range $[\omega_l,\omega_h]$; gain k is adjusted so that the approximation shall have unit gain at 1 rad/sec; the number of poles and zeros N is chosen beforehand (low values resulting in simpler approximations but also causing the appearance of a ripple in both gain and phase behaviours); frequencies of poles and zeros are given by

$$\alpha = \left(\frac{\omega_h}{\omega_l}\right)^{\frac{q}{N}} \tag{10}$$

$$\eta = \left(\frac{\omega_h}{\omega_l}\right)^{\frac{1-q}{N}} \tag{11}$$

$$\omega_{z1} = \omega_l\sqrt{\eta} \tag{12}$$

$$\omega_{zn} = \omega_{p,n-1}\eta, \quad n = 2,\dots,N \tag{13}$$

$$\omega_{pn} = \omega_{z,n-1}\alpha, \quad n = 1,\dots,N \tag{14}$$

The case $q<0$ may be dealt with inverting (9).

In Table 1, approximations of $1/s^q$ have been given for $q\in\{0.1,0.2,\dots,0.9\}$ with maximum discrepancy of 2 dB within (0.01, 100) rad/sec frequency range (Ahmad & Sprott, 2003).

q	Approximated transfer function
0.1	$\frac{1584.8932(s+0.1668)(s+27.83)}{(s+0.1)(s+16.68)(s+2783)}$
0.2	$\frac{79.4328(s+0.05623)(s+1)(s+17.78)}{(s+0.03162)(s+0.5623)(s+10)(s+177.8)}$
0.3	$\frac{39.8107(s+0.0416)(s+0.3728)(s+3.34)(s+29.94)}{(s+0.02154)(s+0.1931)(s+1.73)(s+15.51)(s+138.9)}$
0.4	$\frac{35.4813(s+0.03831)(s+0.261)(s+1.778)(s+12.12)(s+82.54)}{(s+0.01778)(s+0.1212)(s+0.8254)(s+5.623)(s+38.31)(s+261)}$
0.5	$\frac{15.8489(s+0.03981)(s+0.2512)(s+1.585)(s+10)(s+63.1)}{(s+0.01585)(s+0.1)(s+0.631)(s+3.981)(s+3.981)(s+25.12)(s+158.5)}$
0.6	$\frac{10.7978(s+0.04642)(s+0.3162)(s+2.154)(s+14.68)(s+100)}{(s+0.01468)(s+0.1)(s+0.631)(s+4.642)(s+31.62)(s+215.4)}$
0.7	$\frac{9.3633(s+0.06449)(s+0.578)(s+5.179)(s+46.42)(s+416)}{(s+0.01389)(s+0.1245)(s+1.116)(s+10)(s+89.62)(s+803.1)}$
0.8	$\frac{5.3088(s+0.1334)(s+2.371)(s+42.17)(s+749.9)}{(s+0.01334)(s+0.2371)(s+4.217)(s+74.99)(s+1334)}$
0.9	$\frac{2.2675(s+1.292)(s+215.4)}{(s+0.01292)(s+2.154)(s+359.4)}$

Table 1. Approximation of $1/s^q$ for different q values

3. The Ninteger toolbox

Ninteger is a toolbox for MATLAB intended to help developing fractional-order controllers and assess their performance. It is freely downloadable from the internet and implements fractional-order controllers both in the frequency and the discrete time domains. This toolbox includes about thirty methods for implementing approximations of fractional-order and three identification methods. The Ninteger toolbox allow us to implement, simulate and analyze FOPID controllers easily via its functions. In the rest of this chapter, all the simulation studies have been carried out using the Ninteger toolbox.

In order to use this toolbox in our simulation studies, the function *nipid* is suitable for implementing FOPID controllers. The toolbox allow us to implement this function either from *command window* or *SIMULINK*. In order to use *SIMULINK*, a library is provided called *Nintblocks*. In this library, one can find the *Fractional PID* block which implements FOPID controllers. We can specify the following parameters of a FOPID via *nipid* function or *Fractional PID* block:

- proportional gain
- derivative gain
- fractional derivative order
- integral gain
- fractional integral order

- bandwidth of frequency domian approximation
- number of zeros and poles of the approximation
- the approximating formula

It was pointed out in (Oustaloup et al., 2000) that a band-limit implementation of fractional order controller is important in practice, and the finite dimensional approximation of the fractional order controller should be done in a proper range of frequencies of practical interest. This is true since the fractional order controller in theory has an infinite memory and some sort of approximation using finite memory must be done.

In the simulation studies of this chapter, we will use the *Crone* method within the frequency range (0.01, 100) rad/s and the number of zeros and poles are set to 10.

4. Fractional-order Proportional-Integral-Derivative controller

The most common form of a fractional order PID controller is the $PI^{\lambda}D^{\mu}$ controller (Podlubny, 1999a), involving an integrator of order λ and a differentiator of order μ where λ and μ can be any real numbers. The transfer function of such a controller has the form

$$G_c(s) = \frac{U(s)}{E(s)} = k_P + k_I \frac{1}{s^{\lambda}} + k_D s^{\mu}, \quad (\lambda, \mu > 0) \tag{15}$$

where $G_c(s)$ is the transfer function of the controller, $E(s)$ is an error, and $U(s)$ is controller's output. The integrator term is $1/s^{\lambda}$, that is to say, on a semi-logarithmic plane, there is a line having slope -20λ dB/decade. The control signal $u(t)$ can then be expressed in the time domain as

$$u(t) = k_P e(t) + k_I D^{-\lambda} e(t) + k_D D^{\mu} e(t) \tag{16}$$

Fig. 1 is a block-diagram configuration of FOPID. Clearly, selecting $\lambda = 1$ and $\mu = 1$, a classical PID controller can be recovered. The selections of $\lambda = 1$, $\mu = 0$, and $\lambda = 0$, $\mu = 1$ respectively corresponds conventional PI & PD controllers. All these classical types of PID controllers are the special cases of the fractional $PI^{\lambda}D^{\mu}$ controller given by (15).

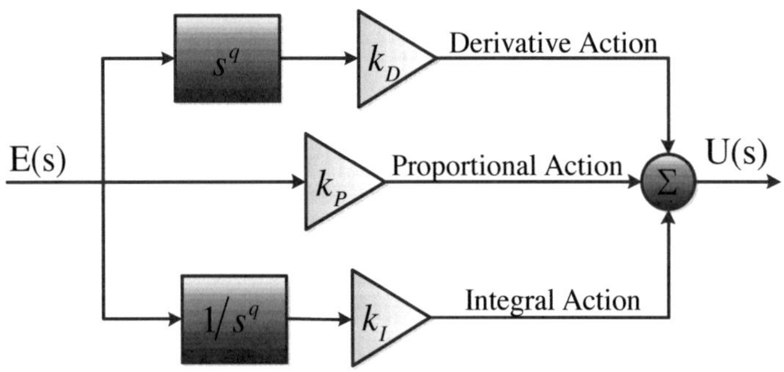

Fig. 1. Block-diagram of FOPID

It can be expected that the $PI^{\lambda}D^{\mu}$ controller may enhance the systems control performance. One of the most important advantages of the $PI^{\lambda}D^{\mu}$ controller is the better control of dynamical systems, which are described by fractional order mathematical models. Another advantage lies in the fact that the $PI^{\lambda}D^{\mu}$ controllers are less sensitive to changes of parameters of a controlled system (Xue et al., 2006). This is due to the two extra degrees of freedom to better adjust the dynamical properties of a fractional order control system. However, all these claimed benefits were not systematically demonstrated in the literature. In the next sections, different design methods of FOPID controllers are discussed. In all cases, we considered the unity feedback control scheme depicted in Fig.2.

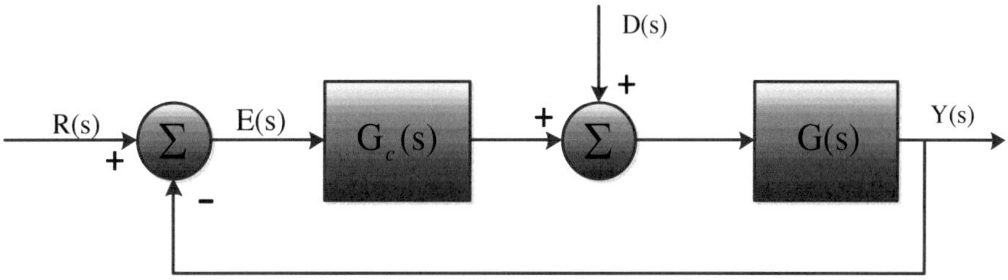

Fig. 2. The considered control scheme; G(s) is the process, $G_c(s)$ is the FOPID controller, R(s) is the reference input, E(s) is the error, D(s) is the disturbance and Y(s) is the output

5. Tuning by minimization

In (Monje et al., 2004) an optimization method is proposed for tuning of FOPID controllers. The analytic method, that lies behind the proposed tuning rules, is based on a specified desirable behavior of the controlled system. We start the section with basic concepts of this design method, and then control pH neutralization process is presented as an illustrative example.

5.1 Basic concepts

In this method, the desirable dynamics is described by the following criteria:

1. No steady-state error:

Properly implemented a fractional integrator of order $k+\lambda$, $k \in N$, $0 < \lambda < 1$, is, for steady-state error cancellation, as efficient as an integer order integrator of order $k+1$.

2. The gain-crossover frequency ω_{cg} is to have some specified value

$$\left|G_c(j\omega_{cg})G(j\omega_{cg})\right| = 0 \text{ dB} \tag{17}$$

3. The phase margin φ_m is to have some specified value

$$-\pi + \varphi_m = \arg\left(G_c(j\omega_{cg})G(j\omega_{cg})\right) \tag{18}$$

4. So as to reject high-frequency noise, the closed loop transfer function must have a small magnitude at high frequencies; thus it is required that at some specified frequency ω_t its magnitude be less than some specified gain

$$\left|T(j\omega) = \frac{G_c(j\omega)G(j\omega)}{1+G_c(j\omega)G(j\omega)}\right| < A \text{ dB } \forall\, \omega \geq \omega_t \rightarrow \left|T(j\omega)\right| = A \text{ dB} \tag{19}$$

5. So as to reject output disturbances and closely follow references, the sensitivity function must have a small magnitude at low frequencies; thus it is required that at some specified frequency ω_s its magnitude be less than some specified gain

$$\left|S(j\omega) = \frac{1}{1+G_c(j\omega)G(j\omega)}\right| < B\ \text{dB}\ \forall\ \omega \leq \omega_s \rightarrow |S(j\omega)| = B\ \text{dB} \tag{20}$$

6. So as to be robust in face of gain variations of the plant, the phase of the open-loop transfer function must be (at least roughly) constant around the gain-crossover frequency

$$\frac{d}{d\omega}\arg\left(G_c(j\omega)G(j\omega)\right)|_{\omega=\omega cg} = 0 \tag{21}$$

A set of five of these six specifications can be met by the closed-loop system, since the FOPID has five parameters to tune. The specifications 2-6 yield a robust performance of the controlled system against gain changes and noise and the condition of no steady-state error is fulfilled just with the introduction of the fractional integrator properly implemented, as commented before.

In (Monje et al., 2004), the use of numerical optimization techniques is proposed to satisfy the specifications 2-6. Motivated from the fact that the complexity of a set of five nonlinear equations (17-21) with five unknown parameters (k_P, k_I, k_D, λ and μ) is very significant, the optimization toolbox of MATLAB has been used to reach out the better solution with the minimum error. The function used for this purpose is called *fmincon*, which finds the constrained minimum of a function of several variables. In this case, the specification in Eq. (17) is taken as the main function to minimize, and the rest of specifications (18-21) are taken as constrains for the minimization, all of them subjected to the optimization parameters defined within the function *fmincon*.

5.2 Example: pH neutralization process

The pH dynamic model of a real sugar cane raw juice neutralization process can be modelled by the following FOPDT dynamic:

$$G(s) = \frac{0.55e^{-s}}{62s+1} \tag{22}$$

Assume that the design specifications are as follows:

- Gain crossover frequency $\omega_{cg} = 0.08$
- Phase margin $\varphi_m = 0.44\pi$
- Robustness to variations in the gain of the plant must be fulfilled.
- $|T(j\omega)| \leq -20$ dB, $\forall\ \omega \geq \omega_t = 10$ rad/sec
- $|S(j\omega)| \leq -20$dB, $\forall\ \omega \leq \omega_s = 0.01$ rad/sec

Using the function *fmincon*, the FOPID controller to control the plant is

$$G_c(s) = 7.9619 + \frac{0.2299}{s^{0.9646}} + 0.1594\ s^{0.0150} \tag{23}$$

Simulation block-diagram of the system is depicted in Fig. 3 and the step response of the closed-loop system is illustrated in Fig. 4.

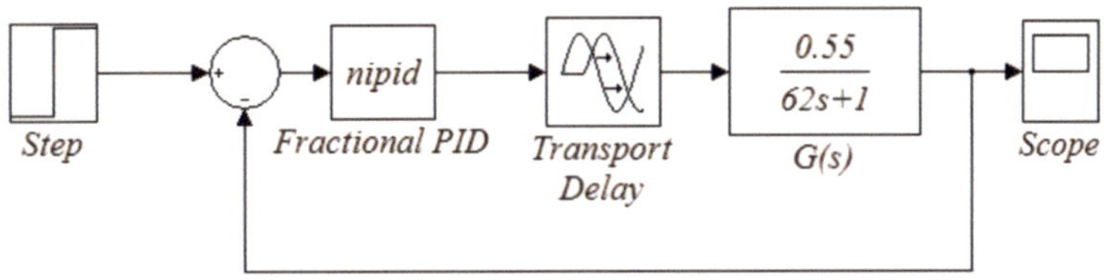

Fig. 3. Simulation block-diagram for control of pH neutralization process

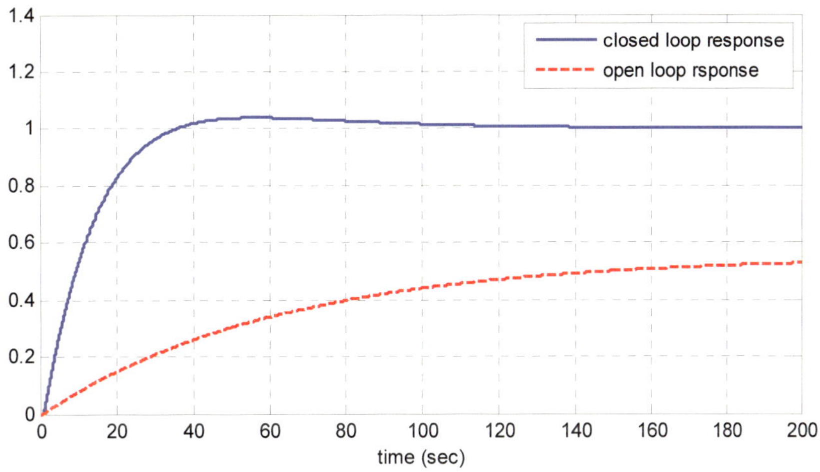

Fig. 4. Step responses of closed loop and open loop pH neutralization process

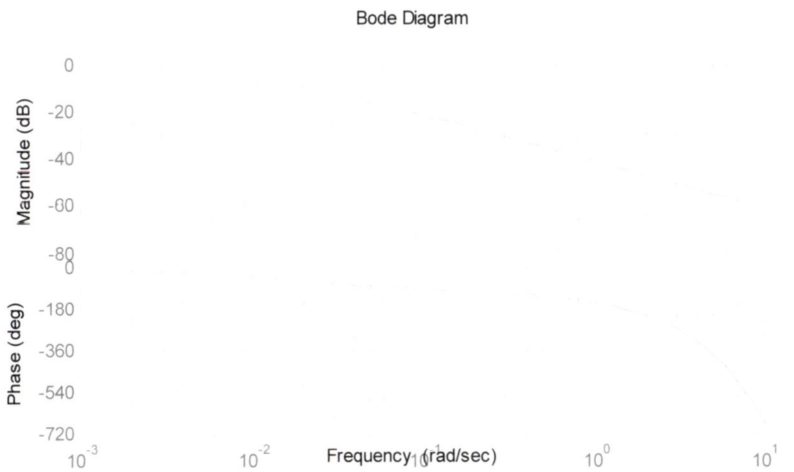

Fig. 5. Bode plot of pH neutralization process

As shown in the Fig.4 the closed loop step response has no steady state error and a fulfilling rise time in the comparison of the open loop response. In order to evaluate the effect of FOPID in frequency response of the process, let us consider Fig.5 as bode plot of the open loop pH neutralization process. The diagram is provided via "Control System Toolbox" of MATLAB. The bode diagram of the FOPID defined in (23) is also depicted in Fig. 6 and finally, the bode plot of $G(s)G_c(s)$ is depicted in Fig. 7.

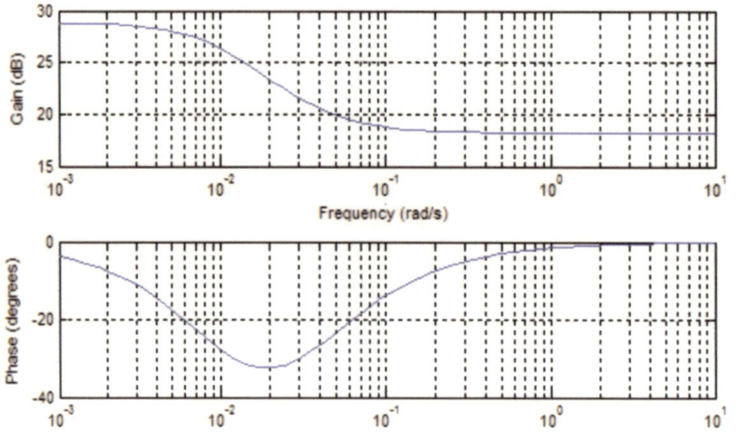

Fig. 6. Bode plot of FOPID controller designed for pH neutralization process

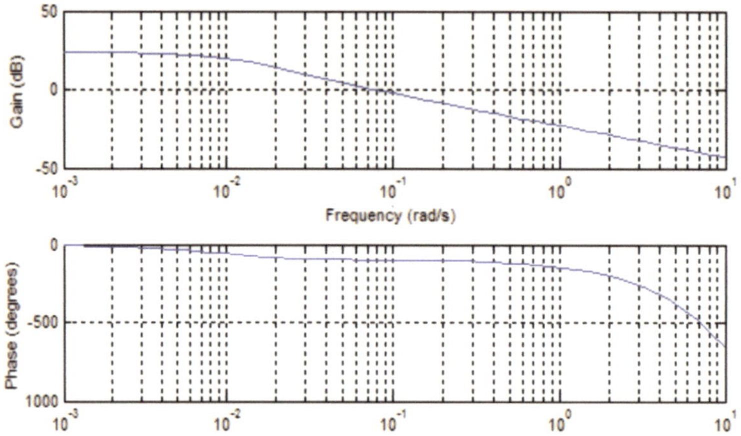

Fig. 7. Bode plot of pH neutralization process when the controller is applied

6. Ziegler-Nichols type tuning rules

In the previous section, a tuning method based on optimization techniques is proposed. The method is effective but allows local minima to be obtained. In practice, most solutions found with this optimization method are good enough, but they strongly depend on initial estimates of the parameters provided. Some may be discarded, because they are unfeasible or lead to unstable loops, but in many cases it is possible to find more than one acceptable FOPID. In others, only well-chosen initial estimates of the parameters allow finding a solution. Motivated from the fact that the optimization techniques depend on initial estimates, Valerio and Costa have introduced some Ziegler-Nichols-type tuning rules for FOPIDs. In this section, we will explain these tuning rules, and two illustrative examples will be presented. These tuning rules are applicable only for systems that have S-shaped step response. The simplest plant to have S-shaped step response can be described by

$$G(s) = \frac{K}{Ts+1}e^{-sL} \tag{24}$$

Valerio and Costa have employed the minimisation tuning method to plants given by (24) for several values of L and T, with $K = 1$. The parameters of FOPIDs thus obtained vary in a regular manner. Having translated the regularity into formulas, some tuning rules are obtained for particular desired responses.

6.1 First set of tuning rules

A first set of rules is given in Tables 2 and 3. These are to be read as

$$\mathrm{P} = -0.0048 + 0.2664\mathrm{L} + 0.4982\mathrm{T} + 0.0232\mathrm{L}^2 - 0.0720\mathrm{T}^2 - 0.0348\mathrm{TL} \tag{25}$$

and so on. They may be used if $0.1 \le \mathrm{T} \le 50, \mathrm{L} \le 2$ and were designed for the following specifications:

- $\omega_{cg} = 0.5\ \mathrm{rad/sec}$
- $\varphi_m = 2/3\ \mathrm{rad}$
- $\omega_t = 10\ \mathrm{rad/sec}$
- $\omega_s = 0.01\ \mathrm{rad/sec}$
- $\mathrm{A} = -10\ d\mathrm{B}$
- $\mathrm{B} = -20\ d\mathrm{B}$

	k_P	k_I	λ	k_D	μ
1	-0.0048	0.3254	1.5766	0.0662	0.8736
L	0.2664	0.2478	-0.2098	-0.2528	0.2746
T	0.4982	0.1429	-0.1313	0.1081	0.1489
L^2	0.0232	-0.1330	0.0713	0.0702	-0.1557
T^2	-0.0720	0.0258	0.0016	0.0328	-0.0250
LT	-0.0348	-0.0171	0.0114	0.2202	-0.0323

Table 2. Parameters for the first set of tuning rules when $0.1 \le \mathrm{T} \le 5$

	k_P	k_I	λ	k_D	μ
1	2.1187	-0.5201	1.0645	1.1421	1.2902
L	-3.5207	2.6643	-0.3268	-1.3707	-0.5371
T	-0.1563	0.3453	-0.0229	0.0357	-0.0381
L^2	1.5827	-1.0944	0.2018	0.5552	0.2208
T^2	0.0025	0.0002	0.0003	-0.0002	0.0007
LT	0.1824	-0.1054	0.0028	0.2630	-0.0014

Table 3. Parameters for the first set of tuning rules when $5 \le \mathrm{T} \le 50$

6.2 Second set of tuning rules

A second set of rules is given in Table 4. These may be applied for $0.1 \le T \le 50$ and $L \le 0.5$. Only one set of parameters is needed in this case because the range of values of L these rules cope with is more reduced. They were designed for the following specifications:

- $\omega_{cg} = 0.5$ rad/sec
- $\varphi_m = 1$ rad
- $\omega_t = 10$ rad/sec
- $\omega_s = 0.01$ rad/sec
- A = -20 dB
- B = -20 dB

	k_P	k_I	λ	k_D	μ
1	-1.0574	0.6014	1.1851	0.8793	0.2778
L	24.5420	0.4025	-0.3464	-15.0846	-2.1522
T	0.3544	0.7921	-0.0492	-0.0771	0.0675
L^2	-46.7325	-0.4508	1.7317	28.0388	2.4387
T^2	-0.0021	0.0018	0.0006	-0.0000	-0.0013
LT	-0.3106	-1.2050	0.0380	1.6711	0.0021

Table 4. Parameters for the second set of tuning rules

6.3 Example: High-order process control

Consider the following high-order process

$$G(s) = \frac{1}{(s+1)^4} \tag{26}$$

The transfer function of the process is not on the form of FOPDT. In order to control the process via FOPID, let us approximate the process by a FOPDT model. The process can be approximated by the following model (see (Astrom & Hagglund, 1995))

$$G(s) = \frac{1}{2s+1} e^{-2s} \tag{27}$$

where K=1, L=2 and T=2. Fig.8 shows the step response of the process (26) and its approximated model. As we see, the model can approximate the process with satisfying accuracy. The step response of the process is of S-shaped type and we can use the Ziegler-Nichols type tuning rules for our FOPID controller.

Using the first set of tuning rules, one can obtain the following FOPID controller.

$$G_c(s) = 1.1900 + 0.6096 \frac{1}{s^{1.2316}} + 1.0696 s^{0.8686} \tag{28}$$

The closed step response of the system is depicted in Fig. 9.

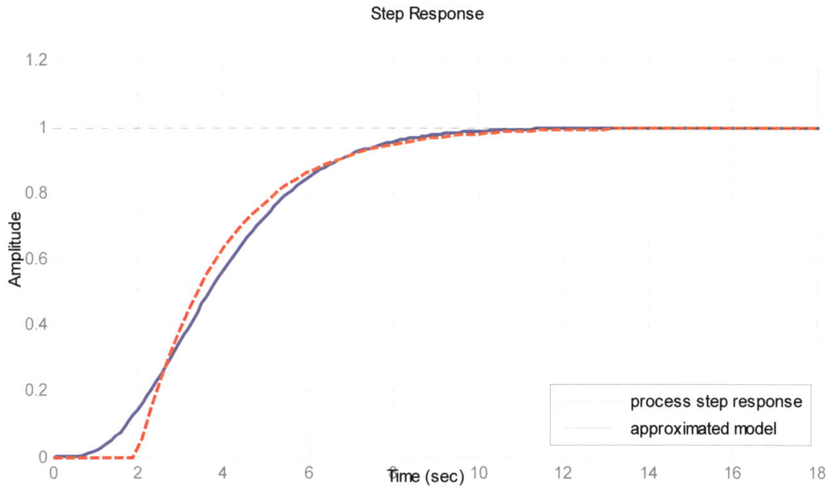

Fig. 8. Step response of the process and its approximated model

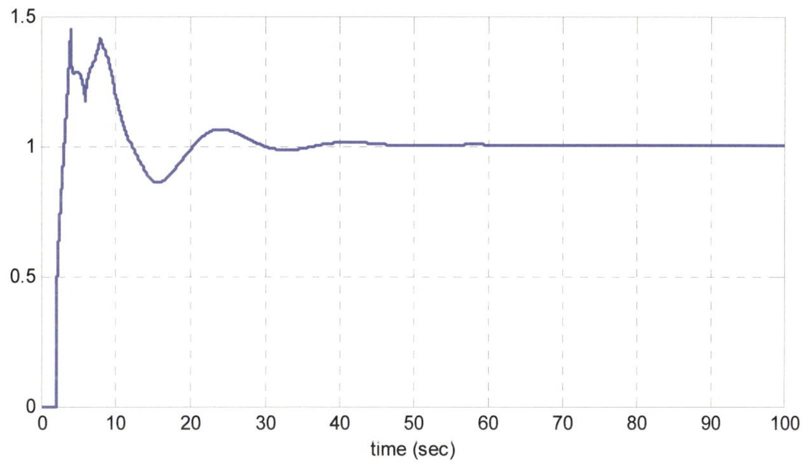

Fig. 9. Step response of high order process controlled by FOPID

6.4 Example: Non-minimum phase process control

When the transfer function of a process is not a FOPDT model, an approximated FOPDT model can be developed; this fact was shown in the previous example. Here, we consider a Non-Minimum phase process. We need to approximate a FOPDT model in order to use Ziegler-Nichols tuning rules. The following non-minimum phase process is considered

$$G(s) = \frac{1-s}{(s+0.5)(s+2)} \tag{29}$$

The process can be approximated by the following model

$$G(s) = \frac{1}{1.8s + 1} e^{-1.7s} \tag{30}$$

The step response of the transfer function (30) is compared with the process (29) and depicted in Fig. 10. As we see, the FOPDT model of the process presents a good accuracy.

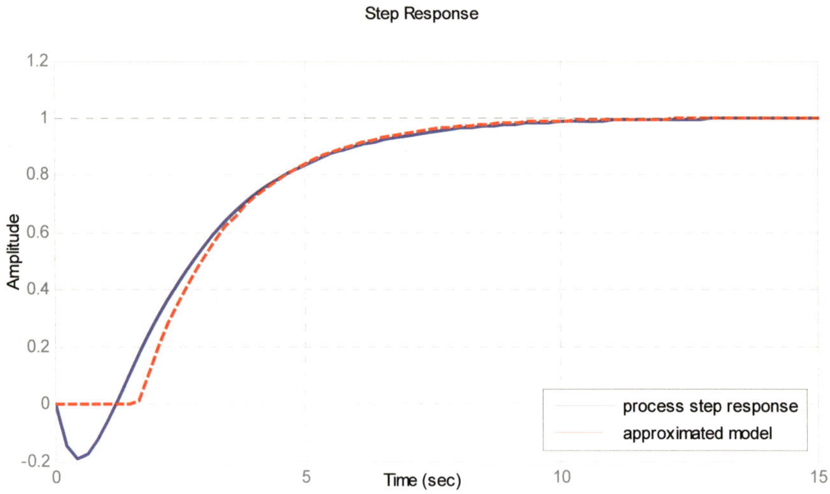

Fig. 10. Step response of the process and its approximated model

After having approximated the process with a FOPDT transfer function, application of the first set of tuning rules gives the following FOPID controller

$$G_c(s) = 1.0721 + 0.6508 \frac{1}{s^{1.2297}} + 0.8140 s^{0.9786} \tag{31}$$

while the step response of the closed loop control system for set point and is depicted in Fig. 11.

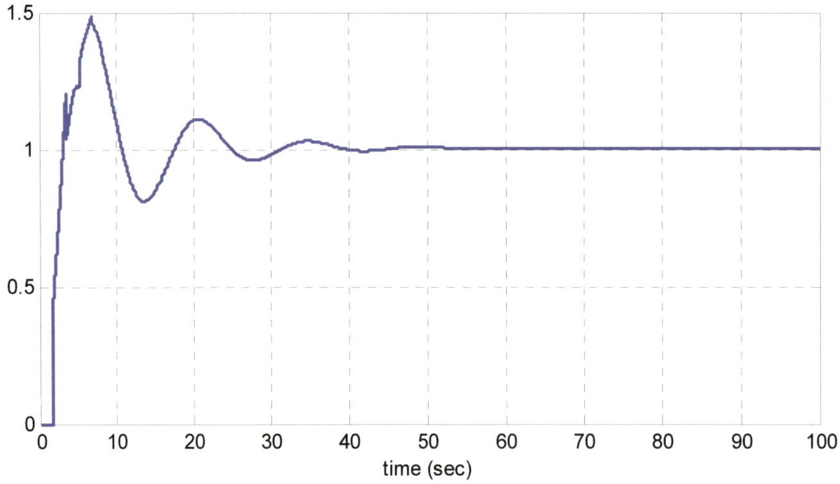

Fig. 11. Step response of non-minimum phase process controlled by FOPID

7. The Padula & Visioli method

In (Padula & Visioli, 2010a), a new set of tuning rules are presented for FOPID controllers. Based on FOPDT models, the tuning rules have been devised in order to minimise the integrated absolute error with a constraint on the maximum sensitivity. In this section, the tuning rules are presented and then the problem of heat exchanger temperature is given.

7.1 Tuning rules

Let us consider a process defined by FOPDT model as one given by Eq. (24). The process dynamics can be conveniently characterised by the normalised dead time and defined as

$$\tau = \frac{L}{L+T} \tag{32}$$

which represents a measure of difficulty in controlling the process. The proposed tuning rules are devised for values of the normalised dead time in the range $0.05 \le \tau \le 0.8$. In fact, for values of $\tau < 0.05$ the dead time can be virtually neglected and the design of a controller is rather trivial, while for values of $\tau > 0.8$ the process is significantly dominated by the dead time and therefore a dead time compensator should be employed. By the methodology developed in (Padula & Visioli, 2010a), the FOPID controller is modeled by the following transfer function

$$G_c(s) = K_p \frac{K_i s^{\lambda} + 1}{K_i s^{\lambda}} \frac{K_d s^{\mu} + 1}{\frac{K_d}{N} s^{\mu} + 1} \tag{33}$$

The major difference of FOPID defined by (33) with the standard form of FOPID defined by (15) is that an additional first-order filter has been employed in (33) in order to make the controller proper. The parameter N is chosen as $N = 10T^{(\mu-1)}$. The performance index is integrated absolute error which is defined as follows

$$IAE = \int_0^{\infty} |e(t)| dt \tag{34}$$

Using Eq.(34) as performance index yields a low overshoot and a low settling time at the same time (Shinskey, 1994). The maximum sensitivity (Astrom and Hagglund, 1995) is defined as

$$M_s = \max\left\{ \frac{1}{1 + G_c(s)G(s)} \right\} \tag{35}$$

which represents the inverse of the maximum distance of the Nyquist plot from the critical point (-1,0). Obviously, the higher value of M_s yields the less robustness against uncertainties. Tuning rules are devised such that the typical values of M_s = 1.4 and M_s = 2.0 are achieved. If only the load disturbance rejection task is addressed, we have

$$K_p = \frac{1}{K}\left(a\tau^{b} + c\right) \tag{36}$$

$$K_i = T\left(a\left(\frac{L}{T}\right)^b + c\right) \tag{37}$$

$$K_d = T\left(a\left(\frac{L}{T}\right)^b + c\right) \tag{38}$$

where the values of the parameters are shown in Tables 5-8.

	a	b	c
k_P	0.2776	-1.097	-0.1426
k_D	0.6241	0.5573	0.0442
k_I	0.4793	0.7469	-0.0239

Table 5. Tuning rules for k_P, k_D and k_I when $M_s = 1.4$

λ	μ
1	1.0 if $\tau < 0.1$ 1.1 if $0.1 \le \tau < 0.4$ 1.2 if $0.4 \le \tau$

Table 6. Tuning rules for λ and μ when $M_s = 1.4$

	a	b	c
k_P	0.164	-1.449	-0.2108
k_D	0.6426	0.8069	0.0563
k_I	0.5970	0.5568	-0.0954

Table 7. Tuning rules for k_P, k_D and k_I when $M_s = 2.0$

λ	μ
1	1.0 if $\tau < 0.2$ 1.1 if $0.2 \le \tau < 0.6$ 1.2 if $0.6 \le \tau$

Table 8. Tuning rules for λ and μ when $M_s = 2.0$

7.2 Example: Heat exchanger temperature control

A chemical reactor called "stirring tank" is depicted in Fig. 12. The top inlet delivers liquid to be mixed in the tank. The tank liquid must be maintained at a constant temperature by varying the amount of steam supplied to the heat exchanger (bottom pipe) via its control valve. Variations in the temperature of the inlet flow are the main source of disturbances in this process.

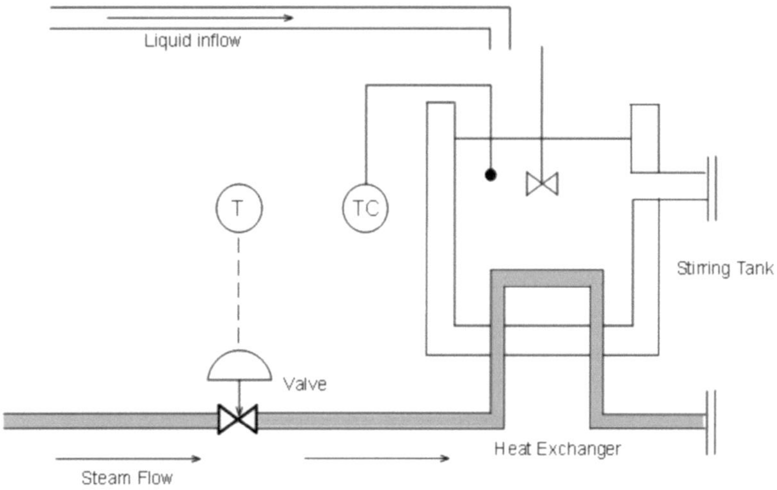

Fig. 12. Stirring Reactor with Heat Exchanger

The process can be modelled adequately by FOPDT models as shown in the Fig. 13.

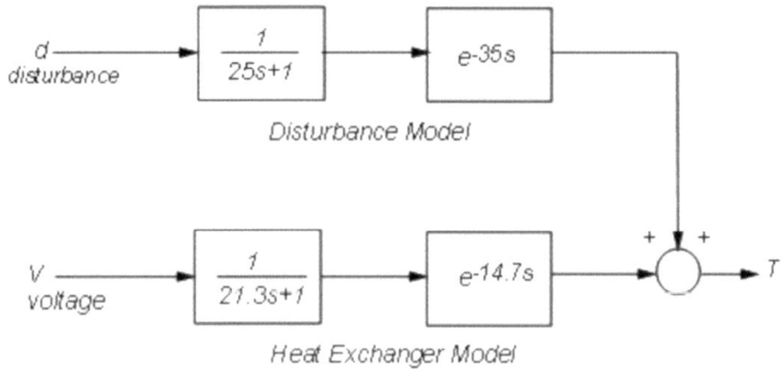

Fig. 13. Open loop process model

The transfer function

$$G(s) = \frac{e^{-14.7s}}{21.3s + 1} \tag{38}$$

models how a change in the voltage V driving the steam valve opening effects the tank temperature T, while the transfer function

$$G_d(s) = \frac{e^{-35s}}{25s + 1} \tag{39}$$

models how a change d in inflow temperature affects T.
The control problem is to regulate tank temperature T around a given setpoint. From Eq. (32), the normalized dead-time of the process (38) is obtained as 0.4083 which implies

that we can utilize the proposed tuning rules. From tuning table 5 and 6, the following FPOID can be obtained for the case of $M_s = 1.4$

$$G_{c1}(s) = 0.3511\frac{11.7527s+1}{11.7527s}\frac{7.2300s^{1.2}+1}{0.3923s^{1.2}+1} \tag{40}$$

And for the case of $M_s = 2$, from tables 7 and 8 we have

$$G_{c2}(s) = 0.1400\frac{11.3467s+1}{11.3467s}\frac{8.3116s^{1.1}+1}{0.4509s^{1.1}+1} \tag{41}$$

Simulation results are presented in Fig. 14. It is assumed that a load disturbance is applied at t=500 seconds, and the disturbance rejection of both controllers are verified. Simulations also show that the transient states of both controllers are approached.

9. Conclusion

In this chapter, some of the well-known tuning methods of FOPID controllers are presented and several illustrative examples, verifying the effectiveness of the methods are given.

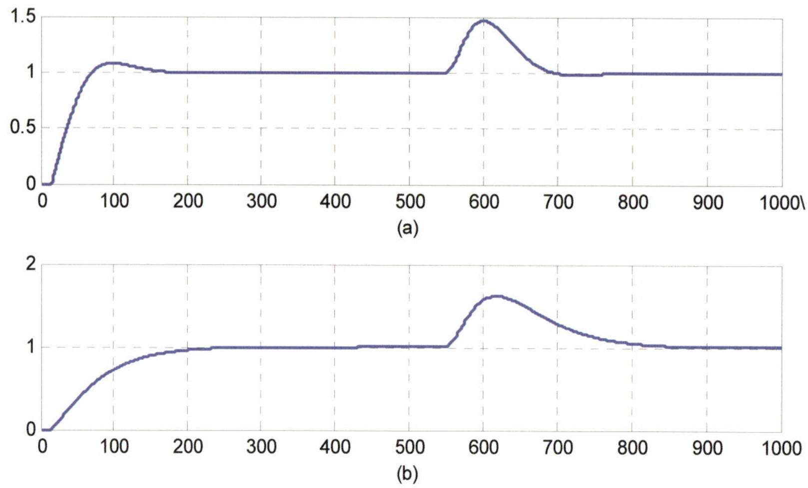

Fig. 13 Closed response of heat exchanger system and disturbance rejection of controllers (a) $G_{c1}(s)$ (b) $G_{c2}(s)$

Simulations have been carried out using *MATLAB/SIMULINK* software via Ninteger toolbox. After discussion on fractional calculus and its approximation methods, the Ninteger toolbox is introduced briefly. Then optimization methods, Ziegler-Nichols tuning rules and a new tuning method were introduced. We have considered control of pH neutralization process, high-order process, Non-Minimum phase process and temperature control of heat exchanger as case studies. In spite of extensive research, tuning the parameters of a FOPID controller remains an open problem. Other analytical methods and new tuning rules may be further studied.

10. References

Ahmad, W.M., Sprott, J.C., (2003). Chaos in fractional-order autonomous nonlinear systems, *Chaos, Solitons & Fractals* Vol. 16, 2003, pp.339–351.

Åström, K.J., Hägglund, T., (1995) PID Controllers: Theory, Design and Tuning, *ISA Press*, Research Triangle Park, 1995

Charef, A., Fergani, N. (2010). $PI^{\lambda}D^{\mu}$ Controller Tuning For Desired Closed-Loop Response Using Impulse Response, *Proceedings of Fractional Differentiation and its Applications*, Badajoz, Spain, October 2010

Delavari, H., Ghaderi, R., Ranjbar, A., Hosseinnia, S.H., Momani S., (2010). Adaptive Fractional PID Controller for Robot Manipulator, *Proceedings of Fractional Differentiation and its Applications*, Badajoz, Spain, October 2010

Domingues, J., Vale´rio, D., Costa, J.S. (2010). Rule-based fractional control of an irrigation canal, *ASME Journal of Computational and Nonlinear Dynamics*, 2010. Accepted.

Jesus, I.S., Machado, J.A.T. (2008). Fractional control of heat diffusion systems, *Nonlinear Dynamics*, Vol. 54, pp. 263-282

Karimi, M., Zamani, M., Sadati, N., Parniani, M. (2009). An Optimal Fractional Order Controller for an AVR System Using Particle Swarm Optimization Algorithm, *Control Engineering Practice*, Vol. 17, pp. 1380–1387

Maiti, D., Biswas, S., Konar, K. (2007). Design of a Fractional Order PID Controller Using Particle Swarm Optimization Technique, *Proceedings of 2nd National Conference on Recent Trends in Information Systems*, 2008

Monje, C.A., Vinagre, B.M. , Chen, Y.Q. , Feliu, V., Lanusse, P. , Sabatier, J. (2004). Proposals for fractional $PI^{\lambda}D^{\mu}$ tuning, *Proceedings of Fractional Differentiation and its Applications*, Bordeaux, 2004

Oustaloup, A. (1991). La commande CRONE: commande robuste d'ordre non entier. Hermès, Paris, 1991

Oustaloup, A., Levron, F. , Mathieu, B. , Nanot, F.M. ,(2000). Frequency-band complex noninteger differentiator: characterization and synthesis, *IEEE Transactions on Circuits and Systems I*, Vol. 47, 2000, pp. 25-39.

Padula, F., Visioli, A., (2010a). Tuning rules for optimal PID and fractional-order PID controllers, *Journal of Process Control*, doi:10.1016/j.jprocont.2010.10.006

Padula, F., Visioli, A., (2010b). Set-point Weighting for Fractional PID Controllers, *Proceedings of Fractional Differentiation and its Applications*, Badajoz, Spain, October 2010

Padula, F., Visioli, A., (2010c). Tuning of Fractional PID Controllers for Integral Processes, *Proceedings of Fractional Differentiation and its Applications*, Badajoz, Spain, October 2010

Podlubny, I. (1999a). Fractional-Order Systems and $PI^{\lambda}D^{\mu}$ Controllers, *IEEE Transactions on Automatic Control*, Vol. 44, No. 1, January 1999, pp. 208-214

Podlubny, I. (1999b). Fractional Differential Equations, *Academic Press*, USA

Podlubny, I., Dorcak, L., Kostial, I. (1997). On Fractional Derivatives, Fractional-Order Dynamic Systems and $PI^{\lambda}D^{\mu}$ controllers, *Proceedings of the 36th Conference on Decision & Control*, San Diego, California, USA, December 1997

Shinskey, F.G. (1994). Feedback Controllers for the Process Industries, *McGraw-Hill*, New York, USA

Tabatabaei, M., Haeri, M., (2010). Loop Shaping Design of Fractional PD and PID Controllers, *Proceedings of Fractional Differentiation and its Applications*, Badajoz, Spain, October 2010

Vale´rio, D., Costa, J.S. (2004). NINTEGER: A Non-Integer Control Toolbox for MATLAB, *Proceedings of Fractional Differentiation and its Applications*, Bordeaux, 2004

Vale´rio, D., Costa, J.S. (2006). Tuning of fractional PID controllers with Ziegler–Nichols-type rules, *Signal Processing*, Vol. 86, pp. 2771–2784

Vinagre, B. M., Podlubny, I., Dorcak, L., Feliu, V. (2000). On Fractional PID Controllers: A Frequency Domain Approach, *Proceedings of IFAC Workshop on Digital Control: Past, Present and Future of PID Control*. Terrasa, Spain, pp. 53—58.

Xue, D., Zhao, C., Chen, Y.Q., (2006). Fractional Order PID Control of A DC-Motor with Elastic Shaft: A Case Study, *Proceedings of the 2006 American Control Conference*, Minneapolis, Minnesota, USA, June, 2006

Yeroglu, C., Özyetkin, M. M., Tan, N. (2010). Design of Robust $PI^{\lambda}D^{\mu}$ Controller for FOPDT Systems, *Proceedings of Fractional Differentiation and its Applications*, Badajoz, Spain, October 2010

14

Design Methodology with System Generator in Simulink of a FHSS Transceiver on FPGA

Santiago T. Pérez[1], Carlos M. Travieso[1], Jesús B. Alonso[1] and José L. Vásquez[2]
[1]*Signals and Communications Department, University of Las Palmas de Gran Canaria*
[2]*Department of Computer Science, University of Costa Rica*
[1]*Spain*
[2]*Costa Rica*

1. Introduction

This study aims to describe a design method for Field Programmable Gate Array (FPGA) (Maxfield, 2004) applied, in particular, to the design of a Frequency Hopping Spread Spectrum (FHSS) transceiver (Simon et al., 1994). Simulink (MathWorks, 2011) is a tool integrated in Matlab, which allows the design of systems using block diagrams in a fast and flexible way. Xilinx is one of the most important FPGA manufacturers and provides System Generator (Xilinx, 2011), it is a design environment over Simulink for FPGA based on the method described. The design is based on a previous FHSS transceiver designed for indoor wireless optical communications made with discrete components (Pérez et al., 2003). One of the improvements in the proposed system is the physical integration.

2. The physical device

Initially, there were several alternatives for the system hardware. In principle, an Application Specific Integrated Circuit (ASIC) can be used (Maxfield, 2004), but to configure these devices must be sent to the manufacturer, which increases development time and makes more expensive the prototype. This technology achieves good physical performances: low area, low power consumption and minimal delays.
At the other extreme Digital Signal Processor (DSP) can be used which are very cheap (Maxfield, 2004). The DSPs do not have the best physical performances; normally they occupy maximum area, have high power consumption and maximum delay. In fact, when the volume of calculus is high, easily they do not have real time response. This is because the architecture is rigid, in both data and operations formats.
In the middle are FPGA, which have a reasonable cost for the design of prototypes; in general an intermediate cost to the two previous cases. The FPGA have significant physical benefits, without reaching the performances of ASIC. FPGAs have benefits outweigh the

DSP because the FPGA final architecture can be configured in a fully flexible way, in both data and operations size.

It must be emphasized that FPGA are integrated circuits reprogrammable by the designer and can be used for different projects, or in a project during its different phases. The FPGAs are also available in the market on printed circuit boards, with power and programming connectors, auxiliary memories and input-output pins; this avoid to design and construct the printed circuit board, and makes it ideal for prototyping design.

3. Design methodology

A transceiver can be designed using discrete electronic components. In general, the overall design is not flexible and highly dependent on technology and available devices, has long design time, occupies large area, has high power consumption and high delays and low maximum operating frequency.

In general, the trend is to integrate the design in a digital integrated circuit and place around the necessary external components; this eliminates the previous inconveniences. It must be emphasized that these designs can be easily portable between devices, even from different manufacturers. This portability is possible because the design can be described with a standard hardware description language (HDL).

In digital systems, when floating point arithmetic is used, the range and precision can be adjusted with the number of bits of exponent and mantissa, it is then possible to obtain a wide range and high precision in this type of representation. However, floating point operations require many hardware resources and long time execution (Hauck & DeHon, 2008). On the other hand, the fixed point arithmetic requires fewer hardware resources, but the range and precision can be improved only by increasing the number of bits. If the number of bits is constant, to increase the range causes a decrease in the precision. It is possible to use fixed point arithmetic in most applications when the range of signals is known or can be determined by statistical methods. In fixed point arithmetic the 2's complement representation is used because its arithmetic rules are simpler than the 1's complement representation.

Ordinarily the systems can be designed using a standard hardware description language: VHDL (Very High Speed Integrated Circuit Hardware Description Language) (Pedroni, 2004) or Verilog (Palnitkar, 2003). Manual coded of complex systems using one of these languages is little flexible and has a great design time. To solve these problems several design programs have been developed. One of them is the System Generator from Xilinx, which is installed in Simulink.

3.1 System generator

When System Generator is installed some Blocksets (Fig. 1) are included in Simulink of Matlab. Each block is configured after opening its dialog window, this permits fast and flexible designs. Basically, System Generator allows minimizing the time spent by the designer for the description and simulation of the circuit. On the other hand, the design is flexible; it is possible to change the design parameters and check quickly the effect on the performances and the architecture of the system. The functional simulation is possible even before the compilation of the model designed. The compilation generates the files of the structural description of the system in a standard hardware description language for the Integrated System Environment (ISE) for Xilinx FPGAs.

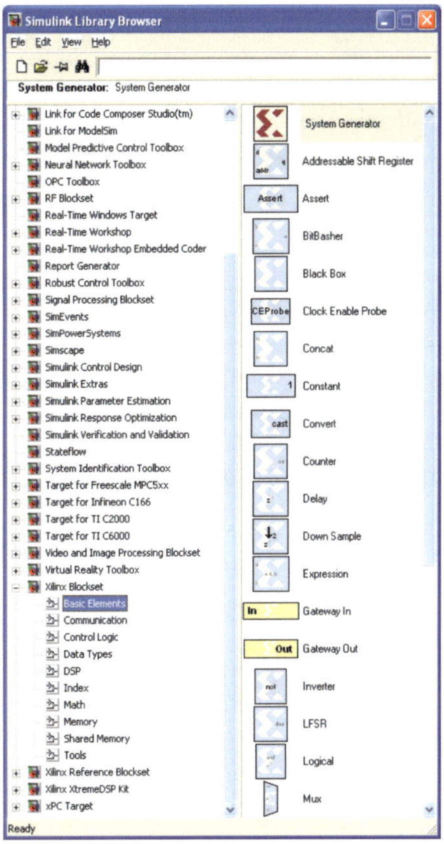

Fig. 1. System Generator Blocksets in Simulink

The FPGA boundary in the Simulink model is defined by Gateway In and Gateway Out blocks. The Gateway In block converts the Simulink floating point input to a fixed point format, saturation and rounding modes can be defined by the designer. The Gateway Out block converts the FPGA fixed point format to Simulink double numerical precision floating point format.

In the System Generator the designer does not perceive the signals as bits; instead, the bits are grouped in signed or unsigned fixed point format. The operators force signals to change automatically to the appropriate format in the outputs. A block is not a hardware circuit necessarily; it relates with others blocks to generate the appropriate hardware. The designer can include blocks described in a hardware description language, finite state machine flow diagram, Matlab files, etc. The System Generator simulations are bit and cycle accurate, this means results seen in a simulation exactly match the results that are seen in hardware. The Simulink signals are shown as floating point values, which makes easier to interpret them. The System Generator simulations are faster than traditional hardware description language simulators, and the results are easier for analyzing. Otherwise, the VHDL and Verilog code are not portable to other FPGA manufacturers. The reason is that System Generator uses Xilinx primitives which take advantages of the device characteristics.

System Generator can be used for algorithm exploration or design prototyping, for estimating the hardware cost and performance of the design. Other possibility is using

System Generator for designing a portion of a big system and joining with the rest of the design. Finally, System Generator can implement a complete design in a hardware description language. Designs in System Generator are discrete time systems; the signals and blocks generate automatically the sample rate. However, a few blocks set the sample rate implicitly or explicitly. System Generator supports multirate circuits and some blocks can be used for changing the sample rate.

Often an executable specification file is created using the standard Simulink Blocksets (see Fig. 2). The specification file can be designed using floating point numerical precision and not hardware detail. Once the functionality and basic dataflow have been defined, System Generator can be used to specify the hardware implementation details for the Xilinx devices. System Generator uses the Xilinx DSP Blockset from Simulink and will automatically invoke Xilinx Core Generator to generate highly optimized netlists for the building blocks. System Generator can execute all the downstream implementation tools to get a bitstream file for programming the FPGA device. An optional testbench can be created using test vectors extracted from the Simulink environment for using with Integrated System Environment simulators.

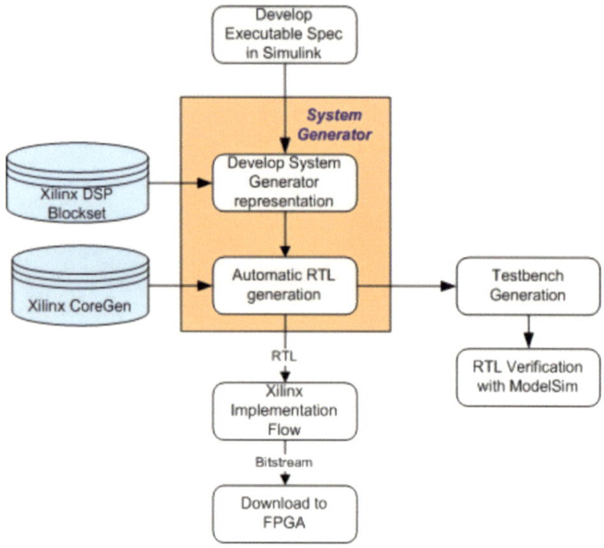

Fig. 2. System Generator design flow (download from www.xilinx.com)

Every system designed with System Generator must contain a System Generator block (Fig. 3); this block specifies how simulation and code generator can be used. Firstly, the type of compilation in the System Generator block can be specified to obtain: HDL netlist, Bitstream for programming, etc. Secondly, the FPGA type can be chosen. The target directory defines where the compilation writes the files of Integrated System Environment project. The synthesis tool specifies which tool is chosen for synthesizing the circuit: Synplify, Synplify Pro or Xilinx Synthesis Tool (XST). In the hardware description language the designer can choose between VHDL and Verilog. Finally, clock options defines the period of the clock, its input pin location, the mode of multirate implementation and the Simulink system period, which is the greatest common divisor of the sample periods that appear in the system. In the block icon display, the type of information to be displayed is specified.

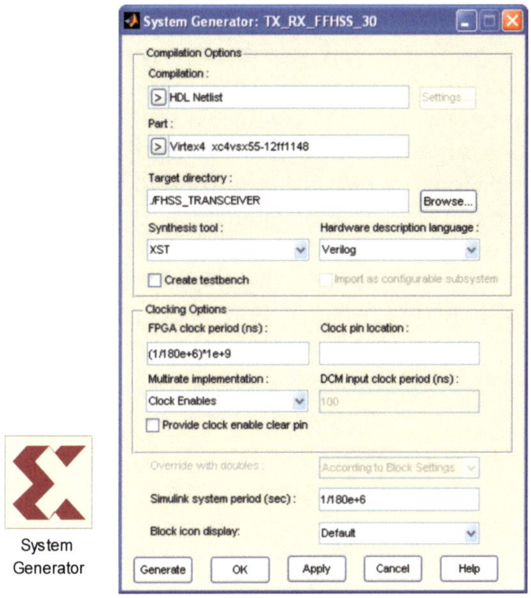

Fig. 3. System Generator block and its dialog window

3.2 Integrated system environment

In Xilinx Integrated System Environment it is possible to compile the hardware description language files, and simulate the system behavioral or timing analysis. Also the occupancy rate, power consumption and operating temperature of the FPGA are obtained. Afterwards the program file can be generated for the chosen device; this file can be downloaded from the computer to the board where the FPGA is included. Finally, the performance of the design system must be checked with electronic measure equipment.

When the designer clicks on Generate in dialog window of System Generator block, the structural description files in a hardware description language are obtained, and a project is created for Integrated System Environment. Now it is possible to check the syntax of the hardware description language files (Fig. 4). The first step in the compilation process is synthesizing the system. The synthesis tool used is Xilinx Synthesis Tool, it is an application that synthesizes hardware description language designs to create Xilinx specific netlist files called NGC (Native Generic Circuit) files. The NGC file is a netlist that contains both logical design data and constraints. The NGC file takes the place of both Electronic Data Interchange Format (EDIF) and Netlist Constraints File (NCF) files. In synthesis options optimization goal for area or speed can be fixed; by default, this property is set to speed optimization. Similarly, optimization effort can be established as normal or high effort; in the last case additional optimizations are performed to get best result for the target FPGA device. Synthesis report can be analyzed by the designer; moreover, the designer can view Register Transfer Level (RTL) schematic or technology schematic. After synthesizing the system, the design is implemented in four stages: translate, map, place and route. The translation process merges all the input netlists and design constraint information and outputs a Xilinx Native Generic Database (NGD) file. Then the output NGD file can be mapped to the targeted FPGA device family. The map process takes the NGD file, runs a design rule checker and maps the logic design to a Xilinx FPGA device. The result appears in a Native Circuit Design (NCD) file, which is used for placing and routing. The place and route process takes a NCD file and produces a new NCD file to be used by the programming file generator. The generator programming file process runs the Xilinx bitstream generation program BitGen to produce a bit file for Xilinx device configuration. Finally, the configuration target device process uses the bit file to configure the FPGA target device. Behavioral simulations are possible in the design before synthesis with the simulate behavioral model process. This first pass simulation is typically performed to verify the Register Transfer Level or behavioral code and to confirm the designed function. Otherwise, after the design is placed and routed on the chip, timing simulations are possible. This process uses the post place and route simulation model and a Standard Delay Format (SDF) file. The SDF file contains true timing delay information of the design.

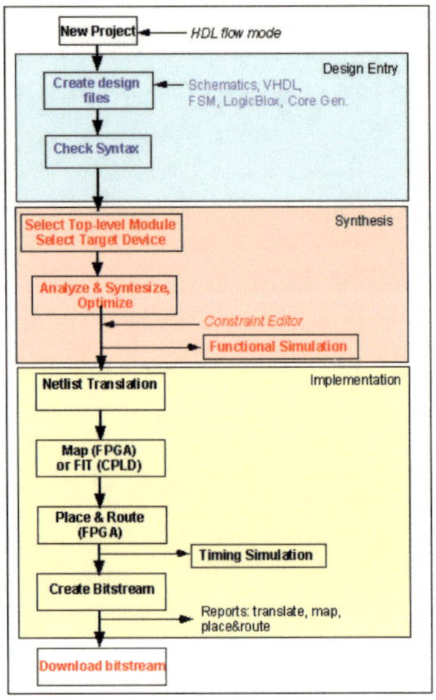

Fig. 4. Overview of design flow of Integrated System Environment (download from www.xilinx.com)

4. The transceiver

This chapter is based on a previous FHSS transceiver (Fig. 5) for wireless optical communications. The FHSS and analog synchronization signals were emitted by two separated Light Emitting Diodes (LED) to avoid adding them with discrete analog circuits.

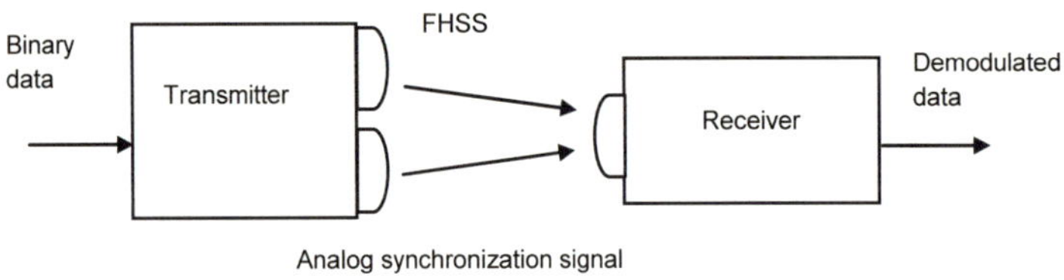

Fig. 5. Block diagram with FHSS transceiver designed previously

The core of the transmitter was a discrete Direct Digital Synthesizer (DDS) AD9851 from Analog Devices (Analog Devices, 2011). The discrete DDS (Fig. 6) is a digital system excepting the final Digital to Analog Converter; its output signal is a sinusoidal sampled signal at 180 MHz. The emitted FHSS signal was smoothed by the 100 MHz bandwidth of the optical emitter. In the DDS used, the output frequency is fixed by the expression (1), where f_{DDS_CLK} is the frequency of the DDS clock (180 MHz), N is the number of bits of the tuning word (32 bits) and Word is the decimal value of 32 bit frequency tuning word.

$$f_{out}=(Word \cdot f_{DDS\_CLK})/2^{N} \tag{1}$$

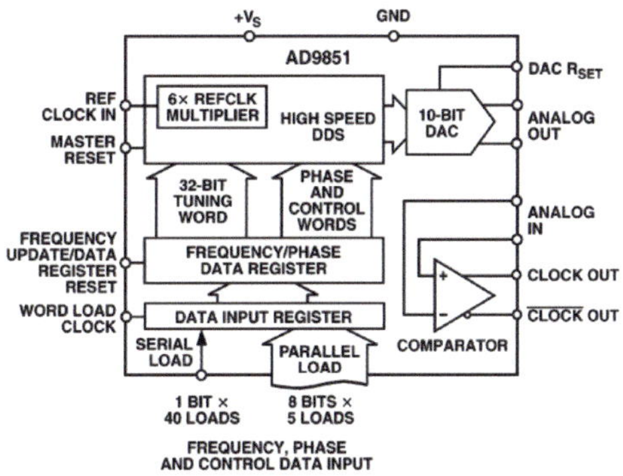

Fig. 6. Block diagram of discrete DDS AD9851 from Analog Devices (download from www.analog.com)

In the demodulator of the receiver, two similar discrete DDS were used as local oscillators. In the new design, the full transceiver with the previous methodology is described. The modulator matches with the transmitter designed previously, excepting the optical emitters and the output Digital to Analog Converter of the discrete DDS. In the same way, the two DDS in the demodulator were integrated in the FPGA. In the previous design, discrete analog filters were used. In the new design, these filters were integrated in the FPGA as digital filters. The new design methodology is improved by DDS block and filter design capabilities in System Generator. The Fig. 7 shows the new FHSS transceiver. In Fig. 8, the data in the transmitter and the demodulated data are shown. After the synchronization is reached in the receiver, the demodulation is executed perfectly.

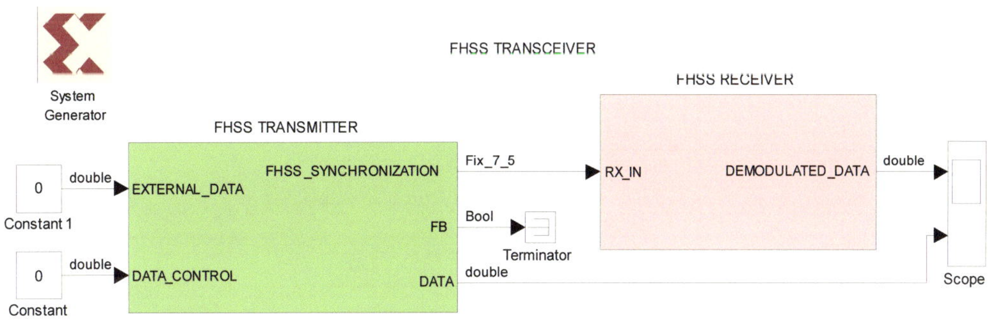

Fig. 7. Frequency Hopping Spread Spectrum transceiver

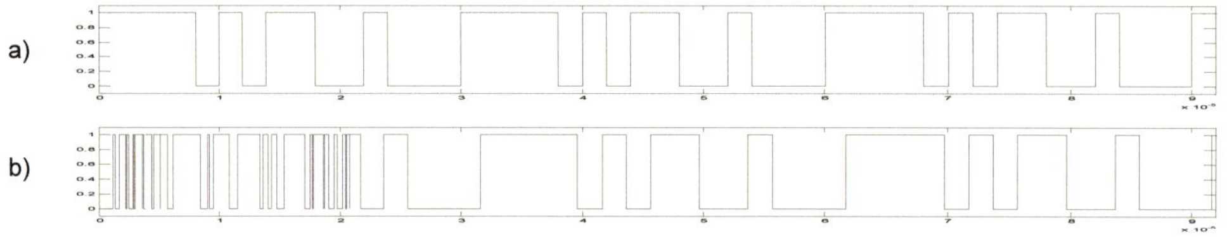

Fig. 8. Data signals in the transceiver: a) transmitted data, b) demodulated data

If Port Data Type is enabled in Simulink, after the system simulation the data types are shown in every point of the design. It can be: Bool (boolean); double, Simulink floating point format; UFix_m_n, unsigned m bits two's complement fixed point format with n fractional bits; Fix_m_n, signed m bits two's complement fixed point format with n fractional bits. Otherwise, the signals can be analyzed in different ways using Simulink Sinks blockset. First, the Scope block can be used; this was the method used for adjusting the transceiver, it is quick but not convenient for capturing signals. Secondly, signals can be captured with the To Workspace block, but these signals are only stored temporarily in Matlab. Finally, To File block keeps the captured signals in a mat file permanently; for this reason To File block was used to capture and present simulations of this design.

5. The transmitter

The block diagram of the designed transmitter is drawn in Fig. 9. It is composed of an internal data generator, a pseudorandom code generator, and two DDS, used to generate the FHSS and synchronization signals. An external clock of 180 MHz is needed for the system. In this transmitter it is possible to choose between internal or external binary data.

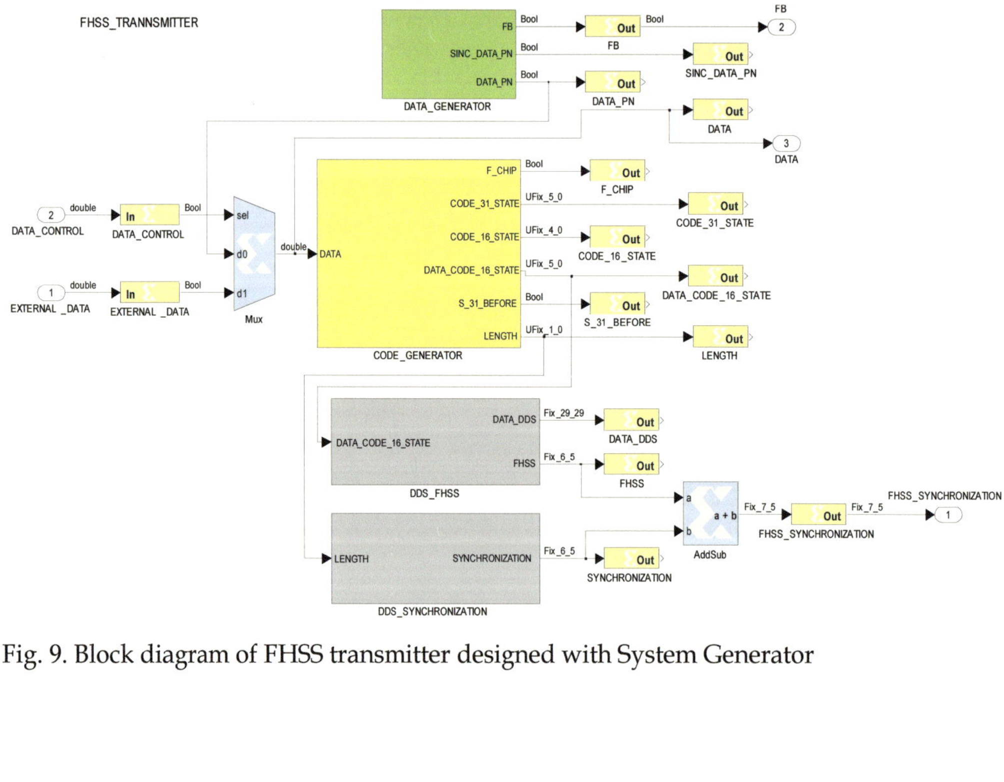

Fig. 9. Block diagram of FHSS transmitter designed with System Generator

5.1 Pseudorandom data generator

Application of the internal data generator (Fig. 10) avoids using an external data source; it was designed using a Linear Feedback Shift Register (LFSR) block as pseudorandom generator of 15 bits long at 500 kilobits per second. A pulse in the pseudorandom data generator is formed each time the sequence begins; this provides a high quality periodic signal to synchronize the oscilloscope. The LFSR block is configured with the dialog windows (Fig. 11). The clock, the data synchronization pulse and the pseudorandom data are shown in Fig. 12.

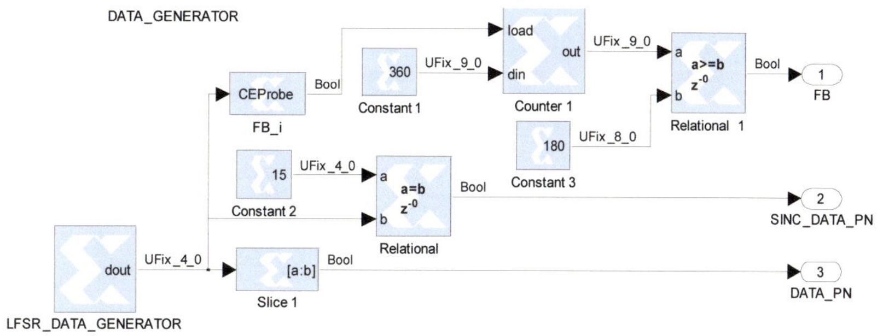

Fig. 10. Internal pseudorandom data generator

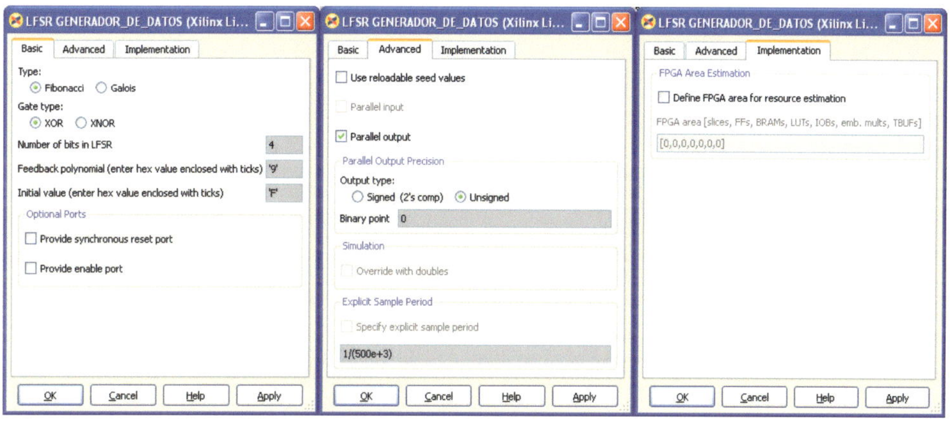

Fig. 11. Linear Feedback Shift Register dialog windows

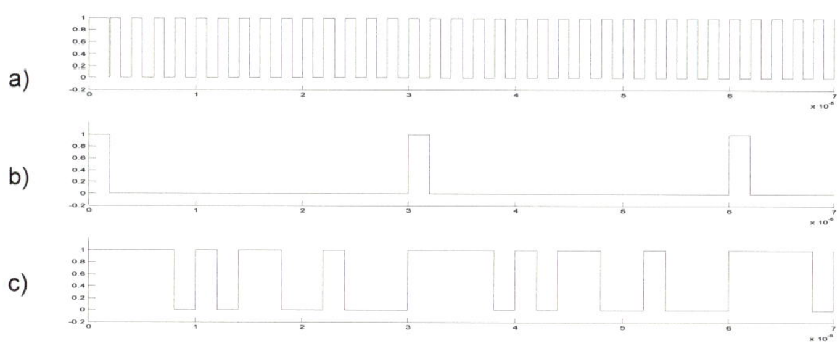

Fig. 12. Pseudorandom data generator signals: a) clock at bit rate, b) the data synchronization pulse, c) the pseudorandom binary data

5.2 Pseudorandom code generator

The pseudorandom code generator and its Simulink simulation signals are shown in Figures 13 and 14. The code rate is called chip frequency; its value is 1.5 Megachips per second. Consequently, three codes are generated by each data bit. The code generator is based on a Linear Feedback Shift Register of 31 states. In the pseudorandom code generator, a pulse is generated each time the sequence begins. A five bits word is obtained with the four most significant bits of the pseudorandom code generator and the data bit as most significant bit.

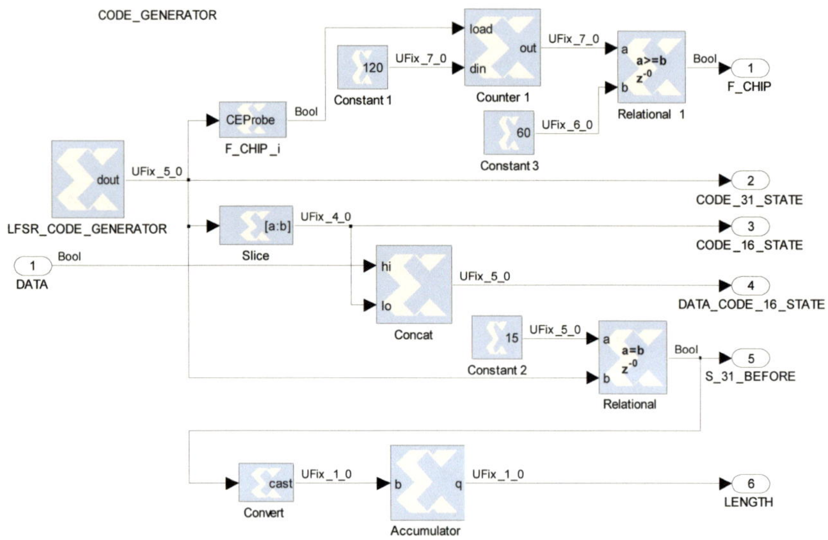

Fig. 13. Pseudorandom code generator

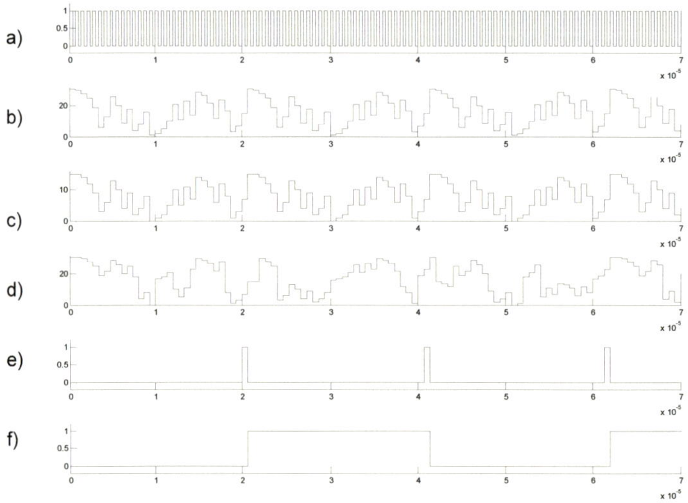

Fig. 14. Pseudorandom code generator signals: a) chip frequency, b) pseudorandom code 5 bits width, c) 4 most significant bits of pseudorandom code 5 bits width, d) data joined with 4 most significant bits, e) the stage previous to "11111", f) square signal which marks the code length

5.3 Frequency hopping spread spectrum signal generation

For each group of five bits (signal d in Fig. 14) a sampled sinusoidal signal is generated according to Table 1.

Code	Frequency (MHz)	Code	Frequency (MHz)
00000	24.384	10000	48.960
00001	25.920	10001	50.496
00010	27.456	10010	52.032
00011	28.992	10011	53.568
00100	30.528	10100	55.104
00101	32.064	10101	56.640
00110	33.600	10110	58.176
00111	35.136	10111	59.712
01000	36.672	11000	61.248
01001	38.208	11001	62.784
01010	39.744	11010	64.320
01011	41.280	11011	65.856
01100	42.816	11100	67.392
01101	44.352	11101	68.928
01110	45.888	11110	70.464
01111	47.424	11111	72.000

Table 1. Transmitted frequencies for the FHSS signal

In Fig. 15, the DDS generating the FHSS signal is shown. The DDS clock is the system clock (180 MHz). Therefore, a pure sinusoidal signal with an external filter can be synthesized until a bit less than 90 MHz.

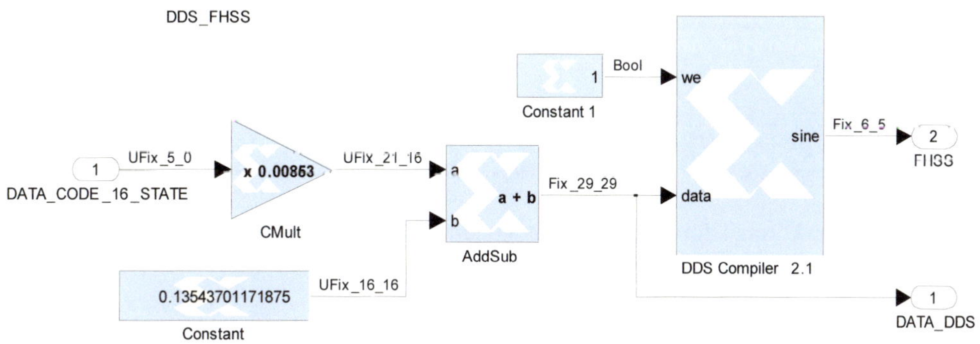

Fig. 15. Direct Digital Synthesizer generating the FHSS signal

The input data for the Xilinx DDS block is the synthesized frequency divided by the DDS clock. The equation (2) shows the meaning of this relation. Consequently, the DDS block fixes the number of N bits according to the rest of the DDS parameters: spurious free dynamic range, resolution, implementation mode, etc.

$$data = f_{out}/f_{DDS\_CLK} = Word/2^{N} \qquad (2)$$

Fig. 16 shows the dialog windows of the DDS block, where the designer can fix its parameters. This DDS acts like a frequency modulator.

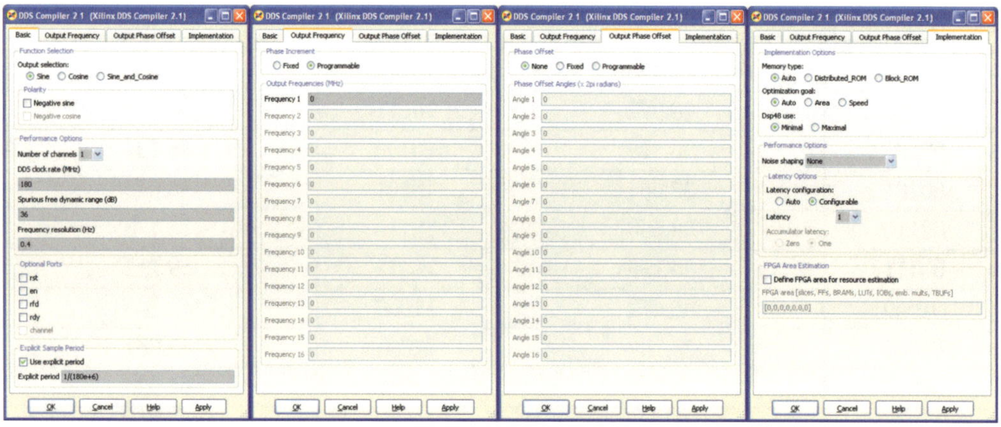

Fig. 16. Direct Digital Synthesizer block dialog windows for FHSS signal

The five bits input signal is transformed to the format of the input DDS block. The last operation is an unsigned fixed point integer to unsigned fixed point decimal conversion. In Fig. 17, five chip times of FHSS signal are shown. Three frequencies are generated by each data bit, therefore this is a Fast Frequency Hopping Spread Spectrum modulation.

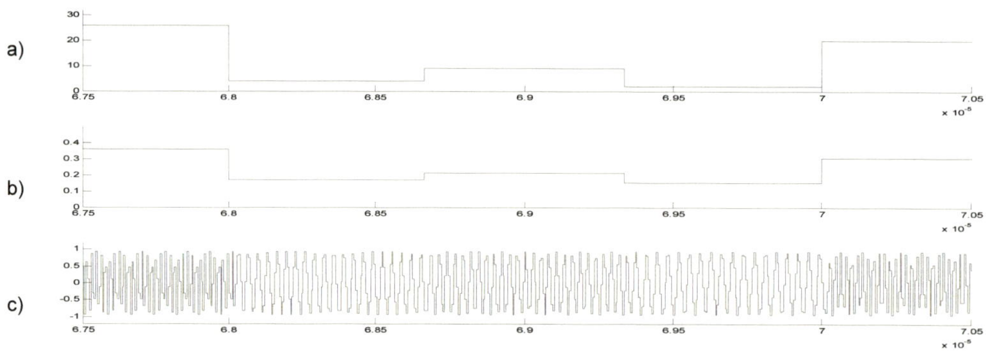

Fig. 17. Signals in Direct Digital Synthesizer generating the FHSS signal: a) five bits DDS input, b) input for Xilinx DDS block, c) FHSS signal

5.4 Synchronization signal generation and final adder

In the pseudorandom code generator, a square signal is generated with a 50% duty cycle (signal f in Fig. 14). This square signal has a semi-period with the same duration as the pseudorandom code length. The square signal is the DDS input (Fig. 18), it modulates in phase to a 9 MHz carrier (Fig. 19). The phase modulated signal carries information about the beginning of the pseudorandom code; and about its chip frequency, because its carrier is a multiple of 1.5 MHz.

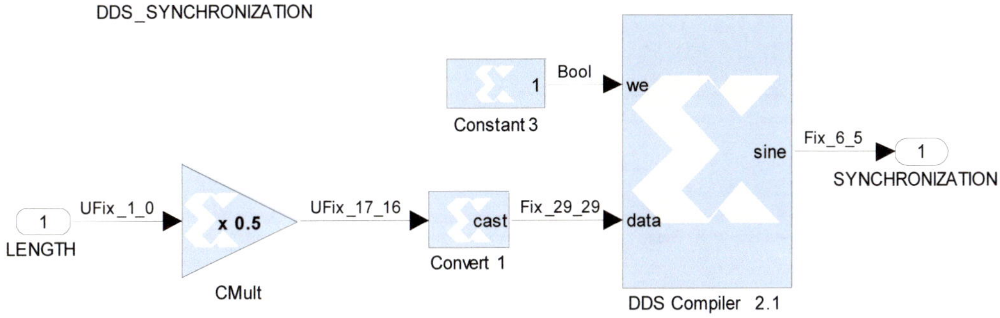

Fig. 18. Direct Digital Synthesizer for synchronization generation

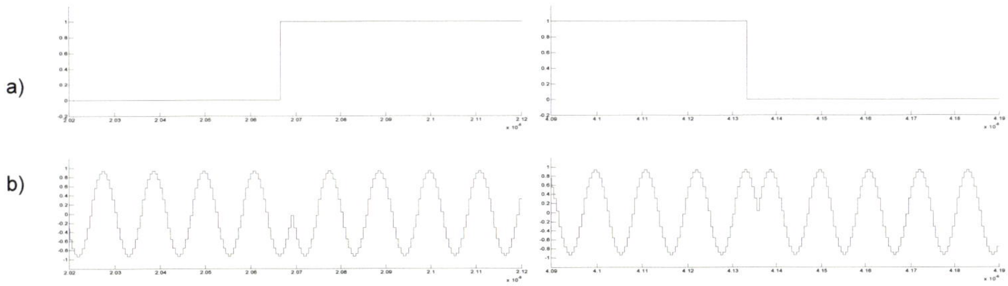

Fig. 19. Signals in Direct Digital Synthesizer that generates the synchronization signal: a) square input signal, b) synchronization signal

The Fig. 20 shows the dialog window of the DDS block. This Direct Digital Synthesizer acts like a phase modulator. In both Xilinx DDS blocks, the latency configuration is fixed to 1 for keeping the DDS delays to the minimum same value, this parameter specifies the delay as number of clock cycles.

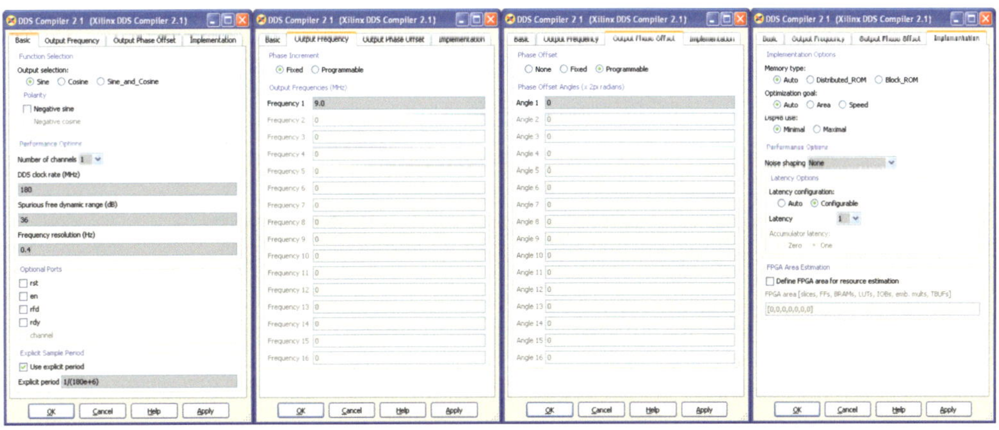

Fig. 20. Direct Digital Synthesizer block dialog windows for synchronization signal

Finally, the FHSS and the synchronization signals are added with an AddSub block, this new signal is the transmitter output (Fig. 21).

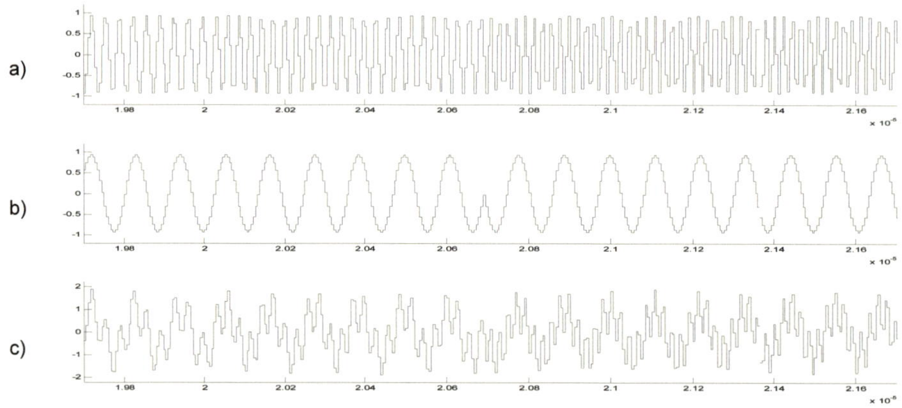

Fig. 21. Inputs and output of final adder: a) FHSS signal, b) synchronization signal, c) the above signals added together

6. The receiver

The receiver block diagram is shown in Fig. 22. The signal received from the transmitter enters in the splitting filter, FHSS and synchronization signals can be separated because they are multiplexed in frequency. The filtered synchronization signal is the input of the synchronization recovery, where the code is obtained in the receiver. The code recovered synchronizes the local oscillators. Finally, the local oscillators outputs and the FHSS filtered are introduced to the double branch data demodulator.

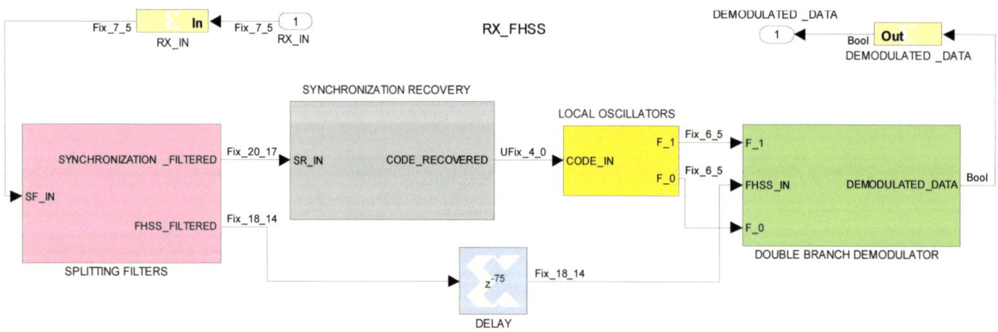

Fig. 22. Block diagram of FHSS receiver designed with System Generator

6.1 Splitting filters

The splitting filters block diagram and signals are drawn in Fig. 23 and 24 respectively. A Finite Impulse Response (FIR) high pass filter recovers the FHSS signal. It was designed using the Filter Design and Analysis Tool (Fig. 25), the filter's coefficients are used by Xilinx FIR Compiler block for being synthesized. In the same way, a band pass filter is designed to obtain the synchronization signal.

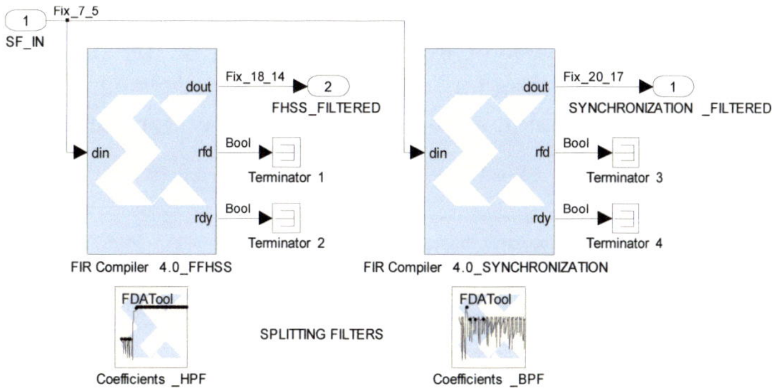

Fig. 23. Splitting filters block diagram

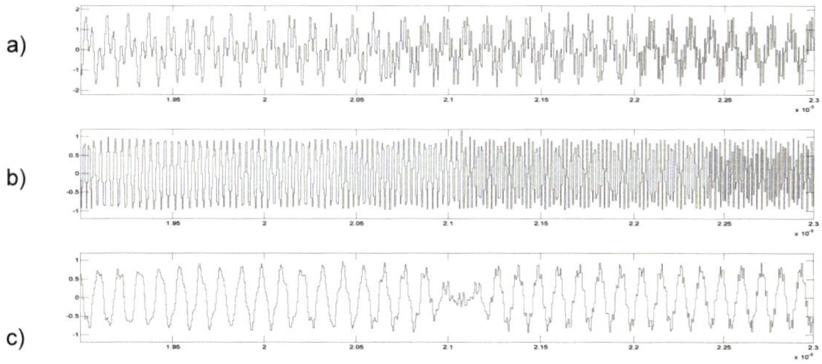

Fig. 24. Splitting filters signals: a) input, b) FHSS filtered, c) synchronization filtered

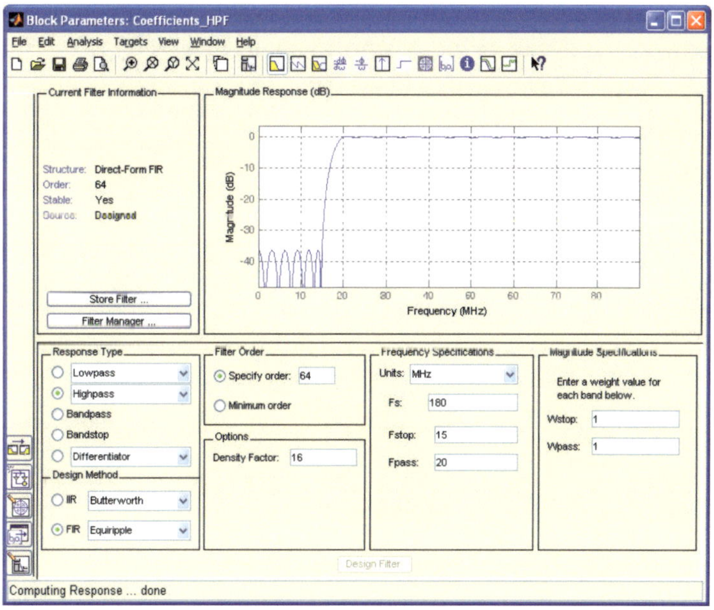

Fig. 25. Filter Design and Analysis Tool dialog window

6.2 Synchronization recovery

The input of this system is the synchronization filtered, in its output gets the most significant four bits of the pseudorandom code (Fig. 26). It is formed (Fig. 27) by a 9 MHz recover, a synchronous demodulator, a load and enable generators, and a Linear Feedback Shift Register code generator.

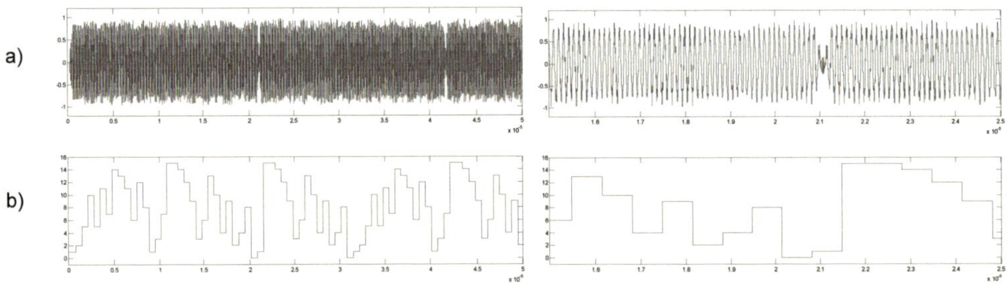

Fig. 26. Synchronization recovery signals: a) synchronization filtered, b) code recovered

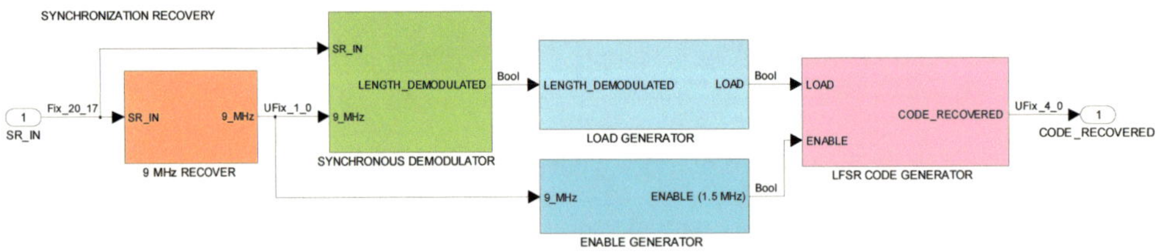

Fig. 27. Synchronization recovery block diagram

6.2.1 Carrier recover (9 MHz)

This system recovers the carrier of the synchronization signal (Fig. 28). Initially the phase-modulated signal is squared and filtered to get double the carrier frequency with an 18 MHz band pass filter (Fig. 29); the sample frequency is 180 MHz. The 18 MHz signal is squared by a comparator and a pulse is generated with each rising edge. Finally, an accumulator generates a 9 MHz squared signal with 50% duty cycle.

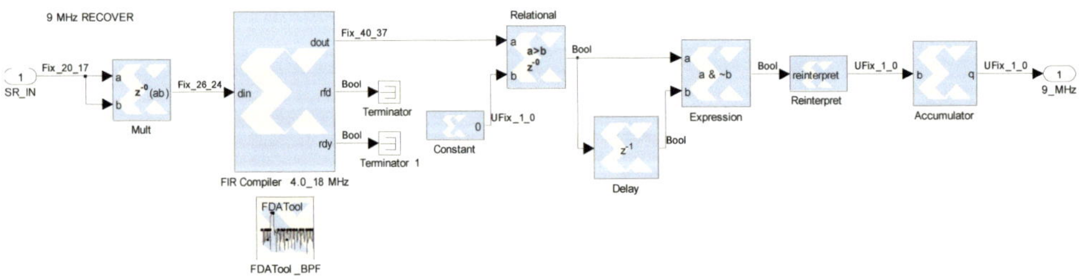

Fig. 28. Carrier recovery of 9 MHz block diagram

6.2.2 Synchronous demodulator

The block in Fig. 30 is a phase demodulator of the synchronization signal. The output indicates the length of the code with two consecutive edges of the signal (Fig. 31). The unipolar square 9 MHz carrier is converted to bipolar; in this way, the multiplier output assumes non-zero values in each semicycle. The delay block for the carrier ensures the synchronous demodulation. The output of the low pass filter is introduced to a comparator to get the length signal demodulated.

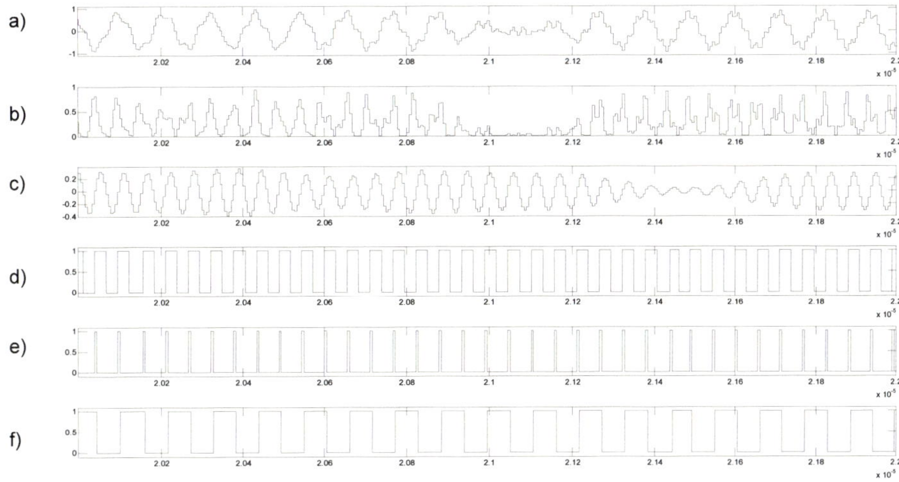

Fig. 29. Carrier recovery signals: a) synchronization filtered input, b) squared signal, c) 18 MHz filtered, d) 18 MHz square wave, e) pulse with rising edge, f) 9 MHz square wave

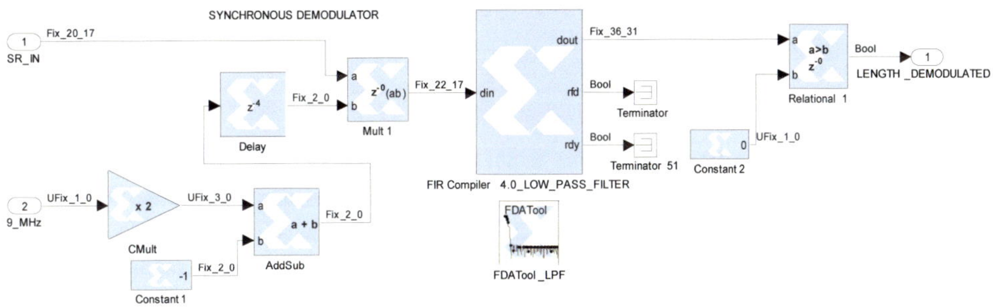

Fig. 30. Synchronous demodulator block diagram

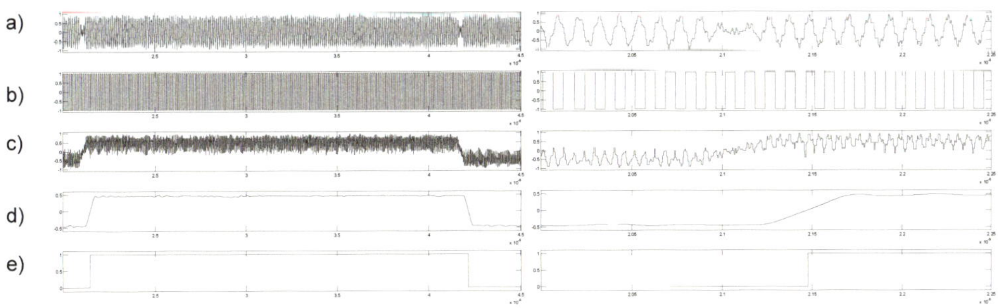

Fig. 31. Synchronous demodulator signals: a) synchronization input, b) 9 MHz multiplier input, c) multiplier output, d) filter output, e) length demodulated

6.2.3 Load generator

The circuit in Fig. 32 produces a pulse with the rising or falling edge at the input (Fig. 33). The output signal loads the initial value "11111" in the Linear Feedback Shift Register of the code generator in the receiver.

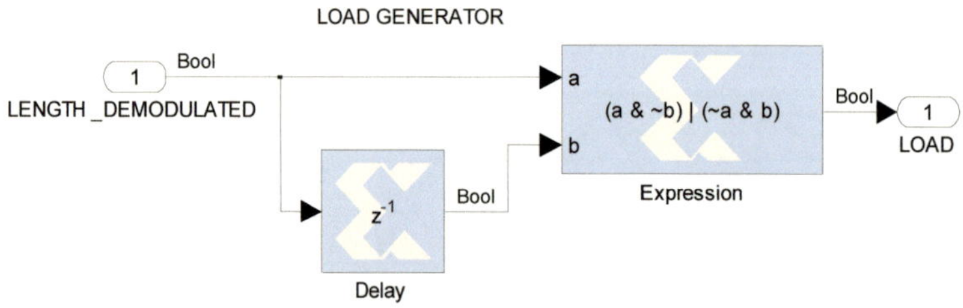

Fig. 32. Load generator

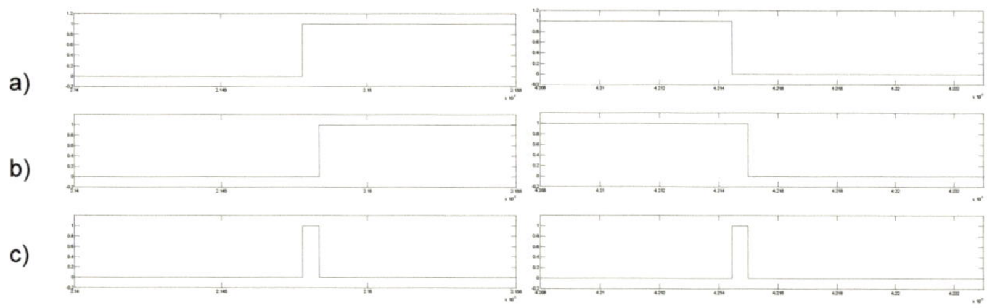

Fig. 33. Load generator signals: a) input, b) delayed input, c) output

6.2.4 Enable generator

The input of this system (Fig. 34) is the 9 MHz square carrier and generates a 1.5 MHz enable signal. A pulse is obtained with the rising edge at the input (Fig. 35). This signal is used as enable signal in a six states counter; a comparator checks when the counter output is zero. Finally, a pulse is generated with each rising edge of the comparator output. The output signal has the chip frequency, it will be used as input in a Linear Feedback Shift Register to recover the pseudorandom code.

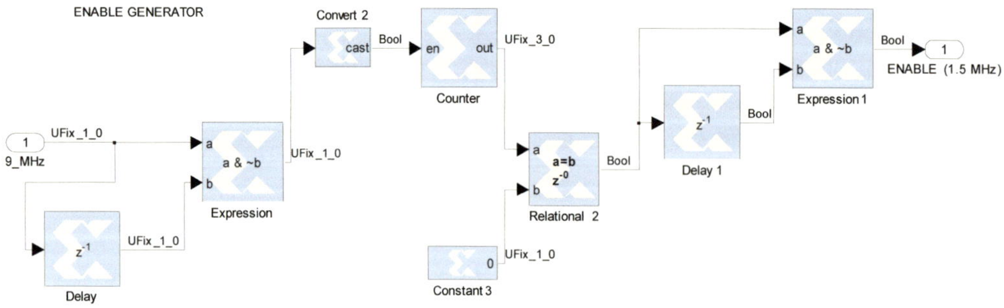

Fig. 34. Enable generator block diagram

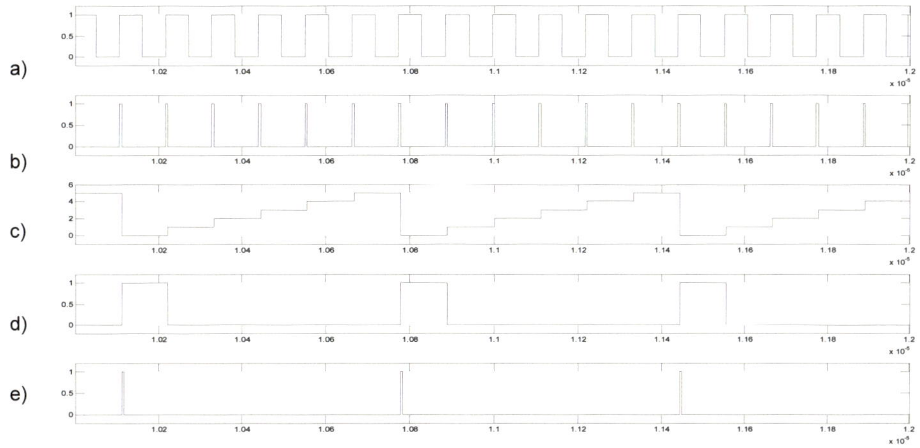

Fig. 35. Enable generator signals: a) 9 MHz input, b) internal pulse with the input rising edge, c) counter output, d) zero value in the counter output, e) enable generator output

6.2.5 Linear feedback shift register code generator

This system is a LFSR similar to the code generator in the transmitter (Fig. 36); with the exceptions of the load signal to initialize the "11111" value and the enable signal to generate the 1.5 MHz output rate. A delay block synchronizes the load and enable signal. The LFSR inputs and the value of the code recovered are shown in Fig. 37.

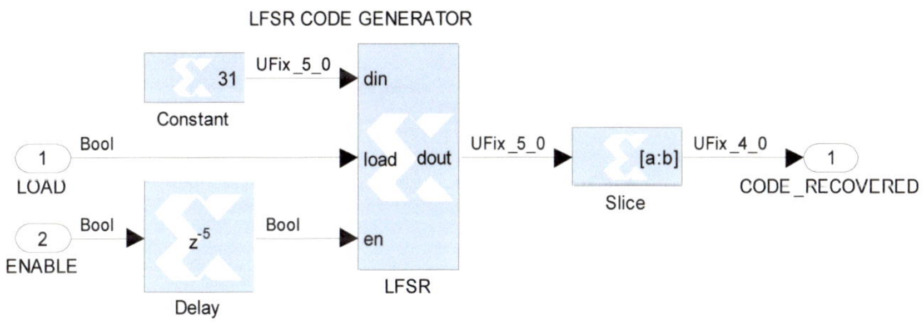

Fig. 36. Linear Feedback Shift Register code generator block diagram

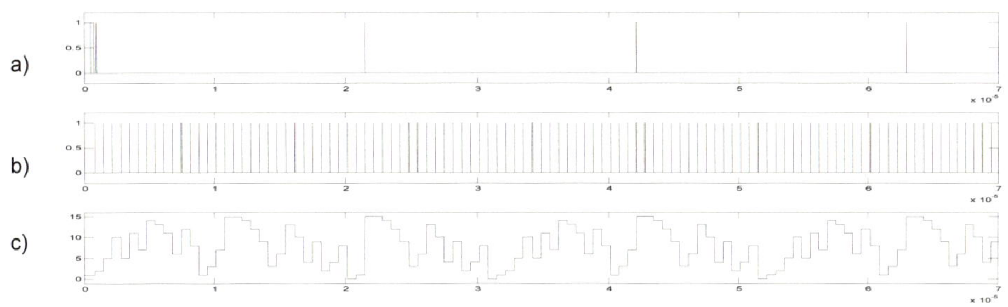

Fig. 37. Linear Feedback Shift Register code generator signals: a) LFSR load input, b) LFSR enable input, c) code recovered

6.3 Local oscillators

The code recovered is the local oscillators input (Fig. 38). The two oscillators were designed using two Direct Digital Synthesizer blocks, and the four bits input code must be converted to the input format of the DDS block. The frequency of the oscillator F_0 output (Fig. 39) is the transmitted frequency if the data in the transmitter is "0" minus 10.7 MHz; in other words, the left side of Table 1 minus 10.7 MHz. Consequently the value of the intermediate frequency in the receiver is 10.7 MHz. Similarly, the frequency of the oscillator F_1 output is the transmitted frequency if the data in the transmitter is "1" minus 10.7 MHz; in the same way, the right side of Table 1 minus 10.7 MHz.

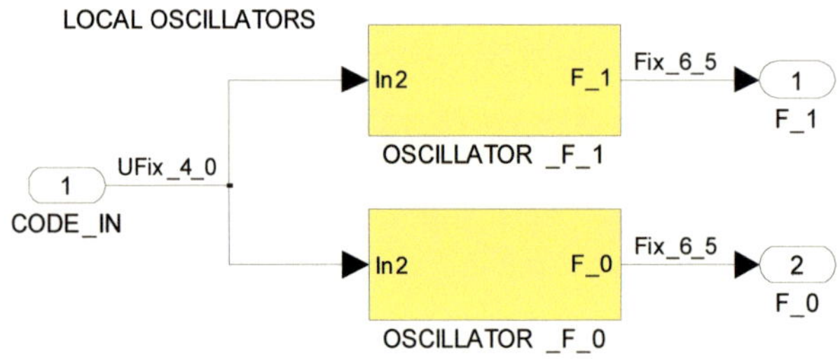

Fig. 38. Local oscillators block diagram

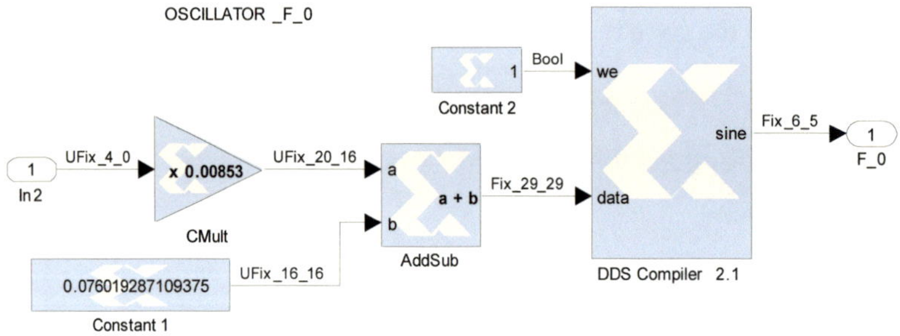

Fig. 39. Oscillator F_0 block diagram

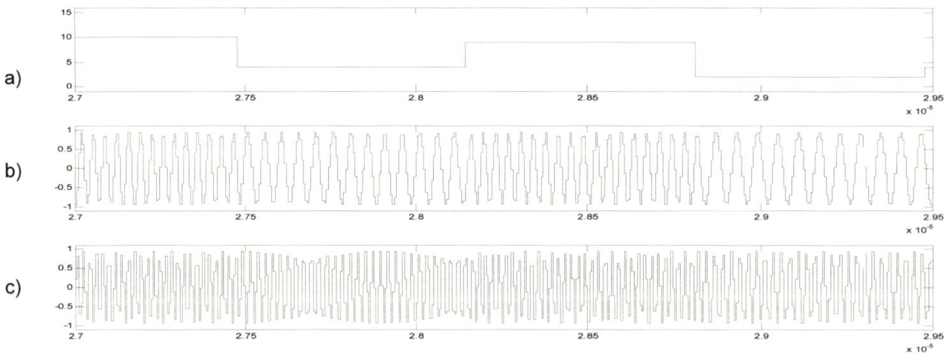

Fig. 40. Local oscillators signals: a) local oscillators input, b) oscillator F_0 output, c) oscillator F_1 output

6.4 Double branch demodulator

This demodulator is formed by two similar envelope detectors (Fig. 41). The inputs are the FHSS filtered signal and the local oscillators outputs. The FHSS filtered signal is delayed to keep the synchronization with the local oscillators frequencies. The top branch gets the waveform of the data and the bottom branch the inverter data. Lastly, the two outputs are compared and final output is the binary demodulated data.

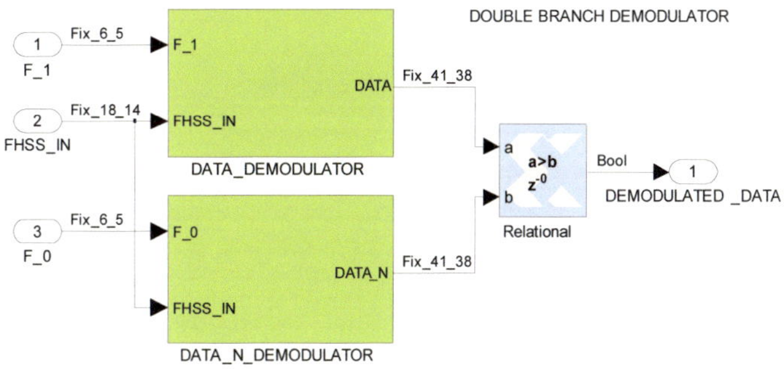

Fig. 41. Double branch demodulator block diagram

The Fig. 42 is the top branch block diagram. The mixer of the branch is the first multiplier and the intermediate frequency band pass filter. The second multiplier and the low pass filter is the envelope detector. The Fig. 43 shows the signals in the demodulator.

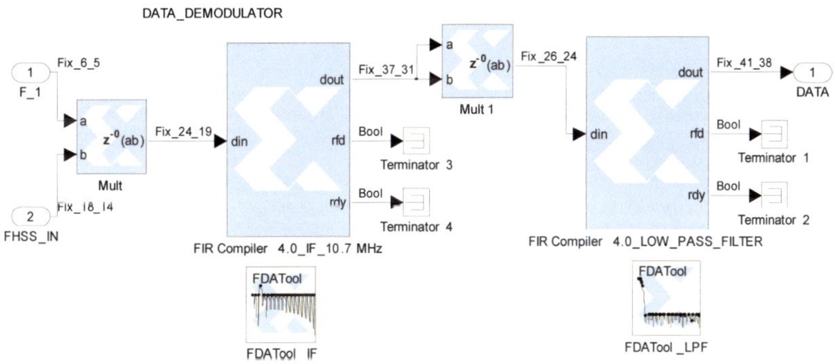

Fig. 42. Top branch demodulator block diagram

7. Channel simulation

Once the design of the transceiver has been finished, the performances can be tested inserting a channel between the transmitter and the receiver. For this purpose, an Additive White Gaussian Noise (AWGN) Simulink channel was chosen (Fig. 44). In this channel, the signal-to-noise power ratio is fixed by the designer. The Bit Error Rate (BER) was measured with the Error Rate Calculation block, where the delay between the data must be specified. Besides, the instant of synchronization in the receiver (20 microseconds) is indicated to start the bit error counter. This block generates three values: the first is the Bit Error Rate, the second is the number of errors, and the third is the number of bits tested. Finally, the BER is represented versus the signal-to-noise power ratio (Fig. 45).

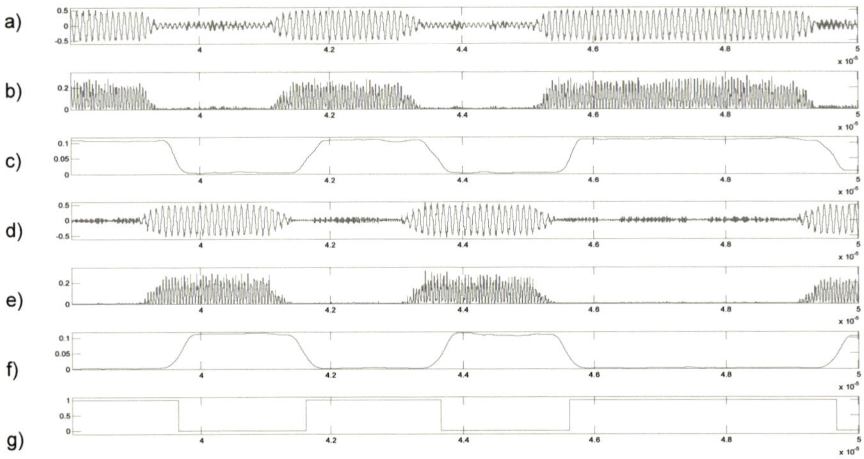

Fig. 43. Double branch demodulator signals: a) intermediate frequency filter output in the top branch, b) squared signal in the top branch, c) low pass filter output in the top branch, d) intermediate frequency filter output in the bottom branch, e) squared signal in the bottom branch, f) low pass filter output in the bottom branch, g) demodulated output

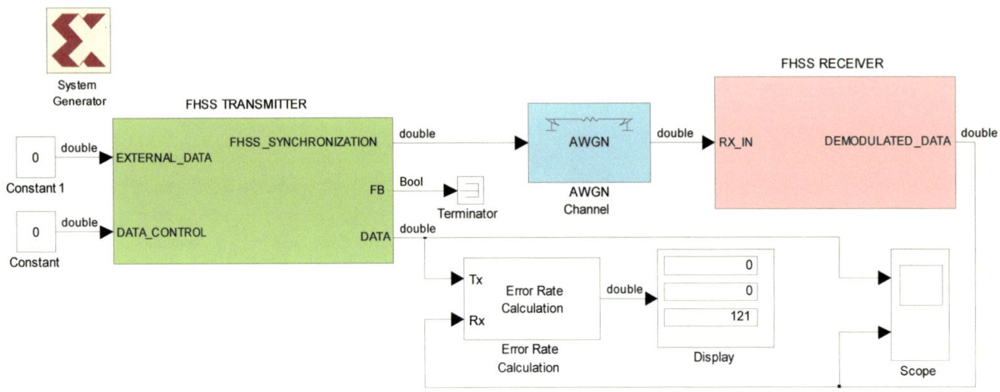

Fig. 44. Error rate calculation in presence of Additive White Gaussian Noise

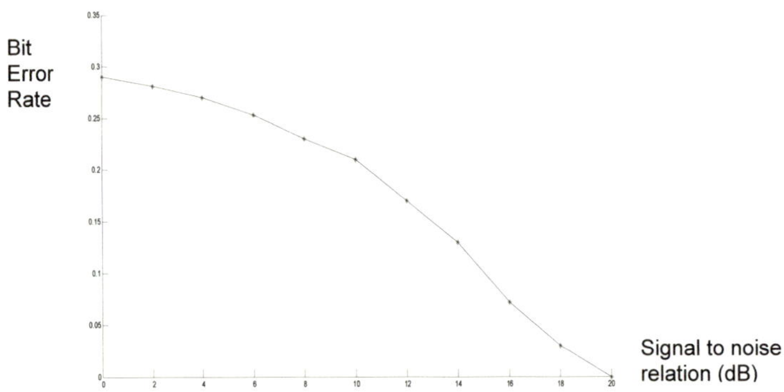

Fig. 45. Bit Error Rate represented versus the signal-to-noise power ratio (decibels)

8. Simulation and compilation with ISE

After the system has been simulated with Simulink, it can be compiled with System Generator. The chosen device is a Virtex 4 FPGA, and the hardware description language is Verilog. A project is then generated for Integrated System Environment, which includes the files for the structural description of the system. The syntax of the Verilog files can be checked, and the synthesis and behavioral simulation of the system can be executed (Fig. 46). Thereafter, the implementation of the design allows the timing simulation of the transceiver (Fig. 47). Lastly, the programming file is generated for the chosen FPGA.

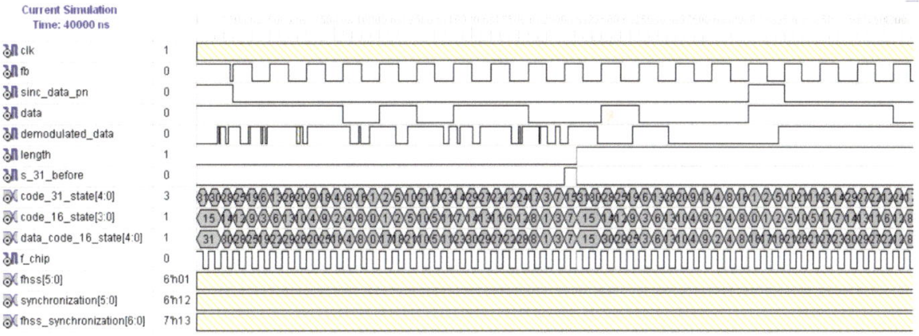

Fig. 46. A long behavioral simulation of the FHSS transceiver using ISE (40 microseconds)

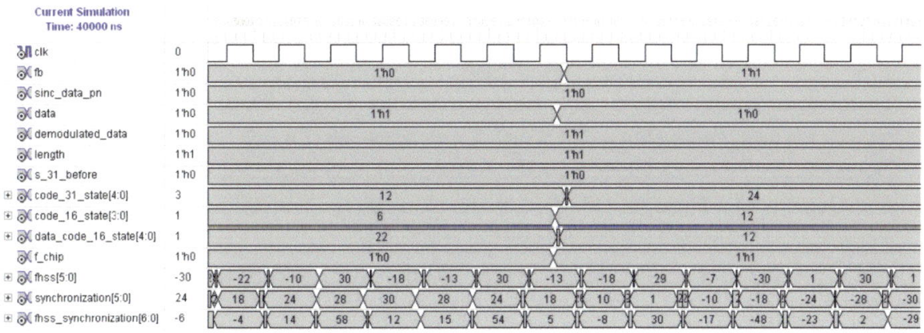

Fig. 47. Timing simulation of the FHSS transceiver using ISE (80 nanoseconds)

The Integrated System Environment software provides a power estimator that indicates a dissipation of 0.52 watts in the FPGA, and an estimated temperature of 31.4 degrees centigrade. The FPGA core is supplied with 1.2 volts and the input-output pins support the Low Voltage Complementary Metal Oxide Semiconductor (LVCMOS) volts standard. The design uses 491 of the 521 FPGA multipliers. The occupation rate of input-output pins in the FPGA is about 12.3%. However, this occupation rate can be reduced until 3.3% if internal signals are not checked.

9. Conclusions and future work

With this design methodology the typical advantageous features of using programmable digital devices are reached. Repeating a design consists in reprogramming the FPGA in the chosen board. The design and simulation times are decreased, consequently the time to market is minimizing. The used tool permits great flexibility; in others words, the design parameters can be changed and new features can be checked within several minutes. The flexibility allows to change the Direct Digital Synthesizers and filters parameters and to check its performances. The Simulink simulations are easy to run, and the signals are shown in floating point format which make easier its analysis. These simulations are possible even before the compilation of the System Generator blocks to obtain the hardware description language files. With the System Generator it is possible to simulate the full transceiver, the transmitter and the receiver can be connected through a channel. Moreover, it is possible to simulate the transmission in presence of interference, distortion, multipath and other spread spectrum signals using different codes.

10. References

Analog Devices (2011). AD9851 DDS. URL: www.analog.com/static/imported-files/data_sheets/AD9851.pdf, active on April 2011

Hauck, S. & DeHon, A. (2008). *Reconfigurable Computing*, Elsevier, ISBN 978-0-12-370522-8, USA

MathWorks. (2011). Simulink. URL: www.mathworks.com/products/simulink, active on April 2011

Maxfield, C. (2004). *The Design Warrior's Guide to FPGAs*, Elseiver, ISBN 0750676043, New York, USA

Palnitkar, S. (2003). *Verilog HDL*. Prentice Hall, ISBN 9780130449115, USA

Pedroni, V. (2004). *Circuit Design with VHDL*, The MIT Press, ISBN 0-262-16224-5, USA

Pérez, S.; Rabadán, J.; Delgado, F.; Velázquez, J & Pérez, R. (2003). Design of a synchronous Fast Frequency Hopping Spread Spectrum transceiver for indoor Wireless Optical Communications based on Programmable Logic Devices and Direct Digital Synthesizers, *Proceedings of XVIII Conference on Design of Circuits and Integrated Systems*, pp. 737-742, ISBN 84-87087-40-X, Ciudad Real, Spain, November, 2003.

Simon, M.; Omura, J.; Scholtz, R. & Levitt, B. (1994). *Spread Spectrum Communications Handbook*, McGraw-Hill Professional, ISBN 0071382151, USA

Xilinx (2011). System Generator. URL: www.xilinx.com/tools/sysgen.htm, active on April 2011

15

Modeling and Control of Mechanical Systems in Simulink of Matlab

Leghmizi Said and Boumediene Latifa
College of Automation, Harbin Engineering University
China

1. Introduction

Mechanical systems are types of physical systems. This is why it is important to study and control them using information about their structure to describe their particular nature. Dynamics of Multi-Body Systems (MBS) refers to properties of the mechanical systems. They are often described by the second-order nonlinear equations parameterized by a configuration-dependent inertia matrix and the nonlinear vector containing the Coriolis and centrifugal terms. These equations are the cornerstone for simulation and control of these systems, and then many researchers have attempted to develop efficient modeling techniques to derive the equations of motion of multi-body systems in novel forms. Furthermore, to prove the efficiency of these models and simulate them, efficient software for modeling is needed.

In the last few years, Simulink has become the most widely used software package in academia and industry for modeling and simulating mechanical systems. Used heavily in industry, it is credited with reducing the development of most control system projects. Simulink (**Simu**lation and **Link**) is an extension of MATLAB by Mathworks Inc. It works with MATLAB to offer modeling, simulation, and analysis of mechanical systems under a graphical user interface (GUI) environment. It supports linear and nonlinear systems, modelled in continuous time, sampled time, or a hybrid of the two. Systems can also be multirate, i.e., have different parts that are sampled or updated at different rates. It allows engineers to rapidly and accurately build computer models of mechanical systems using block diagram notation. It also includes a comprehensive block library of sinks, sources, linear and nonlinear components, and connectors. Moreover it can allow the users to customize and create their own blocks.

Using Simulink we can easily build models from presentative schemes, or take an existing model and add to it. Simulations are interactive, so we can change parameters "on the fly" and immediately see the results. As Simulink is an integral part of MATLAB, it is easy to switch back and forth during the analysis process and thus, the user may take full advantage of features offered in both environments. So we can take the results from Simulink and analyze them in Matlab workspace.

In this chapter we present the basic features of Simulink focusing on modeling and control of mechanical systems. In the first part, we present the method for creating new Simulink models using different toolboxes to customize their appearance and use. Then in the second part, we discuss Simulink and MATLAB features useful for viewing and analyzing simulation results. In the third part, we present different types of modeling of mechanical systems used in Simulink. Finally, we give two examples of modeling and control, illustrating the methods presented in the previous parts. The first example describes the Stewart platform and the second one describes a three Degree of Freedom (3-Dof) stabilized platform.

2. Getting started with Simulink

Simulink is a software package for modeling, simulating, and analyzing dynamical systems. It supports linear and nonlinear systems, modeled in continuous time, sampled time, or a hybrid of the two. Systems can also be multirate, i.e., have different parts that are sampled or updated at different rates (Parlos, 2001).
For modeling, Simulink provides a graphical user interface (GUI) for building models as block diagrams, using click-and-drag mouse operations. With this interface, we can draw the models just as we would with pencil and paper (or depict them as it is done in most textbooks). Simulink includes a comprehensive block library of sinks, sources, linear and nonlinear components, and connectors. We can also customize and create our own blocks.
Models are hierarchical. This approach provides an insight how a model is organized and how its parts interact. After we define a model, we can simulate it, using a choice of different methods, either from the Simulink menus or by entering commands in MATLAB's command window. The menus are particularly convenient for interactive work, while the command-line approach is very useful for running a batch of simulations (for example, if we are doing Monte Carlo simulations or want to sweep a parameter across a range of values). Using scopes and other display blocks, we can see the simulation results while the simulation is running. In addition, we can change parameters and immediately see what happens, for "what if" exploration. The simulation results can be put in the MATLAB workspace for post processing and visualization. And because MATLAB and Simulink are integrated, we can simulate, analyze, and revise our models in either environment at any point (Parlos, 2001).

2.1 Starting Simulink

To start a Simulink session, we'd need to bring up Matlab program first (Nguyen, 1995).
From Matlab command window, enter:
>> simulink
Alternately, we may click on the Simulink icon located on the toolbar as shown:

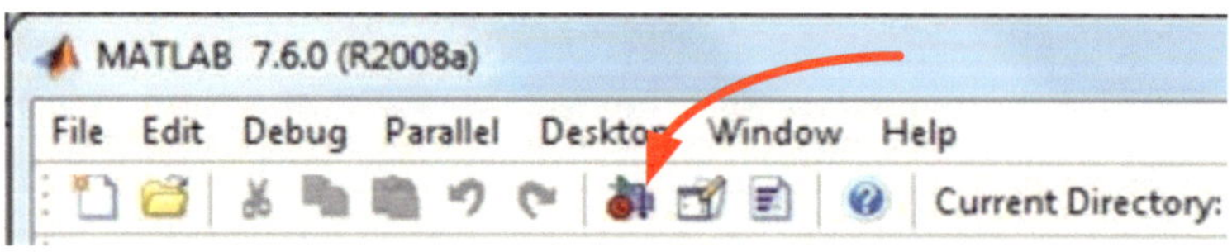

Fig. 1. Simulink icon in Matlab window

Simulink's library browser window like one shown below will pop up presenting the block set for model construction.

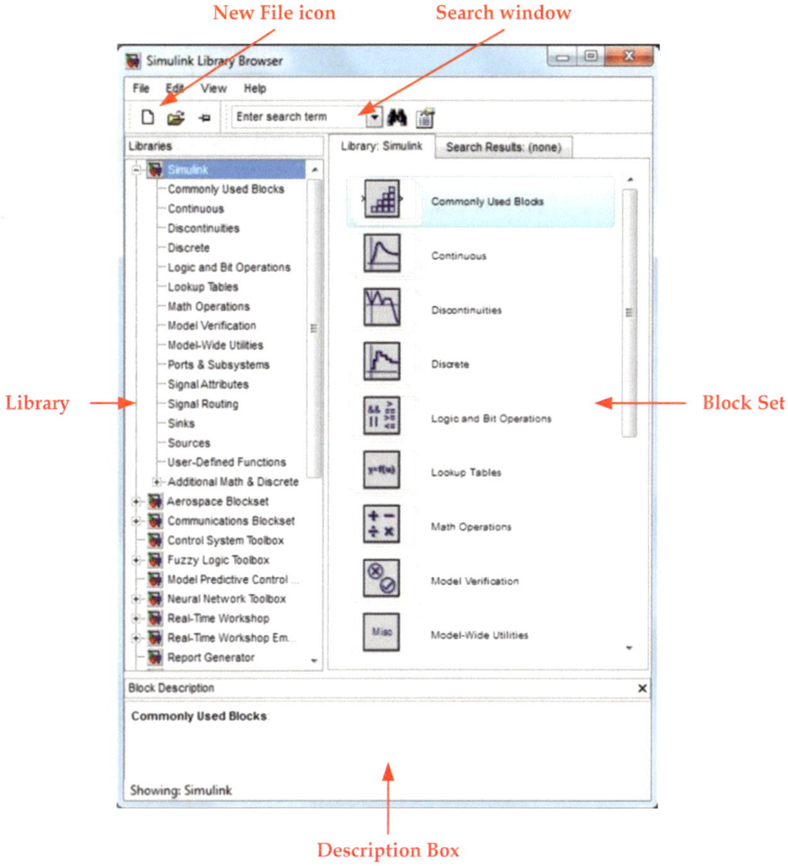

Fig. 2. Simulink's library browser

To see the content of the blockset, click on the "+" sign at the beginning of each toolbox.
To start a model click on the NEW FILE ICON as shown in the screenshot above.
Alternately, we may use keystrokes CTRL+N.
A new window will appear on the screen. We will be constructing our model in this window. Also in this window the constructed model is simulated. A screenshot of a typical working (model) window looks like one shown below:

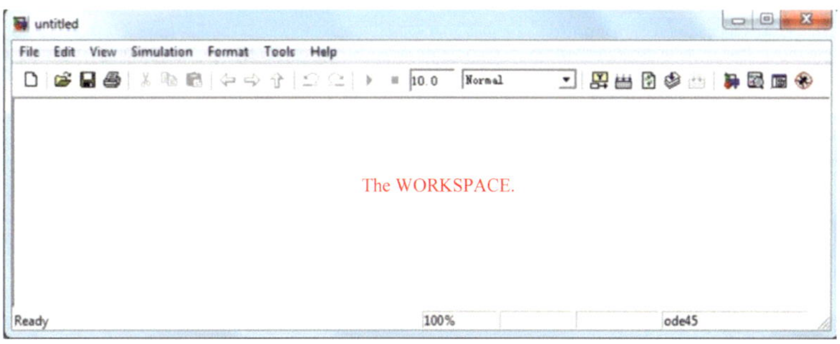

Fig. 3. Simulink workspace

To be more familiarized with the structure and the environment of Simulink, we are encouraged to explore the toolboxes and scan their contents. We may not know what they are all about but perhaps we could catch on the organization of these toolboxes according to the category. For an instant, we may see Control System Toolbox to consist of the Linear Time Invariant (LTI) system library and the MATLAB functions can be found under Function and Tables of the Simulink main toolbox. A good way to learn Simulink (or any computer program in general) is to practice and explore it. Making mistakes is a part of the learning curve. So, fear not, we should be (Nguyen, 1995).

A simple model is used here to introduce some basic features of Simulink. Please follow the steps below to construct a simple model.

Step 1. Creating Blocks.

From BLOCK SET CATEGORIES section of the SIMULINK LIBRARY BROWSER window, click on the "+" sign next to the Simulink group to expand the tree and select (click on) Sources.

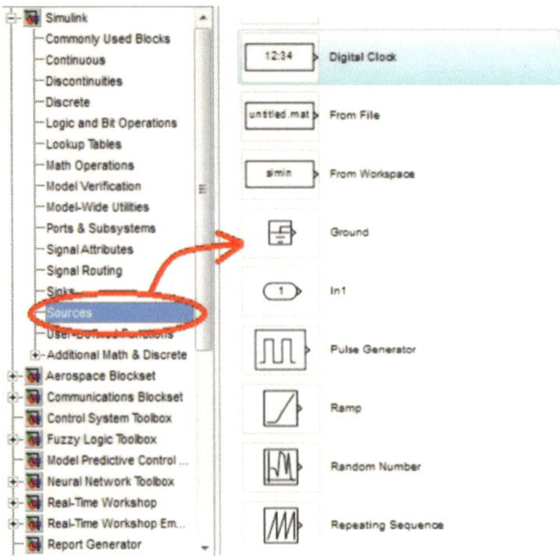

Fig. 4. Sources Block sets

A set of blocks will appear in the BLOCKSET group. Click on the Sine Wave block and drag it to the workspace window (also known as model window).

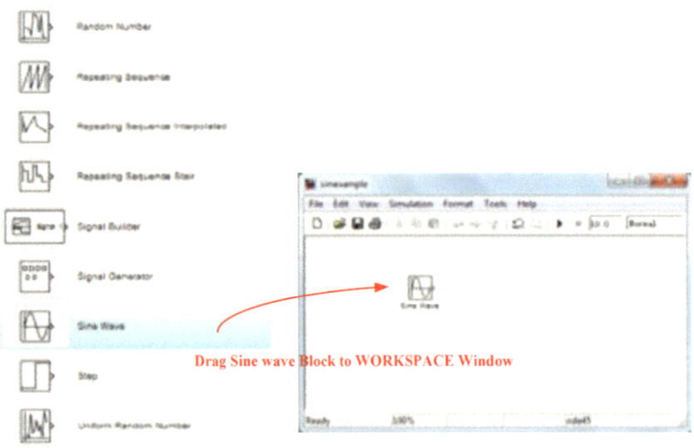

Fig. 5. Adding Blocks to Workspace

Now we have established a source of our model.

To save a model, click on the floppy diskette icon or from FILE menu, select Save or CTRL+S. All Simulink model files will have an extension ".mdl". Simulink recognizes the file with .mdl extension as a simulation model (similar to how MATLAB recognizes files with the extension .m as an MFile).
Continue to build the model by adding more components (or blocks) to the model window. We will add the Scope block from Sinks library, an Integrator block from Continuous library, and a Mux block from Signal Routing library.
NOTE: If we wish to locate a block knowing its name, we may enter the name in the SEARCH WINDOW (at Find prompt) and Simulink will bring up the specified block.
To move the blocks around, click on them and drag to a desired location.
Once all the blocks are dragged over to the work space, we may remove (delete) a block, by clicking on it once to turn on the "select mode" (with four corner boxes) and use the DEL key or keys combination CTRL-X.
Step 2. Making connections.
To establish connections between the blocks, move the cursor to the output port represented by ">" sign on the block. Once placed at a port, the cursor will turn into a cross "+" enabling us to make connection between blocks.
To make a connection: left-click while holding down the control key (on the keyboard) and drag from source port to a destination port.
The connected model is shown below.

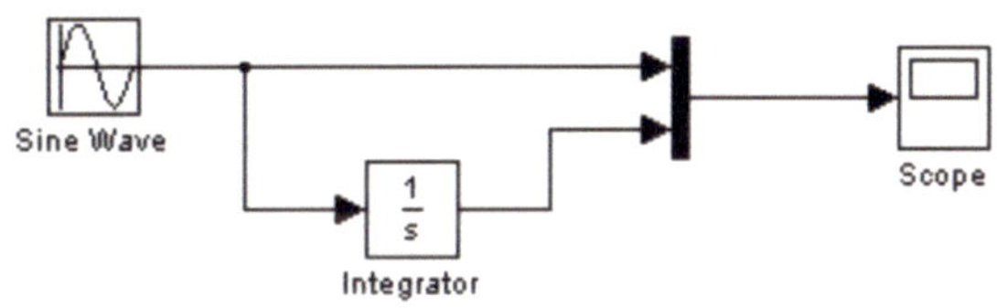

Fig. 6. Block diagram for Sine simulation

A sine signal is generated by the Sine Wave block (a source) and displayed on the scope (fig. 7). The integrated sine signal is sent towards the scope, to display it along with the original signal from the source via the Mux, whose function is to multiplex signals in form of scalar, vector, or matrix into a bus.

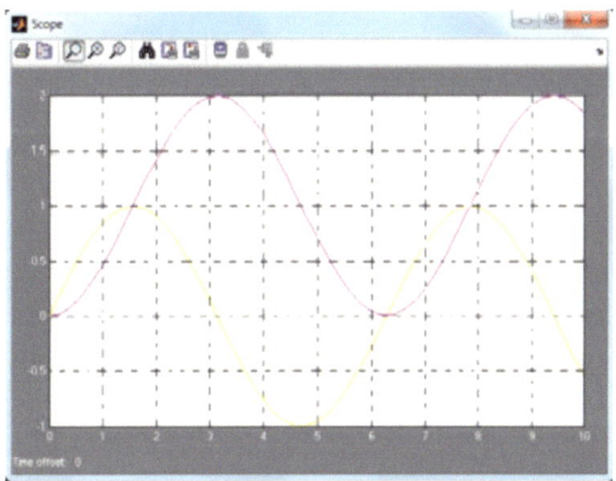

Fig. 7. Scope appearance

Step 3. Running simulation.
Now the simulation of the simple system above can be run by clicking on the play button (▶, alternatively, we may use key sequence CTRL+T, or choose Start submenu under Simulation menu).
Double click on the Scope block to display of the scope.
To view/edit the parameters, simply double click on the block of interest.

2.2 Handling of blocks and lines

The table below describes the actions and the corresponding keystrokes or mouse operations (Windows versions) (Nguyen, 1995).

Actions	Keystrokes or Mouse Actions
Copying a block from a library	Drag the block to the model window with the left mouse button on the OR use choose between select the COPY and PASTE from EDIT menu.
Duplicating blocks in a model	Hold down the CTRL key and select the block. Drag the block to a new location with the left mouse button.
Display block's parameters	Click doubly on the bloc.
Flip a block	CTRL-F
Rotate a block	CTRL-R
Changing blocks' names	Click on block's label and position the cursor to desired place.
Disconnecting a block	Hold down the SHIFT key and drag the block to a new location.
Drawing a diagonal line	Hold down the SHIFT key while dragging the mouse with the left button.
Dividing a line	Move the cursor to the line to where we want to create the vertex and use the left button on the mouse to drag the line while holding down the SHIFT key.

Table 1. The actions and the corresponding keystrokes or mouse operations.

2.3 Simulink block libraries

Simulink organizes its blocks into block libraries according to their behaviour.
The **Simulink** window displays the block library icons and names:

- The Sources library contains blocks that generate signals.
- The Sinks library contains blocks that display or write block output.
- The Discrete library contains blocks that describe discrete-time components.
- The Linear library contains blocks that describe linear functions.
- The Nonlinear library contains blocks that describe nonlinear functions.
- The Connections library contains blocks that allow multiplexing and demultiplexing, implement external Input/Output, pass data to other parts of the model, create subsystems, and perform other functions.
- The Blocksets and Toolboxes library contains the Extras block library of specialized blocks.
- The Demos library contains useful MATLAB and Simulink demos.

3. Viewing and analyzing simulation results

Output trajectories from Simulink can be plotted using one of three methods (The MathWorks, 1999):

- Feeding a signal into either a Scope or an XY Graph block
- Writing output to return variables and using MATLAB plotting commands
- Writing output to the workspace using To Workspace blocks and plotting the results using MATLAB plotting commands

3.1 Using the scope block

We can use display output trajectories on a Scope block during a simulation.
This simple model shows an example of the use of the Scope block:

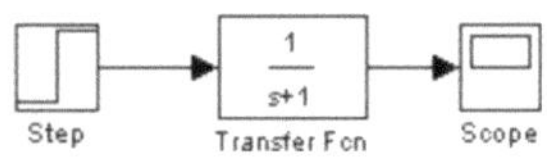

Fig. 8. Block diagram for Scope displaying

The display on the Scope shows the output trajectory. The Scope block enables to zoom in on an area of interest or save the data to the workspace.
The XY Graph block enables to plot one signal against another.
These blocks are described in Chapter 9.

3.2 Using return variables

By returning time and output histories, we can use MATLAB plotting commands to display and annotate the output trajectories.

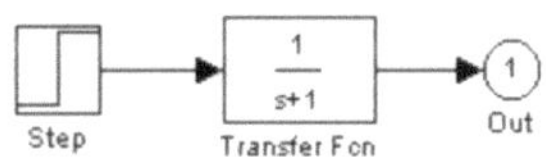

Fig. 9. Block diagram for output displaying

The block labelled **Out** is an Outport block from the Connections library. The output trajectory, yout, is returned by the integration solver. For more information, see Chapter 4.
This simulation can also be run from the Simulation menu by specifying variables for the time, output, and states on the Workspace I/O page of the Simulation Parameters dialog box. then these results can be plot using:
plot (tout,yout)

3.3 Using the To Workspace block

The **To Workspace** block can be used to return output trajectories to the MATLAB workspace. The model below illustrates this use:

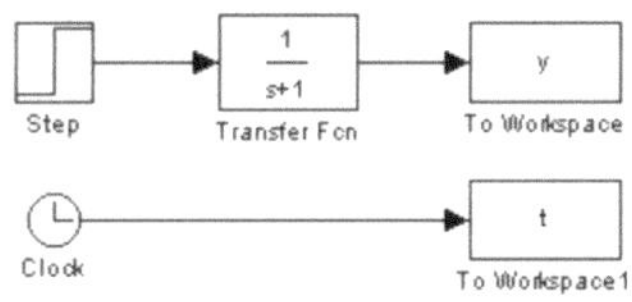

Fig. 10. Block diagram for Workspace displaying

The variables y and t appear in the workspace when the simulation is complete. The time vector is stored by feeding a Clock block into a To Workspace block. The time vector can also be acquired by entering a variable name for the time on the Workspace I/O page of the Simulation Parameters dialog box for menu-driven simulations, or by returning it using the sim command (see Chapter 4 for more information).
The **To Workspace** block can accept a vector input, with each input element's trajectory stored as a column vector in the resulting workspace variable.

4. Modeling mechanical systems with Simulink

Simulink's primary design goal is to enable the modeling, analysis, and implementation of dynamics systems so then mechanical systems. The mechanical systems consist of bodies, joints, and force elements like springs. Modeling a mechanical system need the equations of motion or the mechanical structure. Thus in general mechanical systems can be simulated by two ways:

- Using graphical representation of the mathematical model.
- Drawing directly the mechanical system using SimMechanics.

4.1 Modeling using graphical representation:

The equations of motion of mechanical systems have undergone historical development associated with such distinguished mathematicians as Newton, D'Alembert, Euler, Lagrange, Gauss, and Hamilton, among others (Wood & Kennedy, 2003). While all made significant contributions to the formulation's development of the underlying equations of motion, our interest here is on the computational aspects of mechanical simulation in an existing dynamic simulation package. Simulink is designed to model systems governed by these mathematical equations. The Simulink model is a graphical representation of mathematical operations and algorithm elements. Simulink solves the differential equation by evaluating the individual blocks according to the sorted order to compute derivatives for the states. The solver uses numeric integration to compute the evolution of states through time. Application of this method is illustrated in the first example of the section 5.

4.2 Modeling using SimMechanics

SimMechanics™ software is a block diagram modeling environment for the engineering design and simulation of rigid body machines and their motions, using the standard Newtonian dynamics of forces and torques. Instead of representing a mathematical model of the system, we develop a representation that describes the key components of the mechanical system. The base units in SimMechanics are physical elements instead of algorithm elements. To build a SimMechanics model, we must break down the mechanical system into the building blocks that describe it (Popinchalk, 2009).
After building the mechanical representation using SimMechanics, to study the system's response to and stability against external changes, we can apply small perturbations in the motion or the forces/torques to a known trajectory and force/torque set. SimMechanics software and Simulink® provide analysis modes and functions for analyzing the results of perturbing mechanical motion. To use these modes, we must first build a kinematic model of the system, one that specifies completely the positions, velocities, and accelerations of the system's bodies. We create a kinematic model by interconnecting blocks representing the

bodies and joints of the system and then connecting actuators to the joints to specify the motions of the bodies. Application of this method is illustrated in the second example of the section 5.

5. Examples of modeling and control of mechanical systems

5.1 Dynamics modeling for satellite antenna dish stabilized platform

The stabilized platform is the object which can isolate motion of the vehicle, and can measure the change of platform's motion and position incessantly, exactly hold the motorial gesture benchmark, so that it can make the equipment which is fixed on the platform aim at and track object fastly and exactly. In the stabilized platform systems, the basic requirements are to maintain stable operation even when there are changes in the system dynamics and to have very good disturbance rejection capability.

The objective of this example is to develop the dynamics model simulation for satellite antenna dish stabilized platform. The dynamic model of the platform is a three degree of freedom system. It is composed of, the four bodies which are: case, outer gimbal, inner gimbal and platform as shown in fig. 11. Simulink is used to simulate the obtained dynamic model of the stabilized platform. The testing results can be used to analyze the dynamic structure of the considered system. In addition, these results can be applied to the stabilization controller design study (Leghmizi et al., 2011).

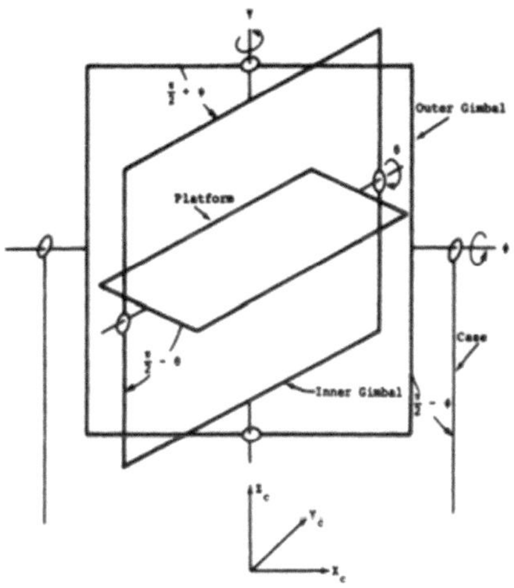

Fig. 11. The system structure

The mathematical modeling was established using Euler theory. The Euler's moment equations are

$$\overrightarrow{M} = i\overrightarrow{H} \tag{1}$$

The net torque $\overrightarrow{M}$ consists of driving torque applied by the adjacent outer member and reaction torque applied by the adjacent inner member.

$$i\overrightarrow{H} = \frac{dH}{dt} = m\overrightarrow{H} + \overrightarrow{\omega_m} \times \overrightarrow{H} \tag{2}$$

$i\vec{\dot{H}}$: Inertial derivative of the vector $\vec{H}$;

$m\vec{\dot{H}}$: Derivative of H calculated in a rotating frame of reference;

$\vec{\omega_m}$: Absolute rotational rate of the moving reference frame;

$\vec{H}$: Inertial angular momentum;

$\vec{M}$: External torque applied to the body.

By applying equation (2) on the different parts of the platform system , the system may be expressed as a set of second-order differential equations in the state variables. Solving this system of equations we obtain:

$$\ddot{\phi} = \frac{C_i B_o - C_o B_i}{A_i B_o - A_o B_i} \tag{3}$$

$$\ddot{\psi} = \frac{C_o A_i - C_i A_o}{A_i B_o - A_o B_i} \tag{4}$$

$$\ddot{\theta} = \frac{C_p}{B_p} - \frac{A_p}{B_p} * \frac{C_i B_o - C_o B_i}{A_i B_o - A_o B_i} \tag{5}$$

Where

$$A_p = \sin\psi$$

$$B_p = 1$$

$$C_p = \frac{M^*_{Ipy} - MPY}{I_{py}}$$

$$A_i = \cos\psi\cos\theta\sin\theta\left[\frac{I_{px} - I_{pz}}{I_{iz}}\right]$$

$$B_i = \left[1 + \sin^2\theta\frac{I_{px}}{I_{iz}} + \cos^2\theta\frac{I_{px}}{I_{iz}}\right]$$

$$C_i = \frac{M^*_{oiz} - MIZ}{I_{iz}}$$

$$A_o = 1 + \cos^2\psi\left[\frac{I_{ix} + I_{px}\cos^2\theta + I_{pz}\sin^2\theta}{I_{ox}}\right] + \sin^2\psi\left[\frac{I_{iy}}{I_{ox}}\right]$$

$$B_o = \cos\theta\sin\theta\cos\psi\left[\frac{I_{px} - I_{pz}}{I_{ox}}\right]$$

$$C_o = \frac{M^*_{cox} - MCX}{I_{ox}}$$

Detailed equations computation is presented in the paper (Leghmizi, 2010, 2011).

Here, it suffices to note that designing a simulation for the system based on these complete nonlinear dynamics is extremely difficult. It is thus necessary to reduce the complexity of the problem by considering the linearized dynamics (Lee et al., 1996). This can be done by noting that the gimbal angles variations are effectively negligible and that the ship velocities effect is insignificant. Applying the above assumptions to the nonlinear dynamics, the following equations are obtained.

$$\ddot{\phi} = \frac{D_{co}}{I_{px} + I_{ix} + I_{ox}}\dot{\phi} - \frac{1}{I_{px} + I_{ix} + I_{ox}}F_{co}(\operatorname{sgn}\dot{\phi}) - \frac{I_{pz} - I_{py} + I_{px}}{I_{px} + I_{ix} + I_{ox}}\dot{\psi}\dot{\theta} - T_{oo} \tag{6}$$

$$\ddot{\psi} = \frac{D_{oi}}{I_{pz} + I_{iz}}\dot{\psi} - \frac{1}{I_{pz} + I_{iz}}F_{oi}(\operatorname{sgn}\dot{\psi}) - \frac{I_{py} - I_{px} + I_{pz}}{I_{pz} + I_{iz}}\dot{\theta}\dot{\phi} - T_{mm} \tag{7}$$

$$\ddot{\theta} = \frac{D_{ip}}{I_{py}}\dot{\theta} - \frac{1}{I_{py}}F_{ip}(\operatorname{sgn}\dot{\theta}) - \frac{I_{px} - I_{pz} + I_{py}}{I_{py}}\dot{\psi}\dot{\phi} - T_{II} \tag{8}$$

5.1.2 Modeling the equations of motion with Simulink

The model in fig. 12 is the graphical representation of equations (6), (7) and (8). It's obtained by using the **Simulink toolbox**.

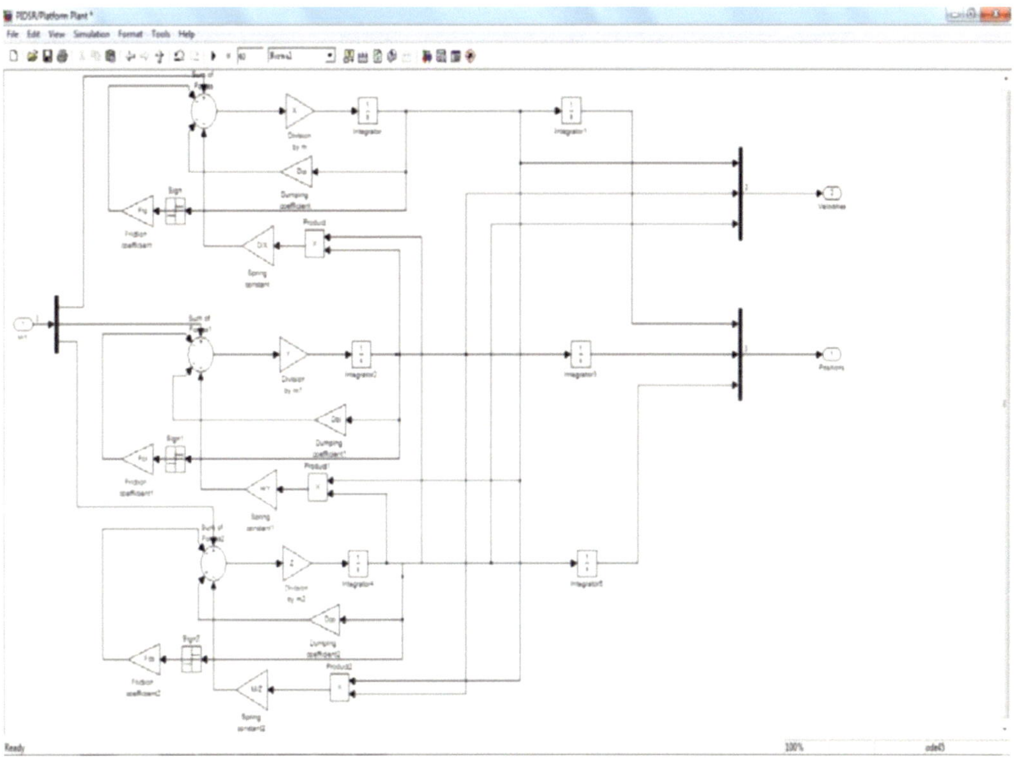

Fig. 12. The platform plant simulation

In order to enhance our understanding of the system, we performed a simulation in closed-loop mode. After that, a PID controller was applied to the closed-loop model. The PID controlled parameters was calculated using the Ziegler–Nichols method (Moradi, 2003). The obtained Simulink model is presented in the fig. 13.

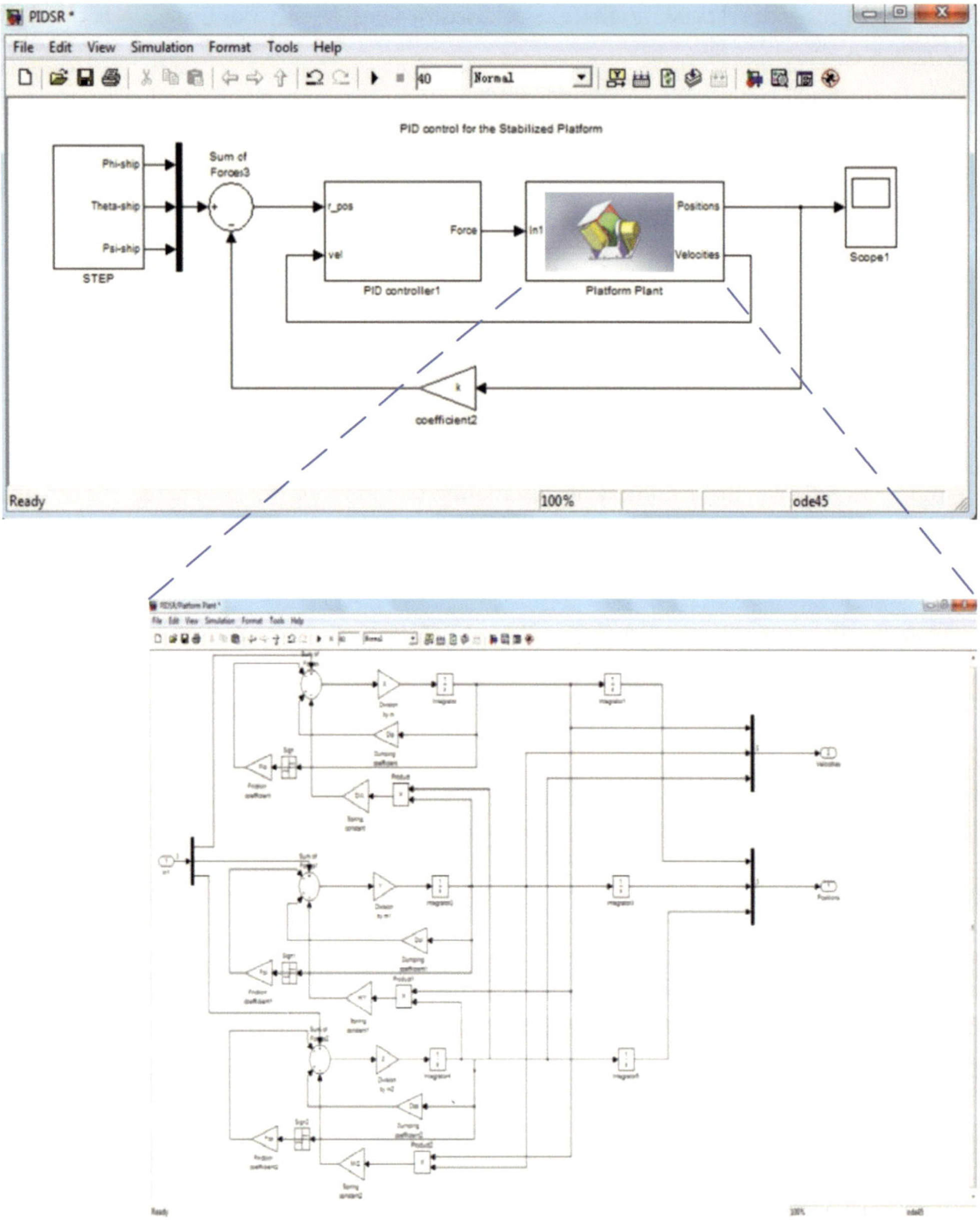

Fig. 13. Simulation model by Simulink

This simulation was particularly useful to recognize the contribution of each modelled effect to the dynamics of the system. Also, knowing the natural behavior of the system could be useful for establishing adapted control laws. Simulation results will be presented to illustrate the gimbals behaviour to different entries. They are presented in fig. 14, which contains the impulsion and step responses of the closed-loop system using the PID controller. Each graph superimposes the angular position on the X axes (blue), the Y axes (green) and the Z axes (red).

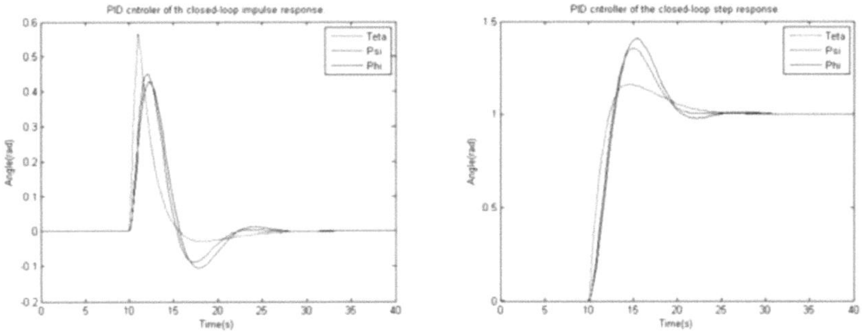

Fig. 14. The closed-loop system impulsion and step responses using the PID controller

5.2 Modeling a Stewart platform

The Stewart platform is a classic design for position and motion control, originally proposed in 1965 as a flight simulator, and still commonly used for that purpose (Stewart, 1965). Since then, a wide range of applications have benefited from the Stewart platform. A few of the industries using this design include aerospace, automotive, nautical, and machine tool technology. Among other tasks, the platform has been used, to simulate flight, model a lunar rover, build bridges, aid in vehicle maintenance, design crane and hoist mechanisms, and position satellite communication dishes and telescopes (Matlab Help).

The Stewart platform has an exceptional range of motion and can be accurately and easily positioned and oriented. The platform provides a large amount of rigidity, or stiffness, for a given structural mass, and thus provides significant positional certainty. The platform model is moderately complex, with a large number of mechanical constraints that require a robust simulation. Most Stewart platform variants have six linearly actuated legs with varying combinations of leg-platform connections. The full assembly is a parallel mechanism consisting of a rigid body top or mobile plate connected to an immobile base plate and defined by at least three stationary points on the grounded base connected to the legs.

The Stewart platform used here is connected to the base plate at six points by universal joints as shown in fig. 15. Each leg has two parts, an upper and a lower, connected by a cylindrical joint. Each upper leg is connected to the top plate by another universal joint. Thus the platform has 6*2 + 1 = 13 mobile parts and 6*3 = 18 joints connecting the parts.

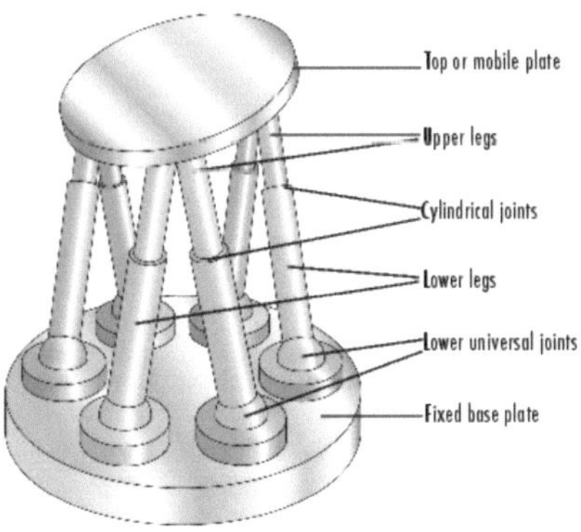

Fig. 15. Stewart platform

5.2.1 Modeling the physical Plant with SimMechanics

The Plant subsystem models the Stewart platform's moving parts, the legs and top plate. The model in the fig. 16 is obtained by using the SimMechanics toolbox. From the Matlab demos we can open this subsystem.

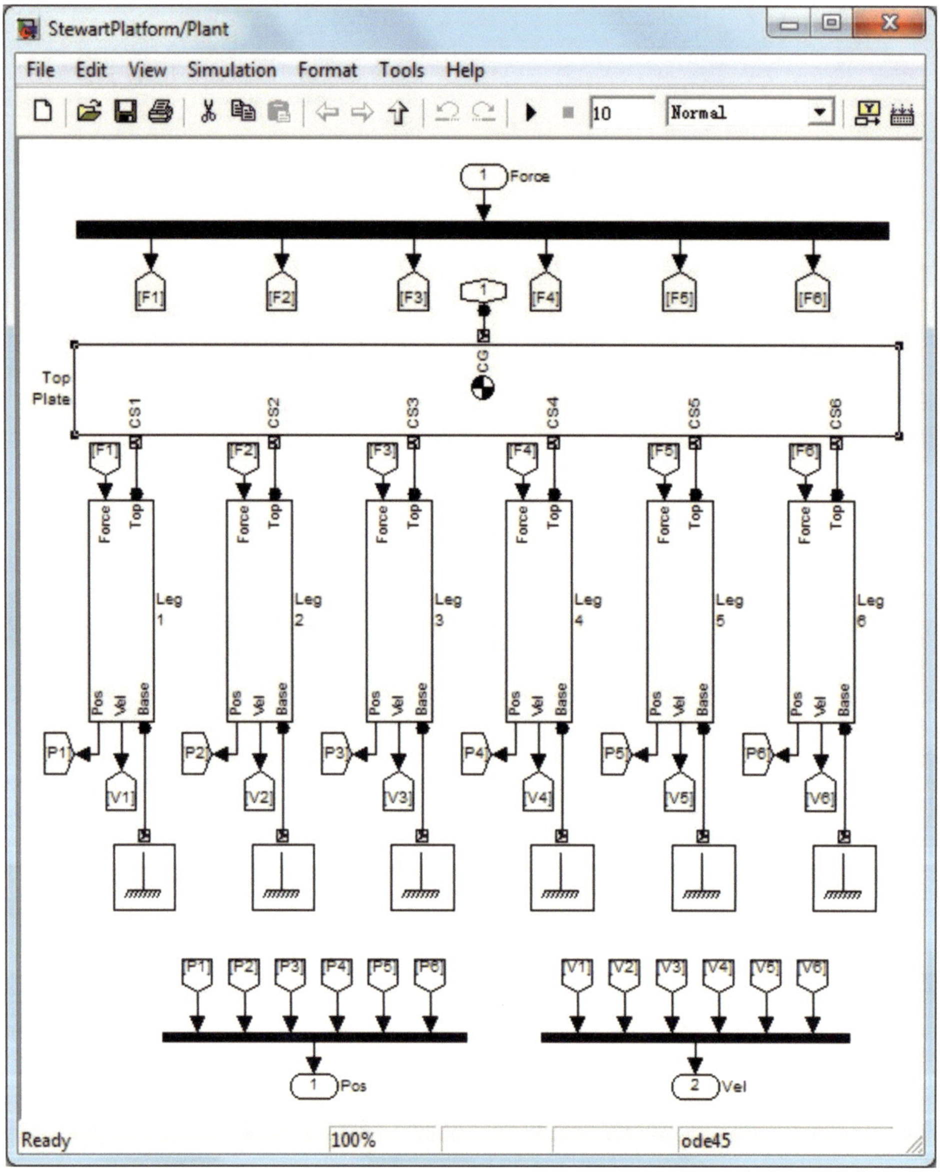

Fig. 16. Stewart platform plant representation with SimMechanics

The entire Stewart platform plant model is contained in a subsystem called **Plant**. This subsystem itself contains the base plate (the ground), the Top plate and the six platform legs. Each of the legs is a subsystem containing the individual Body and Joint blocks that make up the whole leg (see fig. 17).

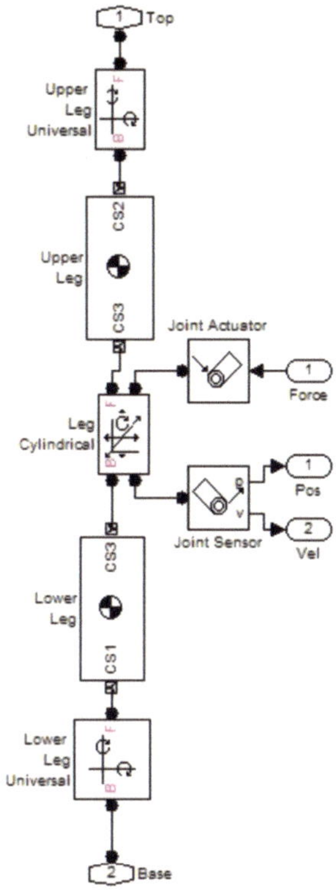

Fig. 17. Leg Subsystem content

To visualise the content of this subsystem, select one of the leg subsystems and right-click select **Look Under Mask**.

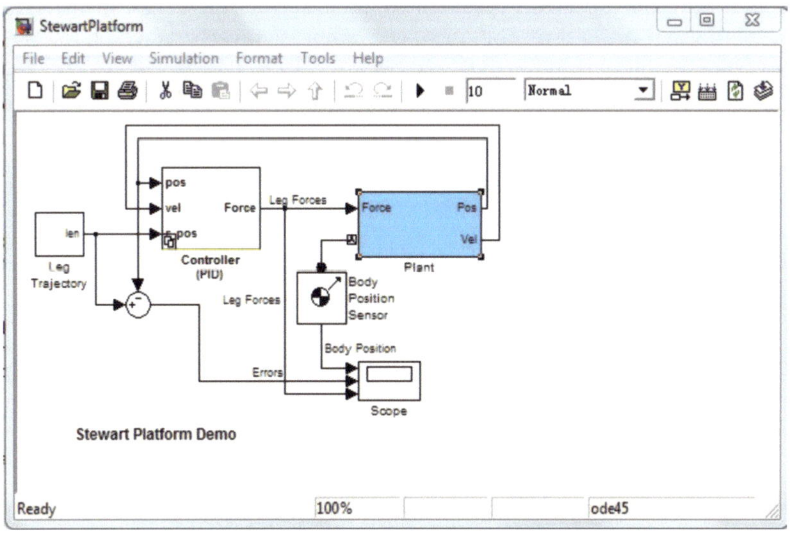

Fig. 18. Stewart Platform Control Design Model

The blue subsystem contains the Stewart platform plant presented in fig. 18. The simulation model in fig. 18 is the control of the Stewart platform's motion with the linear proportional-integral-derivative (PID) feedback system presented in fig. 19.

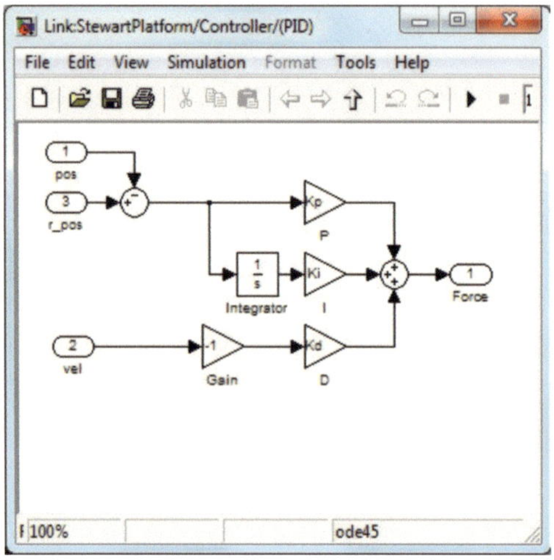

Fig. 19. Stewart Platform PID Controller Subsystem

The control transfer function of the PID linear feedback control system has the form $K_i/s + K_d.s + K_p$. The control gains Ki, Kp, and Kd in their respective blocks refer to the variables K_i, K_p, K_d defined in the workspace. Check their initialized values:

$K_i = 10000$

$K_p = 2000000$

$K_d = 45000$

To simulate the Stewart platform with the PID controller:

- Open the Scope and start the simulation.
- Observe the controlled Stewart platform motion. The Scope results given in fig. 20 show how the platform initially does not follow the reference trajectory, which starts in a position different from the platform's home configuration. The motion errors and forces on the legs are significant. Observe also that the leg forces saturate during the initial transient.

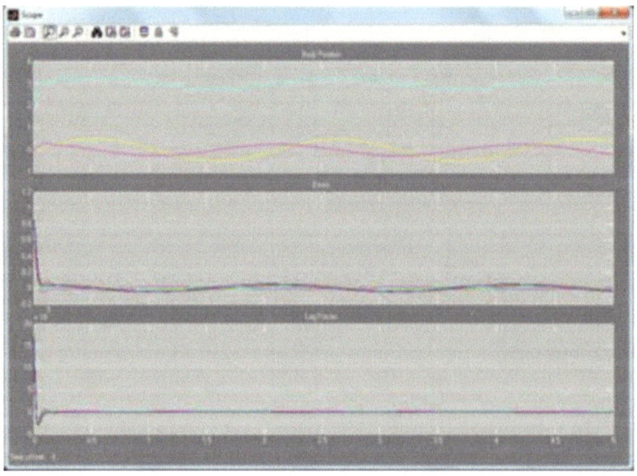

Fig. 20. Simulation results

The platform moves quickly to synchronize with the reference trajectory, and the leg forces and motion errors become much smaller.

6. Conclusion

The modeling of mechanical systems requires a language capable to describe physical phenomena in multiple energy domains, in continuous time or discrete time. Recent advances in modeling have resulted in several languages satisfying these requirements. Simulink of Matlab is one of such languages. Simulink is a software package that enables to model, simulate, and analyze dynamic systems, i.e., the systems with outputs and states changing with time. Simulating a mechanical system is a two-step process with Simulink involved. First, we create a graphical model of the system to be simulated, using the Simulink model editor. Then, we use Simulink to simulate the behavior of the system over a specified time span.

In this Chapter, using Simulink of Matlab, two examples of modeling and simulation were presented. We focused on the Simulation methods used to represent the dynamics of the mechanical systems. For this reason, in this chapter we explain the two methods used for modeling these systems. This chapter featured an explanation in what manner a mechanical system is simulated.

The models achieved in Matlab/Simulink and their simulations allow to study the mechanical system behavior, and to recognize the contribution of each modelled effect to the dynamics of the system. The results obtained could be useful for establishing adapted control laws.

7. References

Lee, T H.; Koh, E K. & Loh M K. (1996). Stable adaptive Control of Multivariable Servomechanisms, with Application to passive line-of-Sight Stabilization System, *IEEE Transactions on Industrial Electronics*, Vol. 43, No.1, pp. 98-105, February 1996.

Leghmizi, S. & Liu, S. (2010). Kinematics Modeling for Satellite Antenna Dish Stabilized Platform, *2010 International Conference on Measuring Technology and Mechatronics Automation*, pp. 558 – 563, Changsha, China, March 13 – 14, 2010

Leghmizi, S.; Fraga, R.; Liu, S.; Later, K.; Ouanzar, A. & Boughelala, A. (2011). Dynamics Modeling for Satellite Antenna Dish Stabilized Platform, *2011 International Conference on Computer Control and Automation*, Jeju Island, South Korea, 1st-3rd,May 2011

Moradi, M.H. (2003). New techniques for PID controller design, Proceeding of IEEE International Conference on Control Applications, Vol. 2, pp. 903 - 908, 2003

Matlab Help documentation

Nguyen, T. (1995) SIMULINK A Tutorial, available from: http://edu.levitas.net/Tutorials/Matlab/about.html

Parlos, AG. (2001). Introduction to Simulink, In: Department of Mechanical Engineering Student Information Retrieval System Texas A&M University, September 13th 2009, Available from: http://www1.mengr.tamu.edu/aparlos/MEEN651/SimulinkTutorial.pdf

Popinchalk, S. (2009). Modeling Mechanical Systems: The Double Pendulum, In: *Mathworks Blogs Seth on Simulink*, February 26th 2009, Available from: http://blogs.mathworks.com/seth/2009/02/26/modeling-mechanical-systems-the-double-pendulum/

Stewart, D. (1965). A platform with six degrees of freedom, *Proceedings of the Institution of Mechanical Engineers*, Vol.180, pp. 371-386, ISSN 0020-3483

The MathWorks, Inc. (1990- 1999). The Student Edition of Simulink Dynamic System Simulation for Matlab User's Guide

Wood, GD.; Kennedy, DC. (2003). Simulating mechanical systems in Simulink with SimMechanics, in: *Technical report of The MathWorks, Inc.*, Available from: www.mathworks.com.

16

Generalized PI Control of Active Vehicle Suspension Systems with MATLAB

Esteban Chávez Conde[1], Francisco Beltrán Carbajal[2]
Antonio Valderrábano González[3] and Ramón Chávez Bracamontes[4]
[1]*Universidad del Papaloapan, Campus Loma Bonita*
[2]*Universidad Autónoma Metropolitana, Plantel Azcapotzalco, Departamento de Energía*
[3]*Universidad Politécnica de la Zona Metropolitana de Guadalajara*
[4]*Instituto Tecnológico de Cd. Guzmán*
México

1. Introduction

The main objective on the active vibration control problem of vehicles suspension systems is to get security and comfort for the passengers by reducing to zero the vertical acceleration of the body of the vehicle. An actuator incorporated to the suspension system applies the control forces to the vehicle body of the automobile for reducing its vertical acceleration in active or semi-active way.

The topic of active vehicle suspension control system has been quite challenging over the years. Some research works in this area propose control strategies like LQR in combination with nonlinear backstepping control techniques (Liu et al., 2006) which require information of the state vector (vertical positions and speeds of the tire and car body). A reduced order controller is proposed in (Yousefi et al., 2006) to decrease the implementation costs without sacrificing the security and the comfort by using accelerometers for measurements of the vertical movement of the tire and car body. In (Tahboub, 2005), a controller of variable gain that considers the nonlinear dynamics of the suspension system is proposed. It requires measurements of the vertical position of the car body and the tire, and the estimation of other states and of the profile of the ride.

This chapter proposes a control design approach for active vehicle suspension systems using electromagnetic or hydraulic actuators based on the Generalized Proportional Integral (GPI) control design methodology, sliding modes and differential flatness, which only requires vertical displacement measurements of the vehicle body and the tire. The profile of the ride is considered as an unknown disturbance that cannot be measured. The main idea is the use of integral reconstruction of the non-measurable state variables instead of state observers. This approach is quite robust against parameter uncertainties and exogenous perturbations. Simulation results obtained from Matlab are included to show the dynamic performance and robustness of the proposed active control schemes for vehicles suspension systems.

GPI control for the regulation and trajectory tracking tasks on time invariant linear systems was introduced by Fliess and co-workers in (Fliess et al., 2002). The main objective is to avoid the explicit use of state observers. The integral reconstruction of the state variables is carried out by means of elementary algebraic manipulations of the system model along with suitable invocation of the system model observability property. The purpose of integral reconstructors is to get expressions for the unmeasured states in terms of inputs, outputs, and sums of a finite number of iterated integrals of the measured variables. In essence, constant errors and iterated integrals of such constant errors are allowed on these reconstructors. The current states thus differ from the integrally reconstructed states in time polynomial functions of finite order, with unknown coefficients related to the neglected, unknown, initial conditions. The use of these integral reconstructors in the synthesis of a model-based computed stabilizing state feedback controller needs suitable counteracting the effects of the implicit time polynomial errors. The destabilizing effects of the state estimation errors can be compensated by additively complementing a pure state feedback controller with a linear combination of a sufficient number of iterated integrals of the output tracking error, or output stabilization error. The closed loop stability is guaranteed by a simple characteristic polynomial assignment to the higher order compensated controllable and observable input-output dynamics. Experimental results of the GPI control obtained in a platform of a rotational mechanical system with one and two degrees of freedom are presented in (Chávez-Conde et al., 2006). Sliding mode control of a differentially flat system of two degrees of freedom, with vibration attenuation, is shown in (Enríquez-Zárate et al., 2000). Simulation results of GPI and sliding mode control techniques for absorption of vibrations of a vibrating mechanical system of two degrees of freedom were presented in (Beltrán-Carbajal et al., 2003).

This chapter is organized as follows: Section 2 presents the linear mathematical models of suspension systems of a quarter car. The design of the controllers for the active suspension systems are introduced in Sections 3 and 4. Section 5 divulges the use of sensors for measuring the variables required by the controller while the simulation results are shown in Section 6. Finally, conclusions are brought out in Section 7.

2. Quarter-car suspension systems

2.1 Mathematical model of passive suspension system

A schematic diagram of a quarter-vehicle suspension system is shown in Fig. 1(a). The mathematical model of passive suspension system is described by

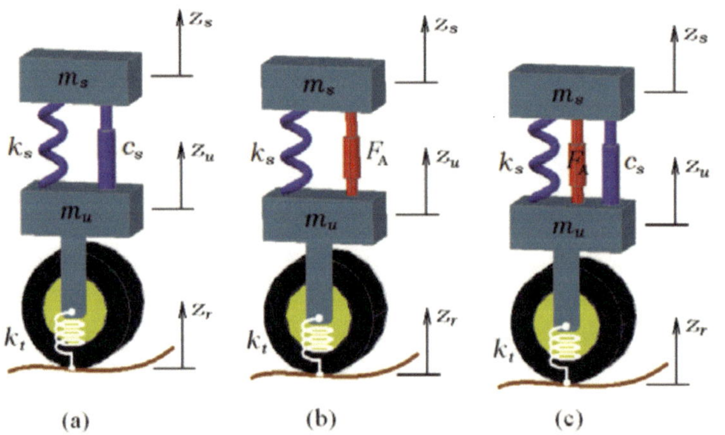

Fig. 1. Quarter-car suspension systems: (a) Passive Suspension System, (b) Active Electromagnetic Suspension System and (c) Active Hydraulic Suspension System.

$$m_s\ddot{z}_s + c_s(\dot{z}_s - \dot{z}_u) + k_s(z_s - z_u) = 0 \tag{1}$$

$$m_u\ddot{z}_u - c_s(\dot{z}_s - \dot{z}_u) - k_s(z_s - z_u) + k_t(z_u - z_r) = 0 \tag{2}$$

where m_s represents the sprung mass, m_u denotes the unsprung mass, c_s is the damper coefficient of suspension, k_s and k_t are the spring coefficients of suspension and the tire, respectively, z_s is the displacements of the sprung mass, z_u is the displacements of the unsprung mass and z_r is the terrain input disturbance.

2.2 Mathematical model of active electromagnetic suspension system

A schematic diagram of a quarter-car active electromagnetic suspension system is illustrated in Fig.1 (b). The electromagnetic actuator replaces the damper, forming a suspension with the spring (Martins et al., 2006). The friction force of an electromagnetic actuator is neglected. The mathematical model of electromagnetic active suspension system is given by

$$m_s\ddot{z}_s + k_s(z_s - z_u) = F_A \tag{3}$$

$$m_u\ddot{z}_u - k_s(z_s - z_u) + k_t(z_u - z_r) = -F_A \tag{4}$$

where m_s, m_u, k_s, k_t, z_s, z_u and z_r represent the same parameters and variables as ones described for the passive suspension system. The electromagnetic actuator force is represented here by F_A, which is considered as the control input.

2.3 Mathematical model of hydraulic active suspension system

Fig. 1(c) shows a schematic diagram of a quarter-car active hydraulic suspension system. The mathematical model of this active suspension system is given by

$$m_s\ddot{z}_s + c_s(\dot{z}_s - \dot{z}_u) + k_s(z_s - z_u) = -F_f + F_A \tag{5}$$

$$m_u\ddot{z}_u - c_s(\dot{z}_s - \dot{z}_u) - k_s(z_s - z_u) + k_t(z_u - z_r) = F_f - F_A \tag{6}$$

where m_s, m_u, k_s, k_t, z_s, z_u and z_r represent the same parameters and variables shown for the passive suspension system. The hydraulic actuator force is represented by F_A, while F_f represents the friction force generated by the seals of the piston with the cylinder wall inside the actuator. This friction force has a significant magnitude ($> 200N$) and cannot be ignored (Martins et al., 2006; Yousefi et al., 2006). The net force given by the actuator is the difference between the hydraulic force F_A and the friction force F_f.

3. Control of electromagnetic suspension system

The mathematical model of the active electromagnetic suspension system, illustrated in Fig. 1(b) is given by the equations (3) and (4). Defining the state variables $x_1 = z_s$, $x_2 = \dot{z}_s$, $x_3 = z_u$ and $x_4 = \dot{z}_u$, the representation in the state-space is,

$$\dot{x}(t) = Ax(t) + Bu(t) + Ez_r(t); \qquad x(t) \in \mathbb{R}^4, A \in \mathbb{R}^{4\times4}, B \in \mathbb{R}^{4\times1}, E \in \mathbb{R}^{4\times1}, \tag{7}$$

$$\begin{bmatrix} \dot{x}_1 \\ \dot{x}_2 \\ \dot{x}_3 \\ \dot{x}_4 \end{bmatrix} = \begin{bmatrix} 0 & 1 & 0 & 0 \\ -\frac{k_s}{m_s} & 0 & \frac{k_s}{m_s} & 0 \\ 0 & 0 & 0 & 1 \\ \frac{k_s}{m_u} & 0 & -\frac{k_s + k_t}{m_u} & 0 \end{bmatrix} \begin{bmatrix} x_1 \\ x_2 \\ x_3 \\ x_4 \end{bmatrix} + \begin{bmatrix} 0 \\ \frac{1}{m_s} \\ 0 \\ -\frac{1}{m_u} \end{bmatrix} u + \begin{bmatrix} 0 \\ 0 \\ 0 \\ \frac{k_t}{m_u} \end{bmatrix} z_r \tag{8}$$

The force provided by the electromagnetic actuator as the control input is $u = F_A$.
The system is controllable with controllability matrix,

$$C_k = \begin{bmatrix} 0 & \frac{1}{m_s} & 0 & -(\frac{k_s}{m_s^2} + \frac{k_s}{m_s m_u}) \\ \frac{1}{m_s} & 0 & -(\frac{k_s}{m_s^2} + \frac{k_s}{m_s m_u}) & 0 \\ 0 & -\frac{1}{m_u} & 0 & (\frac{k_s}{m_s m_u} + \frac{k_s + k_t}{m_u^2}) \\ -\frac{1}{m_u} & 0 & (\frac{k_s}{m_s m_u} + \frac{k_s + k_t}{m_u^2}) & 0 \end{bmatrix}, \tag{9}$$

and flat (Fliess et al., 1993; Sira-Ramírez & Agrawal, 2004), with the flat output given by the following expression relating the displacements of both masses (Chávez et al., 2009):

$$F = m_s x_1 + m_u x_3$$

For simplicity, in the analysis of the differential flatness for the suspension system we have assumed that $k_t z_r = 0$. In order to show the differential parameterization of all the state variables and control input, we first formulate the time derivatives up to fourth order for F, resulting,

$$\begin{aligned} F &= m_s x_1 + m_u x_3 \\ \dot{F} &= m_s x_2 + m_u x_4 \\ \ddot{F} &= -k_t x_3 \\ F^{(3)} &= -k_t x_4 \\ F^{(4)} &= \frac{k_t}{m_u} u - \frac{k_s k_t}{m_u}\left(x_1 - x_3\right) + \frac{k_t^2}{m_u} x_3 \end{aligned}$$

Then, the state variables and control input are parameterized in terms of the flat output as follows

$$x_1 = \frac{1}{m_s}\left(F + \frac{m_u}{k_t}\ddot{F}\right)$$

$$x_2 = \frac{1}{m_s}\left(\dot{F} + \frac{m_u}{k_t}F^{(3)}\right)$$

$$x_3 = -\frac{1}{k_t}\ddot{F}$$

$$x_4 = -\frac{1}{k_t}F^{(3)}$$

$$u = \frac{m_u}{k_t}F^{(4)} + \left(\frac{k_s m_u}{k_t m_s} + \frac{k_s}{k_t} + 1\right)\ddot{F} + \frac{k_s}{m_s}F$$

3.1 Integral reconstructors

The control input u in terms of the flat output and its time derivatives is given by

$$u = \frac{m_u}{k_t}F^{(4)} + \left(\frac{k_s m_u}{k_t m_s} + \frac{k_s}{k_t} + 1\right)\ddot{F} + \frac{k_s}{m_s}F \tag{10}$$

where $F^{(4)} = v$ defines an auxiliary control input variable. The expression (10) can be rewritten of the following form:

$$u = d_1 F^{(4)} + d_2 \ddot{F} + d_3 F \tag{11}$$

where

$$d_1 = \frac{m_u}{k_t}$$

$$d_2 = \frac{k_s m_u}{k_t m_s} + \frac{k_s}{k_t} + 1$$

$$d_3 = \frac{k_s}{m_s}$$

An integral input-output parameterization of the state variables is obtained from equation (11), and given by

$$\widehat{F}^{(3)} = \frac{1}{d_1}\int u - \frac{d_2}{d_1}\widehat{\dot{F}} - \frac{d_3}{d_1}\int F$$

$$\widehat{\ddot{F}} = \frac{1}{d_1}\int^{(2)} u - \frac{d_2}{d_1}F - \frac{d_3}{d_1}\int^{(2)} F$$

$$\widehat{\dot{F}} = \frac{1}{d_1}\int^{(3)} u - \frac{d_2}{d_1}\int F - \frac{d_3}{d_1}\int^{(3)} F$$

For simplicity, we will denote the integral $\int_0^t \phi(\tau)d\tau$ by $\int\phi$ and $\int_0^t\int_0^{\sigma 1}\cdots\int_0^{\sigma n-1}\phi(\sigma_n)d\sigma_n\cdots d\sigma_1$ by $\int^{(n)}\phi$ with n a positive integer.

The relations between the state variables and the integrally reconstructed states are given by

$$F^{(3)} = \widehat{F}^{(3)} + \frac{1}{2}F^{(3)}(0)t^2 + \ddot{F}(0)t + F^{(3)}(0) + \dot{F}(0)$$
$$\ddot{F} = \widehat{\ddot{F}} + F^{(3)}(0)t + \ddot{F}(0)$$
$$\dot{F} = \widehat{\dot{F}} + \frac{1}{2}F^{(3)}(0)t^2 + \ddot{F}(0)t + \dot{F}(0)$$

where $F^{(3)}(0)$, $\ddot{F}(0)$ and $\dot{F}(0)$ are all real constants depending on the unknown initial conditions.

3.2 Sliding mode and GPI control

GPI control is based on the use of integral reconstructors of the unmeasured state variables and the output error is integrally compensated. The sliding surface inspired on the GPI control technique can be proposed as

$$\widehat{\sigma} = \widehat{F}^{(3)} + \alpha_5\widehat{\ddot{F}} + \alpha_4\widehat{\dot{F}} + \alpha_3 F + \alpha_2\int F + \alpha_1\int^{(2)} F + \alpha_0\int^{(3)} F \tag{12}$$

The last integral term yields error compensation, eliminating destabilizing effects, those of the structural estimation errors. The ideal sliding condition $\widehat{\sigma} = 0$ results in a sixth order dynamics,

$$F^{(6)} + \alpha_5 F^{(5)} + \alpha_4 F^{(4)} + \alpha_3 F^{(3)} + \alpha_2\ddot{F} + \alpha_1\dot{F} + \alpha_0 F = 0 \tag{13}$$

The gains of the controller $\alpha_5,\ldots,\alpha_0$ are selected so that the associated characteristic polynomial $s^6 + \alpha_5 s^5 + \alpha_4 s^4 + \alpha_3 s^3 + \alpha_2 s^2 + \alpha_1 s + \alpha_0$ is Hurwitz. As a consequence, the error dynamics on the switching surface $\hat{\sigma} = 0$ is globally asymptotically stable.
The sliding surface $\hat{\sigma} = 0$ is made globally attractive with the continuous approximation to the discontinuous sliding mode controller as given in (Sira-Ramírez, 1993), i.e., by forcing to satisfy the dynamics,

$$\dot{\widehat{\sigma}} = -\mu[\widehat{\sigma} + \gamma sign(\widehat{\sigma})] \tag{14}$$

where μ and γ denote real positive constants and "sign" is the standard signum function.

The sliding surface is globally attractive, $\widehat{\sigma}\dot{\widehat{\sigma}} < 0$ for $\widehat{\sigma} \neq 0$, which is a very well known condition for the existence of sliding mode presented in (Utkin, 1978). Then the following sliding-mode controller is obtained

$$u = d_1 v + d_2\widehat{\ddot{F}} + d_3 F \tag{15}$$

with

$$v = -\alpha_5\widehat{F}^{(3)} - \alpha_4\widehat{\ddot{F}} - \alpha_3\widehat{\dot{F}} - \alpha_2 F - \alpha_1\int F - \alpha_0\int^{(2)} F - \mu[\widehat{\sigma} + \gamma sign(\widehat{\sigma})]$$

This controller requires only the measurement of the variables of state z_s and z_u corresponding to the vertical displacements of the body of the car and the wheel, respectively.

4. Control of hydraulic suspension system

The mathematical model of active suspension system shown in Fig. 1(c) is given by the equations (5) and (6). Using the same state variables definition than the control of electromagnetic suspension system, the representation in the state space form is as follows:

$$\begin{bmatrix}\dot{x}_1\\ \dot{x}_2\\ \dot{x}_3\\ \dot{x}_4\end{bmatrix}=\begin{bmatrix}0 & 1 & 0 & 0\\ -\frac{k_s}{m_s} & -\frac{c_s}{m_s} & \frac{k_s}{m_s} & \frac{c_s}{m_s}\\ 0 & 0 & 0 & 1\\ \frac{k_s}{m_u} & \frac{c_s}{m_u} & -\frac{k_s+k_t}{m_u} & -\frac{c_s}{m_u}\end{bmatrix}\begin{bmatrix}x_1\\ x_2\\ x_3\\ x_4\end{bmatrix}+\begin{bmatrix}0\\ \frac{1}{m_s}\\ 0\\ -\frac{1}{m_u}\end{bmatrix}u+\begin{bmatrix}0\\ 0\\ 0\\ \frac{k_t}{m_u}\end{bmatrix}z_r \tag{16}$$

The net force provided by the hydraulic actuator as control input $u=F_A-F_f$, is the difference between the hydraulic force F_A and the frictional force F_f.
The system is controllable and flat (Fliess et al., 1993; Sira-Ramírez & Agrawal, 2004), with positions of the body of the car and wheel as output $F=m_sx_1+m_ux_3$, (Chávez et al., 2009). The controllability matrix and coefficients are:

$$C_k=\begin{bmatrix}c_{11} & c_{12} & c_{13} & c_{14}\\ c_{21} & c_{22} & c_{23} & c_{24}\\ c_{31} & c_{32} & c_{33} & c_{34}\\ c_{41} & c_{42} & c_{43} & c_{44}\end{bmatrix} \tag{17}$$

$$c_{11}=0,\quad c_{12}=c_{21}=\frac{1}{m_s},\quad c_{13}=c_{22}=-(\frac{c_s}{m_s^2}+\frac{c_s}{m_sm_u}),$$

$$c_{14}=c_{23}=(\frac{c_s^2}{m_s^2}+\frac{c_s^2}{m_sm_u}-\frac{k_s}{m_s})\frac{1}{m_s}-(-\frac{c_s^2}{m_s^2}-\frac{c_s^2}{m_sm_u}+\frac{k_s}{m_s})\frac{1}{m_u},$$

$$c_{24}=[\frac{c_sk_s}{m_s^2}-\frac{c_s}{m_s}(\frac{c_s^2}{m_s^2}+\frac{c_s^2}{m_sm_u}-\frac{k_s}{m_s})+\frac{c_sk_s}{m_sm_u}+\frac{c_s}{m_s}(-\frac{c_s^2}{m_s^2}-\frac{c_s^2}{m_sm_u}+\frac{k_s}{m_s})]\frac{1}{m_s}$$
$$-[-\frac{c_sk_s}{m_s^2}-\frac{c_s}{m_s}(-\frac{c_s^2}{m_s^2}-\frac{c_s^2}{m_sm_u}+\frac{k_s}{m_s})-\frac{c_sk_s}{m_sm_u}+\frac{c_s}{m_s}(\frac{c_s^2}{m_s^2}+\frac{c_s^2}{m_sm_u}-\frac{k_s+k_t}{m_s})]\frac{1}{m_s},$$

$$c_{31}=0,\quad c_{32}=c_{41}=-\frac{1}{m_u},\quad c_{33}=c_{42}=(\frac{c_s}{m_u^2}+\frac{c_s}{m_sm_u}),$$

$$c_{34}=c_{43}=(-\frac{c_s^2}{m_s^2}-\frac{c_s^2}{m_sm_u}+\frac{k_s}{m_u})\frac{1}{m_s}-(\frac{c_s^2}{m_s^2}+\frac{c_s^2}{m_sm_u}-\frac{k_s+k_t}{m_u})\frac{1}{m_u},$$

$$c_{44}=[-\frac{c_sk_s}{m_sm_u}+\frac{c_s}{m_u}(\frac{c_s^2}{m_s^2}+\frac{c_s^2}{m_sm_u}-\frac{k_s}{m_s})-\frac{c_s}{m_u^2}(k_s+k_t)-\frac{c_s}{m_u}(-\frac{c_s^2}{m_u^2}-\frac{c_s^2}{m_sm_u}+\frac{k_s}{m_u})]\frac{1}{m_s}$$
$$-[\frac{c_sk_s}{m_sm_u}+\frac{c_s}{m_u}(-\frac{c_s^2}{m_s^2}-\frac{c_s^2}{m_sm_u}+\frac{k_s}{m_s})+\frac{c_s}{m_u^2}(k_s+k_t)-\frac{c_s}{m_u}(\frac{c_s^2}{m_u^2}+\frac{c_s^2}{m_sm_u}-\frac{k_s+k_t}{m_u})]\frac{1}{m_u}$$

It is assumed that $k_t z_r = 0$ in the analysis of the differential flatness for the suspension system. To show the parameterization of the state variables and control input, we first formulate the time derivatives for $F = m_s x_1 + m_u x_3$ up to fourth order, resulting,

$$\begin{aligned}
F &= m_s x_1 + m_u x_3 \\
\dot{F} &= m_s x_2 + m_u x_4 \\
\ddot{F} &= -k_t x_3 \\
F^{(3)} &= -k_t x_4 \\
F^{(4)} &= \frac{k_t}{m_u} u - \frac{c_s k_t}{m_u}(x_2 - x_4) - \frac{k_s k_t}{m_u}(x_1 - x_3) + \frac{k_t^2}{m_u} x_3
\end{aligned}$$

Then, the state variables and control input are parameterized in terms of the flat output as follows

$$x_1 = \frac{1}{m_s}\left(F + \frac{m_u}{k_t}\ddot{F}\right), \quad x_2 = \frac{1}{m_s}\left(\dot{F} + (\frac{m_u}{k_t})F^{(3)}\right)$$

$$x_3 = -\frac{1}{k_t}\ddot{F}, \qquad x_4 = -\frac{1}{k_t}F^{(3)}$$

$$u = \frac{m_u}{k_t}F^{(4)} + \left(\frac{c_s m_u}{k_t m_s} + \frac{c_s}{k_t}\right)F^{(3)} + \left(\frac{k_s m_u}{k_t m_s} + \frac{k_s}{k_t} + 1\right)\ddot{F} + \frac{c_s}{m_s}\dot{F} + \frac{k_s}{m_s}F$$

4.1 Integral reconstructors

The control input u in terms of the flat output and its time derivatives is given by

$$u = \frac{m_u}{k_t}v + \left(\frac{c_s m_u}{k_t m_s} + \frac{c_s}{k_t}\right)F^{(3)} + \left(\frac{k_s m_u}{k_t m_s} + \frac{k_s}{k_t} + 1\right)\ddot{F} + \frac{c_s}{m_s}\dot{F} + \frac{k_s}{m_s}F \tag{18}$$

where $F^{(4)} = v$, defines the auxiliary control input. Expression (19) can be rewritten in the following form:

$$u = \eta_1 v + \eta_2 F^{(3)} + \eta_3 \ddot{F} + \eta_4 \dot{F} + \eta_5 F \tag{19}$$

where

$$\begin{aligned}
\eta_1 &= \frac{m_u}{k_t} \\
\eta_2 &= \frac{c_s m_u}{k_t m_s} + \frac{c_s}{k_t} \\
\eta_3 &= \frac{k_s m_u}{k_t m_s} + \frac{k_s}{k_t} + 1 \\
\eta_4 &= \frac{c_s}{m_s}, \quad \eta_5 = \frac{k_s}{m_s}
\end{aligned}$$

An integral input-output parameterization of the state variables is obtained from equation (20), and given by

$$\begin{aligned}
\widehat{F}^{(3)} &= \frac{1}{\eta_1}\int u - \frac{\eta_2}{\eta_1}\hat{\ddot{F}} - \frac{\eta_3}{\eta_1}\hat{\dot{F}} - \frac{\eta_4}{\eta_1}F - \frac{\eta_5}{\eta_1}\int F \\
\hat{\ddot{F}} &= \frac{1}{\eta_1}\int^{(2)} u - \frac{\eta_2}{\eta_1}\hat{\dot{F}} - \frac{\eta_3}{\eta_1}F - \frac{\eta_4}{\eta_1}\int F - \frac{\eta_5}{\eta_1}\int^{(2)} F \\
\hat{\dot{F}} &= \frac{1}{\eta_1}\int^{(3)} u - \frac{\eta_2}{\eta_1}F - \frac{\eta_3}{\eta_1}\int F - \frac{\eta_4}{\eta_1}\int^{(2)} F - \frac{\eta_5}{\eta_1}\int^{(3)} F
\end{aligned}$$

For simplicity, we have denoted the integral $\int_0^t \phi(\tau)d\tau$ by $\int \phi$ and $\int_0^t\int_0^{\sigma 1}\cdots\int_0^{\sigma n-1}\phi(\sigma_n)d\sigma_n\cdots d\sigma_1$ by $\int^{(n)}\phi$ with n as a positive integer.

The relationship between the state variables and the integrally reconstructed state variables is given by

$$\begin{aligned}
F^{(3)} &= \widehat{F}^{(3)} + F^{(3)}(0)t^2 + F^{(3)}(0)t + 2\ddot{F}(0)t + \ddot{F}(0) + 2\dot{F}(0) \\
\ddot{F} &= \hat{\ddot{F}} + \frac{1}{2}F^{(3)}(0)t^2 + F^{(3)}(0)t + \ddot{F}(0)t + \ddot{F}(0) + \dot{F}(0) \\
\dot{F} &= \hat{\dot{F}} + \frac{1}{2}F^{(3)}(0)t^2 + \ddot{F}(0)t + \dot{F}(0)
\end{aligned}$$

where $F^{(3)}(0)$, $\ddot{F}(0)$ and $\dot{F}(0)$ are all real constants depending on the unknown initial conditions.

4.2 Sliding mode and GPI control

The sliding surface inspired on the GPI control technique is proposed according to equations (12), (13), and (14). This sliding surface is globally attractive (Utkin, 1978). Then the following sliding-mode controller is obtained:

$$u = \eta_1 v + \eta_2 \widehat{F}^{(3)} + \eta_3 \hat{\ddot{F}} + \eta_4 \hat{\dot{F}} + \eta_5 F \tag{20}$$

With

$$v = -\alpha_5 \widehat{F}^{(3)} - \alpha_4 \hat{\ddot{F}} - \alpha_3 \hat{\dot{F}} - \alpha_2 F - \alpha_1 \int F - \alpha_0 \int^{(2)} F - \mu[\hat{\sigma} + \gamma\, sign(\hat{\sigma})]$$

This controller requires only the measurement of the variables of state z_s and z_u corresponding to the vertical positions of the body of the car and the wheel, respectively.

5. Instrumentation of active suspension system

5.1 Measurements required

The only variables required for implementation of the proposed controllers are the vertical displacement of the body of the car z_s, and the vertical displacement of the wheel z_u. These variables are needed to be measured by sensors.

5.2 Using sensors

In (Chamseddine et al., 2006), the use of sensors in experimental vehicle platforms, as well as in commercial vehicles is presented. The most common sensors, used for measuring the vertical displacement of the body of the car and the wheels, are laser sensors. This type of sensor could be used to measure the variables z_s and z_s needed for implementation of the controllers. Accelerometers or other types of sensors are not needed for measuring the variables $\dot{z}_s$ and $\dot{z}_u$; these variables are estimated with the use of integral reconstruction from knowledge of the control input, the flat output and the differentially flat system model.
The schematic diagram of the instrumentation of the active suspension system is illustrated in Fig. 2.

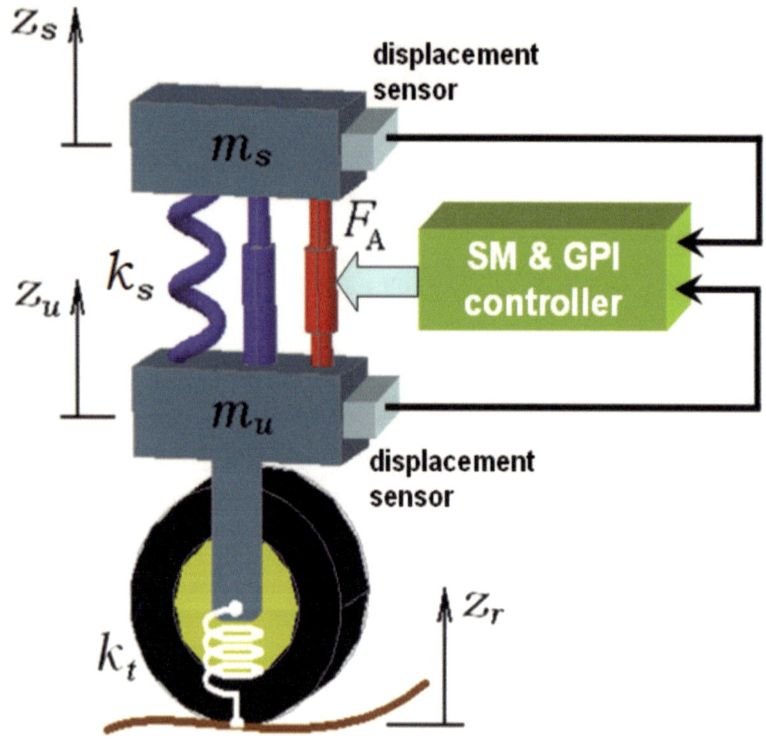

Fig. 2. Schematic diagram of the instrumentation of the active suspension system.

6. Simulation results with MATLAB/Simulink

The simulation results were obtained by means of MATLAB/Simulink®, with the Runge-Kutta numerical method and a fixed integration step of $1\,ms$.

6.1 Parameters and type of road disturbance

The numerical values of the quarter-car suspension model parameters (Sam & Hudha, 2006) chosen for the simulations are shown in Table 1.

Parameter	Value
Sprung mass, m_s	$282\,[kg]$
Unsprung mass, m_u	$45\,[kg]$
Spring stifness, k_s	$17900\,[\frac{N}{m}]$
Damping constant, c_s	$1000\,[\frac{N \cdot s}{m}]$
Tire stifness, k_t	$165790\,[\frac{N}{m}]$

Table 1. Vehicle suspension system parameters for a quarter-car model.

In this simulation study, the road disturbance is shown in Fig. 3 and set in the form of (Sam & Hudha, 2006):

$$z_r = a\frac{1-cos(8\pi t)}{2}$$

with $a = 0.11$ [m] for $0.5 \le t \le 0.75$, $a = 0.55$ [m] for $3.0 \le t \le 3.25$ and 0 otherwise.

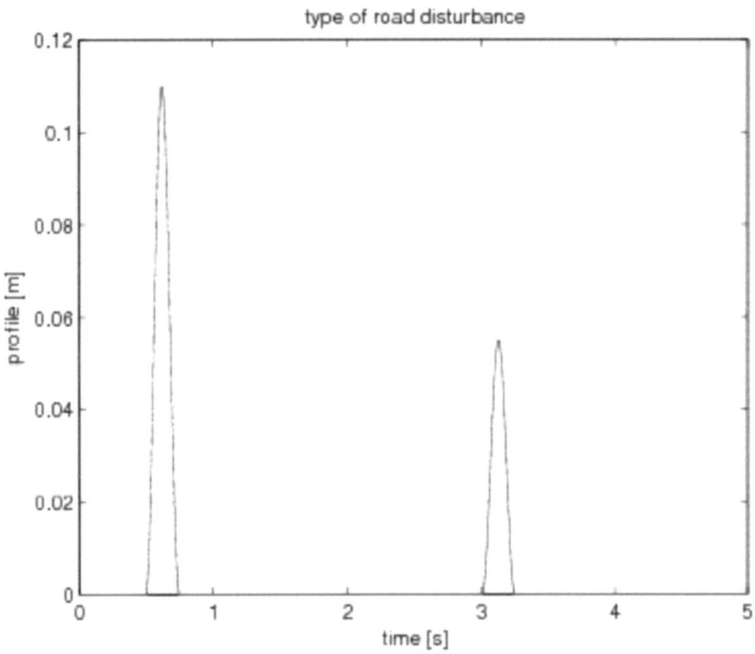

Fig. 3. Type of road disturbance.

The road disturbance was programmed into Simulink blocks, as shown in Fig. 4. Here, the block called "conditions" was developed as a Simulink subsystem block Fig. 5.

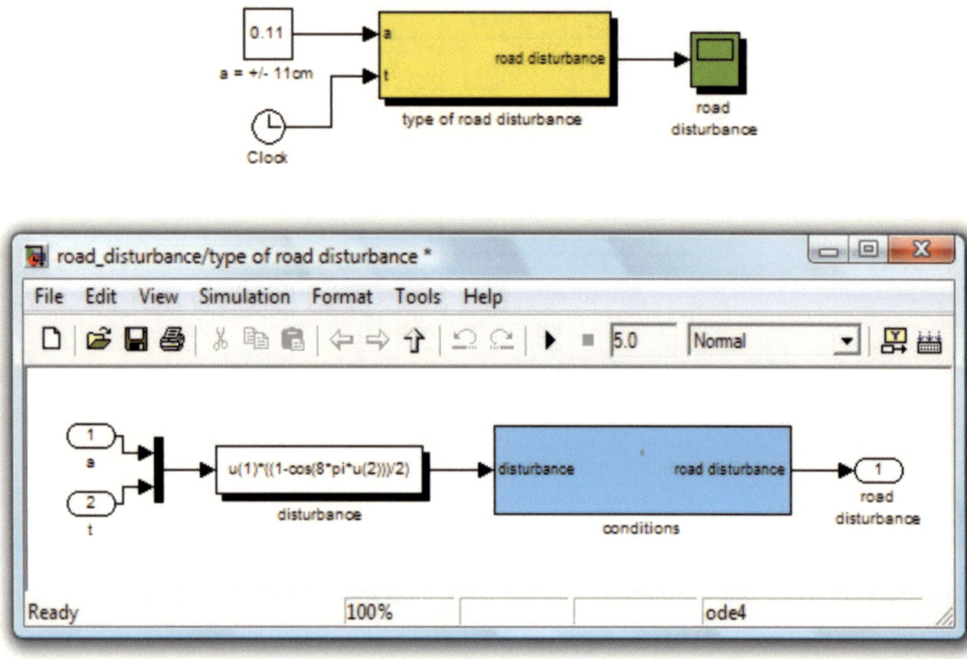

Fig. 4. Type of road disturbance in Simulink.

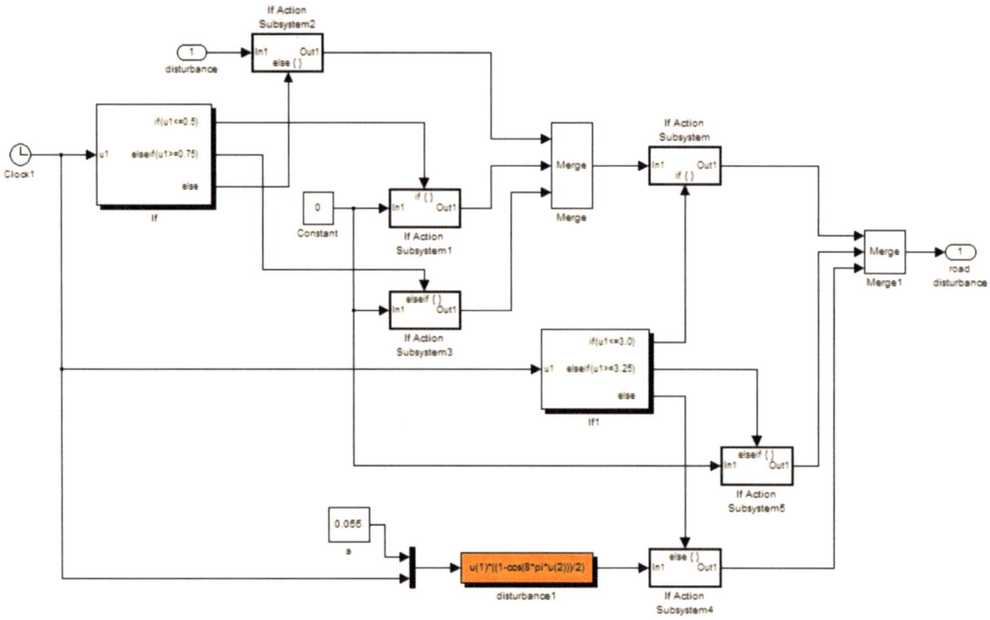

Fig. 5. Conditions of road disturbance in Simulink.

6.2 Passive vehicle suspension system

Some simulation results of the passive suspension system performance are shown in Fig. 6. The Simulink model of the passive suspension system used for the simulations is shown in Fig. 7.

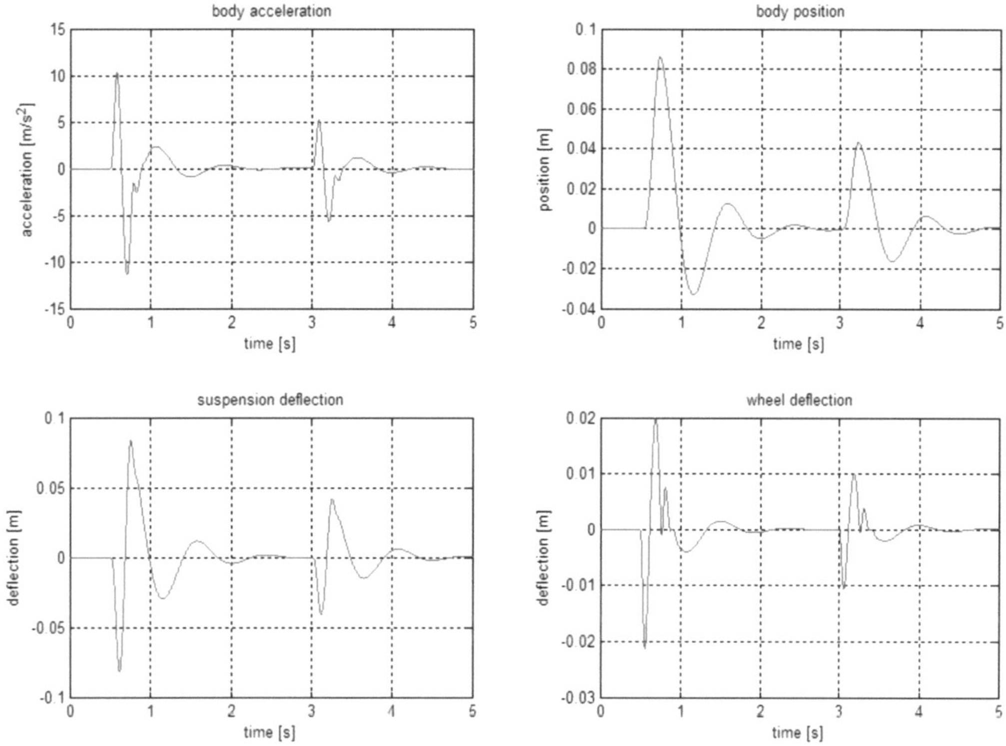

Fig. 6. Simulation results of passive suspension system, where the suspension deflection is given by ($z_s - z_u$) and the tire deflection by ($z_u - z_r$).

6.3 Control of electromagnetic suspension system

It is desired to stabilize the system at the positions $z_s = 0$ and $z_u = 0$. The controller gains were obtained by forcing the closed loop characteristic polynomial to be given by the following Hurwitz polynomial:

$$p_{d1}(s) = (s + p_1)(s + p_2)(s^2 + 2\zeta_1\omega_{n1}s + \omega_{n1}^2)^2$$

with $p_1 = 90$, $p_2 = 90$ $\zeta_1 = 0.7071$, $\omega_{n1} = 80$, $\mu = 95$ y $\gamma = 95$.

The Simulink model of the sliding mode based GPI controller of the active suspension system is shown in Fig. 8. The simulation results are illustrated in Fig. 9 It can be seen the high vibration attenuation level of the active vehicle suspension system compared with the passive counterpart.

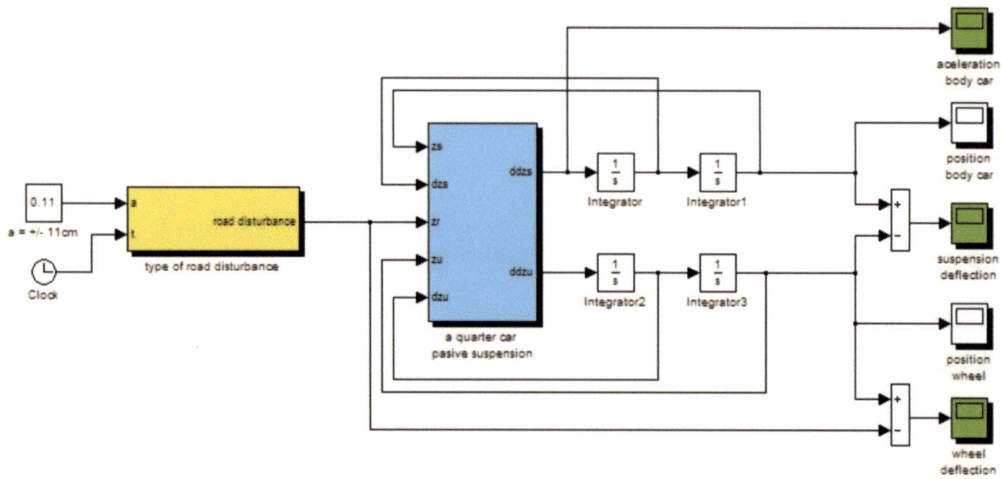

Fig. 7. Simulink model of the passive suspension system.

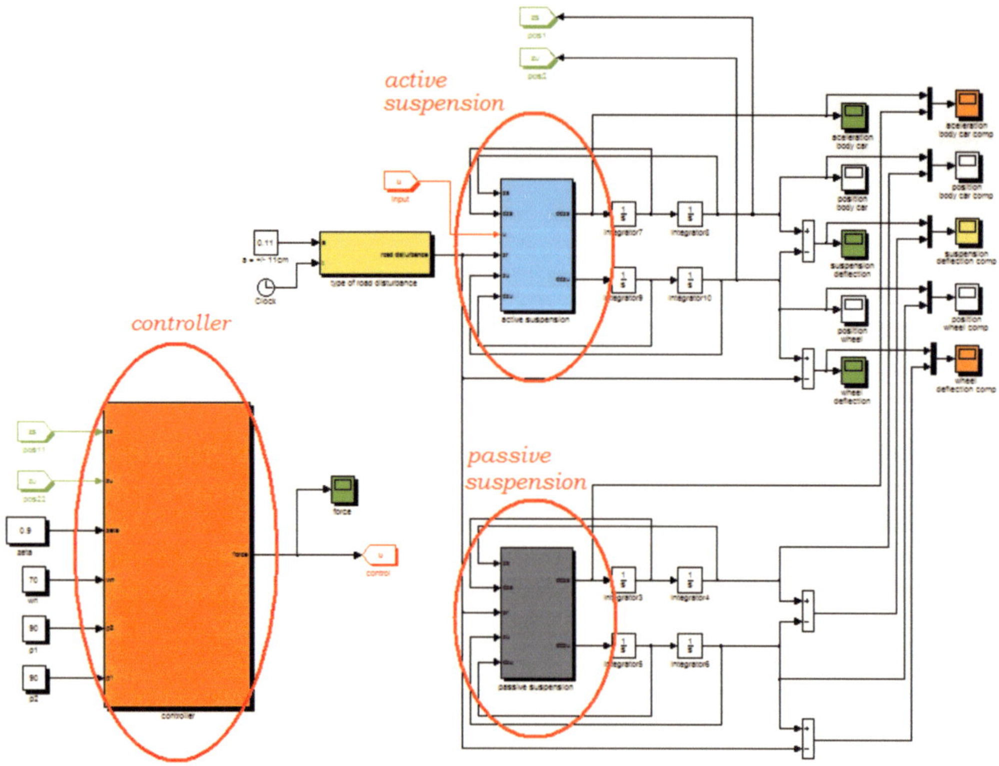

Fig. 8. Simulink model of the sliding mode based GPI controller.

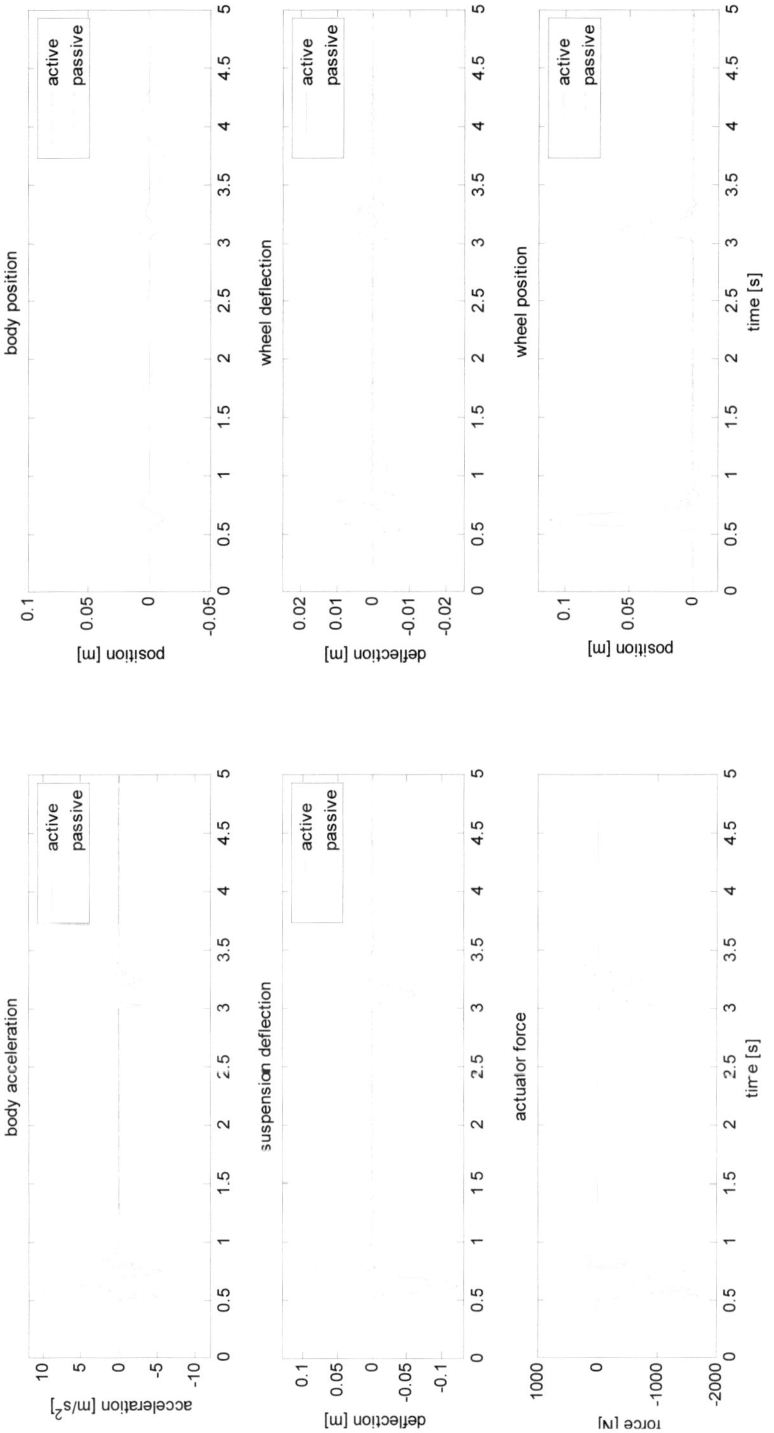

Fig. 9. Simulation results of the sliding mode based GPI controller of the electromagnetic suspension system.

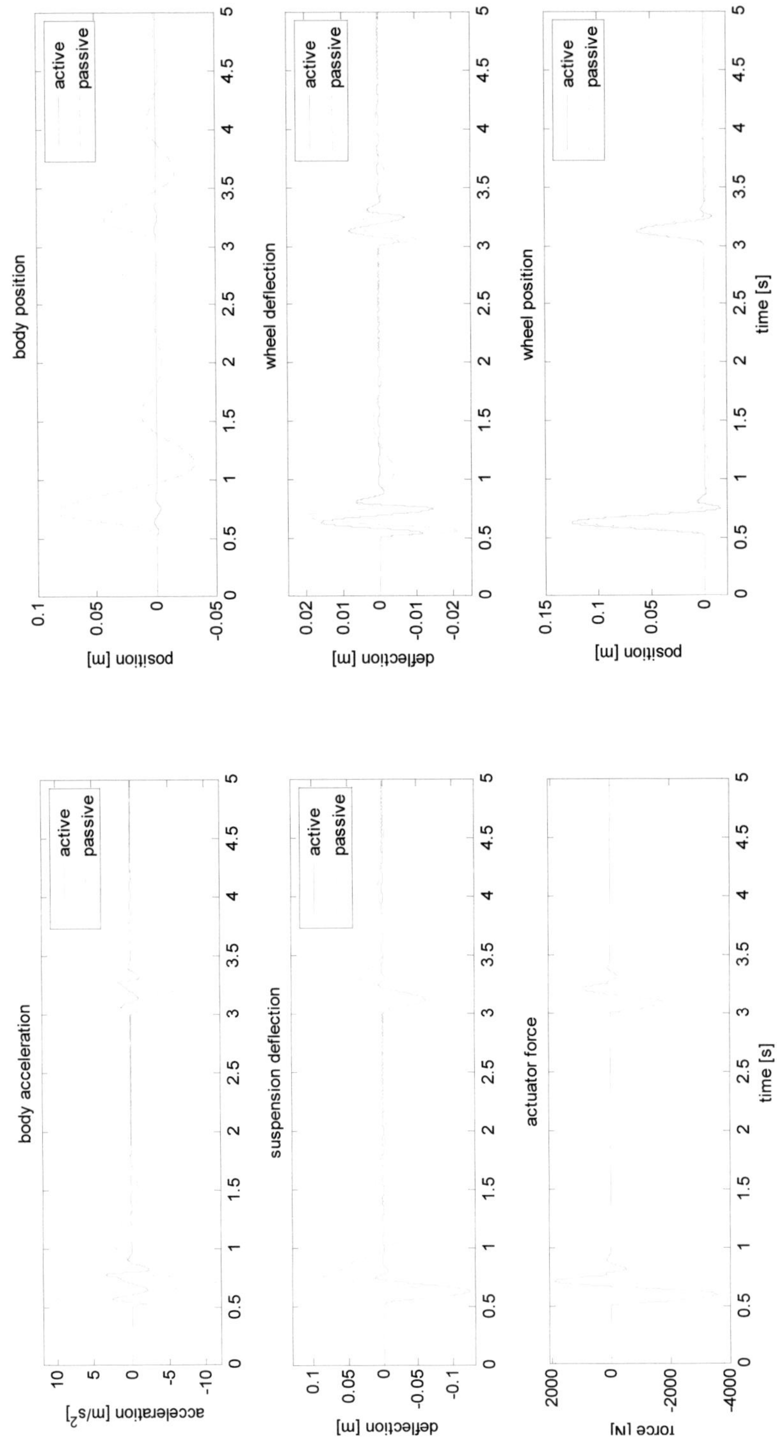

Fig. 10. Simulation results of sliding mode based GPI controller of hydraulic suspension system.

6.3 Control of hydraulic suspension system

It is desired to stabilize the system in the positions $z_s = 0$ and $z_u = 0$. The controller gains were obtained by forcing the closed loop characteristic polynomial to be given by the following Hurwitz polynomial:

$$p_{d2}(s) = (s + p_3)(s + p_4)(s^2 + 2\zeta_2\omega_{n2}s + \omega_{n2}^2)^2$$

with $p_3 = 90$, $p_4 = 90$, $\zeta_2 = 0.9$, $\omega_{n2} = 70$, $\mu = 95$ and $\gamma = 95$. The performance of the sliding mode based GPI controller is depicted in Fig. 10. One can see the high attenuation level of road-induced vibrations with respect to passive suspension system.

The same Matlab/Simulink simulation programs were used to implement the controllers for the electromagnetic and hydraulic active suspension systems. For the electromagnetic active suspension system, it is assumed that $c_z = 0$.

7. Conclusions

In this chapter we have presented an approach of robust active vibration control schemes for electromagnetic and hydraulic vehicle suspension systems based on Generalized Proportional-Integral control, differential flatness and sliding modes. Two controllers have been proposed to attenuate the vibrations induced by unknown exogenous disturbance excitations due to irregular road surfaces. The main advantage of the controllers proposed, is that they require only measurements of the position of the car body and the tire. Integral reconstruction is employed to get structural estimates of the time derivatives of the flat output, needed for the implementation of the controllers proposed. The simulation results show that the stabilization of the vertical position of the quarter of car is obtained within a period of time much shorter than that of the passive suspension system. The fast stabilization with amplitude in acceleration and speed of the body of the car is observed. Finally, the robustness of the controllers to stabilize to the system before the unknown disturbance is verified.

8. References

Beltrán-Carbajal, F.; Silva-Navarro G.; Sira-Ramírez, H. "Active Vibration Absorbers Using Generalized PI And Sliding-Mode Control Techniques", 39th IEEE American Control Conference. pp. 791-796, Denver, Colorado, June 4-6, 2003.

Chamseddine, Abbas; Noura, Hassan; Raharijaona, Thibaut "Control of Linear Full Vehicle Active Suspension System Using Sliding Mode Techniques", 2006 IEEE International Conference on Control Applications. pp. 1306-1311, Munich, Germany, October 4-6, 2006.

Chávez-Conde, E.; Beltrán-Carbajal, F.; Blanco-Ortega, A. and Méndez-Azúa, H. "Sliding Mode and Generalized PI Control of Vehicle Active Suspensions", Proceedings of 18th IEEE International Conference on Control Applications, pp. 1726-1731, Saint Petersburg, Russia, 2009.

Chávez-Conde, E.; Sira-Ramírez H.; Silva-Navarro, G. "Generalized PI Control and On-line Identification of a Rotational Mass Spring System", 25th IASTED Conference International Modelling, Identification and Control. No. 500-107, pp. 467-472. Lanzarote, Canary Islands, Spain, February 6-8, 2006.

Enríquez-Zárate, J.; Silva-Navarro, G.; Sira-Ramírez, H. "Sliding Mode Control of a Differentially Flat Vibrational Mechanical System: Experimental Results", 39th IEEE Conference on Decision and Control. pp. 1679-1684, Sydney, Australia, December 2000.

Fliess, M.; Lévine, J.; Martin, P. and Rouchon P. "Flatness and defect of nonlinear systems: Introductory theory and examples", Int. J. of Control, 61(6), pp. 1327-1361. ISSN: 0020-7179. 1993.

Fliess, M.; Márquez, R.; Delaleau E.; Sira-Ramírez, H. "Correcteurs Proportionnels-Integraux Généralisés", ESAIM Control, Optimisation and Calculus of Variations. Vol. 7, pp. 23-41, 2002.

Liu, Zhen; Luo, Cheng; Hu, Dewen, "Active Suspension Control Design Using a Combination of LQR and Backstepping", 25th IEEE Chinese Control Conference, pp. 123-125, Harbin, Heilongjiang, August 7-11, 2006.

Martins, I.; Esteves, J.; Marques, D. G.; Da Silva, F. P. "Permanent-Magnets Linear Actuators Applicability in Automobile Active Suspensions", IEEE Trans. on Vehicular Technology. Vol. 55, No. 1, pp. 86-94, January 2006.

Sam, Y. M.; Hudha, K. "Modelling and Force Tracking Control of Hydraulic Actuator for an Active Suspension System", IEEE ICIEA, 2006.

Sira-Ramírez, H. "A dynamical variable structure control strategy in asymptotic output tracking problems", IEEE Trans. on Automatic Control. Vol. 38, No. 4, pp. 615-620, April 1993.

Sira-Ramírez, H.; Agrawal, Sunil K. "Differentially Flat Systems", Marcel Dekker, N.Y., 2004.

Tahboub, Karim A. "Active Nonlinear Vehicle-Suspension Variable-Gain Control", 13th IEEE Mediterranean Conference on Control and Automation, pp. 569-574, Limassol, Cyprus, June 27-29, 2005.

Tahboub, Karim A. "Active Nonlinear Vehicle-Suspension Variable-Gain Control", 13th IEEE Mediterranean Conference on Control and Automation, pp. 569-574, Limassol, Cyprus, June 27-29, 2005.

Utkin,V. I. "Sliding Modes and Their Applications in Variable Structure Systems". Moscow: MIR, 1978.

Yousefi, A.; Akbari, A and Lohmann, B., "Low Order Robust Controllers for Active Vehicle Suspensions", IEEE International Conference on Control Applications, pp. 693-698, Munich, Germany, October 4-6, 2006.

17

Control Laws Design and Validation of Autonomous Mobile Robot Off-Road Trajectory Tracking Based on ADAMS and MATLAB Co-Simulation Platform

Yang. Yi, Fu. Mengyin, Zhu. Hao and Xiong. Guangming
School of Automation, Beijing Institute of Technology, China

1. Introduction

Autonomous automobile technology is a rapidly developing field, with interest in both academia and industry. Outdoor navigation of autonomous vehicles, especially for rough-terrain driving, has already been a new research focus. DARPA Grand Challenge and LAGR program stand for the top development level in this research region. Rough-terrain driving research offers a challenge that the in-vehicle control system must be able to handle rough and curvy roads, and quickly varying terrain types, such as gravel, loose sand, and mud puddles - while stably tracking trajectories between closely spaced hazards. The vehicle must be able to recover from large disturbances, without intervention (Gabriel, 2007).
Since robotics autonomous navigation tasks in outdoor environment can be effectively performed by skid-steering vehicles, these vehicles are being widely used in military affairs, academia research, space exploration, and so on. In reference (Luca, 1999), a model-based nonlinear controller is designed, following the dynamic feedback linearization paradigm. In reference (J.T. Economou, 2000), the authors applied experimental results to enable Fuzzy Logic modelling of the vehicle-ground interactions in an integrated manner. These results illustrate the complexity of systematic modeling the ground conditions and the necessity of using two variables in identifying the surface properties. In reference (Edward, 2001), the authors described relevant rover safety and health issues and presents an approach to maintaining vehicle safety in a navigational context. Fuzzy logic approaches to reasoning about safe attitude and traction management are presented. In reference (D. Lhomme-Desages, 2006), the authors introduced a model-based control for fast autonomous mobile robots on soft soils. This control strategy takes into account slip and skid effects to extend the mobility over planar, granular soils. Different from above researches, which control the robots on the tarmac, grass, sand, gravel or soil, this chapter focuses on the motion control for skid-steering vehicles on the bumpy and rocklike terrain, and presents novel and effective trajectory tracking control methods, including the longitudinal, lateral, and sensors pan-tilt control law. Furthermore, based on ADAMS&MATLAB co-simulation platform, iRobot ATRV2 is

modelled and the bumpy off-road terrain is constructed, at the same time, trajectory tracking control methods are validated effectively on this platform.

2. Mobile robot dynamic analysis

To research on the motion of skid-steering robots, the 4-wheeled differentially driven robot, which is moving on the horizontal road normally without longitudinal wheel slippage, is analyzed for kinematics and dynamics. As shown in Fig. 1 (a), global Descartes frame and in-vehicle Descartes frame are established. In Global frame $OXYZ$, its origin O is sited on the horizontal plane where the robot is running, and Z axis is orthogonal to the plane; in in-vehicle frame $oxyz$, its origin o is located at the robot center of mass, z axis is orthogonal to the chassis of robot, x axis is parallel to the rectilinear translation orientation of the robot and y axis is orthogonal to the translation orientation in the plane of the chassis. The robot wheelbase is A and the distance between the left and right wheels is B. According to the relation between $OXYZ$ and $oxyz$, the kinematics equation is as follows.

$$\begin{bmatrix} \dot{X} \\ \dot{Y} \end{bmatrix} = \begin{bmatrix} \dot{x}\cos\theta - \dot{y}\sin\theta \\ \dot{x}\sin\theta + \dot{y}\cos\theta \end{bmatrix} = \begin{bmatrix} \cos\theta & -\sin\theta \\ \sin\theta & \cos\theta \end{bmatrix} \begin{bmatrix} \dot{x} \\ \dot{y} \end{bmatrix} \tag{1}$$

The derivative of equation (1) with respect to time is

$$\begin{aligned} \begin{bmatrix} \ddot{X} \\ \ddot{Y} \end{bmatrix} &= \begin{bmatrix} \cos\theta & -\sin\theta \\ \sin\theta & \cos\theta \end{bmatrix} \begin{bmatrix} \ddot{x} - \dot{y}\dot{\theta} \\ \ddot{y} - \dot{x}\dot{\theta} \end{bmatrix} \\ &= \begin{bmatrix} \cos\theta & -\sin\theta \\ \sin\theta & \cos\theta \end{bmatrix} \begin{bmatrix} a_x \\ a_y \end{bmatrix} \end{aligned} \tag{2}$$

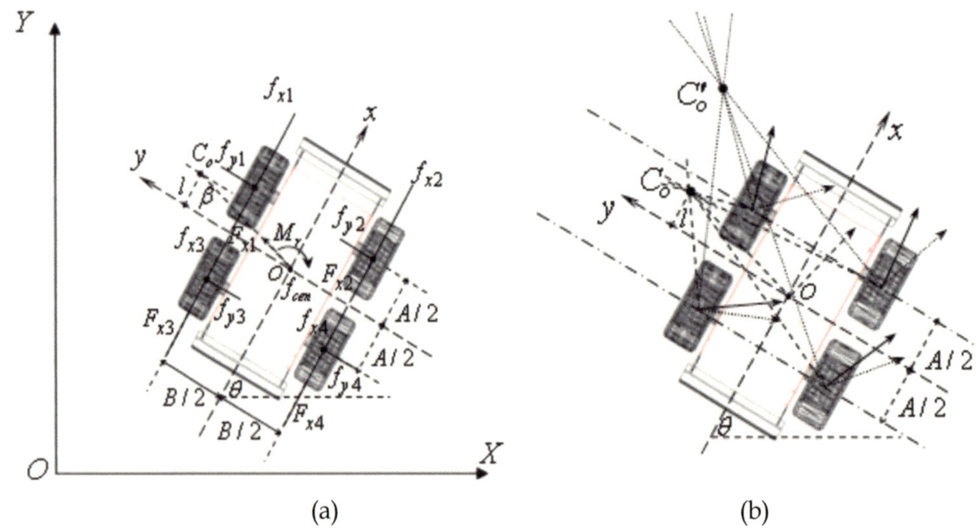

Fig. 1. Dynamics analysis of the robot and the motion constraint about C_o

In the above equations, $\dot{X}, \dot{Y}, \ddot{X}, \ddot{Y}$ represent the absolute longitudinal and lateral velocities, and the absolute longitudinal and lateral accelerations respectively; θ is the angle between x and X axes. $\dot{x}, \dot{y}, \dot{\theta}$ denote longitudinal, lateral and angular velocities in in-vehicle frame, respectively; a_x, a_y are the longitudinal and lateral acceleration respectively in in-vehicle frame. The equations of the robot motion are as follows:

$$\begin{cases} ma_x = \sum_{i=1}^{4} F_{xi} - \sum_{i=1}^{4} f_{xi} \\ ma_y = -\sum_{i=1}^{4} f_{yi} \\ J\ddot{\theta} = (B/2)((-F_{x1} - F_{x3}) + (F_{x2} + F_{x4})) - M_r \end{cases} \tag{3}$$

where J is the moment of inertia of the robot; F_{xi} denotes the tractive force produced by the i-th wheel, and composes the outside tractive force $F_{outside}$ and the inside F_{inside}; f_{xi} is the longitudinal resistance of the i-th wheel; f_{yi} is the lateral resistance of the i-th wheel; M_r is the resistive moment around the center of o.
During the turning, the robot is subject to the centripetal force f_{cen}, the equation of which is,

$$f_{cen} \cos\beta = f_{y3} + f_{y4} - f_{y1} - f_{y2} \tag{4}$$

Let μ_r and μ_s be the coefficient of longitudinal rolling resistance and the coefficient of lateral friction respectively. In (4), β is the angle between $\overrightarrow{C_o o}$ and y axis. Accordingly, when the centripetal acceleration is considered, assume $\beta \approx 0$, then the equation of the tractive force of the robot is,

$$\begin{cases} F_{outside} = (\frac{mg}{2} + \frac{hma_y}{B})\mu_r + \frac{ma_y x_{co}}{2R} + \frac{\mu_s mgA}{4B}\left[1 - \left(\frac{a_y}{g\mu_s}\right)^2\right] \\ F_{inside} = (\frac{mg}{2} - \frac{hma_y}{B})\mu_r + \frac{ma_y x_{co}}{2R} - \frac{\mu_s mgA}{4B}\left[1 - \left(\frac{a_y}{g\mu_s}\right)^2\right] \end{cases} \tag{5}$$

where h is the height of the robot center of mass, the distance between the robot center of mass and the ground, and R is the radius of the robot turning (J. Y. Wong, 1978).
In the context of the robot motion around instantaneous, fixed-axis rotation, the straight line motion of the robot can be referred to $R = \infty$. C_o is the instantaneous center of the rotation, and the coordinates of C_o can be expressed as

$$\begin{bmatrix} x_{C_O} & y_{C_O} \end{bmatrix}^T = \begin{bmatrix} \frac{-\dot{y}}{\dot{\theta}} & \frac{\dot{x}}{\dot{\theta}} \end{bmatrix}^T.$$

In Fig. 1 (b), the real line arrowheads represent the transfer orientations of the four wheels of the robot, that is C_o moves within the wheelbase range of the robot; the dashed arrowheads stand for the transfer orientations of the four wheels of the robot, when C_o, that is C_o', moves beyond the wheelbase range of the robot. Clearly, if C_o moves out of the wheelbase range, the lateral transfer orientations of four wheels are the same; as a result, the motion of the robot will be out of control. The motion constraint is as follows,

$$[-\sin\theta \quad \cos\theta \quad l]\begin{bmatrix}\dot{X}\\ \dot{Y}\\ \dot{\theta}\end{bmatrix}=0 \quad (|l|<A/2\ ) \tag{6}$$

where l is the distance from C_o to y axis. According to Fig. 1 (a) and equation (5), it is $l = Aa_y\cos\beta/2\mu_s g$ that can be obtained. Therefore, the constraint of the motion, shown as follow, is imperative.

$$(\dot{x})^2/R<\mu_s g \text{ or } (\dot{\theta})^2 R<\mu_s g \tag{7}$$

In this paper, a description of trajectory space (Matthew Spenko, 2006) is presented according to the robot's dynamic analysis, which is defined as the two-dimensional space of the robot's turning angular speed $\dot{\theta}$ and longitudinal velocity V_{long}, $(V_{long}=\dot{x})$. This kind of description is very useful during motion control. Consider inequalities (7): $(V_{long}(t))^2/R<\mu_s g$ or $(\dot{\theta}(t))^2 R<\mu_s g$, it is easy to get $|V_{long}(t)|<\sqrt{\mu_s gR}$ or $|\dot{\theta}(t)|<\sqrt{\mu_s g/R}$, then take another constraint into consideration, $V_{long}=\dot{\theta}R$, now a figure of the robot's $(V,\dot{\theta})$ space (see Fig. 2.) can be obtained. The boundary curve in the figure satisfies $V_{long}(t)\cdot\dot{\theta}(t)=\mu_s g$. When the robot's $(V,\dot{\theta})$ state is in the shadow region, that's to say $V_{long}(t)\cdot\dot{\theta}(t)<\mu_s g$, the robot is safe, which means the hazardous situation like side slippage won't occur. As a result, inequalities (7) is crucial for control decision making.

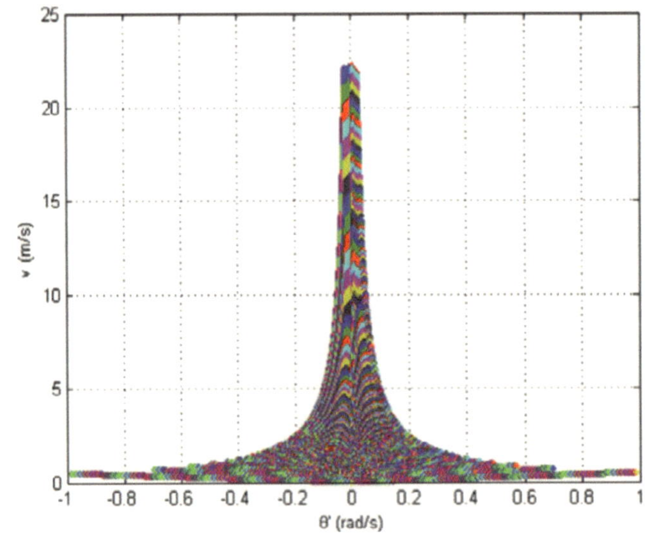

Fig. 2. The $(V,\dot{\theta})$ space of motion control of the robot. (In this figure, $\mu_s=0.49$ and $g=9.8m/s^2$)

3. Trajectory tracking control laws design

Autonomous mobile robot achieves outdoor navigation by three processes, including the environment information acquired by the perception module, the control decision made by the planner module, and the motion plan performed by the motion control module (Gianluca, 2007). Consequently, for safe and accurate outdoor navigation it is vital to harmonize the three modules performance. In this paper, the emphasis is focused on the decision of control laws of the robot, and these controlled objects include the longitudinal velocity, the lateral velocity, and the angles of sensor pan-tilts.

As shown in Fig. 3, in an off-road environment, the robot uses laser range finder (LRF) with one degree of freedom (DOF) pan-tilt (only tilt) to scan bumpy situation of the close front ground, on which the robot is moving, and employs stereo vision with two DOF pan-tilt to perceive drivable situation of far front ground. With the data accessed from laser and vision sensors, the passable path can be planned, and the velocities of left and right robot's sides can be controlled to track the path, consequently, the robot off-road running is completed.

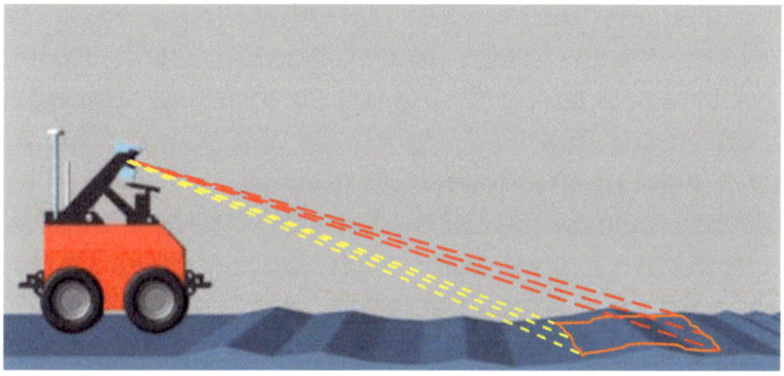

Fig. 3. Off-road driving of the robot

3.1 Longitudinal control law

In this section, a kind of humanoid driving longitudinal control law based on fuzzy logic is proposed. First, the effect factors to the longitudinal velocity are classified. As shown in Fig. 4,

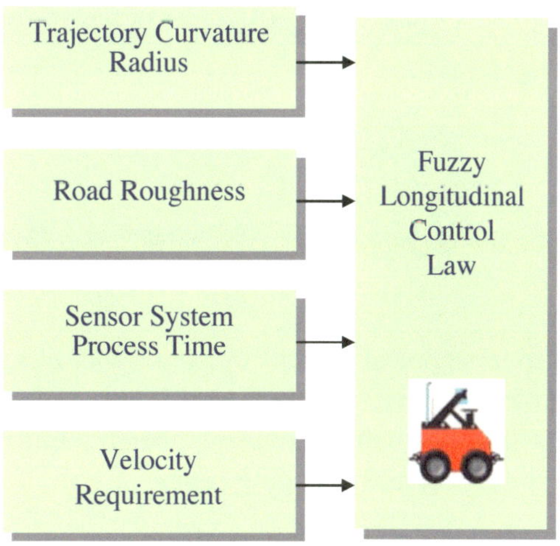

Fig. 4. The longitudinal control law of the robot

these factors include curvature radius of trajectory, road roughness, process time of sensors and speed requirement. Based on the four factors and the analysis of kinematics and dynamics, the longitudinal velocity equation can be given,

$$V_{long} = \left(\mu_{cv}(r_c) + \mu_{rr}(R_{rough})\right)\mu_t(T_{sen})\mu_v(V_{re})V_{re} \tag{8}$$

where V_{long} is longitude velocity command, μ_{cv}, μ_{rr}, μ_t and μ_v are the weight factors of the curvature radius of trajectory r_c, road roughness R_{rough}, processing time of sensors T_{sen} and speed requirement V_{re} respectively. The weight factors can vary within $[0,1]$.

3.2 Lateral control law

Autonomous vehicle off-road driving is a special control problem because mathematical models are highly complex and can't be accurately linearized. Fuzzy logic control, however, is robust and efficient for non-linear system control (Gao Feng, 2009), and a well-tested method for dealing with this kind of system, provides good results, and can incorporate human procedural knowledge into control algorithms. Also, fuzzy logic lets us mimic human driving behavior to some extent (José E. Naranjo, 2007). Therefore, the paper has presented a kind of novel fuzzy lateral control law for the robot off-road running.
Thereafter, the lateral control law is designed for the purpose of position tracking by adjusting navigation orientation to reduce position error.
Definition: When the robot moves toward the trajectory, the orientation angle of the robot is positive, whichever of the two regions, namely left error region and right error region of the tracking position, the robot is in. When the robot moves against the trajectory, the angle is negative. When the robot motion is parallel to the trajectory, the angle is zero.

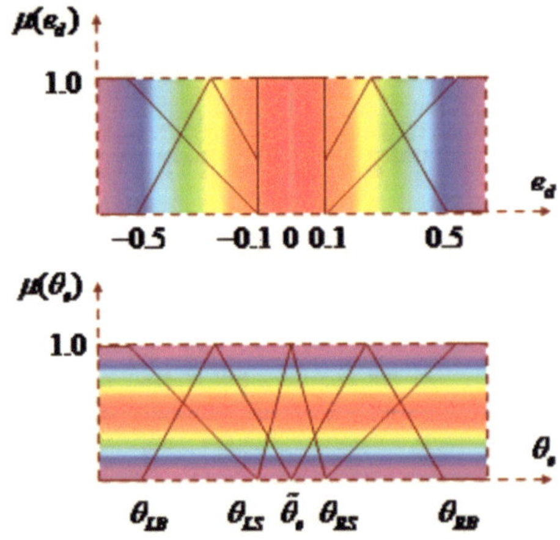

Fig. 5. Plots of membership functions of e_d and θ_e. The upper plot stands for $\mu(e_d)$. $[-0.1,0.1]$ is the range of the *center* region, $\mu(e_d) = 1.0$ in this region. The lower plot expresses $\mu(\theta_e)$, which is indicated with triangle membership function. In this figure, the colorful bands represent the continuous changing course of e_d.

In the course of trajectory tracking of the robot, **position error** e_d and **orientation error** θ_e, which are the error values between the robot and the trajectory, are the inputs of the lateral controller. First, the error inputs, including the position error and the orientation error, are pre-processed to improve steady precision of the trajectory tracking, and restrain oscillation of that. The error E can be written as $E = \overline{E} + \Delta E$, where $\overline{E}$ is the result of smoothing filter about E, i.e.

$$\overline{E} = \sum_{i-n+1}^{i} e_i \Big/ n\,;$$

ΔE forecasts the error produced in the next system sample time,

$$\Delta E = \sum_{i-n+1}^{i} k_{ei} e_i \Big/ n \ (i > n)\,.$$

As a result,

$$E = \sum_{i-n+1}^{i} (1+k_{ei}) e_i \Big/ n \ \ (i > n)\,,\ n = 4\,,\ k_{ei} = f_{ei}(\dot{x}, T_s)\,,$$

T_s represents system sample time. Second, the error inputs, after being pre-processed, are fuzzyfication-processed. As shown in Fig. 5, degree of membership $\mu(e_d)$ and $\mu(\theta_e)$ are indicated in terms of triangle and rectangle membership functions:
Part One: the space of e_d is divided into LB, LS, MC, RS, RB. According to the result of the e_d division, the phenotype rules of the lateral fuzzy control law hold.
Part Two: the space of θ_e is also divided into LB, LS, MC, RS, RB. According to the result of the θ_e division, the recessive rules of the control law are obtained.
It is necessary to explain that the phenotype rules are the basis of the recessive rules, namely each phenotype rule possesses a group of relevant recessive rules. Each phenotype rule has already established their own expectation orientation angle $\tilde{\theta}_e$, that is to say the robot is expected to run on this orientation angle, $\tilde{\theta}_e$, and this angle is the very center angle of this group recessive rules. When the center angle, $\tilde{\theta}_e$, of each group of recessive rules is varying, the division of θ_e of each group recessive rules changes accordingly.
All of the control rules can be expressed as continuous functions: f_{LB}, f_{LS}, f_{MC}, f_{RS}, f_{RB}, and, consequently, the global continuity of the control rules is established.
The functions, f_{LB}, f_{LS}, f_{RS}, f_{RB}, which express the rule functions of the $non-center$ region of e_d, are as follows:

$$\dot{\theta} = \frac{k_{\tilde{\theta}_e} k_t (\tilde{\theta}_e - \theta_e)}{T_s} + k_t \dot{\tilde{\theta}}_{tr} \tag{9}$$

In (9), $\tilde{\theta}_e$ is the expectation tracking-angle in the current position-error region, and $\tilde{\theta}_e$ is monotonically increasing with e_d. $\tilde{\theta}_e$ can be given by this formula

$$\tilde{\theta}_e = \arctan\frac{k_{e_d} e_d}{V_{long}}\,,\ k_{e_d} = \mu_{DL}(e_d) k_{DL} + \mu_{DS}(e_d) k_{DS}\,,$$

where μ_{DL} stands for the large error region, including LB and RB, membership degree of e_d, and μ_{DS} represents the small error region, including LS and RS, membership degree of e_d. $\dot{\theta}_{tr}$ is the estimation of the trajectory-angle rate. $k_{\tilde{\theta}_e}$ can be worked out by this equation:

$$k_{\tilde{\theta}_e} = \mu_{\theta L}(\theta_e)k_{\theta L} + \mu_{\theta S}(\theta_e)k_{\theta S},$$

where $\mu_{\theta L}$ stands for the large error region, including LB and RB, membership degree of θ_e, and $\mu_{\theta S}$ denotes the small error region, including LS and RS, membership degree of θ_e. k_{DL} and $k_{\theta L}$ express the standard coefficients of the large error region of e_d and θ_e; k_{DS} and $k_{\theta S}$ indicate the small error region of e_d and θ_e, respectively. k_t is the proportional coefficients of the system sample time T_S.
f_{MC} is deduced as follows:

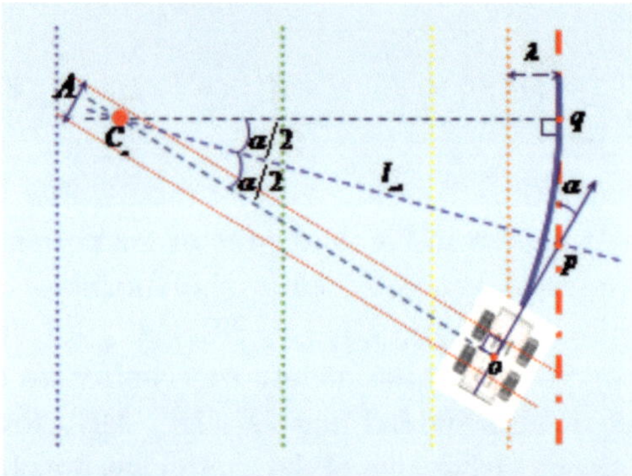

Fig. 6. Tracking trajectory of the robot. In this Figure, the red dashdotted line stands for the trajectory tracked by the robot. The different color dotted lines represent the bounderies of the different error regions of e_d.

When the robot moves into the *center* region at the orientation of α, the motion state of the robot can be divided into two kinds of situations.
Situation One: Assume that α has decreased into the rule admission angular range of *center* region, i.e. $0 \le \alpha \le \theta_{cent}$, where θ_{cent}, which is subject to (7), is the critical angle of *center* region. To make the robot approach the trajectory smoothly, the planner module requires the robot to move along a certain circle path. As the robot moves along the circle path in Fig. 6, the values of e_d and θ_e decrease synchronously. In Fig. 6, λ is the variety range of e_d in the *center* region. α is the angle between the orientation of the robot and the trajectory when the robot just enters the *center* region. $R \approx 2\lambda/\alpha^2$ can be worked out by geometry, and in addition, the value of α is very small, so the process of approaching trajectory can be represented as

$$\Delta\alpha = \alpha\frac{\Delta\lambda}{\lambda}.$$

Situation Two: When $\alpha < 0$ or $\alpha > \theta_{cent}$. If the motion decision from the planner module were the same as Situation One, the motion will not meet (7). According to the above

analysis, the error of tracking can not converge until the adjusted $\tilde{\theta}_e$ makes α be true of Situation One. Therefore, the purpose of control in Situation Two is to decrease θ_e.
Based on the above deduction, f_{MC} is as follow:

$$\dot{\theta} = \frac{k_t(\tilde{\theta}_e - \theta_e)}{T_s} + k_t\dot{\tilde{\theta}}_{tr} \tag{10}$$

Where

$$\tilde{\theta}_e = \frac{e_d \theta_{cent}}{\lambda},$$

λ is the variety range of e_d in the *center* region, $[-0.1m,0]or[0,0.1m]$. $\dot{\theta}$ is the output of (9) and (10), at the same time, $\dot{\theta}$ is subject to (7), consequently, $(\dot{\theta})^2 R < \mu_s g$ is required by the control rules.
The execution sequence of the control rules is as follows:
First, the phenotype control rules are enabled, namely to estimate which error region (LB, LS, MC, RS, RB) the current e_d of the robot belongs to, and to enable the relevant recessive rules; Second, the relevant recessive rules are executed, at the same time, $\tilde{\theta}_e$ is established in time.
The lateral control law is exemplified in Fig. 7. In this figure, the different color concentric circle bands represent the different position error e_d. From the outermost circle band to the

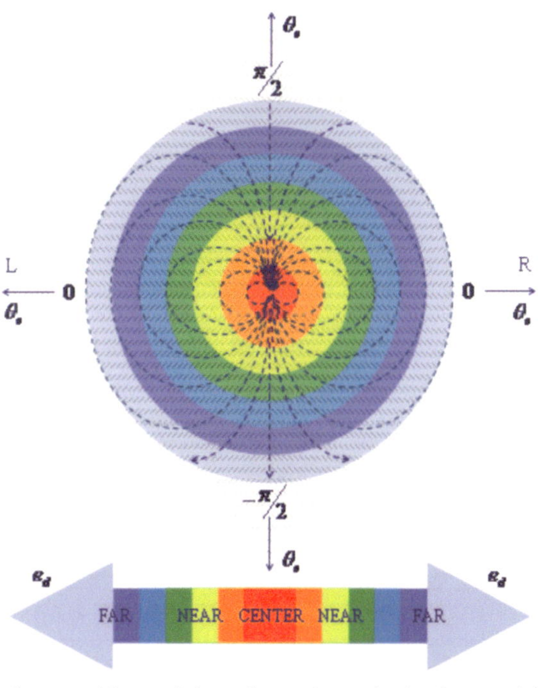

Fig. 7. Plot of the lateral control law of the robot. These dasheds stand for the parts of the performance result of the control law.

center round, the values of e_d is decreasing. The red center round stands for MC of e_d, that is the *center* region of e_d. At the center point of the red round, $e_d = 0$. According to the above definition, the orientation range of the robot is $(-\pi, \pi]$, and the two 0 degree axes of θ_e stand for the 0 degree orientation of the left and right region of the trajectory, respectively. At the same time, $\pi/2$ axis and $-\pi/2$ axis of θ_e are two common axes of the orientation of the robot in the left and right region of the trajectory. In the upper sub-region of 0 degree axes, the orientation of the robot is toward the trajectory, and in the lower sub-region, the orientation of the robot is opposite to the trajectory. The result of the control rules converges to the center of the concentric circle bands according to the direction of the arrowheads in Fig. 7. Based on the analysis of the figure, the global asymptotic stability of the lateral control law can be established, and if $e_d = 0$ and $\theta_e = 0$, the robot reaches the only equilibrium zero. The proving process is shown as follow:

Proof: From the kinematic model (see Fig. 8.), it can be seen that the position error of the robot e_d satisfies the following equation,

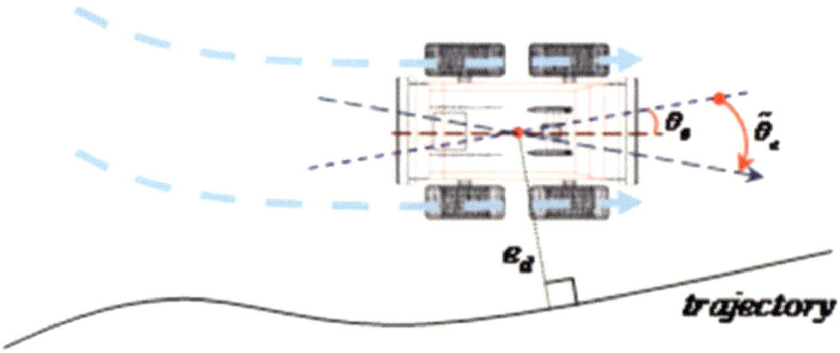

Fig. 8. Trajectory Tracking of the mobile robot

$$\dot{e}_d(t) = -V_{long}(t)\sin(\tilde{\theta}_e(t)) \tag{11}$$

a. When the robot is in the *non – center* region, a controller is designed to control the robot's lateral movement:

$$\tilde{\theta}_e(t) = \arctan\frac{k_{e_d} e_d(t)}{V_{long}(t)} \tag{12}$$

Combining Equations (11) and (12), we get

$$\dot{e}_d(t) = -V_{long}(t)\sin(\arctan(\tilde{\theta}_e(t))) = \frac{-k_{e_d} e_d(t)}{\sqrt{1+\left(\dfrac{k_{e_d} e_d(t)}{V_{long}(t)}\right)^2}} \tag{13}$$

Fig. 9. LRF Pan-Tilt and Stereo Viszion Pan-Tilt motion

As the sign of $\dot{e}_d$ is always opposite that of e_d, e_d will converge to 0. In equation (11), $|\dot{e}_d(t)| \approx V_{long}(t)$, and $|\dot{e}_d(t)| \approx k_{e_d} e_d(t)$ can formed by equation (13). Therefore the convergence rate of e_d is between linear and exponential. When the robot is far away from the trajectory, it's heading for trajectory vertically, then

$$\tilde{\theta}_e = \frac{\pi}{2},\ \dot{e}_d(t) = -V_{long}(t),\ e_d(t) = -V_{long}(t) + e_d(t_0);$$

when the robot is near the trajectory, $e_d \approx 0$, then in equation (12),

$$\sqrt{1+\left(\frac{k_{e_d} e_d(t)}{V_{long}(t)}\right)^2} \approx 1,\ \dot{e}_d(t) = -k_{e_d} e_d(t).$$

According to equation (12), e_d and $\tilde{\theta}_e$ can converge to 0 simultaneously.

b. When the robot enters the *center* region, another controller is designed,

$$\tilde{\theta}_e(t) = \frac{e_d(t)\theta_{cent}}{\lambda} \tag{14}$$

Combining Equations (11) and (14), we get

$$\dot{e}_d = -V_{long} \sin\left(\frac{e_d \theta_{cent}}{\lambda}\right).$$

In this region, e_d is very small, and consequently, $\frac{e_d\theta_{cent}}{\lambda}$ will also be very small, and then

$$\sin(\frac{e_d\theta_{cent}}{\lambda}) \approx \frac{e_d\theta_{cent}}{\lambda}$$

is derived. Therefore,

$$\dot{e}_d = -V_{long}\frac{e_d\theta_{cent}}{\lambda} = -\frac{V_{long}\theta_{cent}}{\lambda}e_d \text{, and then } e_d(t) = e_d(t_1)\exp\{-\frac{V_{long}\theta_{cent}}{\lambda}\},$$

where t_1 is the time when the robot enters the *center* region. In other word, e_d converges to 0 exponentially. Then, according to

$$\tilde{\theta}_e(t) = \frac{e_d\theta_{cent}}{\lambda}, \ \tilde{\theta}_e(t) \text{ converges to } 0.$$

So the origin is the only equilibrium in the $(e_d, \tilde{\theta}_e)$ phase space.

3.3 LRF Pan-tilt and stereo vision pan-tilt control

Perception is the key to high-speed off-road driving. A vehicle needs to have maximum data coverage on regions in its trajectory, but must also sense these regions in time to react to obstacles in its path. In off-road conditions, the vehicle is not guaranteed a traversable path through the environment, thus better sensor coverage provides improved safety when traveling. Therefore, it is important for off-road driving to apply active sensing technology. In the chapter, the angular control of the sensor pan-tilts assisted in achieving the active sensing of the robot. Equation (15) represents the relation between the angles measured, i.e. φ_c, γ_c and γ_l, of the sensors mounted on the robot and the motion state, i.e. θ_e and $\dot{x}$, of the robot.

$$\begin{bmatrix} \varphi_c \\ \gamma_c \\ \gamma_l \end{bmatrix} = \begin{bmatrix} k_{\varphi c} & 0 & 0 \\ 0 & k_{\gamma c} & 0 \\ 0 & 0 & k_{\gamma c} \end{bmatrix} \begin{bmatrix} \theta_e \\ \dot{x} \\ \dot{x} \end{bmatrix} \quad (15)$$

In (15), φ_c, γ_c are the pan angle and tilt angle of the stereo vision respectively. γ_l is the tilt angle of the LRF; $k_{\varphi c}$, $k_{\gamma c}$ and $k_{\gamma l}$ are the experimental coefficients between the angles measured and the motion state, and they are given by practical experiments of the sensors and connected with the measurement range requirement of off-road driving. At the same time, the coordinates of the scanning center are $x_{ec} = x_c + h_c \cot\gamma_c \cos\varphi_c$, $y_{ec} = y_c + h_c \cot\gamma_c \sin\varphi_c$; and $x_{el} = x_l + h_l \cot\gamma_l$, $y_{el} = 0$. In the above equations, x_c, y_c, x_l, y_l, respectively, are the coordinates of the sense center points of the stereo vision and LRF in in-vehicle frame. As shown in Fig. 9, h_c and h_l are their height value, to the ground, accordingly.

The angular control and the longitudinal control are achieved by *PI* controllers, and they are the same as the reference (Gabriel, 2007).

4. Simulation tests

4.1 Simulation platform build

In this section, ADAMS and MATLAB co-simulation platform is built up. In the course of co-simulation, the platform can harmonize the control system and simulation machine system, provide the $3D$ performance result, and record the experimental data. Based on the analysis of the simulation result, the design of experiments in real world can become more reasonable and safer.

First, based on the character data of the test agent, ATRV2, such as the geometrical dimensions $(HLW65 \times 105 \times 80cm)$, the mass value $(118Kg)$, the diameter of the tire $(\Phi 38cm)$ and so on, the simulated robot vehicle model is accomplished, as shown in Fig.10.

Fig. 10. ATRV2 and its model in ADAMS

Second, according to the test data of the tires of ATRV2, the attribute of the tires and the connection character between the tires and the ground are set. The ADAMS sensor interface module can be used to define the motion state sensors parameters, which can provide the information of position and orientation to ATRV2.

It is road roughness that affects the dynamic performance of vehicles, the state of driving and the dynamic load of road. Therefore, the abilities of overcoming the stochastic road roughness of vehicles are the key to test the performance of the control law during off-road driving. In the paper, the simulation terrain model is built up by Gaussian-distributed pseudo random number sequence and power spectral density function (Ren, 2005). The details are described as follows:

a. Gaussian-distributed random number sequence $x(t)$, whose variance $\sigma = 18$ and mean $E = 2.5$, is yielded;
b. The power spectral $S_X(f)$ of $x(t)$ is worked out by Fourier transform of $R_X(\tau)$, which is the autocorrelation function of σ,

$$\begin{aligned} S_X(f) &= \int_{-\infty}^{+\infty} R_X(\tau) e^{-j2\pi f\tau} d\tau \\ &= T\sigma^2 \left(\frac{\sin \pi fT}{\pi fT} \right)^2 \end{aligned} \tag{16}$$

where T is the time interval of the pseudo random number sequence;

c. Assume the following,

$$y(t) = x(t) * h(t) = \int_{-\infty}^{+\infty} x(\tau)h(t-\tau)d\tau \tag{17}$$

$$h(t) = \int_{-\infty}^{+\infty} H(f)e^{j2\pi ft}df \tag{18}$$

where $h(t)$ is educed by inverse Fourier transform from $H(f)$, and they both are real even functions, then,

$$H(f) = \sqrt{\frac{S_Y(f)}{S_X(f)}} \tag{19}$$

$$\begin{aligned} y_k &= y(kT) \\ &= T\sum_{-M}^{+M} x(rT)h(kT - rT) = T\sum_{-M}^{+M} x_r h_{k-r} \end{aligned} \tag{20}$$

where $S_Y(f)$ is the power spectral of $y(t)$, y_k is the pseudo random sequence of $S_Y(f)$, $k = 0,1,2\ldots,N$, and M can be established by the equation $\lim_{m \to M} h_m = h(MT) = 0$;

d. Assign a certain value to the road roughness and adjust the parameters of the special points on the road according to the test design, and the simulation test ground is shown in Fig. 11.

Fig. 11. The simulation test ground in ADAMS

4.2 Simulation tests

In this section, the control law is validated with the ADAMS&MATLAB co-simulation platform.

Based on the position-orientation information provided by the simulation sensors and the control law, the lateral, longitudinal motion of the robot and the sensors pan-tilts motion are achieved. The test is designed to make the robot track two different kinds of trajectories, including the straight line path, sinusoidal path and circle path. In Test One, the tracking trajectory consists of the straight line path and sinusoidal path, in which the wavelength of the sinusoidal path is $5\pi m$, the amplitude is $3m$. The simulation result of Test One is shown in Fig. 12. In Test Two, the tracking trajectory contains the straight line path and circle path, in which the radius of the circle path is $5m$. The simulation result of Test Two is shown in Fig. 13.

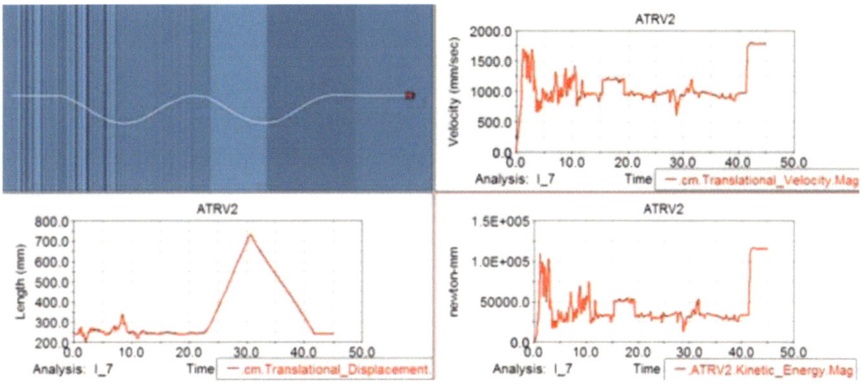

(a)

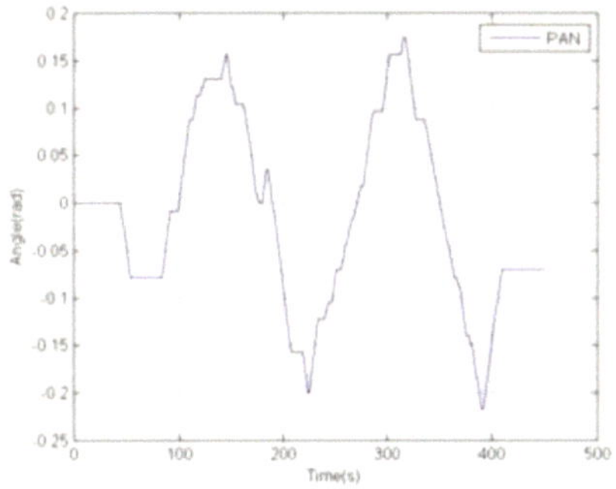

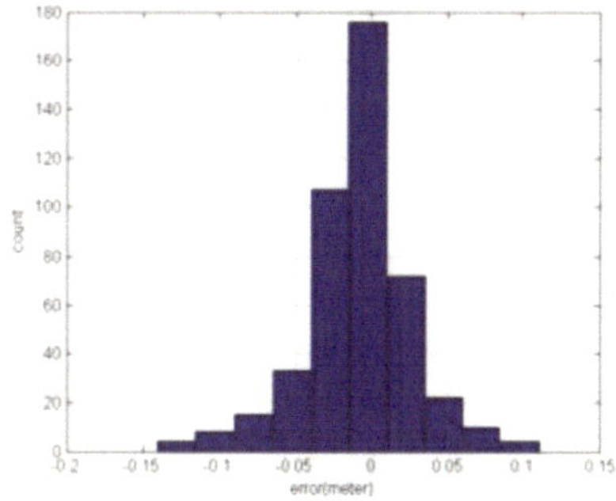

(b) (c)

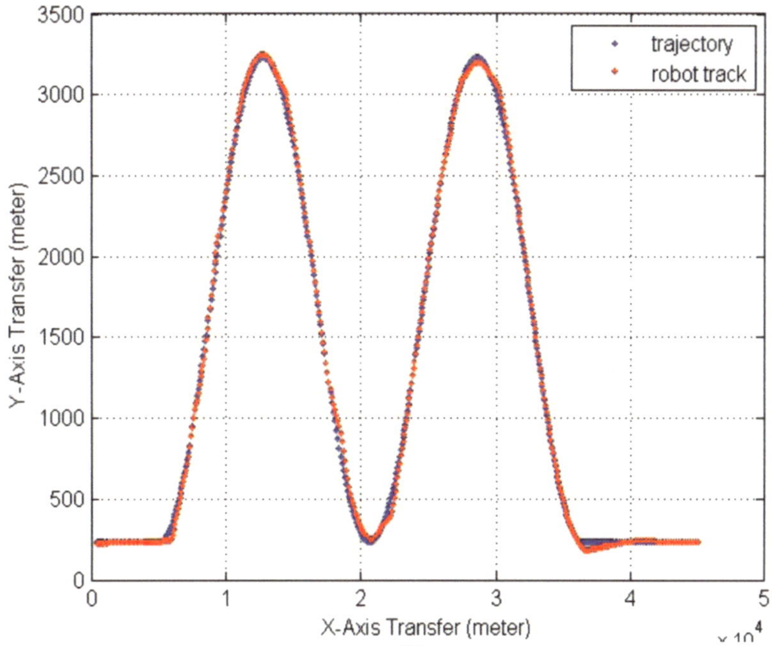

(d)

Fig. 12. Plots of the result of Test One $(T_s = 0.05s)$

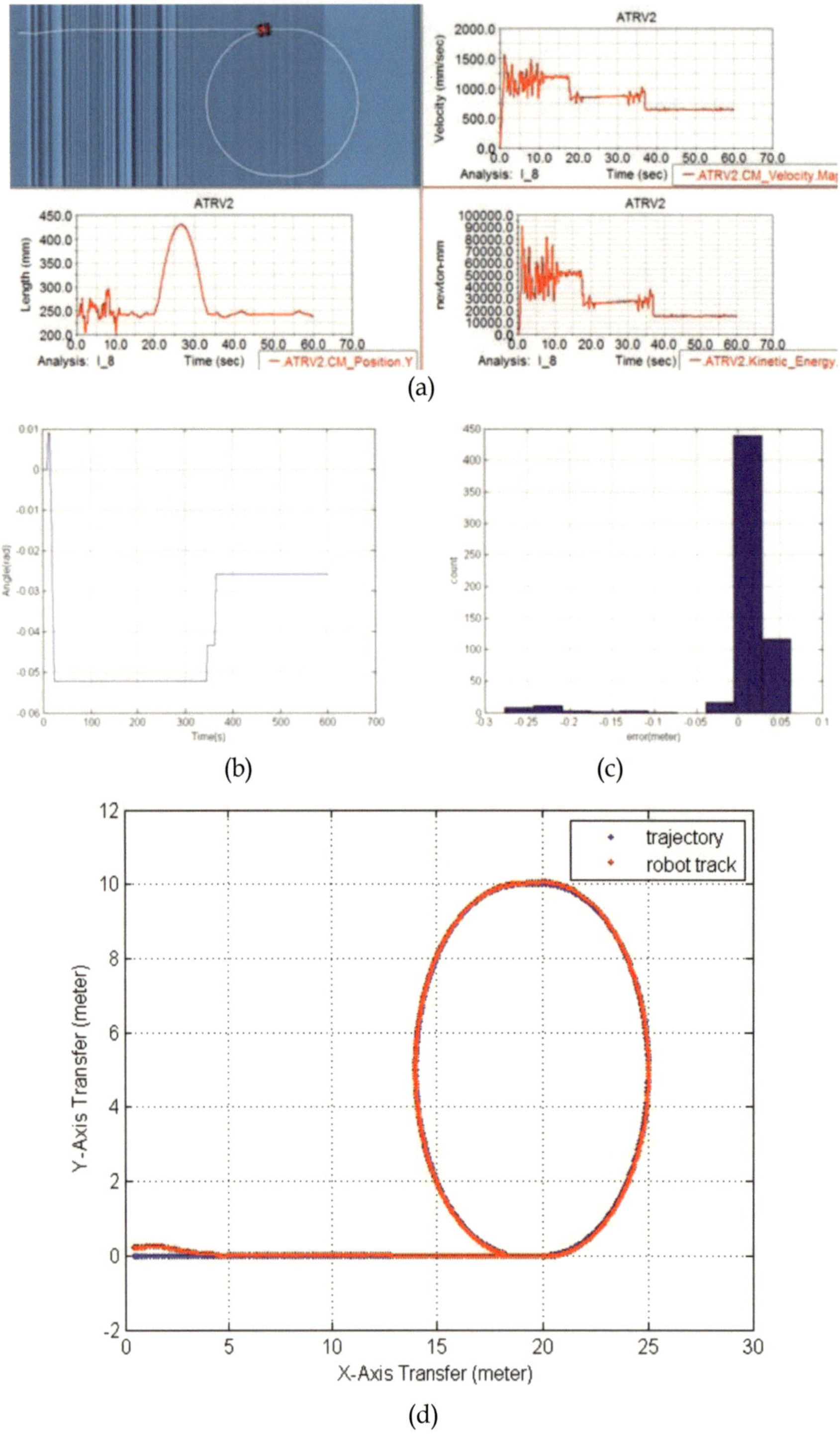

Fig. 13. Plots of the result of Test Two ($T_s = 0.05s$)

In Fig. 12, which is the same as Fig. 13, sub-figure **a** is the simulation data recorded by ADAMS. In sub-figure **a**, the upper-left part is the *3D* animation figure of the robot off-road driving on the simulation platform, in which the white path shows the motion trajectory of the robot. The upper-right part is the velocity magnitude figure of the robot. It is indicated that the velocity of the robot is adjusted according to the longitudinal control law. In addition, it is clear that the longitudinal control law, whose changes are mainly due to the curvature radius of the path and the road roughness, can assist the lateral control law to track the trajectory more accurately. In Test One, the average velocity approximately is $1.2m/s$, and in Test Two, the average velocity approximately is $1.0m/s$. The bottom-left part presents the height of the robot's mass center during the robot's tracking; in the figure, the road roughness can be implied. The bottom-right part shows that the kinetic energy magnitude is required by the robot motion in the course of tracking. In Sub-figure **b**, the angle data of the stereo vision pan rotation is indicated. The pan rotation angle varies according to the trajectory. Sub-figure **c** is the error statistic figure of trajectory tracking. As is shown, the error values almost converge to 0. The factors, which produce these errors, include the roughness and the curvature variation of the trajectory. In Fig. 13 (**d**), the biggest error is yielded at the start point due to the start error between the start point and the trajectory. Sub-figure **d** is the trajectory tracking figure, which contains the objective trajectory and real tracking trajectory. It is obvious that the robot is able to recover from large disturbances, without intervention, and accomplish the tracking accurately.

5. Conclusions

The ADAMS&MATLAB co-simulation platform facilitates control method design, and dynamics modeling and analysis of the robot on the rough terrain. According to the practical requirement, the various terrain roughness and obstacles can be configured with modifying the relevant parameters of the simulation platform. In the simulation environment, the extensive experiments of control methods of rough terrain trajectory tracking of mobile robot can be achieved. The experiment results indicate that the control methods are robust and effective for the mobile robot running on the rough terrain. In addition, the simulation platform makes the experiment results more vivid and credible.

6. References

D. Lhomme-Desages, Ch. Grand, J-C. Guinot, "Model-based Control of a fast Rover over natural Terrain," Published in the Proceedings of CLAWAR'06: Int. Conf. on Climbing and Walking Robots, Sept 2006.

Edward Tunstel, Ayanna Howard, Homayoun Seraji, "Fuzzy Rule-Based Reasoning for Rover Safety and Survivability," Proceedings of the 2001 IEEE International Conference on Robotics & Automation, pp. 1413-1420, Seoul, Korea • May 21-26, 2001.

Gabriel M. Hoffmann, Claire J. Tomlin, Michael Montemerlo, and Sebastian Thrun (2007). Autonomous Automobile Trajectory Tracking for Off-Road Driving: Controller Design, Experimental Validation and Racing. *Proceedings of the 2007 American Control Conference*, 2296-2301. New York City, USA.

Gao Feng, "A Survey on Analysis and Design of Model-Based Fuzzy Control Systems," IEEE Transactions on Fuzzy Systems, Vol. 14, No. 5, pp. 676-697, 2006.

Gianluca Antonell, Stefano Chiaverini, and Giuseppe Fusco. "A Fuzzy-Logic-Based Approach for Mobile Robot Path Tracking," IEEE Transactions on Fuzzy Systems, Vol. 15, No. 2, pp. 211-221, 2007.

José E. Naranjo, Carlos González, Ricardo García, and Teresa de Pedro, "Using Fuzzy Logic in Automated Vehicle Control. IEEE Intelligent Systems," Vol. 22, No. 1, pp. 36-45, 2007.

J.T. Economou, R.E. Colyer, "Modelling of Skid Steering and Fuzzy Logic Vehicle Ground Interaction," Proceedings of the American Control Conference, pp. 100-104, Chicago, Illinois June 2000.

J. Y. Wong, "Theory of Ground Vehicles," John Wiley and Sons, New York, USA, 1978.

Luca Caracciolo, Alessandro De Luca, and Stefano Iannitti, "Trajectory Tracking Control of a Four-Wheel Differentially Driven Mobile Robot," Proceedings of the 1999 IEEE International Conference on Robotics & Automation, pp. 2632-2638. Detroit, Michigan, USA.

Matthew Spenko, Yoji Kuroda,Steven Dubowsky, and Karl Iagnemma, "Hazard avoidance for High-Speed Mobile Robots in Rough Terrain", Journal of Field Robotics, Vol. 23, No. 5, pp. 311–331, 2006.

Ren Weiqun. Virtual Prototype in Vehicle-Road Dynamics System, Chapter Four. Publishing House of Electronics Industry, Beijing, China.

18

A Virtual Tool for Computer Aided Analysis of Spur Gears with Asymmetric Teeth

Fatih Karpat[1], Stephen Ekwaro-Osire[2] and Esin Karpat[1]
[1]*Department of Mechanical Engineering, Uludag University, Bursa,*
[2]*Department of Mechanical Engineering, Texas Tech University, Lubbock,*
[1]*Turkey*
[2]*USA*

1. Introduction

1.1 Background

There is an industrial demand in the increased performance of mechanical power transmission devices. This need in high performance is driven by high load capacity, high endurance, low cost, long life, and high speed. For gears, this has lead to development of new designs, such as gears with asymmetric teeth. The geometry of these teeth is such that the drive side profile is not symmetric to the coast side profile. This type of geometry is beneficial for special applications where the loading of the gear is uni-directional. In such an instance, the loading on the gear tooth is not symmetric, thus calling for asymmetric teeth. Since one of the situations that demand high performance is the high rotational speeds, there is a need to understand the dynamic behavior of the gears with asymmetric teeth at such speeds. Such knowledge would shed light on detrimental characteristics like dynamic loads and vibrations. An efficient way in performing studies on the dynamic behavior of gears is using computer aided analysis on numerical models.

A number of studies on the design and stress analysis of asymmetric gears are available in literature. A large number of studies have been performed over the last two decades to assess whether asymmetric gears are an alternative to conventional gears in applications requiring high performance. In these studies, some standards (i.e., ISO 6336, DIN 3990), analytical methods (i.e., the Direct Gear Design method, the tooth contact analysis), and numerical methods (e.g., Finite element method) have been used to compare the performance of conventional and asymmetric gears under the same conditions (Cavdar et al., 2005; Kapelevich, 2000, Karpat, 2005; Karpat et al., 2005; Karpat & Ekwaro-Osire, 2008; Karpat et al., 2008; Karpat & Ekwaro-Osire, 2010). In the last ten years, the researches conducted in the area of gears with asymmetric teeth point to the potential impact of asymmetric gears on improving the reliability and performance requirements of gearboxes. The benefits of asymmetric gears which have been offered by researchers are: higher load capacity, reduced bending and contact stress, lower weight, lower dynamic loads, reduced wear depths on tooth flank, higher reliability, and higher efficiency. Each of the benefits can be obtained due to asymmetric teeth designed correctly by designers.

1.2 Dynamic analysis of involute spur gears with symmetric teeth

Gear dynamics has been a subject of intense interest to the gearing area during the last few decades. The dynamic response of a gear transmission system is becoming essential due to increased requirements for high speed, low vibration and heavy load in gear design. However, the numerous design parameters, manufacturing and assembly errors, tooth modifications, etc. make difficult to understand gear dynamic response. The dynamic load reducing in a gear pair may decrease noise, increase efficiency, improve pitting fatigue life, and prevent gear tooth failures. Thus far, many researchers have conducted theoretical and experimental studies on gear dynamics. Most of literature on mathematical models used to predict the gear dynamics have been reviewed by (Ozguven & Houser, 1988; Parey & Tandon, 2003). In these reviews, the theoretical studies use a numerical method which included the excitation terms due to errors and periodic variation of the mesh stiffness. This method was used by many researchers to calculate the dynamic contact load or the torsional response, depending on different gear parameters, i.e., tooth errors, addendum modification, mesh stiffness, lubrication, damping factor, gear contact factor, and friction coefficient.

In dynamic analysis of gears, the dynamic factor and static transmission are the two most important definitions. The dynamic factor is defined as the ratio of the maximum dynamic load to the maximum static load on the gear tooth. Dynamic loads of gears with low contact ratio (between 1 and 2) are affected by several parameters, namely: time-varying mesh stiffness, tooth profile error, contact ratio, friction, and sliding. Static transmission errors, which are defined as the difference between the position of an actual gear tooth and that of an idealized gear tooth, and dynamic loads, affect the gear vibrations, acoustic emissions, tooth fatigue, and surface failure. The static transmission errors change in a periodic manner, due to the variation of gear mesh stiffness during contact. This is the source of vibratory excitation in gear dynamics. The static transmission error has basic periodicities related to the shaft rotational frequencies and the gear mesh frequency. The mesh frequency and its first harmonics are the predominant contributors to the generation of noise. The Fast Fourier Transform (FFT) can be used to perform the frequency analysis of static transmission error.

1.3 Motivation and objectives

Involute spur gears with asymmetric teeth provide flexibility to designers for different application areas due to non-standard design. If they are correctly designed, they can make important contributions to the improvement of designs in aerospace industry, automobile industry, and wind turbine industry. This often relates to improving the performance, increasing the load capacity, reduction of acoustic emission, and reduction of vibration. In the past, most of the analysis of gears with asymmetric teeth has been limited to cases under static loading.

Dynamic loads and vibration are a major concern for gears running at high speeds. Therefore, dynamic behavior should be analyzed to determine the feasibility of asymmetric gears in different applications. In order to utilize asymmetric gear designs more effectively, it is imperative to perform analyses of these gears under dynamic loading. This study offers designers preliminary results for understanding the response of asymmetric gears under dynamic loading. The effect of some design parameters, such as pressure angle or tooth height on dynamic loads, is shown. The asymmetric gears considered will have a larger pressure angle on the drive side compared to the coast side. In this study, to investigate the response of asymmetric gears under dynamic loading, the dynamic loads and static transmission errors were used. The first objective of this chapter is to use dynamic analysis

to compare conventional spur gears with symmetric teeth and spur gears with asymmetric teeth. The second objective is to develop a MATLAB-based virtual tool to analyze dynamic behavior of spur gears with asymmetric teeth. For this purpose a MATLAB based virtual tool called DYNAMIC is developed.
The first part of the study is focused on assymetric gear modelling. The second part focuses on the virtual tool parameters. In the third and the last part, the simulation results are given for different asymmetric gear parameters.

2. Dynamic model for involute spur gears with asymmetric teeth

There is an essential need to find the equations of motion for a gear tooth pair during a mesh to determine the variation of dynamic load with the contact position. A single-degree-of-freedom model of the gear system consists of a gear and a pinion shown in Fig. 1. The equations of motion can be expressed as follows:

$$J_g\ddot{\theta}_g = r_{bg}(F_I + F_{II}) \pm \rho_{gI}\,\mu_I F_I \pm \rho_{gII}\,\mu_{II} F_{II} - r_{bg} F_D \tag{1}$$

$$J_p\ddot{\theta}_p = r_{bp}F_D - r_{bp}(F_I + F_{II}) \pm \rho_{pI}\,\mu_I\,F_I \pm \rho_{pII}\,\mu_{II} F_{II} \tag{2}$$

where J_p and J_g represent the polar mass moments of inertia of the pinion and gear, respectively. The dynamic contact loads are F_I and F_{II}, while μ_I and μ_{II} are the instantaneous coefficients of friction at the contact points. θ_p and θ_g represent the angular displacements of pinion and gear. The radii of the base circles of the engaged gear pair are r_{bp} and r_{bg}, while the radii of curvature at the mating points are $\rho_{p\,I,II}$ and $\rho_{g\,I,II}$.

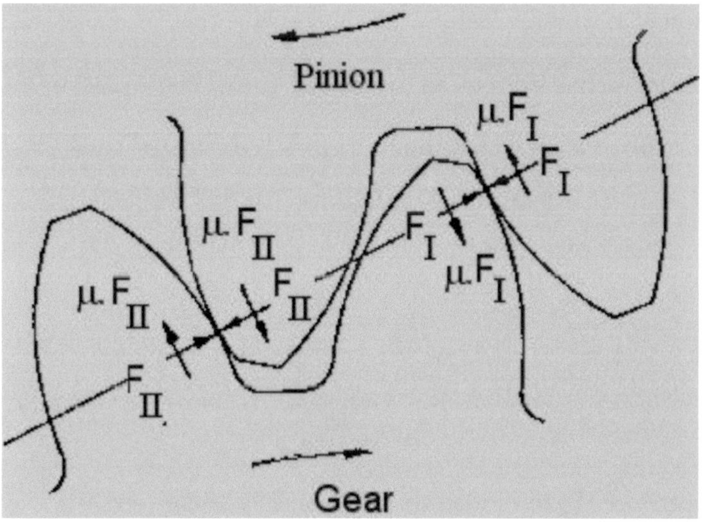

Fig. 1. The free body diagram of an engaging teeth pairs

The static tooth load is defined as:

$$F_D = \frac{T_p}{r_{bp}} = \frac{T_g}{r_{bg}} \tag{3}$$

The relative displacement, velocity, and acceleration can be writtehn as follows:

$$x_{\mathrm{r}} = y_{\mathrm{p}} - y_{\mathrm{g}} \tag{4}$$

$$\dot{x}_{\mathrm{r}} = \dot{y}_{\mathrm{p}} - \dot{y}_{\mathrm{g}} \tag{5}$$

$$\ddot{x}_{\mathrm{r}} = \ddot{y}_{\mathrm{p}} - \ddot{y}_{\mathrm{g}} \tag{6}$$

The effective gear masses are:

$$M_{\mathrm{p}} = \frac{J_{\mathrm{p}}}{r_{\mathrm{bp}}^2} \tag{7}$$

$$M_{\mathrm{g}} = \frac{J_{\mathrm{g}}}{r_{\mathrm{bg}}^2} \tag{8}$$

Including viscous damping, the equations of motion are reduced to:

$$\ddot{x}_{\mathrm{r}} + 2\omega\xi\dot{x}_{\mathrm{r}} + \omega^2 x_{\mathrm{r}} = \omega^2 x_{\mathrm{s}} \tag{9}$$

$$\omega^2 = \frac{K_I\left(S_{\mathrm{pI}}M_{\mathrm{g}} + S_{\mathrm{gI}}M_{\mathrm{p}}\right) + K_{\mathrm{II}}\left(S_{\mathrm{pII}}M_{\mathrm{g}} + S_{\mathrm{gII}}M_{\mathrm{p}}\right)}{M_{\mathrm{g}}M_{\mathrm{p}}} \tag{10}$$

$$\omega^2 x_{\mathrm{s}} = \frac{(M_{\mathrm{g}} + M_{\mathrm{p}})F_{\mathrm{D}} + K_{\mathrm{I}}\lambda_{\mathrm{I}}\left(S_{\mathrm{pI}}M_{\mathrm{g}} + S_{\mathrm{gI}}M_{\mathrm{p}}\right) + K_{\mathrm{II}}\lambda_{\mathrm{II}}\left(S_{\mathrm{pII}}M_{\mathrm{g}} + S_{\mathrm{gII}}M_{\mathrm{p}}\right)}{M_{\mathrm{g}}M_{\mathrm{p}}} \tag{11}$$

The loaded static transmission errors can be obtained by dividing Eq. (11) by Eq. (10) to yield:

$$x_{\mathrm{s}} = \frac{(M_{\mathrm{g}} + M_{\mathrm{p}})F_{\mathrm{D}} + K_{\mathrm{I}}\lambda_{\mathrm{I}}\left(S_{\mathrm{pI}}M_{\mathrm{g}} + S_{\mathrm{gI}}M_{\mathrm{p}}\right) + K_{\mathrm{II}}\lambda_{\mathrm{II}}\left(S_{\mathrm{pII}}M_{\mathrm{g}} + S_{\mathrm{gII}}M_{\mathrm{p}}\right)}{K_I\left(S_{\mathrm{pI}}M_{\mathrm{g}} + S_{\mathrm{gI}}M_{\mathrm{p}}\right) + K_{\mathrm{II}}\left(S_{\mathrm{pII}}M_{\mathrm{g}} + S_{\mathrm{gII}}M_{\mathrm{p}}\right)} \tag{12}$$

The equivalent stiffness of meshing tooth pairs, in Eq. (10) through (12), can be written as:

$$K_{\mathrm{I}} = \frac{k_{\mathrm{pI}}k_{\mathrm{gI}}}{k_{\mathrm{pI}} + k_{\mathrm{gI}}} \tag{13}$$

$$K_{\mathrm{II}} = \frac{k_{\mathrm{pII}}k_{\mathrm{gII}}}{k_{\mathrm{pII}} + k_{\mathrm{gII}}} \tag{14}$$

The friction experienced by the pinion and the gear can be expressed as:

$$S_{\mathrm{pI}} = 1 \pm \frac{\mu_{\mathrm{I}}\rho_{\mathrm{pI}}}{r_{\mathrm{bp}}} \tag{15}$$

$$S_{\mathrm{gI}} = 1 \pm \frac{\mu_{\mathrm{I}}\rho_{\mathrm{gI}}}{r_{\mathrm{bd}}} \tag{16}$$

$$S_{\mathrm{pII}} = 1 \pm \frac{\mu_{\mathrm{II}} \rho_{\mathrm{pII}}}{r_{\mathrm{bp}}} \tag{17}$$

$$S_{\mathrm{gII}} = 1 \pm \frac{\mu_{\mathrm{II}} \rho_{\mathrm{gII}}}{r_{\mathrm{bd}}} \tag{18}$$

The signs in the above expressions are positive (+) for the approach and negative (–) for the recess.
The coefficient of friction is expressed by formula:

$$\mu_{\mathrm{I,II}} = 18.1 \nu^{-0.15} \left(\frac{v_{\mathrm{g\,I,II}} + v_{\mathrm{p\,I,II}}}{\left| v_{\mathrm{g\,I,II}} - v_{\mathrm{p\,I,II}} \right|} \right)^{-0.15} \left(\left| v_{\mathrm{g\,I,II}} - v_{\mathrm{p\,I,II}} \right| \right)^{-0.5} \left(\frac{\rho_{\mathrm{g\,I,II}} \rho_{\mathrm{p\,I,II}}}{\rho_{\mathrm{g\,I,II}} + \rho_{\mathrm{p\,I,II}}} \right)^{-0.5} \tag{19}$$

where ν is the viscosity of lubricant (cSt). And $v_{\mathrm{pI,II}}$ and $v_{\mathrm{gI,II}}$ are the surface velocities (mm/s), which can be formulated as follows:

$$v_{\mathrm{pI,II}} = V \left(\frac{L_{\mathrm{p\,I,II}} \cos \alpha_{\mathrm{d}}}{r_{\mathrm{bp}}} + \sin \alpha_{\mathrm{d}} \right) \tag{20}$$

$$v_{\mathrm{g\,I,II}} = V \left(-\frac{L_{\mathrm{g\,I,II}} \cos \alpha_{\mathrm{d}}}{r_{\mathrm{bg}}} + \sin \alpha_{\mathrm{d}} \right) \tag{23}$$

where $L_{\mathrm{pI,II}}$ and $L_{\mathrm{gI,II}}$ are the distances between the contact point and the pitch point along the line of action for pinion and gear, respectively, and V is the tangential velocity on the pitch circle.
The value of the damping ratio, ξ, in Eq. (9), is commonly recommended in literature as one between 0.1 and 0.2. In this study, a constant value of 0.17 proposed in literature for the damping ratio, ξ, was adapted in the solution of equations.
The dynamic contact loads, which include tooth profile error, can then be written as:

$$F_{\mathrm{I}} - K_{\mathrm{I}}(x_{\mathrm{r}} - \lambda_{\mathrm{I}}) \tag{21}$$

$$F_{\mathrm{II}} = K_{\mathrm{II}}(x_{\mathrm{r}} - \lambda_{\mathrm{II}}) \tag{22}$$

where λ_{I} and λ_{II} are the tooth profile errors. In this study, the effects of profile errors on the dynamic response of gears are not considered. Thus, the tooth profile errors are assumed to be zero. The developed computer program has a capability of using any approach for the determination of errors.
It should be noted that the above equations are valid only when there is contact between two gears. When separation occurs between two gears, because of the relative errors between the teeth of gears, the dynamic load will be zero and equation of motion will be given by:

$$T \ddot{x}_{\mathrm{r}} = F_{\mathrm{D}} \tag{23}$$

The meshing conditions are described as follows:

If $x_r > \lambda_I$; $x_r > \lambda_{II}$	F_I, $F_{II} > 0$	Double tooth contact
If $x_r \leq \lambda_I$; $x_r \leq \lambda_{II}$	$F_I = F_{II} = 0$	Tooth separation
If $\lambda_I < x_r \leq \lambda_{II}$	$F_I > 0$ and $F_{II} = 0$	Single tooth contact
If $\lambda_{II} < x_r \leq \lambda_I$	$F_I = 0$ and $F_{II} > 0$	Single tooth contact

3. Tooth stiffness

According to Equations (13) and (14), in order to calculate the equivalent stiffness of a meshing tooth pair, the tooth stiffness has to be known beforehand. In this study, a 2-D finite element model was developed to calculate the deflections of both the asymmetric and the symmetric gear teeth. By using this model, nodal deflections are calculated for pre-determined contact points. The load applied for each contact point is taken as a constant in order to determine tooth deflection under unit load. By putting the calculated nodal deflection values into Equations (24-27), the tooth stiffness are calculated and then the approximate curves for the single tooth stiffness along the contact line are obtained with respect to the radius of the gears. This process was repeated for each gear previously designed for different gear parameters.

$$k_{p1} = \frac{F}{\delta_{pI}} \tag{24}$$

$$k_{g1} = \frac{F}{\delta_{gI}} \tag{25}$$

$$k_{pII} = \frac{F}{\delta_{pII}} \tag{26}$$

$$k_{gII} = \frac{F}{\delta_{gII}} \tag{27}$$

where F is the load applied, and δ_{pI}, δ_{pII}, δ_{gI}, and δ_{gII} are the deflections of the teeth in the direction of this load.

4. Computational procedure

The reduced equation of motion is solved numerically using a method that employs a linear iterative procedure. This involves dividing the mesh period into many equal intervals. In this study, the flowchart of this computational procedure developed in MATLAB, used for calculating the dynamic responses of spur gears, is shown in Fig. 2. The time interval, between the initial contact point and the highest point of single contact, is considered as a mesh period. In the numerical solution, each mesh period is divided into 200 intervals for good accuracy. Within each of the sub-intervals thus obtained, various parameters of equations of motion are taken as constants, and an analytical solution is obtained. The calculated values of the relative displacement and the relative velocity after one mesh period are compared with the initial values x_r and v_r. Unless the differences between them are smaller than a preset tolerance (0.000001), the iteration procedure is repeated by taking the previously calculated values of x_r and v_r at the end point of single pair of teeth contact as the new initial conditions. Then the dynamic loads are calculated by using the calculated relative displacement values. After the gear dynamic load has been calculated, the dynamic load factor can be determined by dividing the maximum dynamic load along the contact line to the static load.

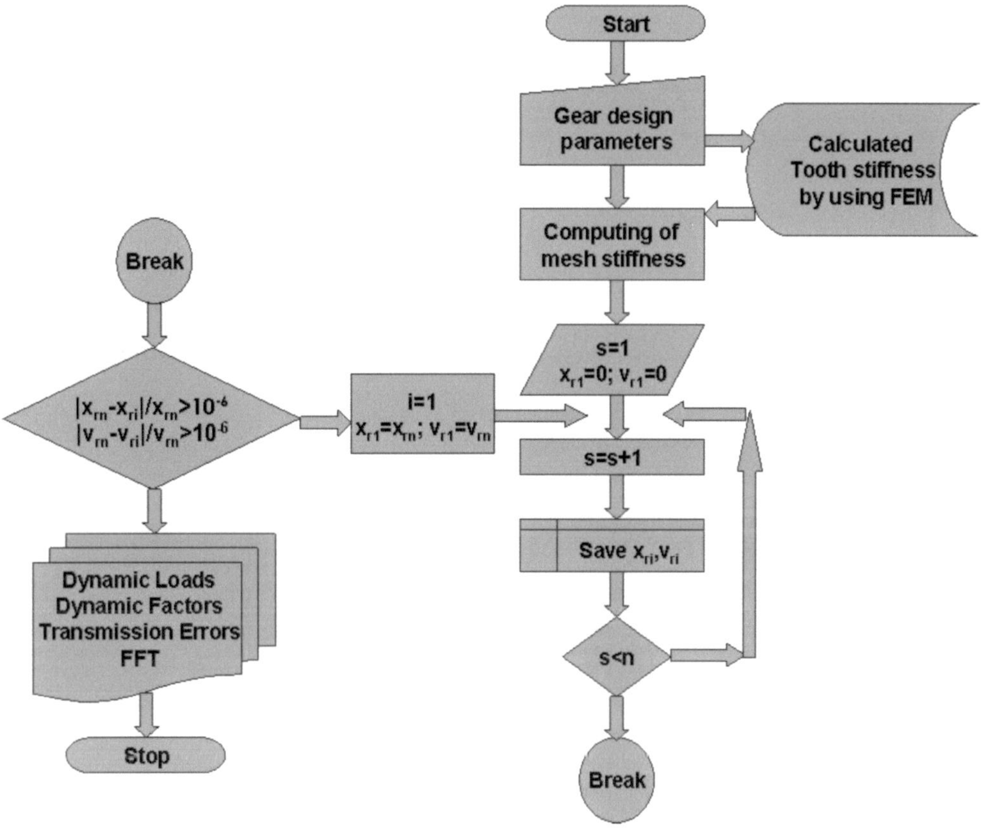

Fig. 2. Flowchart of the developed computer program in MATLAB

5. DYNAMIC virtual tool

Physics-based modeling and simulation is important in all engineering problems. The current mature stage of computer software and hardware makes it possible complex mechanical problems, such as gear design, to be solved numerically. In-house prepared codes to handle individual research projects, graduate, and/or PhD studies; commercial packages for engineers in industry are widely used to solve almost every engineering problem. Tailored with graphical user interfaces (GUIs) and easy-to-use design steps, anyone-even a beginner- can design a gear pair and obtain results, e.g Dynamic Load,

Transmitted Torque, Static Transmission Error as a function of time, and Static Transmission Error Harmonics etc., just by pressing a command button. Lecturers have been increasingly using these packages to increase their teaching performance and student understanding.
Based on and triggered by these thoughts, a virtual tool DYNAMIC is prepared that can be used for educational and research purposes. The DYNAMIC is a general purpose gear analyzing tool (Fig. 3).

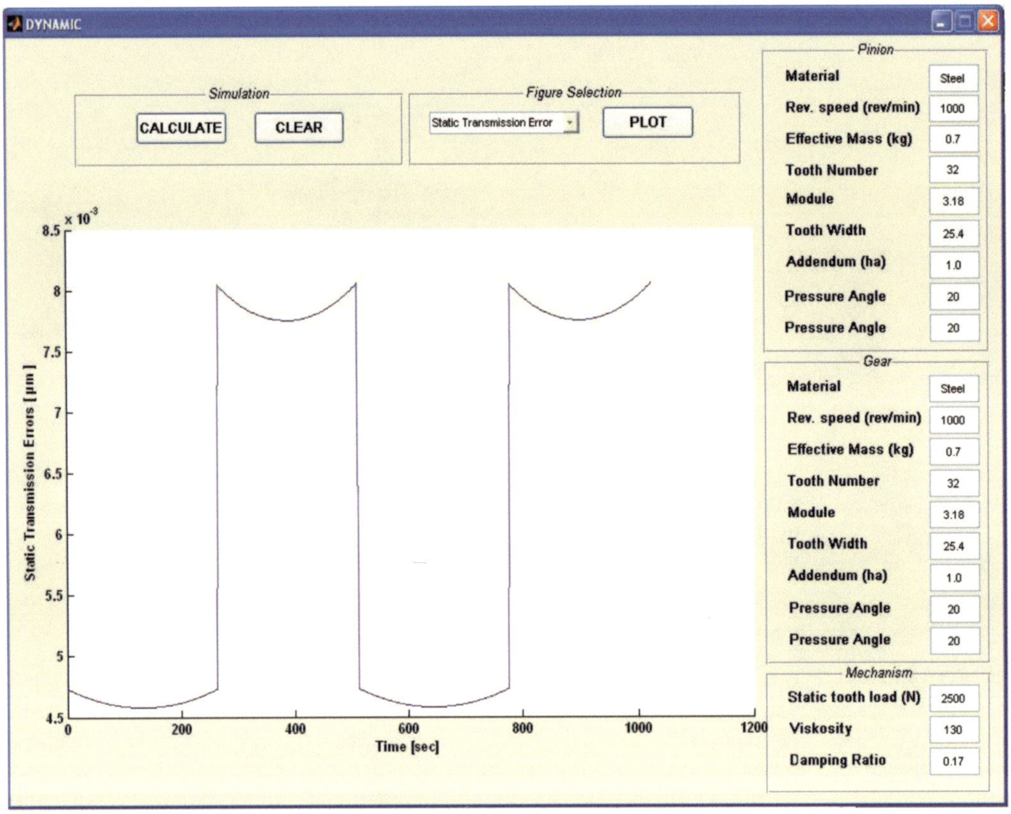

Fig. 3. The Front panel of the DYNAMIC tool

There are six blocks and a figure block on the front panel of the tool. Three blocks on the right side of the front panel, belong to the parameters which will be defined by the users (Fig. 2 a, b). *Pinion* and *Gear* blocks are reserved for the tooth parameters and *Mechanism* block is for the parameters related to the mechanical variables. Material is set to "Steel" by default and can not be changed by the user.
The two blocks above the figure are *Simulation* and *Figure Selection* panels (Fig 3a). Once the user inputs the needed parameters, he/she clicks the CALCULATE pushbutton to obtain the solution for the specified parameters. In the *Figure Selection* block, from the pop-up menu, user can select which solution to be plotted: Dynamic Load, Transmitted Torque, Static Transmission Error or Static Transmission Error Harmonics (Fig 3b). Then the required figure can be plotted with the PLOT button. Once the solutions are calculated, it is not needed to run the program again and again for each figure option. CLEAR is to clean the figure axes before each plot.

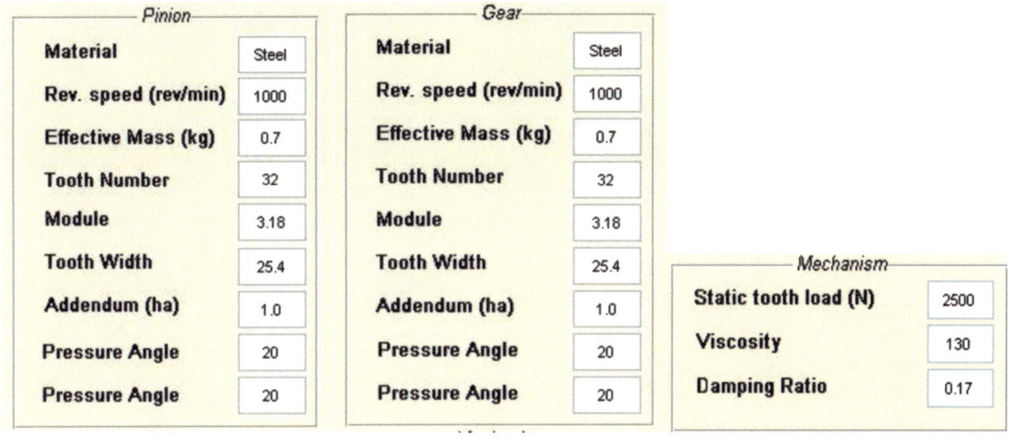

(a) (b) (c)

Fig. 4. Variable input blocks: a) pinion, b) gear, c) mechanism

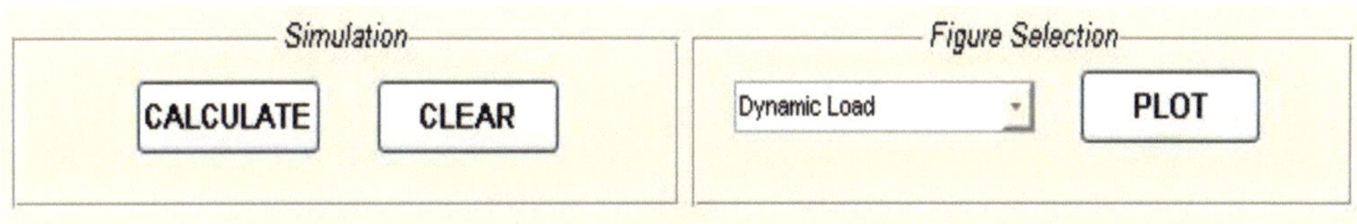

(a)

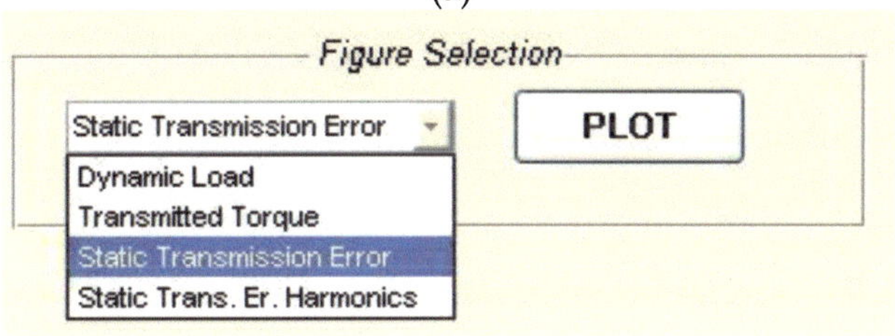

(b)

Fig. 5. Simulation command blocks

The variation of dynamic load with respect to time can be seen in Fig. 6. The solutions for different variables can be plotted in one figure, for comparison. In Fig. 6 two different solutions for dynamic load are plotted for different revolution speed. Fig. 7 is an example for Transmitted Torque solution.

6. Results and discussions

The computer program developed has been used for the dynamic analysis of spur gears with symmetric and asymmetric teeth. In this study, seven different gear pairs are considered for the dynamic analysis of spur gears with asymmetric teeth. In order to simplify the analysis, all gear parameters are kept constant, apart from the pressure angle on the drive side and the tooth height. Since the effects of the tooth profile errors are not considered in this study, the analyzed gears are assumed to be "perfect gears" without tooth errors. The properties of these gear pairs are provided in Table.

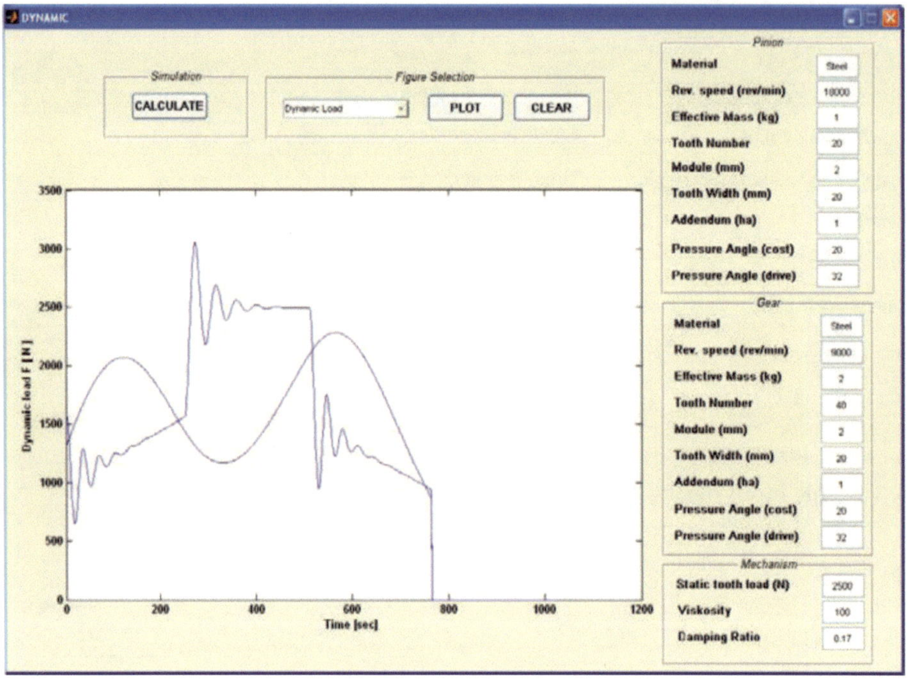

Fig. 6. The comparison of variation of dynamic load for different rotational speeds

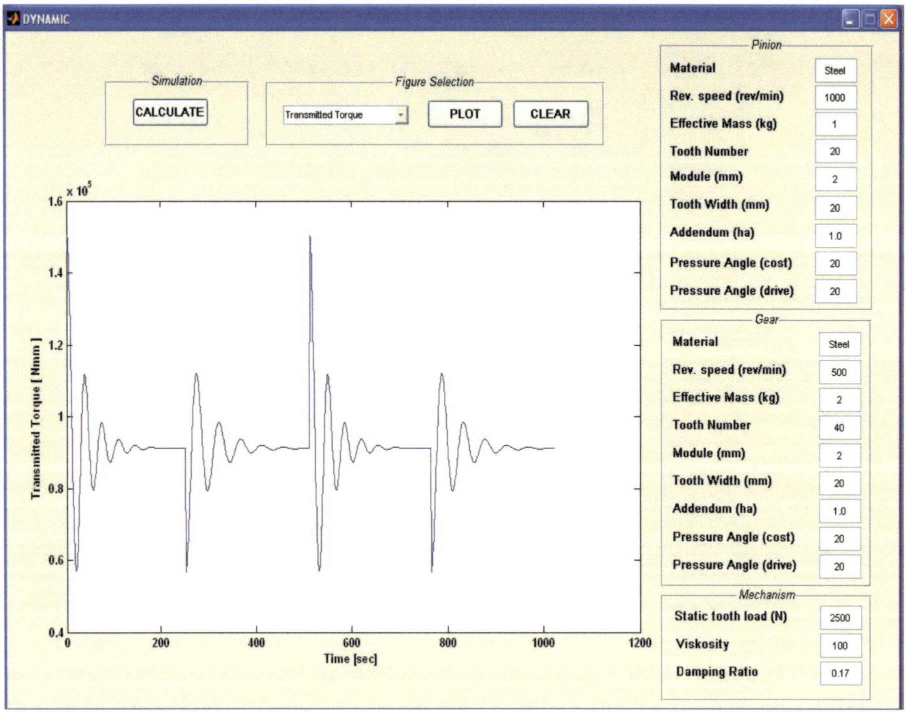

Fig. 7. An example of transmitted torque solution

In a previous work (Karpat, 2005), different approaches for minimizing the dynamic factors and the static transmission errors, in low-contact ratio gears, were reviewed in details. In one of the approaches discussed, the usage of high gear contact ratio was included. It was observed that increasing the gear contact ratio reduced the dynamic load. In literature, minimum dynamic loads were obtained for contact ratios between 1.8 and 2.0. A way of increasing the contact ratio is by using higher addendum values. It should be noted that increasing the value of the addendum leads to a reduction in the bending stress at the tooth root. This occurs through the lowering of the location of the highest point of single tooth contact (HPSTC). The other gear characteristics impacted by high addendum are the thickness of tooth tip and undercut. In this study, for asymmetric gears, high addenda are analyzed, as a means of minimizing the dynamic factors and the static transmission errors (Gear Pair 4 and 5).

	Gear Pair				
	1	2	3	4	5
Module m_n	2 mm	2 mm	2 mm	2 mm	2 mm
Teeth number of pinion z_{n1}	20	20	32	32	32
Pressure angle on coast side α_c	20°	20°	20°	20°	20°
Pressure angle on drive side α_d	20°	24°	32°	24°	32°
Gear ratio	2	2	2	2	2
Mass of pinion M_p	1 kg	1 kg	1 kg	1 kg	1 kg
Mass of gear M_g	2 kg	2 kg	2 kg	2 kg	2 kg
Material	Steel	Steel	Steel	Steel	Steel
Kinematic viscosity	100 cSt	100 cSt	100 cSt	100 cSt	100 cSt
Damping ratio	0,17	0,17	0,17	0,17	0,17
Tooth width	20 mm	20 mm	20 mm	20 mm	20 mm
Addendum h_a	1 m_n	1 m_n	1 m_n	1.32 m_n	1.17 mn
Contact ratio	1.64	1.49	1.31	1.90	1.52

Table 1. The data of the gear pairs

For the sample gear pair whose dimensions and properties are given in Table 1, variations of dynamic loads are determined for various pinion speeds between 1000 rpm and 20 000 rpm. As an example, the dynamic load variation of gear pair 1 for 1000 rpm, 3000 rpm, 10 000 rpm and 18 000 rpm is shown in Figure 8.

Fig. 9 shows the relationship between the dynamic factors and the rotational speed. When comparing the maximum dynamic factors in the corresponding gear pairs in Fig. 9. (e.g., Gear Pair 1 versus Gear Pair 3), it is generally stated that the dynamic factor for spur gears with asymmetric teeth increases with increasing pressure angles on the drive side. Furthermore, it is obvious that the sample Gear Pair 4, which is the gear pair with the highest gear contact ratio 1.90, has a lower dynamic load, at all speeds; this indicates that the impact of gear contact ratio on dynamic loads. The highest dynamic factor is observed at the resonant rotational speed (about 12 000). Beyond this speed, the asymmetric teeth have consistently higher dynamic factors than symmetric teeth. One of reasons for that may be the effect of contact ratio on dynamic loads. As the pressure angle on drive side increases, the contact ratio decreases. However, the dynamic factor in gear systems decreases with increasing the contact ratio. This result may be due to the narrow single contact zone. Because of the narrow single contact zone, this zone is passed speedily as gear rotate and system can not respond. Other reason may be seen by analyzing the variation of mesh stiffness with respect to time. As can be seen from this figure, in the single contact zone, the asymmetric gear (Gear Pair 4) has higher mesh stiffness than the symmetric gear (Gear Pair 1). The high mesh stiffness is one of the reasons for the high dynamic factor observed in Fig.9.

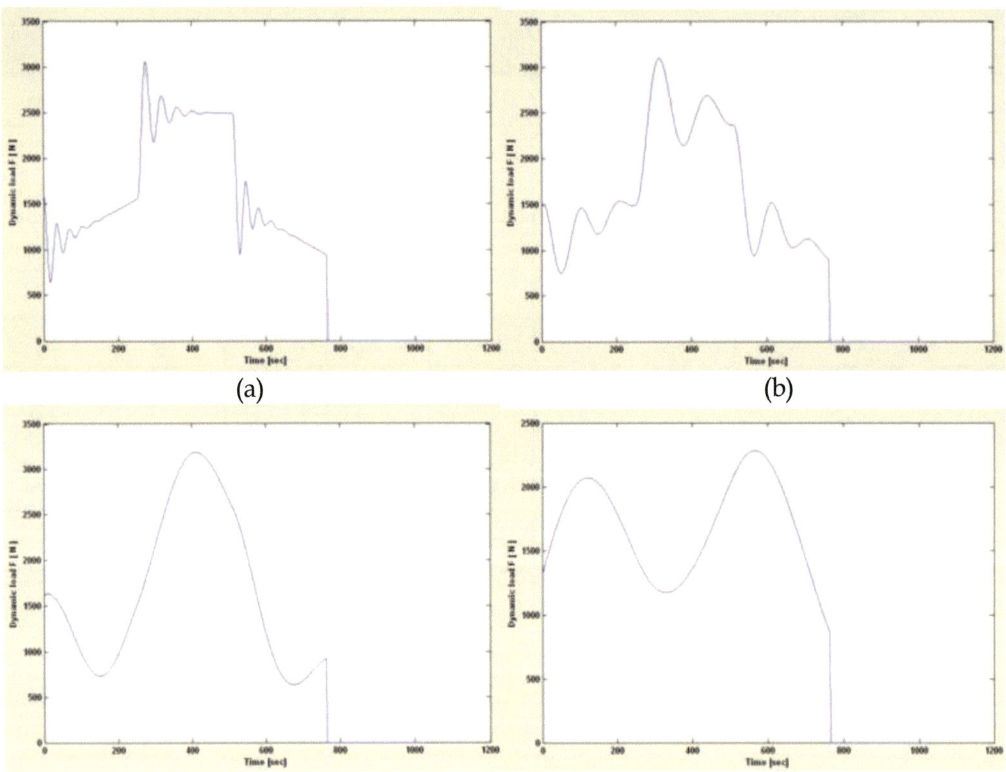

(a) (b) (c) (d)

Fig. 8. Variation of dynamic load with rotational speed of pinion: a) 1000 rpm b) 3000 rpm c) 10 000 d) 18 000 rpm

Fig. 10 shows the impact of increasing the pressure angle, on the drive side, on the static transmission error. Generally, changing the pressure angle will impact the tooth mesh characteristics, such as the tooth contact zone and contact ratio. Fig. 11 indicates that the single tooth contact zone increases with increased pressure angle. Thus, compared to gears with symmetric teeth, gears with asymmetric teeth have a larger single tooth contact zone.

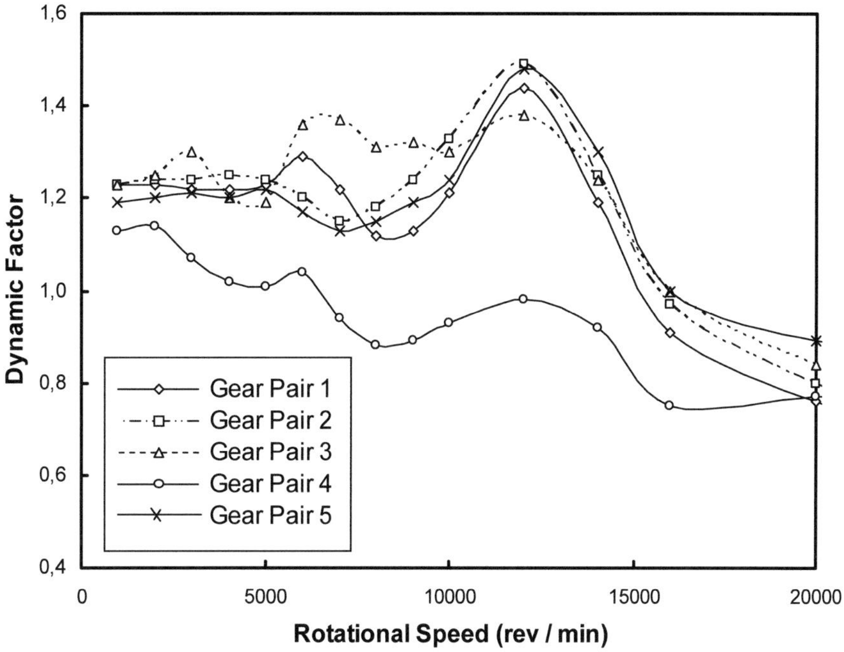

Fig. 9. The maximum dynamic factors with respect to rotational speeds

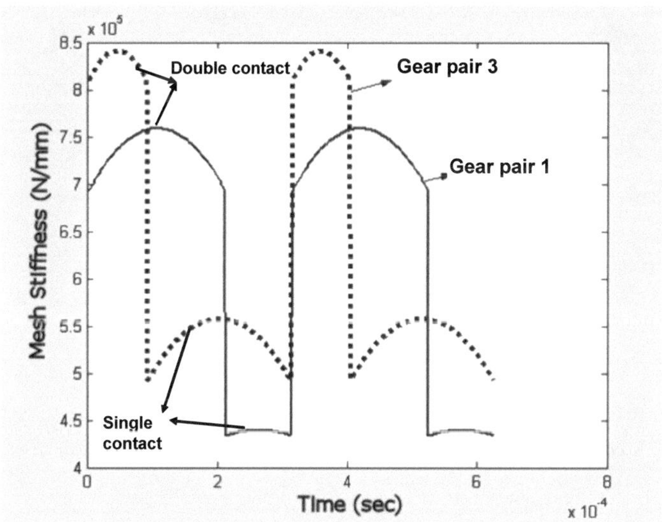

Fig. 10. The variation of mesh stiffness with respect to time for Gear Pair 1 (symmetric teeth) and Gear Pair 3 (asymmetric teeth)

Furthermore, the static transmission error, at the center of the single tooth contact zone, decreases with increasing of pressure angle. The frequency spectra of the static transmission errors are depicted in Fig. 11. In these figures, the sum of first five harmonics slightly increases with increasing pressure angle.

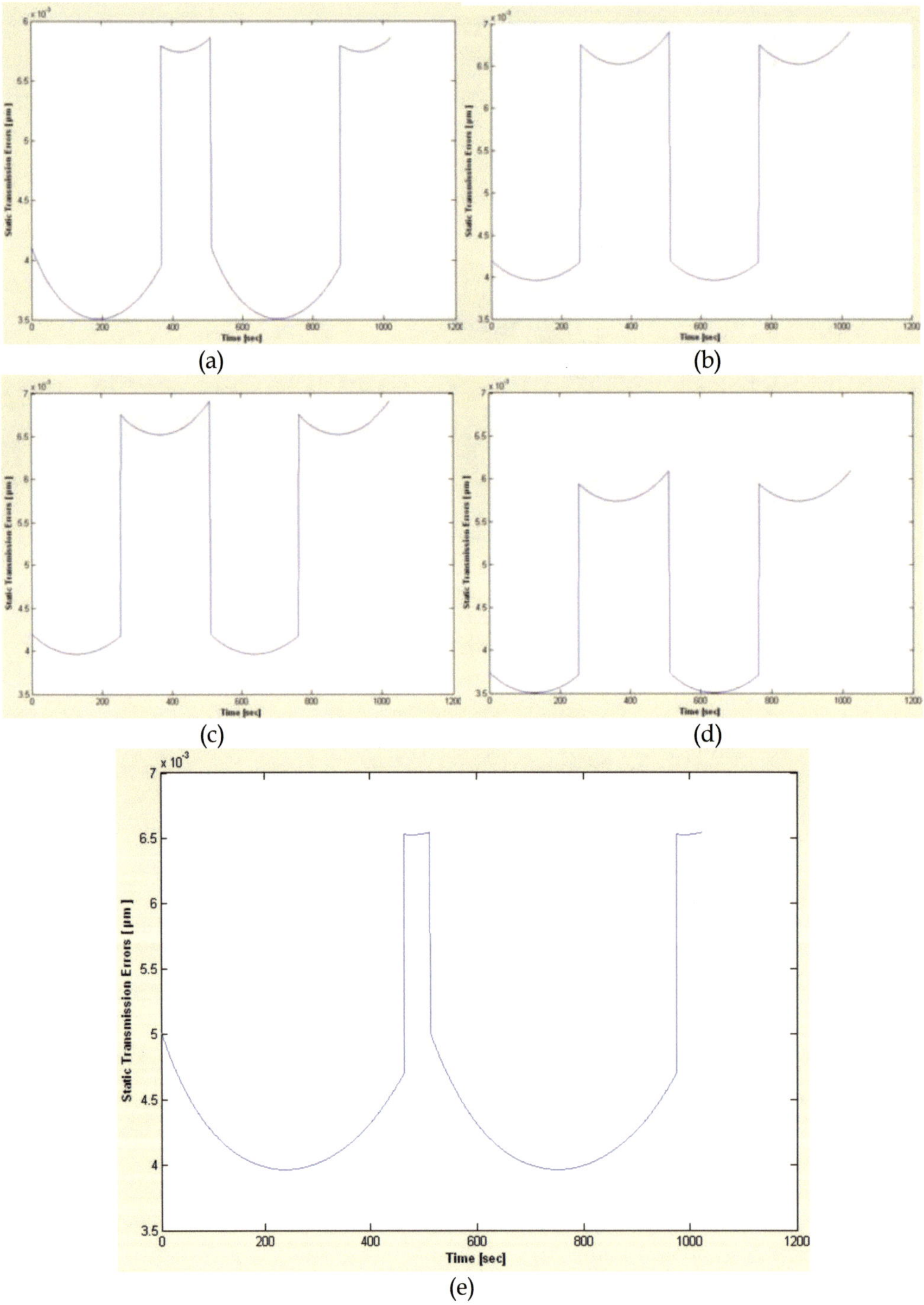

Fig. 11. Static transmission errors (a) Gear Pair 1 ($\alpha_c = 20°$, $\alpha_d = 20°$), (b) Gear Pair 2 ($\alpha_c = 20°$, $\alpha_d = 24°$), (c) Gear Pair 3 ($\alpha_c = 20°$, $\alpha_d = 32°$), (d) Gear Pair 4 ($\alpha_c = 20°$, $\alpha_d = 24°$), (d) Gear Pair 5 ($\alpha_c = 20°$, $\alpha_d = 32°$)

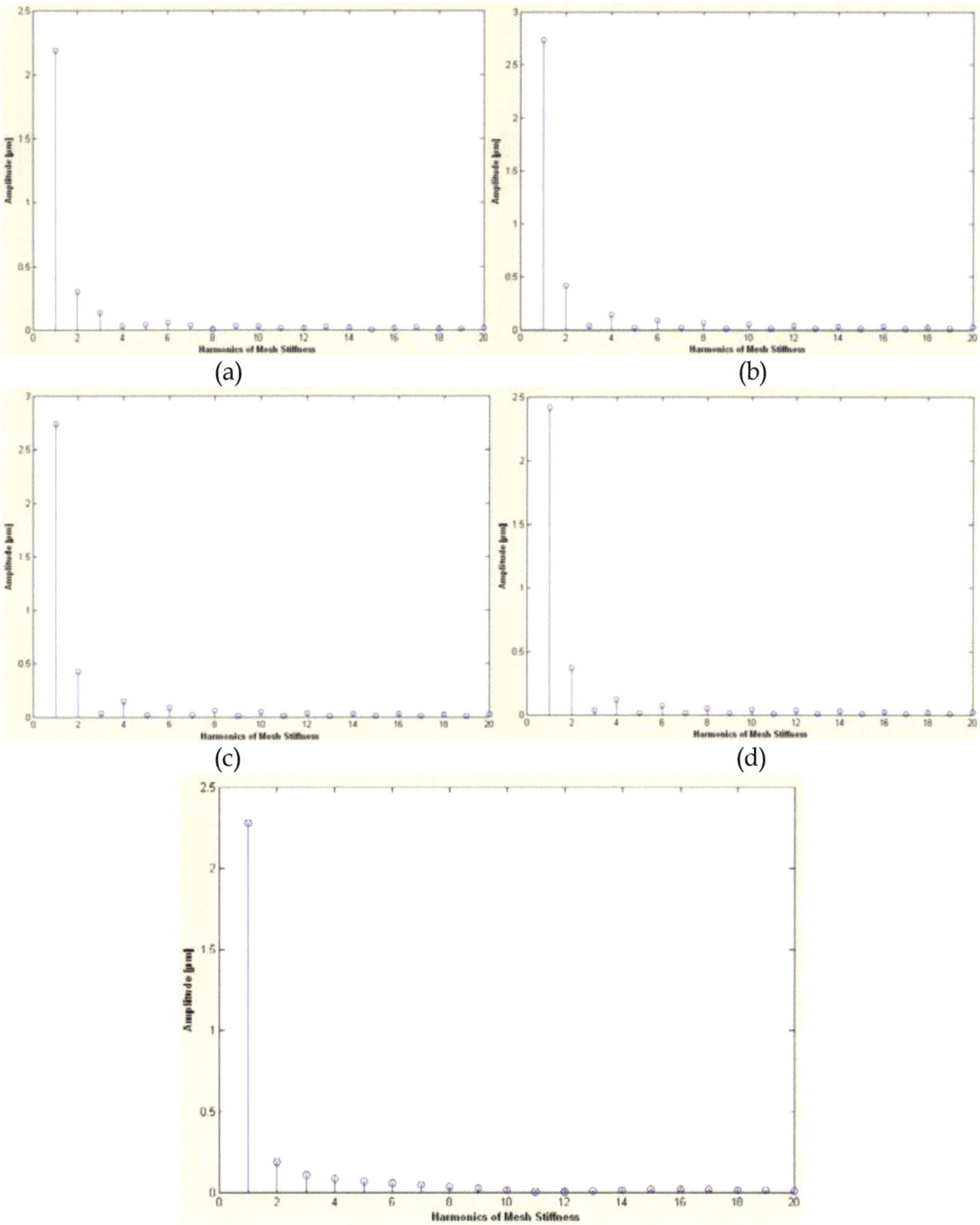

Fig. 12. Frequency spectra of the static transmission errors (a) Gear Pair 1 ($\alpha_c = 20°$, $\alpha_d = 20°$), (b) Gear Pair 2 ($\alpha_c = 20°$, $\alpha_d = 24°$), (c) Gear Pair 3 ($\alpha_c = 20°$, $\alpha_d = 32°$), (d) Gear Pair 4 ($\alpha_c = 20°$, $\alpha_d = 24°$), (e) Gear Pair 5 ($\alpha_c = 20°$, $\alpha_d = 32°$)

Fig. 12 (d) and (e) shows the static transmission error for increased values of addendum for asymmetric teeth. Increasing the addendum, the amplitude of the static transmission errors is decreased for a comparable pressure angle. Additionally, the single tooth contact zone decreased for a comparable pressure angle. In Fig. 12 (d), it is noted that the asymmetric tooth with $h_{ap} = 1.32m_n$, $\alpha_c = 20°$, and $\alpha_d = 24°$, has the lowest static transmission error. Furthermore, the difference in the magnitude of the error, in the single tooth contact and double teeth contact zones, is also smallest for this tooth configuration. In Fig. 12 (d), the amplitudes of harmonics of static transmission errors are significantly reduced when asymmetric teeth with long addendum, providing high gear contact ratio close to 2.0 are used. By referring to Fig. 12, it can be inferred that when designing asymmetric gears, for achieving reduced dynamic response, one may consider using a high addendum. In summary, for asymmetric teeth, increasing the addendum leads to a significant decrease in the dynamic factor. The maximum reduction of the dynamic factor is achieved for a gear contact ratio of about 2.0. The result implies that the usage of long addendum for involute spur gears with asymmetric teeth may be an alternative way to reduce the dynamic response as well decreasing tooth stress at root.

7. Conclusions

Virtual tools have become very effective in teaching engineering problems. The user need not to know graphical user interface details, programming tips, etc. Instead, such tools have the capability of handling a variety of different gear problems.

A MATLAB-based virtual tool, DYNAMIC, is introduced to analyze dynamic behavior of spur gears with asymmetric tooth design. The DYNAMIC is used to compare conventional spur gears with symmetric teeth and spur gears with asymmetric teeth in this study. The results for dynamic load, dynamic factor, transmitted torque, static transmission error and static transmission error harmonics are obtained for various tooth parameters to show the powerful aspects of asymmetric teeth.

8. References

Ozguven HN., and Houser DR. (1988). The mathematical models used in gear dynamics - A review. *Journal of Sound and Vibration*;121(3):383-411.

Parey A., and Tandon N. (2003). Spur gear dynamic models including defects: A review. *Shock Vibration Digest*;35(6):465-78.

Cavdar K., Karpat F., and Babalik FC. (2005). Computer aided analysis of bending strength of involute spur gears with asymmetric profile. *Journal of Mechanical Design* - T ASME;127(3):477-84.

Kapelevich A. (2000). Geometry and design of involute spur gears with asymmetric teeth. *Mechanism and Machine Theory*;35(1):117-30.

Karpat F. (2005). Analysis of Involute Spur Gears with Asymmetric Teeth. Ph.D Thesis [Bursa-Turkey: Uludag University.

Karpat F., and Ekwaro-Osire S. (2010). Influence of Tip Relief Modification on the Wear of Spur Gears with Asymmetric Teeth, *Tribology & Lubrication Technology*, Vol. 66, No. 6, pp. 50–60.

Karpat F., Ekwaro-Osire S., Cavdar K., and Babalik F.C. (2008). Dynamic Analysis of Involute Spur Gears with Asymmetric Teeth, *International Journal of Mechanical Sciences*, 50 (12) 1598-1610.

Karpat F., and Ekwaro-Osire S. (2008). Influence of Tip Relief Modification on the Wear of Spur Gears with Asymmetric Teeth, *Tribology Transactions*, Volume 51, Issue 5 , pages 581- 588.

Karpat F., Ekwaro-Osire S., and Khandaker M.P.H. (2008). Probabilistic Analysis of MEMS Asymmetric Gear Tooth, *Journal of Mechanical Design*, Volume 130, Issue 4.

19

The Use of Matlab in Advanced Design of Bonded and Welded Joints

Paolo Ferro
University of Padova
Italy

1. Introduction

From a mathematical viewpoint, welding can be considered as a transient boundary problem in which the thermal input varies in space and time. Thermal coefficients involved with heat lost by convection and radiation, are usually temperature-dependent; displacement constraint conditions are also imposed on the geometry. Temperature and stress development in the material are steered by the well know differential equations of heat exchange and elasto-plastic equilibrium. Two complications in the models are due to the microstructure transformations (which influence the mechanical behaviour of the joint), and to the filler metal (which influences also the chemical composition of the parent metal and the temperature distribution). It should be noted that coupled phenomena are involved because the latent heat of phase transformation influences the temperature distribution due to the welding source. Moreover, the constitutive relations which connect stresses to strains are both temperature and phase dependent.

The development of new models for joint planning is of great importance in the industrial and research fields. The prediction of residual stresses, temperature distributions, phase transformations, asymptotic stress fields near the weld toe or near the interface between the matrix and the adhesive in bonded joints, may be of fundamental importance for a good joining plan and operation. In this chapter, some models developed for bonded and welded joints and solved by means of Matlab program, are presented. In the first part, models for temperture ditributions and phase transformations diagrams are considered with particular attention, referred both to conventional and innovative welding precesses, such as laser and friction stir welding. In the second part, mechanical models are described with particolar attention put on residual stress calculation and advanced joints planning methodologies.

Only analytical or semi-analyitical models are taken into account due to their efficiency compared to Finite Element models. As a matter of fact, by using analytical models for temperature distributions prediction it is possible to optimize the process parameters such as power source, welding speed and pre-heating temperature, with low effort in terms of time and cost. Such models offer also the possibility to predict the fusion zone (FZ) and heat affected zone (HAZ) extension and, finally, to perform a parametric sudy of welding. In this work, the Rosenthl solution (Rosenthal, 1941; Rosenthal and Shamerber, 1938) of the welding thermal problem, will be described. Moving point source, linear source or combinations of the last two are used to reproduce the fusion zone shape of the joint,

leading to good results in a very short time. Referring to the residual stresses calcualtion, the "rod model" by Cañas et al. will be presented. In this model, the equations referred to the problem under consideration, are written in matrix notation and advantageously used in an efficient algorithm solved with Matlab. As refers to phase transformations, the possibility to calculate the Time-Temperature Transformation (TTT) and Continuous Cooling Transformation (CCT) diagrams of steels with use of the Kirkaldy model is also proved.
In the matter of advanced joint planning, it was shonwn that better predictions of static and fatigue resitance are possible if the intensity of the asymptotic stress fields is taken into account. Dealing with the fatigue strength of welded joints, such local approach models the weld toe region as a sharp, zero radius, V-shaped notch. Under these conditions, the intensity of asymptotic stress distribuions, obeying Williams' solution, are quantified by means of the notch stress intensity factors (NSIFs). The formulation of this method is completed analytically and the resulting set of ordinary differential equations is solved numerically by means of Matlab. In this chapter it is described with a particular attention put on bonded joints.

2. Thermo-metallurgical analysis

The thermal history induced by a welding process can be calculated by solving the fundamental equation of heat transfer (1):

$$\rho C_p \dot{T} = \nabla \cdot k \nabla T - \sum_{i<j} L_{ij}(T) p_{ij} \tag{1}$$

where ρ is the material density, C_p is the specific heat capacity of the material (weighted according to proportions of various phases), k is the thermal conductivity of material (weighted according to proportions of various phases), T is the temperature, $\dot{T}$ is the temperature rate (Newton's notation is used for the time derivative of a function), $L_{ij}(T)$ is the latent heat (at temperature T) of the $i \rightarrow j$ transformation, p_{ij} is the phase proportion of i-th phase which is transformed into j-th phase in the time unit, and

$$\nabla = \mathbf{i}_1 \frac{\partial}{\partial x_1} + \mathbf{i}_2 \frac{\partial}{\partial x_2} + \mathbf{i}_3 \frac{\partial}{\partial x_3}$$

is the 3D gradient vector operator. The heat transfer boundary conditions of the problem are

$$q = -k \nabla T \tag{2}$$

where q is the heat flux at the boundary which, in the welding process, consists of a prescribed function of the time and space (heat source), convective and radiative heat loss, and zero flux in a symmetry plane.
The Rosenthal solution of Eq. (1) is described both for fusion and friction stir welding with some guidelines put on its practical use in welding process plan.

2.1 Temperature distribution and cooling rate in fusion welding

The analytical solution of Eq. (1) was given by Rosenthal (1941), who considered a point source moving on a semi-infinite plate under steady-state conditions, with temperature-independent material properties, at convective and radiative heat loss and phase transformations neglected. In a reference system linked to the source, this solution is given by the following equation:

$$T - T_0 = \frac{Q}{2\pi k} e^{-\lambda v \xi} \frac{e^{-\lambda v R}}{R} \tag{3}$$

where T_0 is the reference temperature, $R=(\xi^2 + y^2 + z^2)^{1/2}$ is the radial distance of a point of the plate from the source axis, v is the welding speed, t is the time, $\xi = x - vt$ is a moving co-ordinate, $\lambda = 1/(2a)$ (where a is the diffusivity), and Q is the effective thermal power absorbed by the material. In the case of a line source in a plate of thickness H, the relation (3) becomes:

$$T - T_0 = \frac{Q}{2\pi k} e^{-\lambda v \xi} \frac{K_0(\lambda v r)}{H} \tag{4}$$

where K_0 is the modified Bessel function of the second kind and zero order. In the case of arc welding, the effective thermal power equals to

$$Q = \eta V I \tag{5}$$

where V is the arc voltage, I is the current intensity, and η is the arc efficiency. Eq. (4) can be easily solved by means of Matlab. Figure 1 shows a 3D representation of Eq. (4) and a comparison between analytical and Finite Element (FE) solution (Ferro et al., 2002). It can be observed that the asymptotic solution at the centre of the source gives non-realistic results (asymptotic temperature distribution). This means that Eqs. (3) and (4) are valid only when referred to the points distant from the heat source axis.

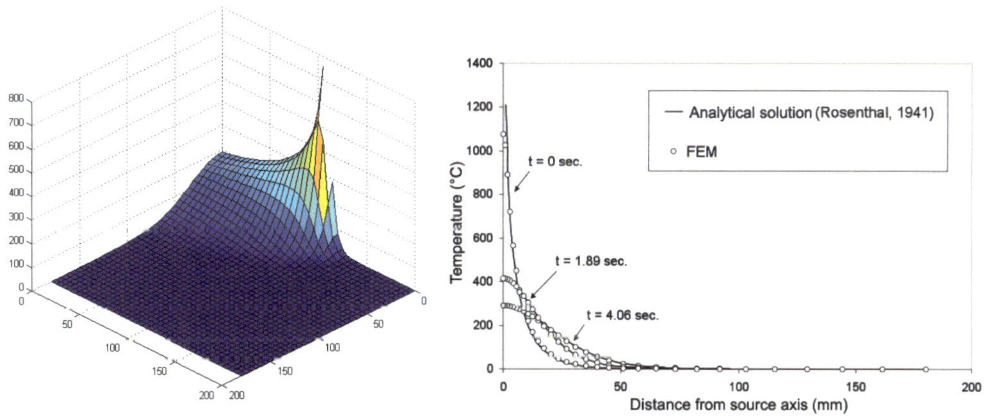

(a) (b)

Fig. 1. Thermal analytical solution (Rosenthal, 1941) (a); comparison between FE and analytical thermal solution (b). Material: AA-5083-O, welding technology: GMAW, voltage = 23.4 V, current = 170 A, welding speed: 11 mm/s

The time derivative of Eq. (3) gives an estimation of the cooling rate (at the point of its maximum value (y = z = 0)) and $\xi < 0$):

$$\frac{\partial T}{\partial t} = -\frac{2\pi k}{Q} v (T - T_0)^2 \qquad (6)$$

Equation (6) shows the strong (squared) dependence of the pre-heating (T-T_0) on cooling rate compared to the others process parameters such as welding speed and power. It means that pre-heating is the most efficient variable, in the case of steel welding, which can be modified in order to obtain sound welds. Knowing the critical cooling rate of the steel, it is possible to estimate, by using Eq. (6), the pre-heating value needed to avoid a martensitic microstructure in the weld bead.

2.2 Temperature distribution in Friction Stir Welding

The main difficulty in the formulation of any model for friction stir welding (FSW) is due to the high coupling between thermal and mechanical phenomena. Thus, in Ferro et al. (2010), the solution of the formulated equation was obtained by a numerical routine written in Matlab code under the simplification of isothermal condition at the matrix/tool interface. The formulation of heat flow is based on Rosethal's solution, while the heat generation is described as a surface flux, which depends on the variation of the shear yield stress with temperature.

2.2.1 Governing equations

As proposed by P. Vilaca et al. (2007), the heat source can be considered to be concentrated at the mid-thickness of the plate, simulating the typical location of the nugget centre and travelling with a constant linear velocity (v) (fig. 2)(Eq. 3).

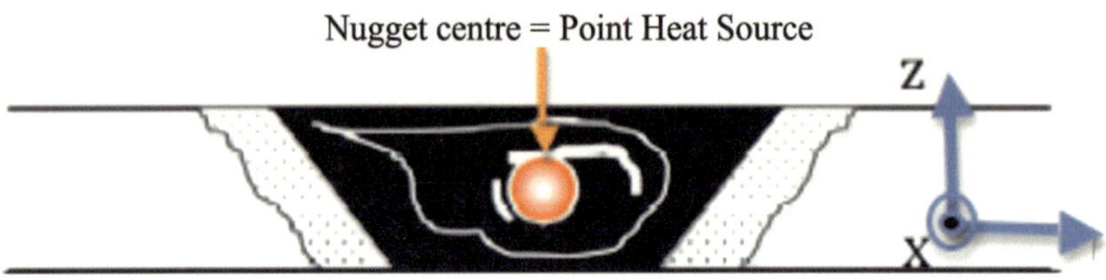

Fig. 2. Point Heat Source located at the nugget centre.

In this case, in Eq. (3), Q is the total heat generation due to frictional and plastic dissipation. Eq. (3) gives good results in case of thick plates. For medium thick plates, good results can be obtained by using eq. (7) (Ferro et al. (2010)):

$$T - T_0 = \frac{Q}{2\pi k} e^{-v\xi/2\alpha} \left(\sum_{i=-\infty}^{i=+\infty} \frac{1}{r_i} e^{-\frac{v}{2\alpha} r_i} \right) \qquad (7)$$

where $r_i = \sqrt{\xi^2 + y^2 + (z - 2iH)^2}$ and H is the thickness of the plates. Finally, if thin plates has to be modelled, the best results can be found by using linear heat source (Eq. (4)) instead of point-source.

The heat flux in FSW is primarily generated by the friction and the deformation process. However, the mechanical loads applied by the pin tool to the workpiece result in a yielded region only in the immediate vicinity of the former while most of the workpiece remains unyielded. Thus, idealizing the localized yielded region as being coincident with the tool surface and treating the workpiece as a rigid matter, the heat generation originated from both frictional and plastic dissipation, can be modelled via surface flux boundary condition at tool/matrix interface (Schmidt et al., 2008, Perivilli et al., 2008). It can be found (Ferro et al., 2010) that the heat generated is expressed by the formula:

$$Q_{workpiece} = \frac{2}{3}\pi\eta\omega\tau_0\left(1-\frac{T^*}{T_M}\right)\left[(R_{sh}^{\ 3}-R_p^{\ 3})(1+\tan\beta)+R_p^{\ 3}+3R_p^{\ 2}H_p\right] \tag{8}$$

where β is the tool shoulder cone angle, H_p is the tool pin height, R_{sh} and R_p are the shoulder and pin radius respectively (Fig. 3), T_M is the melting temperature, τ_0 is a fitting material parameter, η is the thermal efficiency of the process, ω is the angular velocity of the tool and T^* is the temperature at the tool/matrix interface. Thus, in the case of thick plates, the temperature field induced by friction stir welding under steady-state conditions can be described by eq. (9):

$$T = T_0 + \frac{\frac{2}{3}\pi\eta\omega\tau_0\left(1-\frac{T^*}{T_M}\right)\left[(R_{sh}^{\ 3}-R_p^{\ 3})(1+\tan\beta)+R_p^{\ 3}+3R_p^{\ 2}H_p\right]}{2\pi k}e^{-v\xi/2\alpha}\frac{e^{-\frac{v}{2\alpha}r}}{r} \tag{9}$$

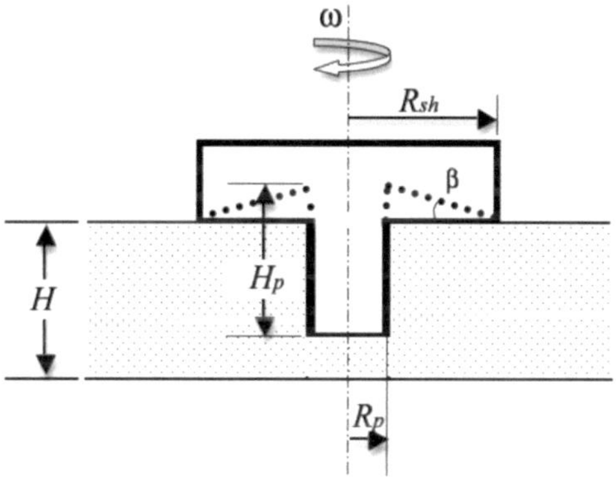

Fig. 3. Schematic representation of the tool geometry.

(Ferro et al., 2010). The unknown parameters in Eqs. (8) and (9) are: η and T^*, showing the coupled thermo-mechanical characteristic of the problem under consideration. However, Eq. (9) can be solved by using a simple numerical routine, as one described in the flow chart of Fig. 5 where ΔT is the temperature increment and T^*_{trial} is an interface trial temperature value. This routine was written in Matlab code. Finally, the thermal efficiency (η) is calculated by a reverse analysis as in any other analytical or phenomenological numerical model of welding process. Because of the temperature singualrity of the Rosenthal's solution, the validity of Eq. (9) is limited to a zone sufficentely far from the source centre. Moreover, in order to obtain a numerical solution of Eq. (9), in the proposed model, T^* refers to the temperature reached at a distance R^* close to R_{sh} (Fig. 4). Good results were obtained with $R^*=R_{sh}$ for aluminum alloys. The modelling procedure, although not perfect, is belived to be a reasonable approach. Finally, since the Rosenthal solution depends on the thickness of the plates (Eqs. (3, 4,7)), the correct formulation has to be used according to the analysed plates thickness.

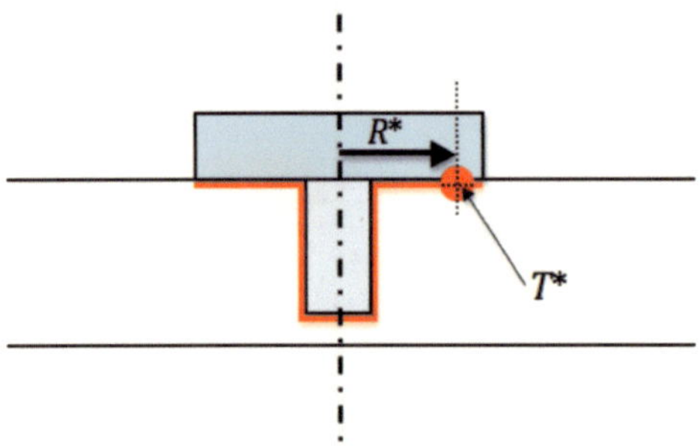

Fig. 4. Schematic representation of the tool/matrix interface temperature and R^* parameter

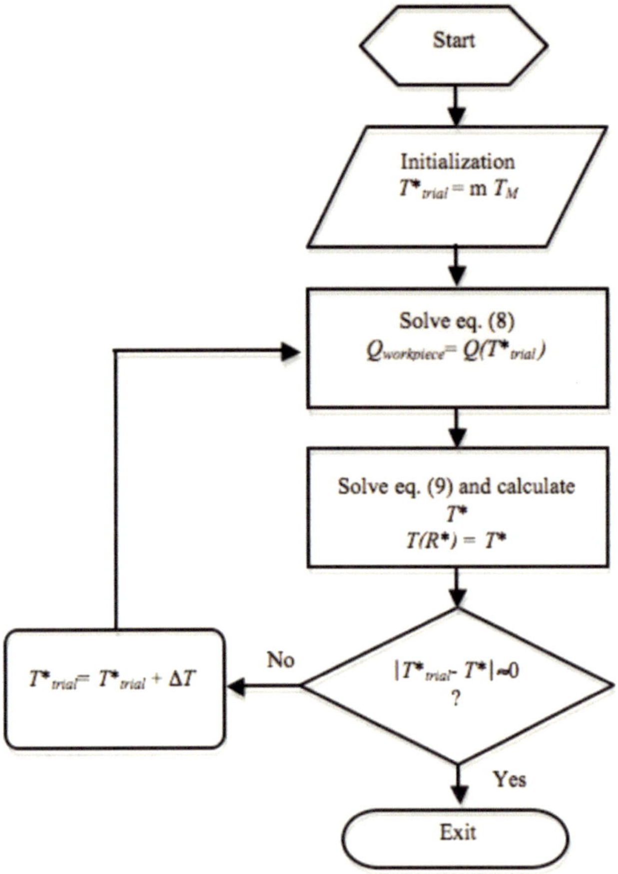

Fig. 5. Flow chart of the numerical routine written in Matlab code

The model was validated by comparison with different experimental data found in literature (Ferro et al., 2010). In Fig. 6 it can be observed that the thermal history calculated by the model is in good agreement with that measured experimentally.

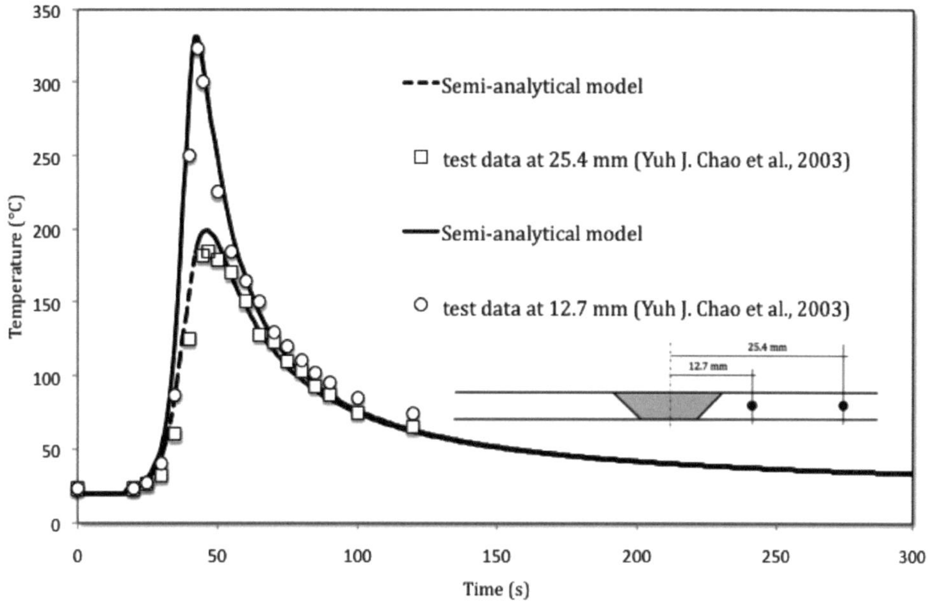

Fig. 6. Variation of transient temperature at different locations of the thermocouples for rotational speed of 240 rpm, welding speed 3.32 mm/s (η=0.5, $R^*=R_{sh}$, τ_0=51.56 MPa) (lines: Semi-analytical solution, symbols: test data (Chao et al. (2003)))

2.3 TTT and CCT diagrams calculation

The Time-Temperature Transformation (TTT) and Continuous Cooling Transformation (CCT) diagrams are useful tools in thermomechanical processing of steels. Such diagrams depend on a so great number of variables that it is impossible to produce enough experimental diagrams for generalised use. For this reason, significant work has been undertaken to develop models that can calculate TTT and CCT diagrams for steels.

Starting from Kirkaldy's model, the general formulation of TTT diagrams is described by the relation (10):

$$\tau(X,T) = \frac{F(C,Mn,Si,Ni,Cr,Mo,N)}{\Delta T^n \exp(-Q_{eff} / RT)} S(X) \tag{10}$$

where τ is the time needed to transform X volume fraction of austenite, T is the temperature, F is a function of steel composition (expressed in wt%), N is the prior austenite grain size (ASTM number), ΔT is the undercooling, Q_{eff} is the effective activation energy for diffusion, and the exponent n is an empirical constant, determined by the effective diffusion mechanism; n = 2 for volume and n = 3 for boundary diffusion. $S(X)$ is the reaction rate term, which approximates the sigmoidal effect of phase transformation. In the work of Victor Li at al. (1998), $S(X)$ is expressed as follows:

$$S(X) = \int_0^X \frac{dX}{X^{0.4(1-X)}(1-X)^{0.4X}} \tag{11}$$

In a TTT diagram, the location of the 'nose' of each C curve correlates to the maximum reaction rate. The exact locations of the nose are jointly determined by the values of n and Q. From Eq. (10), at the nose temperature the denominator has to be maximum, thus:

$$\frac{d}{dT}\left(\Delta T^n \exp(-Q_{eff} / RT)\right) = 0 \tag{12}$$

which lead to the relationship:

$$Qeff = \frac{nRT_{Nose}^2}{\Delta T} \tag{13}$$

where T_{Nose} is the temperature at the nose position. Eq. (13) can be calibrated by using experimental data taken from literature and getting good estimations of the optimal value of Q_{eff}. It was found in Victor et al. (1998) that the Q_{eff} values have a median value of 27500 kcal/mol °C. For simplicity, this value is used for each diffusion-controlled phase transformation. The kinetic coefficients of alloying elements in Eq. (10) are then determined by calibrating such equation with TTT diagrams in the open literature. Under isothermal conditions, the ferrite transformation can be represented by:

$$\tau_F = \frac{\exp(1.00 + 6.31C + 1.78Mn + 0.31Si + 1.12Ni + 2.70Cr + 4.06Mo)}{2^{0.41N}(Ae_3 - T)^3 \exp(-27500 / RT)} S(X) \tag{14}$$

the pearlite transformation is represented by

$$\tau_P = \frac{\exp(-4.25 + 4.12C + 4.36Mn + 0.44Si + 1.71Ni + 3.33Cr + 5.19\sqrt{Mo})}{2^{0.32N}(Ae_1 - T)^3 \exp(-27500 / RT)} S(X) \tag{15}$$

and the bainite transformation under isothermal condition is represented by

$$\tau_B = \frac{\exp(-10.23 + 10.18C + 0.85Mn + 0.55Ni + 0.90Cr + 0.36Mo)}{2^{0.29N}(B_S - T)^2 \exp(-27500 / RT)} S(X) \tag{16}$$

where

$$B_s(°C) = 637 - 58C - 35Mn - 15Ni - 34Cr - 41Mo \tag{17}$$

While, the martensite start temperature can be expressed by the following equation:

$$M_s(°C) = 539 - 423C - 30.4Mn - 17.7Ni - 12.1Cr - 7.5Mo + 10Co - 7.5Si \tag{18}$$

Once the TTT diagram is calculated, it is possible to transform it into a CCT diagram using the well-established additivity rule:

$$\int_0^t \frac{dt}{\tau^{TTT}(X,T(t))} = \int_0^t \frac{\Delta T^n \exp(-Q / RT)}{F(C,Mn,Si,Ni,Cr,Mo,G)S(X)} dt = 1 \tag{19}$$

where $\tau^{TTT}(X,T(t))$ represents the isothermal transformation time for X at temperature T, and t is the total non-isothermal transformation time. Fig. 7 shows an example of TTT diagram computed with Matlab, starting from Eqs. (14-18).

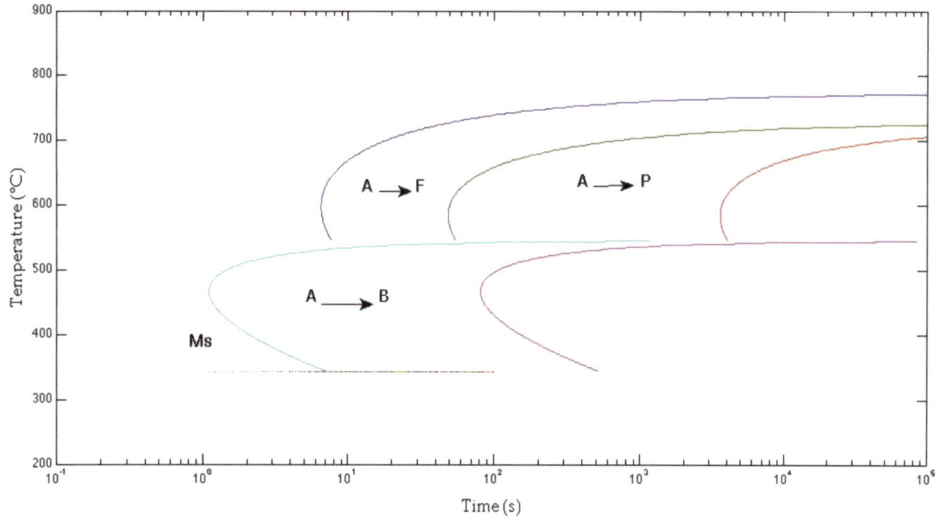

Fig. 7. Calculated TTT diagrams; steel composition (wt%): C 0.37, Mn 0.77, Si 0.15, Ni 0.04, Cr 0.98, Mo 0.21; ASTM grain size number: 7; A= Austenite, F = Ferrite, P = Pearlite, B = Bainite, Ms = martensite start temperature.

The above described model is limited to carbon and low-alloy steels. However, efforts are made in literature in order to develop models for general steels, including medium to high alloy types, tool steels, 13%Cr steels etc.

2.4 Practical use of thermo-metallurgical models for welding

An efficient recognition of the thermal field induced by a welding process, offers the possibility to make a parametric study of welding in order to check the influence of process, material and geometrical parameters on the temperature distribution within the plates. Fig. 8 shows an example of influence of the welding speed on the temperature distribution during the welding. It is clear that the lower the velocity the wider the HAZ.

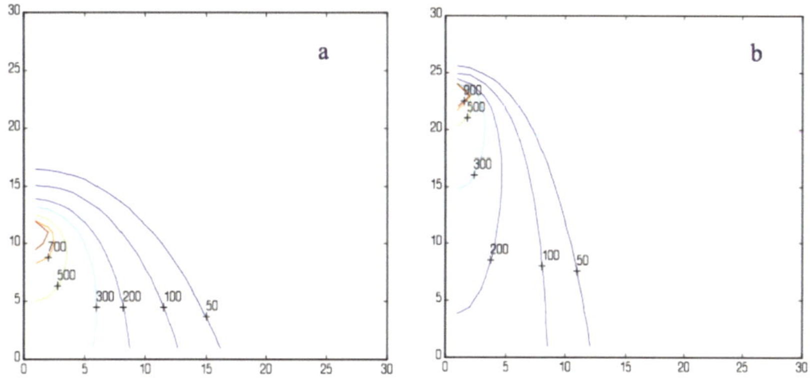

Fig. 8. Isotherms [°C]: at I = 170 A, V = 23.4 Volt, H = 6.6 mm, T_0 = 0 °C and a) v = 5 mm/s b) v = 11 mm/s [Material: AA-5083-O, welding technology: GMAW]

By comparing the solidus temperature isotherm width with that of FZ, it is also possible to estimate the thermal efficiency of the welding process. Finally, by using the CCT diagram and Eq. (6), it is possible to evaluate the pre-heating temperature needed to avoid a martensitic microstructure in the weld bead.

3. Mechanical analysis

3.1 Residual stresses calculation on butt-welded joints

High thermal gradients occurred during a welding process make thermal stresses in welded plates, that develop, after cooling, a state of permanent stress, generally defined as residual stresses. The magnitude of this residual stress state is so great that the mechanical behaviour of the welded joint, and in particular: fatigue, fracture, instability strength and stress corrosion, may be compromised. Thus the knowledge and, above all, the prediction of residual stresses is very important for a correct choice of parameters of the welding process and a good planning of welded joints. Unfortunately, the evaluation of thermal and residual stresses is not an easy task because of the complexity of the phenomena. However, in the case of simple shapes like butt or edge welded plates, some simplifications are possible. In such instances, one can calculate the residual stress field induced by a welding operation by using simple equations which can be solved with an iterative procedure with high time efficiency. The use of such analytical models were already been proposed by several authors. In particular, Goff (1979) simplified the problem assuming temperature-independent materials properties and a linear temperature distribution in the transversal direction of the plate. Using the singular Rosenthal solution of the thermal field, Tall (1964) suggested a step by step trial and error method in which at any temperature increment one had to determinate the equilibrium of thermal stress seen as the summation of temperature and equilibrium stresses; thermal stresses due to the temperature increment were summed to stresses calculate at the previous time step. Agapakis and Masubuchi (1984) developed the previous work by Tall, solving the equilibrium and stress-strain consititutive relations by an iterative procedure. Finally, Cañas *et al* (1996), proposed a 'rod model' in which the previous equations were written in matrix form and advantageously used in an efficient algorithm.

In what follows a model for residual stresses calcualtion in butt-welded joints is described. The equations which solve the problem are written in matrix form like in Cañas's work (1996). The thermal field induced by welding is given by Eq. (4) in which some fundamental assumptions are made:

1. the plate is infinitely large and very thin;
2. Eq. (4) describes a line source and then no temperature gradient exists through the thickness of the plate;
3. steady-state conditions;
4. for the stress calculation it is assumed that at time t, each longitudinal section is a part of an infinitely long plate subject to the same temperature distribution over its entire length (T=T(x,t)) (Fig. 9).

Moreover, plates without lateral constraints are considered so that longitudinal stresses are much greater than the transversal ones which are for this reason neglected. In order to write the equations in matrix form the welded plates are divided into n bars as shown in Fig. 9.

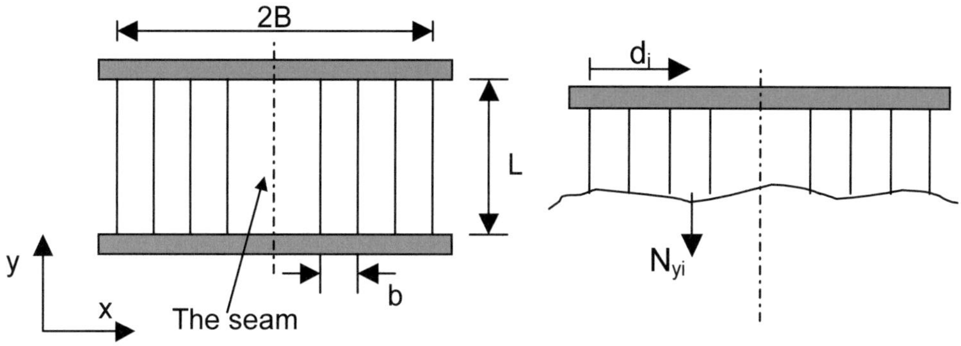

Fig. 9. Schematic representation of welded plates (plate thickness: h)

According to the configuration shown in Fig. 9, the conditions of equilibrium of forces and moments, written in matricial form, are:

$$\mathbf{C}^{\mathrm{T}}\mathbf{N}_y = \mathbf{0} \tag{20}$$

where **C** and $\mathbf{N}_y$ represent the following matrixes:

$$\mathbf{C} = \begin{bmatrix} 1 & d_1 \\ \dots & \dots \\ 1 & d_i \\ \dots & \dots \\ 1 & d_n \end{bmatrix} \quad \mathbf{N}_y = \begin{bmatrix} N_{y1} \\ \dots \\ N_{yi} \\ \dots \\ N_{yn} \end{bmatrix} \tag{21}$$

N_{yi} is the axial force of the bar i and n is the total number of bars employed to represent the welded plates. Assuming an ideal elasto-plastic non-holonomic material behaviour the constitutive equations are:

$$\mathbf{q}^y = \mathbf{q}^y{}_{\mathrm{e}} + \mathbf{q}^y{}_{\mathrm{t}} + \mathbf{q}^y{}_{\mathrm{p}} + \Delta\mathbf{q}^y{}_{\mathrm{p}} \tag{22}$$

where

- $\mathbf{q}^y$ represents the elongation vector in y direction (q_i^y is the elongation of the bar i in y direction);
- $q_{ei}{}^y = \dfrac{L}{E(T_i)h}\left(\dfrac{N_{yi}}{b}\right)$ is the elastic elongation of the bar i in y direction (Hooke's law);
- $q_{ti}{}^y = L\alpha(T_i)(T_i - T_0)$ is the thermal elongation of the bar i
- $q_{pi}{}^y$ is the accumulated inelastic elongation of the bar i during the previous time increments;
- $\Delta q_{pi}{}^y$ is the change of inelastic elongation of the bar i in y direction during the current time increment;

The compatibility equations are:

$$\mathbf{q}^y = \mathbf{Cu} \tag{22}$$

where **u** is the displacement vector associated to the degrees of freedom δ and θ to which the equilibrium conditions are applied (fig. 10).

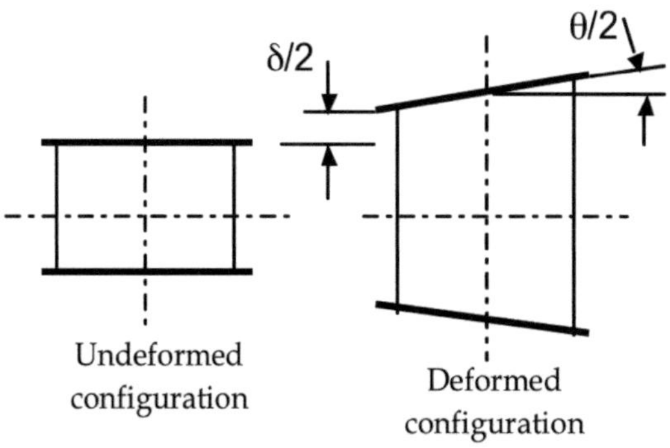

Fig. 10. Scheme of welded general plate deformation.

3.1.1 Field equations reduction

Eq. (22) can be written as:

$$\mathbf{q}^y = \mathbf{A}\mathbf{N}_y + \mathbf{A}_t(\mathbf{T}-\mathbf{T}_0) + \mathbf{q}_p{}^y + \Delta\mathbf{q}_p{}^y \tag{23}$$

where **A** is a diagonal matrix, each element of it representing the flexibility coefficient of the bar i (L/(E(Ti)hb), with E = Young's modulus), $\mathbf{A}_t$ is another diagonal matrix where each element of it is $L\alpha(T_i)$ and **T** is the temperature vector.

Now by using Eqs. (22) and (23), the vector $\mathbf{N}_y$ turns out to be:

$$\mathbf{N}_y = \mathbf{K}(\mathbf{C}\mathbf{u} - \mathbf{A}_t(\mathbf{T}-\mathbf{T}_0) - \mathbf{q}_p{}^y - \Delta\mathbf{q}_p{}^y) \tag{24}$$

where $\mathbf{K} = [\mathbf{A}]^{-1}$. From Eqs. (24) and (20):

$$\mathbf{u} = [\mathbf{C}^T\mathbf{K}\mathbf{C}]^{-1}\mathbf{C}^T\mathbf{K}(\mathbf{A}_t(\mathbf{T}-\mathbf{T}_0) + \mathbf{q}_p{}^y + \Delta\mathbf{q}_p{}^y) \tag{25}$$

Now, the only unknown terms are the current plastic elongations ($\Delta q_{pi}{}^y$) but a convergence procedure may be used to calculate them. At each time step, the temperature vector ($\mathbf{T}$-$\mathbf{T}_0$) can be first calculated by Eq. (4) and thus the temperature dependent material characteristics ($E(T_i)$ etc). The matrixes, **K**, **A** and $\mathbf{A}_t$ ($\mathbf{q}_p{}^y$ is known from the previous time step) may be then determined. Initially assuming that no plastic elongation exists, Eqs. (24) and (25) can be used for a first approximation of $\mathbf{N}_y$. Imposing

$$|N_i^y| \le N_{pi} \text{ for i =1...n} \tag{26}$$

where N_{pi} is the yield force of the bar i, a first approximation of $\Delta\mathbf{q}_p{}^y$ can be obtained by using the previous value of **u** and Eqs. (22) and (23). In this way a second approximation of $\mathbf{N}_y$ can be obtained by means of Eqs. (24), (25) and (26) and this procedure can be repeated until convergence is reached for the current time step. A program for the automatic solution of such iterative procedure can be easily written in Matlab code. The input data requested are: the net energy (Q) of the heat source, the welding speed (v), the liquidus and reference temperature, plates dimensions (L, 2B, h), the total number of bars (n). Figure 11 shows an example of the computed residual stresses in a butt welding joint and the comparison with Finite Element and experimental results.

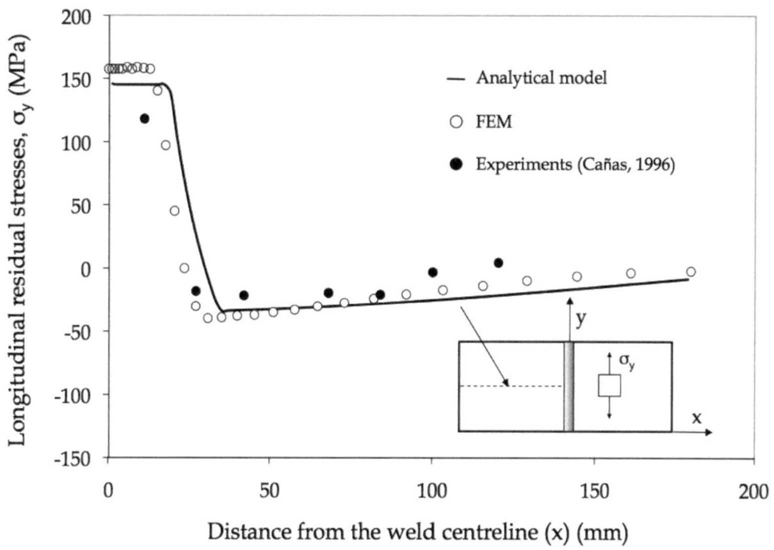

Fig. 11. Residual stresses along the centre line transverse to welding direction: analytical solution (Material: AA-5083-O. Geometrical parameters: h = 0.66 cm, 2B = 36 cm, L = 25 cm. Welding procedure: GMAW; Welding voltage: 23.4 V; Welding current: 170 A; Arc efficiency: 0.64; Welding speed: 11 mm s^{-1}; Filler wire diameter: 1.2 mm; Number of passes: 1; Shielding gas: Argon; Shielding gas flow rate: 0.21 s^{-1})

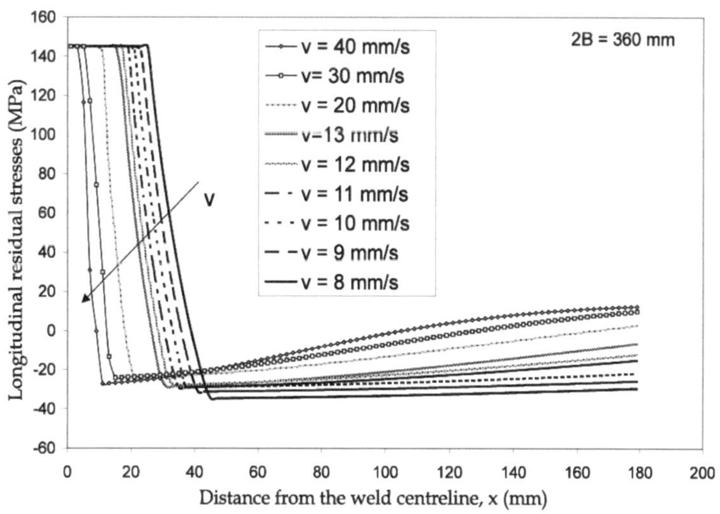

Fig. 12. Influence of welding speed (v) on residual stresses

The analytical model is very cost-effective in its computer implementation. Therefore, it allows for a series of parametric analyses to be performed and the relative importance of various parameters to be easily investigated. Fig. 12 shows, for example, the influence of welding speed on the residual stress field in welded plate without lateral constraints. Because of the heat input reduction, a decrement of plastic zone when welding speed increases is found.

3.2 Asymptotic stress distributions in welded and bonded joints

It is well know that fatigue resistance in mecahical components is controlled above all by the singular stress fields which arise near the gemetric discontinuities such as the wleld toe in welded joints (Livieri at al. (2005)) (Fig. 13) or the interface between the substrate and the adhesive in bonded joints (Lazzarin et al. (2002)).

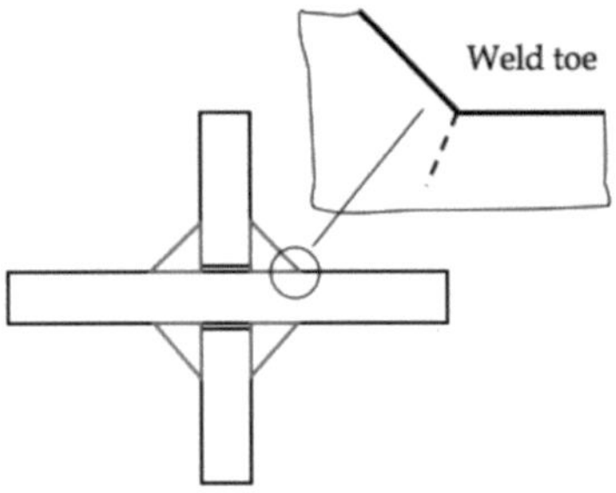

Fig. 13. Welded joint geometry and weld toe.

In several works (Lazzarin at al., 1998; Livieri et al, 2005) the weld toe region is modelled as a sharp, zero radius, V-shaped notch and the intensity of asymptotic stress distributions obeying Williams' solution (Williams, 1952) are quantified by means of the Notch Stress Intensity Factors (NSIFs). When the constancy of the angle included between weld flanks and main plates is assured and the angle is large enough to make mode II contribution non-singular, mode I NSIF can be directly used to summarised the fatigue strength of welded joints having very different geometry (Livieri et al, 2005). Furthermore, the NSIFs parameters can be used also for the evaluation of thermal fatigue resistance of different components (Ferro et al., 2006; Ferro et al., 2009).

The same approach is used for the advanced planning of bonded joints (Lazzarin et al., 2002). Adhesively bonded joints inevitably present high stress concentration zones, due to the different elastic properties of the connected materials. While in a homogeneous material, linear elastic stress distributions need the presence of a V-shaped corner to become singular (Williams, 1952), in the bi-material problems stress singularity arises, as well known, also in absence of any geometrical discontinuity (Bogy, 1968).

Strength evaluation needs both the order and the intensity of the stress singularity to be quantified in terms of joint geometry, material elastic properties and applied load. Several researchers (Gradin, (1982); Adams, et. al (1987); Groth, (1988); Hattory et al., (1988); Hattory, (1991); Reedy, (1990)) have used H (or other symbols, as K or Q) as a "generalised" stress intensity factor suitable as a failure criterion for bonded joints made of dissimilar materials. In the work of Hattory et al. (1991), for example, the stress field parameter (denoted Q_{xy}) was determined on the basis of the singular distribution of the shear stress σ_{xy}

present at the interface of Large Scale Integrated (LSI) electronic circuit devices subjected to thermal stresses. The critical value of Q_{xy} (able to provoke delamination in the components) was plotted against the order of the singularity γ. Different values of γ were obtained by using various configurations of epoxy/Fe-Ni blocks bonded together. Previously, Q_{xy} had already been used by Gradin (1982), by introducing his static criterion for brittle edge-bonded bi-material bodies.

More recently, a H-based approach has also been used by Lefrebvre and Dillard (1999) to predict the fatigue crack initiation in epoxy-aluminium wedge specimens, in a manner similar to the use of the Notch Stress Intensity Factors in welded structures (Lazzarin at al., 1998).

In view of the use of stress fields and stress intensity factors to predict the fatigue life at crack initiation, it is important to have the complete and correct description of the stress field very near to the apex. A method for the evaluation of the singular stress field in bonded joints of different geometry is presented and solved with Matlab; the stress distributions are represented by a two terms stress expansion, under the hypothesis that both first and second terms are in the variable separable form and therefore each term can be represented by a radial component with unknown exponent (eigenvalue) and an angular function also unknown.

The resulting analytical formulation of the stress distributions can be given as:

$$\sigma_{ij}(r,\vartheta) = H_0\, r^s\, f_{ij}^{(0)}(\vartheta) + H_1\, r^t\, f_{ij}^{(1)}(\vartheta) \tag{27}$$

The method is based on the numerical solution of the ordinary differential equation (ODE) system that, under the hypothesis of plane strain state, derives from the equilibrium and compatibility equations of a bonded joint or, more generally, of a bi-material body.

The capability of the formulation to account for the actual elastic properties of the substrates, allows us to obtain the accurate description of the stress field even in the case of joints made of materials with comparable elastic properties. It is worth noting that the "stress function approach" (where the formulation is completed analytically and the resulting set of equations is solved numerically) has already been used successfully by many researchers, mainly engaged with in-plane crack and notch problems in materials obeying a power-hardening law (Lazzarin et al., 2001).

3.2.1 Analytical frame

Let us consider the problem of the elastic equilibrium in a bi-material joint, in presence of a V-shaped corner with an opening angle $(\vartheta_1 + \vartheta_2)$ as shown in Figure 14. Both materials are thought of as homogeneous and isotropic and subjected to plane strain conditions. Under linear elastic hypothesis, strains components are:

$$\varepsilon_{ij} = \frac{1+\nu_m}{E_m}\sigma_{ij} - \frac{\nu_m}{E_m}\sigma_{kk}\delta_{ij} \tag{28}$$

where subscript m =1, 2 denotes the material, δ_{ij} is the Kroneker delta, and summation convention is used for repeated indexes.

In writing the problem of the elastic equilibrium we can now consider separately the two materials and later find the solution by applying the boundary conditions at the traction free surfaces and at the interface. It is possible therefore to omit, from now on and until not differently evidenced, the material subscript m, being the equations valid for the both substrates.

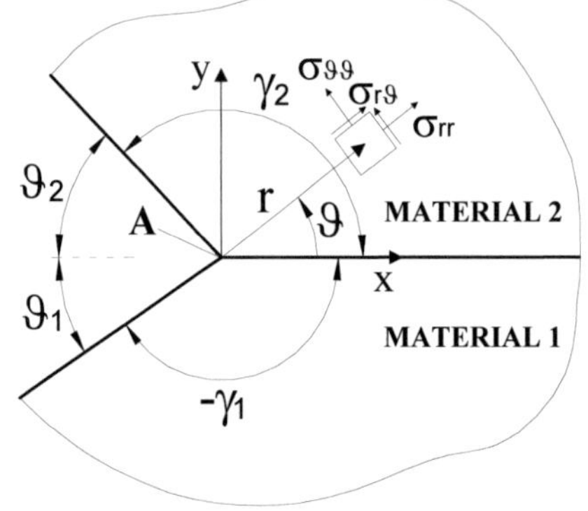

Fig. 14. Schematic view of the singular zone showing the cartesian and polar coordinate systems.

By assuming a polar coordinate system, in absence of body forces, the equilibrium conditions can be written as:

$$\frac{\partial \sigma_{rr}}{\partial r}+\frac{1}{r}\frac{\partial \sigma_{r\vartheta}}{\partial \vartheta}+\frac{\sigma_{rr}-\sigma_{\vartheta\vartheta}}{r}=0 \tag{29}$$

$$\frac{1}{r}\frac{\partial \sigma_{\vartheta\vartheta}}{\partial \vartheta}+\frac{\partial \sigma_{r\vartheta}}{\partial r}+\frac{2}{r}\sigma_{r\vartheta}=0 \tag{30}$$

The compatibility equations between strains and displacements are:

$$\varepsilon_{rr}=\frac{\partial U_r}{\partial r} \tag{31}$$

$$\varepsilon_{\vartheta\vartheta}=\frac{U_r}{r}+\frac{1}{r}\frac{\partial U_\vartheta}{\partial \vartheta} \tag{32}$$

$$\varepsilon_{r\vartheta}=\frac{1}{2}\left(\frac{1}{r}\frac{\partial U_r}{\partial \vartheta}+\frac{\partial U_\vartheta}{\partial r}-\frac{U_\vartheta}{r}\right) \tag{33}$$

where U_r and U_ϑ are the displacement components.
According to the direct approach, first suggested by Ponte Castanêda (1985) and then used also in (Yuan et al., (1994); Lazzarin et al. (2001)), a variable separable two term expansion is used for the stresses:

$$\sigma_{ij}(r,\vartheta)=r^s f_{ij}^{(0)}(\vartheta)+r^t f_{ij}^{(1)}(\vartheta) \tag{34}$$

where the exponent s is to be thought of as negative to give a stress field singular and, moreover, it is stated for hypothesis that $s < t$.
It should be noted that in Eq. (34) the generalised stress intensity factors H_0 and H_1, related to the first and second order component of the stress distribution respectively, are, for the time being, included in the angular stress distribution functions f_{ij} which are always defined within a constant value. Such a value is to be later determined by means of FE analyses.

Substitution of Eq. (34) into (28) gives the following expressions for strains:

$$\varepsilon_{ij}(r,\vartheta) = r^s \varepsilon_{ij}^{(0)}(\vartheta) + r^t \varepsilon_{ij}^{(1)}(\vartheta) \tag{35}$$

where:

$$\varepsilon_{ij}^{(0)}(\vartheta) = \frac{1+\nu}{E} f_{ij}^{(0)}(\vartheta) - \frac{\nu}{E} f_{kk}^{(0)}(\vartheta)\cdot\delta_{ij} \tag{36}$$

$$\varepsilon_{ij}^{(1)}(\vartheta) = \frac{1+\nu}{E} f_{ij}^{(1)}(\vartheta) - \frac{\nu}{E} f_{kk}^{(1)}(\vartheta)\cdot\delta_{ij} \tag{37}$$

The relevant displacement components are:

$$U_i(r,\vartheta) = r^{s+1} U_i^{(0)}(\vartheta) + r^{t+1} U_i^{(1)}(\vartheta) \tag{38}$$

As it is known, the exponents depend on the combination of the material elastic properties. In the close neighbourhood of the singularity point (r which tends towards zero), the first term of the stress distribution becomes dominant. Let us consider, therefore, in the stress and strain expansions only the leading-order term, s being the relevant exponent.
Substitution of Eqs. (34), (35) and (38) into Eqs. (29) to (33), together with the plane strain conditions

$$f_z^{(0)}(\vartheta) = \nu[f_{rr}^{(0)}(\vartheta) + f_{\vartheta\vartheta}^{(0)}(\vartheta)] \tag{39}$$

gives the following system:

$$\begin{aligned}
(s+1)f_{rr}^{(0)}(\vartheta) + f_{r\vartheta,\vartheta}^{(0)}(\vartheta) - f_{\vartheta\vartheta}^{(0)}(\vartheta) &= 0\\
f_{\vartheta\vartheta,\vartheta}^{(0)}(\vartheta) + (s+2)f_{r\vartheta}^{(0)}(\vartheta) &= 0\\
(s+1)U_r^{(0)}(\vartheta) - \frac{1+\nu}{E} f_{rr}^{(0)}(\vartheta) + \frac{\nu}{E}[f_{rr}^{(0)}(\vartheta)(1+\nu) + f_{\vartheta\vartheta}^{(0)}(\vartheta)(1+\nu)] &= 0\\
U_r^{(0)}(\vartheta) + U_{\vartheta,\vartheta}^{(0)}(\vartheta) - \frac{1+\nu}{E} f_{\vartheta\vartheta}^{(0)}(\vartheta) + \frac{\nu}{E}[f_{rr}^{(0)}(\vartheta)(1+\nu) + f_{\vartheta\vartheta}^{(0)}(\vartheta)(1+\nu)] &= 0\\
\frac{1}{2}[U_{r,\vartheta}^{(0)}(\vartheta) + sU_\vartheta^{(0)}(\vartheta)] - \frac{1+\nu}{E} f_{r\vartheta}^{(0)}(\vartheta) &= 0
\end{aligned} \tag{40}$$

where $f_{,\vartheta}$ and $U_{,\vartheta}$ mean $\frac{\partial f}{\partial \vartheta}$ and $\frac{\partial U}{\partial \vartheta}$, respectively.

The boundary conditions, at the traction free surface and at the interface between the two materials, are as follows:

$$\begin{aligned}
f_{\vartheta\vartheta}^{mat.1}(-\gamma_1) &= f_{\vartheta\vartheta}^{mat.2}(+\gamma_2) = 0\\
f_{r\vartheta}^{mat.1}(-\gamma_1) &= f_{r\vartheta}^{mat.2}(+\gamma_2) = 0\\
f_{\vartheta\vartheta}^{mat.1}(0) &= f_{\vartheta\vartheta}^{mat.2}(0)\\
f_{r\vartheta}^{mat.1}(0) &= f_{r\vartheta}^{mat.2}(0)\\
U_\vartheta^{mat.1}(0) &= U_\vartheta^{mat.2}(0)\\
U_r^{mat.1}(0) &= U_r^{mat.2}(0)
\end{aligned} \tag{41}$$

By using the third equation of the system 40 to eliminate the $U_r^{(0)}(\vartheta)$, the problem gives four differential equations for the material 1 and four differential equations for the material 2. The angular stress and displacement components $f_{\vartheta\vartheta}$, $f_{r\vartheta}$, f_{rr} and U_ϑ are the eigenfunctions of the problem, which will be given to within a constant value, as the problem is homogeneous.
A PC-based application has been developed for the solution of the system, by using the MATLAB® program and, particularly, its ODE45® routine.
According to the procedure illustrated in the flowchart of Figure 15, the solution begins with the introduction of an arbitrary value for $U_\vartheta(-\gamma_1)$ (for example, $10^{-4} \div 10^{-6}$) together with a couple of **s** and $f_{rr}(-\gamma_1)$ guess values and proceeds in iterative form till up:

$$abs\left\{ f_{\vartheta\vartheta}^{mat.2}(\gamma_2) \right\} + abs\left\{ f_{r\vartheta}^{mat.2}(\gamma_2) \right\} \leq tolerance \tag{42}$$

the tolerance value being usually set equal to 10^{-15}, while the angular stress components are close to the unity.

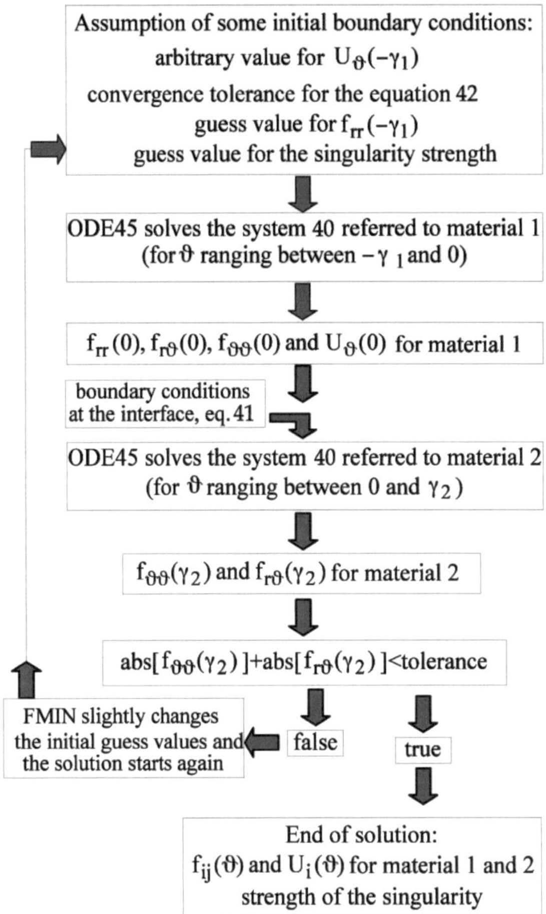

Fig. 15. Procedure for the solution of the ODE system (40).

To obtain the solution, the MATLAB® FMIN® function can, automatically, slightly modify the guessed values and restart the procedure. In cases where the convergence is not reached within a certain number of iterations, substantially different guessed values have to be chosen and the solution to be restarted.
As the stress expansion is in a variable separable form, and due also to the hypothesis of linear elastic behaviour, if we consider, in the stress and strain expansions, only the second term and the associated **t** order exponent, the system solution provides the related eigenfunctions.
Once the solution of the ODE system (40) is completed, the eigenfunctions, that is the angular stress and displacement distribution functions, and also the singularity strength for both the leading and second order term and for material 1 and 2 are available.
For the complete description of the stress field, according to Eq. (27), the generalised stress intensity factors H_0 and H_1 have still to be determined and this can be done through FE analyses, by minimising, for a generic ϑ^* direction (arbitrarily chosen on the steel side), the following error function:

$$E.F.(H_0,H_1)=\sum_{r,min}^{r,max} abs.[H_0 r^s f_{ij}^{(0)}(\vartheta^*)+H_1 r^t f_{ij}^{(1)}(\vartheta^*)-\sigma_{ij}(FE)] \tag{43}$$

being the r_{min} and r_{max} values usually set to 10^{-4} mm and one tenth of the substrate thickness, respectively. It is important to note that, kept constant the mesh refinement, the adhesive and substrate thickness varied from model to model, being 0.5-1.0 mm and 2.0-4.0 mm, respectively, their more typical value ranges. Fig. 16 shows the asymptotic stress distribution near the interface between the adhesive and the substrate in bonded joints obtained with Matlab.

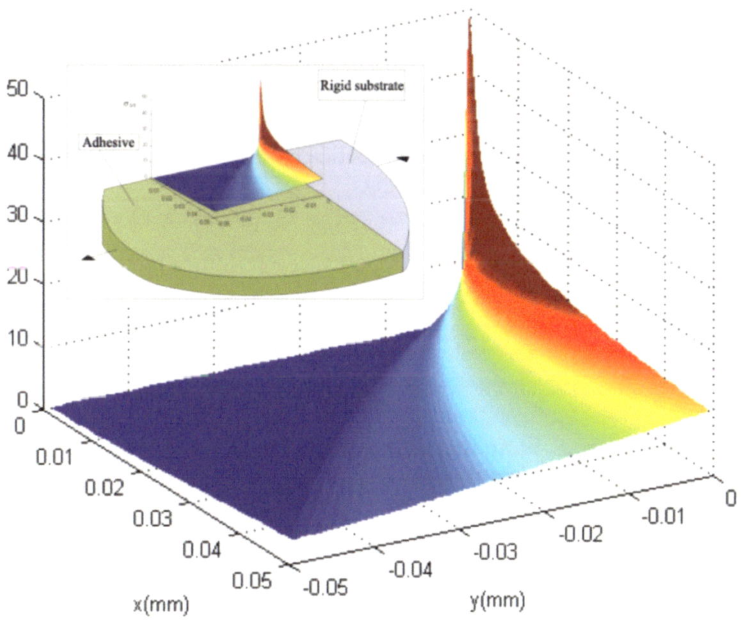

Fig. 16. Asymptotic stress distribution near the interface between the adhesive and the substrate in bonded joints

4. Conclusion

Different thermal and mechanical models solved with Matlab were presented which are very useful for a good planning of welded or bonded joints. About the thermal and residual stress fields predictions, some limitations are due to the geometry and material properties, but, compared to the finite element models, they are more user friendly and more efficient in terms of computational time; thus they can be used both for a rapid check of the thermal and stress filed induced by welding and for a parametric study of the process.
The 'stress field approach' for fatigue resistance prediction of welded and bonded joints was also presented. In particular, an analytical method for the description of the singular stress distributions on bonded joints of different geometry has been developed. The stress distributions near the singularity have been assumed to be represented by a power series expansion in the variable separable form as usually done in the elastoplastic analyses; under the further hypothesis of plane strain state, applying the equilibrium and compatibility conditions results in a ordinary differential equation system, which has been numerically solved by using a "shooting" technique.

5. References

Rosenthal, D. (1941). Mathematical theory of heat distribution during welding and cutting, *Weld. J. Res. Supp.*, 20, 220s.

Rosenthal, D. and Shamerber, H. (1938). Thermal study of Arc Welding. Experimental Verification of Theoretical Formulas. *The Welding Journal Res. Suppl.*, Vol. 17, No. 4, pp. 2-8.

Ferro, P., Tiziani, A., Bonollo, F. (2002). Analisi numerica e teorica del campo di tensioni residue indotte dal processo di saldatura in piastre in lega leggera. *Proceedings of XXXI AIAS Conference*, Parma, Italy, September 18-21, 2002.

Ferro, P., Bonollo, F. (2010). A Semianalytical Thermal Model for Friction Stir Welding. *Metallurgical and Material transaction A*, Vol. 41A, pp. 440 -449.

Vilaca, P., Quintino, L., dos Santos, J.F., Zettler, R., Sheikhi, S. (2007). Quality assessment of friction stir welding joints via an analytical thermal model, iSTIR'. *Materials Science and Engineering A*, 445-446 pp. 501-508.

Victor Li, M., Niebuhr, V., Meekisho, L., Atteridge, G. (1998). A Computational Model for the Prediction of Steel Hardenability. *Metallurgical and Materials Transactions B*, Vol. 29B, pp. 661-672.

Schmidt, H.B.,. Hattel. J.H. (2008). Thermal modelling of friction stir welding'. *Scripta Materialia,* Vol 58, pp. 332-337.

Perivilli, S., Peddieson, J., Cui, J. (2008). Simplified Two-Dimensional Analytical Model for Friction Stir Welding heat Transfer. *Journal of Heat Transfer*, Vol. 130, pp 1-9.

Goff, R. F. D. Porter. (1979). A Simplified Analysis of the Residual Longitudinal Stresses and Strains Due to the Gas-Cutting and Welding of Thin Steel Plate. *Int. J. Mech. Sci.* Vol. 21, pp. 287-300.

Chao, Y.J., Qi, X., Tang., W. (2003). Heat Transfer in Friction Stir welding - experimental and Numerical Studies. *Transaction of ASME*, Vol 125, pp 138-145.

Tall, L. (1964). Residual Stresses in Welded plates – a Theoretical Study. *Weld. J. Res. Supp.* Vol. 43, 10s.

Agapakis, J. E., Masubuchi, K. (1984). Analytical Modeling of Thermal Stress Relieving in Stainless and High Strength Steel Weldments", *Weld J. Res. Suopp.* 36, 187s.

Cañas, J., Picòn, R., París, F., Blazquez A., Marín, J. C. (1996). A Simplified Numerical Analysis of Residual Stresses in Aluminium Welded Plates, *Computers & Structures*, Vol. 58 No. 1, pp. 59-69

Cañas, J., Picòn, R., París F., Del Río, J. I. (1996). A One-Dimensional Model for the Prediction of Residual Stress and its Relief in Welded Plates, *Int. J. Mech. Sci.* Vol. 38, pp. 735-751.

Lazzarin, P., Quaresimin, M., Ferro, P. (2002). A two terms stress function approach to evaluate stress distributions in bonded joints of different geometry, *Journal of Strain Analysis for Engineering Design*, Vol 37 No 5, pp. 385-398

Livieri, P., Lazzarin, P. (2005). Fatigue strength of steel and aluminium welded joints based on generalised stress intensity factors and local energy values, International Journal of Fracture, Vol. 133, pp. 247-276

Williams, M.L. (1952). Stress singularities resulting from various boundary conditions in angular corners of plates in exstension. *Journal of Applied Mechanics*, Vol 19, pp. 526-528

Bogy, D.B. (1968) Edge-bonded dissimilar orthogonal elastic wedges under normal and shear loading. *J. Appl. Mechanics*, Vol 35, pp. 460-466

Gradin, P.A. (1982). A fracture criterion for edge-bonded bi-material bodies. *J. Composite Mater.*, Vol. 16, pp. 448-456

Adams, R.D. and Harris, J.A., (1987). The influence of local geometry on the strength of adhesive joints. *Int. J. Adhes. Adhes.*, Vol. 7, pp. 69-80

Groth, H.L. (1988). Stress singularities and fracture at interface corners in bonded joints, *Int. J. Adhes. Adhes.*, , Vol. 8, pp. 107-113

Hattory, T., Sakata, S., Hatsuda, T. and Murakami, G. (1988). A stress singularity parameter approach for evaluating adhesives strength. *JSME Int. J., Series I*, Vol. 31, pp. 718-723

Hattory T. (1991). A stress singularity parameter approach for evaluating the adhesives strength of single lap joint. *JSME. Int. J., Series I*, Vol. 34 , pp. 326-331

Reedy, Jr E.D. (1990). Intensity of stress singularity at the interface-corner between a bonded elastic and rigid layer. *Engng Fracture Mechanics*, Vol. 36, pp. 575-583

Lefebvre, D.R. and Dillard, D.A. (1999). A stress singularity approach for the prediction of fatigue crack initiation in adhesive bonds. PART 1: Theory. *J. Adhesion*, Vol. 70, pp. 119-138

Lazzarin, P. and Tovo, R. (1998). A Notch Stress Intensity Factor Approach to the Stress Analysis of Welds. *Fatigue Fracture Engng Mater. Structs*, Vol. 21, pp. 1089-1104

Lazzarin, P., Zambardi, R. and Livieri, P. (2001). Plastic Notch Stress Intensity Factors for Large V-Shaped Notches under Mixed Load Conditions. *Int. J. Fracture*, Vol. 107, pp. 361-377

Ponte Castañeda, P. (1985). Asymptotic fields in steady crack growth with linear strain-hardening. *J. Mech. Phys. Solids*, Vol. 35, pp. 227-268

Yuan, H. and Lin, G. (1994). Analysis of elastoplastic sharp notches. *Int. J. Fracture*, , Vol. 67, pp. 187-216

Ferro, P., Petrone, N. (2009). Asymptotic Thermal and Residual Stress Distributions due to Transient thermal Loads. *Fatigue and Fracture of Engineering Materials and Structures*. Vol. 32, pp. 936-948

Ferro, P., Berto, F., Lazzarin, P. (2006). Generalized stress intensity factors due to steady and transient thermal loads with applications to welded joints. *Fatigue Fract. Engng. Mater. Struct*, Vol. 29, pp. 440-453.

20

ISPN: Modeling Stochastic with Input Uncertainties Using an Interval-Based Approach

Sérgio Galdino and Paulo Maciel
Polytechnic School of Pernambuco University
& Federal University of Pernambuco
Brazil

1. Introduction

Analytic techniques are frequently used for performance analysis of discrete event systems. Conventional models have a set of single value input parameters (such as mean resource demands) and give single value results for each performance index of interest (such as mean system throughput). However, this single point characterization of parameters is insufficient when uncertainties and variabilities are related with system parameters. As an application domain, we may highlight software performance engineering, which accomplishes performance modelling in several phases design-cycle and throughout implementation (Girault & Valk, 2003; Smith, 1990). Even if uncertainties and variabilities may be associated with one or more parameters of the system in early stages of system design, the expert designer might have a suitable guess related to the interval of values associated with these parameters due to previous experience.
The current availability of software tools for performance evaluation allows one to hide the technicalities from the end-user. Users specify their performance model using some high-level modeling language supported by tools such as PEPSY-QNS, TimeNET 4.0, SPNP 6.0, GreatSPN 2.0, or PEPA, in which the underlying mathematical model is automatically generated and analyzed. We propose the adoption of intervals to represent the uncertainties in the parameters of ISPN (Interval Stochastic Petri Net) models (Galdino & Maciel, 2006; Galdino et al., 2007a;b). Therefore, the set of methods considered for Markov chain steady-state analysis have to be adapted for taking into account interval arithmetic. In ISPN the exponential transition rates and immediate transition weights are represented by intervals. This chapter focuses on ISPN using MATLAB with INTLAB toolbox. We briefly introduce the interval arithmetic. Afterwards, we describe the ISPN and outline the approach adopted to the respective interval steady state analysis. We present two ISPN system models and the respective results of analysis. Further possibilities of the method are also suggested.

2. Background

Prior to present the ISPN, this section introduces some basic concepts needed to understand how interval arithmetics may be used for evaluating system's metrics. Hence, we initially introduce some concepts on interval arithmetics.

2.1 Notation

Throughout this paper, all scalar variables are denoted by ordinary lowercase letters (a). Interval variables are enclosed in square brackets ([a]). Underscores and overscores denote lower and upper bounds, respectively.
A real interval $[x]$ is a nonempty set of real numbers

$$[x] = [\underline{x}, \overline{x}] = \{\tilde{x} \in \mathbb{R} : \underline{x} \leq \tilde{x} \leq \overline{x}\} \tag{1}$$

where $\underline{x}$ and $\overline{x}$ are called the *infimum (inf)* and *supremum (sup)*, respectively, and $\tilde{x}$ is a point value belonging to an interval variable $[x]$.
The set of all intervals $\mathbb{R}$ is denoted by $I(\mathbb{R})$ where

$$I(\mathbb{R}) = \{[\underline{x}, \overline{x}] : \underline{x}, \overline{x} \in \mathbb{R} : \underline{x} \leq \overline{x}\} \tag{2}$$

2.2 Interval arithmetic

Let $+$, $-$, $\times$, and $\div$ denote the arithmetic operations. If $\bullet$ denotes any of these arithmetic operation for real numbers x and y, then the corresponding operation for arithmetic on interval numbers $[x]$ and $[y]$ is

$$[x] \bullet [y] = \{x \bullet y | x \in [x], y \in [y]\}.$$

Thus the interval $[x] \bullet [y]$ resulting from the operations contain every possible number that can be found as $x \bullet y$ for each $x \in [x]$, and each $y \in [y]$.
A form of interval arithmetic perhaps first appeared in 1924 and 1931 in (Chen & van Emden, 1995; Young, 1931), then later in (Ullrich, 1990). Modern development of interval arithmetic began with R. E. Moore's dissertation (Moore, 1962) as a method for determining absolute errors of an algorithm, considering all data errors and rounding, after R.E. Moore introduced interval analysis (Moore, 1966). Interval arithmetic is an arithmetic defined on sets of intervals, rather than sets of real numbers. The power of interval arithmetic lies in its implementation on computers. In particular, outwardly rounded computations allows rigorous enclosures.
An important result is the inclusion property theorem . Rall aptly calls this the fundamental theorem of interval analysis (Hansen & Walster, 2004; Rall, 1969).

Theorem 2.1 (Fundamental Theorem). *If the function $f([x]_1, [x]_2, [x]_3, \cdots [x]_n)$ is an expression with a finite number of intervals $[x]_1, [x]_2, [x]_3, \cdots [x]_n \in I(\mathbb{R})$ and interval operations $(+, -, \times, \div)$, and if $[w]_1 \subseteq [x]_1, [w]_2 \subseteq [x]_2, [w]_3 \subseteq [x]_3, \cdots, [w]_n \subseteq [x]_n$ then $f([w]_1, [w]_2, [w]_3, \cdots, [w]_n) \subseteq f([x]_1, [x]_2, [x]_3, \cdots, [x]_n)$.*

2.3 Enclosures for the range of function

Consider a function f from $\mathbb{R}^n$ to $\mathbb{R}$. The interval function [f] from $I(\mathbb{R}^n)$ to $I(\mathbb{R})$ is an inclusion function [f] if

$$\forall [\mathbf{x}] \in I(\mathbb{R}^n),\ f([\mathbf{x}]) \subset [f]([\mathbf{x}])$$

Interval analyses provides, for a large class of functions f, inclusion functions such that $[f]([\mathbf{x}]$ is not too large.
An inclusion function for $f : \mathbb{R}^n \to \mathbb{R}$ is obtained with two optimizations to compute the *infimum* anad *supremum* of f. However, these optimization problems are far from trivial in general. An more tractable approach uses the following theorem (Jaulin et al., 2001), which is a direct consequence of Theorem 2.1.

Theorem 2.2 (Natural Inclusion Function Theorem). *Consider a function*

$$f : \mathbb{R}^n \to \mathbb{R}, (x_1, x_2, x_3, \cdots x_n) \mapsto f(x_1, x_2, x_3, \cdots x_n),$$

expressed as a finite composition of the operators $+$, $-$, $\times$, and $\div$ and elementary functions (sin, cos, exp, sqr, ...). An inclusion monotonic and thin (degenerated) inclusion function $[f] : I(\mathbb{R})^n \to I(\mathbb{R})$ for f is obtained by replacing each real variable x_i by an interval variable $[x_i]$ and each operator or function by its interval counterpart. This function is called the natural inclusion function of f. If f involves only continuous operators and continuous elementary functions, the [f] is convergent.If, moreover, each of the variables $(x_1, x_2, x_3, \cdots x_n)$ occurs at most once in the formal expression of f then $[f]$ is minimal.

Natural inclusion functions are not minimal in general, because of the dependence problem. The accuracy of the resulting interval strongly depends on the expression of f. The use of natural inclusion functions is not always the best choice. An important field of interval analysis is the use other types of inclusion functions that would provide best enclosures.

3. ISPN formalism

Petri Nets (PNs) represent a family of forms of graphical representation for description of systems whose dynamics are characterized by concurrency, synchronization, mutual exclusion, and conflict, which are typical features of distributed environments (Murata, 1989). PNs incorporate a notion of local state and a rule for state change (transition firing) that allow them to capture both the static and the dynamic characteristics of a real system being explicit about time considerations. The introduction of timing concepts into PN models were proposed later by Ramchandani (Ramchandani, 1974), Merlin (Merlin & Farber, 1976), and Sifakis (Sifakis, 1978) from distinct viewpoints. Molloy (Molloy, 1981) as well as Florin (Florin & Natkin, 1989) proposed PN models in which stochastic timing was considered. These works opened the possibility of connecting PN theory and stochastic modeling. Nowadays, these models as well as their extensions are generically named Stochastic Petri nets (SPN).

ISPN is an extension of GSPN (*Generalized Stochastic Petri Nets*) model in order to introduce the interval analysis (Galdino & Maciel, 2006) and has a lot of potential to practical applications. As part of the contribution in the development of this work, the authors also brought out its related practical applications in performance and dependability evaluation (Galdino & Maciel, 2006; Galdino et al., 2007a;b). GSPN is a particular timed PN (**Petri Net**) that incorporates both stochastic timed transitions (represented as white boxes) and immediate transitions (represented as thin black bars). Timed transitions have an exponentially distributed firing time and immediate transitions fire in zero time. GSPNs were originally defined (Marsan, Balbo & Conte, 1984) and later modified as described in (Brinksma, 2001). A formal definition of ISPN is provided below. This definition keeps to the SPN definition presented in (German, 2000), but considers real intervals assigned to transition delays and weights instead of adopting real single values.

Let $ISPN = (P, T, I, O, \Pi, G, M_0, Atts)$ be an interval stochastic Petri net, where

- $P = \{p_1, p_2, \cdots p_n\}$ is the set of places,
- $T = \{t_1, t_2, \cdots t_m\}$ is the set of transitions,
- $I \in (\mathbb{N}^n \to \mathbb{N})^{n \times m}$ is a matrix of marking-dependent multiplicities of input arcs, where the i_{jk} entry of I gives the possibly marking-dependent arc multiplicity of input arcs from place p_j to transition t_k $[A \subset (P \times T) \cup (T \times P) - set\ of\ arcs]$,

- $O \in (\mathbb{N}^n \rightarrow \mathbb{N})^{n \times m}$ is a matrix of marking-dependent multiplicities of output arcs, where o_{jk} entry of O gives the possibly marking-dependent arc multiplicity of output arcs from transition t_j to place p_k,
- $H \in (\mathbb{N}^n \rightarrow \mathbb{N})^{n \times m}$ is a matrix of marking-dependent multiplicities of inhibitor arcs, where h_{jk} entry of H gives the possibly marking-dependent arc multiplicity of inhibitor arcs from place p_j to transition t_k,
- $G \in (N^n \rightarrow \{true, false\})^m$ is a vector that assigns a guard condition related to place markings to each transition,
- $M_0 \in \mathbb{N}^n$ is a vector that assigns the initial marking of each place (initial state),
- $Atts = (Dist, W, Markdep, Police, Concurrency)^m$ comprises the set of attributes for transitions, where
  - $[Dist] \in \mathbb{N}^m \rightarrow [\mathcal{F}]$ is a possible marking-dependent firing interval distribution function (the domain of $[\mathcal{F}]$ is $[0, \infty)$),
  - $[W] \in \mathbb{N}^m \rightarrow I(\mathbb{R}^+)$ is a possible marking-dependent interval weight,
  - $Markdep \in \{constant, enabdep\}$ where the transition interval firing timing distribution could be marking independent $(constant)$ or enabling dependent ($enabdep$ - the distribution depends on the actual enabling condition),
  - $Police \in \{prd, prs\}$ is the preemption policy (*prd- preemptive repeat different* means that when a preempted transition becomes enabled again the previous elapsed firing time is lost; *prs- preemptive resume*, in which the firing time related to a preempted transition is resumed when the transition becomes enabled again),
  - $Concurrency \in \{ss, is\}$ is the degree of concurrency of transitions, where ss represents single server semantics and is depicts infinite-server semantics.

It is worth noting that if only point intervals are assigned to delays and immediate transition weights the model is reduced to a GSPN. This case the ISPN analysis provides GSPN verified results.

3.1 ISPN steady state analysis

ISPN is considered to be a high-level formalism for ICTMC (Interval Continuous Time Markov Chain) generation Galdino et al. (2007b). The classical algorithms found in literature (Bolch et al., 2006) are adapted to take into account the interval coefficients of the ISPN model. This is a contribution to analysis of models ISPN that will be presented in sequel. The analysis of models using ISPN is accomplished in four subtasks:

- generation of the IERG (Interval Extended Reachability Graph),
- elimination of vanishing markings and the corresponding state transitions,
- interval steady-state analysis,
- computation of measures. Standard measures such as the average number of tokens in places and the throughput of timed transitions are computed using interval arithmetic.

3.1.1 Generation of the IERG

The first of four steps of ISPN analysis is the IERG generation (*interval extended reachability graph*). From the IERG the set of markings $\mathcal{M} = \mathcal{T} \cup \mathcal{V}$ is divided into set of tangible markings $\mathcal{T}$ and vanishing $\mathcal{V}$. Through the elimination of vanishing markings discussed below, using methods of interval analysis, we obtain the infinitesimal generator matrix $[Q]$ of ICTMC underlying an ISPN model.

From a given ISPN, an interval extended reachability graph (IERG) is generated containing markings as nodes and interval stochastic information attached to arcs so as to relate markings to each other. The ISPN reachability graph is a directed graph $RG(ISPN) = (V, E)$, where $V = RS(ISPN)$ and $E = \left\{\langle \mathbf{m}, t, \mathbf{m}' \rangle \mid \mathbf{m}, \mathbf{m}' \in RS(ISPN) \;\; and\; \mathbf{m} \xrightarrow{t} \mathbf{m}'\right\}$ are the set of nodes and edges, respectively. If an ISPN model is bounded, the $RG(ISPN)$ is finite and it can be constructed, for example, based on Algorithm 5.1: *Computation of the Reachability Graph* p. 61 from (Girault & Valk, 2003).

The $RG(ISPN)$ is constructed, in this work, using the **Algorithm 1** below. The activity defined in Step 2.1 ensures that no marking is visited more than once. Each visited marking is labeled (Step 2.1), and Step 2.2.3 ensures that only unique added markings to V are those that were not previously added. When the marking is visited, only those edges that represents the firing of an enabled transition are added to the set E (Step 2.2.4).

==

Algorithm 1

(IERG generation **)**

Input - A ISPN model.
Output - A directed graph $RG(ISPN) = (V, E)$ of a limited network system.

1. Initialize $RG(ISPN) = (\{\mathbf{m}_0\}, \emptyset)$; $\mathbf{m}_0$ is unlabelled.
2. **while** there are an unlabeled node **m** in V **do**
   2.1 Select an unlabeled node $\mathbf{m} \in V$ label it
   2.2 **for** each enabled transition **t** in **m** **do**
      2.2.1 Calculate $\mathbf{m}'$ such that $\mathbf{m} \xrightarrow{t} \mathbf{m}'$;
      2.2.2 **if** there are $\mathbf{m}'' \in V$ such that $\mathbf{m}'' \xrightarrow{\sigma} \mathbf{m}'$ and $\mathbf{m}'' \leq \mathbf{m}'$
            then the algorithm fails and ends;
               (no limitation condition was detected).
      2.2.3 **if** there is no $\mathbf{m}'' \in V$ such that $\mathbf{m}'' = \mathbf{m}'$
            then $V := V \cup \{\mathbf{m}'\}$; ($\mathbf{m}'$ é um nó não etiquetado).
      2.2.4 $E := E \cup \{\langle \mathbf{m}; t; \mathbf{m}' \rangle\}$
3. The algorithm is successful and RG(ISPN) is the interval extended reachability graph.

==

3.1.2 Elimination of vanishing markings

The second of four steps of ISPN analysis is the elimination of vanishing markings, which is the step for generating the ICTMC from a given ISPN. Once the IERG has been generated, it is transformed into an ICTMC by the use of matrix algorithms Bolch et al. (2006).

The markings set $\mathcal{M} = \mathcal{V} \cup \mathcal{T}$ in the reachability set of an ISPN is partitioned into two sets, the vanishing markings $\mathcal{V}$ and the tangible markings $\mathcal{T}$. Let:

$$[\mathbf{P}]^{\mathcal{V}} = [\mathbf{P}]^{\mathcal{V}\mathcal{V}} \mid [\mathbf{P}]^{\mathcal{V}\mathcal{T}} \tag{3}$$

denote an interval matrix, where

- $[\mathbf{P}]^{\mathcal{VV}}$ - denotes the interval transition probabilities between vanishing markings,
- $[\mathbf{P}]^{\mathcal{VT}}$ - denotes the interval transition probabilities from vanishing markings to the tangible markings.

Furthermore, let

$$[\mathbf{U}]^{\mathcal{T}} = [\mathbf{U}]^{\mathcal{TV}} \mid [\mathbf{U}]^{\mathcal{TT}} \tag{4}$$

denote an interval matrix, where

- $[\mathbf{U}]^{\mathcal{TV}}$- represents interval transition rates from tangible to vanishing markings;
- $[\mathbf{U}]^{\mathcal{TT}}$- represents interval transition rates between tangible markings.

Now, we obtain the interval rate matrix $[\mathbf{U}]$. This matrix has dimensions $|\mathcal{T}| \times |\mathcal{T}|$, where $\mathcal{T}$ denotes the set of tangible markings.

$$[\mathbf{U}] = [\mathbf{U}]^{\mathcal{TT}} + [\mathbf{U}]^{\mathcal{TV}}(1 - [\mathbf{P}]^{\mathcal{VV}})^{-1}[\mathbf{P}]^{\mathcal{VT}} \tag{5}$$

The interval matrix of the infinitesimal generator is $[\mathbf{Q}] = [q]_{ij}$, where its entries are given by:

$$[q]_{ij} = \begin{cases} [u]_{ij} \;\; if\ i \neq j \\ -\sum_{\substack{k \in \mathcal{T} \\ k \neq i}} [u]_{ik} \;\; if\ i = j \end{cases} \tag{6}$$

where $\mathcal{T}$ denotes the set of tangible markings.

3.1.3 Steady-state probability vector evaluation

Now we describe the third of four steps of ISPN analysis. The steady-state solution of the ICTMC model underlying the ISPN is obtained by solving the interval linear system of equations with as many equations as the number of tangible markings.

$$\begin{cases} [\pi] \cdot [\mathbf{Q}] = \mathbf{0} \\ \sum_{M \in \mathcal{T}} [\pi]\,(M) = 1 \end{cases} \tag{7}$$

$[\pi]$ is the interval vector for the equilibrium pmf (probability mass function) over the reachable tangible markings, and we write $[\pi]\,(M)$ for the interval steady-state probability of a given tangible marking M.
Once the interval generator matrix $[\mathbf{Q}]$ of the ICTMC associated with a ISPN model has been derived, the steady state probability is calculated so that other respective metrics might be subsequently computed.
ISPN models deal with system uncertainties by considering intervals for representing time as well as weights assigned to transition models. The proposed model and the respective methods, adapted to take interval arithmetic into account, allow the influence of simultaneous parameters and variabilities on the computation of metrics to be considered, thereby providing rigorously bounded metric ranges. It is also important to stress that even when only taking into account thin intervals, one may make use of the proposed model, since rounding and truncation errors are naturally dealt with in interval arithmetic, so that the metrics results obtained are certain to belong to the intervals computed.

3.1.4 Interval performance indices

The computation of performance indices (metrics) of interest is the fourth and final step in the analysis ISPN. In the case of ISPN steady state analysis, where interval p.m.f. has already been obtained, indices are calculated by interval function evaluation. Interval performance indices are interval functions extended on classical indices (Marsan, Bobbio, Conte & Cumani, 1984).

4. Examples of ISPN models

The purpose of this section is to present clearly all steps of ISPN analysis. Two examples are used. One is very simple and can be followed up and have calculations performed without using a computer. The second case, however, you must use a software with an interval arithmetic library as a tool to carry out by all his calculations. Example 1 has only two tangible markings and two vanishing markings. Example 2 has sixteen tangible markings and twelve vanishing markings. The performance evaluations are carried out in MATLAB with the INTLAB toolbox (MATLAB *toolbox* INTLAB framework). The ISPN model analysis considering only degenerated intervals (points) leads to the classic model GSPN, with verified computations (self-validating).

4.1 Example 1: ISPN analysis of a single machine

The model depicted in Figure 1 represents a failure prone machine and finite capacity buffer (Desrochers & Al-Jaar, 1994). Table 1 presents (degenerated) interval rates of timed transition firing per unit time, where $[\nu]$ represents the production rate interval, $[\lambda]$ represents the failure rate interval, and $[\mu]$ represents the repair rate interval. Here we have a model equivalent to the GSPN model, because there are only degenerate interval parameters.

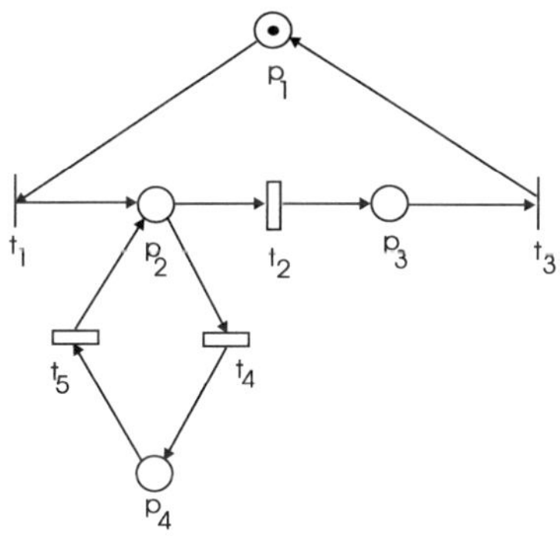

Fig. 1. The Single Machine module.

Transition	Value ($[t]^{-1}$)	Symbol
$[t_2]$	[10, 10]	$[\nu]$
$[t_4]$	[3, 3]	$[\mu]$
$[t_5]$	[5, 5]	$[\lambda]$

Table 1. Transition Firing Rates (degenerated intervals) for the Single Machine One-Buffer Transfer Line.

As a result of the first step of ISPN analysis we obtain the reachability set (Table 2), and the reachability graph (Figure 2).

State	Marking (m_1, m_2, m_3, m_4)
1	$M_0 = (1, 0, 0, 0)$
2	$M_1 = (0, 1, 0, 0)$
3	$M_2 = (0, 0, 1, 0)$
4	$M_3 = (0, 0, 0, 1)$

Table 2. Reachability set and distribution markings from ISPN of Figure 1.

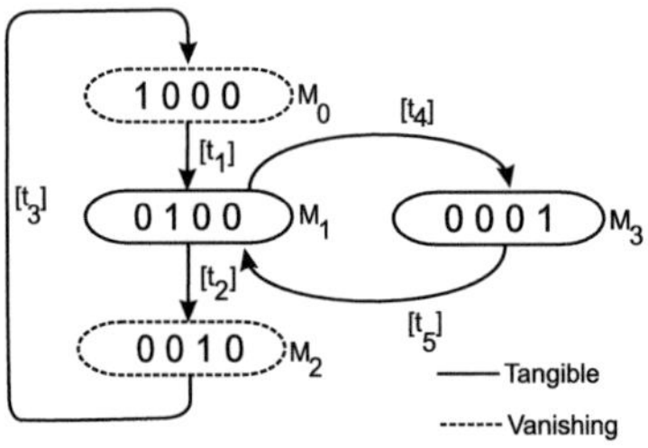

Fig. 2. Reachability graph and interval embedded Markov chain

Finally, we obtain the matrices $[\mathbf{P}]^{\mathcal{VV}}$, $[\mathbf{P}]^{\mathcal{VT}}$, $[\mathbf{U}]^{\mathcal{TV}}$ and $[\mathbf{U}]^{\mathcal{TT}}$:

$$[\mathbf{P}]^{\mathcal{VV}} = \begin{pmatrix} [0,\ 0] & [0,\ 0] \\ [1,\ 1] & [0,\ 0] \end{pmatrix} \quad [\mathbf{P}]^{\mathcal{VT}} = \begin{pmatrix} [1,\ 1] & [0,\ 0] \\ [0,\ 0] & [0,\ 0] \end{pmatrix}$$

$$[\mathbf{U}]^{\mathcal{TT}} = \begin{pmatrix} [0,\ 0] & [5,\ 5] \\ [3,\ 3] & [0,\ 0] \end{pmatrix} \quad [\mathbf{U}]^{\mathcal{TV}} = \begin{pmatrix} [0,\ 0] & [10,\ 10] \\ [0,\ 0] & [0,\ 0] \end{pmatrix}.$$

Afterwards, carry out the elimination of vanishing markings (Equation 5) to obtain the matrix of rate intervals $[U]$. The matrix of rate intervals represents an IREMC (*Interval Reduced Embedded Markov Chain* on Figure 3):

$$[\mathbf{U}] = \begin{pmatrix} [10,\ 10] & [5,\ 5] \\ [3,\ 3] & [0,\ 0] \end{pmatrix}.$$

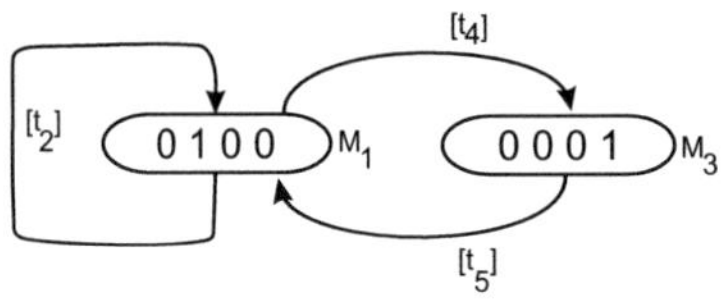

Fig. 3. Interval Reduced Embedded Markov Chain

Finally, using Equation 6, we find the infinitesimal generator interval matrix:

$$[\mathbf{Q}] = \begin{pmatrix} [-5,\ -5] & [5,\ 5] \\ [3,\ 3] & [-3,\ -3] \end{pmatrix}.$$

The third step of ISPN analysis solves the system of interval linear equations described by Equation (7). The interval linear equations solution is carried out by the verifylss function of the MATLAB *toolbox* INTLAB. Substituting the last equation of system $([\pi]_1, [\pi]_2) \cdot [\mathbf{Q}] = 0$ by the normalization condition $[\pi]_1 + [\pi]_2 = 1$, the linear system $([\pi]_1, [\pi]_2) \cdot [\mathbf{A}] = [\mathbf{b}]$ is obtained. The solution of this system directly provides the steady state probabilities of tangible states. Considering

$$[\mathbf{A}] = \begin{pmatrix} -3 & 5 \\ 1 & 1 \end{pmatrix} \text{ and } [\mathbf{b}] = \begin{pmatrix} 0 \\ 1 \end{pmatrix}$$

the M-file MATLAB toolbox INTLAB **case1v.m**, used for calculating verified probabilities and machine production rate, is given bellow:

```
%       INPUT:     A coeffifiente matrix
%                  b right hand side vector
%       OUTPUT:    x interval probabilities vector solution
%                  P machine production rate
format long
intvalinit('displayinfsup')
A=intval([-3,5;1,1])
b=[0;1]
x=verifylss(A,b)
P=10*x(1)
```

Executing **case1v.m** yields:

```
>> case1v
===> Default display of intervals by infimum/supremum (e.g. [ 3.14 , 3.15 ])
intval A =
[ -3.00000000000000, -3.00000000000000] [ 5.00000000000000, 5.00000000000000]
[  1.00000000000000,  1.00000000000000] [ 1.00000000000000, 1.00000000000000]
b =
     0
     1
intval x =
[   0.62499999999998,    0.62500000000001]
[   0.37499999999999,    0.37500000000001]
intval P =
[   6.24999999999998,    6.25000000000001]
>>
```

The verified interval bounds of each state probabilities on tangible states are:

$$[\pi]_{(1)} = [\,0.62499999999998,\ 6.25000000000001]$$

and

$$[\pi]_{(2)} = [\,0.37499999999999,\ 0.37500000000001].$$

Finally we can make the fourth and final step of analysis ISPN, computation of metrics. The machine production rate is

$$[P] = [\,6.24999999999998,\ 6.25000000000001]$$

(calculated with the formula $[P] = [\pi]_{(1)} \cdot [t_2]$). This results exhibit the enclosure of exact value obtained by GSPN analysis. The ISPN analysis results give us verified results, ensuring that the exact value is certain to belong to the intervals computed. One can, for example, to compare this result with interval $P = 6.25$ exact value in this simple case.

Introducing parameters with input uncertainties

Now we calculate a solution in which the parameters are not known exactly, but it is known that they are within certain intervals. Lets consider that rates are $[\mu] = 3 \pm 0.01 = [2.99,\ 3.01]$ and $[\lambda] = 5 \pm 0.01 = [4.99,\ 5.01]$ intervals.

As a result from the first step of analysis (by-product of the reachability set), we obtain the matrices $[\mathbf{P}]^{\mathcal{VV}}$, $[\mathbf{P}]^{\mathcal{VT}}$, $[\mathbf{U}]^{\mathcal{TV}}$ e $[\mathbf{U}]^{\mathcal{TT}}$:

$$[\mathbf{P}]^{\mathcal{VV}} = \begin{pmatrix} [\,0,\ 0] & [\,0,\ 0] \\ [\,1,\ 1] & [\,0,\ 0] \end{pmatrix} \qquad [\mathbf{P}]^{\mathcal{VT}} = \begin{pmatrix} [\,1,\ 1] & [\,0,\ 0] \\ [\,0,\ 0] & [\,0,\ 0] \end{pmatrix}$$

$$[\mathbf{U}]^{\mathcal{TT}} = \begin{pmatrix} [\,0,\ 0] & [\,4.99,\ 5.01] \\ [\,2.99,\ 3.01] & [\,0,\ 0] \end{pmatrix} \quad [\mathbf{U}]^{\mathcal{TV}} = \begin{pmatrix} [\,0,\ 0] & [\,10,\ 10] \\ [\,0,\ 0] & [\,0,\ 0] \end{pmatrix}.$$

Afterwards, carry out the elimination of vanishing markings (Equation 5), to obtain the matrix of rate intervals $[U]$:

$$[\mathbf{U}] = \begin{pmatrix} [\,10,\ 10] & [\,4.99,\ 5.01] \\ [\,2.99,\ 3.01] & [\,0,\ 0] \end{pmatrix}.$$

Finally, using Equation 6, we find the infinitesimal generator interval matrix:

$$[\mathbf{Q}] = \begin{pmatrix} [\,\text{-}5.01,\ \text{-}4.99] & [\,4.99,\ 5.01] \\ [\,2.99,\ 3.01] & [\,\text{-}3.01,\ \text{-}2.99] \end{pmatrix}.$$

Considering

$$[\mathbf{A}] = \begin{pmatrix} -3 & 5 \\ 1 & 1 \end{pmatrix} \ \mathit{and}\ [\mathbf{b}] = \begin{pmatrix} 0 \\ 1 \end{pmatrix}$$

the M-file MATLAB toolbox INTLAB **case1i.m**, used for calculating verified probabilities and machine production rate, is given bellow:

```
%        INPUT:     A coeffifiente matrix
%                   b right hand side vector
%        OUTPUT:    x interval probabilities vector solution
%                   P machine production rate
format long
intvalinit('displayinfsup')
A=infsup([-3.01,4.99;1,1],[-2.99,5.01;1,1])
b=[0;1]
x=verifylss(A,b)
P=10*x(1)
```

Executing **case1i.m** yields:

```
>> case1i
===> Default display of intervals by infimum/supremum (e.g. [ 3.14 , 3.15 ])
intval A =
[ -3.01000000000000, -2.99000000000000] [ 4.99000000000000, 5.01000000000000]
[  1.00000000000000,  1.00000000000000] [ 1.00000000000000, 1.00000000000000]
b =
     0
     1
intval x =
[    0.62374656249999,    0.62625343750001]
[    0.37374656249998,    0.37625343750001]
intval P =
[    6.23746562499999,    6.26253437500001]
>>
```

The interval bounds of each state probabilities on tangible states are:

$$[\pi]_{(1)} = [\,0.62374656249999,\ 0.62625343750001]$$

and

$$[\pi]_{(2)} = [\,0.37374656249998,\ 0.37625343750001].$$

Finally we can make the computation of machine production rate:

$$[P] = [\,6.23746562499999,\ 6.26253437500001]$$

(calculated with the formula $[P] = [\pi]_{(1)} \cdot [t_2]$). This result represents the variabilities when the rates are in $[\mu] = [2.99,\ 3.01]$ and $[\lambda] = [4.99,\ 5.01]$ intervals.

4.2 Example 2: ISPN analysis of Two-Machine One-Buffer Transfer Line Model

Consider the Two-Machine One-Buffer Transfer Line Model in Figure 4 (Desrochers & Al-Jaar, 1994). Table 3 presents (degenerated) interval rates of timed transition firing per unit time, where $[\nu_i]$ represents the production rate intervals, $[\lambda_i]$ represents the failure rate intervals, and $[\mu_i]$ represents the repair rate intervals. Here we have a model equivalent to the GSPN model, because there are only degenerate interval parameters.

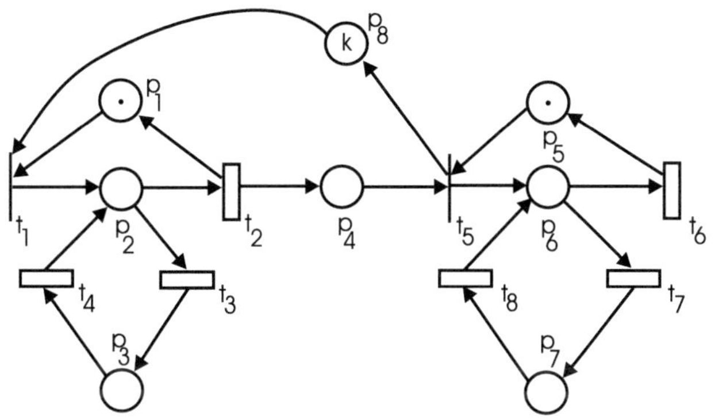

Fig. 4. Two-Machine One-Buffer Transfer Line Model ($k = 3$)

Transition	Value $([t]^{-1})$	Symbol
$[t_2]$	[1, 1]	$[\nu_1]$
$[t_3]$	[3, 3]	$[\lambda_1]$
$[t_4]$	[5, 5]	$[\mu_1]$
$[t_6]$	[2, 2]	$[\nu_2]$
$[t_7]$	[4, 4]	$[\lambda_2]$
$[t_8]$	[6, 6]	$[\mu_2]$

Table 3. Interval transition firing rates for the Two-Machine One-Buffer Transfer Line model.

As a result of the first step of ISPN analysis we obtain the reachability set (Table 4) and the reachability graph (Table 5).

Markings enabling the transitions t_1 and t_5 are vanishing, because enabled transitions are immediate (state changes that take negligible amounts of time to occur). Can be identified twelve vanishing markings M_0, M_2, M_4, M_5, M_7, M_{12}, M_{13}, M_{17}, M_{19}, M_{22}, M_{24}, M_{26} (firing of immediate transitions t_1 and t_5) and other markings are tangibles.

State	Marking[1]	State	Marking[1]
1	$M_0 = [1,0,0,0,1,0,0,3]$	15	$M_{14} = [0,0,1,1,0,1,0,1]$
2	$M_1 = [0,1,0,0,1,0,0,2]$	16	$M_{15} = [0,1,0,1,0,0,1,1]$
3	$M_2 = [1,0,0,1,1,0,0,2]$	17	$M_{16} = [0,1,0,2,0,1,0,0]$
4	$M_3 = [0,0,1,0,1,0,0,2]$	18	$M_{17} = [0,0,1,1,1,0,0,1]$
5	$M_4 = [0,1,0,1,1,0,0,1]$	19	$M_{18} = [0,0,1,1,0,0,1,1]$
6	$M_5 = [1,0,0,0,0,1,0,3]$	20	$M_{19} = [1,0,0,2,0,0,1,1]$
7	$M_6 = [0,1,0,0,0,1,0,2]$	21	$M_{20} = [1,0,0,3,0,1,0,0]$
8	$M_7 = [1,0,0,1,0,1,0,2]$	22	$M_{21} = [0,0,1,2,0,1,0,0]$
9	$M_8 = [0,0,1,0,0,1,0,2]$	23	$M_{22} = [0,1,0,2,1,0,0,0]$
10	$M_9 = [0,1,0,0,0,0,1,2]$	24	$M_{23} = [0,1,0,2,0,0,1,0]$
11	$M_{10} = [0,1,0,1,0,1,0,1]$	25	$M_{24} = [1,0,0,3,1,0,0,0]$
12	$M_{11} = [0,0,1,0,0,0,1,2]$	26	$M_{25} = [1,0,0,3,0,0,1,0]$
13	$M_{12} = [1,0,0,1,0,0,1,2]$	27	$M_{26} = [0,0,1,2,1,0,0,0]$
14	$M_{13} = [1,0,0,2,0,1,0,1]$	28	$M_{27} = [0,0,1,2,0,0,1,0]$

1- $Marking = [\ m_1, m_2, m_3, m_4, m_5, m_6, m_7, m_8\ ]$

Table 4. Reachability set and distribution markings from ISPN of Figure 4.

Marking $\vert$ *Firing of transition* $\rangle$ *New marking*				
$M_0\,\vert t_1\rangle\,M_1$	$M_1\,\vert T_2\rangle\,M_2$	$M_1\,\vert T_3\rangle\,M_3$	$M_2\,\vert t_1\rangle\,M_4$	$M_2\,\vert t_5\rangle\,M_5$
$M_3\,\vert T_4\rangle\,M_1$	$M_4\,\vert t_5\rangle\,M_6$	$M_5\,\vert t_1\rangle\,M_6$	$M_6\,\vert T_2\rangle\,M_7$	$M_6\,\vert T_3\rangle\,M_8$
$M_6\,\vert T_6\rangle\,M_1$	$M_6\,\vert T_7\rangle\,M_9$	$M_7\,\vert t_1\rangle\,M_{10}$	$M_8\,\vert T_4\rangle\,M_6$	$M_8\,\vert T_6\rangle\,M_3$
$M_8\,\vert T_7\rangle\,M_{11}$	$M_9\,\vert T_2\rangle\,M_{12}$	$M_9\,\vert T_3\rangle\,M_{11}$	$M_9\,\vert T_8\rangle\,M_6$	$M_{10}\,\vert T_2\rangle\,M_{13}$
$M_{10}\,\vert T_3\rangle\,M_{14}$	$M_{10}\,\vert T_6\rangle\,M_4$	$M_{10}\,\vert T_7\rangle\,M_{15}$	$M_{11}\,\vert T_4\rangle\,M_9$	$M_{11}\,\vert T_8\rangle\,M_8$
$M_{12}\,\vert t_1\rangle\,M_{15}$	$M_{13}\,\vert t_1\rangle\,M_{16}$	$M_{14}\,\vert T_4\rangle\,M_{10}$	$M_{14}\,\vert T_6\rangle\,M_{17}$	$M_{14}\,\vert T_7\rangle\,M_{18}$
$M_{15}\,\vert T_2\rangle\,M_{19}$	$M_{15}\,\vert T_3\rangle\,M_{18}$	$M_{15}\,\vert T_8\rangle\,M_{10}$	$M_{16}\,\vert T_2\rangle\,M_{20}$	$M_{16}\,\vert T_3\rangle\,M_{21}$
$M_{16}\,\vert T_6\rangle\,M_{22}$	$M_{16}\,\vert T_7\rangle\,M_{23}$	$M_{17}\,\vert t_5\rangle\,M_8$	$M_{18}\,\vert T_4\rangle\,M_{15}$	$M_{18}\,\vert T_8\rangle\,M_{14}$
$M_{19}\,\vert t_1\rangle\,M_{23}$	$M_{20}\,\vert T_6\rangle\,M_{24}$	$M_{20}\,\vert T_7\rangle\,M_{25}$	$M_{21}\,\vert T_4\rangle\,M_{16}$	$M_{21}\,\vert T_6\rangle\,M_{26}$
$M_{21}\,\vert T_7\rangle\,M_{27}$	$M_{22}\,\vert t_5\rangle\,M_{10}$	$M_{23}\,\vert T_2\rangle\,M_{25}$	$M_{23}\,\vert T_3\rangle\,M_{27}$	$M_{23}\,\vert T_8\rangle\,M_{16}$
$M_{24}\,\vert t_5\rangle\,M_{13}$	$M_{25}\,\vert T_8\rangle\,M_{20}$	$M_{26}\,\vert t_5\rangle\,M_{14}$	$M_{27}\,\vert T_4\rangle\,M_{23}$	$M_{27}\,\vert T_8\rangle\,M_{21}$

Table 5. Literal description of reachability graph from ISPN of Figure 4.

Finally, we obtain the matrices $[\mathbf{P}]^{\mathcal{VV}}$, $[\mathbf{P}]^{\mathcal{VT}}$, $[\mathbf{U}]^{\mathcal{TV}}$ and $[\mathbf{U}]^{\mathcal{TT}}$:

$$[\mathbf{P}]^{\mathcal{VV}} = \begin{pmatrix}
[0,0] & [0,0] & [0,0] & [0,0] & [0,0] & [0,0] & [0,0] & [0,0] & [0,0] & [0,0] & [0,0] & [0,0] \\
[0,0] & [0,0] & [0{,}5,0{,}5] & [0{,}5,0{,}5] & [0,0] & [0,0] & [0,0] & [0,0] & [0,0] & [0,0] & [0,0] & [0,0] \\
[0,0] & [0,0] & [0,0] & [0,0] & [0,0] & [0,0] & [0,0] & [0,0] & [0,0] & [0,0] & [0,0] & [0,0] \\
[0,0] & [0,0] & [0,0] & [0,0] & [0,0] & [0,0] & [0,0] & [0,0] & [0,0] & [0,0] & [0,0] & [0,0] \\
[0,0] & [0,0] & [0,0] & [0,0] & [0,0] & [0,0] & [0,0] & [0,0] & [0,0] & [0,0] & [0,0] & [0,0] \\
[0,0] & [0,0] & [0,0] & [0,0] & [0,0] & [0,0] & [0,0] & [0,0] & [0,0] & [0,0] & [0,0] & [0,0] \\
[0,0] & [0,0] & [0,0] & [0,0] & [0,0] & [0,0] & [0,0] & [0,0] & [0,0] & [0,0] & [0,0] & [0,0] \\
[0,0] & [0,0] & [0,0] & [0,0] & [0,0] & [0,0] & [0,0] & [0,0] & [0,0] & [0,0] & [0,0] & [0,0] \\
[0,0] & [0,0] & [0,0] & [0,0] & [0,0] & [0,0] & [0,0] & [0,0] & [0,0] & [0,0] & [0,0] & [0,0] \\
[0,0] & [0,0] & [0,0] & [0,0] & [0,0] & [0,0] & [0,0] & [0,0] & [0,0] & [0,0] & [0,0] & [0,0] \\
[0,0] & [0,0] & [0,0] & [0,0] & [0,0] & [0,0] & [1,1] & [0,0] & [0,0] & [0,0] & [0,0] & [0,0] \\
[0,0] & [0,0] & [0,0] & [0,0] & [0,0] & [0,0] & [0,0] & [0,0] & [0,0] & [0,0] & [0,0] & [0,0]
\end{pmatrix}$$

$$[\mathbf{P}]^{\mathcal{V}\mathcal{T}} = \left(\begin{array}{cccccccccccccccc}
[1, 1] & [0, 0] & [0, 0] & [0, 0] & [0, 0] & [0, 0] & [0, 0] & [0, 0] & [0, 0] & [0, 0] & [0, 0] & [0, 0] & [0, 0] & [0, 0] & [0, 0] & [0, 0] \\
[0, 0] & [0, 0] & [0, 0] & [0, 0] & [0, 0] & [0, 0] & [0, 0] & [0, 0] & [0, 0] & [0, 0] & [0, 0] & [0, 0] & [0, 0] & [0, 0] & [0, 0] & [0, 0] \\
[0, 0] & [0, 0] & [1, 1] & [0, 0] & [0, 0] & [0, 0] & [0, 0] & [0, 0] & [0, 0] & [0, 0] & [0, 0] & [0, 0] & [0, 0] & [0, 0] & [0, 0] & [0, 0] \\
[0, 0] & [0, 0] & [1, 1] & [0, 0] & [0, 0] & [0, 0] & [0, 0] & [0, 0] & [0, 0] & [0, 0] & [0, 0] & [0, 0] & [0, 0] & [0, 0] & [0, 0] & [0, 0] \\
[0, 0] & [0, 0] & [0, 0] & [0, 0] & [0, 0] & [1, 1] & [0, 0] & [0, 0] & [0, 0] & [0, 0] & [0, 0] & [0, 0] & [0, 0] & [0, 0] & [0, 0] & [0, 0] \\
[0, 0] & [0, 0] & [0, 0] & [0, 0] & [0, 0] & [0, 0] & [0, 0] & [0, 0] & [1, 1] & [0, 0] & [0, 0] & [0, 0] & [0, 0] & [0, 0] & [0, 0] & [0, 0] \\
[0, 0] & [0, 0] & [0, 0] & [0, 0] & [0, 0] & [0, 0] & [0, 0] & [0, 0] & [0, 0] & [1, 1] & [0, 0] & [0, 0] & [0, 0] & [0, 0] & [0, 0] & [0, 0] \\
[0, 0] & [0, 0] & [0, 0] & [1, 1] & [0, 0] & [0, 0] & [0, 0] & [0, 0] & [0, 0] & [0, 0] & [0, 0] & [0, 0] & [0, 0] & [0, 0] & [0, 0] & [0, 0] \\
[0, 0] & [0, 0] & [0, 0] & [0, 0] & [0, 0] & [0, 0] & [0, 0] & [0, 0] & [0, 0] & [0, 0] & [0, 0] & [0, 0] & [0, 0] & [1, 1] & [0, 0] & [0, 0] \\
[0, 0] & [0, 0] & [0, 0] & [0, 0] & [0, 0] & [1, 1] & [0, 0] & [0, 0] & [0, 0] & [0, 0] & [0, 0] & [0, 0] & [0, 0] & [0, 0] & [0, 0] & [0, 0] \\
[0, 0] & [0, 0] & [0, 0] & [0, 0] & [0, 0] & [0, 0] & [0, 0] & [0, 0] & [0, 0] & [0, 0] & [0, 0] & [0, 0] & [0, 0] & [0, 0] & [0, 0] & [0, 0] \\
[0, 0] & [0, 0] & [0, 0] & [0, 0] & [0, 0] & [0, 0] & [0, 0] & [1, 1] & [0, 0] & [0, 0] & [0, 0] & [0, 0] & [0, 0] & [0, 0] & [0, 0] & [0, 0]
\end{array}\right)$$

$$[\mathbf{U}]^{\mathcal{T}\mathcal{T}} = \left(\begin{array}{cccccccccccccccc}
[0, 0] & [3, 3] & [0, 0] & [0, 0] & [0, 0] & [0, 0] & [0, 0] & [0, 0] & [0, 0] & [0, 0] & [0, 0] & [0, 0] & [0, 0] & [0, 0] & [0, 0] & [0, 0] \\
[5, 5] & [0, 0] & [0, 0] & [0, 0] & [0, 0] & [0, 0] & [0, 0] & [0, 0] & [0, 0] & [0, 0] & [0, 0] & [0, 0] & [0, 0] & [0, 0] & [0, 0] & [0, 0] \\
[2, 2] & [0, 0] & [0, 0] & [3, 3] & [4, 4] & [0, 0] & [0, 0] & [0, 0] & [0, 0] & [0, 0] & [0, 0] & [0, 0] & [0, 0] & [0, 0] & [0, 0] & [0, 0] \\
[0, 0] & [2, 2] & [5, 5] & [0, 0] & [0, 0] & [0, 0] & [4, 4] & [0, 0] & [0, 0] & [0, 0] & [0, 0] & [0, 0] & [0, 0] & [0, 0] & [0, 0] & [0, 0] \\
[0, 0] & [0, 0] & [6, 6] & [0, 0] & [0, 0] & [0, 0] & [3, 3] & [0, 0] & [0, 0] & [0, 0] & [0, 0] & [0, 0] & [0, 0] & [0, 0] & [0, 0] & [0, 0] \\
[0, 0] & [0, 0] & [0, 0] & [0, 0] & [0, 0] & [0, 0] & [0, 0] & [3, 3] & [4, 4] & [0, 0] & [0, 0] & [0, 0] & [0, 0] & [0, 0] & [0, 0] & [0, 0] \\
[0, 0] & [0, 0] & [0, 0] & [6, 6] & [5, 5] & [0, 0] & [0, 0] & [0, 0] & [0, 0] & [0, 0] & [0, 0] & [0, 0] & [0, 0] & [0, 0] & [0, 0] & [0, 0] \\
[0, 0] & [0, 0] & [0, 0] & [0, 0] & [0, 0] & [5, 5] & [0, 0] & [0, 0] & [0, 0] & [0, 0] & [4, 4] & [0, 0] & [0, 0] & [0, 0] & [0, 0] & [0, 0] \\
[0, 0] & [0, 0] & [0, 0] & [0, 0] & [0, 0] & [6, 6] & [0, 0] & [0, 0] & [0, 0] & [0, 0] & [3, 3] & [0, 0] & [0, 0] & [0, 0] & [0, 0] & [0, 0] \\
[0, 0] & [0, 0] & [0, 0] & [0, 0] & [0, 0] & [0, 0] & [0, 0] & [0, 0] & [0, 0] & [0, 0] & [0, 0] & [1, 1] & [3, 3] & [4, 4] & [0, 0] & [0, 0] \\
[0, 0] & [0, 0] & [0, 0] & [0, 0] & [0, 0] & [0, 0] & [0, 0] & [6, 6] & [5, 5] & [0, 0] & [0, 0] & [0, 0] & [0, 0] & [0, 0] & [0, 0] & [0, 0] \\
[0, 0] & [0, 0] & [0, 0] & [0, 0] & [0, 0] & [0, 0] & [0, 0] & [0, 0] & [0, 0] & [0, 0] & [0, 0] & [0, 0] & [0, 0] & [0, 0] & [4, 4] & [0, 0] \\
[0, 0] & [0, 0] & [0, 0] & [0, 0] & [0, 0] & [0, 0] & [0, 0] & [0, 0] & [0, 0] & [5, 5] & [0, 0] & [0, 0] & [0, 0] & [0, 0] & [0, 0] & [4, 4] \\
[0, 0] & [0, 0] & [0, 0] & [0, 0] & [0, 0] & [0, 0] & [0, 0] & [0, 0] & [0, 0] & [6, 6] & [0, 0] & [0, 0] & [0, 0] & [0, 0] & [1, 1] & [3, 3] \\
[0, 0] & [0, 0] & [0, 0] & [0, 0] & [0, 0] & [0, 0] & [0, 0] & [0, 0] & [0, 0] & [0, 0] & [0, 0] & [6, 6] & [0, 0] & [0, 0] & [0, 0] & [0, 0] \\
[0, 0] & [0, 0] & [0, 0] & [0, 0] & [0, 0] & [0, 0] & [0, 0] & [0, 0] & [0, 0] & [0, 0] & [0, 0] & [0, 0] & [6, 6] & [5, 5] & [0, 0] & [0, 0]
\end{array}\right)$$

$$
[\mathbf{U}]^{\mathcal{TV}} = \begin{pmatrix}
[0, 0] & [1, 1] & [0, 0] & [0, 0] & [0, 0] & [0, 0] & [0, 0] & [0, 0] & [0, 0] & [0, 0] & [0, 0] & [0, 0] \\
[0, 0] & [0, 0] & [0,0] & [0, 0] & [0, 0] & [0, 0] & [0, 0] & [0, 0] & [0, 0] & [0, 0] & [0, 0] & [0, 0] \\
[0, 0] & [0, 0] & [0, 0] & [0, 0] & [1, 1] & [0, 0] & [0, 0] & [0, 0] & [0, 0] & [0, 0] & [0, 0] & [0, 0] \\
[0, 0] & [0, 0] & [0, 0] & [0, 0] & [0, 0] & [0, 0] & [0, 0] & [0, 0] & [0, 0] & [0, 0] & [0, 0] & [0, 0] \\
[0, 0] & [0, 0] & [0, 0] & [0, 0] & [0, 0] & [1, 1] & [0, 0] & [0, 0] & [0, 0] & [0, 0] & [0, 0] & [0, 0] \\
[0, 0] & [0, 0] & [2, 2] & [0, 0] & [0, 0] & [0, 0] & [1, 1] & [0, 0] & [0, 0] & [0, 0] & [0, 0] & [0, 0] \\
[0, 0] & [0, 0] & [0, 0] & [0, 0] & [0, 0] & [0, 0] & [0, 0] & [0, 0] & [0, 0] & [0, 0] & [0, 0] & [0, 0] \\
[0, 0] & [0, 0] & [0, 0] & [0, 0] & [0, 0] & [0, 0] & [0, 0] & [2, 2] & [0, 0] & [0, 0] & [0, 0] & [0, 0] \\
[0, 0] & [0, 0] & [0, 0] & [0, 0] & [0, 0] & [0, 0] & [0, 0] & [0, 0] & [1, 1] & [0, 0] & [0, 0] & [0, 0] \\
[0, 0] & [0, 0] & [0, 0] & [0, 0] & [0, 0] & [0, 0] & [0, 0] & [0, 0] & [0, 0] & [2, 2] & [0, 0] & [0, 0] \\
[0, 0] & [0, 0] & [0, 0] & [0, 0] & [0, 0] & [0, 0] & [0, 0] & [0, 0] & [0, 0] & [0, 0] & [0, 0] & [0, 0] \\
[0, 0] & [0, 0] & [0, 0] & [0, 0] & [0, 0] & [0, 0] & [0, 0] & [0, 0] & [0, 0] & [0, 0] & [2, 2] & [0, 0] \\
[0, 0] & [0, 0] & [0, 0] & [0, 0] & [0, 0] & [0, 0] & [0, 0] & [0, 0] & [0, 0] & [0, 0] & [0, 0] & [2, 2] \\
[0, 0] & [0, 0] & [0, 0] & [0, 0] & [0, 0] & [0, 0] & [0, 0] & [0, 0] & [0, 0] & [0, 0] & [0, 0] & [0, 0] \\
[0, 0] & [0, 0] & [0, 0] & [0, 0] & [0, 0] & [0, 0] & [0, 0] & [0, 0] & [0, 0] & [0, 0] & [0, 0] & [0, 0] \\
[0, 0] & [0, 0] & [0, 0] & [0, 0] & [0, 0] & [0, 0] & [0, 0] & [0, 0] & [0, 0] & [0, 0] & [0, 0] & [0, 0]
\end{pmatrix}
$$

Afterwards, carry out the elimination of vanishing markings (Equation 5), to obtain the matrix of rate intervals $[U]$ representing the IREMC:

$$
[\mathbf{U}] = \left(\begin{matrix}
[0, 0] & [3, 3] & [1, 1] & [0, 0] & [0, 0] & [0, 0] & [0, 0] & [0, 0] & [0, 0] & [0, 0] & [0, 0] & [0, 0] \\
[5, 5] & [0, 0] & [0, 0] & [0, 0] & [0, 0] & [0, 0] & [0, 0] & [0, 0] & [0, 0] & [0, 0] & [0, 0] & [0, 0] \\
[2, 2] & [0, 0] & [0, 0] & [3, 3] & [4, 4] & [1, 1] & [0, 0] & [0, 0] & [0, 0] & [0, 0] & [0, 0] & [0, 0] \\
[0, 0] & [2, 2] & [5, 5] & [0, 0] & [0, 0] & [0, 0] & [4, 4] & [0, 0] & [0, 0] & [0, 0] & [0, 0] & [0, 0] \\
[0, 0] & [0, 0] & [6, 6] & [0, 0] & [0, 0] & [0, 0] & [3, 3] & [0, 0] & [1, 1] & [0, 0] & [0, 0] & [0, 0] \\
[0, 0] & [0, 0] & [2, 2] & [0, 0] & [0, 0] & [0, 0] & [0, 0] & [3, 3] & [4, 4] & [1, 1] & [0, 0] & [0, 0] \\
[0, 0] & [0, 0] & [0, 0] & [6, 6] & [5, 5] & [0, 0] & [0, 0] & [0, 0] & [0, 0] & [0, 0] & [0, 0] & [0, 0] \\
[0, 0] & [0, 0] & [0, 0] & [2, 2] & [0, 0] & [5, 5] & [0, 0] & [0, 0] & [0, 0] & [0, 0] & [4, 4] & [0, 0] \\
[0, 0] & [0, 0] & [0, 0] & [0, 0] & [0, 0] & [6, 6] & [0, 0] & [0, 0] & [0, 0] & [0, 0] & [3, 3] & [0, 0] \\
[0, 0] & [0, 0] & [0, 0] & [0, 0] & [0, 0] & [2, 2] & [0, 0] & [0, 0] & [0, 0] & [0, 0] & [0, 0] & [1, 1] \\
[0, 0] & [0, 0] & [0, 0] & [0, 0] & [0, 0] & [0, 0] & [0, 0] & [6, 6] & [5, 5] & [0, 0] & [0, 0] & [0, 0] \\
[0, 0] & [0, 0] & [0, 0] & [0, 0] & [0, 0] & [0, 0] & [0, 0] & [0, 0] & [0, 0] & [2, 2] & [0, 0] & [0, 0] \\
[0, 0] & [0, 0] & [0, 0] & [0, 0] & [0, 0] & [0, 0] & [0, 0] & [2, 2] & [0, 0] & [5, 5] & [0, 0] & [0, 0] \\
[0, 0] & [0, 0] & [0, 0] & [0, 0] & [0, 0] & [0, 0] & [0, 0] & [0, 0] & [0, 0] & [6, 6] & [0, 0] & [0, 0] \\
[0, 0] & [0, 0] & [0, 0] & [0, 0] & [0, 0] & [0, 0] & [0, 0] & [0, 0] & [0, 0] & [0, 0] & [0, 0] & [6, 6] \\
[0, 0] & [0, 0] & [0, 0] & [0, 0] & [0, 0] & [0, 0] & [0, 0] & [0, 0] & [0, 0] & [0, 0] & [0, 0] & [0, 0]
\end{matrix} \right.
$$

$$
\left. \begin{matrix}
[0, 0] & [0, 0] & [0, 0] & [0, 0] \\
[0, 0] & [0, 0] & [0, 0] & [0, 0] \\
[0, 0] & [0, 0] & [0, 0] & [0, 0] \\
[0, 0] & [0, 0] & [0, 0] & [0, 0] \\
[0, 0] & [0, 0] & [0, 0] & [0, 0] \\
[0, 0] & [0, 0] & [0, 0] & [0, 0] \\
[0, 0] & [0, 0] & [0, 0] & [0, 0] \\
[0, 0] & [0, 0] & [0, 0] & [0, 0] \\
[0, 0] & [1, 1] & [0, 0] & [0, 0] \\
[3, 3] & [4, 4] & [0, 0] & [0, 0] \\
[0, 0] & [0, 0] & [0, 0] & [0, 0] \\
[0, 0] & [0, 0] & [4, 4] & [0, 0] \\
[0, 0] & [0, 0] & [0, 0] & [4, 4] \\
[0, 0] & [0, 0] & [1, 1] & [3, 3] \\
[0, 0] & [0, 0] & [0, 0] & [0, 0] \\
[6, 6] & [5, 5] & [0, 0] & [0, 0]
\end{matrix} \right).
$$

Finally, using Equation 6, we find the infinitesimal generator interval matrix:

$$
[\mathbf{Q}] = \left(\begin{array}{cccccccccccccccc}
[-4,-4] & [3,3] & [1,1] & [0,0] & [0,0] & [0,0] & [0,0] & [0,0] & [0,0] & [0,0] & [0,0] & [0,0] & [0,0] & [0,0] & [0,0] & [0,0] \\
[5,5] & [-5,-5] & [0,0] & [0,0] & [0,0] & [0,0] & [0,0] & [0,0] & [0,0] & [0,0] & [0,0] & [0,0] & [0,0] & [0,0] & [0,0] & [0,0] \\
[2,2] & [0,0] & [-10,-10] & [3,3] & [4,4] & [1,1] & [0,0] & [0,0] & [0,0] & [0,0] & [0,0] & [0,0] & [0,0] & [0,0] & [0,0] & [0,0] \\
[0,0] & [2,2] & [5,5] & [-11,-11] & [0,0] & [0,0] & [4,4] & [0,0] & [0,0] & [0,0] & [0,0] & [0,0] & [0,0] & [0,0] & [0,0] & [0,0] \\
[0,0] & [0,0] & [6,6] & [0,0] & [-10,-10] & [0,0] & [3,3] & [0,0] & [1,1] & [0,0] & [0,0] & [0,0] & [0,0] & [0,0] & [0,0] & [0,0] \\
[0,0] & [0,0] & [2,2] & [0,0] & [0,0] & [-10,-10] & [0,0] & [3,3] & [4,4] & [1,1] & [0,0] & [0,0] & [0,0] & [0,0] & [0,0] & [0,0] \\
[0,0] & [0,0] & [0,0] & [6,6] & [5,5] & [0,0] & [-11,-11] & [0,0] & [0,0] & [0,0] & [0,0] & [0,0] & [0,0] & [0,0] & [0,0] & [0,0] \\
[0,0] & [0,0] & [0,0] & [2,2] & [0,0] & [5,5] & [0,0] & [-11,-11] & [0,0] & [0,0] & [4,4] & [0,0] & [0,0] & [0,0] & [0,0] & [0,0] \\
[0,0] & [0,0] & [0,0] & [0,0] & [0,0] & [6,6] & [0,0] & [0,0] & [-10,-10] & [0,0] & [3,3] & [0,0] & [0,0] & [1,1] & [0,0] & [0,0] \\
[0,0] & [0,0] & [0,0] & [0,0] & [0,0] & [2,2] & [0,0] & [0,0] & [0,0] & [-10,-10] & [0,0] & [1,1] & [3,3] & [4,4] & [0,0] & [0,0] \\
[0,0] & [0,0] & [0,0] & [0,0] & [0,0] & [0,0] & [0,0] & [6,6] & [5,5] & [0,0] & [-11,-11] & [0,0] & [0,0] & [0,0] & [0,0] & [0,0] \\
[0,0] & [0,0] & [0,0] & [0,0] & [0,0] & [0,0] & [0,0] & [0,0] & [0,0] & [2,2] & [0,0] & [-6,-6] & [0,0] & [0,0] & [4,4] & [0,0] \\
[0,0] & [0,0] & [0,0] & [0,0] & [0,0] & [0,0] & [0,0] & [2,2] & [0,0] & [5,5] & [0,0] & [0,0] & [-11,-11] & [0,0] & [0,0] & [4,4] \\
[0,0] & [0,0] & [0,0] & [0,0] & [0,0] & [0,0] & [0,0] & [0,0] & [0,0] & [6,6] & [0,0] & [0,0] & [0,0] & [-10,-10] & [1,1] & [3,3] \\
[0,0] & [0,0] & [0,0] & [0,0] & [0,0] & [0,0] & [0,0] & [0,0] & [0,0] & [0,0] & [0,0] & [6,6] & [0,0] & [0,0] & [-6,-6] & [0,0] \\
[0,0] & [0,0] & [0,0] & [0,0] & [0,0] & [0,0] & [0,0] & [0,0] & [0,0] & [0,0] & [6,6] & [5,5] & [0,0] & [-11,-11] & [0,0] & [0,0]
\end{array}\right)
$$

out by the verifylss function of the MATLAB

The third step of ISPN analysis solves the system of interval linear equations described by Equation (7). The interval linear equations solution is carried out by the verifylss function of the MATLAB *toolbox* INTLAB. Substituting the last equation of system $[\vec{\pi}] \cdot [\mathbf{Q}] = 0$ by the normalization condition $\sum_{i=1}^{16} [\pi]_i = 1$, the linear system $([\pi]_1, [\pi]_2) \cdot [\mathbf{A}] = [\mathbf{b}]$ is obtained. The solution of this system directly provides the steady state probabilities of tangible states:

$$[\vec{\pi}]^t = \begin{pmatrix} [\,0.30162341059172. & 0.30162341059173] \\ [\,0.20129241213850. & 0.20129241213851] \\ [\,0.10001579083719. & 0.10001579083720] \\ [\,0.05079591445866. & 0.05079591445867] \\ [\,0.05701697985273. & 0.05701697985274] \\ [\,0.05122652318522. & 0.05122652318523] \\ [\,0.03402132703571. & 0.03402132703572] \\ [\,0.02728986215974. & 0.02728986215975] \\ [\,0.03607316886026. & 0.03607316886027] \\ [\,0.02968055852738. & 0.02968055852739] \\ [\,0.01976172320179. & 0.01976172320180] \\ [\,0.02527256969829. & 0.02527256969830] \\ [\,0.01396928749535. & 0.01396928749536] \\ [\,0.02086458086920. & 0.02086458086922] \\ [\,0.02032580994373. & 0.02032580994374] \\ [\,0.01077008114445. & 0.01077008114446] \end{pmatrix}.$$

Finally we can make the fourth (final) step of analysis ISPN, i.e. computation of metrics. The average utilization of machines, i.e., the probability that a machine is processing a part are:

$$[UM_1] = [prob](m(p_2) = 1) \;\; and \;\; [UM_2] = [prob](m(p_6) = 1).$$

The evaluation result provides the following values:

$$[UM_1] = [0.59650101272372, 0.59650101272374] \;\; and$$

$$[UM_2] = [0.29825050636186, 0.29825050636187].$$

These results gives interval bounds to exact value and can be used to verify conventional analysis of GSPN results.

Experiment for Two-Machine One-Buffer Transfer Line Model

Table 6 shows the average machine utilization, UM_1 and UM_2, for three μ_1 rate intervals (degenerated intervals). ISPN analysis results, provided by ISPN MATLAB toolbox INTLAB, are GSPN ordinary results with verified interval bounds.

Interval rate $[\mu_1]$	**Machine utilization**	
	$[UM_1]$	$[UM_2]$
[0.1E2, 0.1E2]	[0.11946700722573, 0.11946700722574]	[0.59733503612865, 0.59733503612866]
[0.1E1, 0.1E1]	[0.59650101272372, 0.59650101272374]	[0.29825050636186, 0.29825050636187]
[0.2E0, 0.2E0]	[0.62490104707753, 0.62490104707755]	[0.06249010470775, 0.06249010470776]

Table 6. Experiment for Two-Machine One-Buffer Transfer Line Model for three MR (Machining Rate) = μ_1 (degenerated interval). Results obtained with ISPN MATLAB toolbox INTLAB Prototype Tool.

Interval rate $[\mu_1]$	**Machine utilization**	
	$[UM_1]$	$[UM_2]$
$[0.099E2, 0.101E2]$ = $0,100E2 \pm 0,001E2$	[0.11399679921745, 0.12493721523401] = 0.11946700722573± 0.00547020800828	[0.57960670982656, 0.61506336243075] = 0.59733503612865± 0.01772832630210
$[0.099E1, 0.101E1]$ = $0,100E1 \pm 0,001E1$	[0.49611631459760, 0.69688571084986] = 0.59650101272373± 0.10038469812613	[0.22827877740233, 0.36822223532140] = 0.29825050636187± 0.06997172895954
$[0,199E0, 0,201E0]$ = $0,200E0 \pm 0,001E0$	[0.54449037658809, 0.70531171756699] = 0.62490104707754± 0.08041067048945	[0.02346019982939, 0.10152000958611] = 0.06249010470775± 0.03902990487836

Table 7. The average machine utilization results obtained with ISPN MATLAB toolbox INTLAB Prototype Tool to Two-Machine One-Buffer Transfer Line Model for three μ_1 rate intervals.

Introducing parameters with input uncertainties:

In sequel, the variations in the rates of exponential transitions are considered. To avoid redundancy, will not be displayed detailing of ISPN analysis as in previous examples. Table 7 shows the average machine utilization, UM_1 and UM_2 for three $[\mu_1]$ rate intervals. All exponential rate variabilities have ± 1 as errors in the 3rd significant digits:

ISPN.m Line 59 modification for each experiment:

- AT(3,1)= [infsup(0.099E2,0.101E2),infsup(2.99,3.01),infsup(4.99,5.01),infsup(1.99,2.01), infsup(3.99,4.01),infsup(5.99,6.01)];
- AT(3,1)= [infsup(0.099E1,0.101E1),infsup(2.99,3.01),infsup(4.99,5.01),infsup(1.99,2.01), infsup(3.99,4.01),infsup(5.99,6.01)];
- AT(3,1)= [infsup(0.199E0, 0.201E0),infsup(2.99,3.01),infsup(4.99,5.01),infsup(1.99,2.01), infsup(3.99,4.01),infsup(5.99,6.01)];

5. ISPN MATLAB toolbox INTLAB prototype tool

ISPN M-file MATLAB toolbox INTLAB is a prototype for the modeling and evaluation of ISPNs in which exponential transition rates and immediate transition weights may be represented by intervals. Models are specified by matrix input/output arc multiplicity of transitions as a direct mapping of usual graphical Petri Nets representation description of systems. The stationary analysis is based on Markov theory. An interval embedded Markov chain (IEMC), constructed and solved by interval methods, allow us computation metrics. The current prototype is still being used but **ISPN.n** will allow you to write your own features and to tailor ISPNs to your own needs.

The **ISPN.m** used for calculating verified probabilities and the machine utilization rate from ISPN model of Figure 4, is given bellow:
Uncomment specified lines to display:

- **Line 191:** Reachability set and distribution markings from ISPN model (Table 4)
- **Line 192:** Literal description of reachability graph from ISPN model (Table 4)
- **Line 213:** $[P]^{\mathcal{VV}}$
- **Line 218:** $[P]^{\mathcal{VT}}$
- **Line 223:** $[U]^{\mathcal{TV}}$
- **Line 229:** $[U]^{\mathcal{TT}}$
- **Line 237:** $[U]$
- **Line 237:** $[Q]$

```
1. %
2. %  ISPN prototype tool
3. %
4. %  INPUT MODEL : Two-Machine One-Buffer Transfer Line Model ( Fig. 4 )
5. %
6. %  Obs: Using matrix notation of ISPN model
7. datestr(now,0)
8. format long
9. clear At % Clear variable At
10. % input arc multiplicity of immediate transitions, (-) minus means input
11. At(1,1)= {[-1, 0;   % P1
12.             0, 0;   % P2
13.             0, 0;   % P3
14.             0,-1;   % P4
15.             0,-1;   % P5
16.             0, 0;   % P6
17.             0, 0;   % P7
18.            -1, 0]}; % P8
19. % labels of immediate transition
20. At(2,1)={ ['t1';'t5']};
21. % weight of immediate transition
22. At(3,1)= {[1,1]};
23. % celldisp(At) % uncomment display cell array contents
24. clear AtO %  Clear variable AtO
25. % output arc multiplicity of immediate transitions
26. AtO(1,1)= {[ 0, 0;   % P1
27.              1, 0;   % P2
28.              0, 0;   % P3
29.              0, 0;   % P4
30.              0, 0;   % P5
31.              0, 1;   % P6
32.              0, 0;   % P7
33.              0, 1]}; % P8
34. % celldisp(AtO) % uncomment display cell array contents
35. clear Ai % Clear variable Ai
36. % arc multiplicity of inhibitor arcs (associeted to immediate transitions)
37. Ai(1,1)= {[0, 0;   % P1
38.            0, 0;   % P2
39.            0, 0;   % P3
40.            0, 0;   % P4
41.            0, 0;   % P5
42.            0, 0;   % P6
43.            0, 0;   % P7
44.            0, 0]}; % P8
45. % celldisp(Ai) % uncomment display cell array contents
46. clear AT % Clear variable AT
47. % input arc multiplicity of timed transitions, ( - )  minus means input
```

```
AT(1,1)= {[ 0, 0, 0, 0, 0, 0;
           -1,-1, 0, 0, 0, 0;
            0, 0,-1, 0, 0, 0;
            0, 0, 0, 0, 0, 0;
            0, 0, 0, 0, 0, 0;
            0, 0, 0,-1,-1, 0;
            0, 0, 0, 0, 0,-1;
            0, 0, 0, 0, 0, 0]};
% labels of timed transitions
AT(2,1)={ ['T2';'T3';'T4';'T6';'T7';'T8']};
% interval rate  of timed transitions (degenereted)
AT(3,1)= {[1,3,5,2,4,6]};
% server semantics of timed transitions
AT(4,1)= {['SS';'SS';'SS';'SS';'SS';'SS']};
% celldisp(AT) % uncomment display cell array contents
clear ATO  % Clear variable ATO
ATO(1,1)= {[1, 0, 0, 0, 0, 0;
            0, 0, 1, 0, 0, 0;
            0, 1, 0, 0, 0, 0;
            1, 0, 0, 0, 0, 0;
            0, 0, 0, 1, 0, 0;
            0, 0, 0, 0, 0, 1;
            0, 0, 0, 0, 1, 0;
            0, 0, 0, 0, 0, 0]};
% celldisp(ATO)  % uncomment display cell array contents
clear M % Clear variable M
clear d % Clear variable d
% Initial marking of each place (initial state)
M(1,1)={ [1;0;0;0;1;0;0;3] };
M(2,1)={ 'M0' };
im=0;
ivm=1;
itm=1;
n=size(At{1},2); % number of columns of At
nT=size(AT{1},2); % number of columns of  AT
m=size(AT{1},1);  % number of rows of AT
id=1;
ic=1;
Q=infsup(0.0,0.0);
while im < size(M,2)
    j=0;
    t=0;
    tvm=1;
    mx=M{1,im+1};
    for i=1:n
        mt=At{1,1} (1:end,i);
        ai=0;
        mi=Ai{1,1} (1:end,i);
        mi=mx-mi;
        if mi==mx | min(mi)<0
            ai=1;
        end
        md=mx+mt;
        if min(md)>=0 & ai==1
            d{id,1}=strcat(M{2,1+im} (1:end),'|', At{2} (i,1:end),'>');
            md=md+AtO{1,1} (1:end,i);
            t=1;
            tvm=0;
            id=id+1;
            c=size(M,2);
            xt='new';
            for ix = 1:c
                if md == M{1,ix}
                    x=M{2,ix};
                    d{id-1,2}=x;
                     xt='old';
                     Q(im+1,ix)=At{3,1} (i);
                    break
```

```
                end
            end
            if xt=='new'
                strx=strcat('M',num2str(c));
                d{id-1,2}=strx;
                M{1,c+1} =md;
                M{2,c+1}= strx;
                Q(im+1,c+1)=At{3,1} (i);
            end
        end
    end
    % If there is no firing of immediate transitions so we try
    % to firing timed transitions
    if t==0
        for i= 1:nT
           mt=AT{1,1} (1:end,i);
           md=mx+mt;
           min(md);
           if min(md) >= 0
             d{id,1}=strcat(M{2,1+im} (1:end),'|', AT{2} (i,1:end),'>');
             md=md+ATO{1,1} (1:end,i);
             ma=md;
             ga=0;
             while min(ma)>=0
                 ma=ma+AT{1,1} (1:end,i);
                 ga=ga+1;
             end
             t=1;
             id=id+1;
             c=size(M,2);
             xt='new';
             for ix = 1:c
                    if md == M{1,ix}
                        x=M{2,ix};
                        d{id-1,2}=x;
                        xt='old';
                        if AT{4} (i,1:end) == 'SS'
                              Q(im+1,ix)=AT{3,1} (i);
                        end
                        if AT{4} (i,1:end) == 'IS'
                            Q(im+1,ix)=ga*AT{3,1} (i);
                        end
                        break
                    end
                end
               if xt=='new'
                    strx=strcat('M',num2str(c));
                    d{id-1,2}=strx;
                    M{1,c+1} =md;
                    M{2,c+1}= strx;
                    if AT{4} (i,1:end) == 'SS'
                              Q(im+1,c+1)=AT{3,1} (i);
                          end
                    if AT{4} (i,1:end) == 'IS'
                              Q(im+1,c+1)=ga*AT{3,1} (i);
                    end
               end
            end
        end
    end
    im=im+1; % provoca termino do loop while
    if tvm==0
        vm(ivm)=im-1;
        ivm=ivm+1;
    else
        tm(itm)=im-1;
        itm=itm+1;
    end
```

```
end
clear At % Clear variable At
clear At0 % Clear variable At0
clear AT % Clear variable AT
clear AT0 % Clear variable AT0
clear Ai % Clear variable Ai
%==========================================
% celldisp(M);  % uncomment display reachability set and distribution markings from ISPN = ( Table 4 )
% d % uncomment display literal description of reachability graph from ISPN = ( Table 5 )
% vm % uncomment display vanishing markings index vector
% tm % uncomment display tangible markings index vector
%==========================================
% 'number of vanishing markings'
ivm=ivm-1;
% 'number of tangible markings'
itm=itm-1;
n=ivm+itm;
clear PVV % Clear variable PVV
PVV=intval(zeros(ivm,ivm));
i = (1:ivm);
j=(1:ivm);
PVV(i,j)=Q(vm(i)+1,vm(j)+1);
% weigths uniformization of immediate transitions
for i= 1:ivm
    s=sum(PVV(i,1:ivm));
    if s>1
        PVV(i,1:ivm)=PVV(i,1:ivm)/s;
    end
end
% PVV % uncomment display PVV
clear PVT % Clear variable PVV
i = (1:ivm);
j=(1:itm);
        PVT(i,j)=Q(vm(i)+1,tm(j)+1);
% PVT % uncomment display PVT
clear UTV % Clear variable UTV
i = (1:itm);
j=(1:ivm);
      UTV(i,j)=Q(tm(i)+1,vm(j)+1);
% UTV % uncomment display UTV
clear UTT  % Clear variable UTT
i = (1:itm);
j=(1:itm);
    UTT(i,j)=Q(tm(i)+1,tm(j)+1);
clear Q % Clear variable Q
% UTT % uncomment display UTT
% 'Calculating X=eye(size(PVV,1))-PVV'
X=eye(size(PVV,1))-PVV;
clear PVV % Clear variable PVV
% 'Calculating X=inv(X)'
X=inv(X);
% 'Calculating  U=UTT+UTV*X*PVT'
U=UTT+UTV*X*PVT;
% U % uncomment display U
clear PVT % Clear variable PVT
clear UTT % Clear variable UTT
clear UTV % Clear variable UTV
clear X % Clear variable X
n=size(U,1);
t=sum(U.');
    for i=1:n
        U(i,i)=-t(i);
    end
Q=U;
% Q  % uncomment display Q
clear U % Clear variable U
```

```
QZ=Q.';
clear Q % Clear variable Q
m=size(QZ,1);
j= 1:m;
QZ(m,j)=1;
QZ;
Z(m)=1;
Z=Z.';
% 'Calculating x=verifylss(QZ,Z)'
x=verifylss(QZ,Z)
% [UM1] = [prob](m(p_{2}) = 1)
'UM1'
 s1=0;
 for i= 1:n
    if M{1,tm(i)+1} (2) >0
                s1=s1+x(i);
    end
end
intvalinit('displaymidrad')
s1
intvalinit('displayinfsup')
s1
% [UM2] = [prob](m(p_{6}) = 1)
'UM2'
s1=0;
for i= 1:n
   if M{1,tm(i)+1} (6) >0
                s1=s1+x(i);
   end
end
intvalinit('displaymidrad')
s1
intvalinit('displayinfsup')
s1
datestr(now,0)
```

Executing **ISPN.m** yields:

```
>> ISPN
ans =
01-Apr-2011 23:59:14
intval x =
[   0.30162341059172,   0.30162341059173]
[   0.20129241213850,   0.20129241213851]
[   0.10001579083719,   0.10001579083720]
[   0.05079591445866,   0.05079591445867]
[   0.05701697985273,   0.05701697985274]
[   0.05122652318522,   0.05122652318523]
[   0.03402132703571,   0.03402132703572]
[   0.02728986215974,   0.02728986215975]
[   0.03607316886026,   0.03607316886027]
[   0.02968055852738,   0.02968055852739]
[   0.01976172320179,   0.01976172320180]
[   0.02527256969829,   0.02527256969830]
[   0.01396928749535,   0.01396928749536]
[   0.02086458086920,   0.02086458086922]
[   0.02032580994373,   0.02032580994374]
[   0.01077008114445,   0.01077008114446]
ans =
UM1
===> Default display of intervals by midpoint/radius (e.g. < 3.14 , 0.01 >)
intval s1 =
<   0.59650101272373,  0.00000000000001>
===> Default display of intervals by infimum/supremum (e.g. [ 3.14 , 3.15 ])
intval s1 =
[   0.59650101272372,   0.59650101272374]
ans =
```

```
UM2
===> Default display of intervals by midpoint/radius (e.g. < 3.14 , 0.01 >)
intval s1 =
<   0.29825050636187,  0.00000000000001>
===> Default display of intervals by infimum/supremum (e.g. [ 3.14 , 3.15 ])
intval s1 =
[   0.29825050636186,   0.29825050636187]
ans =
01-Apr-2011 23:59:14
>>
```

6. Concluding remarks

In this chapter, ISPN is used as an approach to ISPN performance analysis in which the exponential rates fall within pre-assumed intervals. ISPN is mainly applied in modeling, where input data are known within definite interval of accuracy. Such uncertainties include the errors involved with experimental data obtained from measurements. This framework provides a way to formalize and study problems related to the presence of uncertainties. Such uncertainties include data errors occurring during data measurements and rounding errors generated during calculations. The model proposed and the related method of analysis, involves the case of simultaneous variability in values of parameters. As an immediate consequence, the ISPN analysis, designed for evaluation of results obtained from measurements, may appear to be useful for engineers and technicians as a tool for decision making. As future works, methods for interval transient analysis and simulation should considered. Furthermore, other case studies should also be take into account. ISPN MATLAB toolbox INTLAB Prototype Tool will allow you to specify your own ISPNs. We plan to post future developments of ISPN MATLAB toolbox INTLAB Prototype Tool.

7. References

Bolch, G., Greiner, S. & Trived, K. (2006). *Queueing networks and Markov chains: modeling and performance evaluation with computer science applications*, A Wiley-Inerscience publication, John Wiley and Sons, Inc, Second Edition.

Brinksma, E. (2001). *Lectures on formal methods and performance analysis: revised lectures/ First EEF Summer School on Trends in Computer Science. Berg en Dal, The Netherlands, July 3 - 7, 2000. 9ed.*, Springer, Ed Brinksma (editor).

Chen, H. M. & van Emden, M. H. (1995). Adding interval constraints to the moore skelboe global optimization algorithm, *in* V. Kreinovich (ed.), *Extended Abstracts of APIC'95, International Workshop on Applications of Interval Computation*, Reliable Computing (Supplement), pp. 54–57.

Desrochers, A. & Al-Jaar, R. (1994). *Applications of Petri nets in manufacturing systems: modeling, control, and performance analysis*, IEEE Press, Piscataway, NJ, USA.

Florin, G. & Natkin, S. (1989). Matrix product form solution for closed synchronized queueing networks, In In Proc. 3rd Intern. Workshop on Petri Nets and Performance Models, pp. 29–39.

Galdino, S. & Maciel, P. (2006). Interval generalized stochastic petri net models in performance evaluation, *IEEE International Conference on Systems, Man, and Cybernetics 2006*, Taiwan, pp. 2723– 2728.

Galdino, S., Maciel, P. & Rosa, N. S. (2007a). Interval generalized stochastic petri net models in dependability evaluation, *IEEE International Conference on Systems, Man, and Cybernetics 2007*, Montreal, pp. 2502–2507.

Galdino, S., Maciel, P. & Rosa, N. S. (2007b). Interval markovian models in dependability evaluation, *International Journal of Pure and Applied Mathematics* Vol. 41(No. 2): 151–176.

German, R. (2000). *Performance Analysis of Communicating Systems - Modeling with Non-Markovian Stochastic Petri Nets*, Wiley.

Girault, C. & Valk, R. (2003). *Petri Nets for Systems Engineering: a guide to modeling, verification, and applications*, Springer.

Hansen, E. & Walster, G. (2004). *Global Optimization Using Internal Analysis*, Second Edition, Revised and Expanded, Marcel Dekker, Inc., New York.

Jaulin, L., Kieffer, M., Didrit, O. & Walter, E. (2001). *Applied Interval Analysis: with Examples in Parameter and State Estimation, Robust Control and Robotics*, Springer-Verlag.

Marsan, M., Balbo, G. & Conte, G. (1984). A class of generalized sthochastic petri nets for the performance evaluation of multiprocessor systems, *ACM Transactions on Computer Systems* 2: 93–122.

Marsan, M., Bobbio, A., Conte, G. & Cumani, A. (1984). Performance analysis of degradable multiprocessor systems using generalized stochastic petri nets, *IEEE Computer Society Newsletters, 6 SI-* 1: 47–54.

Merlin, P. & Farber, D. (1976). Recoverability of communication protocols: Implications of a theoretical study, Vol. 24, No. 9, IEEE Trans. Comm., pp. 1036–1043.

Molloy, M. (1981). *On the Integration of Delay and Throughput Measures in Distributed Processing Models*, PhD thesis, UCLA, Los Angeles, CA.

Moore, R. E. (1962). *Interval Arithmetic and Automatic Error Analysis in Digital Computing*, PhD thesis, Stanford University.

Moore, R. E. (1966). *Interval Analysis*, Prentice Hall, Englewood Clifs, NJ, USA.

Murata, T. (1989). Petri nets: Properties, analysis and application (an invited survey paper), *Proceedings of the IEEE* 77: 541–580.

Rall, L. (1969). *Computacional Solution of Nonlinear Operator Equations*, Wiley, New York.

Ramchandani, C. (1974). *Analysis of Asynchronous Concurrent Systems by Timed Petri Nets*, PhD thesis, MIT, Cambridge, MA.

Sifakis, J. (1978). Petri nets for performance evaluation, In 3rd Intern. Symp. IFIP, pp. 75–93.

Smith, C. U. (1990). *Petri Nets for Systems Engineering: a guide to modeling, verification, and applications*, Addison-Wesley, Reading, MA.

Ullrich, C. (1990). *in* C. Ullrich (ed.), *Contributions to Computer Arithmetic and Self-Validating Numerical Methods*, Vol. 7, J. C. Baltzer AG, Scientific Publishing Co.

Young, R. C. (1931). The algebra of many-valued quantities, *Math. Ann.* 104: 260–290.

Classifiers of Digital Modulation Based on the Algorithm of Fast Walsh-Hadamard Transform and Karhunen-Loeve Transform

Richterova Marie and Mazalek Antonin
University of Defence
Czech Republic

1. Introduction

Automatic recognition of modulation is rapidly evolving area of signal analysis. In recent years, much interest by academic and military research institutes has focused around the research and development of recognition algorithms modulation. There are two mains reasons to know the correct modulation type of a signal: to preserve the signal information content and to decide the suitable counter action such as jamming (Nandi & Azzouz, 1998), (Grimaldi et al, 2007), (Park & Dae, 2006).

From this viewpoint, considerable attention is being paid to the research and development of algorithms for the recognition of modulated signals. The need of practice made it necessary to solve the questions of automatic classification of samples of received signals with use of computers and available software.

In this chapter, a new original configuration of subsystems for the automatic modulation recognition of digital signals is described. The signal recognizer being developed consists of five subsystems: (1) adaptive antenna arrays, (2) pre-processing of signals, (3) key features extraction, (4) modulation recognizer and (5) output stage.

This chapter describes the use of Walsh–Hadamard transform (WHT) and Karhunen-Loeve transform (KLT) for the modulation recognition in high frequency (HF) and very high frequency (VHF) bands. The input real signal is pre-processed and converted to the "phase image". The WHT and KLT is applied and the dimensionality reduction is implemented and the classifier recognized the signal. The clustering analysis method was chosen by acclamation for 2-class and 3-class recognition of 2-FSK, 4-FSK and PSK signals. The 2-class and 3-class minimum-distance modulation classifier was created in the MATLAB programme. The tests of designed algorithm were implemented on real signal patterns.

2. Orthogonal transforms used for modulation recognition

The utilization of orthogonal transforms for the recognition of various types of modulated signals is described in a number of reference sources. Fourier transform (Ahmed & Rao, 1975), (Jondral, 1991), Haar transform (Ahmed & Rao, 1975), discrete cosine transform (Ahmed & Rao, 1975), (Jondral, 1991), Walsh–Hadamard transform (WHT) (Ahmed & Rao, 1975), (Richterova, 1997, 2001) and Karhunen–Loeve transform (KLT) (Hua & Liu, 1998),

(Richterova, 2001), (Richterova & Juracek, 2006) belong to the most frequently exploited and recommended orthogonal transforms. In this chapter, the use of WHT and KLT for the recognition of the frequency shift keying (2–FSK and 4–FSK) signals and the phase shift keying (2–PSK and 4–PSK) signals will be described.

2.1 Walsh-Hadamard transform

The Walsh–Hadamard transform (WHT) is perhaps the most well-known of the nonsinusoidal orthogonal transforms. The WHT has gained prominence in various digital signal processing applications, since it can essentially be computed using additions and subtractions only. WHT is used for the Walsh representation of the data sequences. Their basis functions are sampled Walsh functions which can be expressed in terms of the Hadamard matrix. The WHT is defined by relation (Ahmed & Rao, 1975),

$$B(N)=\frac{1}{N}H(N)\cdot X(N), \tag{1}$$

where :
B(N) - coefficients of WHT,
N - order of the WHT,
H(N) - N–order Hadamard matrix,
X(N) - signal vector.
An algorithm for the WHT was realized in the MATLAB programme.

2.2 Karhunen-Loeve transform

The Karhunen-Loeve transform (Hua & Liu, 1998) (named after Kari Karhunen and Michel Loeve) is a representation of a stochastic process as an infinite linear combination of orthogonal functions, analogous to a Fourier series representation of a function on a bounded interval.

In contrast to a Fourier series, where the coefficients are real numbers and the expansion basis consists of sinusoidal functions (that is, sine and cosine functions), the coefficients in the Karhunen-Loeve transform are random variables and the expansion basis depends on the process. In fact, the orthogonal basis functions used in this representation are determined by the covariance function of the process. The KLT is a key element of many signal processing and communication tasks.

The Karhunen-Loeve Transform (KLT), also known as Hotelling Transform and Eigenvector Transform, is closely related to the Principal Component Analysis (PCA) and widely used in many fields of data analysis.

Let Φ_k be the eigenvector corresponding to the kth eigenvalue λ_k of the covariance matrix $\sum_x$, i.e.,

$$\sum\nolimits_x \Phi_k=\lambda_k\Phi_k \quad (k=0,\cdots,N-1) \tag{2}$$

or in matrix form:

$$\begin{bmatrix} \cdots & \cdots & \cdots \\ \cdots & \sigma_{ij} & \cdots \\ \cdots & \cdots & \cdots \end{bmatrix} \begin{bmatrix} \\ \Phi_k \\ \\ \end{bmatrix} = \lambda_k \begin{bmatrix} \\ \Phi k \\ \\ \end{bmatrix} \quad (k=0,\cdots N-1) \tag{3}$$

As the covariance matrix $\sum_x = \sum_x^T$ is symmetric (Hermitian if $\bar{x}$ is complex), its eigenvectors Φ_i are orthogonal:

$$\left(\Phi_i,\Phi_j\right)=\Phi_i^T\Phi_j=\begin{cases}1 & i=j\\ 0 & i\neq j\end{cases} \tag{4}$$

and we can construct an $N\times N$ orthogonal (unitary) matrix Φ

$$\Phi\cong\left[\Phi_0,\cdots,\Phi_{N-1}\right] \tag{5}$$

satisfying

$$\Phi^T\Phi=I, ie., \quad \Phi^{-1}=\Phi^T \tag{6}$$

The N eigenequations above can be combined to be expressed as:

$$\sum\nolimits_x\Phi=\Phi\Lambda \tag{7}$$

or in matrix form:

$$\begin{bmatrix}\cdots & \cdots & \cdots\\ \cdots & \sigma_{ij} & \cdots\\ \cdots & \cdots & \cdots\end{bmatrix}\left[\Phi_0,\cdots,\Phi_{N-1}\right] = \left[\Phi_0,\cdots,\Phi_{N-1}\right]\begin{bmatrix}\lambda_0 & 0 & \cdots & 0\\ 0 & \lambda_1 & 0 & \vdots\\ \vdots & 0 & \ddots & 0\\ 0 & \cdots & 0 & \lambda_{N-1}\end{bmatrix} \tag{8}$$

Here Λ is a diagonal matrix $\Lambda=diag\left(\lambda_0,\cdots,\lambda_{N-1}\right)$. Left multiplying $\Phi^T=\Phi^{-1}$ on both sides, the covariance matrix $\sum_x$ can be diagonalized:

$$\Phi^T\sum\nolimits_x\Phi=\Phi^{-1}\sum\nolimits_x\Phi=\Phi^{-1}\,\Phi\,\Lambda=\Lambda \tag{9}$$

Now, given a signal vector $\bar{x}$, we can define the orthogonal (unitary if $\bar{x}$ is complex) Karhunen-Loeve Transform of $\bar{x}$ as:

$$y=\begin{bmatrix}y_0\\ y_1\\ \vdots\\ y_{N-1}\end{bmatrix} = \Phi^T x = \begin{bmatrix}\Phi_0^T\\ \Phi_1^T\\ \vdots\\ \Phi_{N-1}^T\end{bmatrix}x \tag{10}$$

where the ith component y_i of the transform vector is the projection of $\bar{x}$ onto Φ_i:

$$y_i=\left(\Phi_i,x\right)=\Phi_i^T\,x \tag{11}$$

Left multiplying $\Phi=\left(\Phi^T\right)^{-1}$ on both sides of the transform $y=\Phi T x$, we get the inverse transform:

$$x = \Phi\, y = \left[\Phi_0, \Phi_1, \cdots, \Phi_{N-1}\right] \begin{bmatrix} y_0 \\ y_1 \\ \vdots \\ y_{N-1} \end{bmatrix} = \sum_{i=0}^{N-1} y_i \Phi_i \qquad (12)$$

By this transform we see that the signal vector $\bar{x}$ is now expressed in an N-dimensional space spanned by the N eigenvectors Φ_i $(i = 0, \cdots, N-1)$ as the basis vectors of the space. An algorithm for the KLT was realized in the MATLAB programme.

3. Principle of the recognition of FSK and PSK signals

The common fundamental diagram for recognition of 2-FSK, 4-FSK and PSK signals is introduced in Fig. 1 (Richterova, 1999, 2001). General principle of this system for recognition will be described in next text.

The inquiry analog signal $x(t)$ enters into an A/D converter, where it subjects sampling, quantization and make-up into matrix 32x32. This way, we obtain a "phase image" of the inquiry input signal $x(t)$. The orthogonal transform (KLT or WHT) is implemented on this matrix of "phase image" with the aim to emphasize important elements image and at the same time to suppress the circumstantial and disturbing elements and the components.

The property of Karhunen-Loeve transform will be used for the recognition of 2-FSK, 4-FSK and PSK signals. All samples of signal pattern are not needed to the proper recognition; it is possible to use the dimensional reduction of the matrix. The proper classification of signal and his enlistment into corresponding group of signals follow up the block of orthogonal transform.

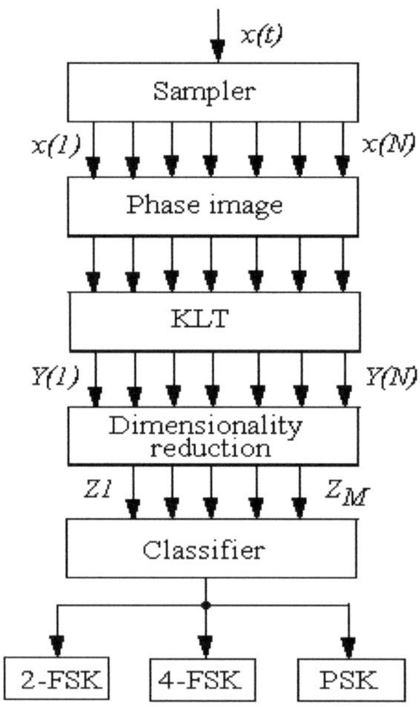

Fig. 1. Block diagram for recognition of digital modulated signals

The minimum distance classifier will be used for the solution of the problem of the recognition of 2-FSK, 4-FSK and PSK signals. The principle of minimum distance classifier will be described in the next section.

3.1 Phase image

The input signal is given by sequence of the samples corresponding to the digital form of recognition signal. The input vector has the length of 2048 samples. The "phase image" of modulated signal is composed so, that they are generated of points about "the coordinates" - the value of sample and the difference between samples.

These points are mapping into the rectangular net about proportions 32 x 32 so, that a relevant point of net is allocated the number one. If more points fall through into the identical node, then is adding the number one next. These output values are standardized and quantized (Richterova, 1997, 1999, 2001), (Richterova & Juracek, 2006). The "phase images" of 2-FSK and 4-FSK signals are presented on Fig. 2.

Lower frequency of FSK signal corresponds to the ellipse, which lies near to centre of image. Higher frequency of FSK signal corresponds to the ellipse, which is on the margin of image. The "phase image" of PSK is one ellipse.

3.2 The 3-class minimum-distance classifier

The minimum-distance classifier is designed to operate on the following decision rule (Ahmed & Rao, 1975), (Richterova, 2001), (Richterova & Juracek, 2006):

A given pattern Z belongs to C_i, if Z is closest to $\overline{Z}_i, i=1,2,3$ ....

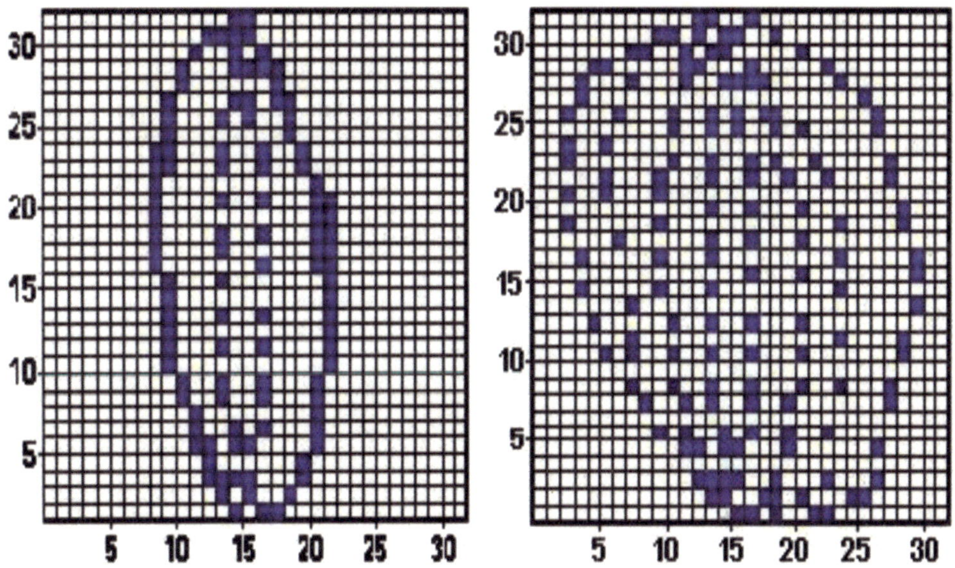

Fig. 2. "Phase images" of 2-FSK signal and "phase image" of 4-FSK signal

Let D_i denote the distance of Z from $\overline{Z}_i, i=1,2,3$. Then we have [see Fig 3]

$$D_i^2 = \|Z - \bar{Z}_i\|^2 = (Z - \bar{Z}_i)'(Z - \bar{Z}_i), \tag{13}$$

Simplification of D_i yields

$$D_i^2 = \|Z\|^2 - 2 \cdot \left(\bar{Z}_i Z - \frac{1}{2}\|\bar{Z}_i\|^2 \right), \tag{14}$$

Clearly, D_i^2 is a minimum, when the quantity $\left(\bar{Z}_i Z - \frac{1}{2}\|\bar{Z}_i\|^2 \right)$ is a maximum. Thus, rather than having the classifier computes D_i^2 in Eq. (13), it is simpler to require it to compute the quantity $\left(\bar{Z}_i Z - \frac{1}{2}\|\bar{Z}_i\|^2 \right)$. The classifier is then described by the discriminant functions

$$g_i(Z) = \bar{Z}_i' Z - \frac{1}{2}\|\bar{Z}_i\|^2, \qquad i = 1,2,3 \tag{15}$$

The classifier thus computes three numbers $g_1(Z)$, $g_2(Z)$, $g_3(Z)$ as shown in Fig. 3 and then compares them. It assigns Z to C_1 if $g_1(Z)$ is maximum, to C_2 if $g_2(Z)$ is maximum and to C_3 if $g_3(Z)$ is maximum.

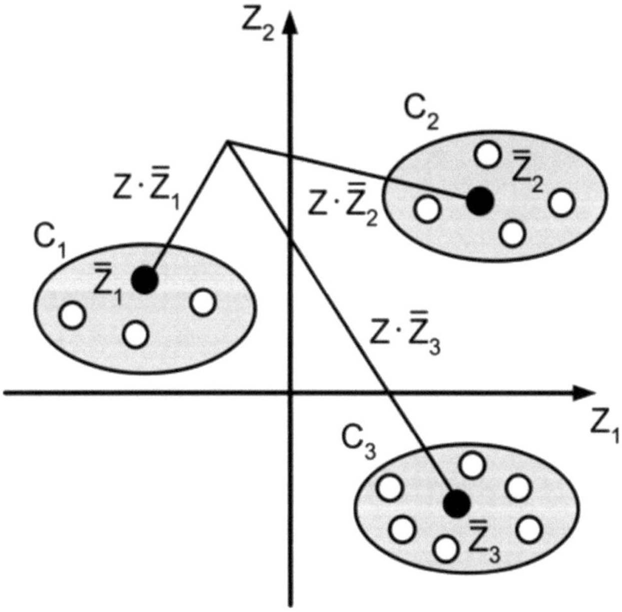

Fig. 3. 3-class classifier of FSK and PSK signals

3.3 The 2–class minimum–distance classifier

The process of the recognition of 2–FSK and 4–FSK signals by means of the 2-class minimum distance classifier is shown in Fig.4.

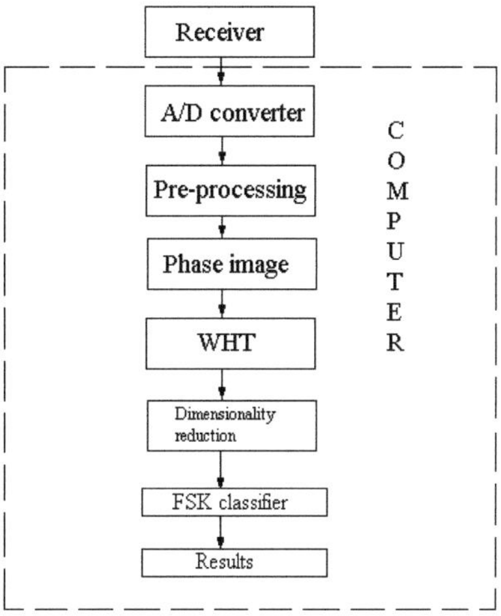

Fig. 4. Simplified block scheme of a recogniser of 2-FSK and 4-FSK signals

Now we briefly describe the block scheme from Fig. 4. A real signal inputs from a receiver via an A/D converter into a computer, where it is processed and stored in the data format WAV. Then block is pre-processed and used for the filtering and scaling of the input vector of real pattern of 2-FSK or 4-FSK signal. The scaling of real pattern signal is performed in this case and the spectral power density signal is calculated by means of the function PSD, which is implemented in the MATLAB programme. By testing of PSD waveform is proccesed the classification in to FSK or PSK signals.

The phase image (Fig. 2) of the processed pattern of real signal is created by means of algorithms described in (Richterova, 1997, 2001).

The feature vector is a result of the pre-processing of the real signal pattern. The feature vector is classified via a minimum-distance classifier.

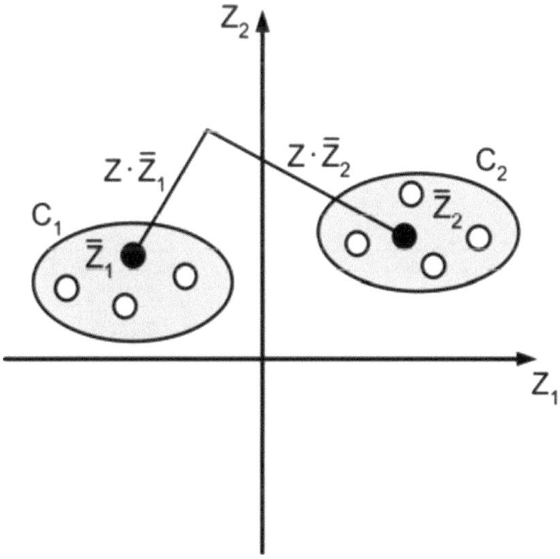

Fig. 5. A 2-class classifier of FSK or PSK signals

Two 2-class minimum-distance classifiers for 2-FSK and 4-FSK signals and two 2-class minimum-distance classifiers for 2-PSK and 4-PSK signals were designed and realized via the learning process. The learning process and the working principle of these minimum-distance classifiers are described in (Ahmed & Rao, 1975), (Richterova, 1997, 2001). The practical application of 2-class minimum-distance classifiers is presented in (Richterova, 1997, 2001).

4. Experimental results for 2-class classifier

The performance evaluations of the proposed 2-class minimum-distance classifier (see Fig.4) are introduced for 2-FSK and 4-FSK signals and for 2-PSK and 4-PSK. We have classified 42 real patterns of FSK signals. Parameters of real FSK signal patterns, which were used to experimental process, are presented in Table 1.

Modulation type	Carrier frequency [Hz]	Sampling frequency [Hz]	Modulation velocity [Bd]
2-FSK	2400	44100	150
4-FSK	4800	44100	150
2-FSK	4800	44100	100
4-FSK	2400	44100	100
2-FSK	1200	44100	50
4-FSK	4800	44100	200

Table 1. Parameters of real 2-FSK and 4-FSK patterns

We have classified 32 real patterns of PSK signals. Parameters of real PSK signal patterns, which were used to experimental process, are presented in Table 2.

Modulation type	Carrier frequency [Hz]	Sampling frequency [Hz]	Modulation velocity [Bd]
2-PSK	2400	44100	150
4-PSK	4800	44100	150
2-PSK	4800	44100	100
4-PSK	2400	44100	100
2-PSK	4800	44100	200
4-PSK	4800	44100	200

Table 2. Parameters of real 2-PSK and 4-PSK patterns

The results of the performance are summarized in Table 3 for the classifier based on the WHT and FSK signals.

Real pattern signals	Classified modulation type [%]	
	2-FSK	4-FSK
2-FSK	87,0	13,0
4-FSK	15,0	85,0

Table 3. Performance of the 2-class minimum-distance classifier of FSK based on the WHT

The results of the performance are presented in Table 4 for the classifier based on the WHT and PSK signals.

Real pattern signals	Classified modulation type [%]	
	2-PSK	4-PSK
2-FSK	77,0	23,0
4-FSK	25,0	75,0

Table 4. Performance of the 2-class minimum-distance classifier of PSK signals based on the WHT

The results of the performance are summarized in Table 5 for the classifier based on the KLT and FSK signals.

Real pattern signals	Classified modulation type [%]	
	2-FSK	4-FSK
2-FSK	87,0	13,0
4-FSK	15,0	85,0

Table 5. Performance of the 2-class minimum-distance classifier of FSK based on the KLT

The results of the performance are presented in Table 6 for the classifier based on the KLT and PSK signals.

Real pattern signals	Classified modulation type [%]	
	2-PSK	4-PSK
2-FSK	77,0	23,0
4-FSK	25,0	75,0

Table 6. Performance of the 2-class minimum-distance classifier of PSK signals based on the KLT

5. Experimental results for a 3-class classifier

The learning process of the 3-class minimum-distance classifier was effected for 30 realizations of the simulation patterns of 2-FSK, 4-FSK, 2-PSK and 4-PSK signals with the modulation velocity 50, 100, 150 and 200 Bd and SNR 15, 20, 30 [dB].
The experimental tests for the 3-class minimum-distance classifier were implemented on 200 realizations of real patterns of 2-FSK, 4-FSK, 2-PSK and 4-PSK signals. Parameters of real signal patterns, which were used to experimental process, are presented in Table 7.
The results of classification of modulation type for 200 realizations of 2-FSK, 4-FSK, 2-PSK and 4-PSK signals are introduced in Table 8.

Modulation type	Carrier frequency [Hz]	Sampling frequency [Hz]	Modulation velocity [Bd]
2-FSK	2400	44100	150
4-FSK	4800	44100	150
2-PSK	2400	44100	100
4-PSK	2400	44100	100

Table 7. Parameters of real digital modulation patterns

Modulation type	Correct classification in [%] for KLT	Correct classification in [%] for WHT
2-FSK	75	78
4-FSK	72	76
PSK	64	62

Table 8. Results of classification of modulation type by 3-class minimum-distance classifier for 200 realizations

The results of classification of PSK signal show, that the classifier based on orthogonal transform have not optimal solution for problems of classification of real PSK signals. We are explored other solution of classification of PSK signals. We want to introduce simple classifier of PSK signal based on cyclostationary feature detection.
This next section introduced the basic cyclostationary descriptors and on simply experiments demonstrates the effectiveness of this approach and its resistance against additive white Gaussian noise (AWGN). The high resistance level results from correlation principle of cyclostationary method because mean value of correlation of AWGN signal is zero.
There are many important aspects in cyclostationary measurement and application; one of them is high sensitivity of obtained results on input parameters that is to say the input sequence length and required cyclic and frequency resolution. In some applications, the input signal pre-processing is necessary. The future research will be focused on automatic modulation recognition.

6. Cyclostationary signals descriptors

A random process x(t) is said to be Nth order cyclostationary in the strict sense if its Nth order distribution function exhibits periodicity in time with period T (Gardner et al., 2006)

$$F(x_1,x_2,...,x_n;t_1,t_2,...,t_n)=F(x_1,x_2,...,x_n;t_1+mT,t_2+mT,...,t_n+mT) \tag{16}$$

In practice it is often sufficient to use only second order statistics which leads to the definition of second-order cyclostationarity in wide sense. The key second order statistical characteristic is instantaneous autocorrelation function Rxx(t,τ). So, the process x(t) is said to be cyclostationary in a wide sense if its autocorrelation function is periodic in time with period T

$$R_{xx}(t,\tau)=R_{xx}(t+mT,\tau) \tag{17}$$

where the instantaneous autocorrelation function is defined as (Semmlow, 2004)

$$R_{xx}(t,\tau)=x(t+\tau/2)x^*(t-\tau/2) \tag{18}$$

where τ is the time lag and * represents the complex conjugate of the signal x(t). Because the instantaneous autocorrelation function is periodic in time (for all τ) it can be expanded as Fourier series

$$R_{xx}(t,\tau)=\sum_{n=-\infty}^{+\infty} R_{xx}^{\alpha}(\tau)e^{i2\pi\alpha t} \tag{19}$$

where $\alpha = n / T$ are called cyclic frequencies, and $R_{xx}^{\alpha}(\tau)$ are the Fourier coefficients of the instantaneous autocorrelation function that are also referred to as cyclic autocorrelation function

$$R_{xx}^{\alpha}(\tau) = \frac{1}{T} \int_{-\frac{T}{2}}^{\frac{T}{2}} R_{xx}(t,\tau) e^{-i2\pi\alpha t} dt \tag{20}$$

The cyclic autocorrelation function presents the key descriptor of cyclostationary signals in two-dimensional time domain. When we reformulate the equation (20) by substitution (18) we obtained (Gardner, 1991)

$$\begin{aligned} R_{xx}^{\alpha}(\tau) &= \frac{1}{T} \int_{-\frac{T}{2}}^{\frac{T}{2}} x(t+\tau/2) x^{*}(t-\tau/2) e^{-i2\pi\alpha t} dt = \\ &= \frac{1}{T} \int_{-\frac{T}{2}}^{\frac{T}{2}} \left\langle \left[x(t+\tau/2) e^{-i2\pi\alpha(t+\tau/2)} \right] \left[x(t-\tau/2) e^{+i2\pi\alpha(t-\tau/2)} \right]^{*} \right\rangle dt = E\{u(t)v(t)\}. \end{aligned} \tag{21}$$

Now it is possible to bring out two others, but equivalent, definitions of cyclostationary signals (Gardner, 1991). Firstly, the signal x(t) appears the second order periodicity (x(t) is cyclostationary signal) if and only if the power spectral density of the delay-product signal (18) for some delays τ contains spectral lines at some nonzero frequencies $\alpha \neq 0$, that is if and only if $R_{xx}^{\alpha}(\tau) \neq 0$ is satisfied. Secondly, the multiplication with $e^{\pm i\pi\alpha t}$ shifts the signal x(t) in the frequency domain of $\pm\alpha / 2$. The third definition of cyclostationarity is described in (Gardner, 1991); the cyclic autocorrelation function of a signal x(t) is equivalent to cross-correlation function of the frequency shifted versions u(t) and v(t) of the same signal x(t). The signal x(t) exhibits second order cyclostationary if and only if the all vector of signal x(t) is frequency shifted and correlated with each other vector; that is if $E\{u(t)v(t)\} = R_{xx}^{\alpha}(\tau)$ is not zero as a function of τ for some $\alpha \neq 0$.

Cyclic autocorrelation function is the descriptor in time domain. For many applications, it is more useful and convenient to apply the descriptor in frequency domain. The well-known is the Wiener-Khinchin theorem that determines the power spectral density by applying Fourier transform on autocorrelation function. When we apply the Fourier transform on the cyclic autocorrelation function, we obtain the so-called spectral correlation density function $S_{x}^{\alpha}(f)$ (SCDF), which represents the key descriptor of cyclostationary signals in frequency domain

$$S_{x}^{\alpha}(f) = F\left\{R_{xx}^{\alpha}(\tau)\right\} = \int_{-\infty}^{\infty} R_{xx}^{\alpha}(\tau) e^{-i2\pi f\tau} d\tau \tag{22}$$

It is convenient to use the form (23) for the real calculation of SCDF

$$S_x^{\alpha}(f) = \lim_{\Delta t \to \infty} \lim_{T \to \infty} \frac{1}{\Delta t} \frac{1}{T} \int_{-\Delta t/2}^{\Delta t/2} X_T(t, f + \frac{\alpha}{2}) X_T^*(t, f - \frac{\alpha}{2}) dt \tag{23}$$

where

$$X_T(t,f) = \int_{t-T/2}^{t+T/2} x(u) e^{-i2\pi f u} du, \tag{24}$$

is spectral component of x(t) at frequency f with bandwidth 1/T.
In the next sections, there will be shown simple application of cyclostationary descriptors on the tasks of symbol timing recovery and modulation recognition. In both cases the resistibility of this approach against additive white Gaussian noise will be investigated. The experiments were simulated in the MATLAB by partial usage the MATLAB code published in (Costa, 1996).

7. Symbol timing recovery experiment

The symbol timing recovery plays the critical role for reliable data detection in the digital communication receiver. In most cases the timing signal is derived from the demodulated signal received x(t) (Barry et all, 2004). One of the methods used is based on spectral-line generation by applying nonlinear transformation. Because the timing signal usually has phase jitter, the phase lock loop (PLL) is used often to reduce it to the level desired. The general form of symbol timing recovery system based on spectral-line generation is shown in Fig. 6.

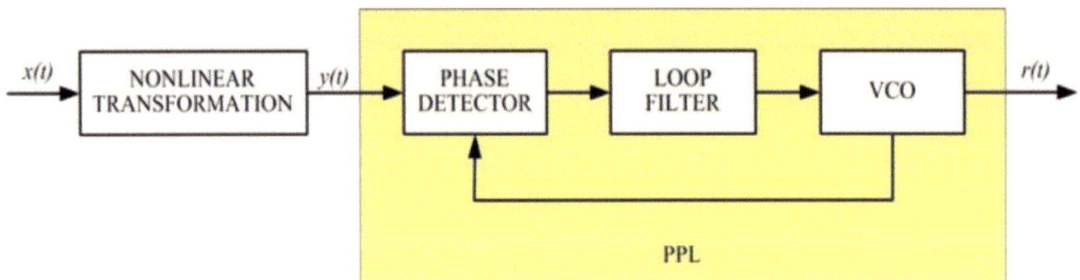

Fig. 6. General form of symbol timing recovery subsystem based on spectral line generation.

Some subsystems of symbol timing recovery exploit squaring of signal as nonlinear transformation. But squaring transformation works well only for certain types of data coding. For example, if signal x(t) represents binary data with levels ±1, the square transform generates constant output signal $y(t) = x^2(t) = 1$ for all t (Gardner, 1991,1994). A more general is the quadratic transformation involving delays

$$y(t) = x(t)x(t-\tau) \tag{25}$$

where $x(t-\tau)$ is nonzero delay τ of signal x(t). However, the relation (25) is equivalent to relation (18) for certain time lag τ. It is obvious that square transformation is a special case $y(t) = x(t+0)x^*(t-0) = x^2(t)$ of relation (18) too. So cyclic autocorrelation function is suitable for symbol timing recovery.

Next problem is to determine the optimal delay τ or by considering CAF optimal cyclic frequency α. It depends on particular modulation format as well as the pulse shape and data correlation. The mathematical derivations for some modulation types are described in (Gardner, 1986), (Lopez-Salcedo & Vazquez, 2003).
An experiment in the SIMULINK was simulated to show the timing recovery of BPSK modulated signal based on multiplication of demodulated signal and its delayed version (the delay equals to half of symbol period $\tau = T/2$). The schema of simulated system is shown in Fig. 7.

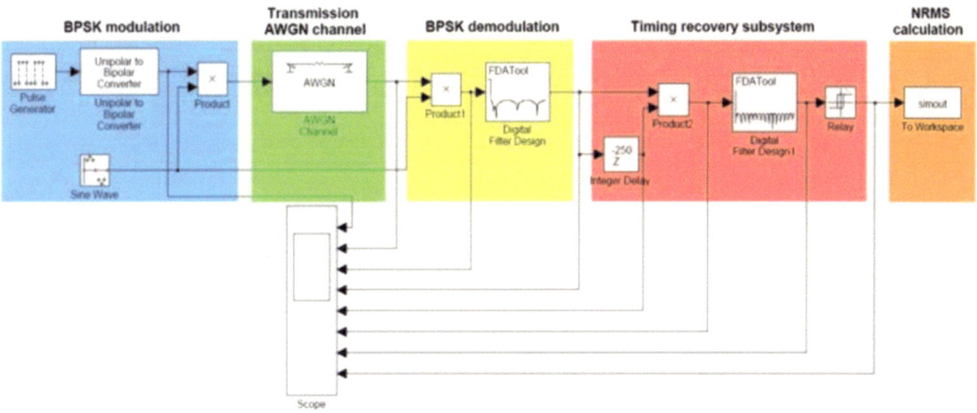

Fig. 7. The structure of simulated system in SIMULINK.

Appropriate timing behaviour of signals are displayed in Fig. 8.
Further, the simulation of timing recovery performance depending on AWGN in transmission channel was done. To the solution this problem, the ideal modulation data generated by the pulse generator (instead of random generator) were be used. The level of AWGN (E_b / N_0) in channel were adjusted from 50 to 5 dB. The difference of time position of rising edge of recovered timing signal and the ideal time position were be measured on the output y(t). The method of normalized root mean square (RMS) of timing difference was been used as evaluation criteria. The results are shown in Fig. 9.

8. Modulation recognition experiment

The spectral correlation density function provides convenient classification criteria to be applied for modulation recognition. In contrast to traditional power spectral density function, which is often identical for different modulation type (example for BPSK, QPSK), SCDF can lead to different graphs (Gardner et all, 1987). Many works dealing with this problem were published (Gardner et all, 1987), (Qi et all, 2009). So, we try to simulate the SCDF of modulated signals BPSK and QPSK in MATLAB. Both signals were created with following parameters:

- sampling frequency 8192 Hz,
- carrier frequency 2048 Hz,
- symbol rate 512 b/s,
- data length 1024.

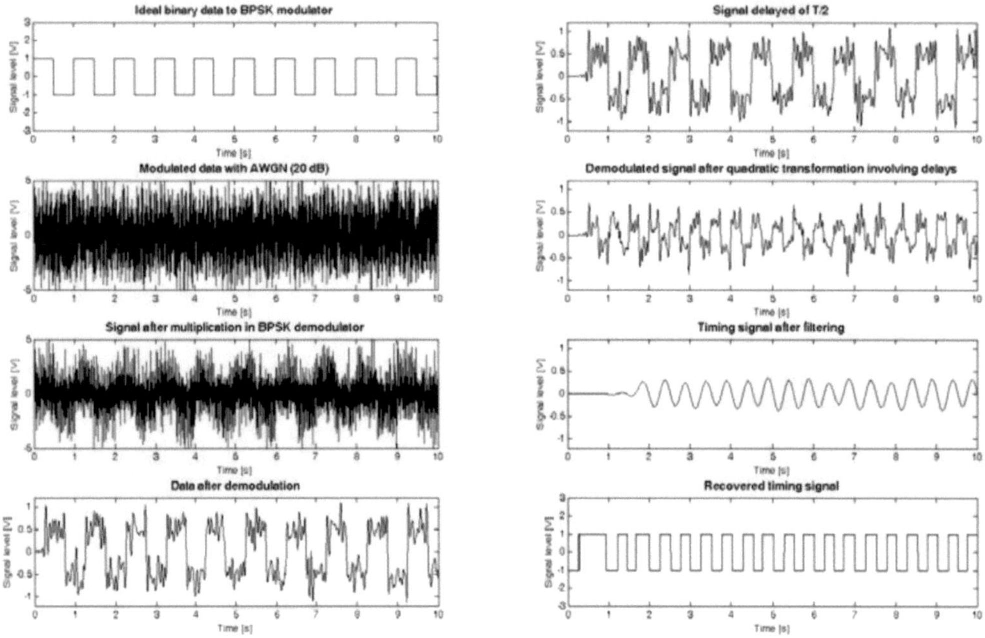

Fig. 8. Time behaviour of simulated signals.

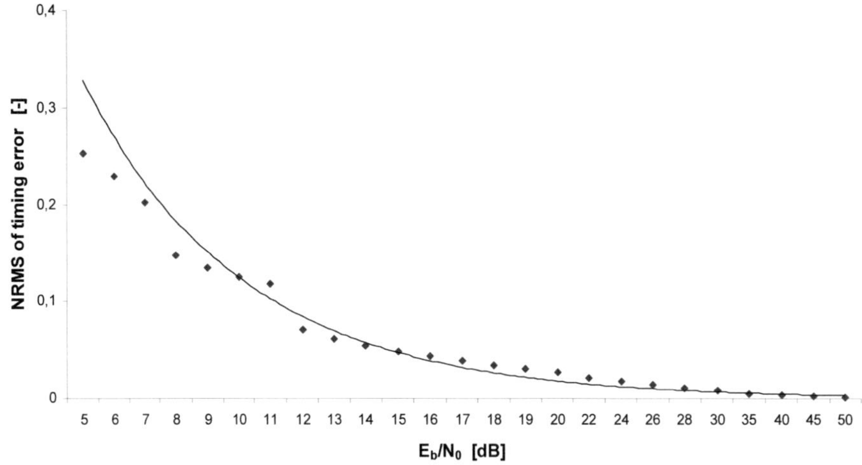

Fig. 9. Normalized RMS of timing error versus AWGN.

Obtained SCDF functions are shown in Fig. 10. Although PSK and QPSK signals have the same spectral density function, the graphic difference of both results (spectral correlation density functions of PSK and QPSK signal) is evident. We can split the graph to standard four quadrants and investigate the magnitude of maximum peak in each quadrant separately. While PSK signal has the equivalent level of magnitude for all peaks (quadrants), QPSK signal reaches in two opposed quadrants only about 50% of maximum. Exact value is dependant on statistical character of just utilized data and oscillates for each simulation.

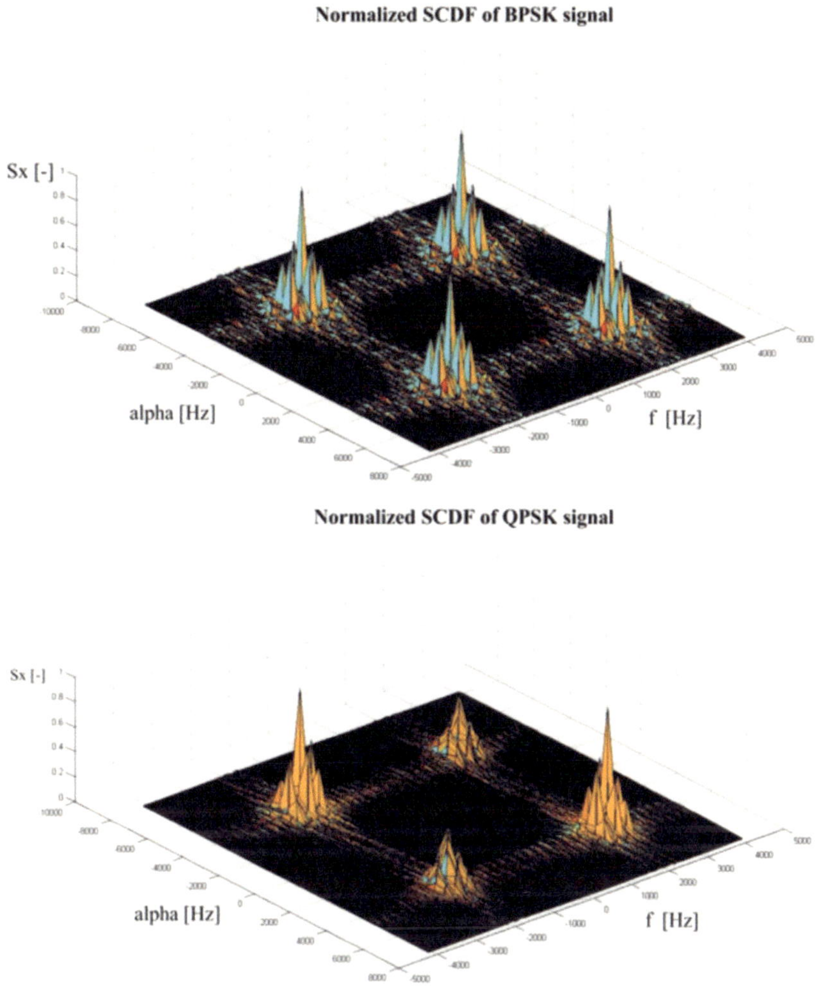

Fig. 10. Spectral Correlation Density Functions of PSK and QPSK signals

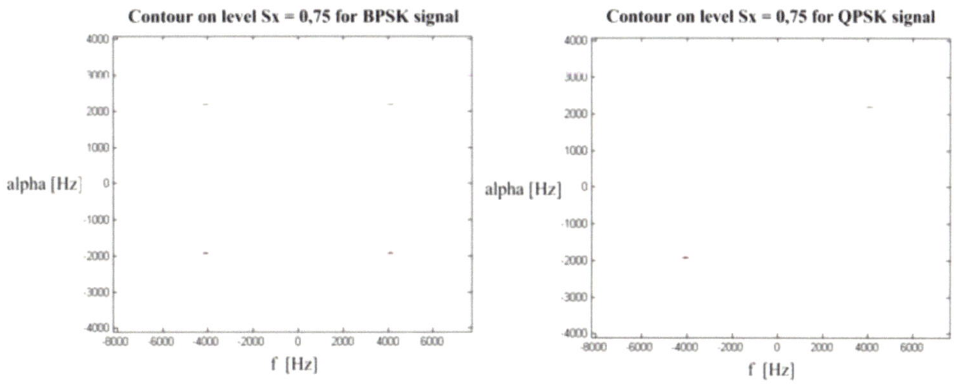

Fig. 11. Contours of normalized SCDF for modulation recognition

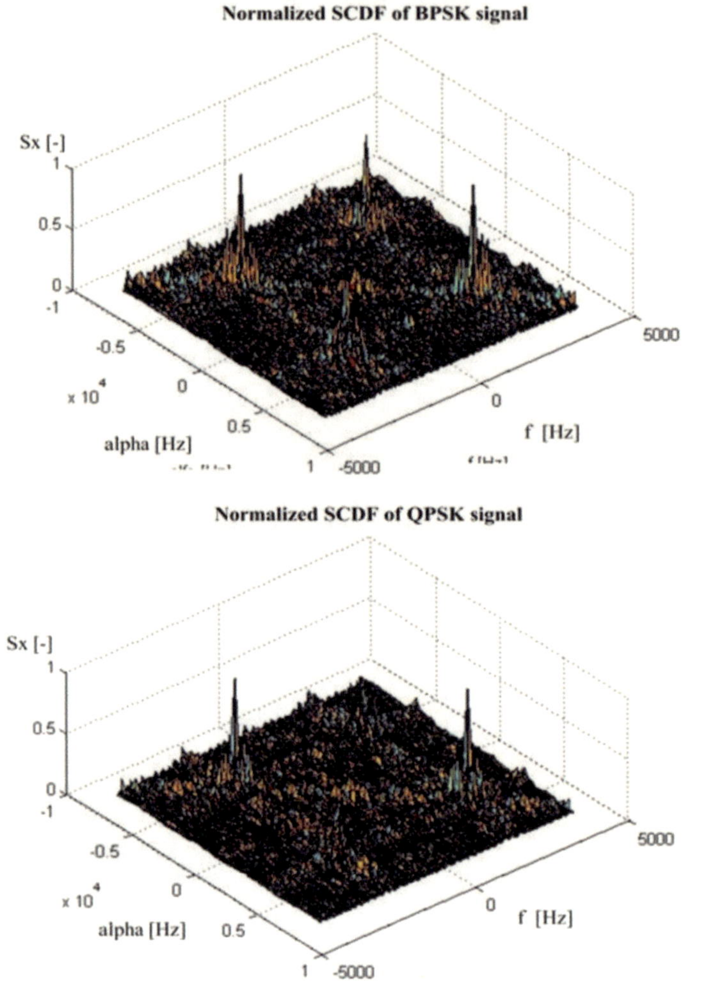

Fig. 12. Spectral Correlation Density Functions of PSK and QPSK signals for SNR = - 3 dB

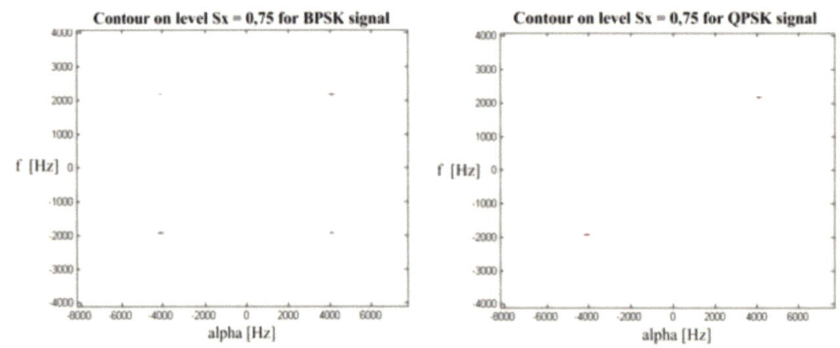

Fig. 13. Contours of normalized SCDF for modulation recognition for SNR = - 3 dB

Now we select very simply decision criteria for modulation recognition. If we make a contour of normalized SCDF on level 0,75 we obtain different results for each type modulation type.

For PSK signal it has four products while for QPSK signal it has only two products. The situation illustrate Fig. 11.
What can be more surprising is that this simply decision criteria works well under low level of signal to noise ratio (SNR). If we add to the signals additive white Gaussian noise it will work well. The results of simulation for SNR = - 3 dB are shown on Fig. 12 and Fig. 13.

9. Conclusion

The operation of the 2–class minimum–distance classifier of 2–FSK and 4–FSK signals has been verified by means of practical programming realized in the MATLAB programme. Results of the classification show that the Walsh–Hadamard transform has better properties for the recognition of FSK compared to Karhunen–Loeve transform (Richterova & Juracek, 2006). The classification efficiency of the 2–class minimum–distance classifier is superior to the linear classifier and quadratic classifier as presented in (Richterova, 2001). Experimental results show that the principal block scheme for the recognition of real pattern of 2–FSK and 4–FSK signals can be used for the special signal analysis in the areas where it is necessary to know or recognize the signal modulation type.
The experimental results indicate, that the 3-class minimum-distance classifier based on Karhunen-Loeve transform and the 3-class minimum-distance classifier based on Walsh-Hadamard transform are able recognize of three types of digital modulated signals. The number of correct classification for real patterns of FSK signals reachs approximately 70 %. The real patterns of PSK signals are classified correctly about 60 %. The designed classifiers are not able recognize modulation type 2-PSK and 4-PSK because the characteristic features of modulation type 2-PSK and 4-PSK are very similar. If we want recognize the groups of 2-PSK and 4-PSK, we must propose other type of modulation classifier.
The practical programming solution and performed experiments were verified a working 3-class minimum-distance classifier for the recognition of 2-FSK, 4-FSK and PSK signals. Results of the classification show that the Walsh–Hadamard transform has better properties for the recognition of FSK compared to Karhunen–Loeve transform. The results show, that this principle can be used for the technical analysis of signals in the branch, where necessary is obtained the information about the modulation type in the automatic system.
Although the theory of cyclostationary signals is known for several decades the practical research in this field still grows. New applications in cognitive radio (Sebesta, 2010), in military field (for example cyclostationary can be used to detect and identify ships, submarines or torpedoes in the ocean (Costa, 1996)) or in other scientific areas are investigated. This paper introduced the basic cyclostationary descriptors and on simply experiments demonstrates the effectiveness of this approach and its resistance against AWGN noise. The high resistance level results from correlation principle of cyclostationary method (useful signal) because mean value of AWGN correlation is zero.
There are many important aspects in cyclostationary measurement and application that were not mentioned here because of bounded length of paper. One of them is high sensitivity of obtained results on input parameters that is to say the input sequence length and required cyclic and frequency resolution. In some applications this leads on necessity of input signal pre-processing. The future research will be focus on automatic modulation recognition.

10. References

Ahmed, N.; Rao, K., R. (1975). *Orthogonal Transforms for Digital Signal Processing*. Springer–Verlag, Berlin, Germany.

Barry, J. R.; Lee, E. A ; Messerschmitt, D. G. (2004). Digital Communication. (Third edition). Kluwer Academic Publishers, Dordrecht ISBN 0-7923-75483.

Costa, E. L. (1996). *Detection and identification of cyclostationary signals.* (Ph.D. Thesis). Naval postgraduate school, Monterey, California.

Gardner, W. A. The Role of Spectral Correlation in Design and Performance Analysis of Synchronizers. *IEEE Transactions on Communications,* vol. 34, no. 11., (November 1986), pp.1089-1095. ISSN 0090-6778.

Gardner, W. A. *Exploitation of Spectral Redundancy in Cyclostationary Signals. IEEE Signal Processing Magazine,* vol. 8, no. 2, (April 1991), pp. 14-36, ISSN 1053-5888.

Gardner, W. A. (1994) *Cyclostationarity in Communications and Signal Processing*. IEEE Press, New York, USA, ISBN 0-7803-1023-3.

Gardner, W. A.; Brown, W.; Chin-Kang, C. Spectral Correlation of Modulated Signals:Part II-Digital Modulation. *IEEE Transactions on Communications,* vol. 35, no. 6, (June 1987), pp. 595-601, ISSN 0096-2244.

Gardner, W.; Napolitano, A.; Paura, L. Cyclostationarity: Half a century of research. *Signal processing,* vol. 86, no. 4, (2006), pp. 639-697, ISSN 0165-1684.

Grimaldi, D.; Rapuano, S.; De Vito, L. An Automatic Digital Modulation Classifier for Measurement on Telecommunication Networks. *IEEE Transactions on Instrumentation and Measurement,* vol. 56, no. 5, (2007), pp. 1711-1720.

Hua, Y.; Liu, W. Generalized Karhunen-Loeve transform. *IEEE on Signal Processing Letters,* vol. 5, no. 6, (1998), pp. 141-142.

Jondral, F. (1991). *Funksignalanalyse*. Teubner, Stuttgart, Germany.

Lopez-Salcedo, J., A.; Vazquez, G. Stochastic Approach to Square Timing Estimation with Frequency Uncertainty. *Proceedings of IEEE International Conference on Communications (ICC'03),* vol. 5, pp. 3555–3559, ISBN 0-7803-7802-4, Anchorage, AK, May 2003.

Nandi, A, K.; Azzouz, E.E. Algorithms for Automatic Modulation Recognition of Communication Signals. *IEEE Transactions on Communications,* vol. 46, no. 4., (1998), pp. 431 - 436.

Park, Ch.-S.; Dae, Y., K. A Novel Robust Feature of Modulation Classification for Reconfigurable Software Radio. *IEEE Transactions on Consumer Electronics,* vol. 52, no. 4, (2006), pp. 1193-1200.

Qi, Y., Peng, T., Wang, W., Luo, S. Cyclostationary signature design for common control channel of cognitive radio. *The Journal of China Universities of Posts and Telecommunications,* vol. 16, no. 2, (April 2009), pp. 42-46, ISSN 1005-8885.

Richterova, M.; Juracek, D. Modulation classifiers based on orthogonal transforms. *Proceedings of the ITTE International Conference "C2 Systems and NATO NEC",* pp. 14-18, University of Defence, Brno, Czech Republic, May 10-11, 2006.

Richterova, M. (2001) *Contribution to recognition of data modulated signals* (in Czech). (PhD Thesis). Military Academy, Brno, Czech Republic, 2001.

Richterova, M. A 2-class classifier of FSK signals. signals (in Czech), *Proceedings of STO-6,* pp. 22-27, Military Academy, Brno, Czech Republic, September 22-23, 1997.

Richterova, M. Modulation Recognition in Radiocommunication Systems. *Proceedings of. A XXVIII. Sesiune de Comunicari Stiintifice cu Participare Internationala,* pp.36-42, ATM, Bucharest, Romania, October 1999.

Semmlow, J. L. (2004) *Biosignal and Biomedical Image Processing. MATLAB-Based Applications.* CRC Press, New York, USA, ISBN 0–8247-4803–4.

Sebesta, V. Estimating a Spectral Correlation Function under the Conditions of Imperfect Relation between Signal Frequencies and a Sampling Frequency. *Radioengineering,* vol. 19, no. 1, (2010), ISSN 1210-2512.

22

Novel Variance Based Spatial Domain Watermarking and Its Comparison with DIMA and DCT Based Watermarking Counterparts

Rajesh Kannan Megalingam, Mithun Muralidharan Nair, Rahul Srikumar, Venkat Krishnan Balasubramanian and Vineeth Sarma Venugopala Sarma
Amrita Vishwa Vidyapeetham, Amritapuri Campus
India

1. Introduction

Most computers and systems are dealing with huge volumes of digital data. Major part of these digital data deals with multimedia, images and videos. The storage and secure transfer of this class of data is a burden for both individuals and organizations. Data authentication, data security and data compression are the primary requisites for any class of digital data in communication systems. Due to widespread and unrestricted use of the internet, multimedia data are available to everyone. For the protection of the author copyrights, image authentication is extremely important in present-day day communication systems. In image processing, authentication is implemented by using watermarking techniques. Nevertheless, whatever be the technique of watermarking, one of the important factors to be considered is robustness. In this chapter, novel methods for digital image watermarking and digital image compression are discussed. A novel method for digital watermarking in spatial domain, called as the (VB)2 (Variance Based Variable Block) Algorithm, will be discussed. The comparison in robustness of the spatial domain algorithm called as the DIMA (Diversified Intensity Matrix Algorithm) with our DCT-based frequency domain algorithm has been presented in [2]. The proposed work compares all watermarking techniques and determines the method with the highest robusteness. Additionally, a compression technique to address the problem of multimedia data storage and management is also proposed. This compression is brought about by a variance based algorithm.

2. Digital watermarking

Digital watermarking is about embedding digital information into another information/data, which can be reversible or irreversible. The information can be audio, video or images. Digital watermarking can be visible or invisible and the visibility of the watermark can be varied according to the wish of the owner. Major applications of watermarking include copyright protection and steganography. In steganography, people communicate secretly with their information embedded in digital signals, which have been in use for a long time. Watermaking can be done using software or hardware. But the efficiency of the watermarking technique is found out with the capacity, robustness and perceptibility of the method. Watermarking that we have done is purely image watermarking, both visible and invisible and this finds its potent applications in copyright authentication. Any method in frequency domain can be used for watermarking which can be based on Discrete Cosine Transform (DCT), Discrete Wavelet Transform (DWT), Discrete Hartley Transform (DHT), etc. Watermarking can also be done using the conventional spatial domain techniques. In this chapter, we discuss an improved version of the spatial domain watermarking.

While working with images, there comes another dilemma of dealing with copyright protection. Due to the widespread accessibility of Internet, multimedia data (or images) are available everywhere with minimum effort. It becomes easier for anyone to tamper with any image according to their whims and fancies. Therefore, it becomes mandatory to provide authors of images with appropriate copyright protection. One of the methods to provide image copyright protection is to embed a watermark in the parent image. Such methods are broadly called as watermarking schemes.

3. Compressed variance-based block type spatial domain watermarking technique

Images form an integral part of all information systems. Visual information perceived by the eyes are easily registered and recollected by the brain in contrast to other sources of information. Thus, transmitting, receiving, storing and processing images become extremely important. At the same time, images require higher bandwidths for transmission and greater memory for storage. Therefore, any technique that can bring forth a significant reduction in the memory requirement of images without affecting their integrity would be extremely useful in both transmission and storage of images. Such methods are broadly known as compression methods.

3.1 Compression

Compression is the process of reducing the number of pixels in an image without affecting the overall information content. As a result, the amount of memory required to store an image is reduced significantly. In our proposed work, a novel and efficient method for compression is discussed.

In this method, an $M=2^a$ x $N=2^b$ image is divided into X blocks, each of size $P=2^c$ x $Q=2^d$, where

$$X = \frac{M*N}{P*Q} = 2^{a-c+b-d} \tag{1}$$

If the image matrix and the block matrix are square matrices, i.e., $M = N = 2^a$ and $P = Q = 2^b$, the equation can be simplified as below

$$X = 2^{2a-2b} = 2^{2(a-b)} \tag{2}$$

The next step involves computation of mean and variance of each of the X number of blocks. This step enables identification of the blocks, having the least variance values. Small value of variance in a particular block signifies the fact that pixels of the corresponding block are closely related in magnitude and that the information content in the block is less. Thus, replacing the original pixel values of various blocks with their respective mean values will not distort the image significantly. i.e., the image can be recovered efficiently. Therefore, it suffices to transmit the mean value of a block instead of the entire block itself, thereby providing unparalleled compression in the image.

After the blocks with the smallest set of variance are identified, a threshold variance V_t is chosen. Those pixels of blocks having a variance V less than V_t , are replaced by their corresponding means and transmitted. The pixels of blocks having a variance V greater than V_t , are kept unchanged from that of the parent image and transmitted. The transmitted image is recovered and its integrity to that of the parent image is measured, using a parameter called the PSNR (Peak Signal to Noise Ratio). The PSNR is a measure of the robustness of an image and its resemblance to the parent image.
In the proposed image compression technique, an instance of a 512*512 Lena Image was used. During the first analysis, this image was divided into 64 blocks each of size 64*64. The next step involved the computation of mean and variance for the 64 blocks and replacing the blocks having the minimum set of variance with their corresponding mean values. The reconstructed image showed minimum distortion as the chosen threshold value for variance was decreased. The first analysis brought about a conclusion that higher the size of each block formed during the division of an image, higher will be the chances of distortion in the reconstructed image.
In order to overcome the distortion effects, we decided to delve deep into the block division process. This enabled us to come up with an idea to construct blocks of much smaller sizes. Therefore, a compression method involving blocks of size 16*16 was devised. After forming 16*16 blocks from the Lena Image, the mean and consequently the variance of each block were computed. The analysis was done by choosing threshold variances, V_t = 10, 20, 50, 100, 200 and 300 respectively, and transmitting only the means of those blocks whose variances were less than V_t while transmitting the other blocks unchanged. The reconstructed Lena images, with compressed blocks whose variances were less than V_t , are given in Fig. 1.

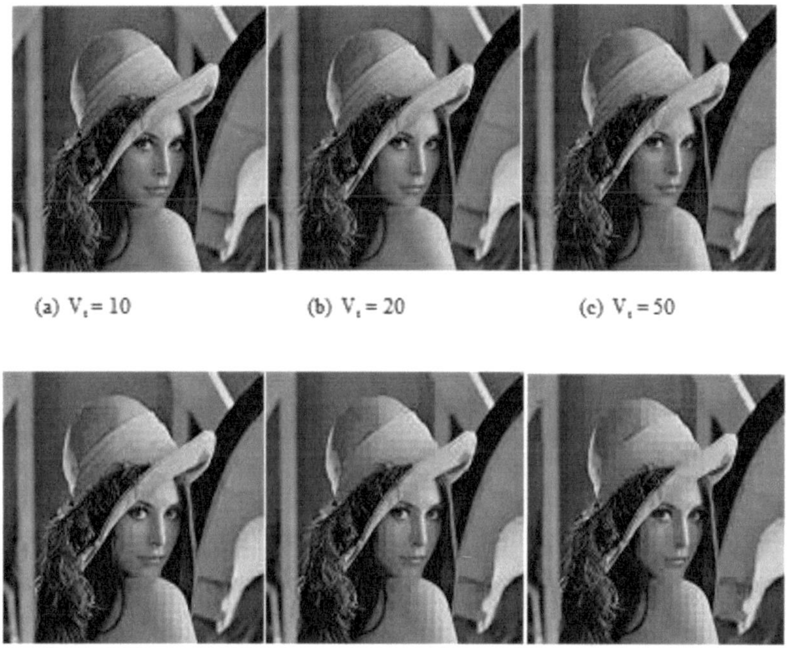

(a) $V_t = 10$ (b) $V_t = 20$ (c) $V_t = 50$

(d) $V_t = 100$ (e) $V_t = 200$ (f) $V_t = 300$

Fig. 1. Reconstructed Lena images with compressed 16*16 blocks with different threshold variances V_t.

The PSNR between the original and compressed reconstructed images for varying threshold variances, V_t are tabulated in Table 1.

Compression type(Variance)	**PSNR b/w original and compressed(Lena) in dB**
10	49.0054
20	44.5549
50	39.5507
100	36.0901
200	33.2333
300	31.7445

Table 1. PSNR between original and reconstructed images for different values of V_t.

The amount of compression achieved from this variance based compression technique is tabulated in Table 2.

Compression type(Variance)	**Percentage compression (%)**
10	10.35
20	20.11
50	33.88
100	45.41
200	55.27
300	59.86

Table 2. Amount of compression achieved for varying V_ts.

By scrupulous analysis of the findings in Tables 1 and 2, it can be inferred that at V_t= 300, the compression obtained is ~60% and the PSNR is also quite high (31.74). However, if one needs to bring in more clarity in the reconstructed image, V_t = 100 can be chosen. This gives a compression of 45.5% and a PSNR of 36.1, which indicates high amount of robustness in the received image.
From Tables 1 and 2, it is possible to derive a 2nd order regression equation with PSNR as the dependent and percentage compression as the independent variable. The equation can be formulated using the following equations.

$$PSNR = a * (\%\,Compression)^2 + b * (\%\,Compression) + c \qquad (3)$$

Performing summation on both sides of equation (3), we get

$$\sum PSNR = a * \sum(\%Compression)^2 + b * \sum(\%\,Compression) + c * N \qquad (4)$$

Multiplying $\sum(\%\,Compression)$ on both sides of equation (3), we get

$$\sum(\%\,Compression)*PSNR = \\ a*\sum(\%Compression)^3 + b*\sum(\%Compression)^2 + c*\sum\%Compression \qquad (5)$$

Multiplying $(\sum\%\,Compression^2)$ on both sides of equation (3), we get

$$\sum\left(\%\ Compression^2\right)*PSNR = a*\sum(\%Compression)^4 + b*\sum(\%Compression)^3 + c*\sum(\%Compression)^2 \quad (6)$$

By determining the values of the various summation factors and solving equations (4), (5) and (6), the parameters a, b and c are obtained as follows.

a = 1.95*10^ (-3); b = - 0.48 ; c = 53.613.

Therefore, equation (3) can be re-written as

$$PSNR = 1.95 * 10^{-3} * (\%\ Compression)^2 - 0.48 * (\%\ Compression) + 53.613 \quad (7)$$

The above equation is a theoretical approximation of the dependence of % compression on PSNR of images subjected to compression derived from the findings in Tables 1 and 2.
This equation can be used to estimate the PSNR in dB of the compressed Lena image to that of the original image for any percentage compression. A compression of 60% gives a PSNR of 31 dB.

3.2 Watermarking

The process of embedding an image or text into another image for the purpose of copyright protection, security or data authentication is known as watermarking. The image into which another image is embedded is called the parent image and the image used for the embedding process is called the watermark.

Fig. 2. Watermarked images for varying compression rates defined by the threshold variances (V_t).

Consider the image to be watermarked, I and the watermark, W. In our work, we have used the Lena Image (I) as the image to be watermarked and an Amrita Logo (W) as the watermark. In the technique of watermarking, both the image and the watermark are scaled by factors α and β such that the intensity of the original image is significantly prominent (α > β) when compared to that of the watermark. The values of α and β were obtained by trial and error method to be 0.97 and 0.15 respectively. The Image obtained after watermarking would be a linear combination of scaled I and scaled W represented as given below.

$$Watermarked\ Image = 0.97 * I + 0.15 * W \tag{8}$$

The watermarked image is transmitted and then received. After reception of the watermarked image, α*I is subtracted from the received image and multiplied by (1/ β) to obtain the watermark. The watermarking process is repeated using compressed images for all the afore-mentioned threshold variances (V_t) from 10 to 300 in the previous section. The robustness of the retrieved watermark is measured using the PSNR (Peak Signal to Noise Ratio).

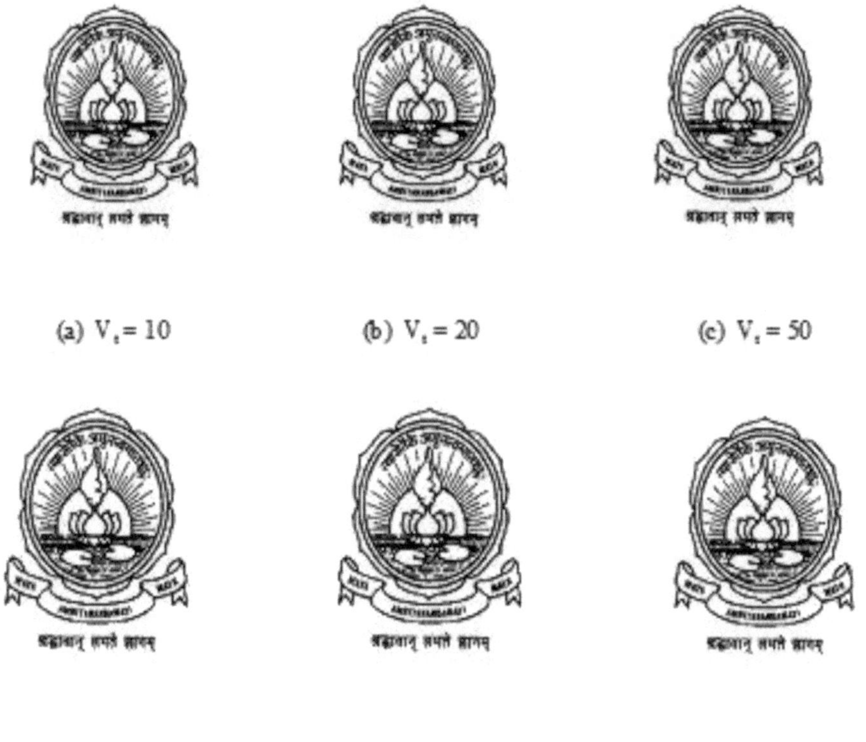

(a) $V_t = 10$ (b) $V_t = 20$ (c) $V_t = 50$

(d) $V_t = 100$ (e) $V_t = 200$ (f) $V_t = 300$

Fig. 3. Reconstructed watermarks for varying watermarking schemes compressed using threshold variances, V_t = 10, 20, 50, 100, 200 and 300.

Table 3 tabulates PSNR between original and compressed Lena images for varying threshold variances V_t.

Compression type (Variance V_t)	PSNR between original and Compressed Images (Amrita Logo)(dB)
10	57.0258
20	56.5360
50	52.6592
100	50.6900
200	47.8014
300	46.0550

Table 3. PSNR between original and compressed watermark images for varying V_ts.

Table 4 shows PSNR between original and reconstructed watermarks for varying threshold variances V_t.

Compression type(Variance V_t)	PSNR b/w original and reconstructed Images(Amrita Logo)(dB)
10	49.1933
20	49.1086
50	48.1102
100	47.3150
200	45.7512
300	44.5842

Table 4. PSNR between original and reconstructed watermarks for varying V_ts.

By heedful analysis of Tables 3 and 4, it can be observed that, as the threshold variance for compression is increased, the dip in PSNR is found to be decreasing. At V_t = 300, the dip in PSNR is about 1.47 dB (46.0550 - 44.5842). This enables us to arrive at a conclusion that at higher compression rates using the proposed method, the PSNR dip is almost insignificant. In other words, the proposed method helps to achieve high rates of compression without compromising PSNR, a technique of very high robustness and significant compression.

4. DCT based watermarking

Several frequency domain methods can be used in watermarking which can be based on Discrete Cosine Transform (DCT), Discrete Wavelet Transform (DWT), Discrete Hartley Transform (DHT), etc. The discrete cosine transform (DCT) and the inverse discrete cosine transform (IDCT) are substantial performance bottlenecks in image watermarking, since the time taken to watermark the image depends on the time required to get the DCT/IDCT of the images.

4.1 Two dimensional DCT

A DCT expresses finite number of data points in terms of sum of cosine functions oscillating at different frequencies. The method that we used for digital image watermarking is based on DCT, where the 2D DCT of the images are determined and added to watermark an image. This needs the 2-dimensional DCT of the images for the watermarking to be performed. 2-D DCT is represented by the equation (1), where n1 and n2 vary from 0 to 7 for a 8x8 block of data. The value of the constants k1 and k2 also vary from 0 to 7.

$$X(k1,k2) = \sum_{n1=0}^{N1}\sum_{n2=0}^{N2} x(n1,n2)Cos(\left(\left(\frac{\pi}{N1}\right)+0.5\right)k1)Cos(\left(\left(\frac{\pi}{N2}\right)+0.5\right)k2)$$

There are many methods for finding the 2D DCT of which the transpose method is the most common method.

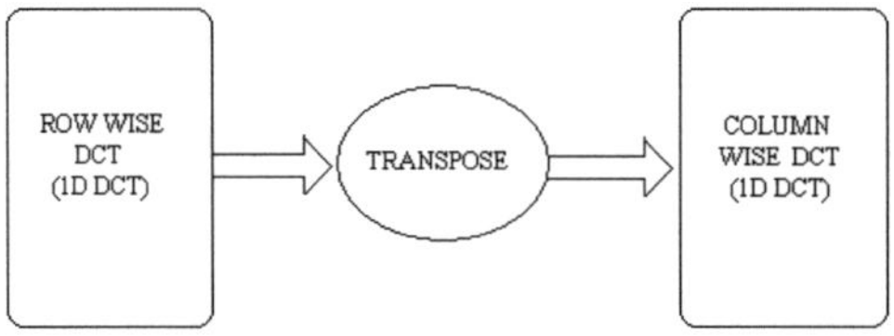

Fig. 4. 2D-DCT using 1D-DCT

The digital data of the image is made into several 8X8 blocks and the 1D DCT of each block is found out. Then the transpose of the 8x8 block is taken and again the 1D DCT is found out, which when applied to all the blocks of the image gives the 2D DCT of the whole image. In other words, the row wise block DCT is first found, followed by the column wise DCT which gives the 2D DCT. Suppose that the image under consideration is of size 512x512, and then the image, when divided into 8x8 blocks gives, 4096 blocks. The block wise DCT is found out for each block. The "Fig.1" illustrates the method of finding the 2D DCT of an 8x8 block of data. The same procedure is repeated for all the 8x8 block of data.
From the above explanation it is quite evident that the implementation of digital watermarking needs an efficient algorithm to find the 2D DCT/IDCT, for which we need the implementation of 1D DCT. So the implementation of 1D DCT has been discussed in the next section.

4.2 One dimensional DCT implementation

The 1-D DCT of a sequence of length N is given by

$$C(u) = \alpha(u) \sum_{x=0}^{N-1} f(x)\cos\left[\pi(2x+1)u/2N\right] \tag{10}$$

For u=0, 1, 2, 3..... (N-1) and in the similar way the 1-D IDCT is defined as

$$f(x) = \alpha(u) \sum_{u=0}^{N-1} \alpha(u)\ C(u)\ \cos\left[\pi(2x+1)u/2N\right] \tag{11}$$

For x=0, 1, 2, 3.... (N-1) and for both the equations

$$\alpha(u) = (1/N)^{0.5} \quad \text{for } u=0$$

$$= (2/N)^{0.5} \quad \text{for } u\neq 0$$

Here we consider an 8X8 block of data and for this we will have to find the 1D-DCT for each row of 8 elements and each column of 8 elements separately. The major concern in finding the 1D DCT/IDCT is the number of multipliers and the adders that had to be used.

$$\begin{bmatrix} y0 \\ y1 \\ y2 \\ y3 \\ y4 \\ y5 \\ y6 \\ y7 \end{bmatrix} = \frac{1}{2} \begin{bmatrix} c4 & c4 & c4 & c4 & c4 & c4 & c4 & c4 \\ c1 & c3 & c5 & c7 & -c7 & -c5 & -c3 & -c1 \\ c2 & c4 & c6 & -c2 & -c2 & -c6 & c6 & c2 \\ c3 & -c7 & -c1 & -c5 & -c5 & c1 & c7 & -c3 \\ c5 & -c1 & c7 & c3 & -c3 & -c7 & c1 & -c5 \\ c6 & -c2 & c2 & -c6 & -c6 & c2 & -c2 & c6 \\ c7 & -c5 & c3 & -c1 & c1 & -c3 & c5 & -c7 \end{bmatrix} \begin{bmatrix} x0 \\ x1 \\ x2 \\ x3 \\ x4 \\ x5 \\ x6 \\ x7 \end{bmatrix}$$

Fig. 5. Matrix method of implementing 1D-DCT/IDCT

4.3 Watermarking

Watermarking of an image can be done using the DCTs of the images to be used. The DCT of both the images are taken and the intensity of the image that has to appear as the water mark, can be varied by the proportion in which the DCT is added. The basic process that takes place, is the addition of DCTs followed by the IDCT of the result, which gives the watermarked image.

$$V_i'=V_i * (1+ \alpha * (X_i + \beta * W_i)) \tag{13}$$

Where Vi' is the result of the added DCT of the two images. X_i is the DCT value of the image on which the watermarking is done and W_i is the DCT of the logo, which is watermarked on the image. The constants α, β, affect the visibility of the watermark. For very small β value, a watermark is invisible and as the visibility increases by growth of β value. For extraction of a watermark, the values of α and β have to be known and hence the extraction of the watermarking cannot be done by anyone who does not know these values. To increase security, there are methods where in the values of α, β are varied for each block, which are known only to the owner. This is the principle used in image authentication or copyright.

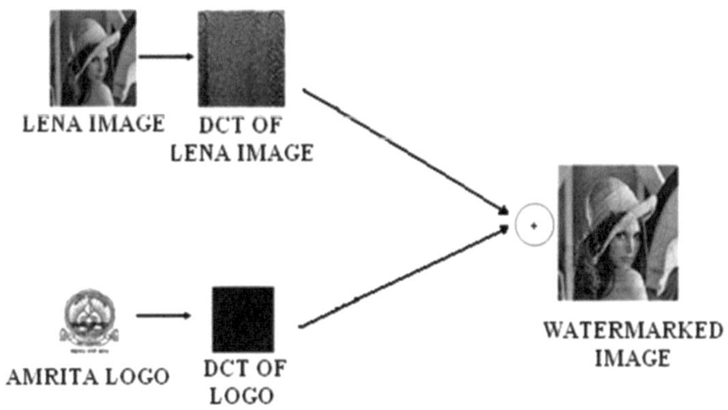

Fig. 6. DCT/IDCT based digital watermarking.

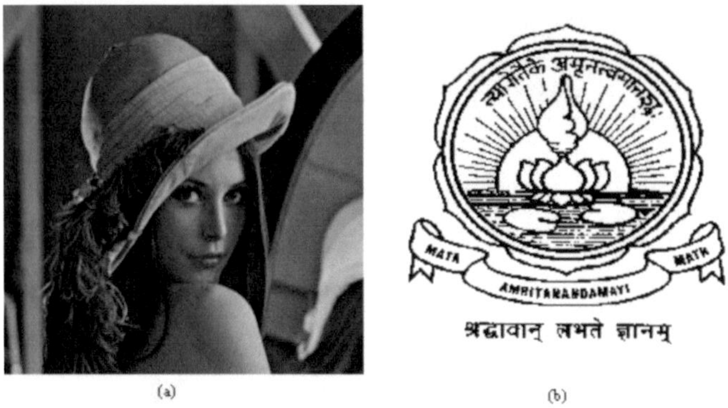

Fig. 7. (a) Lena image (b) logo to be watermarked

Fig. 8. The images obtained after watermarking (a) for α=.97 and β=.07 (b) for α=.97 and β=.17 (c) for α=.97 and β=.27 (d) invisible watermarking

5. Watermarking in spatial domain

Conventional Spatial domain watermarking is generally not in use due to its least reliability. In the spatial domain, pixels in randomly selected regions of the image are modified according to the signature or logo desired by the author of the product. This method involves modifying the pixel values of the original image where the watermark should be embedded. Fig. 2 shows the block diagram of a spatial-domain data embedding system.

Randomly selected image data are dithered by a small amount according to a predefined algorithm, whose complexity may vary in practical systems. The algorithm defines the intensity and the position of the watermark on the original image. One of the major disadvantages of the conventional watermarking is that it can be easily extracted from the original image which makes this technique unsuitable for copyright authentication.
There are three factors that determine the parameters of the algorithm applied in the spatial domain watermarking. The three factors are:

- The information associated with the signature. Basically, the signature is the watermark embedded on the original image. The information of the signature is closely related to the size and quality of the signature.
- The secret random key. The secret key may be included in the process of watermarking to improve the security during transmission. If a key is also included, only the receiver who knows the key can extract the watermark, and not any intruders.
- The masking property of the image. The masking property of the image is also related to the quality and composition of the image which signifies the clarity of the watermark on the original image.

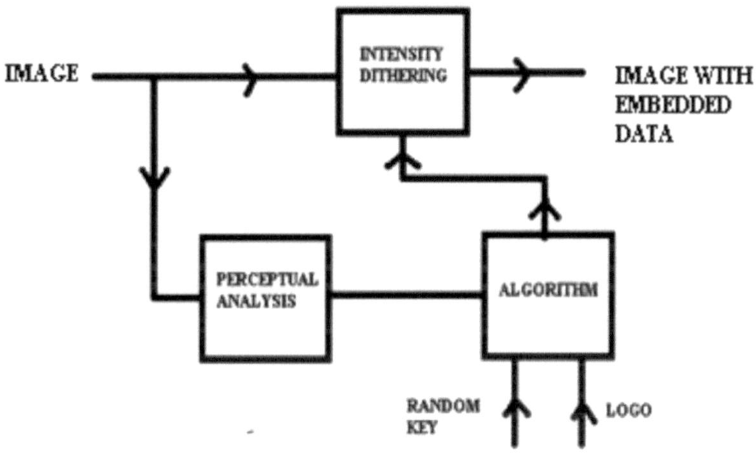

Fig. 9. Spatial domain data embedding system.

One form of the data embedding algorithm is given by the equation (14),

$$\hat{y}=y+\alpha I \quad (14)$$

where *y(i,j)*, is the original image intensity at pixel position *(i,j)*, ŷ is the marked image, and *αI* represents the embedded data in the form of small changes in intensity levels. The author of the watermark holds two keys:

- The region of the image where the mark is hidden and
- The information in the watermark, *αI*.

Given the marked image, the original owner will be able to recover the watermark by comparing the marked image with the original. In the reconstruction of the embedded watermark, the following computation is made,

$$I= (\hat{y}-y)/\alpha \quad (15)$$

This is the simplest watermarking technique that can be used.

5.1 Diversified intensity matrix

The pixel intensity matrix of the original image is compared with four predetermined constant terms.These constants for 8-bit encoded pixel data are: 63, 127, 191 and 255. The four diversified pixel intensity matrices are named as lowest intensity matrix(LL), Intermediate Intensity Matrix(LH) ,Higher Intensity Matrix(HL) and the Highest Intensity Matrix(HH), as shown in Fig 3.

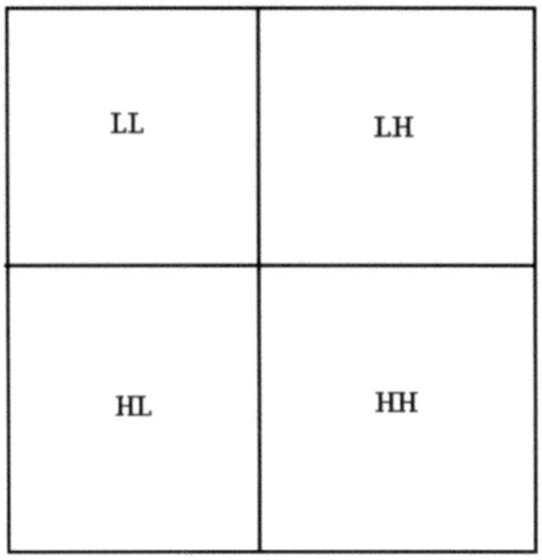

Fig. 10. Diversified pixel intensity matrices

Each pixel value is compared with these four constants and sorted into corresponding matrices as given in Table 5. The matrices thus obtained have one fourth the size of the original image matrix.

Category	**Pixel value range (P)**	**Diversified intensity matrix**
1	$0 < P \leq 63$	LL
2	$64 \leq P \leq 127$	LH
3	$128 \leq P \leq 191$	HL
4	$192 \leq P \leq 255$	HH

Table 5. Diversified Intensity Matrices

5.2 Novel spatial domain watermarking algorithm

The methodology that we used in the spatial domain watermarking involves the following steps. The first step involves the computation of the four diversified pixel intensity matrices for the original image, as well as the watermark to be embedded as shown in Fig. 11. This is done by the comparator technique mentioned in the previous section.Once these eight matrices have been obtained, the four diversified pixel intensity matrices of the watermark is scaled by a constant, a.

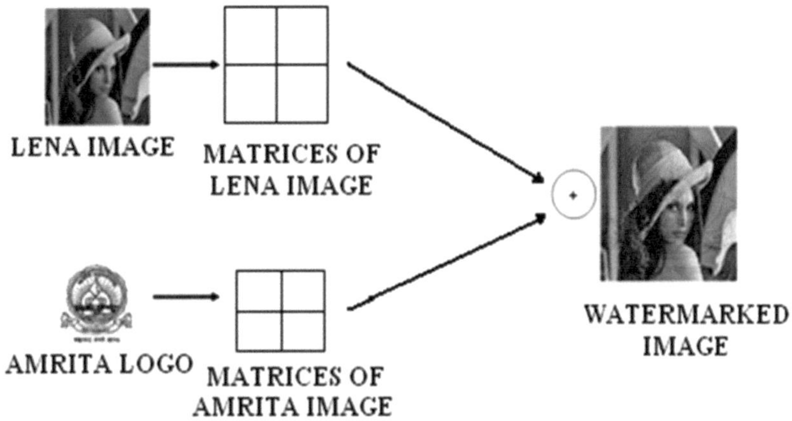

Fig. 11. Spatial domain digital watermarking with two images.

Similarly, the four diversified intensity matrices of the original image to be watermarked is scaled by another factor β. Once these scaled matrices are obtained, one can do both visible as well as invisible watermarking.

A. Visible watermarking

The eight matrices obtained after scaling are added together to obtain the Watermarked Image, $\hat{y}$. The visibility of the watermark can be varied by changing the value of a and β. Prior to the above addition, the values of the scaling factors, a and β were experimentally determined to be 0.12 and 0.97 respectively.

B. Invisible watermarking

The advantage of this type of watermarking is that one cannot identify the watermark that is embedded in the image. This is most commonly used for secret communication . For the process of invisible watermarking, the scaling factors, α and β , were experimentally found to be 0.005 and 0.97.

C. Robustness of the watermarking technique

Digital image watermarking can be done for copyright authentication or secret communication. The former can be achieved by the invisible watermarking done by the novel method proposed. The latter should be tested for its robustness and hence we used Pseudo Random Noise for the security purpose. This noise was added to the watermarked image as a key with the intention of bringing about a variation in the pixel values. Robustness was checked by adding random noise along with the scaled and added versions of the diversified intensity matrices and then transmitted. To check the security aspect, we tried to extract the watermark without using the key, which was not possible. The normal watermark can be extracted out from the conventional spatial domain watermarked image just by subtracting the original image (Lena image) from the watermarked image. The security is ensured by the fact that direct subtraction of the original image from the watermarked image by an eavesdropper results in an unrecoverable blurred image with no resemblance to that of the watermark. Only the intended user can extract the watermark by using the same key at the receiver end. So this would prevent any eavesdropper from extracting the information embedded in the watermark, which makes the method suitable in security aspect as well.

Robustness of this watermarking technique can also be verified by use of pseudo random noise with the watermarked image. In this case, an intruder who does not know the proper key that is multiplied with the image cannot extract the watermark.

5.3 Results

Fig.5 shows the results of implementation, using the standard 'Lena' image, which is the original image used and the the logo of our university, Amrita Vishwa Vidyapeetham, the watermark used. Fig.6 (c) shows the watermarked 'Lena' image using the proposed methodology of watermarking. For visible watermarking we have used $\alpha = 0.9$ and $\beta = 0.12$. Fig.6(d) shows the result of the invisible watermarking done where we chose $\alpha = 0.9$ and $\beta = 0.005$.

The invisible watermarking is implemented by adding a different scaled version of the image to be watermarked to the original image. Finally, it is retrieved by using a secret floating point number. The algorithm is implemented in Verilog HDL. The applicability of this method for any image is also verified using another standard image, which is the 'Cameraman' image. The watermarking is done using 'Lena' image as the base image and 'Cameraman' image is watermarked onto it. The results thus obtained are as shown in Fig.7. Here the original image is again the 'Lena image'. Since similar results are obtained for both set of images, we can conclude that this method guarantees an average PSNR for any image that we consider.

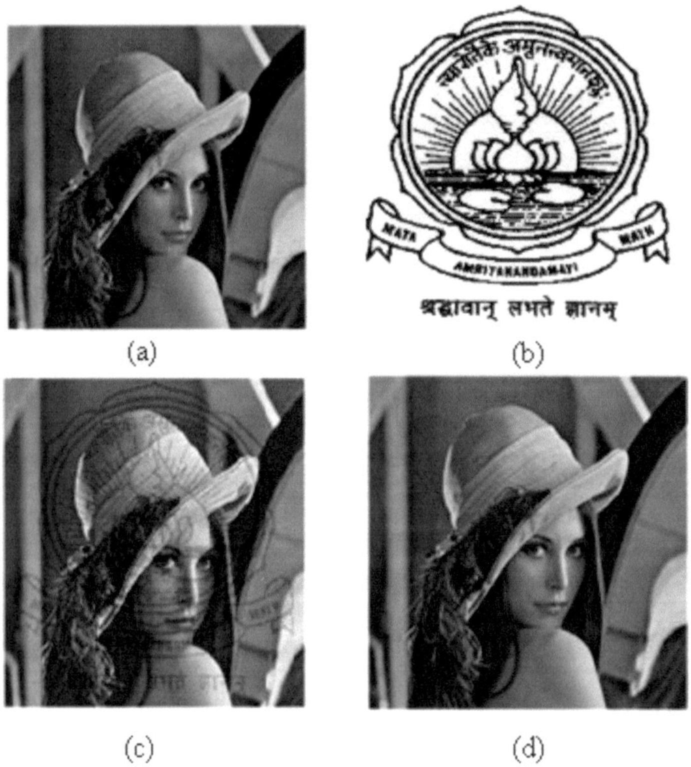

Fig. 12. The figure shows (a) the original Lena image (b) the logo to be watermarked (c) visible watermarked image and (d) invisible watermarked image.

Fig. 13. The figure shows (a) the Lena image (b) the original Cameraman image to be watermarked (c) visible watermarked image and (d) the retrieved cameraman image.

Domain	PSNR (dB)
Spatial	29.66
Frequency	33.16

Table 6. Comparison Of PSNR Values In Spatial And Transform Domains

The robustness of the method is given by the Peak Signal to Noise Ratio (PSNR) value of the retrieved image with respect to that of the original image. The value of PSNR for the proposed method is found out experimentally. The digital image watermarking was done by the proposed method and noise was added to it. We did the retrieval of the watermark from the watermarked image and the mean square error and the PSNR is found out. The Mean Square error, M.E and the PSNR of the retrieved image can be calculated by using the following equations (4) & (5).

$$M.E = (1/(m*n))*\sum i \sum j \, (I_1(i,j)-I_2(i,j))^2 \qquad (16)$$

$$PSNR = 10*\log\,(\max(I_1(i,j))^2)/M.E) \;\; dB \qquad (17)$$

where m and n are the pixel dimensions of the image, and I1 and I2 are the original and retrieved images respectively.

The results of the calculations for the proposed spatial domain watermarking and a standard frequency domain watermarking using DCT are as given in Table 1. It can be seen that the PSNR value of the proposed method is comparable to the PSNR that can be obtained by the frequency domain watermarking which is most commonly used. The DCT based watermarking could give a PSNR of 33.16 and the novel spatial domain gives a PSNR of 29.66 dB which shows that our method is reliable and robust. The comparison is made with the implementation done using DCT algorithm [1].

From Table 2 it is clear that the proposed method of digital image watermarking is reliable to a good extent since it gives a PSNR value comparable to the PSNR value that can be obtained by the frequency domain watermarking for the same set of images used.

6. Comparison and results

From the above results, it can be concluded that the Compressed Variance-Based Block Type Spatial Domain Watermarking Technique is having the required amount of robustness and is able to give a good amount of compression.

The digital image watermarking using diversified intensity matrices and using discrete cosine transform is also robust. But higher robustness can be achieved using the present method as per the requirements by using equation (7). If watermarking demands a minimum robustness of X dB, put X in equation 7 and find the maximum compression that can be achieved and then do the watermarking. Hence, this is a flexible and efficient method capable of doing significant compression and robust watermarking.

7. Acknowledgment

We gratefully acknowledge the Almighty GOD who gave us strength and health to successfully complete this venture. The authors wish to thank Amrita Vishwa Vidyapeetham, in particular the Digital library, for access to their research facilities and for providing us the laboratory facilities for conducting the research.

8. References

[1] Rajesh Kannan Megalingam, Vineeth Sarma.V , Venkat Krishnan.B , Mithun.M, Rahul Srikumar, Novel Low Power, High Speed Hardware Implementation of 1D DCT/IDCT using Xilinx FPGA.

[2] Rajesh Kannan Megalingam, Venkat Krishnan.B, Vineeth Sarma.V, Mithun.M, Rahul Srikumar, Hardware Implementation of Low Power, High Speed DCT/IDCT Based Digital Image Watermarking International Journal of Computer Theory and Engineering, Vol. 2, No. 4, August, 2010.

[3] Khurram Bukhari, Georgi Kuzmanov and Stamatis Vassiliadis, DCT and IDCT Implementations on Different FPGA Technologies.

[4] S. An C. Wang, Recursive algorithm, architectures and FPGA implementation of the two-dimensional discrete cosine transform.

[5] Cayre F, Fontaine C, Furon T. Watermarking security: theory and practice. IEEE Transactions on Signal Processing, 2005, 53 (10) :3976-3987.

[6] W. N. Cheung, Digital Image Watermarking In Spatial and Transform Domains.

[7] M. Barni, F. Bartolini, and T. Furon, "A general framework for robust watermarking security," Signal Process., vol. 83, no. 10, pp. 2069- 2084, Oct. 2003, to be published.
[8] A. Kerckhoffs, "La cryptographie militaire," J. Des Sci. Militaires, vol.9, pp. 5-38, Jan. 1883.
[9] C. E. Shannon, "Communication theory of secrecy systems," Bell Syst.Tech. J., vol. 28, pp. 656–715, Oct. 1949.
[10] W. Diffie and M. Hellman, "New directions in cryptography," IEEE Trans. Inf. Theory, vol. IT-22, no. 6, pp. 644–654, Nov. 1976.
[11] Liu Jun, Liu LiZhi, An Improved Watermarking Detect Algorithm for Color Image in Spatial Domain, 2008 International Seminar on Future BioMedical Information Engineering.
[12] B. Smitha and K.A. Navas, Spatial Domain- High Capacity Data Hiding in ROI Images, IEEE - ICSCN 2007.
[13] Amit Phadikar Santi P. Maity Hafizur Rahaman, Region Specific Spatial Domain Image Watermnarking Scheme, 2009 IEEE International Advance Computing Conference (IACC 2009).
[14] Houtan Haddad Larijani, Gholamali Rezai Rad, A New Spatial Domain Algorithm for Gray Scale Images Watermarking, Proceedings of the International Conference on Computer and Communication Engineering 2008.
[15] Irene G. Karybali, Efficient Spatial Image Watermarking via New Perceptual Masking and Blind Detection Schemes, IEEE transactions on information forensics and security.
[16] Dipti Prasad Mukherjee, Spatial Domain Digital Watermarking of Multimedia Objects for Buyer Authentication, IEEE Transactions on multimedia.
[17] D.W. Trainor J.P. Heron" and R.F. Woods," Implementation of the 2D DCT using a XILINX XC6264 FPGA, "0-7803-3806-5/97.
[18] S. Musupe and is Arslun, Low power DCT implementation approach for VLSI DSP processors, 0-7803-5471 -0/99.
[19] S. An C. Wang "Recursive algorithm, architectures and FPGA implementation of the two- dimensional discrete cosine transform", The Institution of Engineering and Technology 2008.
[20] Saied Amirgholipour Kasmani, Ahmadreza Naghsh-Nilchi, " A New Robust Digital Image Watermarking Technique Based On Joint DWTDCT Transformation", Third 2008 International Conference on Convergence and Hybrid Information Technology.
[21] A.Aggoun and I. Jalloh "Two-dimensional DCT/SDCU architecture", 2003 IEE proceedings online no. *20030063, DOI:* 10.1049/ip-edt:20030063.
[22] Syed Ali Khayam, "The Discrete Cosine Transform (DCT): Theory and Application", Department of Electrical & Computer Engineering, Michigan State University.
[23] Kuo-Hsing Cheng, Chih-Sheng Huang and Chun-Pin lin "The Design and implementation of DCT/IDCT Chip with Novel Architecture" , ISCAS 2000 - IEEE international symposium on circuits and systems, may 28-31, 2000, Geneva, Switzerland.

[24] Christoph Loeffler, Adriaan Lieenberg, and George s. Moschytz, "Practical fast 1-d DCT algorithms With 11 multiplications ", ch2673-2/89/0000-0098.

[25] Archana Chidanandan, Joseph Moder, Magdy Bayoumi "Implementation of neda-based DCT architecture using even-odd decomposition of the 8 x 8 DCT matrix", 1-4244-0173-9/06.

[26] Archana Chidanandan, Magdy Bayoumi, "Area-efficient neda architecture for the 1-D DCT/IDCT", 142440469x/06/.

23

Quantitative Analysis of Iodine Thyroid and Gastrointestinal Tract Biokinetic Models Using MATLAB

Chia Chun Hsu[1,3], Chien Yi Chen[2] and Lung Kwang Pan[1]
[1]*Central Taiwan University of Science and Technology*
[2]*Chun Shan Medical University*
[3]*Buddhist Tzu Chi General Hospital, Taichung Branch*
Taiwan

1. Introduction

This chapter quantitatively analyzed the biokinetic models of iodine thyroid and the gastrointestinal tract (GI tract) using MATLAB software. Biokinetic models are widely used to analyze the internally absorbed dose of radiation in patients who have undergone a nuclear medical examination, or to estimate the dose of I-131 radionuclide that is absorbed by a critical organ in patients who have undergone radiotherapy (ICRP-30, 1978). In the specific biokinetic model, human organs or tissues are grouped into many compartments to perform calculations. The defined compartments vary considerably among models, because each model is developed to elucidate a unique function of the human metabolic system.
The solutions to the time-dependent simultaneous differential equations that are associated with both the iodine and the GI tract model, obtained using the MATLAB default programming feature, yield much medical information, because the calculations that are made using these equations provide not only the precise time-dependent quantities of the radionuclides in each compartment in the biokinetic model but also a theoretical basis for estimating the dose absorbed by each compartment. The results obtained using both biokinetic models can help a medical physicist adjust the settings of the measuring instrumentation in the radioactive therapy protocol or the radio-sensitivity of the dose monitoring to increase the accuracy of detection and reduce the uncertainty in practical measurement.
In this chapter, MATLAB algorithms are utilized to solve the time-dependent simultaneous differential equations that are associated with two biokinetic models and to define the correlated uncertainties that are related to the calculation. MATLAB is seldom used in the medical field, because the engineering-based definition of the MATLAB parameters reduces its ease of use by unfamiliar researchers. Nevertheless, using MATLAB can greatly accelerate analysis in a practical study. Some firm recommendations concerning future studies on similar topics are presented and a brief conclusion is drawn.

2. Iodine thyroid model

2.1 Biokinetic model

The iodine model simulates the effectiveness of healing by patients following the post-surgical administering of ^{131}I for the ablation of residual thyroid. Following initial treatment (a near-total or total thyroidectomy), most patients are treated with ^{131}I for ablation of the residual thyroid gland (De Klerk *et al.*, 2000; Schlumberger 1998). However, estimates of cumulative absorbed doses in patients and people close to them remains controversial, despite the establishment of the criteria for applying the iodine biokinetic model to a healthy person from the ICRP-30 report. Conversely, the biokinetic model of iodine that is applied following the remnant ablation of the thyroid must be reconsidered from various perspectives, because the gland that is designated as dominant, the thyroid, in (near-) total thyroidectomy patients is the remnant gland of interest (Kramer *et al.*, 2002; North *et al.*, 2001).

According to the ICRP-30 report in the biokinetic model of iodine, a typical human body can be divided into five major compartments. They are (1) stomach, (2) body fluid, (3) thyroid, (4) whole body, and (5) excretion as shown in Fig. 1. Equations 1-4 are the simultaneous differential equations for the time-dependent correlation among iodine nuclides in the compartments

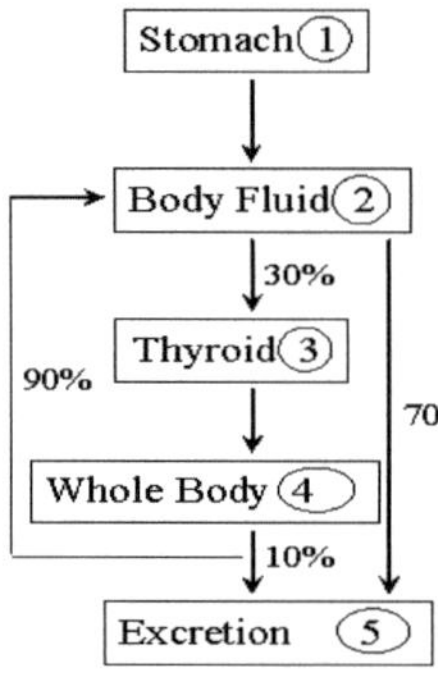

Fig. 1. Biokinetic model of Iodine for a standard healthy man. The model was recommended by ICRP-30.

$$\frac{d}{dt}q_{ST} = -(\lambda_R + \lambda_{ST})q_{ST} \tag{1}$$

$$\frac{d}{dt}q_{BF} = \lambda_{ST}q_{ST} - (\lambda_R + \lambda_{BF1} + \lambda_{BF2})q_{BF} + \lambda_{WB2}q_{WB} \tag{2}$$

$$\frac{d}{dt}q_{Th} = \lambda_{BF1}q_{BF} - (\lambda_R + \lambda_{Th})q_{Th} \tag{3}$$

$$\frac{d}{dt}q_{WB} = \lambda_{Th}q_{Th} - (\lambda_R + \lambda_{WB2} + \lambda_{WB1})q_{WB} \tag{4}$$

The terms q_i and λ_i are the time-dependent quantity of ^{131}I in all compartments and the decay constants between pairs of compartment, respectively (R: physical half life, ST: stomach, BF: body fluid, Th: thyroid, WB: whole body). Accordingly, the quantity of iodine nuclide in the stomach decreases regularly, whereas the quantity change inside the body fluid is complicated because the iodine can be transported from either stomach or whole body into the body fluid and then removed outwardly also from two channels (to thyroid or to excretion directly). The quantity change of iodine nuclides in either thyroid or whole body is comparatively direct since only one channel is defined for inside or outside [Fig. 1]. Since the biological half-lives of iodine, as recommended by ICRP-30 for the stomach, body fluid, thyroid and whole body, are 0.029d, 0.25d, 80d and 12d, respectively, the corresponding decay constants for each variable can be calculated [Tab. 1]. Additionally, the time-dependent quantity of iodine in each compartment is depicted in Fig. 2, and the initial time is the time when the ^{131}I is administered to the patient.

λ	coeff.	Derivation
λ_R	0.0862 d^{-1}	ln2 / 8.0
λ_{ST}	24 d^{-1}	ln2 / 0.029
λ_{BF1}	0.832 d^{-1}	0.3xln2 / 0.25
λ_{BF2}	1.940 d^{-1}	0.7xln2 / 0.25
λ_{Th}	0.0058 d^{-1}	ln2 / 120
λ_{WB2}	0.052 d^{-1}	0.9xln2 / 12
λ_{WB1}	0.0052 d^{-1}	0.1xln2 / 12

Table 1. The coefficients of variables for simultaneous differential equations as adopted in this work. The calculation results are theoretical estimations of the time-dependent quantity of iodine in various compartments for a typical body. Additionally, the decay constant for physical half-life of ^{131}I is indicated as λ_R and the physical half-life is 8.0 d.

2.2 MATLAB algorithms

Eqs 1-4 can be reorganized as below and solved by the MATLAB program.

$$\begin{bmatrix} dN_{ST}/dt \\ dN_{BF}/dt \\ dN_{Th}/dt \\ dN_{WB}/dt \end{bmatrix} = \begin{bmatrix} -(\lambda_{ST}+\lambda_R) & 0 & 0 & 0 \\ \lambda_{ST} & -(\lambda_{BF1}+\lambda_{BF2}+\lambda_R) & 0 & \lambda_{WB2} \\ 0 & \lambda_{BF} & -(\lambda_{Th}+\lambda_R) & 0 \\ 0 & 0 & \lambda_{Th} & -(\lambda_{WB1}+\lambda_{WB2}+\lambda_R) \end{bmatrix} \begin{bmatrix} N_{ST} \\ N_{BF} \\ N_{Th} \\ N_{WB} \end{bmatrix}$$

The MATLAB program is depicted as below;

```
#################################################################
A=[-24.086 0 0 0;24 -2.859 0 0.052; 0 0.832 -0.0922 0; 0 0 0.0058 -0.144];
x0 = [1 0 0 0]';
B = [0 0 0 0]';
C = [1 0 0 0];
D = 0;
for i = 1:101,
  u(i) = 0;
  t(i) = (i-1)*0.1;
end;
sys=ss(A,B,C,D);
[y,t,x] = lsim(sys,u,t,x0);
plot(t,x(:,1),'-',t,x(:,2),'-.',t,x(:,3),'--',t,x(:,4),'--',t,x(:,2)+x(:,4),':')
semilogx(t,x(:,1),'-',t,x(:,2),'-.',t,x(:,3),'--',t,x(:,4),'--',t,x(:,2)+x(:,4),':')
legend('ST','BF','Th','WB','BF+WB')
```

```
% save data
n = length(t);
fid = fopen('44chaineq.txt','w'); % Open a file to be written
for i = 1:n,
  fprintf(fid,'%20.16f  %20.16f  %20.16f %20.16f %20.16f
%20.16f\n',t(i),x(i,1),x(i,2),x(i,3),x(i,4),x(i,2)+x(i,4)); % Saving data
end
fclose(fid);
save 44chaineq.dat -ascii t,x
###############################################################
```

Figure 2 plots the derived time-dependent quantities of iodine in various compartments in the biokinetic model. The solid dots represent either the sum of quantities in the body fluid and the whole body, or the thyroid gland. The practical measurement made regarding body fluid and whole body cannot be separated out, whereas the data concerning the thyroid gland are easily identified data collection.

2.3 Experiment

2.3.1 Characteristics of patients

Five patients (4F/1M) aged 37~46 years underwent one to four consecutive weeks of whole body scanning using a gamma camera following the post-surgical administration of ^{131}I for ablation of the residual thyroid. An iodine clearance measurement was made on all five patients before scanning to suppress interference with the data.

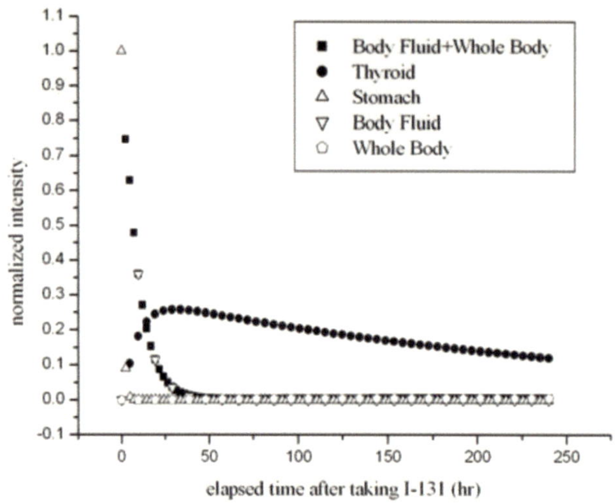

Fig. 2. The theoretical estimation for time-dependent quantities of iodine in various compartments of the biokinetic model.

2.3.2 Gamma camera

The gamma camera (SIEMENS E-CAM) was located at Chung-Shan Medical University Hospital (CSMUH). The gamma camera's two NaI 48x33x0.5 cm^3 plate detectors were positioned 5 cm above and 6 cm below the patient's body during scanning. Each plate was connected to a 2"-diameter 59 Photo Multiplier Tube (PMT) to record the data. Ideally, the two detectors captured ~70% of the emitted gamma ray. Each patient scanned was given a 1.11GBq (30 mCi) ^{131}I capsule for thyroid gland remnant ablation. The ^{131}I capsule was carrier-free with a radionuclide purity that exceeded 99.9% and radiochemical purity that exceeded 95.0%. All radio pharmaceutical capsules were fabricated by Syncor Int., Corp. The coefficient of variance (%CV) of the activity of all capsules from a single batch was less than 1.0%, as verified by spot checks (Chen *et al.*, 2003). Therefore, the position-sensitive gamma ray emitted from the ^{131}I that was administered to patient could be analyzed and plotted.

2.3.3 Whole body scanning of patients

Each patient was treated with 1.11 GBq ^{131}I once weekly for four consecutive weeks, to ensure ablation of the residual thyroid gland. This treatment suppressed the rapid absorption of ultra high doses by normal organs. Post treatment ^{131}I was typically administered six weeks after the thyroidectomy operation. However, thyroid medication was discontinued during the sixth week to reduce the complexity of any side effects. Care was taken to ensure that drugs that were administrated one week before scanning contained no iodine or radiographic contrast agent. Table 2 presents the measured data and the scanning schedule for the first subject for the first week. The schedules for other patients were similar, with only minor modifications. The final column in Tab. 2 presents data obtained from the thigh as ROI. This area was used to determine the pure background for the NaI counting system. Additionally, the body fluid and whole body compartments were treated as a single compartment and re-defined as "remainder" in the empirical evaluation since *in-vivo* measurements of these compartments were not separable. Therefore, the net counts for the ROI (either the remainder or the thyroid) were simply determined by subtracting either the count in the thigh region plus that in the thyroid areas or that in the thigh area only from the total counts from the entire whole body.

2.4 Data analysis

Data for each patient are analyzed and normalized to provide initial array in MATLAB output format to fit the optimal data for Eqs. 1-4. Additionally, to distinguish between the results fitted in MATLAB and the practical data from each subject, a value, Agreement (AT), is defined as

$$AT = \sqrt{\frac{\sum_{i=1}^{n}[Y_i(nor.\ iten.) - Y_i(MATLAB)]^2}{N}} \times 100\% \tag{5}$$

where Y_n(nor. iten.) and Y_n(MATLAB) are the normalized intensity that were practically obtained from each subject in the n_{th} acquisition, and that data computed using MATLAB, respectively. N is defined to be between 11 and 17, corresponding to the different counting schedules of the subjects herein.

An AT value of zero indicates perfect agreement between analytical and empirical results. Generally, an AT value of less than 5.00 can be regarded as indicating excellent consistency between computational and practical data, whereas an AT within the range 10.00-15.00 may still offer reliable confidence in the consistency between analytical and empirical results (Pan *et al.*, 2000; 2001). Table 3 shows the calculated data for five subjects over four weeks of whole body scanning. As shown in Tab. 3, the $T_{1/2}$(thy.) and $T_{1/2}$(BF) are changed from 80d and 0.25d to 0.66±0.50d and 0.52±0.23d, respectively. Yet, the branching ratio from the body fluid compartment to either the thyroid compartment ($I_{thy.}$) or the excretion compartment ($I_{exc.}$) is changed from 30% or; 70%, respectively to 11.4±14.6% or; 88.4±14.6%, respectively. A shorter biological half-life (80d→0.66d) and a smaller branching ratio from body fluid to remnant thyroid gland (30%→11.4%) also reveal the rapid excretion of the iodine nuclides by the metabolic mechanism in thyroidectomy patients.

Figure 3 presents the results computed using MATLAB along with practical measurement for various subjects, to clarify the evaluation of the ^{131}I nuclides of either the thyroid compartment or the remainder. As clearly shown in Fig. 3, the consistency between each calculated curve and practical data for various subjects reveals not only the accuracy of calculation but also the different characteristics of patients' biokinetic mechanism, reflecting the real status of remnant thyroid glands.

2.5 Discussion

Defining the biological half-life of iodine in the thyroid compartment without considering the effects of other compartments in the biokinetic model remains controversial. For healthy people, the thyroid compartment dominates the biokinetic model of iodine. In contrast, based on the analytical results, for (near) total thyroidectomy patients, both the body fluid and the thyroid dominate the revised biokinetic model. Additionally, the biological half-life of iodine in the thyroid of a healthy person can be evaluated directly using the time-dependent curve. The time-dependent curve for thyroidectomy patients degrades rapidly because of iodine has a short biological half-life in the remnant thyroid gland. Withholding iodine from the body fluid compartment of thyroidectomy patients rapidly increases the percentage of iodine nuclides detected in subsequent *in-vivo* scanning.

counting No.	elapsed time(hrs)	whole body	thyroid	thigh
1	0.05	21504618	355224	101133
2	0.25	19894586	434947	219306
3	0.5	22896468	754599	308951
4	0.75	23417836	834463	298034
5	1.00	23645836	944563	316862
6	2.00	21987448	1014885	311113
7	3.00	18901178	1124704	260065
8	4.00	18997956	1329043	245960
9	5.00	19006712	1297005	242498
10	6.00	16861720	1247396	204844
11	7.00	16178016	1334864	191212
12	8.00	14884935	1222750	175766
13	32.00	7810032	1080369	70999
14	56.00	3709699	949135	17926
15	80.00	2100217	673606	7377
16	104.00	1639266	540182	4627
17	128.00	1477639	429230	5457

Table 2. The time schedule for, and measured data from, whole body scanning of patient case 5. The last column presents data for the thigh area. This specific area simulated the pure background for the NaI counting system.

In a further examination of the theoretical biokinetic model, since 90% of the administered ^{131}I to the whole body (compartment 4) feeds back to the body fluid (compartment 2) and only 30% of the administered ^{131}I in the body fluid flows directly into the thyroid (compartment 3) [Fig. 1], the cross-links between compartments make obtaining solutions to Eqs. 1-4 extremely difficult. Just a small change in the biological half-life of iodine in the thyroid compartment significantly affects the outcomes for all compartments in the biokinetic model. Moreover, the effect of the stomach (compartment 1) on all compartments is negligible in this calculation because the biological half-life of iodine in the stomach is a mere 0.029 day (~40min). The scanned gamma camera counts from the stomach yield no useful data two hours after I-131 is administered, since almost 90% of all of the iodine nuclides are transferred to other compartments. Therefore, analysis of the calculated ^{131}I nuclides in the biokinetic model remains in either the remainder or the thyroid compartment only (Chen *et al.*, 2007).

Case No.	week	$T_{1/2}$(thy.) (d)	$T_{1/2}$(BF)(d)	I_{thy} (%)	I_{exc} (%)	AT_{thy}	AT_{BF}
ICRP-30		80	0.25	30	70		
1	1	1.10	0.65	12.5	87.5	1.74	31.22.
	2	0.50	0.50	5.0	95.0	0.60	12.58
	3	0.50	0.50	5.0	95.0	0.60	12.10
	4	0.50	0.50	5.0	95.0	0.55	6.23
2	1	1.70	1.20	55.0	45.0	4.34	7.56
	2	1.25	0.80	32.5	67.5	5.24	25.38
	3	1.10	0.55	12.5	87.5	3.21	30.13
	4	0.50	0.30	5.0	95.0	1.20	35.90
3	1	0.15	0.40	5.0	95.0	0.53	8.93
	2	0.15	0.40	5.0	95.0	0.22	2.07
	3	0.15	0.40	5.0	95.0	0.10	3.64
	4	0.15	0.40	5.0	95.0	0.70	7.56
4	1	0.25	0.25	5.0	95.0	0.62	27.65
5	1	1.25	0.50	5.0	95.0	1.74	5.79
Average		0.66±0.50	0.52±0.23	11.4±14.6	88.4±14.6	1.52±1.54	14.05±11.01

Table 3. The reevaluated results for five patients in this work. The theoretical data quoted from ICRP-30 report is also listed in the first row for comparing.

3. Gastrointestinal tract model

The gastric emptying half time (GET) of solid food in 24 healthy volunteers is evaluated using the gamma camera method. The GET of solids is used to screen for gastric motor disorders and can be determined using many approaches, among which the gamma camera survey is simple and reliable. Additionally, scintigraphic gastric emptying tests are used extensively in both academic research and clinical practice, and are regarded as the gold-standard for evaluating gastric emptying (Minderhoud *et al.*, 2004; Kim *et al.*, 2000). The GET can also be estimated by monitoring the change in the concentration of an ingested tracer in the blood, urine, or breath, since the tracer is rapidly absorbed only after it leaves the stomach. The tracer, the paracetamol absorption approach and the ^{13}C-octanoate breath test (OBT), all support convenient means of evaluating GET. However, the breath test yields only a convolution index of GE, although it requires no gamma camera and can be performed at the bedside (Sanaka *et al.*, 1998; 2006).

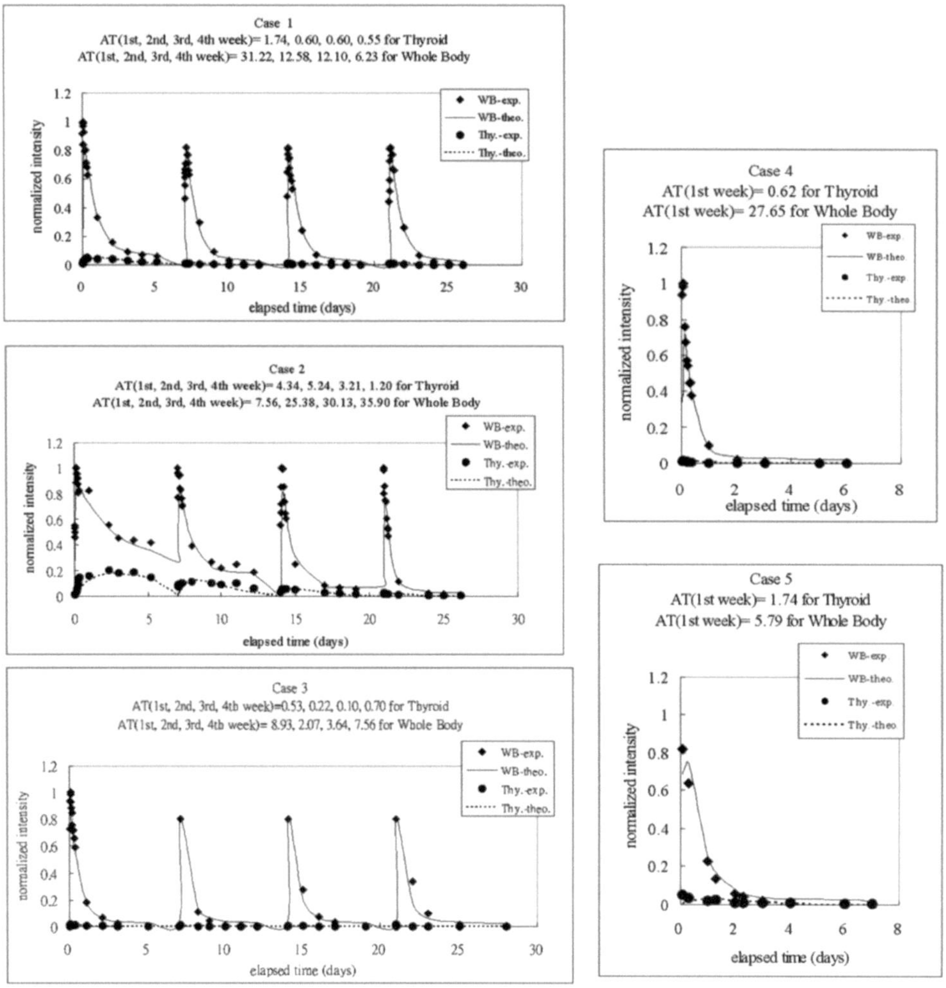

Fig. 3. The time-dependent intensity of either whole body plus body fluid compartments or thyroid compartment from the optimized results of revised biokinetic model of iodine. The various data from *in-vivo* scanning of 5 patients are also included.

The use of a gamma camera to survey the absorption by subjects of Tc-99m radionuclide-labeled products satisfies the criteria for the application of the GI tract biokinetic model, because the short physical half life of Tc-99m is such that a limited dose is delivered. In this study, the revised GET of solids is determined from several *in-vivo* measurements made of healthy volunteers. Twenty-four healthy volunteers underwent a 5 min. scan from neck to knee once every 30 min. for six hours using a gamma camera. Measured data were analyzed and normalized as input data to a program in MATLAB. The revised GET of solids for volunteers differed significantly from those obtained using a theoretical simulation that was based on the ICRP-30 recommendation.

3.1 Biokinetic model

According to the ICRP-30 report, the biokinetic model of the GI tract divides a typical human body into five major compartments, which are (1) stomach (ST), (2) small intestine (SI), (3) upper large intestine (ULI), (4) lower large intestine (LLI), and (5) body fluid (BF), as shown in Fig. 4. Equations 6-9 are the simultaneous differential equations that specify the time-dependent correlation among the quantities of the radio-activated Tc-99m nuclides in the compartments.

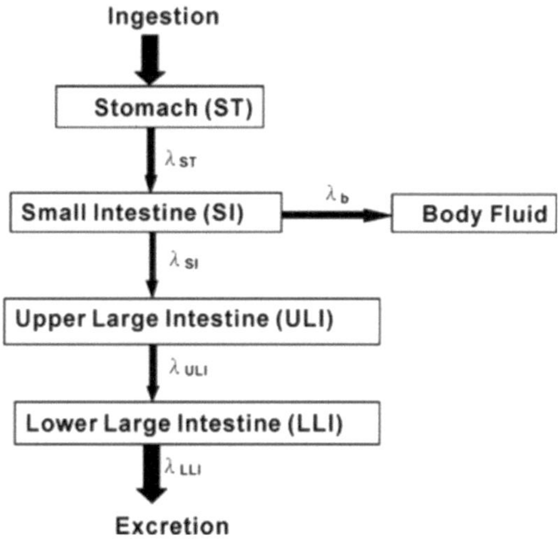

Fig. 4. Biokinetic model of Gastric Intestine Tract for a standard healthy man. The model is recommended by the ICRP-30 report.

$$\frac{d}{dt}q_{ST} = -(\lambda_{ST} + \lambda_R)\cdot q_{ST} \tag{6}$$

$$\frac{d}{dt}q_{SI} = -(\lambda_{SI} + \lambda_b + \lambda_R)\cdot q_{SI} + \lambda_{ST}\cdot q_{ST} \tag{7}$$

$$\frac{d}{dt}q_{ULI} = -(\lambda_{ULI} + \lambda_R)\cdot q_{ULI} + \lambda_{SI}\cdot q_{SI} \tag{8}$$

$$\frac{d}{dt}q_{LLI} - -(\lambda_{LLI} + \lambda_R)\cdot q_{LLI} + \lambda_{ULI}\cdot q_{ULI} \tag{9}$$

The terms q_i and λ_i are defined as the time-dependent quantities of radionuclide, Tc-99m, and the biological half-emptying constants, respectively, for the compartments. λ_R is the physical decay constant of the Tc-99m radionuclide.
Since the biological half lives of Tc-99m, given by ICRP-30, in the stomach, small intestine, upper large intestine and lower large intestine are 0.029d, 0.116d, 0.385d and 0.693d, respectively, the corresponding half-emptying constants can be calculated, and are presented in Fig. 4. Additionally, λ_b is the metabolic removal rate and equals $[f_1\times\lambda_{SI}/(1-f_1)]$. This term varies with the chemical compound and is 0.143 for Tc-99m nuclides.

λ	Half-emptying constant	Derivation
λ_R	2.77 d^{-1}	(ln2 / 6.0058) × 24
λ_{ST}	24 d^{-1}	ln 2 / 0.029
λ_{SI}	6 d^{-1}	ln 2 / 0.116
λ_{ULI}	1.8 d^{-1}	ln 2 / 0.385
λ_{LLI}	1 d^{-1}	ln 2 / 0.693
λ_b	1 d^{-1}	0.143×6 / (1-0.143)

Table 4. The coefficients of variables for simultaneous differential equations as adopted in this work. The calculation results are theoretical estimations of the time-dependent quantity of Tc-99m in various compartments for a typical body. Additionally, the decay constant for physical half life of Tc-99m is indicated as λ_R and the physical half-life is 6.0058 h.

3.2 MATLAB algorithms

Eqs 6-9 can be reorganized again as below and solved by the MATLAB program.

$$\begin{bmatrix} dN_{ST}/dt \\ dN_{SI}/dt \\ dN_{ULI}/dt \\ dN_{LLI}/dt \end{bmatrix} = \begin{bmatrix} -(\lambda_{ST}+\lambda_R) & 0 & 0 & 0 \\ \lambda_{ST} & -(\lambda_{SI}+\lambda_b+\lambda_R) & 0 & 0 \\ 0 & \lambda_{SI} & -(\lambda_{ULI}+\lambda_R) & 0 \\ 0 & 0 & \lambda_{ULI} & -(\lambda_{LLI}+\lambda_R) \end{bmatrix} \begin{bmatrix} N_{ST} \\ N_{SI} \\ N_{ULI} \\ N_{LLI} \end{bmatrix}$$

The MATLAB program is depicted as below;

```
##################################################################
A=[-26.77 0 0 0;24 -9.77 0 0; 0 6 -4.57 0; 0 0 1.8 -3.77];
x0 = [1 0 0 0]';
B = [0 0 0 0]';
C = [1 0 0 0];
D = 0;
for i = 1:101,
  u(i) = 0;
  t(i) = (i-1)*0.01;
end;
sys=ss(A,B,C,D);
[y,t,x] = lsim(sys,u,t,x0);
plot(t,x(:,1),'-',t,x(:,2),'-.',t,x(:,3),'--',t,x(:,4),'--',t,x(:,2)+x(:,3)+x(:,4),':')
semilogx(t,x(:,1),'-',t,x(:,2),'-.',t,x(:,3),'--',t,x(:,4),'--',t,x(:,2)+x(:,3)+x(:,4),':')
legend('ST','SI','ULI','LLI','SI+ULI+LLI')
% save data
n = length(t);
fid = fopen('gi44chaineq.txt','w');  % Open a file to be written
for i = 1:n,
   fprintf(fid,'%10.8f  %20.16f  %20.16f  %20.16f %20.16f
%20.16f\n',t(i),x(i,1),x(i,2),x(i,3),x(i,4),x(i,2)+x(i,3)+x(i,4)); % Saving data
end
```

```
fclose(fid);
save gi44chaineq.dat -ascii t,x
################################################################
```

Figure 5 shows the time-dependent amount of Tc-99m in each compartment, and the initial time is defined as the time when a Tc-99m dose is administered to the volunteer. The results can be calculated and plotted using a program in MATLAB.

3.3 Experiment

3.3.1 Characteristics of volunteers

Twenty-four healthy volunteers (13F/11M) aged 19~75 years underwent six continuous hours of whole body scanning using a gamma camera after they had ingested Tc-99m-labeled phytate with solid food.

3.3.2 Tc-99m-labeled phytate solid food

The test meal comprised solid food and a cup of 150 ml water that contained 5% dextrose. The solid food was two pieces of toast and a two-egg-omelet. The two eggs were broken, stirred and mixed with 18.5 MBq (0.5 mCi) Tc-99m-labeled phytate. Each omelet was baked in an oven for 20 min at 250 ^{0}C, and then served to a volunteer. Each volunteer had fasted for at least eight hours before eating the meal and finished it in 20 minutes, to avoid interference with the data.

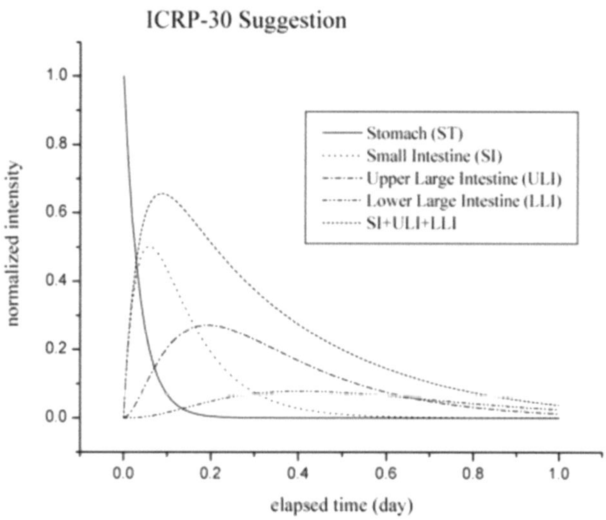

Fig. 5. The theoretical estimation for time-dependent amounts of Tc-99m in various compartments of the biokinetic model.

3.3.3 Gamma camera

The gamma camera (SIEMENS E-CAM) was located at the Department of Nuclear Medicine, TaiChung Veterans General Hospital (TVGH). The camera's two NaI (48×33×0.5 cm^3) plate detectors were positioned 5 cm above and 6 cm below the volunteer's body during scanning. Each plate was connected to a 2"-diameter 59 Photo Multiplier Tube (PMT) to record data. The two detectors captured ~70% of the emitted gamma rays.

3.3.4 Whole body scanning of volunteers

Each volunteer underwent his/her first gamma camera scan immediately after finishing the meal. The scan protocol was as follows; supine position, energy peak of 140 keV (window: 20%), LEHS collimator, 128×128 matrix, and scan speed of 30 cm/min. over a distance of 150 cm (~5 min. scan from neck to knee) for 5 min. every half hour. The complete scan took six hours. Thirteen sets of data were recorded for every volunteer for analysis. The regions of interest (ROIs) of the images in the subsequent analysis were (1) whole body, WB, (2) stomach, ST, and (3) small intestine, upper large intestine and lower large intestine, SI+ULI+LLI. The data that were obtained from SI could not be separated from those obtained from ULI or LLI, whereas the data for ST were easily distinguished during the collection of data. Therefore, the SI, ULI, and LLI data were summed in the data analysis.

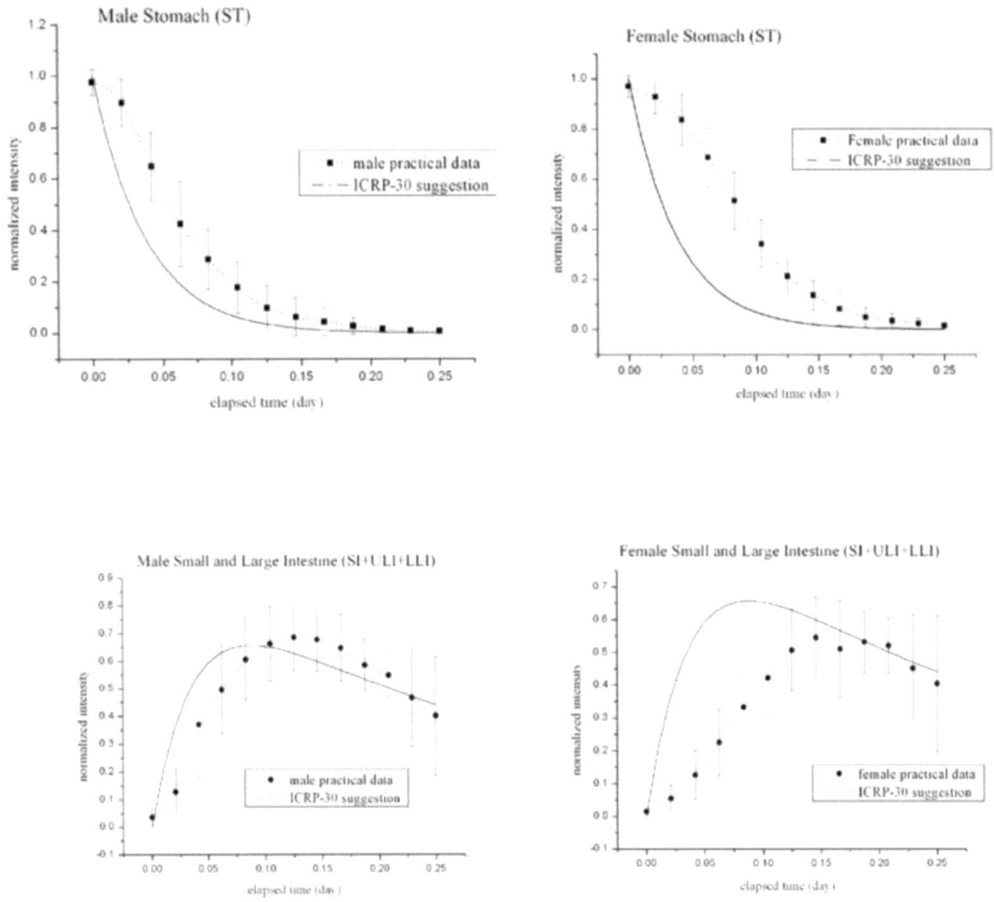

Fig. 6. The time dependent curve of ST and SI+ULI+LLI for males and females, respectively. The inconsistence in comparing the theoretical calculation and practical evaluation is significant.

3.4 Data analysis

Table 5 shows the results that were obtained for 24 healthy volunteers. The first row includes theoretical recommendations in the ICRP-30 report for comparison. The results are grouped into male and female, and each volunteer is indicated. The GET is the effective half life of Tc-99m in the stomach. It equals the reciprocal of the sum of the reciprocal of the biological half life and that of the radiological half life ($GET^{-1} = T_{1/2eff}(ST)^{-1} = [T_{1/2}(Tc\text{-}99m)^{-1} + T_{1/2}(ST)^{-1}]$). The biological half lives in the stomach $T_{1/2}(ST)$ and small intestine $T_{1/2}(SI)$ in

Case No.	Sex	$T_{1/2}(ST)$ Min.	$T_{1/2}(SI)$ Min.	$T_{1/2}(ULI)$ Min.	$T_{1/2}(LLI)$ Min.	$T_{1/2}(b)$ Min.	AT_{ST} %	AT_{LSI} %
ICRP-30		41.8	167.0	554.5	998.0	998.0		
1	F	166.4	199.6	554.5	998.0	1.0E+05	8.4	7.5
2	F	142.6	199.6	554.5	998.0	1.0E+05	10.5	7.3
3	F	110.9	166.4	554.5	998.0	1.0E+05	5.9	7.6
4	F	142.6	199.6	554.5	998.0	1.0E+05	5.9	3.6
5	F	124.8	199.6	554.5	998.0	1.2E+04	11.3	6.9
6	F	166.4	199.6	554.5	998.0	1.0E+05	9.8	8.5
7	F	99.8	332.7	554.5	998.0	1.0E+05	12.7	17.0
8	F	142.6	249.5	554.5	998.0	1.0E+05	14.5	10.6
9	F	99.8	249.5	554.5	998.0	1.0E+05	10.9	14.9
10	F	199.6	166.4	554.5	998.0	1.0E+05	11.9	10.1
11	F	99.8	166.4	554.5	998.0	1.0E+05	8.2	7.6
12	F	124.8	166.4	554.5	998.0	1.0E+05	14.2	9.6
13	F	166.4	199.6	554.5	998.0	1.0E+05	15.8	8.6
Average (1~13)		137.4 ±31.3	207.3 ±46.9	554.5	998.0	9.3E+04± 2.4E+04	10.8± 3.1	9.2 ±3.5
14	M	83.2	199.6	554.5	998.0	1.0E+05	12.1	13.3
15	M	99.8	249.5	554.5	998.0	1.0E+05	11.4	16.3
16	M	99.8	166.4	554.5	998.0	1.0E+05	7.6	8.6
17	M	99.8	249.5	554.5	998.0	1.0E+05	8.1	15.7
18	M	62.4	166.4	554.5	998.0	3.3E+04	3.3	6.5
19	M	142.6	124.8	554.5	998.0	1.0E+05	11.5	6.9
20	M	76.8	166.4	554.5	998.0	1.0E+05	3.7	5.1
21	M	45.4	166.4	554.5	998.0	5.0E+04	10.9	9.6
22	M	62.4	166.4	554.5	998.0	1.0E+05	10.3	9.7
23	M	90.7	166.4	554.5	998.0	1.0E+05	13.8	13.9
24	M	52.5	998.1	554.5	998.0	1.0E+05	10.9	14.4
Average (14~24)		76.7 ±23.0	256.3 ±248.9	554.5	998.0	8.9E+04± 2.4E+04	9.3 ±3.4	10.5 ±4.0

Table 5. The evaluated results for 24 healthy volunteers in this work. The Theoretical recommendation from ICRP-30 report is also listed in the first row for comparing. Either AT_{ST} or AT_{LSI} indicates the curve fitting agreement between theoretical estimation and practical measurement for stomach (ST) or small intestine (SI) + upper large intestine (ULI) + lower large intestine (LLI).

males are 76.7± 23.0 min. and 256.3± 248.9 min. respectively, and in females are 137.4± 31.3 min., 207.3± 46.9 min, respectively. Therefore, the GET and $T_{1/2eff}$(SI) for males are 63.2±18.9 min. and 149.8±145.1 min. and those for females are 99.5±22.6 min. and 131.6±29.8 min., respectively. The values of both $T_{1/2}$(ULI) and $T_{1/2}$(LLI) that were used in the program calculation were those suggested in the ICRP-30 report. The calculated $T_{1/2}$(b) 10,000, is greatly higher that that, 998, recommended by the original ICRP-30 report. The increased half life, associated with metabolic removal (around an order of magnitude greater than its suggested value), indicates that only a negligible amount of Tc-99m phytate is transported to the body fluid (BF).

Both AT_{ST} and AT_{LSI} reveal consistency between the measured and estimated fitted curves for ST and SI+ULI+LLI [Eq. 5]. The ATs are around 3.6~16.3; the average ATs for males are 9.3± 3.4 and 10.5± 4.0 and those for females are 10.8± 3.1 and 9.2± 3.5 [Tab. 5, last two columns]. Twenty-six correlated data are used in the program in MATLAB to find an optimal value of Tc-99m quantities for each volunteer (13×2=26, ST and SI+ULI+LLI). Equations 6-9 must be solved simultaneously and include all four compartments of the GI tract biokinetic model [cf. Fig. 4]. Figure 6 plots the time-dependent curves of ST and SI+ULI+LLI for males and females. The inconsistency between the theoretical and empirical values is significant.

3.5 Discussion

Unlike the thyroid biokinetic model, which includes a feedback loop between the body fluid compartment and the whole body compartment, the GI Tract biokinetic model applies exactly the direct chain emptying principle, and assumes that no equilibrium exists between the parent and daughter compartments, because the parent's (ST) biological half emptying time is shorter than the daughter's (SI+ULI+LLI) biological half emptying time. The unique integration of parent's and daughter's biological half emptying times also reflects the unpredictability of the real GET of the gastrointestinal system. Therefore, a total of 13 groups of data were obtained for each volunteer over six continuous hours of scanning and input to the program in MATLAB to determine the complete correlation between ST and SI+ULI+LLI. Simplifying either the biokinetic model or the calculation may generate errors in the output and conclusion. Very few studies have addressed the time-dependent curve for SI+ULI+LLI, because this curve is not a straight line that is associated with a particular emptying constant (slope) [Fig. 6]. Any two or three sets of discrete measurements cannot provide enough data to yield a conclusive result. The optimal fitted time-dependent SI+ULI+LLI curve is a polynomial function of fourth or fifth order. Therefore, the data must be measured discretely in five or six trials to draw conclusions with a satisfactory confidence level.

The biological half emptying time of SI dominates the time-dependent curve of SI+ULI+LLI, since the SI biological half emptying time, $T_{1/2}$(SI), fluctuates markedly, whereas the values of both $T_{1/2}$(ULI) and $T_{1/2}$(LLI) contribute inconsiderably to solve the simultaneous differential equations in the program in MATLAB [cf. Tab. 5]. Additionally, a close examination of the time-dependent SI+ULI+LLI curve of either males or females reveals that quantities of Tc-99m radionuclides in the SI compartment for males more rapidly approaches saturation than does that for the females, and so the biological half emptying time is shorter in males [cf. Fig. 6]. However, the analyzed results concerning GETs herein do not support this claim (female: 207.3±46.9 min.; male: 256.3±248.9 min.) because the extent of changes of the SI (daughter compartment) is governed by the chain emptying rate from the ST (parent compartment), and the $T_{1/2}$(ST) for males (76.7±23.0 min.) is shorter than that for females (137.4±31.3 min.). Restated, the correct interpretation of the results must be based on the GI Tract biokinetic model and satisfy the simultaneous differential equations, Eqs. 6-9.

4. Recommendation and conclusion

Both the effective half-life of iodine in either the thyroid or the body fluid compartment of (near) total thyroidectomy patients and the gastric emptying half time of solid food in 24 healthy volunteers (11M/13F) were determined using the *in-vivo* gamma camera method. The real images that were captured using the gamma camera provide reliable information for biokinetic model-based analysis, since the easy and accurate positioning feature enables the time-dependent quantities of cumulated gamma rays in various biokinetic compartments to be determined.

MATLAB is rarely used in the medical field because of its complicated demanding programming. However, its powerful ability to define time-dependent simultaneous differential equations and to derive optimal numerical solutions can accelerate correlative analyses in most practical studies. Notably, only an appropriate definition at the beginning of study can ensure a reliable outcome that is consistent with practical measurements. The application of a simplistic or excessively direct hypothesis about any radiological topic can yield very erroneous results.

4.1 Iodine thyroid model

The revised values of T_{eff} of iodine in the thyroid compartment were initially obtained from computations made for each subject using the iodine biokinetic model and averaged over all five subjects. The T_{eff} of iodine in the thyroid compartment was revised from the original 7.3d to 0.61d, while that of iodine in the body fluid compartment was increased from 0.24d to 0.49d. The $I_{thy.}$ and $I_{exc.}$ were revised from the original 30% and 70% to 11.4% and 88.4%, respectively following *in-vivo* measurement. The differences between the results of the original and the revised iodine biokinetic models were used AT to determine the biological half-life of iodine in the thyroid and the remainder. The T_{eff} of the integrated remainder (both body fluid and whole body compartments) remained around 5.8d, since the body fluid and whole body compartment were inseparable in practical scanning of the whole body. The different effective half lies of radioiodine nuclides in thyroidectomy patients had to be considered in evaluating effective dose.

4.2 Gastrointestinal tract model

The results obtained using the program in MATLAB were based on four time-dependent simultaneous differential equations that were derived to be consistent with the measured gamma ray counts in different compartments in the GI Tract biokinetic model. The GET and $T_{1/2eff}$(SI) for males thus obtained were 63.2±18.9 min. and 149.8±145.1 min. and those for females were 99.5±22.6 min. and 131.6±29.8 min. The calculated $T_{1/2}$(b), 10,000 was greatly higher that that, 998, recommended by the original ICRP-30 report. The fact that the half life associated with metabolic removal, $T_{1/2}$(b), was around ten times the original value implied that a negligible amount of Tc-99m phytate was transported to the body fluid.

5. Acknowledgement

The authors would like to thank the National Science Council of the Republic of China for financially supporting this research under Contract No. NSC~93-2213-E-166-004. Ted Knoy is appreciated for his editorial assistance.

6. References

Chen C.Y., Chang P.J., Pan L.K., ChangLai S.P., Chan C.C. (2003) Effective half life of I-131 of whole body and individual organs for thyroidectomy patient using scintigraphic images of gamma-camera. *Chung Shan Medical J, ROC,* Vol.4, pp. 557-565

Chen C.Y., Chang P.J., ChangLai S.P., Pan L.K. (2007) Effective half life of Iodine for five thyroidectomy patients using an *in-vivo* gamma camera approach. *J. Radiation Research,* Vol.48, pp. 485-493

De klerk J.M.H., Keizer B.De., Zelissen P.M.J., Lips C.M.J., Koppeschaar H.P.F. (2000) Fixed dosage of I-131 for remnant ablation in patients with differentiated thyroid carcinoma without pre-ablative diagnostic I-131 scintigraphy. *Nuclear Medicine Communications,* Vol.21, pp. 529-532

ICRP-30 (1978) Limits for intakes of radionuclides by workers. Technical Report ICRP-30, *International commission on radiation protection,* Pergamon Press, Oxford.

Kim D.Y., Myung S.J., Camiller M. (2000) Novel testing of human gastric motor and sensory functions: rationale, methods, and potential applications in clinical practice, *Am J. Gastroenterol,* Vol.95, pp. 3365-3373

Kramer G.H., Hauck B.M., Chamerland M.J. (2002) Biological half-life of iodine in adults with intact thyroid function and in athyreoticpersons. *Radiation Protection Dosimetry,* Vol.102, No.2, pp. 129-135.

Minderhoud I.M., Mundt M.W. Roelofs J.M.M. (2004) Gastric emptying of a solid meal starts during meal ingestion: combined study using ^{13}C-Octanoic acid breath test and Doppler ultrasonography, *Digestion,* Vol.70, pp. 55-60

North D.L., Shearer D.R., Hennessey I.V., Donovan G.L. (2001) Effective half-life of I-131 in thyroid cancer patients. *Health Physics,* Vol.81, No.3, pp. 325-329

Pan L.K. and Tsao C.S. (2000) Verification of the neutron flux of a modified zero-power reactor using a neutron activation method. *Nucl. Sci. and Eng.,* Vol.135, pp. 64-72.

Pan L.K. and Chen C.Y. (2001) Trace elements of Taiwanese dioscorea spp. using instrumental neutron activation analysis. *Food Chemistry,* Vol.72, pp. 255-260.

Sanaka M., Kuyama Y., Yamanaka M. (1998) Guide for judicious use of the paracetamol absorption technique in a study of gastric emptying rate of liquids, *J. Gastroenterol,* Vol.33, pp. 785-791

Sanaka M., Yamamota T., Osaki Y., Kuyama Y. (2006) Assessment of the gastric emptying velocity by the ^{13}C-octanoate breath test: deconvolution versus a Wagner-Nelson analysis, *J. Gastroenterol,* Vol.41, pp.638-646

Schlumberger M.J. (1998) Rapillary and follicular thyroid carcinoma. *New England J. Medicine,* Vol.338, pp. 297-306.

24

Modelling and Simulation of pH Neutralization Plant Including the Process Instrumentation

Claudio Garcia and Rodrigo Juliani Correa De Godoy
Escola Politécnica da Universidade de São Paulo
Brazil

1. Introduction

In this chapter, we aim to show the facilities available in Matlab/Simulink to model control loops. For this, it is implemented a simulator in Matlab/Simulink, which shows details about the modelling of each component in a pH neutralization plant, where pH and tank level are simulated and controlled in a CSTR (Continuous Stirred Tank Reactor). Both loops are modelled considering the plant itself, the measuring and actuating instruments and the control algorithms. The pH neutralization is normally a difficult process to control, due to the non-linearity caused by the titration curve (Asuero & Michalowski, 2011), mainly when strong acids and bases are involved.

It is presented the equations (linear or non-linear) corresponding to the loop elements and how they are translated into a Simulink model and how blocks are created in Simulink to ensemble the components of the loop. Another objective is to show a case in which a P&ID diagram of the control system is presented and how it is used to reach an equivalent Simulink model.

All the model parameters, initial conditions and data related to the simulations are inserted in a Matlab file and it is stressed how it can generate a well-documented project. It is also addressed the option to create a batch in Matlab, which enables to automatically simulate the plant in different conditions and to plot graphs of different responses, in order to compare the behaviour of distinct situations. To exemplify that and validate the model, tests were performed considering set point variations (servo mode) and disturbances (regulatory mode).

2. Process description

The P&ID of the pH neutralization plant is shown in Figure 1 (ISA, 2009). In it, pH is affected by the variations in acid and base flows, where the first is considered a disturbance and the second the manipulated variable. Level is affected by the input and output flows, where the input values are considered disturbances and the output flow is the manipulated variable. This model includes the following items:

a. modeling of pH in the CSTR;

b. modeling of level in the CSTR;
c. modeling of pH (AE/AITY-10) and level (LIT-20) meters;
d. modeling of two kinds of actuators for the pH loop: dosing pump (FZ-11) and control valve (FV-12) driven by an I/P converter (FY-12);
e. modeling of a solenoid valve (LV-20) as the actuator of the level loop;
f. modeling of the meters for measuring the acid flow disturbance (FIT-30) and the base flow (FIT-10); and
g. inclusion of digital PI regulators to control pH (AIC-10) and level (LIC-20).

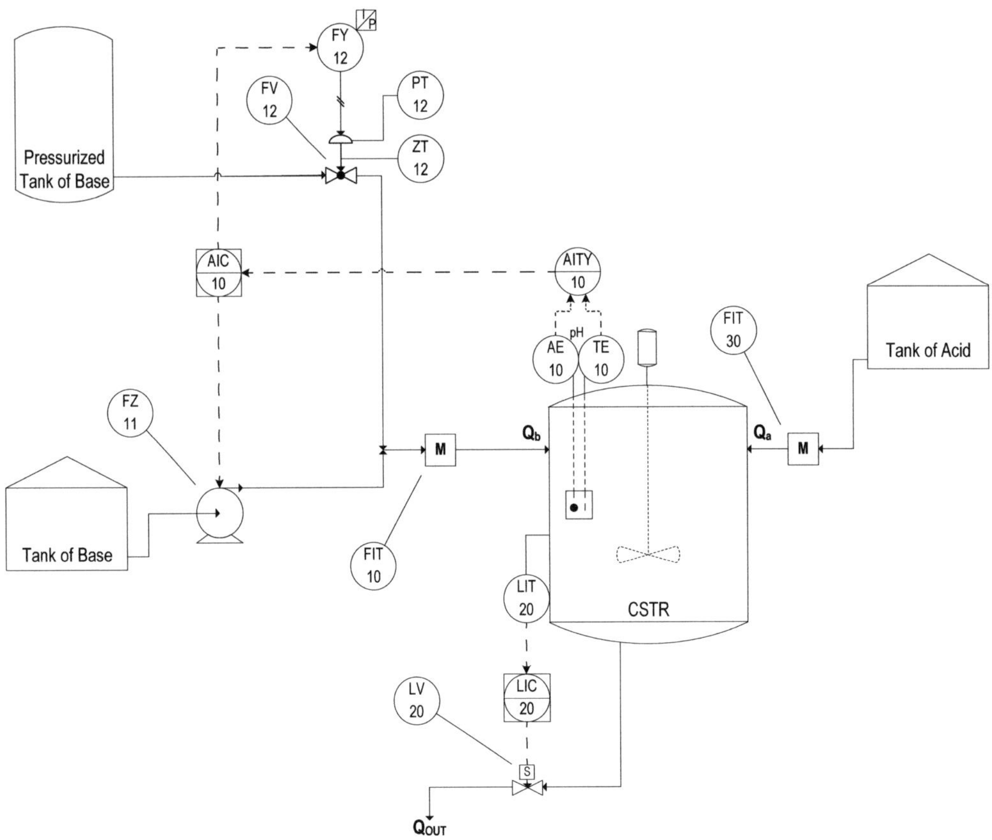

Fig. 1. P&ID of the pH neutralization plant

One important point to be emphasized is that the two kinds of actuators for the pH loop represent a linear one (dosing pump) and a non-linear actuator, as the control valve is modeled considering that it has large friction coefficients, so representing a problematic valve. The idea is to show the effects in the closed loop variability of an actuator (Rinehart & Jury, 1997) which is performing well and another one which needs maintenance. To enable analyzing the friction in the control valve, it is assumed that its stem position (ZT-12) and the actuator pressure (PT-12) are measured.

The P&ID diagram in Figure 1 is converted in the Simulink diagram in Figure 2.

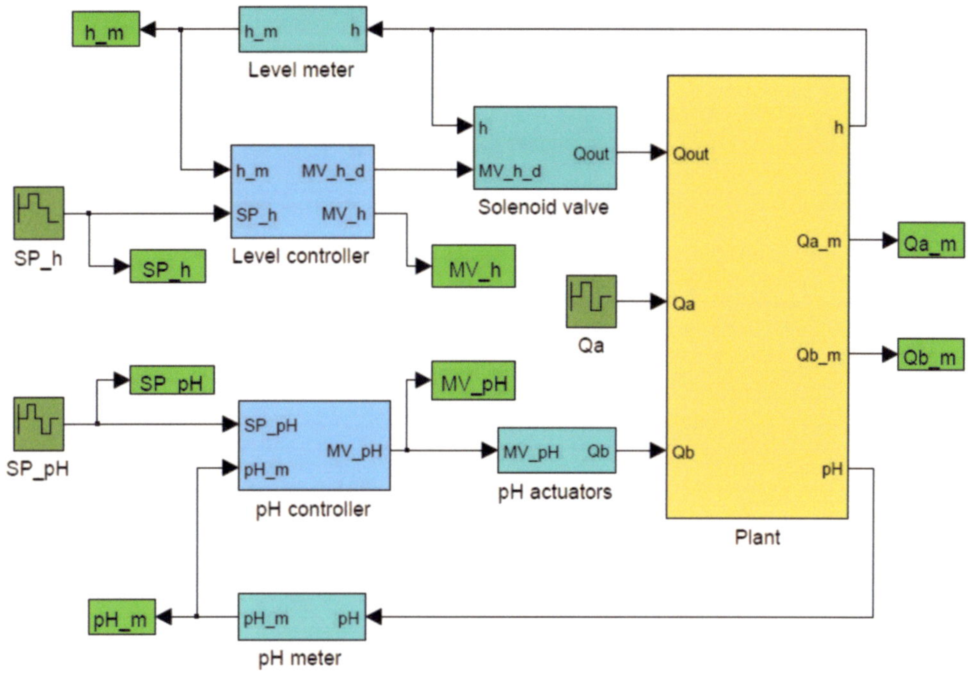

Fig. 2. Representation of the pH neutralization plant model in Simulink.

Each block of this model is individually presented in the next section.

3. Mathematical modelling and implementation in Simulink

Each element of the plant is next modeled (Garcia, 2005).

3.1 pH neutralization process

pH is related to the concentration of the ions [H+] through the following logarithmic function:

$$pH \equiv -\log_{10}[H^+] \tag{1}$$

The process here investigated is the neutralization of a strong acid effluent (HCl) in a CSTR by a strong base (NaOH). This process is modeled according to (Jacobs et al., 1980). They used a first order dynamics model with titration curve as the nonlinearity. The reactions that occur are:

$$\begin{cases} HCl + NaOH \rightarrow H_2O + NaCl \\ H^+ + OH^- \rightarrow H_2O \end{cases} \tag{2}$$

The possible amount of effluent to be neutralized is defined mainly by the concentration of the reactants. If the mixture is perfect and instantaneous, the ionic concentrations $[Cl^-]$ and $[Na^+]$ in the CSTR can be related to the flows of acid Q_a and of base Q_b and to the input concentrations $[Cl_{in}^-]$ and $[Na_{in}^+]$, according to the following equations:

$$V\frac{d}{dt}[Cl^-] = [Cl_{in}^-]\cdot Q_a - [Cl^-]\cdot Q_{out} \tag{3}$$

$$V\frac{d}{dt}[Na^+] = [Na_{in}^+]\cdot Q_b - [Na^+]\cdot Q_{out} \tag{4}$$

where V corresponds to the volume of fluid inside the CSTR.
The concentrations must also satisfy the electro-neutrality equation:

$$[Na^+] + [H^+] = [Cl^-] + [OH^-] \tag{5}$$

which, together with the dissociation equation for water:

$$[H^+]\cdot[OH^-] = k_W = 10^{-14} \tag{6}$$

relates these concentrations to $[H^+]$ and therefore to pH. This relationship is expressed in terms of the difference of the ionic concentrations X:

$$X \equiv [OH^-] - [H^+] \tag{7}$$

that combined with equation (5) results in:

$$X = [Na^+] - [Cl^-] \tag{8}$$

Combining (6) and (7) results in:

$$\begin{cases} [H^+] = \frac{X}{2}\cdot\left(\sqrt{1+\frac{4.k_W}{X^2}}-1\right) & \text{if } X>0 \\ [H^+] = -\frac{X}{2}\cdot\left(\sqrt{1+\frac{4.k_W}{X^2}}+1\right) & \text{if } X<0 \\ [H^+] = \sqrt{k_W} & \text{if } X=0 \end{cases} \tag{9}$$

The equation describing the process dynamics is obtained by subtracting (3) from (4) and using (8), resulting in:

$$V\frac{dX}{dt} = [Na_{in}^+]\cdot Q_b - [Cl_{in}^-]\cdot Q_a - X\cdot Q_{out} \tag{10}$$

The time constant τ of the process is dependent on the residence time and is given by:

$$\tau = \frac{V}{Q_{out}} \tag{11}$$

Equations (1), (9) and (10) correspond to the pH neutralization model. It is considered that the CSTR is at room temperature.
This model, implemented in Simulink, is shown in Figure 3.

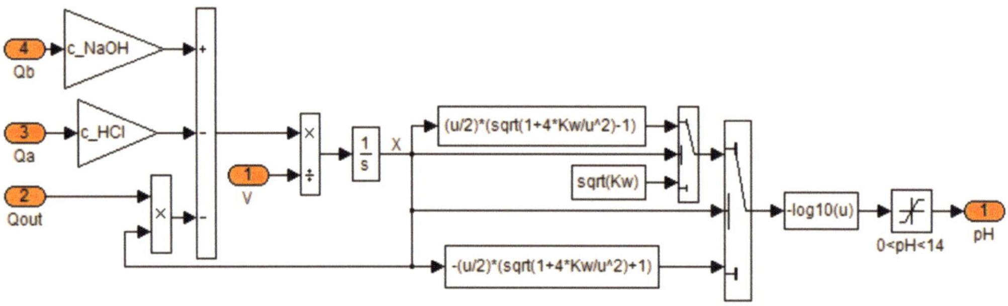

Fig. 3. Model of the pH neutralization process.

3.2 CSTR level

The level h in the CSTR is modeled through a mass balance:

$$\rho \cdot \frac{dV}{dt} = A \cdot \rho \cdot \frac{dh}{dt} = \rho_a \cdot Q_a + \rho_b \cdot Q_b - \rho \cdot Q_{out} \quad (12)$$

where A is the surface area of the CSTR, ρ is the specific mass of the mixture inside the CSTR, ρ_a is the specific mass of the acid solution associated with the acid flow Q_a, ρ_b is the specific mass of the base solution associated with the base flow Q_b and Q_{out} is the output flow of the CSTR.

The implementation of this model in Simulink is presented in Figure 4.

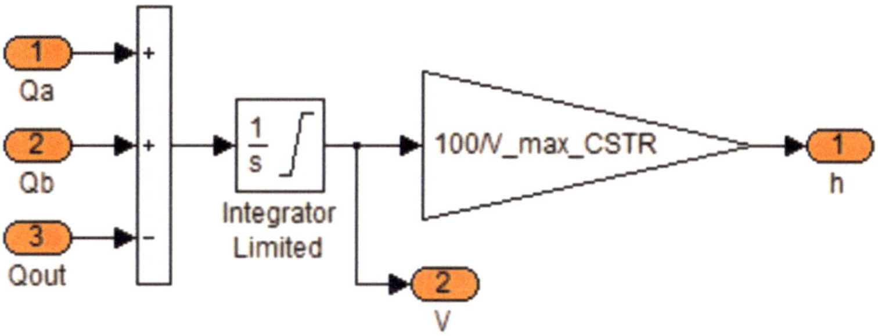

Fig. 4. Model of the level in the CSTR.

The integration of the pH and level models derives the plant model, as shown in Figure 5.

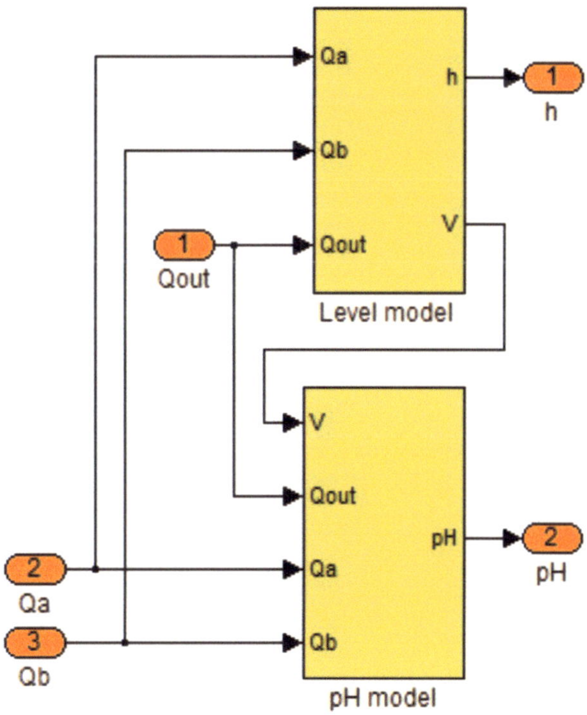

Fig. 5. Model of the plant.

3.3 pH, level and flow meters

All the measuring instruments are modeled considering that their dynamics is described by a first order system:

$$G_{meter}(s) = \frac{Y_{meas}(s)}{Y(s)} = \frac{K_{meter}}{\tau_{metr} \cdot s+1} \quad (13)$$

In (13) Y is the variable to be measured, Y_{meas} is the measured value of the variable Y, K_{meter} is the meter gain and τ_{meter} is the meter constant time. For instance, the level meter is modeled as shown in Figure 6.

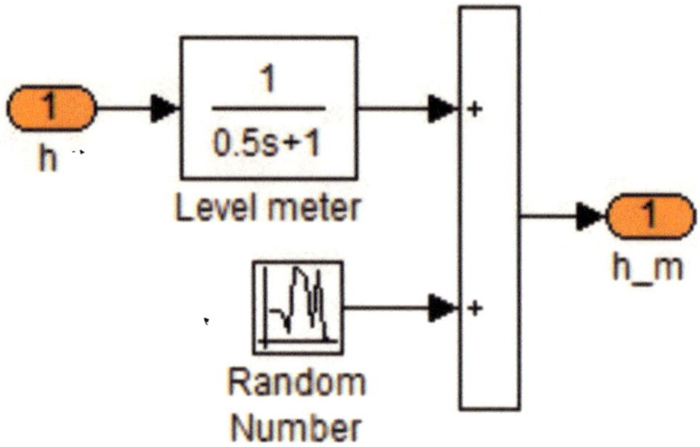

Fig. 6. Model of the lever meter.

It can be noticed in Figure 6 that it is added to the output of the meter a random number, representing measurement noise. In order to show other available forms in Simulink to represent a first order system, the pH meter in Figure 7 is represented through state space.

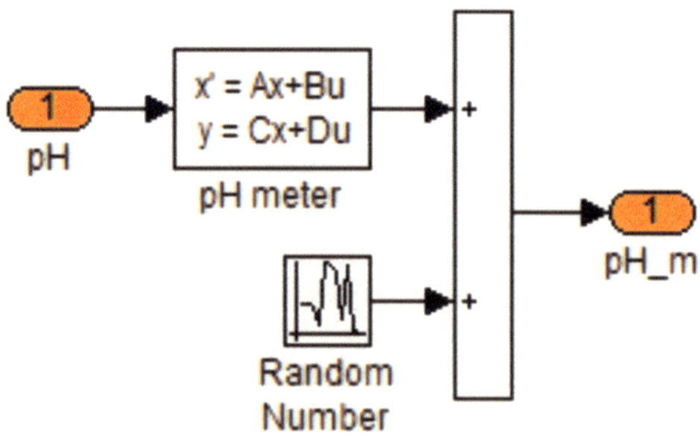

Fig. 7. Model of the pH meter.

An expanded view of the plant in Figure 5 is shown in Figure 8, where the meters of the flows Q_a and Q_b are included.

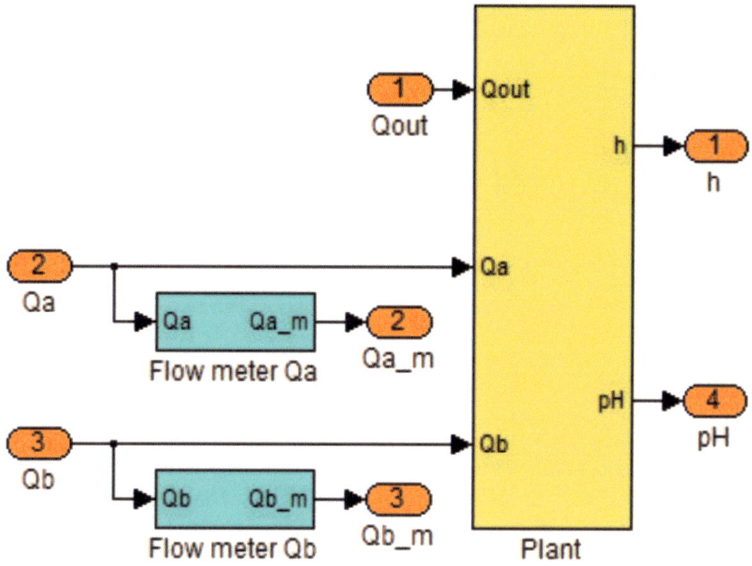

Fig. 8. Model of the plant including the flow meters for flows Q_a and Q_b.

The specific values of K_{meter} and τ_{meter} for each meter is presented in the Matlab file in Section 6.2 that describes the parameters of the plant and of the instruments.

3.4 pH actuators

As seen in Figure 1, the manipulation of the base flow occurs in two different modes: through a pump or via a control valve, as represented in Figure 9.

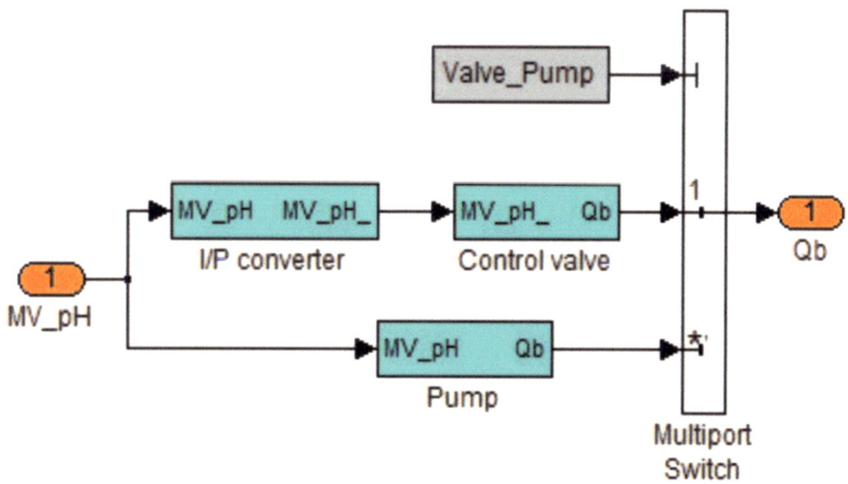

Fig. 9. Representation of the forms of manipulation of the base flow Q_b.

The pump has a linear behavior and its dynamics is very fast, so that it is considered negligible. Its model is presented in Figure 10.

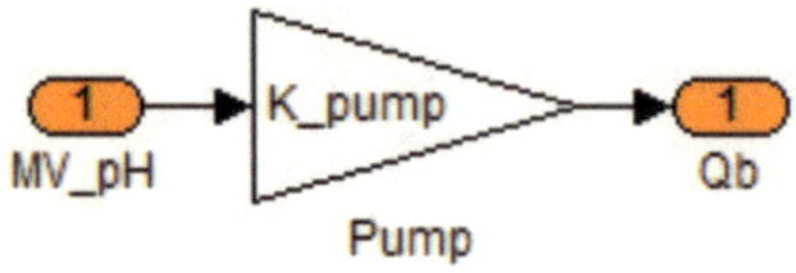

Fig. 10. Model of the pump.

The control valve is pneumatic, thus it needs an I/P converter to transform current into pressure. The model of this I/P converter is shown in Figure 11.

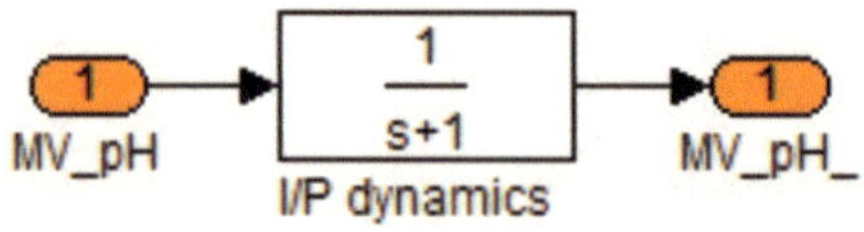

Fig. 11. Model of the I/P converter.

The control valve is modeled in two parts: the first represents its actuator, which is responsible for converting the pressure input signal into the valve stem movement, here denoted by x. This variable is assumed to vary in the range 0 to 1, that is, it is represented in p.u. (per unit). The second part is its body and it converts the valve stem movement x into flow Q_b. The model of the control valve is depicted in Figure 12.

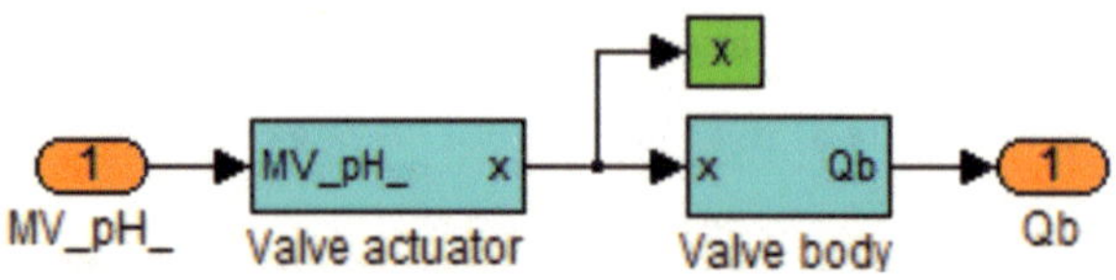

Fig. 12. Parts of the model of the control valve.

The valve actuator model is divided in two parts, as seen in Figure 13. The first part represents the actuator dynamics whereas the second part depicts the effect of the friction in the control valve.

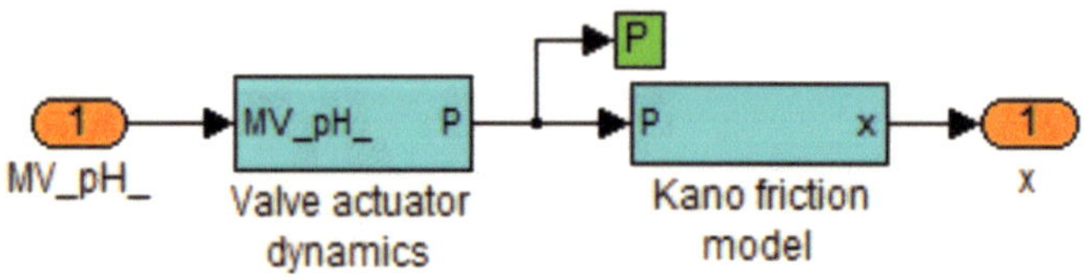

Fig. 13. Parts of the model of the control valve actuator.

The dynamics of the valve actuator is represented by a first order system, as shown in Figure 14.

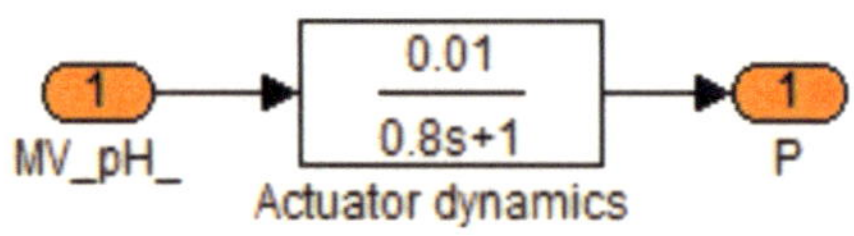

Fig. 14. Dynamics of the control valve actuator.

The Kano friction model, as presented in Figure 15, is one of the possible forms to represent the effects of friction in control valves. For more details about it, consult (GARCIA, 2008).

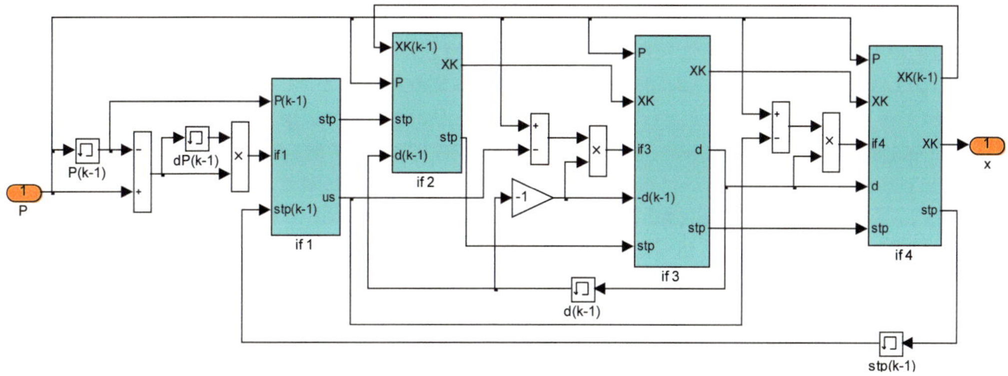

Fig. 15. Kano friction model of the control valve.

To complete the model of the control valve, its body is shown in Figure 16.

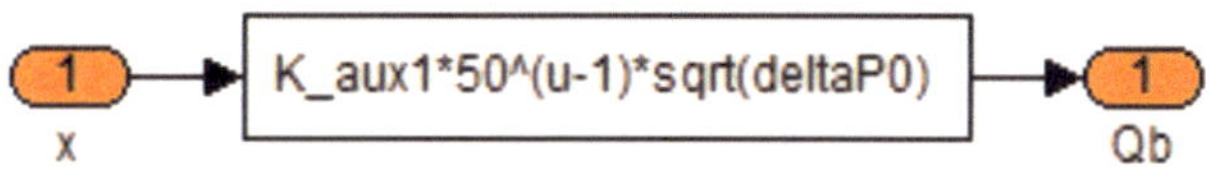

Fig. 16. Equation representing the control valve body.

The equation present in Figure 16 represents an equal percentage valve, which, when dealing with liquids, is described by the following equation:

$$Q_b = k_V \cdot C_V \cdot f(x) \cdot \sqrt{\frac{\Delta P}{\rho}} \tag{14}$$

where k_v is a term to adapt the engineering units of the equation, C_v is the flow coefficient of the valve, $f(x)$ represents how the flow varies as the valve stem position x changes, ΔP is the pressure drop in the control valve and ρ is the specific mass of the fluid in the flowing conditions. As the valve used is an equal percentage, it can be described by $f(x) = R^{x-1}$, where R is the valve rangeability.

3.5 Level actuator

The final control element of the level control loop is a solenoid valve, which model is depicted in Figure 17. It is supposed that its actuation is so fast, that its dynamics is considered negligible.

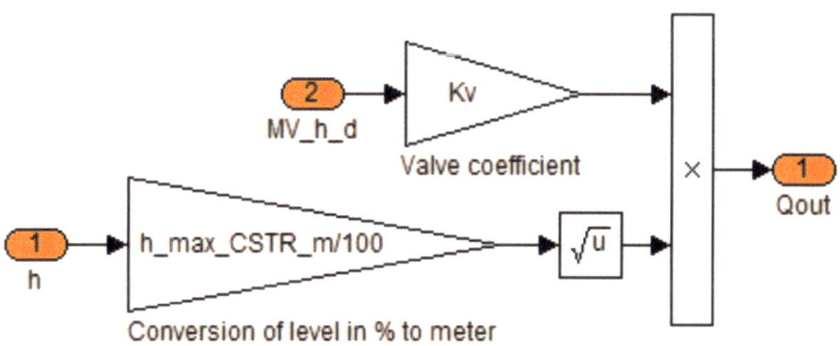

Fig. 17. Model of the solenoid valve.

3.6 pH controller

The acid solution is neutralized by NaOH that enters the CSTR with a flow governed by one of the pH actuators. These actuators are manipulated by a PI digital controller, which receives the pH set point (*SP_pH*) and the pH measured value (*pH_m*). This controller has reverse action and it is implemented through individual blocks of the Simulink, showing that it is possible to mount your own controller. It has the possibility to operate in automatic or manual. Besides, it is included an anti-reset windup algorithm, to avoid saturation of the integral action. Its algorithm is shown in Figure 18.

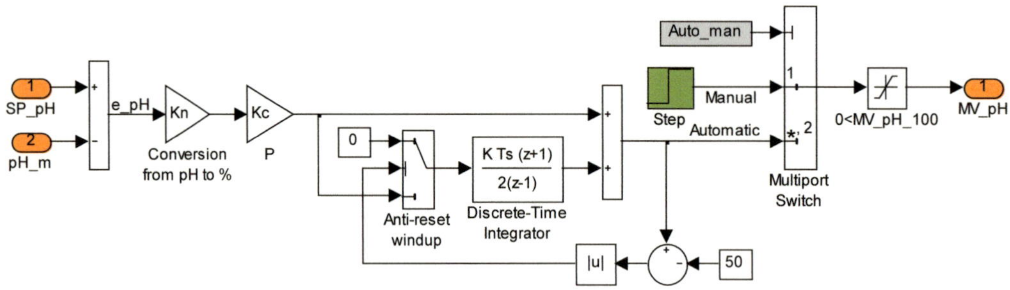

Fig. 18. Algorithm of the PI digital controller of pH.

The tuning parameters of the pH controller are K_c=1.34 and T_i=620 sec/rep.

3.7 Level controller

The level in the CSTR is controlled through the output flow using a solenoid valve, which is manipulated by a PI digital controller, which receives the level set point (*SP_h*) and the level measured value (*h_m*). It has direct action and is implemented through a single block of the Simulink. As the final control element of this loop is a solenoid valve, the continuous output of the PI controller has to converted to a time-discrete signal, operating in two levels: 1 (valve open) and 0 (valve closed). It is performed through a PWM converter. The level controller is shown in Figure 19.

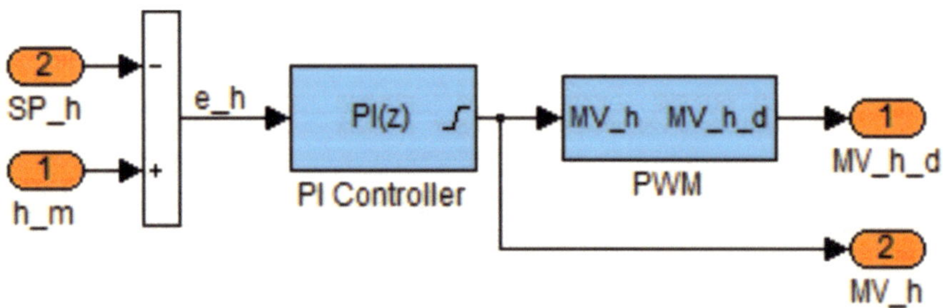

Fig. 19. Level controller with PI and PWM algorithms.

The PI controller is configured to have anti-reset windup by back-calculation and saturation in the output. The tuning parameters of the level controller are K_c=11.65 and T_i=271.52 sec/rep. Its algorithm is shown in Figure 20.

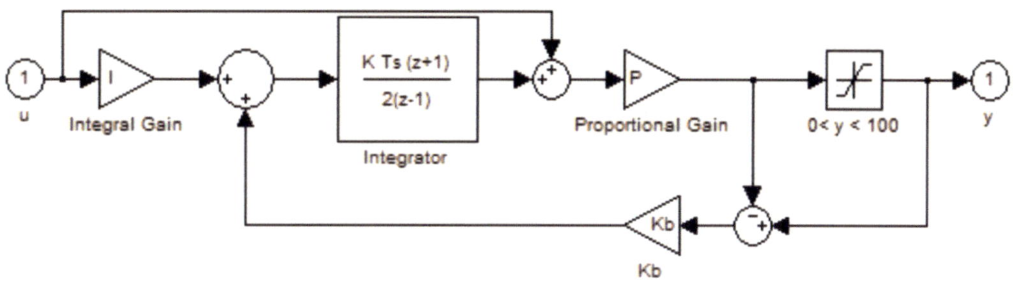

Fig. 20. Algorithm of the PI digital controller of level.

As the final control element of this loop is a solenoid valve, the continuous output of the PI controller has to be converted to a time-discrete signal, operating in two levels: 1 (valve open) and 0 (valve closed). It is performed through the PWM algorithm, as presented in Figure 21.
The PWM algorithm operates as the following equation:

$$\begin{cases} MV\_hd = 1 \text{ for } 0 < t_{PWM} \leq MV\_h \cdot T \\ MV\_hd = 0 \text{ for } MV\_h \cdot T < t_{PWM} \leq T \end{cases} \quad (15)$$

where MV_hd is the valve position (open or closed), T is the PWM duty cycle, set to 10 seconds, MV_h is the continuous signal being transformed, the PI controller output, and t_{PWM} is the internal clock of the PWM.

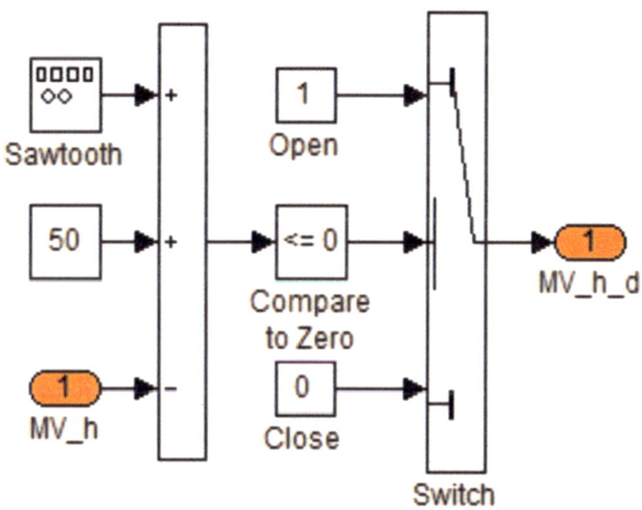

Fig. 21. Algorithm of the PWM block.

4. Model simulation

Here are presented some guidelines on how to create a batch file that configures and runs the model and also manages and presents the simulations results.

First of all, it is recommended to reset Matlab in order to avoid previously loaded data from interfering in the simulation.
Next, the model parameters, as presented in a Matlab script *(Configuring_pH_and_level_model.m)* in Section 6.2, should be loaded to the Workspace.
Following that, configuration parameters for the simulation should be loaded to the Workspace, such as simulation interval, step size of the simulation, set points for the controllers and operation mode selection variables.
The main difference between these two sets, that is, model parameters and simulation parameters, is that the first defines the system and generally is only changed when it is desired to change some characteristic of the model itself, while the later defines an operation mode for the model and are more frequently changed in order to run simulations in different conditions.
With the model implemented in Simulink and its parameters loaded to the Workspace, it is possible to run a simulation directly from Simulink with the start simulation command, or from the Matlab Workspace, with the sim function. However, a more interesting way of simulating the model is from a batch file, automatically running different simulations.
In order not to overwrite simulation results, after each simulation all the relevant variables should be copied to new unique variables.
Another useful hint is to save all generated data, mainly when running long simulations. This can be done through the save function.
After all the simulations are run or after each simulation is concluded, the generated results can be presented in many ways. A very concise and helpful method of presenting results is in graphs, which can be created with the plot function and its variants.
A batch was developed following these guidelines and is presented in a Matlab script (Simulating_pH_and_level_model) in Section 6.1.

5. Simulations results

For the presented model, two simulations are run, one with the dosing pump as the actuator in the pH loop and the other one with the control valve as its actuator. In both simulations the level and pH controllers are tested in servo and regulatory mode. For that, steps are applied to the set point of each controller and to the acid flow, the model disturbance variable.
Figures 22 and 23 show the simulated pH, level and acid flow for the plant with dosing pump and control valve as actuator, respectively. Each simulation was done for a time interval of 500,000 seconds, which correspond to a total of 278 hours or 11.6 days of continuous plant operation. This is one of the main advantages of using a simulator: to generate several hours of estimated system behavior in some seconds or minutes.
As can be seen in Figure 22, the level controller performs quite well, being capable of following the set point (servo mode) and rejecting disturbances (regulatory mode) with a low error. This controller is analyzed in greater detail ahead. It also shows that the pH controller with the dosing pump can follow set points and reject disturbances with no steady state error and fast response.
In Figure 23, the simulation results with the control valve active, it can be seen that the pH control cannot settle in the desired set point, presenting a high variability. This problem is better analyzed ahead. It can also be seen in this figure that the level controller performs well, even with an oscillatory base flow caused by the variability in the pH loop.

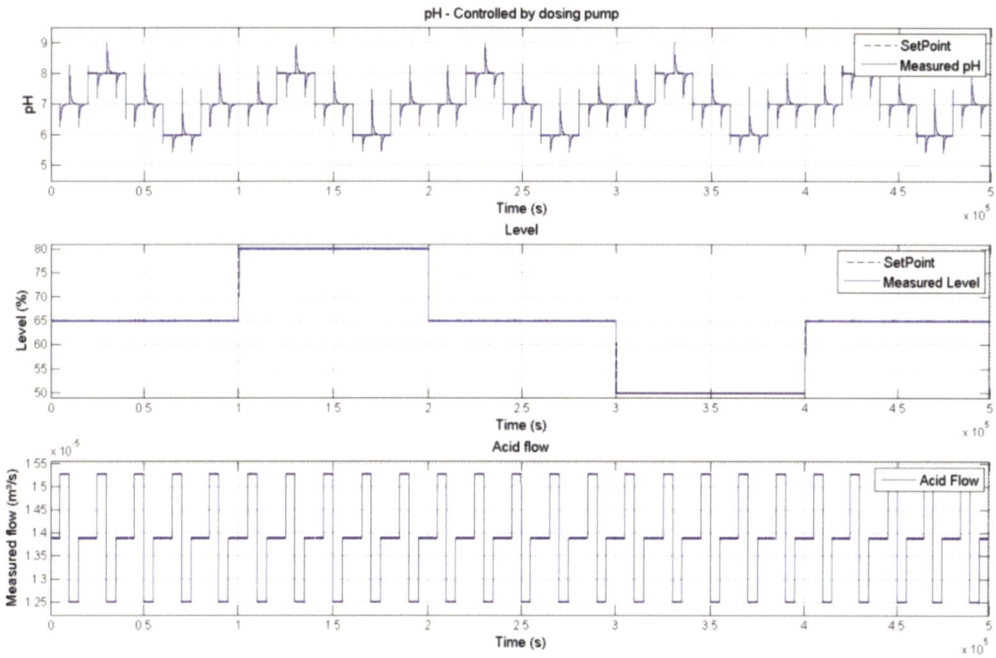

Fig. 22. All simulation results for pH, level and acid flow with dosing pump active.

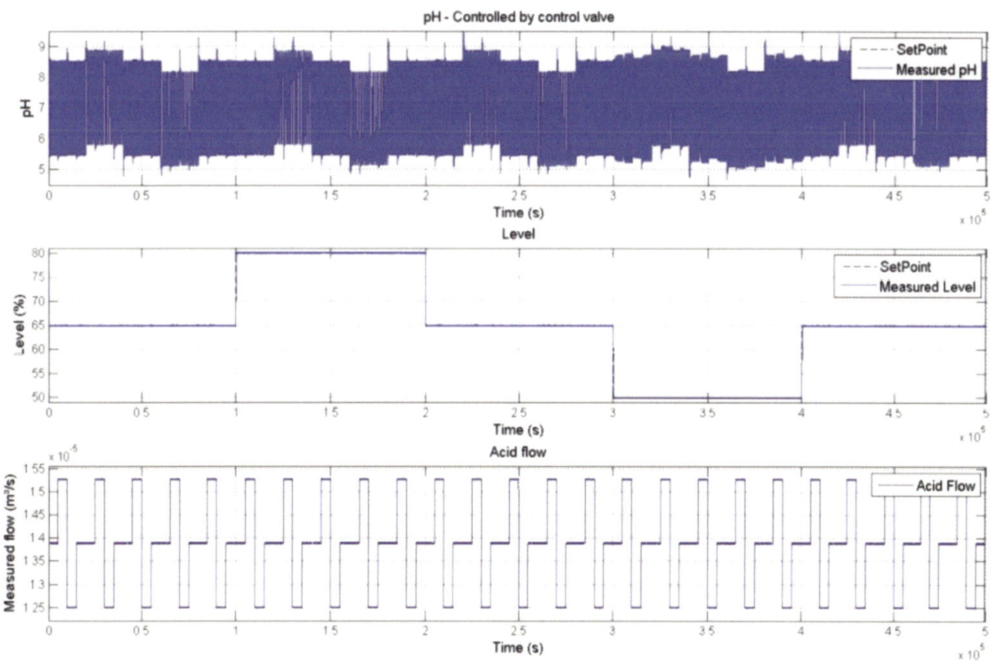

Fig. 23. All simulation results for pH, level and acid flow with control valve enable.

In order to better analyze the level controller performance, its responses with both actuators are plotted and zoomed at the steps in set point in Figure 24. As can be seen in this figure, the level controller performs almost identically in both simulations and does not deviate from the set point when disturbances are applied. This demonstrates a very good performance, either in servo or regulatory mode. The instants of step application are zoomed below the complete response in Figure 24. It can be seen that the settling time of the loop depends on the step direction and the CSTR level. It can also be noticed that there is no overshoot or undershoot in the level response.

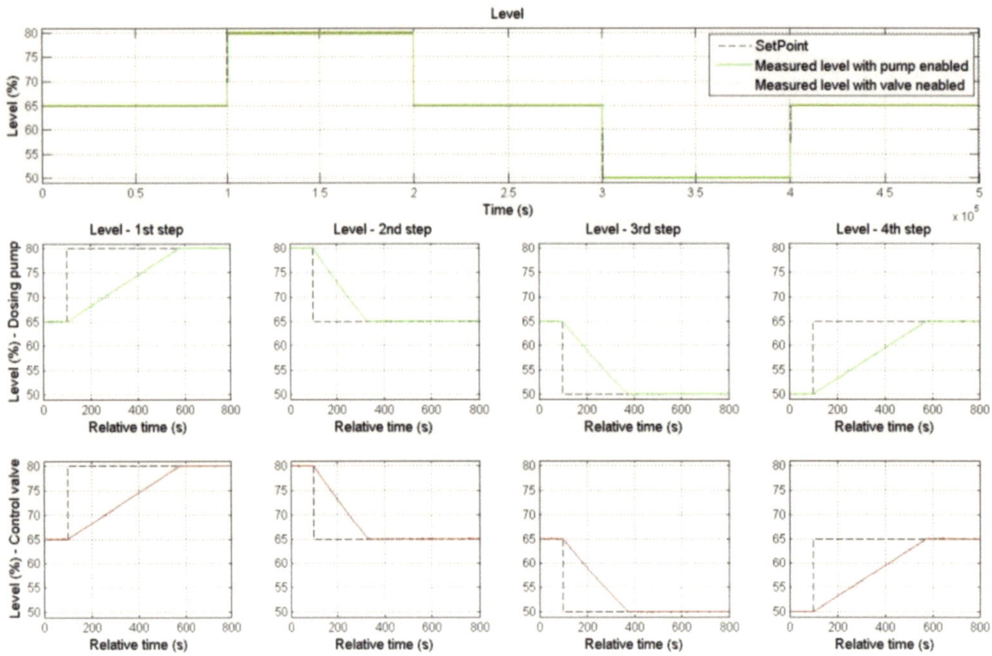

Fig. 24. Level controller response.

In order to analyze the level influence in the pH loop, this loop response with different levels (50%, 65% and 80%) is plotted in Figure25.

As can be noted in the upper graph in Figure 25, the pH response with the pump enabled is not significantly affected by variations in the level in the operation region, since the controller is capable of compensating these changes. With the control valve enabled, however, the pH response is more affected by the CSTR level. As the level decreases, oscillations in the measured pH become greater in amplitude and frequency. It happens because the valve has high friction and does not stop in a fixed position, but remains oscillating around a certain overture.

For a better analysis of the pH controller, Figures 26 and 27 show its response with the CSTR level constant at its nominal value. These figures also show the measured flows of acid and base and the control effort.

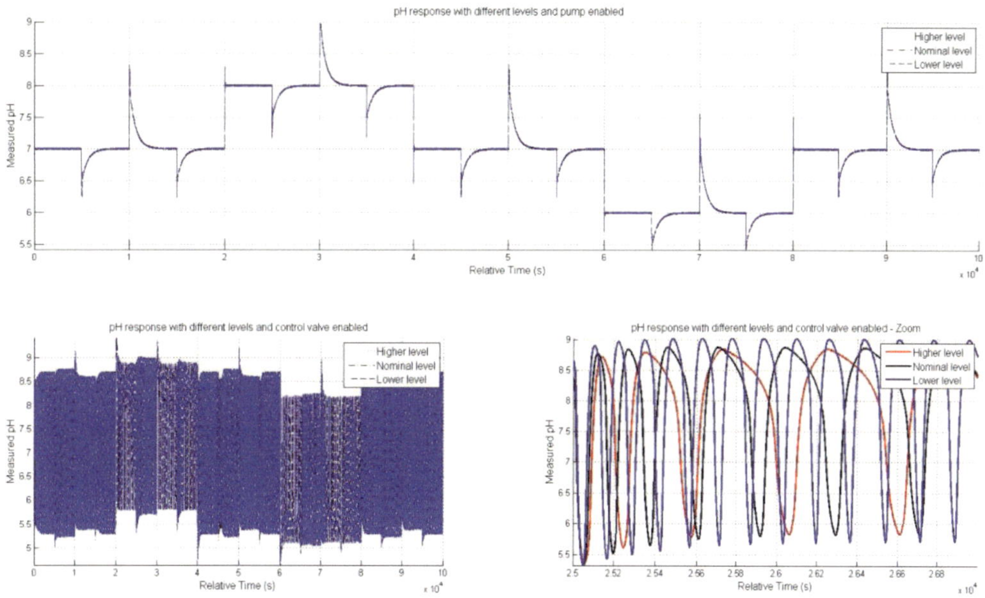

Fig. 25. Level influence in the pH response.

As can be observed in Figure 26, the controller output varies to compensate the pH error and is followed by the base flow, because the dosing pump is a linear and fast actuator.

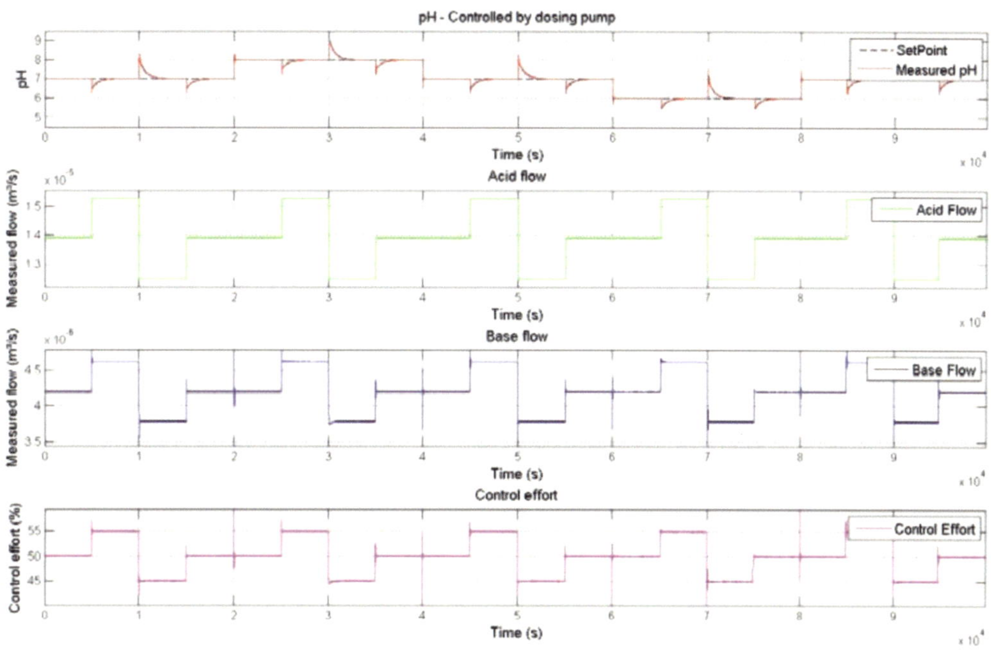

Fig. 26. pH controller response and control effort with dosing pump enabled.

The pH response with the control valve as actuator, shown in Figure 27, is oscillatory due to variability in the loop. As can be noted in the two lower plots, the controller output varies to compensate the pH error but the base flow does not change proportionally.

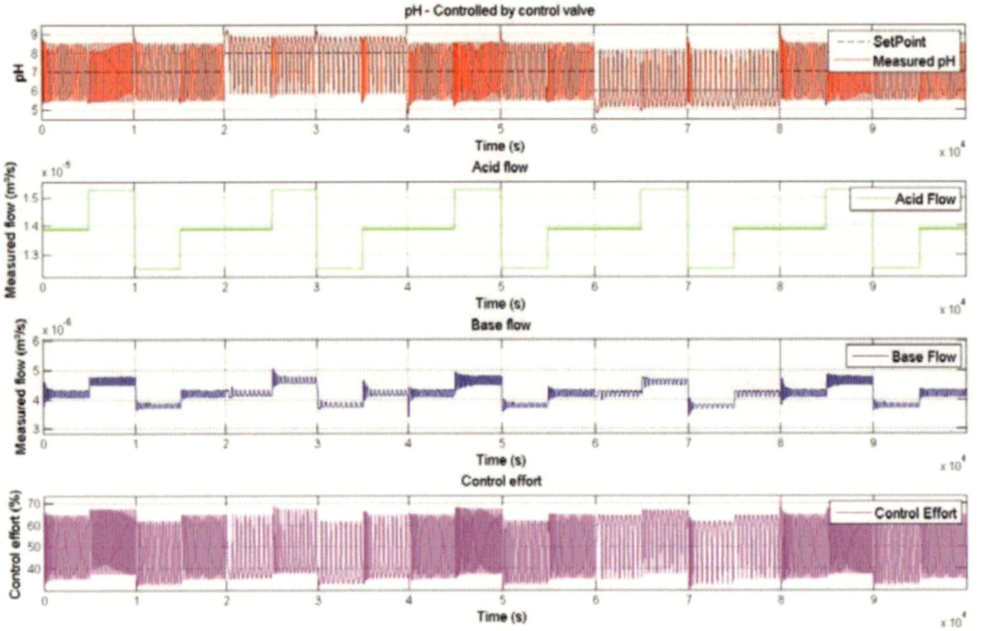

Fig. 27. pH controller response and control effort with control valve enabled.

The effect of the variability in the control loop is observed in greater detail in Figure 28.

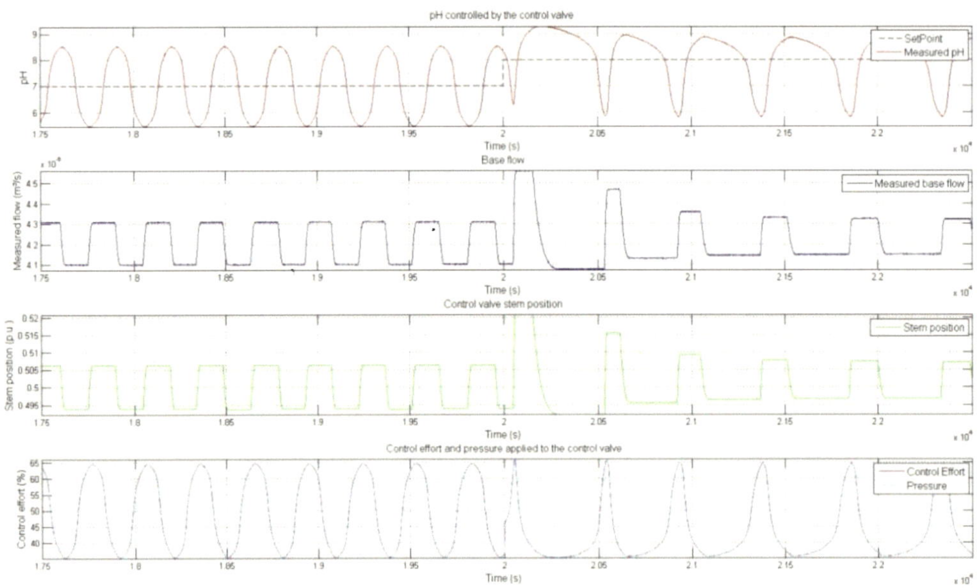

Fig. 28. Control variability due to valve friction.

The pH controller output is shown in the lower plot in Figure 28 together with the pressure applied to the valve by the I/P converter. Since this converter is linear and has a fast response, the pressure virtually follows the controller output.
Despite the efficient operation of the I/P converter, the base flow, shown in the second plot in Figure 28, does not follow the controller output, becoming constant on certain intervals, what causes the variability in the control loop. This effect can be better understood observing the valve stem position, shown in the third plot in this figure. The base flow follows the stem position, since the valve opening is proportional to it, considering that the stem movements are very small, around 1%. The problem of variability arises because the stem position does not strictly follow the changes in the pressure applied to the valve. This happens because of the friction in the valve, which prevents the stem from moving for low changes in pressure, causing the movement seen in the plots and the variability observed in the pH response.

6. Matlab code

Here are presented the Matlab .m files developed to configure and simulate the presented model, and to save and present the results of the simulations.
Seven Matlab files were created, where one of them is the main script that runs all the other files, including the Simulink model. Another file is a script to load the model parameters to the Workspace. Finally, there are five function files that generate graphics with the simulations results. Each of them will be presented and briefly commented, since all the code is documented in detail.

6.1 Simulating pH and level model

Here is presented the main Matlab script (*simulatin_pH_and_level_model.m*). It initializes the Workspace, loads the model parameters, simulates the model and saves and presents the results.
The main point in writing a script instead of manually simulating the model is that it facilitates the model use, making it easier to run several simulations and manage the resulting data.

```
%% Simulation of the pH neutralization plant
% Batch for the simulation of the model
% Authors: Claudio Garcia and Rodrigo Juliani
% ------------------------------------------------------------------------------------------
%% Initialization
% Matlab Workspace is initialized
matlabrc;                                    % Clears all variables in the workspace and reset Matlab
close all;                                   % Closes all figures
clc;                                         % Clears the command window
tic;                                         % Starts Matlab timer
scrsz = get(0,'ScreenSize');                 % Gets the size of the screen
fig_size = [1 1 scrsz(3) scrsz(4)];          % Sets a default size for figures to fit the screen
% ------------------------------------------------------------------------------------------
%% Model Configuration
Configuring_pH_and_level_model               % Model parameters are loaded to the Workspace
% ------------------------------------------------------------------------------------------
%% Simulations Configuration
% Parameters of the simulation
```

```
delta_sim = 0.05;                                          % [s] Fixed step size of the simulation
Ts = 0.5;                                                  % [s] Sampling time of the digital controllers
Decim = Ts/delta_sim;                                      % [adim.] Decimation of the recorded variables
Tsim = 500000;                                             % [s] Simulation interval
% Setpoints and disturbance for the simulation
delta_h = 15;                                              % [%] Step size for the level controller
exc_h = [h_nom h_nom+delta_h h_nom h_nom-delta_h].';       % [%] Vector of setpoins for the level controller
T_h = Tsim/5;                                              % [s] Step times for the level controller setpoints
delta_pH = 1;                                              % [pH] Step size for the pH controller
exc_pH = [pH_nom pH_nom+delta_pH pH_nom pH_nom-delta_pH pH_nom].';% [pH] Vector of setpoints for the pH controller
T_pH = T_h/5;                                              % [s] Step times for the pH controller setpoints
delta_Qa = Qa_nom*0.1;                                     % [m³/s] Step size for the acid flow disturbance
exc_Qa = [Qa_nom Qa_nom+delta_Qa Qa_nom-delta_Qa Qa_nom].'; % [m³/s] Vector of acid feed flow
T_Qa = T_pH/4;                                             % [s] Step times for the acid flow disturbances
% Control mode
Auto_man = 2;                                              % pH controller: Manual =1; Automatic = 2;
% ------------------------------------------------------------------------------------------------------------
%% Simulations
% Process response with pump enabled
Valve_Pump = 2;                                            % pH actuator: Valve = 1; Pump = 2;
sim ('Model_pH_and_level');                                % Simulates the model
 % Simulation results are copied to unique variables
h_pump = h_m;                                              % Measured level
pH_pump = pH_m;                                            % Measured pH
Qa_pump = Qa_m;                                            % Measured acid flow
Qb_pump = Qb_m;                                            % Measured base flow
MV_h_pump = MV_h;                                          % Level control effort
MV_pH_pump = MV_pH;                                        % pH control effort
% Process response with valve enabled
Valve_Pump = 1;                                            % pH actuator: Valve = 1; Pump = 2;
sim ('Model_pH_and_level');                                % Simulates the model
% Simulation results are copied to unique variables
h_valve = h_m;                                             % Measured level
pH_valve = pH_m;                                           % Measured pH
Qa_valve = Qa_m;                                           % Measured acid flow
Qb_valve = Qb_m;                                           % Measured base flow
MV_h_valve = MV_h;                                         % Level control effort
MV_pH_valve = MV_pH;                                       % pH control effort
x_valve = x;                                               % Valve stem position
P_valve = P;                                               % Pressure applied to the control valve
% Saves simulated data
save Simulated_Data;                                       % Saves the simulated data in a .mat file
% ------------------------------------------------------------------------------------------------------------
%% Results
% Complete results
plot_all_data(t, SP_pH, pH_pump, SP_h, h_pump, Qa_pump, Tsim, h_nom,...  % Plots all the simulation data with the
   delta_h, Qa_nom, delta_Qa, 'dosing pump', fig_size);                   % dosing pump enabled
print -djpeg All_data_pump;                                % Saves the figure as a .jpg file
plot_all_data(t, SP_pH, pH_valve, SP_h, h_valve, Qa_valve, Tsim, h_nom,... % Plots all the simulation data with the
   delta_h, Qa_nom, delta_Qa, 'control valve', fig_size);                 % control valve enabled
print -djpeg All_data_valve;                               % Saves the figure as a .jpg file
% Level responses
plot_level_response(t, SP_h, h_pump, h_valve, h_nom, delta_h, Tsim, fig_size);
print -djpeg Level_response;                               % Saves the figure as a .jpg file
% Level influense analysis
plot_level_influence(t, pH_pump, pH_valve, fig_size);
print -djpeg Level_influence;                              % Saves the figure as a .jpg file
% pH responses for nominal level
```

```
plot_pH_response(t(1:length(t)/5), SP_pH(1:length(t)/5), pH_pump(1:length(t)/5), Qa_pump(1:length(t)/5), ...
   Qa_nom, delta_Qa, Qb_pump(1:length(t)/5), MV_pH_pump(1:length(t)/5), 'dosing pump', fig_size);
print -djpeg pH_response_pump;                                  % Saves the figure as a .jpg file
plot_pH_response(t(1:length(t)/5), SP_pH(1:length(t)/5), pH_valve(1:length(t)/5), Qa_valve(1:length(t)/5), ...
  Qa_nom, delta_Qa,Qb_valve(1:length(t)/5), MV_pH_valve(1:length(t)/5), 'control valve', fig_size);
print -djpeg pH_response_valve;                                 % Saves the figure as a .jpg file
% Control valve friction analysis
plot_valve_friction_analysis(t(length(t)/5*0.175:length(t)/5*0.225), SP_pH(length(t)/5*0.175:length(t)/5*0.225),...
   pH_valve(length(t)/5*0.175:length(t)/5*0.225), Qb_valve(length(t)/5*0.175:length(t)/5*0.225), ...
   MV_pH_valve(length(t)/5*0.175:length(t)/5*0.225), x(length(t)/5*0.175:length(t)/5*0.225), ...
   P(length(t)/5*0.175:length(t)/5*0.225), fig_size);
print -djpeg valve_friction_analysis;                           % Saves the figure as a .jpg file
% --------------------------------------------------------------------------------------------------------
%% Execution Time
Execution_time = toc;                                           % Registers the current value in Matlab timer
Execution_time_minutes = floor(Execution_time/60);              % Calculates the number of minutes elapsed
Execution_time_seconds = Execution_time-Execution_time_minutes*60;  % Calculates the number of seconds elapsed
Elapsed_time = [num2str(Execution_time_minutes) ' minutes ' ...
   num2str(Execution_time_seconds) ' seconds'];                 % Creates a string with elapsed time
msgbox(Elapsed_time, 'Elapsed Time');                           % Shows a message box with the elapsed time
```

6.2 Configuring pH and level model

This file (*Configuring_pH_and_level_model.m*) loads all the model parameters to the Workspace.

Although it is easier to set all model parameters directly in the Simulink model, generating it with literal parameters and creating a Matlab script with the parameter values has some advantages, such as making it simpler to locate any parameter, to change its value or to make simulations with different values for certain parameters, as was done for the pH loop actuator.

```
%% Configuring pH and level model
% Data for the simulation of the pH neutralization plant
% Authors: Claudio Garcia and Rodrigo Juliani
% --------------------------------------------------------------------------------------------------------
%% Model parameters are loaded to the Workspace
% Parameters of the reactants
c_NaOH = 0.0185;                                                % [kmol/m³] Molar concentration of the base
c_HCl = 0.0056;                                                 % [kmol/m³] Molar concentration of the acid
Kw = 10^-14;                                                    % [adim.] Dissociation constant of water
% --------------------------------------------------------------------------------------------------------
% Parameters of the reaction tank (CSTR)
D_tank = 0.4;                                                   % [m] Reaction tank (CSTR) diameter
D_pHmeter = 0.03;                                               % [m] pHmeter diameter
D_cond_ext = 0.035;                                             % [m] Instrument external diameter
D_cond_int = 0.030;                                             % [m] Instrument internal diameter
D_cond_inst = 0.01;                                             % [m] Instrument diameter
D_resist = 0.01;                                                % [m] Equipment diameter
D_agit = 0.01;                                                  % [m] Agitator diameter
D_pH_cond = 0.05;                                               % [m] Instrument diameter
A_tank = pi*D_tank^2/4;                                         % [m²] Area of the base of the CSTR
A_inst = pi*(D_pHmeter^2+D_cond_ext^2-D_cond_int^2+D_cond_inst+2*D_resist^2+D_agit^2+D_pH_cond^2)/4;
                                                                % [m²] Area of the instrumentation in the CSTR
A_CSTR = A_tank - A_inst;                                       % [m²] Effective area of the CSTR
h_max_CSTR = 100;                                               % [%] Maximum CSTR level, in percentage
h_max_CSTR_m = 0.5;                                             % [m] Maximum CSTR level, in meters
```

```
h_nom = 65;                                    % [%] Nominal CSTR level
h0_CSTR = h_nom;                               % [%] Initial CSTR level
V_max_CSTR = A_CSTR*h_max_CSTR_m;              % [m³] Effective maximum CSTR volume
V0_CSTR = V_max_CSTR*h0_CSTR/100;              % [m³] Initial CSTR volume
% Parameters of the pressurized base tank
D_press = 0.65;                                % [m] Pressurized base tank diameter
A_press = pi*D_press^2/4;                      % [m²] Base area of the pressurized base tank
H_press_max = 1.05;                            % [m] Maximum height of the base tank
rho = 998.21;                                  % [kg/m3] Mass density of the base at 20oC
Patm = 9.247e5;                                % [Pa] Local atmospheric pressure
P_press = 2.13e4;                              % [Pa] Gauge internal pressure of the pressurized tank
% Parameters of the I/P converter
K_ip = 1;                                      % [adim.] Gain of the I/P converter
tau_ip = 1;                                    % [s] Time constant of the I/P converter
% Parameters of the pHmeter
tau_meter_pH = 10;                             % [s] Time constant of the pH meter
K_meter_pH = 1;                                % [pH/pH] Gain of the pH meter
[A,B,C,D] = tf2ss(K_meter_pH,[tau_meter_pH 1]); % Estimates the state-space representation of the
pHmeter
var_noise_pH = 1E-5;                           % [adim.] Variance of noise in the pHmeter
seed_noise_pH = 67890;                         % [adim.] Seed of the random number generator
% Parameters of the level meter
K_meter_level = 1;                             % [%/%] Gain of the level meter
tau_meter_level = 0.5;                         % [s] Time constant of the level meter
T_noise_level = -1;                            % [s] Period of noise in the level meter
var_noise_level = 1E-4;                        % [adim.] Variance of noise in the level meter
seed_noise_level = 12345;                      % [adim.] Seed of the random number generator
% Parameters of the flow meters
K_meter_flow = 1;                              % [(m³/s)/(m³/s)] Gain of the flow meters
tau_meter_flow = 3;                            % [s] Time constant of the flow meters
var_noise_Qa  = 1E-17;                         % [adim.] Variance of the acid flow meter
seed_noise_Qa = 357;                           % [adim.] Seed fot the random number generator
var_noise_Qb  = 1E-18;                         % [adim.] Variance of the base flow meter
seed_noise_Qb = 159;                           % [adim.] Seed fot the random number generator
% Parameters of the pump
K_pump = 30.3/1000/3600/100;                   % [(m³/s)/%] Gain of the pump
% Parameters of the solenoid valve
Kv = 9.238E-5;                                 % [m³/s/sqrt(m)] Flow coefficient of the valve
% Parameters of the control valve of the pressurized base tank
g = 9.80665;                                   % [m/s²] Standard gravity
Cv = 0.22;                                     % [sqrt(psig)/gpm] Flow coefficient of the valve
deltaP0 = P_press+rho*g*H_press_max;           % [Pa] Maximum differential pressure in the valve
K_aux1 = 2.40153e-5*Cv/sqrt(rho);              % Auxiliar parameter
% Parameters of the control valve actuator
K_at = 0.01;                                   % [p.u./%] Gain of the valve actuator
tau_at = 0.8;                                  % [s] Time constant of the valve actuator
% Nomimal variable values of the pH plant
Qa_nom = 13.8889e-6;                           % [m³/s] Nominal flow of acid
Qb_nom = 4.204e-6;                             % [m³/s] Nominal flow of base
pH_nom = 7;                                    % [pH] Nominal value of pH
X_nom = 0;                                     % [kmol/m³] Nominal value of the
                                               % ionic concentration difference

% Inicialization of the plant variables
mv0 = 50;                                      % [%] Initial output of the pH controller
pH_m0 = pH_nom*K_meter_pH;                     % [%] Initial output of the pH meter
mv_p0 = K_ip*mv0;                              % [%] Initial output of the I/P converter
x0 = mv0*K_at;                                 % [p.u.] Initial opening of the control valve
% Inicialization of the Kano friction model
```

```
J = 0.0;                    % [p.u.] Value of the friction parameter J
S = 0.28;                   % [p.u.] Value of the friction parameter S
d0 = 1;                     % [adim.] Initial value of the friction direction
                            % d=1: positive friction; d=-1: negative friction
u0 = x0;                    % [p.u.] Initial input signal
us0 = u0;                   % [p.u.] Initial value for wich the input moved before
% the stem stopped
u_10 = u0;                  % [p.u.] Initial value for the input signal at t=-1
stp0 = 1;                   % [adim.] Initial value for the stem movement condition
                            % (stp=0: moving stem; stp=1: stopped tem)

% Tuning parameters of the pH controller (PI)
Kn = 100/14;                % [%/pH] Adimensionalization gain
Kc = 1.34;                  % [adim.] Gain of the PI controller
Ti = 620;                   % [adim.] Ti parameter of the PI controller
% Tuning parameters of the level controller (PI)
P_l = 11.65;                % [adim.] Proportional gain of the PI controller
I_l = 271.52;               % [adim.] Integrative gain parameter of the PI controller
T_PWM = 10;                 % [s] Period of the PWM in the level controller
```

6.3 Plot all data

This function (*plot_all_data.m*) plots the controlled variables, pH and level, and the disturbance for both loops, acid flow.
Since it is a Matlab function, it can be used more than once, avoiding repetition of code and making changes to the plots easier to perform.

```
%% Plot all data
% Plots all the simulation data for pH, level and acid flow
% Authors: Claudio Garcia and Rodrigo Juliani
% -----------------------------------------------------------------------------------------------------------
function [] = plot_all_data(t, SP_pH, pH, SP_h, h, Qa, Tsim, h_nom, delta_h, Qa_nom, delta_Qa, actuator, fig_size)
figure_complete = figure('OuterPosition',fig_size);   % Generates a figure with specified size and location
subplot(3,1,1);                       % Creates a plot in the upper part of the figure
stairs(t,SP_pH,'k--');                % Plots the setpoint for the pH controller
hold on;                              % Holds the plot so that other plots can be added to it
plot(t,pH);                           % Plots measured values of the pH
axis ([0 Tsim 4.5 9.5]);              % Sets the plot axis to desired dimensions
grid;                                 % Inserts a grid on the plot
title (['pH - Controlled by ' actuator], 'FontSize', 12),   % Inserts a title in the plot
xlabel ('Time (s)', 'FontSize', 12);  % Inserts a label in the horizontal axis
ylabel ('pH', 'FontSize', 12);        % Inserts a label in the vertical axis
leg = legend ('SetPoint','Measured pH');   % Inserts a legend in the plot
set (leg, 'FontSize', 12);            % Sets the font size in the legend
subplot(3,1,2);                       % Creates a plot in the middle part of the figure
stairs(t,SP_h,'k--');                 % Plots the setpoints for the level controller
hold on;                              % Holds the plot for another plot can be added
plot(t,h);                            % Plots measured values of the level
axis ([0 Tsim h_nom-delta_h-1 h_nom+delta_h+1]);   % Sets the plot axis so that data fits the plot area
grid;                                 % Inserts a grid on the plot
title ('Level', 'FontSize', 12);      % Insert a title in the plot
xlabel ('Time (s)', 'FontSize', 12);  % Inserts a label in the x axis
ylabel ('Level (%)', 'FontSize', 12); % Inserts a label in the vertical axis
leg = legend ('SetPoint','Measured Level');   % Inserts a legend in the plot
set (leg, 'FontSize', 12);            % Sets the font size in the legend
subplot(3,1,3);                       % Creates a plot in the lower part of the figure
plot(t,Qa);                           % Plots measured values of acid flow
axis ([0 Tsim Qa_nom-delta_Qa*1.2 Qa_nom+delta_Qa*1.2]);   % Sets the plot axis so that data fits the plot area
```

```
grid;                                                   % Inserts a grid on the plot
title ('Acid flow', 'FontSize', 12);                    % Insert a title in the plot
xlabel ('Time (s)', 'FontSize', 12);                    % Inserts a label in the x axis
ylabel ('Measured flow (m³/s)', 'FontSize', 12);        % Inserts a label in the vertical axis
leg = legend ('Acid Flow');                             % Inserts a legend in the plot
set (leg, 'FontSize', 12);                              % Sets the font size in the legend
```

6.4 Plot level response

This function (*plot_level_response.m*) generates graphs of the level with both actuators enabled, dosing pump and control valve, for comparison. It also generates plots zoomed on the steps applied to the level controller set point.

```
%% Plot level controller response
% Plots the level controller response for different conditions
% Authors: Claudio Garcia and Rodrigo Juliani
% -----------------------------------------------------------------------------------------------
function [] = plot_level_response(t, SP_h, h_pump, h_valve, h_nom, delta_h, Tsim, fig_size)
figure_complete = figure('OuterPosition',fig_size);     % Generates a figure with specified size and location
%% Level response comparison
subplot(3,1,1);                                         % Creates a plot in the upper part of the figure
stairs(t,SP_h,'k--');                                   % Plots the setpoints for the level controller
hold on;                                                % Holds the plot for another plot to be added
plot(t,h_pump, 'g', t, h_valve, 'r:');                  % Plots measured values of the level
axis ([0 Tsim h_nom-delta_h-1 h_nom+delta_h+1]);        % Sets the plot axis with desired dimensions
grid;                                                   % Adds a grid to the plot
title ('Level', 'FontSize', 12);                        % Inserts a title in the plot
xlabel ('Time (s)', 'FontSize', 12);                    % Inserts a label in the x axis
ylabel ('Level (%)', 'FontSize', 12);                   % Inserts a label in the vertical axis
leg = legend ('SetPoint','Measured level with pump enabled',
  'Measured level with valve neabled');                 % Inserts a legend in the plot
set (leg, 'FontSize', 12);                              % Sets the font size in the legend
%% Parameters for the step response plots
slice = length(h_pump)/5;                               % Determines reference points for the steps
relative_t = t(1:slice*0.008+1);                        % Creates a time vector for the step response plots
axis_values = [0 800 h_nom-delta_h-1 h_nom+delta_h+1];  % Creates a parameter for the following plots axis
%% Pump
subplot(3,4,5);                                         % Creates a plot for the first step
stairs(relative_t,SP_h(slice*0.999:slice*1.007),'k--'); % Plots the setpoint for the level controller
hold on;                                                % Holds the plot for another plot to be added
plot(relative_t,h_pump(slice*0.999:slice*1.007), 'g');  % Plots measured values of the level
axis (axis_values);                                     % Sets the plot axis to desired dimensions
grid;                                                   % Adds a grid to the plot
title ('Level - 1st step', 'FontSize', 12);             % Inserts a title in the plot
xlabel ('Relative time (s)', 'FontSize', 12);           % Inserts a label in the horizontal axis
ylabel ('Level (%) - Dosing pump', 'FontSize', 12);     % Inserts a label in the vertical axis
subplot(3,4,6);                                         % Creates a plot for the second step
stairs(relative_t,SP_h(slice*1.999:slice*2.007),'k--'); % Plots the setpoint for the level controller
hold on;                                                % Holds the plot for another plot to be added
plot(relative_t,h_pump(slice*1.999:slice*2.007), 'g');  % Plots measured values of the level
axis (axis_values);                                     % Sets the plot axis to desired dimensions
grid;                                                   % Adds a grid to the plot
title ('Level - 2nd step', 'FontSize', 12);             % Inserts a title in the plot
xlabel ('Relative time (s)', 'FontSize', 12);           % Inserts a label in the horizontal axis
subplot(3,4,7);                                         % Creates a plot for the third step
stairs(relative_t,SP_h(slice*2.999:slice*3.007),'k--'); % Plots the setpoint for the level controller
hold on;                                                % Holds the plot for another plot to be added
plot(relative_t,h_pump(slice*2.999:slice*3.007), 'g');  % Plots measured values of the level
```

```
axis (axis_values);                                              % Sets the plot axis to desired dimensions
grid;                                                            % Adds a grid to the plot
title ('Level - 3rd step', 'FontSize', 12);                      % Inserts a title in the plot
xlabel ('Relative time (s)', 'FontSize', 12);                    % Inserts a label in the horizontal axis
subplot(3,4,8);                                                  % Creates a plot for the fourth step
stairs(relative_t,SP_h(slice*3.999:slice*4.007),'k--');          % Plots the setpoint for the level controller
hold on;                                                         % Holds the plot for another plot to be added
plot(relative_t,h_pump(slice*3.999:slice*4.007), 'g');           % Plots measured values of the level
axis (axis_values);                                              % Sets the plot axis to desired dimensions
grid;                                                            % Adds a grid to the plot
title ('Level - 4th step', 'FontSize', 12);                      % Inserts a title in the plot
xlabel ('Relative time (s)', 'FontSize', 12);                    % Inserts a label in the horizontal axis
%% Control Valve
subplot(3,4,9);                                                  % Creates a plot for the first step
stairs(relative_t,SP_h(slice*0.999:slice*1.007),'k--');          % Plots the setpoint for the level controller
hold on;                                                         % Holds the plot for another plot to be added
plot(relative_t,h_valve(slice*0.999:slice*1.007), 'r');          % Plots measured values of the level
axis (axis_values);                                              % Sets the plot axis to desired dimensions
grid;                                                            % Adds a grid to the plot
xlabel ('Relative time (s)', 'FontSize', 12);                    % Inserts a label in the horizontal axis
ylabel ('Level (%) - Control valve', 'FontSize', 12);            % Inserts a label in the vertical axis
subplot(3,4,10);                                                 % Creates a plot for the second step
stairs(relative_t,SP_h(slice*1.999:slice*2.007),'k--');          % Plots the setpoint for the level controller
hold on;                                                         % Holds the plot for another plot to be added
plot(relative_t,h_valve(slice*1.999:slice*2.007), 'r');          % Plots measured values of the level
axis (axis_values);                                              % Sets the plot axis to desired dimensions
grid;                                                            % Adds a grid to the plot
xlabel ('Relative time (s)', 'FontSize', 12);                    % Inserts a label in the horizontal axis
subplot(3,4,11);                                                 % Creates a plot for the third step
stairs(relative_t,SP_h(slice*2.999:slice*3.007),'k--');          % Plots the setpoint for the level controller
hold on;                                                         % Holds the plot for another plot to be added
plot(relative_t,h_valve(slice*2.999:slice*3.007), 'r');          % Plots measured values of the level
axis (axis_values);                                              % Sets the plot axis to desired dimensions
grid;                                                            % Adds a grid to the plot
xlabel ('Relative time (s)', 'FontSize', 12);                    % Inserts a label in the horizontal axis
subplot(3,4,12);                                                 % Creates a plot for the fourth step
stairs(relative_t,SP_h(slice*3.999:slice*4.007),'k--');          % Plots the setpoint for the level controller
hold on;                                                         % Holds the plot for another plot to be added
plot(relative_t,h_valve(slice*3.999:slice*4.007), 'r');          % Plots measured values of the level
axis (axis_values);                                              % Sets the plot axis to desired dimensions
grid;                                                            % Adds a grid to the plot
xlabel ('Relative time (s)', 'FontSize', 12);                    % Inserts a label in the horizontal axis
```

6.5 Plot level influence

This funciont (*plot_level_influence.m*) plots the pH response with different levels for both actuators.

```
%% Plot level influence analysis
% Plots the pH response with different levels in the CSTR
% Authors: Claudio Garcia and Rodrigo Juliani
% ---------------------------------------------------------------------------------------------------------------------------
function [] = plot_level_influence(t, pH_pump, pH_valve, fig_size)
figure_level_influence = figure('OuterPosition',fig_size);       % Generates a figure with specified size and location
slice = length(pH_pump)/5;                                       % Determines a slice to separate data with constant level
subplot(2,1,1);                                                  % Creates a plot in the upper half of the figure
hold on;                                                         % Holds the plot so that other plots can be added to it
plot(t((1:slice*1+1)),pH_pump(slice*1:slice*2),'r:');            % Data for high level
```

```
plot(t((1:slice*1+1)),pH_pump(slice*2:slice*3),'k-.');                % Data for nominal level
plot(t((1:slice*1+1)),pH_pump(slice*3:slice*4),'b--');                % Data for low level
axis 'tight'                                                          % Sets the plot axis to desired dimensions
grid;                                                                 % Inserts a grid on the plot
xlabel ('Relative Time (s)', 'FontSize', 12);                         % Inserts a label in the horizontal axis
ylabel ('Measured pH', 'FontSize', 12);                               % Inserts a label in the vertical axis
title ('pH response with different levels and pump enabled', 'FontSize', 12);  % Inserts a title in the plot
leg = legend ('Higher level','Nominal level', 'Lower level');         % Inserts a legend in the plot
set (leg, 'FontSize', 12);                                            % Sets the font size in the legend
subplot(2,2,3);                                                       % Creates a plot in the left part lower half of the figure
hold on;                                                              % Holds the plot so that other plots can be added to it
plot(t((1:slice*1+1)),pH_valve(slice*1:slice*2),'r:');                % Data for high level
plot(t((1:slice*1+1)),pH_valve(slice*2:slice*3),'k-.');               % Data for nominal level
plot(t((1:slice*1+1)),pH_valve(slice*3:slice*4),'b--');               % Data for low level
axis 'tight'                                                          % Sets the plot axis to desired dimensions
grid;                                                                 % Inserts a grid on the plot
xlabel ('Relative Time (s)', 'FontSize', 12);                         % Inserts a label in the horizontal axis
ylabel ('Measured pH', 'FontSize', 12);                               % Inserts a label in the vertical axis
title ('pH response with different levels and control valve enabled', 'FontSize', 12);% Inserts a title in the plot
leg = legend ('Higher level','Nominal level', 'Lower level');         % Inserts a legend in the plot
set (leg, 'FontSize', 12);                                            % Sets the font size in the legend
subplot(2,2,4);                                                       % Creates a plot in the lower half of the figure
hold on;                                                              % Holds the plot so that other plots can be added to it
plot(t((slice*.25:slice*.27)),pH_valve(slice*1.25:slice*1.27),'r','LineWidth',1.5);  % Data for high level
plot(t((slice*.25:slice*.27)),pH_valve(slice*2.25:slice*2.27),'k','LineWidth',1.5);  % Data for nominal level
plot(t((slice*.25:slice*.27)),pH_valve(slice*3.25:slice*3.27),'b','LineWidth',1.5);  % Data for low level
axis 'tight'                                                          % Sets the plot axis to desired dimensions
grid;                                                                 % Inserts a grid on the plot
xlabel ('Relative Time (s)', 'FontSize', 12);                         % Inserts a label in the horizontal axis
ylabel ('Measured pH', 'FontSize', 12);                               % Inserts a label in the vertical axis
title ('pH response with different levels and control valve enabled - Zoom', 'FontSize', 12);
                                                                      % Inserts a title in the plot
leg = legend ('Higher level','Nominal level', 'Lower level');         % Inserts a legend in the plot
set (leg, 'FontSize', 12);                                            % Sets the font size in the legend
```

6.6 Plot pH response

This function (*plot_pH_response.m*) plots the pH response and respective control effort with constant level.

```
%% Plot pH response
% Plots the pH step and disturbance responses
% Authors: Claudio Garcia and Rodrigo Juliani
% -------------------------------------------------------------------------------------------------------------------------------
function [] = plot_pH_response(t, SP_pH, pH, Qa, Qa_nom, delta_Qa, Qb, MV_pH, actuator, fig_size)
figure_complete = figure('OuterPosition',fig_size);                   % Generates a figure with specified size and location
subplot(4,1,1);                                                       % Creates a plot in the upper part of the figure
stairs(t,SP_pH,'k--');                                                % Plots the setpoint for the pH controller
hold on;                                                              % Holds the plot so that other plots can be added to it
plot(t,pH,'r');                                                       % Plots measured values of the pH in red
axis ([0 t(length(t)) 4.5 9.5]);                                      % Sets the plot axis to desired dimensions
grid;                                                                 % Inserts a grid on the plot
title (['pH - Controlled by ' actuator], 'FontSize', 12);             % Inserts a title in the plot
xlabel ('Time (s)', 'FontSize', 12);                                  % Inserts a label in the horizontal axis
ylabel ('pH', 'FontSize', 12);                                        % Inserts a label in the vertical axis
leg = legend ('SetPoint','Measured pH');                              % Inserts a legend in the plot
set (leg, 'FontSize', 12);                                            % Sets the font size in the legend
subplot(4,1,2);                                                       % Creates a plot for the acid flow
```

```
plot(t,Qa,'g');                                                    % Plots measured values of acid flow
axis ([0 t(length(t)) Qa_nom-delta_Qa*1.2 Qa_nom+delta_Qa*1.2]);  % Sets the plot axis to desired dimensions
grid;                                                              % Inserts a grid on the plot
title ('Acid flow', 'FontSize', 12);                               % Insert a title in the plot
xlabel ('Time (s)', 'FontSize', 12);                               % Inserts a label in the x axis
ylabel ('Measured flow (m³/s)', 'FontSize', 12);                   % Inserts a label in the vertical axis
leg = legend ('Acid Flow');                                        % Inserts a legend in the plot
set (leg, 'FontSize', 12);                                         % Sets the font size in the legend
subplot(4,1,3);                                                    % Creates a plot for the base flow
plot(t,Qb,'b');                                                    % Plots measured values of base flow
axis 'tight';                                                      % Sets the plot axis so that data fits the plot area
grid;                                                              % Inserts a grid on the plot
title ('Base flow', 'FontSize', 12);                               % Insert a title in the plot
xlabel ('Time (s)', 'FontSize', 12);                               % Inserts a label in the x axis
ylabel ('Measured flow (m³/s)', 'FontSize', 12);                   % Inserts a label in the vertical axis
leg = legend ('Base Flow');                                        % Inserts a legend in the plot
set (leg, 'FontSize', 12);                                         % Sets the font size in the legend
subplot(4,1,4);                                                    % Creates a plot in the lower part of the figure
plot(t,MV_pH,'m');                                                 % Plots the control efforts
axis 'tight';                                                      % Sets the plot axis so that data fits the plot area
grid;                                                              % Inserts a grid on the plot
title ('Base flow', 'FontSize', 12);                               % Insert a title in the plot
xlabel ('Time (s)', 'FontSize', 12);                               % Inserts a label in the x axis
ylabel ('Control effort (%)', 'FontSize', 12);                     % Inserts a label in the vertical axis
leg = legend ('Control Effort');                                   % Inserts a legend in the plot
set (leg, 'FontSize', 12);                                         % Sets the font size in the legend
```

6.7 Plot valve friction analysis

This function (*plot_valve_friction_analyis.m*) plots the pH with the control valve enabled and respective base flow, valve stem position, pressure applied to the valve actuator and control effort.

```
%% Plot valve friction analysis
% Generates plots for a valve friction analysis
% Authors: Claudio Garcia and Rodrigo Juliani
% ----------------------------------------------------------------------------------------------------------------
function [] = plot_valve_friction_analysis(t, SP_pH, pH, Qb, MV_pH, x, P, fig_size)
figure_complete = figure('OuterPosition',fig_size);               % Generates a figure with specified size and location
subplot(4,1,1);                                                    % Creates a plot in the upper part of the figure
stairs(t,SP_pH,'k--');                                             % Plots the setpoint for the pH controller
hold on;                                                           % Holds the plot so that other plots can be added to it
plot(t,pH,'r');                                                    % Plots measured values of the pH in red
axis 'tight';                                                      % Sets the plot axis so that all data can be seen
grid;                                                              % Inserts a grid on the plot
title ('pH controlled by the control valve', 'FontSize', 12);      % Inserts a title in the plot
xlabel ('Time (s)', 'FontSize', 12);                               % Inserts a label in the horizontal axis
ylabel ('pH', 'FontSize', 12);                                     % Inserts a label in the vertical axis
leg = legend ('SetPoint','Measured pH');                           % Inserts a legend in the plot
set (leg, 'FontSize', 12);                                         % Sets the font size in the legend
subplot(4,1,2);                                                    % Creates a plot for the base flow
plot(t,Qb,'b');                                                    % Plots measured values of base flow
axis 'tight';                                                      % Sets the plot axis so that data fits the plot area
grid;                                                              % Inserts a grid on the plot
title ('Base flow', 'FontSize', 12);                               % Insert a title in the plot
xlabel ('Time (s)', 'FontSize', 12);                               % Inserts a label in the x axis
ylabel ('Measured flow (m³/s)', 'FontSize', 12);                   % Inserts a label in the vertical axis
leg = legend ('Measured base flow');                               % Inserts a legend in the plot
```

```
set (leg, 'FontSize', 12);                     % Sets the font size in the legend
subplot(4,1,3);                                % Creates a plot for the stem position
plot(t,x,'g');                                 % Plots the valve stem position
axis 'tight';                                  % Sets the plot axis so that data fits the plot area
grid;                                          % Inserts a grid on the plot
title ('Control valve stem position', 'FontSize', 12);   % Insert a title in the plot
xlabel ('Time (s)', 'FontSize', 12);           % Inserts a label in the x axis
ylabel ('Stem position (p.u.)', 'FontSize', 12);   % Inserts a label in the vertical axis
leg = legend ('Stem position');                % Inserts a legend in the plot
set (leg, 'FontSize', 12);                     % Sets the font size in the legend
subplot(4,1,4);                                % Creates a plot in for the control effort
plot(t,MV_pH,'m',t,P*100,'c--');               % Plots the control efforts and pressure applied to
                                               % the control valve
axis 'tight';                                  % Sets the plot axis so that data fits the plot area
grid;                                          % Inserts a grid on the plot
title ('Control effort and pressure applied to the control valve', 'FontSize', 12);   % Inserts a title in the plot
xlabel ('Time (s)', 'FontSize', 12);           % Inserts a label in the x axis
ylabel ('Control effort (%)', 'FontSize', 12); % Inserts a label in the vertical axis
leg = legend ('Control Effort', 'Pressure');   % Inserts a legend in the plot
set (leg, 'FontSize', 12);                     % Sets the font size in the legend
```

7. Conclusion

In this chapter it was demonstrated how to build a Simulink model from a P&ID diagram of a plant and from the mathematical model of each of its components.
It has also been shown how to simulate the model, changing operation conditions and grouping several tests.
To test the built model, simulations were made and the results were analyzed, being similar to the expected from the real plant that was used as basis for the modeling method.
The process of building the model was described with enough detail in order to enable the reproduction of the model by the reader and with sufficient generalization so that it can be used as a guide for creating models for other systems.
Finally, all Simulink diagrams and Matlab codes developed were presented for easy consultation, understanding and reproduction of the model and obtained results.

8. References

ANSI/ISA-5.1-2009 (2009). Instrumentation symbols and identification. *American National Standard*. ISBN 978-1-936007-29-5.

Asuero, A. G. & Michalowski, T. (2011). Comprehensive formulation of titration curves for complex acid-base systems and its analytical implications. *Critical Reviews in Analytical Chemistry*, Vol.41, No.2, (May 2011), pp. 151-187, ISSN 1547-6510.

Garcia, C. (2005). *Modelagem e simulação*. (2nd edition), EDUSP, ISBN 85-314-0904-7 , São Paulo, Brazil. /In Portuguese/

Garcia, C. (2008). Comparison of friction models applied to a control valve. *Control Engineering Practice*, Vol.16, No.10, (October 2008), pp. 1231-1243, ISSN 0967-0661.

Jacobs, O. L. R., Hewkin, M. A. & While, C. (1980). Online computer control of pH in an industrial process. *IEE Proceedings D*, Vol.127, No.4, (July 1980), pp. 161-168, ISSN 0143-7054.

Rinehart, N. & Jury, F. (1997). How control valves impact process optimization. *Hydrocarbon Processing*, Vol.76, No.6, (June 1997), pp.53-58, ISSN 0018-8190.